Kant's Transcendental Deduction

Kant's Transcendental Deduction

An Analytical-Historical Commentary

Henry E. Allison

OXFORD
UNIVERSITY PRESS

OXFORD
UNIVERSITY PRESS

Great Clarendon Street, Oxford, OX2 6DP,
United Kingdom

Oxford University Press is a department of the University of Oxford.
It furthers the University's objective of excellence in research, scholarship,
and education by publishing worldwide. Oxford is a registered trade mark of
Oxford University Press in the UK and in certain other countries

First Edition published in 2015
Impression: 1

Published in the United States of America by Oxford University Press
198 Madison Avenue, New York, NY 10016, United States of America

British Library Cataloguing in Publication Data
Data available

Library of Congress Control Number: 2014958033

ISBN: 978-0-19-872485-8 (Hbk.)
ISBN: 978-0-19-872486-5 (Pbk.)

Printed and bound by
CPI Group (UK) Ltd, Croydon, CR0 4YY

Dedicated to the memory of H. J. Paton, whose writings taught me how to read the Transcendental Deduction

Acknowledgments

I wish to express my gratitude to Karl Ameriks, Alison Laywine, and two anonymous readers for Oxford University Press for their many helpful comments and criticisms of central portions of this work. Thanks are also due to Wolfgang Carl, Huaping Lu-Adler, Oliver Sensen, and Christian Wenzel for their comments on specific chapters, to Jay Reuscher for making available to me the typescript of his translation, together with a digest and topical index to the Duisburg Nachlass, to Peter Momtchiloff for his continued support of my work, and to Janum Sethi for undertaking the laborious task of preparing the index.

Finally, I wish to thank Cambridge University Press and the editors and translators for permission to quote from the following works in the *Cambridge Edition of the Works of Immanuel Kant: Critique of Pure Reason*, edited and translated by Paul Guyer and Allen Wood; *Theoretical Philosophy 1755–1770*, edited and translated by David Walford in collaboration with Ralf Meerbote; *Theoretical Philosophy after 1781*, edited and translated by Henry Allison and Peter Heath, translated by Michael Friedman and Gary Hatfield; and *Notes and Fragments*, edited by Paul Guyer and translated by Curtis Bowman, Paul Guyer, and Frederick Rauscher.

Contents

Note on Sources and Key to Abbreviations and Translations

Apart from the *Critique of Pure Reason*, where references are to the standard A and B pagination, all references to Kant are first to the volume and page of *Kant's gesammelte Schriften* (KGS), herausgegeben von der Deutschen (formerly Könligli-chen Preuissischen) Akademie der Wissenschaften, twenty-nine volumes (Berlin Walter de Gruyter (and predecessors), 1902ff) and second (where applicable) to the volume and pagination in *The Cambridge Edition of the Works of Immanuel Kant* (Cambridge: Cambridge University Press, 1998). Translations from the *Groundwork for the Metaphysics of Morals* are my own; although I have consulted most of the already existing English translations.

A   *Anthropologie in pragmatischer Hinsicht = Anthropologie in pragmatischer Hinsicht* (KGS 7: 119–333) *Anthropology from a pragmatic point of view*, translated by Robert B. Louden in *Anthropology, History and Education* (231–429), *The Cambridge Edition of the Works of Immanuel Kant*, edited by Günter Zöller and Robert B. Louden, Cambridge: Cambridge University Press (2007).

AF   *Anthroplogie Friedlander* (KGS 25: 465–728).

AN   *Allgemeine Naturgeschicte und Theorie des Himmels oder Versuch von der Verfassung und dem mechanischen Ursprunge des ganzen Weltgebäudes, nach Newtonischen Grundsätzen abgehandelt* (*General Natural History and Theory of the Heavens or an Essay about the Constitution and Mechanical Origin of the Whole Universe, Created in Conformity with Newtonian Principles*) (KGS 1: 221–368).

AP   *Anthropologie Parrow* (KGS 25: 239–463).

Br   *Kant's Briefwechsel* (KGS 10–12) *Correspondence*, translated and edited by Arnulf Zweig, *The Cambridge Edition of the Works of Immanuel Kant*, Cambridge: Cambridge University Press (1999).

EMB   *Der einzig mögliche Beweisgrund zu einer Demonstration des Daseins Gottes* (KGS 2: 63–163), *The Only Possible Argument in Support of a Demonstration of the Existence of God*, *Theoretical Philosophy 1755–1770*, *The Cambridge Edition of the Works of Immanuel Kant*, translated and edited by David Walford in collaboration with Ralf Meerbote, 362–72, Cambridge: Cambridge University Press (1992).

FI   *Erste Einleitung in die Kritik der Urteilskraft* (KGS 20: 193–251) *First Introduction to the Critique of the Power of Judgment*, translated by Paul Guyer and Eric Matthews, in *Critique of the Power of Judgment, The Cambridge Edition of the Works of Immanuel Kant* (3–51), edited by Paul Guyer, Cambridge: Cambridge University Press (2000).

Fort   *Welches sind die wirklichen Fortschritte, die die Metaphysik seit Leibnitzens und Wolfs Zeiten in Deutchland gemacht hat?* (KGS 20: 255–351) *What Real Progress Has Metaphysics Made in Germany since the Time of Leibniz and Wolff?* Translated by Peter Heath, in *Theoretical Philosophy after 1781, The Cambridge Edition of the Works of Immanuel Kant* (353–424), edited by Henry Allison and Peter Heath, Cambridge: Cambridge University Press (2002).

FS   *Die falsche Spitzfindigkeit der vier syllogistischen Figuren* (KGS 2: 44–61) *The False Subtlety of the Four Syllogistic Figures, Theoretical Philosophy 1755–1770, The Cambridge Edition of the Works of Immanuel Kant*, translated and edited by David Walford in collaboration with Ralf Meerbote (86–105), Cambridge: Cambridge University Press (1992).

G   *Von dem ersten Grunde der Unterschiedes der Gegenden im Raume* (KGS 2, 375–83) *Concerning the Ultimate Ground of the Differentiation of Directions in Space, Theoretical Philosophy 1755–1770, The Cambridge Edition of the Works of Immanuel Kant*, translated and edited by David Walford in collaboration with Ralf Meerbote (362–72), Cambridge: Cambridge University Press (1992).

GTP   *Über den Gebrauch der teleologischer Principien in der Philosophie* (KGS: 157–84) *On the Use of Teleological Principles in Philosophy*, translated by Günter Zöller, in *Anthropology, History and Education* (195–218), *The Cambridge Edition of the Works of Immanuel Kant*, edited by Günter Zöller and Robert B. Louden, Cambridge: Cambridge University Press (2007).

GwS   *Gedanken von den wahren Schätzung der lebendigen Kräfte und Beurtheilung der Beweise, deren sich herr von Leibniz und andere Mechaniker in dieser Streitsache bedient haben, nebst einigen vorhergehenden Betrachtungen, welche die Kraft der Körper überhaupt betreffen* (GMS 1: 7–181) *Thoughts on the True Estimation of Living Forces and Criticism of the Proofs of which Herr von Leibniz and Others Have Made Use in this Controversy, Preceded by a Few Reflections which Concern the Force of Bodies in General*, translated by Jeffrey B. Edwards and Martin Schönfeld, in *Natural Science, The Cambridge Edition of the Works of Immanuel Kant*, edited by Eric Watkins (2012).

ID   *De mundi sensibilis atque intelligibilis forma et principiis* (KGS 2: 385–419) *On the Form and Principles of the Sensible and the Intelligible World* (Inaugural Dissertation), *Theoretical Philosophy 1755–1770, The Cambridge*

Edition of the Works of Immanuel Kant, translated and edited by David Walford in collaboration with Ralf Meerbote (377–416), Cambridge: Cambridge University Press (1992).

JL   JL= *Jäsche Logik* (KGS 9) *The Jäsche Logic*, translated by J. Michael Young, in *Lectures on Logic, The Cambridge Edition of the Works of Immanuel Kant*, edited by J. Michael Young (527–640), Cambridge: Cambridge University Press (1992).

KpV   *Kritik der praktischen Vernunft* (KGS 5: 1–163) *Critique of Practical Reason*, translated by Mary J. Gregor, in *Practical Philosophy, The Cambridge Edition of the Works of Immanuel* Kant (139–271), edited by Mary J. Gregor, Cambridge: Cambridge University Press (1996).

KU   *Kritik der Urtheilskraft* (KGS 5: 165–485), *Critique of the Power of Judgment*, translated by Paul Guyer and Eric Matthews, *The Cambridge Edition of the Works of Immanuel Kant*, edited by Paul Guyer, Cambridge: Cambridge University Press (2000).

LB   *Logik Blomberg* (KGS 24: 16–301) *The Blomberg Logic*, translated by J. Michael Young, in *Lectures on Logic, The Cambridge Edition of the Works of Immanuel Kant*, edited by J. Michael Young (5–246), Cambridge: Cambridge University Press (1992).

LD-W   *Logik Dohna-Wundlacken* (KGS 24: 693–784) *The Dohna-Wundlacken Logic*, translated by J. Michael Young, in *Lectures on Logic, The Cambridge Edition of the Works of Immanuel Kant*, edited by J. Michael Young (431–516), Cambridge: Cambridge University Press (1992).

LBu   *Logik Busolt* (KGS 24: 608–86).

LPh   *Logik Philippi* (KGS 24: 311–496).

LPö   *Logik Pölitz* (KGS 24: 502–602).

LW   *Wiener Logik* (KGS 24: 790–937) *The Vienna Logic*, translated by J. Michael Young, in *Lectures on Logic, The Cambridge Edition of the Works of Immanuel Kant*, edited by J. Michael Young (249–377), Cambridge: Cambridge University Press (1992).

MAN   *Metaphysische Anfangsgründe der Naturwissenschaft* (KGS 4) *Metaphysical Foundations of Natural Science*, translated by Michael Freedman, in *Theoretical Philosophy after 1781, The Cambridge Edition of the Works of Immanuel Kant* (183–270), edited by Henry E. Allison and Peter Heath, Cambridge: Cambridge University Press (2002).

MH   *Metaphysik Herder* (KGS 28: 5–166).

ML_1 Metaphysik L_1 (KGS 28: 195–301), translated by Karl Ameriks and Steve Naragon, in *Lectures on Metaphysics, The Cambridge Edition of the Works of Immanuel Kant* (19–106), edited by Karl Ameriks and Steve Naragon, Cambridge: Cambridge University Press (1997).

MM   *Metaphysik Mrongovius* (KGS 29: 747–940), translated by Karl Ameriks and Steve Naragon, in *Lectures on Metaphysics* (109–286), *The Cambridge Edition of the Works of Immanuel Kant* (19–106), edited by Karl Ameriks and Steve Naragon, Cambridge: Cambridge University Press (1997).

N   *M. Immanuel Kants Nachricht von der Einrichtung seiner Vorlesungen in dem Winterhalbenjahre von 1765–1766* (KGS2: 305–13) *M. Immanuel Kant's Announcement of the Programme of His Lectures for the Winter Semester 1765–1766, Theoretical Philosophy 1755–1770, The Cambridge Edition of the Works of Immanuel Kant*, translated and edited by David Walford in collaboration with Ralf Meerbote (287–300), Cambridge: Cambridge University Press (1992).

ND   *Principiorum Primorum Cognitionis Metaphysicae Nova Dilucidatio* (KGS 1: 385–416) *A New Elucidation of the First Principles of Metaphysical Cognition. Theoretical Philosophy 1755–1770, The Cambridge Edition of the Works of Immanuel Kant*, translated and edited by David Walford in collaboration with Ralf Meerbote, 1–45, Cambridge: Cambridge University Press (1992).

PM   *Metaphysicae cum geometria iunctae usus in philosophia naturali, cuius specimem I. continet Monadologiam Physicam* (KGS 1: 473–87) *The Employment in Natural Philosophy of Metaphysics Combined with Geometry, of which Sample I Contains the Physical Monadology, Theoretical Philosophy 1755–1770, The Cambridge Edition of the Works of Immanuel Kant*, translated and edited by David Walford in collaboration with Ralf Meerbote, 47–66, Cambridge: Cambridge University Press (1992).

PRO   *Prolegomena zu einer jeden künftigen Metaphysik, die als Wissenschaft wird aufterten können* (KGS 4) *Prolegomena to Any Future Metaphysics that Will Be Able to Come Forward as Science*, translated by Gary Hatfield, in *Theoretical Philosophy after 1781, The Cambridge Edition of the Works of Immanuel Kant* (53–169), edited by Henry E. Allison and Peter Heath, Cambridge: Cambridge University Press (2002).

R   *Reflexionen* (KGS 17–19) *Notes and Fragments, The Cambridge Edition of the Works of Immanuel Kant* (301–59), edited by Paul Guyer, translated by Curtis Bowman, Paul Guyer, and Frederick Rauscher, Cambridge: Cambridge University Press (2005).

RHI   *Recension der Herders Ideen zur Philosophie der Geschichte der Menschheit* (KGS 8: 44–66) *Review of Herder's Ideas for the Philosophy of the History of Humanity, Parts 1 and 2*, translated by Allen Wood, in *Anthropology, History and Education* (124–42), *The Cambridge Edition of the Works of*

Immanuel Kant, edited by Günter Zöller and Robert B. Louden, Cambridge: Cambridge University Press (2007).

RP   *Religionslehre Pölitz* (KGS 28: 989–1126) *Lectures on the Philosophical Doctrine of Religion*, translated by Allen Wood in *Religion and Rational Theology, The Cambridge Edition of the Works of Immanuel Kant* (335–451), translated and edited by Allen Wood and George Di Giovani, Cambridge: Cambridge University Press (1996).

T   *Träume eines Geistsehers, erläutert durch Träume der Metaphysik* (KGS 4: 314–73) *Dreams of a Spirit-Seer Elucidated by Dreams of Metaphysics*, in *Theoretical Philosophy, 1755–1770, The Cambridge Edition of the Works of Immanuel Kant* (301–59), translated and edited by David Walford in collaboration with Ralf Meerbote, Cambridge: Cambridge University Press (1992).

U   *Untersuchung über die Deutlichkeit der Gründsatze der natüturlichen Theologie und der Moral* (KGS 2: 273–301) *Inquiry Concerning the Distinctness of the Principles of Natural Theology and Morality*, translated by David Walford in *Theoretical Philosophy, 1755–1770, The Cambridge Edition of the Works of Immanuel Kant* (248–75), translated and edited by David Walford in collaboration with Ralf Meerbote, Cambridge: Cambridge University Press (1992).

UE   *Über eine Entdeckung, nach der alle neue Kritik der reinen Vernunft durch eine ältere entbehrlich gemacht warden soll* (KGS 8) *On a Discovery Whereby Any New Critique of Pure Reason Is to Be Made Superfluous by an Older One*, translated by Henry Allison in *Theoretical Philosophy after 1781, The Cambridge Edition of the Works of Immanuel Kant* (283–336), edited by Henry E. Allison and Peter Heath, Cambridge: Cambridge University Press (2002).

VKK   *Versuch über die Krankheiten des Kopfes* (KGS 2: 259–71), *Essay on the Maladies of the Head*, translated by Holly Wilson in *Anthropology, History and Education* (195–218), *The Cambridge Edition of the Works of Immanuel Kant*, edited by Günter Zöller and Robert B. Louden, Cambridge: Cambridge University Press (2007).

VP   *Vorarbeit zu den Prolegomena zu einer jeden künftigen Metaphysik* (KGS 23: 53–76) *Preliminary to the Prolegomena to Any Future Metaphysics*.

VSgE   *Vorarbeiten zur Schrift gegen Eberhard* (KGS 20: 353–78) *Preliminaries to the Writing against Eberhard*.

WHD   *Was heisst sich im Denken orientieren?* (KGS 8: 133–46) *What Does It Mean to Orient Oneself in Thinking?* Translated by Allen Wood, in *Religion and Rational Theology, The Cambridge Edition of the Works of Immanuel Kant* (7–18), translated and edited by Allen Wood and George Di Giovani, Cambridge: Cambridge University Press (1996).

Introduction

In the preface to the first edition of the *Critique of Pure Reason* Kant remarks:

I am acquainted with no investigations more important for getting to the bottom of that faculty we call the understanding, and at the same time for the determination of the rules and boundaries of its use, than those I have undertaken in the second chapter of the Transcendental Analytic, under the title *Deduction of the Pure Concepts of the Understanding*; they are also the investigations that have cost me the most, but I hope not unrewarded, effort.   (Axvi)

Although lacking the importance of Kant's original project, the labor required to understand and evaluate its results has been recognized and duly noted by generations of commentators. In this work I propose to add my endeavor to theirs, all of whom, including myself, have undoubtedly shared Kant's hope that their efforts will not go unrewarded. The approach will be both analytical and historical. While the main goal is to provide a critical analysis and evaluation of the Transcendental Deduction, as it is found in the first and second editions of the *Critique*, I share with many commentators the view that Kant's argument can best be understood in light of the internal development of his thought, which eventually led him both to the recognition of the need for a transcendental deduction and to the forms that it took in the first two editions of the *Critique*.[1] In short, I believe that in order to understand Kant's novel project it is necessary to traverse the path through which he arrived at his understanding of the problematic to which it is addressed and his method of addressing it.

An analysis of this path is the concern of the first three chapters and of an appendix to Chapter 3, which discusses the relation between Kant's views and those of Tetens. These chapters trace the development of Kant's thought from the 1760s through the end of the so-called "Silent Decade" (the period from 1770–1781), insofar as it bears on the eventual project of a transcendental deduction. Because of the focus on texts that have a significant bearing on the future, not yet envisioned, deduction, there is no attempt to provide anything like a complete survey of Kant's "pre-critical" thought, which is quite wide ranging, encompassing virtually all of the

---

[1] In what follows I shall use the terms "Transcendental Deduction" or simply "Deduction" to refer to the actual texts of Kant's arguments in the *Critique* and "transcendental deduction" or "deduction" to refer to the project in general.

topics with which the "critical" Kant was concerned. Moreover, by beginning with Kant's writings in the 1760s I am ignoring the earliest phase of his work. Kant's first publication was in 1747 (*Thoughts on the True Estimation of Living Forces*) and it dealt with a debate between the Cartesians and the Leibnizians regarding the nature of the fundamental laws of motion. In addition, he composed a number of works in the 1750s dealing with both scientific and more properly philosophical topics, the most important of the latter group being *A New Elucidation of the First Principles of Metaphysical Cognition* (1755). In fact, a recent commentator, Martin Schönfeld, has seen in these works the inception of what he terms Kant's "pre-critical project," which is continued in the writings of the first years of the 1760s. According to Schönfeld, this project consists essentially in an attempt to construct a grand synthesis of the basic principles of Newtonian physics and its model of nature as a thoroughly mechanistic system with certain metaphysical conceptions, most notably free will, the existence of an immaterial mind or soul, mind–body interaction, and the existence of a providential deity.[2]

In neglecting these earlier works, I am not denying either their intrinsic interest or thematic connection with the texts from the 1760s with which Chapter 1 will be primarily concerned, namely, "Inquiry Concerning the Distinctness of the Principles of Natural Theology and Morality" (1764); "An Attempt to Introduce the Concept of Negative Magnitudes into Philosophy (1763)," *The Only Possible Basis for a Demonstration of the Existence of God* (1763), and *Dreams of a Spirit-Seer, Illustrated by Dreams of Metaphysics* (1766). In addition to a desire to avoid unnecessary complication, the main reason for this restriction is that these works provide the first clear expression of a concern that remained central to Kant's thought throughout the remainder of his career and that eventually gave rise to the transcendental deduction project. Although this concern did not constitute a radical departure from that of Kant's earliest writings and his initial project, as described by Schönfeld, it does mark a turn from what one might regard as straightforward metaphysics in the traditional sense, which the "critical" Kant labeled "dogmatic," to a methodological concern with the nature and conditions of the possibility of metaphysics. In short, Kant became and remained throughout his career a practitioner of what is today sometimes called "metametaphysics." Moreover, that Kant thought of his own work in that way is evident from a letter that he sent to Marcus Herz shortly after the initial appearance of the *Critique* in which he remarks that it contains "the metaphysics of metaphysics" (Br 10: 269_{32-3}; 181).[3]

The methodological or metametaphysical focus is particularly evident in the above mentioned writings from the 1760s, which will be discussed in Chapter 1. We shall see that in these works Kant adopted for metaphysics what he termed the "analytic

---

[2]   See Schönfeld (2000). For an excellent earlier account along similar lines, though less detailed, see also Laywine (1994).

[3]   The letter is dated May 11, 1781.

method," which he contrasted with the "synthetic method" of mathematics. Whereas the latter begins with definitions, from which it derives conclusions by logical means, the former begins with a complex phenomenon or state of affairs as given and endeavors to understand it by breaking it up into simple parts and, as it were, reconstituting it in thought. Kant's avowed model for this was the method of Newton in natural philosophy; but we shall see that adopting it for metaphysics, by which Kant, following Baumgarten, understood as "the philosophy of the fundamental principles of our cognition" (U 2: 283_{13-14}; 256), required a significant modification of the analysandum.[4] For Newton this was bodies in motion, from which he ascended inductively to general laws with the help of mathematics; while for Kant it was initially confused concepts and the goal was to ascend from these to clear and self-evident simple concepts, which are contained in them as marks and which neither require nor are capable of further analysis. In short, the analytic method in metaphysics, as Kant understood it at the time, was a form of conceptual analysis which, as such, is quite distinct from the method of natural science adopted by Newton.

Moreover, we shall see that, despite the sharp break with the Wolffians regarding the method of metaphysics and the influence of Crusius, who was the most important anti-Wolffian metaphysician in Germany at the time, Kant's epistemology in the 1760s retained an essential Wolffian feature; viz., the view that the ultimate grounds of judgment are logical. For the Wolffians, who followed the Leibnizian principle that in every true judgment the predicate is contained in the concept of the subject (and in every false judgment excluded from it), this ground was the principle of non-contradiction; whereas for Kant the principle of non-contradiction governed merely negative judgments and the principle of identity positive ones. Accordingly, I characterize Kant's epistemological stance in these writings as based upon an analytic model of cognition (not to be confused with the analytic method in metaphysics), which is a slightly modified version of the Wolffian (logicist) model, and contrast it with the discursive model with which Kant later replaced it and which gives a central place to the distinction between analytic and synthetic judgments and the consequent problem of the synthetic a priori. And since Kant had not yet adopted this model of cognition, he does not appeal in these writings to the analytic-synthetic distinction, which is the distinctive feature of his "critical" epistemology.

In the first three of the forementioned works we find Kant spelling out and applying his self-described analytic method to a range of issues, most notably the reconciliation of the conception of body or material substance, as composed of indivisible particles (physical monads), with the infinite divisibility of space as demonstrated in geometry; the grounds of a real opposition between things, as contrasted with a merely logical opposition between concepts; and the basis for the

---

[4] See Baumgarten (1926), 23; (2013), 99.

demonstration of the existence of an *ens realissimum* as the real ground of possibility. We shall also see, however, that the latest of the above-mentioned writings, which is concerned with pneumatology (the doctrine of the soul), has a quite different tone, since Kant there assumes a decidedly skeptical stance, raising fundamental problems regarding the viability, or at least the scope, of his proposed method in metaphysics.

Chapter 2 is concerned with two published texts: *Concerning the Ultimate Ground of the Differentiation of Directions in Space* (1768) and *On the Form and Principles of the Sensible and the Intelligible World* (1770), which will henceforth be referred to as the *Inaugural Dissertation*, as well as a *Reflexion* of uncertain date in which Kant claims that the year 1769 gave him "great light." We shall see that the illumination that Kant received in 1769 concerned the radical distinction between sensibility and understanding as cognitive faculties and that he put it directly to work the following year in the *Inaugural Dissertation*. Since the latter is by far Kant's most important "pre-critical" publication, its analysis will be the main business of Chapter 2. For the present, however, it must suffice to note two points regarding this work. First, it marks a sharp turn from Newton to Plato, which appears to have been largely the result of the influence of Leibniz's *New Essays*, which was first published in 1765 and which Kant apparently studied soon after its appearance. Second, notwithstanding its strong Platonic element, the *Inaugural Dissertation* continues, albeit in different terms, the methodological concern of the writings of the early 1760s. Thus, rather than being a direct contribution to metaphysics, Kant describes it as a specimen of a "propaedeutic science" (ID 2: 395; 387), with that for which it is a propaedeutic being metaphysics. The governing idea is that the work can fulfill this essentially methodological function because metaphysics is reconceived in a Platonic manner as a science of non-sensible entities; while the sharp separation of the sensible from the intellectual makes it possible to avoid the contagion of the latter by the former, which Kant at the time regarded as the chief source of metaphysical error.

Chapter 3 considers Kant's thought during the lengthy period between the publication of the *Inaugural Dissertation* in 1770 and the first edition of the *Critique* in 1781, which due to the absence of any publications in theoretical philosophy, has come to be known as the "Silent Decade."[5] Notwithstanding the lack of publication, this proved to be the decisive period of Kant's philosophical development, since it was during these years that he fully entered the "critical" path and worked out the basics of the line of thought that eventually led to the Transcendental Deduction in the *Critique*. But while there is a general agreement regarding the broad course of Kant's development during this time, there are many unresolved questions and much disagreement regarding details. At the heart of the problem are the materials on which any attempted reconstruction must rely. Since there are no published texts,

---

[5] During this period Kant published two short pieces, which have no bearing on the problematic of the deduction: "*Von den verschiedenen Racen der Menschen*" (1775) and "*Auffsätze, das philanthropin betreffend*" (1776/77).

these consist solely of correspondence, *Reflexionen*, which are often ambiguous and in most cases notoriously hard to date, and student's notes from Kant's lectures during the period, the proper interpretation of which is also frequently problematic.

Fortunately, however, there are texts, which are datable with various degrees of assurance and which span the entire decade. From the first part of the decade we have Kant's letters to Herz, particularly the famous letter of February 21, 1772, in which he appears to raise the "critical" problem of the possibility of a priori knowledge involving non-empirical concepts, such as those that he had already identified in the *Dissertation*. The crown jewel of the mid-decade is the so-called "*Duisburg Nachlass*," which is a series of related *Reflexionen* that are roughly datable because one of them was written on the back of a letter to Kant dated May 20, 1775. These are of decisive importance because they contain Kant's earliest known discussion of the unity of apperception and a detailed exploration of the function of the relational categories, which anticipates the argument of the Analogies of Experience in the *Critique*. And from the final portion we have a sketch of a transcendental deduction, or at least the elements thereof, known as "*Loses Blatt* B 12," which is closely related to the one contained in the first edition of the *Critique* and is datable because it was likewise scribbled by Kant on the back of an envelope of a letter dated January 20, 1780. By focusing on these texts, supplemented by other, not precisely datable materials from Kant's *Nachlass*, Chapter 3 attempts to provide an overview of Kant's thought during this period, which is informed by, but differs sharply in certain respects from, the complementary accounts of this topic by Wolfgang Carl and Alison Laywine.[6] Finally, since Kant's concern with Tetens is traceable to the last period of the "Silent Decade" (from 1777), a comparison of their views on topics pertaining to the Transcendental Deduction and a consideration of the likely nature and extent of Tetens' influence on Kant is appended to Chapter 3.

After sketching the development of Kant's thought regarding topics bearing on a transcendental deduction of the categories over a period of almost two decades, the remainder of this study will be concerned with an analysis of the versions of the Transcendental Deduction contained in the first two editions of the *Critique* (1781 and 1787), together with texts from the period between the editions, which is here referred to as "The Interlude." Following custom, I shall henceforth refer to the two versions as the A- and the B-Deductions respectively.

The analysis of the A-Deduction consists of three chapters (4–6). Chapter 4 is divided into two parts. The first discusses the section of the Transcendental Analytic entitled "On the Clue to the Discovery of All Pure Concepts of the Understanding," to which Kant refers in the second edition as the Metaphysical Deduction. Although not part of the Transcendental Deduction, it requires consideration because it provides the materials with which the latter is concerned by deriving the categories

---

[6] Carl (1989b) and Laywine (2001), (2003), (2005), and (2006).

from the forms of judgment delineated in general logic. The second part of Chapter 4 is concerned with the first section of the Transcendental Deduction, in which Kant presents his views on the aim of, need for, and strategy of a transcendental deduction in general and of the pure concepts of the understanding or categories in particular. This is the only portion of the A-Deduction that is retained (albeit with some modifications) in the second edition. Chapter 5 is likewise divided into two parts. The first considers the nature and import of the distinction between a subjective and an objective deduction, which Kant draws in the Preface. The second analyzes Kant's preliminary discussion of the central themes of the Deduction in section 2 of the A-Deduction, which we are told is intended "more to prepare than to instruct the reader" (A98). The organizing principle of the latter is Kant's account of a three-fold synthesis, which has both empirical and a priori dimensions and supposedly underlies all cognition. Chapter 6 examines Kant's systematic formulation of the Deduction in section 3, which he divides into an argument "from above" (beginning with pure apperception and descending to the relation between the categories and appearances) and an argument "from below" (beginning with experience and rising to the conditions of its possibility).

Chapters 7–9 deal respectively with the relevant material stemming from the period between the publications of the first two editions of the *Critique* and the two parts into which Kant divides the B-Deduction. Although it includes an analysis of a set of *Reflexionen*, which bear on the problematic of the Transcendental Deduction and are datable as stemming from the Interlude, the twin foci of Chapter 7 are the surrogate for the Transcendental Deduction, which Kant provides in the second part of the *Prolegomena* (1783) and a note added to the Preface to the *Metaphysical First Principles of Natural Science* (1786). The former features the closely related distinctions between the unification of representations in an individual consciousness and in consciousness in general, on the one hand, and between judgments of perception and judgments of experience, on the other. Perhaps its most important claim, however, since it is essential to understanding the argument of the Transcendental Deduction in the *Critique*, is that "[o]bjective validity and necessary universal validity (for everyone) are . . . interchangeable concepts" (Pro 4: 298$_{28-29}$; 93). In the note Kant responds to reservations with respect to the A-Deduction and its counterpart in the *Prolegomena* expressed by his supposed ally and initial commentator, J. G. Schultz, in the latter's review of a work critical of Kant by the Wolffian philosopher August Heinrich Ulrich and points ahead to the centrality to be given to the nature of judgment in the forthcoming B-Deduction.

Chapters 8 and 9 are devoted to the analysis of the two parts of the B-Deduction. As in my previous treatments of the topic, the emphasis is on Kant's claim that the two parts are intended as two steps in a single proof, rather than as either two distinct proofs or two formulations of a single argument.[7] Unlike my previous treatments,

---

[7] These are Allison (1983), 133–72 and (2004), 159–2001.

however, which largely ignored the A-Deduction, I here consider the relation between the two versions of the Deduction and the nature and the significance of the changes that Kant made. Whereas in the A-Deduction Kant was concerned from the beginning with the relation between the categories and what is given in perception in accordance with the forms of human sensibility, i.e., appearances in space and time, the B-Deduction adds an extra level of analysis that has no precise counterpart in the initial version. This analysis, which constitutes the first step in the two-step proof, abstracts from these forms of sensibility (on the premise that other forms are at least logically possible), in order to consider the a priori contribution of the understanding to cognition, much as in the Aesthetic Kant isolated sensibility in order to specify its a priori contribution. And it will be argued that what made such a procedure viable for Kant was his underlying assumption, which was the result of the "great light," that sensibility and understanding are two generically distinct cognitive powers, each with its own set of a priori forms. Since Kant regarded the human understanding as discursive, which means not only that cognition consists in the application of concepts but also that it requires data to which these concepts (including the categories) can be applied, he found it impossible to abstract completely from sensibility as the source of these data or the matter of cognition; but he also thought it possible to conduct this analysis on the minimalist assumption that some data are given, without considering how they are given, e.g., as in space and time.

The advantage of this approach is that, given the identification of thinking and judging, which follows from the discursivity thesis, it enabled Kant to link the categories directly to the very capacity to think, through their relation to the forms of judgment, thereby establishing their necessity for the thought of an object in general or as such (*Object überhaupt*). At the same time, however, it has a built-in limitation, since the conception of an object with which it is concerned is defined solely in terms of the requirements of the understanding, which are themselves defined in terms of the conditions of the unity of apperception, i.e., the possibility of the unification (synthesis or combination) of a cognizer's representations being accompanied by an identical "I think," it does not follow that appearances, considered qua given in accordance with our forms of sensibility, necessarily conform to the requirements of the understanding. Kant addresses this limitation in the second part of the B-Deduction, where he argues that the categories necessarily apply to whatever is perceived in accordance with our forms of sensibility.

The main point, however, is that it does not suffice to appeal to the *de facto* conformity of appearances to the requirements of the understanding, since Kant insists that what is needed is a demonstration of their *necessary* conformity. In other words, for Kant the accord of appearances with the requirements of the understanding cannot be considered a merely contingent matter, such as philosophers of Kant's time might attribute to a pre-established harmony and of our time to the process of natural selection or some naturalistic analogue thereof.[8] Moreover, we shall see that for Kant it would not be enough to maintain that this conformity is necessary merely in the hypothetical or conditional sense that it is only to the extent that it occurs that we can apply concepts (including the categories) to nature and have what counts as experience, i.e., empirical cognition. Although it is frequently claimed that this sense of necessity is all that Kant either needs or is entitled to, he maintains that it must be shown to be necessary in a stronger (albeit not logical) sense.

There are two reasons for Kant's insistence upon this necessity. One is obvious and often noted; viz., his underlying metametaphysical project, specifically his endeavor to ground the possibility of what he termed metaphysics "in its first part," in which the objects corresponding to a priori concepts can be given in experience (Bxviii–xix). Since this is a matter of accounting for the possibility of a priori cognition, it requires necessity and universality as the twin criteria of the a priori. And in order to account for this necessity Kant famously appeals to his "Copernican" and transcendentally idealistic thesis that the source of this necessity is the human mind and its scope is limited to objects as they appear under the forms of human sensibility. The other and less well-understood reason is to account for possibility of empirical cognition. At issue are the grounds for the attribution of objective validity to any empirical proposition, which, in Hume's terms, goes "beyond the present testimony of our senses or the records of our memory."[9] Expressed in more Kantian terms, to claim objective validity for such propositions is to claim that the connection of representations they contain hold not only for a particular cognizer at a certain time, but also for the same cognizer at other times and, indeed, for any cognizer, which is to say that, even though the propositions, as empirical, are contingent, their assertion involves an appeal to a kind of necessity.

In his initial presentation of the problem of accounting for this necessity in the introductory portion of the Transcendental Deduction Kant poses it as a worry that,

Appearances could . . . be so constituted that the understanding would not find them in accord with the conditions of its unity, and everything would then lie in such confusion that, e.g., in the succession of appearances nothing would offer itself that would furnish a rule of synthesis and thus correspond to the concept of cause and effect, so that this concept would therefore be entirely empty, nugatory, and without significance. Appearances would nonetheless offer objects to our intuition, for intuition by no means requires the functions of thinking.

(A90–91/B122–23)

I refer to this possibility as a specter because its realization would result in cognitive chaos, and I argue that the Transcendental Deduction can be regarded as Kant's attempt to exorcize it. Although this specter may call to mind the famous Cartesian

---

[8] The latter alternative is suggested by Harrison (1982), 223 and Westphal (1997), 153. It is also noted in passing by Stern (2000), 55.
[9] Hume (1999), 108.

specter that we are being systematically deceived by an evil genius, it is significantly different from it. Whereas the latter, which has its present-day counterpart in the worry that, for all we could know, we might be merely brains in vats, whose thought processes are controlled by a mad scientist, is at bottom a worry about the lack of correspondence between our experiences and a mind-independent reality; the Kantian specter concerns a worry about a cognitive fit between two species of representation. And while the problem in the Cartesian specter is that everything would appear to be exactly as if our experience were genuine, thereby making it impossible to determine the true state of affairs; in the Kantian specter the problem is precisely the opposite, since nothing would be recognizable and our experience would be nothing but what William James famously referred to as "one great blooming, buzzing confusion."[10] Kant does not deny the Cartesian problem, but he assigns its resolution to the Refutation of Idealism. The specter of a cognitive dissonance or lack of cognitive fit is reserved for the Transcendental Deduction, however, since it is directly concerned with the grounds of the possibility of the experience that we do have.

Although both versions of the Deduction are centrally concerned with eliminating this specter, it is more evident in the B-Deduction with its sharp division into two steps, the second of which is devoted to this task. Moreover, it is important to realize that the specter is in a sense a problem of Kant's own making, since it is a direct consequence of the way in which he separates the contributions to cognition of sensibility and understanding. Accordingly, it could not arise, at least not in this form, for either the Leibnizian rationalist, who considers sensible representations as merely obscure forms of what can be clearly and distinctly grasped by the intellect, or the Lockean empiricist, for whom all concepts are ultimately derivable from experience. Simply put, the problem is that Kant not only distinguishes sharply between these two faculties, but also insists that cognition requires their cooperation. And this, again, is clearly not something that would be required by either the Leibnizian rationalist or the Lockean empiricist because for them there is no need for any such "cooperation."

Since the reason why the non-conformity of the sensible with the intellectual conditions of cognition constitutes a specter is that empirical cognition requires their necessary conformity, it behooves us to determine the nature of this necessity. And while it is clear that it is not a logical necessity, since empirical propositions, which presuppose this conformity, can be denied without contradiction and the scenario that Kant describes is not logically impossible, it is far from evident how it should be positively characterized. Basing my analysis largely on Kant's claim in the *Prolegomena* that objective validity and necessary universality are interchangeable concepts, I argue that the kind of necessity that pertains to empirical propositions is normative.

---

[10] James (1890), 488.

In other words, to claim, for example, that ice turns from a liquid to a frozen state at 0 degrees Celsius is to claim not only that every time water is lowered to that temperature it will freeze, but also that everyone *ought* to concur with this proposition. Accordingly, a warrant is required for this epistemic ought, which in this case is provided by an empirical causal law. But following Hume, who in this respect is more a positive influence than an opponent, Kant cannot stop there and needs to supply a second-order warrant for relying upon the first-order warrant provided by empirical laws. For Kant this second-order warrant is conferred by the categories and securing their normative status, which would also eliminate the specter, is the task of the Transcendental Deduction.

Finally, this understanding of the purpose of the Deduction accords, with Henrich's well-known philological thesis that Kant's use of the term "deduction" was borrowed from the legal system of the Holy Roman Empire, where *Deduktionsschriften* were writings issued by the parties involved in legal disputes, most of which involved territorial claims.[11] In short, Kant understood by a deduction not a deductive argument, but, rather, an argument (of whatever form) that endeavors to justify a right to possess and use something, which in the case of the Transcendental Deduction is a set of pure concepts of the understanding or categories. Indeed, Kant himself makes this quite clear, when he writes: "Jurists, when they speak of entitlements and claims, distinguish in a legal matter between the question about what is lawful (*quid juris*) and that which concerns the fact (*quid facti*), and since they demand proof of both, they call the first, that which is to establish the entitlement or legal claim the *deduction*" (A84/B116).

Expressed in present-day philosophical parlance, Kant's Transcendental Deduction may be described as an endeavor to establish a "warranted assertability" with regard to a unique set of concepts, which determines the grounds and boundaries of their legitimate use. Although most of the difficulty concerns the first part of this endeavor, we shall see that these are complementary and equally essential sides of his project, because as a "critical" philosopher Kant regarded all such warrants as limited and was therefore concerned to establish the bounds as well as the right to use the pure concepts of the understanding. We shall further see that, in virtue of the underlying transcendental idealism, these tasks are inseparably linked; for, as Kant notes in the Schematism, "the schemata of sensibility [i.e., the sensible conditions under which the categories apply to appearances] first realize the categories, yet they likewise also restrict them, i.e., limit them to conditions that lie outside the understanding (namely, in sensibility)" (A146/B185–86). And, finally, in view of these and other considerations, it will be argued that the currently popular attempt to save the Transcendental Deduction or some reasonable facsimile thereof, by separating it from this idealism, is bound to fail.

---

[11] Henrich (1989a), esp. 30–40.

1

Kant's Analytic Metaphysics and Model of Cognition in the 1760s

This is the first of three chapters dealing with the development of Kant's thought during the "pre-critical" period insofar as it bears on the problematic of the Transcendental Deduction. The chapter is divided into two parts. The first is concerned with the works written in 1762 and 1763, the most important of which are: "Inquiry concerning the Distinctness of the Principles of Natural Theology and Morality," which is commonly referred to as the "Prize Essay," "An Attempt to Introduce the Concept of Negative Magnitudes into Philosophy," and *The Only Possible Basis for a Demonstration of the Existence of God* or, as it will here be called, the *Beweisgrund*.[1] After a brief discussion of Kant's announcement of proposed metaphysics lectures for the winter term of 1765–66, the remainder of the second part will be devoted to Kant's enigmatic *Dreams of a Spirit-Seer Elucidated by Dreams of Metaphysics* (1766).

I

A) *The Prize Essay*: This compact essay was composed in response to the essay contest proposed by the Berlin Royal Academy of Sciences for the year 1763 on the question:

whether the metaphysical truths in general, and the first principles of *Theologiae naturalis* and morality in particular, admit of distinct proofs to the same degree as geometrical proofs; and if they are not capable of such proofs, one wishes to know what the genuine nature of their certainty is, to what degree the said certainty can be brought, and whether this degree is sufficient for complete conviction.[2]

Kant's essay directly addresses the question posed and is based on a sharp distinction between the methods of mathematics and metaphysics, which determines the nature

---

[1] The term *Beweisgrund* is literally translated as "ground of proof," but is usually rendered as either "basis" or "argument." Of the two English translations, I am following Treash (1979), who renders it in the former manner rather than Walford (1992), who renders it in the latter.

[2] Walford (1992), lxii. Although Kant did not win the prize, which was awarded to Moses Mendelssohn, his essay was commended and published by the academy.

of the evidence and degree of certainty attainable in each science. The method of mathematics is synthetic, by which Kant meant that it begins with arbitrarily chosen definitions from which it deduces consequences by logical means. By contrast, the method of metaphysics and, more generally, of philosophy, which includes natural philosophy or physics, is analytic.[3] By the latter Kant understood the method of Newton, which begins with the observation of particular phenomena and strives to arrive inductively at general conclusions. For a practitioner of the analytic method definitions are a desideratum rather than a condition of explanatory success. As Kant puts it in a passage expressing the gist of his position:

> The true method of metaphysics is basically the same as that introduced by *Newton* into natural science...*Newton*'s method maintains that one ought, on the basis of certain experience and, if need be, with the help of geometry, to seek out the rules in accordance with which certain phenomena of nature occur. Even if one does not discover the fundamental principle of these occurrences in the bodies themselves, it is nonetheless certain that they operate in accordance with this law. Complex natural events are explained once it has been clearly shown how they are governed by these well-established rules. Likewise in metaphysics: by means of certain inner experience, that is to say, by means of an immediate and self-evident [*augenscheinliches*] consciousness, seek out those characteristic marks which are certainly to be found in the concept of any general property. And even if you are not acquainted with the complete essence of the thing, you can still safely employ those characteristic marks to infer a great deal from them about the thing in question.   (U 2: 286$_{7-21}$; 259)

What Kant says about Newton's method reflects his deep acquaintance with the latter's work. The basic point is that, in sharp contrast to mathematical reasoning, one begins with the observation of an occurrence, for example, a body in motion, and on the basis of repeated observations of similar occurrences, combined with relevant mathematical principles, arrives at rules or laws according to which the natural phenomena in question occur. Presumably alluding to Newton's notorious agnosticism regarding the cause of gravity, Kant emphasizes that the failure to find an ultimate explanation does not vitiate the genuineness of the explanation that has been found (the law of universal gravitation), which differs from the situation in mathematics or any bit of purely deductive reasoning, where the conclusion must be completely grounded in the premises.

  Given this, Kant's task is to show that the proper method in metaphysics is more akin to that of Newton than to the method of demonstration in mathematics. To this end, he introduces the conception of an "inner experience," which Kant regards as the metaphysician's counterpart to the observations of the Newtonian physicist. If one is to understand this, however, it is necessary to keep in mind that this inner experience should not be equated with introspection; for while this might yield an

---

[3] For a detailed account of the complex history of the distinction between the analytic and synthetic methods in both mathematics and in philosophy in the eighteenth century prior to Kant, see Tonelli (1976), 178–213.

empirical psychology, it could not provide the basis for metaphysics. Rather, as Kant's reference to an "immediate and self-evident consciousness" indicates, he understood the term as referring to an immediate insight into essential properties and relations, much like an Husserlian "*Wesenschau*" or, to use a loaded phrase for Kantians, an "intellectual intuition."[4]

Moreover, this appeal to a self-certifying intuition is not an isolated occurrence, which might be dismissed as an aberration or explained away as a careless and misleading formulation of what is at bottom an empiricistic thesis in the Lockean mold.[5] In fact, Kant makes basically the same point in somewhat different terms in his 1762 essay on the syllogism. After devoting the bulk of the essay to arguing for the logical thesis that a pure syllogism is possible only in the first of the traditional four figures, in his Concluding Reflection Kant abruptly shifts from logic to epistemology.[6] In an endeavor to distinguish between human and animal mentality, Kant there asserts that distinct concepts and with them genuine cognitions rest on the capacity to judge, which is a capacity that only rational beings possess.

In light of this, Kant states that the key to comprehending the difference between rational beings and those lacking reason lies in "understanding what the mysterious power is which makes judging possible." Although Kant does not venture a definitive explanation of this power, he suggests that his present opinion is that it is inner sense, characterized as the "faculty of making one's own representations the object of one's thought" (FS 2: 60_{13-15}; 104). Presumably, this inner sense, which Kant describes as a fundamental faculty belonging only to rational beings, is equivalent to the "inner experience" of the "Prize Essay."

Accordingly, the objects with which the analytic metaphysician is concerned are not the observed properties and behavior of natural phenomena, which constitute the given data and starting point for the physicist, but the concepts that are to be analyzed. In short, the analysis in which the metaphysician, unlike the physicist, engages is purely conceptual in nature. It consists in clarifying the analysanda by determining the characteristic marks that are already contained in them, albeit in a confused and indistinct manner, and it provides the basis for whatever valid inferences the metaphysician is able to draw from these concepts (U 2: 280_{14-15}; 252).

---

[4] What made the concept of an intellectual intuition problematic for Kant was the distinction between sensibility and understanding. But since this was a product of the "great light" of 1769, it presumably would not have seemed problematic to him at the time.

[5] An empiricist reading of Kant's account has been offered by de Vleeschauwer (1962), 33–7. This has been criticized, however, by Friedman, who warns against being misled by Kant's comments in his introduction that in accordance with the Newtonian method his treatise consists of "secure propositions of experience and the consequences immediately drawn therefrom" (U 2: 275_{17-18}). As Friedman, who also refers to the passage from *The False Subtlety*, noted by the propositions of inner experience Kant means "an immediately evident consciousness." See Friedman (1992a), 24, note 39.

[6] By a "pure syllogism" Kant understands one that is a product of only three propositions. This is contrasted with a "mixed syllogism," which is one that presupposes an additional immediate inference (based either on logical conversion or contraposition). See FS 2: 50_{11-19}.

Kant emphasizes that the process must eventually culminate in unanalyzable concepts and that the propositions based on such concepts are indemonstrable. But by appealing to a self-validating inner experience or inner sense, Kant contends that such propositions can nonetheless be accepted as certain and used as the basis for the demonstration of further propositions. As an illustration of this procedure, he cites the proposition: "all bodies must consist of simple substances" (U 2: 286_{27-8}; 259). Kant notes that the demonstration of this proposition, which he had already sketched at the end of the second section of the First Reflection in terms of the concept of substance (U 2: 279_{11-25}; 259), can dispense with the abstract concept of substance and refer instead merely to simple parts and that it does not require a prior definition of body. His present concern, however, is not with this demonstration itself, but its compatibility with the infinite divisibility of space, the certainty of which is demonstrated in geometry. This worry evidently arises from the fact that bodies occupy space, which Kant here regards as a self-evident intuition. The problem is that if bodies occupy space and space is infinitely divisible, it seems to follow that bodies must likewise be infinitely divisible and therefore cannot be composed of simple parts. Kant's resolution of this problem turns on his dynamical theory of matter, according to which the simple parts of a body, i.e., physical monads, occupy space in virtue of their possession of a repulsive force of impenetrability rather than their extension.

Since our concern here is with the structure of Kant's argument rather than its cogency, there is no need to subject it to further analysis.[7] What is of interest is the inclusion of premises based on a presumably self-evident intuition (bodies occupy space) and mathematics (space is infinitely divisible) in what is supposedly a bit of analytic metaphysics. But inasmuch as geometry is included only because this particular argument makes an essential reference to space and Kant is concerned with a method that supposedly applies to all branches of metaphysics, not simply a metaphysics of corporeal nature, the crucial point is the inclusion of purportedly indemonstrable though self-evident propositions.[8] Kant was, of course, well aware of this and notes that their presupposition occupies the place that definitions have in mathematics (U 2: 296_{3-6}; 269). Accordingly, a central concern of the essay is to justify the attribution of certainty to such propositions, despite their indemonstrability.

---

[7] Kant himself presents this as an illustration of the fruitfulness of the analytic method rather than as an actual demonstration. The latter is to be found in his *Physical Monadology* of 1756. For analyses of this argument, see Friedman (1992a), 5–11 and 23–4 and Schönfeld (2000), 161–79. It should also be noted that the issue reappeared in its "critical" form in the Second Antinomy.

[8] As examples of metaphysical claims grounded in indemonstrable but self-evident premises, which do not involve an appeal to mathematics, Kant cites the proposition that every appetite presupposes the representation of the object of the appetite (U 2: 284_{19-20}) and the fundamental principles of natural theology (U 2: 296–7).

To this end, Kant follows Crusius in distinguishing between formal and material principles of cognition and identifies the latter with these indemonstrable yet certain propositions to which he assigns two roles: (1) providing the initial data for thought (its material or propositional content) and (2) serving as vehicles for drawing inferences from one proposition to another that does not follow immediately from it. At the same time, however, Kant's view of the formal principles marks a sharp break with the views of both the Wolffians and Crusius. And while he incorporates elements of the latter's account of material principles he does not do so uncritically.

Crusius agrees with the Wolffians in regarding the principle of contradiction as the sole *formal* principle; though because of his distinction between formal and material principles he assigns considerably less significant epistemic weight to it. Kant, by contrast, held that there are two logically distinct and independent formal principles: identity and contradiction.[9] The former is the principle of affirmative judgments and it maintains that the judgment is true if the predicate is *identical* with the subject.[10] The latter is the principle of negative judgments and it states that a judgment is true if the affirmation of the predicate *contradicts* the subject (U 2: 294_{17-24}; 268). Accordingly, Kant explicitly rejects the view that the latter is the first principle of all truths, demoting it to the apparently secondary status of being merely the first principle of negative truths (U 2: 294_{26-8}; 268).

Far from being a mere detail, Kant's insistence that identity and contradiction are independent formal principles, each governing one of the two fundamental types of proposition, is an essential ingredient in his epistemology at the time. This is because Kant effectively maintains that these principles are not merely necessary but sufficient marks of truth. Indeed, Kant is completely unambiguous on this point, insisting that they provide the truth conditions of not only demonstrable, but also indemonstrable propositions. As he puts it:

Any proposition is indemonstrable...if it is immediately thought under one of these two supreme principles and if it cannot be thought in any other way. In other words, any proposition is indemonstrable if either the identity or contradiction is to be found immediately

---

[9] For the Wolffians, the principle of contradiction was not only the supreme logical principle, but also the fundamental ontological principle. Herder cites Kant as noting that for Baumgarten the principle of identity can be derived from the principle of contradiction (MH 28: 11). By contrast, Crusius held that the principle of contradiction is an identical proposition and therefore incapable of itself proving anything (1747), 467.

[10] Kant does not mean by this that the predicate must be literally identical with (the very same thing as) the subject, since that would make every true affirmative judgment a tautology. Rather, he is affirming the familiar Leibnizian view that the predicate must be in the subject, which Kant will later claim applies only to analytic judgments. At the time, Kant makes the point by distinguishing between total and partial identity (MH 28: 158). Although this distinction is already found in Baumgarten, according to Herder's transcript, Kant claimed that Baumgarten used the principle of identity to express the former more than the latter (MH 28: 11).

in the concepts, and the identity and the contradiction cannot or may not be understood through analysis by means of intermediate characteristic marks.   (U 2: 294_{28-33}; 268)[11]

This explains why Kant could place such confidence in these indemonstrable propositions; for like the demonstrable ones, they are grounded in the principles of identity and contradiction. The only difference is that in the one case the identity or contradiction is recognized immediately, whereas in the other this recognition requires an intermediate concept through which the logical relation of the other concepts to each other (identity or contradiction) can be cognized through a syllogism (U 2: 295_{16-18}; 268–9).

This also shows, however, that despite his disagreement with the Wolffians regarding the supreme status of the principle of contradiction, Kant was still committed to the analytic model of cognition broadly construed. In other words, while appealing to the analytic method as the model for metaphysics and agreeing with Crusius regarding the importance of indemonstrable propositions and the need to separate certainty from demonstrability, Kant retained an essential ingredient of the Wolffian position.

Moreover, because of this Kant differed with Crusius, who was the more consistent anti-Wolffian, on two fundamental points.[12] First, he finds fault with a number of the indemonstrable propositions for which Crusius claims certainty, including "What I cannot think as existing has never existed" and the notorious "All things must be somewhere and somewhen" (U 2: 294_{2-4}; 268).[13] Whatever epistemic credentials such propositions might possess, they cannot be seen as immediately grounded in either the principle of identity or contradiction. Second, he rejects Crusius' candidate for the supreme material rule governing all cognition, namely, "[W]hat I cannot think as other than true is true" (U 2: 294_2; 268).[14] As Kant points out, it is easy to see

---

[11]   See also MH 28: 158.

[12]   Herder's transcript of Kant's metaphysics lectures includes a comparative analysis of what Kant takes to be the respective strengths and weaknesses of the Wolffian and Crusian positions, which partly corresponds to his assessments in the published writings of the time. Wolff is criticized for his failure to recognize any unanalyzable (*unausflöslichen*) concepts and his view that all can be defined; his failure to recognize many first material principles and his consequent attempt to demonstrate everything in metaphysics on the basis of the law of contradiction; while, somewhat incongruously, he is credited merely with sharpening our endeavors to be able to define. By contrast, Crusius is credited with recognizing unanalyzable concepts and their natural clarity, as well as the existence of numerous fundamental material principles, which are indemonstrable and, accordingly, cannot be derived from the principle of contradiction. But in contrast to what we shall see below, Crusius is there criticized only for his inadequate account of the first principles of mathematics. See MH 28: 156–7.

[13]   See Crusius (1747), 468–9. Among the indemonstrable yet certain propositions that Crusius there mentions are: "Each and every force is in a subject;" "Everything that originates, originates from a sufficient cause;" "Everything, whose not being can be thought has its cause and came into being at one time;" "each and every substance is somewhere;" "Everything that is, is at some time;" "two matters cannot be entirely in one place at the same time;" and "A point of a body cannot be both red and green at the same time."

[14]   See Crusius (1747), 465–6. Crusius' full formulation of his principle is: "that which *we cannot think as other than true is true*, and what we *absolutely cannot think at all, or cannot think as other than false is false*." For Crusius this amounts to an assertion of the reliability of the human understanding, which is itself assured by God.

that this proposition cannot serve as the ground of truth, since it amounts to saying that there is no ground of truth other than a feeling of conviction, which is a matter of psychology (U 2: 295_{27-35}; 269).[15] And instead of Crusius' supreme material principle, Kant affirms the reality of innumerable indemonstrable yet certain propositions, each of which can serve as a material principle, insofar as it provides the basis for the demonstration of other propositions (U2: 295_{3-5}; 268).[16] Accordingly, rather than postulating a supreme material principle or set thereof, Kant may be said to have functionalized the conception of such a principle by characterizing it in terms of what it does, namely, to provide a basis for the demonstration of other propositions, a move which allows him to recognize the existence and importance of material principles without abandoning the analytic model of cognition.[17]

B) *Negative Magnitudes*: Although published before the *Prize Essay*, this piece was evidently written after it and marks a significant development of the line of thought sketched in the latter.[18] Its continuity with the *Prize Essay* is two-fold. First, it applies the analytic method as specified in that work to a specific concept; viz., real opposition, which is mathematically expressed as the contrast between positive and negative magnitudes or quantities. Second, it continues to assume the analytic model of cognition in a modified form, according to which all true propositions, even indemonstrable ones, are ultimately grounded in either the principle of identity or contradiction. Its development beyond the standpoint of the *Prize Essay* consists in the fact that the analysis of the concept of a real (as opposed to a logical) opposition leads to that of a real (as opposed to a logical) ground, which poses a fresh and potentially fatal challenge to this model. In fact, the manifest incompatibility of these real–logical contrasts with the analytical model, according to which all grounds must be regarded as logical, has led some interpreters to maintain that Kant had here already arrived at the distinction between analytic and synthetic judgments, if not the terminology in which it was later expressed.[19] But inasmuch as he still assumes the analytic model of cognition this cannot be correct. As we shall see, it is rather that Kant had arrived at the point from which, when viewed retrospectively,

[15] Kant advances similar criticisms of Crusian epistemology in R4275 17: 492; R4446 17: 554; and JL 9: 21. See also Beck (1969a), 397, note 8.

[16] As an example of such a principle Kant cites: "a body is compound" (U 2 294_{36}; 268). This principle is material rather than formal, since it applies to the nature of body; and while itself indemonstrable, it provides the basis for inferring that bodies are divisible.

[17] As Laywine noted in her comments on an earlier version of this chapter, a curious omission in the *Prize Essay* is any reference to the principle of sufficient reason, which as "the principle of determining reason" played a significant role in the *Nova dilucidatio* and again in the *Beweisgrund*. Her explanation, with which I agree, is that at the time Kant still thought that the principle of sufficient reason could be derived from the principle of contradiction, which implies that it is not a material principle in the sense in which Kant here understood the notion. This also shows the depth of his commitment to the Wolffian analytic model of cognition.

[18] *Negative Magnitudes* was both written and published in 1763, whereas the *Prize Essay*, though only published in 1764, had been completed by the end of 1762. See Walford (1992), lxi.

[19] See Vaihinger (1881), 270 and Henrich (1967), 34–5.

drawing this distinction is precisely the move that is required; though he had not yet realized this.

Whereas in the *Prize Essay* Kant had begun by distinguishing sharply between the methods of mathematics and philosophy, he here commences with a discussion of the possible use of mathematics for philosophy. He suggests that the latter has two possible uses in philosophy: to provide either a method to be imitated or an application of some of its concepts and doctrines. After abruptly rejecting the former for the reasons given in the *Prize Essay*, Kant affirms the latter. And the concept he chose to illustrate this fruitfulness is that of a negative magnitude, which he notes refers not to the negation of magnitude but to something positive in itself, though opposed to the positive magnitude (NG 2: 169$_{17-20}$; 209).

The concept in which Kant is really interested, however, is not the mathematical concept of negative magnitudes or quantities, but its philosophical counterpart: that of a real opposition, which he contrasts with a merely logical opposition. The latter arises when something is simultaneously affirmed and denied of the same thing. Such an opposition is ruled out by the principle of contradiction and its result Kant notes is "*nothing at all (nihil negativum irrepraesentabile)*" (NG 2: 171$_{9-10}$; 211). By contrast, a real opposition occurs when two non-contradictory predicates of a thing are opposed to each other. Although the opposing predicates cancel each other out, in this case the result is something cognizable (*cogitabile*) (NG 2: 171$_{15-18}$; 211). As an example of the latter, Kant cites the opposition between the moving force of a body in one direction and an equal tendency of the same body in the opposite direction. Since these two forces cancel each other out, the body remains at rest; but, unlike a logical opposition, both predicates can be attributed to the body at the same time without any contradiction.

In explicating this concept, Kant offers two rules regarding the determination of a real opposition (*Realentgegensetzung*) or repugnancy, which he treats as equivalent. Although he describes the second rule merely as the reverse of the first (NG 2: 177$_9$; 217), they actually specify respectively the necessary and a sufficient condition of such an opposition. The first rule holds that "A real repugnancy only occurs where there are two things, *as positive grounds*, and where one of them cancels the consequence of the other" (NG 2: 175$_{34-5}$; 215). In explaining this rule, Kant stipulates four conditions of its application: (1) the conflicting determinations must exist in the same subject; (2) the opposed determinations cannot be contradictories; (3) a determination can only negate what is posited in the other; (4) the two determinations cannot both be negative. In sum, a real opposition requires that "the two predicates must both be positive, but positive in such a way that, when they are combined, there is a reciprocal cancellation of the consequences in the same subject" (NG 2: 176$_{13-15}$; 216).

According to the second rule, "wherever there is a positive ground and the consequence is nonetheless zero then there is a real opposition" (NG 2: 177$_{10-11}$; 217).

Although Kant is hardly clear on the matter, the latter rule states merely a sufficient condition of a real opposition, because (as we learn later) there can be a real opposition when the opposing predicates do not *completely* cancel each other out. For example, a balance scale with a one-pound weight placed at one end and a two-pound weight on the other involves a real opposition, which, assuming that the arms are of equal length and the balance is supported from above, does not leave the scale in the same position as it was before adding the weights.

Kant concludes the first part of the essay by using the conception of a real opposition to distinguish two kinds of negation. One, which results from a real opposition, is a deprivation (*Beraubung*) (*privatio*); the other, which does not, is a lack or deficiency (*Mangel*) (*defectus, absentia*) (NG 2: 177_{27}–8_1; 217). This distinction turns out to be of considerable import, because Kant notes that its neglect has led to disastrous consequences, perhaps the most notable of which is the view of evil as consisting simply in a deficiency of goodness (a privation) rather than as a positive reality opposed to the good (NG 2: 182_{12-21}; 221).

The second part of the essay consists mainly of a series of examples of real opposition, of which Kant's favorite seems to be the conflict between attractive and repulsive force. He characterizes the latter as *"negative attraction,"* in order to underscore the fact that it is a real force in its own right and is only characterized in negative terms when contrasted with attraction (NG 2: 179_{24}; 218). In addition, Kant appeals to some other obvious examples from natural science, such as positive and negative electricity and magnetism, which were topics of great interest at the time. Kant does not, however, limit himself to examples from natural science; rather, he cites examples from areas as diverse as psychology, aesthetics, and ethics. Thus, in contrasting pleasure and displeasure, he insists that the latter is not merely a lack or deficiency of pleasure, but a reality in its own right, which he terms *"negative pleasure"* (NG 2: 180_{14}; 219). Similarly, ugliness is not simply a lack of beauty, which would make them contradictory or logical opposites, but a contrasting reality or *"negative beauty"* (NG 2: 182_{4-5}; 221). Finally, Kant notes the usefulness of the notion of real opposition in practical philosophy, for example, with regard to the concept of vice, which is quite distinct from a mere lack of virtue and which he terms *"negative virtue"* (NG 2: 182_{31}; 221).

Kant's aim in the third part is to spell out the philosophical import of the conception of a real opposition, which, following the analytic method, he does by introducing the concept of a real ground. The point is that, since the elements constituting a real opposition are themselves realities, they must have a real ground or cause, which cannot be claimed to be a mere lack. Moreover, in view of his emphasis on the positive or real nature of certain negations, according to which *"every passing-away is a negative coming-to be"* (NG 2: 190_{13}; 228), Kant further insists that a real ground is just as necessary to cancel the existence of something existing as it is to bring into existence something that does not yet exist (NG 2: 190_{13-15}; 228). In the language of the First Analogy, both a coming-to-be and a passing-away are alterations in the state of a substance that endures throughout the change of state.[20] Accordingly, both require a real ground. But whereas in the *Critique* Kant limited this thesis regarding alterations to the physical world, he here insists that it applies to both the physical and the mental domains. The only differences are that in the former the real ground of the alteration is external and in the latter internal and that its applicability in the former is much more evident than in the latter. As Kant puts it,

[I]n what concerns the *cancellation* of an existing *something*, there can be no difference between the accidents of mental natures and the effects of operative forces in the physical world... [A]n inner accident, a thought of the soul, cannot cease to be without a truly active power of exactly the *self-same* thinking subject. The difference here only relates to the different laws governing the two types of being; for the state of matter can only ever be changed by means of an *external cause*, whereas the state of the mind can also be changed by means of an *internal cause*.   (NG 2: 191$_{29}$–2$_4$; 229)

In addition to supplying the usual plethora of examples of this principle, which are intended to illustrate its usefulness in virtually all branches of philosophy, Kant further complicates matters by introducing a modal consideration; claiming that the necessity of a real ground applies to *possible* as well as to *actual* real oppositions. According to Kant, both types of opposition are real in the sense of being distinct from a merely logical opposition and he notes that "both of them are constantly employed in mathematics, and they both deserve to be employed in philosophy as well" (NG 2: 193$_{26}$–$_9$; 231). To cite his own example, two bodies that are moving away from each other along a straight line with equal force (such that one is the negative of the other) are in a potential real opposition, because if either of these bodies were to collide with a body moving in the same direction as the other, it would cancel as much force in it as exists in the other body (NG 194$_{29}$–5$_2$; 232). But, again, Kant is not concerned merely with the application of this modalized conception to physical forces and he devotes the remainder of the section to a consideration of all of the grounds of real opposition in the world. Moreover, in so doing, he formulates two propositions regarding the calculation of the sum of real changes (both positive and negative) and of the real grounds of these changes, the aim of which is to suggest that, if calculated in the way he suggests (by adding together the positive and the negative changes), both the changes and the conflicting grounds would cancel each other out, providing an equilibrium (between action and reaction) in the one case and a sum of positive and negative grounds equal to zero in the other.[21]

  The most important part of this essay, however, is the General Remark, which functions as an appendix to the third part; for it is here that Kant poses the question that arises naturally from his thesis that every real opposition presupposes a real

---

[20] See A177–8/B230–1. For my analysis of this thesis, see Allison (2004, 239–45).
[21] The first proposition is at NG 2: 194$_{19}$–$_{23}$; 232 and the second at NG 2: 197$_6$–$_9$; 234.

ground or cause: "How am I to understand the **fact that, because something is, something else is?**" (NG 2: 202_{20-1}; 239). As Kant points out, the problem arises because, unlike the logical relation between ground and consequent, the real relation cannot be based on the principle of identity, which is to say that it is not a matter of logical entailment. Although Kant's way of posing the problem is reminiscent of Hume, it is not necessary to assume the latter's influence at this point, since the problem can be seen as arising internally to Kant's own thought. Indeed, it becomes evident as soon as one distinguishes between a logical and a real ground. And Kant did not need Hume for this, since the distinction is also found in Crusius.[22]

Kant also criticizes Crusius in the General Remark, however, as he had likewise done in the *Prize Essay*. Kant's criticism turns on the fact that his distinction between the two types of ground is not precisely the same as Crusius'.[23] Thus, while it is again clear that Crusius exercised an important influence on Kant, it did not lead him to adopt the Crusian view whole cloth. The key point is that Crusius distinguished between an ideal (rather than a logical) and a real ground and understood by the former a ground of cognition, which, as Kant notes, is significantly different from his own distinction since, as a ground of cognition, an ideal ground can also be a real ground, which cannot be said of a Kantian logical ground (NG 2: 203_{10-15}; 240).[24]

This serves, however, to sharpen the problem rather than to resolve it; for it now seems that a real opposition is itself inexplicable. Indeed, Kant himself gives expression to the apparent *cul de sac* to which his analysis leads by reformulating the problem with which the General Remark began in its negative form, namely, to explain "how it is that, **because something is, something else is cancelled**, and whether we can say anything more than . . . it simply does not take place in virtue of the law of contradiction" (NG 2: 203_{32-7}; 241). Kant acknowledges having reflected on the question and issues a promissory note to provide one day a detailed account of the fruit of his reflections. But rather than simply leaving the reader completely in the dark regarding the direction of his thought, Kant indicates one of his conclusions: "[T]he relation of a real ground to something, which is either posited or cancelled by it, cannot be expressed by a judgment; it can only be expressed by a concept. That concept can probably be reduced through analysis to simple concepts of real grounds, the relation of which to their consequences cannot be rendered distinct at all" (NG 2: 204_{2-8}; 241).[25] Although it is difficult to determine exactly what Kant had in mind with this hermetic claim, which is followed by a challenge to philosophers to see if

---

[22] See de Vleeschauwer (1934), 111; (1962), 28–9; Beck (1969a), 464–5; (1978), 101–10); and Beiser (1992), 55. It is evident, however, that Hume did become important to Kant by 1766.

[23] Kant had already discussed Crusius' distinction between various types of ground in ND 1: 398; 20, which was written in 1755.

[24] See Crusius (1745), 55 and (1747), 421–3. In both places Crusius insists on the point to which Kant objects; viz., that a real ground can also be an ideal ground (if it is the source of the cognition of its consequence); but he notes that this is not always the case.

[25] Kant makes the same point in MH 28: 24 and R3755 17: 283.

their methods allow for better answers to such enigmatic problems, I believe it is best seen as a last-ditch attempt to deal with the concept of a real ground within the framework of the analytic model of cognition.[26] It is evident the real ground relation cannot be expressed by a judgment; since on this model all judgments are grounded in either the principle of identity or contradiction, there is no place within the conception of judgment to draw a distinction between a real and a merely logical ground. And since the only other element of cognition that this model recognizes is the concept, it follows that the notion of a real ground must find its explication here. This much seems relatively clear. The question concerns how Kant at the time thought that the matter might be dealt with successfully in terms of the theory of concepts associated with the analytic model. And Kant's seemingly tentative suggestion that "The concept [of a real ground] can probably be reduced through analysis to simple concepts of real grounds, the relation of which to their consequences cannot be rendered distinct at all" does not immediately appear to be helpful.

Nevertheless, I think it possible to make some headway in determining what Kant was getting at here by considering the nature of concepts according to the analytic model and the similarities between the concept of a real ground and certain other concepts that Kant appears to have regarded as in some ways analogous it. According to this model, there are two fundamentally different types of concept: those that are simple in the sense of being unanalyzable and those that are analyzable; though the situation is further complicated by the fact that different concepts are subject to different degrees of analysis. Moreover, in the "Prize Essay," where he does not deal explicitly with the concept of a real ground, among the class of unanalyzable concepts Kant cites "being next to" and "being after."[27] Assuming that Kant regarded these as analogs to the concept of a real ground and noting that, as concepts, they are all two-place predicates, the suggestion is that he may have thought that the concept of a real ground could in some way be explicated, though not strictly speaking analyzed, by a comparison with them.[28] The idea is that just as one might maintain that "being next to" or "before" could be explicated as being next to or before x, y, z, so the general concept or predicate "being the real ground of" could be explicated as being the real

[26] de Vleeschauwer characterizes Kant's claim as "enigmatic" and "a veritable crux for the commentators" (1962), 32.

[27] See U 2: 280$_{21-2}$; 252. Kant also includes "representation" as an example of such a concept. Admittedly, in this passage Kant says that these concepts are "scarcely capable of analysis at all" (*beinahe gar nicht aufgelöset werden können*), which might suggest that he is including them among concepts that are capable of some (minimal) analysis rather than regarding them as fully unanalyzable. But I believe that the heading of the section in which Kant introduces these examples ("In Mathematics, Unanalysable Concepts and Indemonstrable Propositions are Few in Number, whereas in Philosophy they are Innumerable") indicates that he considered them unanalyzable. Moreover, in Herder's transcript of Kant's metaphysics lectures he is quite explicit on the matter, referring to "being next to another" and "being after another," as well "being through another," which is presumably equivalent to having a real ground in another, as unanalyzable concepts (MH 28: 158).

[28] Evidence for the supposition that Kant held to such a view at the time is provided by the Herder transcript of Kant's metaphysics lectures. See the preceding note.

ground of x, y, z, etc. Otherwise expressed, it is by recognizing this relation as instantiated in particular cases that we come to understand it, which therefore serves as a surrogate for an analysis.

The above is intended as a somewhat speculative account of what Kant may have thought at the time, but it should in no way be regarded as an attempt to defend the view attributed to him or anything like it. Apart from the endeavor to shed some light on what Kant actually says at the end of *Negative Magnitudes*, the intent is to underscore the tension between the analytic model of cognition and the concept of a real ground. That Kant was aware of this tension is evident from his account and viewed from our vantage point it is easy to see that what is required is the distinction between analytic and synthetic judgments. But, again, contrary to those who see here the origins of the analytic–synthetic distinction, I take the way in which he attempts to deal with the concept of a real ground as a strong indication that he had not yet arrived at this crucial distinction.[29]

C) *The Beweisgrund*: Whereas the *Prize Essay* is a programmatic piece, setting forth the Newtonian methodology that Kant used to construct his analytic metaphysics and *Negative Magnitudes* contains an application of this method to the concept of a real opposition, *Beweisgrund* is a treatise in which this method is used for the construction of a systematic account in which a mechanistic view of nature is grounded in a conception of God as an absolutely necessary being. Our concern with this work, however, will be limited to the first of its three parts, which gives the work its title. And, in order to avoid lengthy digressions, the focus will be on Kant's treatment of the modal concepts of possibility, existence, and necessary existence, since this bears directly on our present concerns.[30]

Kant makes clear in his conclusion to the first part that the argument is based merely on the fact that something is possible and it turns on "the internal characteristic mark of absolute necessity" (EMB 2: 91_{4-8}; 135). Presumably, the former is one of those indemonstrable, yet certain, propositions, while the latter is a piece of conceptual analysis. The actual starting point of Kant's argument, however, is an analysis of the concept of existence. Although Kant emphasizes that for ordinary purposes there is no need for such an analysis, since we all understand what it means to affirm or deny that

---

[29] Since Henrich provides essentially the same analysis of Kant's claim (1967), 32–3, I find it strange that he also claims that Kant was in possession of the distinction between analytic and synthetic judgments at the time.

[30] The second two parts are somewhat loosely connected with the first and are largely concerned with a revised version of physico-theology, which supposedly makes it possible to account for the order of nature without, like the traditional version, having to rely totally on the notion of design. To this end, Kant uses the conception of God as the ground of possibility established in the first part as the basis for his revised physico-theology. This enables him to argue that a mechanistic order is grounded in the very possibility of things, which is an idea that Kant initially expressed in his cosmogonical work the *Universal Natural History* (1755). Moreover, the seventh reflection of the third part of the *Beweisgrund* contains a condensed version of the cosmogony developed in the earlier work.

something exists, he thinks that one is required for philosophical purposes, insofar as one is concerned with the concepts of absolutely necessary and contingent existence.

Nevertheless, this analysis turns out to be relatively meager and does not amount to anything like a definition (*Erklärung*), which would require a complete analysis of the concept.[31] This is because Kant includes existence among those concepts that are "almost unanalyzable" in virtue of their simplicity. Kant characterizes such concepts as those in which "the characteristic marks are only to a very small degree clearer and simpler than the thing itself" (EMB 2: 73_{36}–4_1; 119). This analysis consists of two steps: first Kant tells us what the concept is not, namely, a predicate, and then he specifies what it is, namely, the "absolute positing [*Position*] of a thing" (EMB 2: 73_{20}; 119).[32]

Save for drawing an explicit distinction between a logical and a real predicate or determination of a thing, Kant's argument that "existence" is not a predicate is identical to the one in the *Critique*.[33] In both texts a real predicate is a determination (*Bestimmung*) of the thing of which it is predicated, i.e., some property or relation that is attributed to a thing. Although Kant consistently denied that "existence" is a predicate *in this sense*, he also recognized that it can be predicated of objects in the sense that existential judgments are informative. In view of the purpose to which his analysis is put, Kant connects the notion of a (real) predicate or determination with the conception of possibility, understood in terms of the complete concept that the divine intellect would have of a thing qua possible. The basic idea is that this concept contains all the properties that could be predicated of a thing if it were actual, so that its actualization would not add any further determination.[34]

As in the *Critique*, the upshot of the matter is that, if one wants to determine whether something exists, one should not consult the concept of that thing. Instead, in the case of an empirical concept (Kant's example is that of a sea unicorn or narwal) one should look to experience to see if there is an entity to which the predicate contained in the concept applies. And, on the basis of this, Kant recommends a reformulation of existential claims, which is designed to avoid mistakenly taking existence as a predicate or determination. Thus, rather than saying that "A sea unicorn is an existent animal" one should say that "The predicates, which I think collectively when I think of a sea unicorn, attach to a certain existent sea animal" (EMB 2: 73_{5-8}; 118). Although Kant does not present this as a proposal for the reformation of ordinary language, since for everyday purposes the usual way of

---

[31]   For an account of Kant's view on definitions see Beck (1965b), 61–75.

[32]   Kant uses two terms (*Position* and *Setzung*), which he treats as equivalent and which can be rendered in English as "positing." In contrast to "existence" Kant characterizes "positing" as perfectly simple and therefore incapable of any analysis. He also equates it with the concept of "being as such" (*sein überhaupt*) (EMB 2: 73_{24-5}). This suggests a distinction between "existence" (*Dasein*) and "being" (*Sein*), which to my knowledge Kant failed to develop.

[33]   See A598/B624.

[34]   The point is precisely the same as Kant makes in the *Critique* with his famous discussion of the difference between a hundred real and the same number of imaginary thalers at A599/B627.

speaking about existence is perfectly acceptable, he does think it necessary when philosophers are concerned with topics such as the existence of God.

Inasmuch as he regards the concept of existence as *almost* unanalyzable, Kant admits that his positive characterization of existence as "the absolute positing of a thing" is not very informative. Nevertheless, he insists that it does serve to distinguish it from ordinary concepts. The key is the distinction between an absolute and a relative positing. The latter corresponds to what we understand by predication, i.e., the attribution (or denial) of a property to an entity. Such positing is relative in the sense that it occurs in relation to an entity the existence (actual or possible) of which is already assumed. As Kant notes, it is this sense of positing that is expressed by the copula "is." Correlatively, an absolute positing is one that is not relative in this sense, but, rather, concerns the claim (or denial) that the predicates which determine the concept of an entity are collectively instantiated. Whereas the former involves the copulative use of "is," the latter involves its existential use.

The denial that "existence" is a predicate naturally gives rise to the question of whether it is correct to say that there is more in existence than in mere possibility, which Kant addresses by drawing two overlapping distinctions. The first is between *what* is posited and *how* it is posited (EMB 2: 75_{14}; 120). The second is between positing *in* and positing *through* (EMB 2: 75_{27-30}; 121). Although there is no difference in what is posited in an existent or in a merely possible thing, there is one in the manner in which it is posited and this is equivalent to the difference between a relative and an absolute positing. The former is a positing *in*, since what is posited is included in the concept of an entity as a determination. The latter is a positing *through*, since it is an act through which the existence (or non-existence) of an entity corresponding to the concept is posited.[35] Accordingly, Kant can say that there is more in the positing of existence, than in mere possibility, without acknowledging that this more consists in an additional predicate or determination.[36]

Kant's distinction between different types of positing not only clears the decks for his positive argument by undermining the classical Anselmian-Cartesian version of the ontological argument, it also provides the basis for his own version of the argument, which turns on the necessity of the absolute positing of an *ens realissimum*. The argument amounts to a reflection on the conditions of the possibility of possibility. Although Kant characterizes the sense of possibility with which he is concerned as "internal [*innern*] possibility," by which he understands lack of

---

[35] Although Kant here consistently characterizes positing of both types in positive terms, it seems evident from the account in *Negative Magnitudes* that he regarded his account as applying to negative positings (the denial of a property or existence) as well.

[36] This provides the basis for Kant's critique of the treatment of the concept of existence in Wolff and Baumgarten. As Kant notes (EMB 2: 76; 121), Wolff defines existence as "a completion of possibility," while Baumgarten introduces the concept of "a thoroughgoing internal determination" and maintains that this is what distinguishes the existent from the merely possible. Although Kant offers a further objection based on the law-excluded middle, his main objection to both of these analyses is that they end up treating "existence" as a predicate or determination.

contradiction, the fact that in the heading of the second reflection he specifies that his concern is with this sense of possibility "insofar as it presupposes existence" (EMB 2: 77_{6-7}; 122) indicates that his interest is not in logic per se but ontology. Moreover, this becomes clear with Kant's introduction of a distinction between two elements of this possibility: a formal element and a material one.

The formal element is conceivability or lack of contradiction and whatever violates this condition is deemed "absolutely impossible" (EMB 2: 77_{22-3}; 123). Kant's main concern, however, is with the material element, which he also calls the "real element" in possibility and which he regards as a condition of the possibility of the former. His point is simply that a contradiction presupposes something to contradict. For example, the proposition that a quadrangular triangle exists (or is possible) is ruled out on the grounds of its inconceivability. But the very possibility of such a contradiction presupposes that there is some datum or material to contradict, which in this case is the concept of a triangle.

Given this distinction, Kant proceeds to determine what must be presupposed, if there is to be the required material element. The argument falls into two parts, which constitute the subject matter of the remainder of the second reflection and the bulk of the third. Together they purport to show that possibility presupposes the necessary existence of something as its material or real ground and the identification of the latter with the *ens realissimum*. Kant begins by asserting that the inner possibility (conceivability) of all things presupposes that something or other (*irgend ein Dasein*) exists (EMB 2: 78_{8-9}; 123). Although this may appear to be an extremely weak claim, since it leaves it completely open what this something (or somethings) must be, its actual strength is a function of how one takes the expression "all things" (*alle Dinge*). If it is taken to refer to each and every thing taken individually, it is indeed weak; for it then claims merely that the possibility of each and every thing presupposes something existent, which one could hardly deny, if one accepts Kant's thesis that possibility has a material as well as a formal condition. But if, as seems to be the case, it refers not merely to things taken individually (each and every thing), but also (and primarily) to all things taken collectively, it is quite robust; for it is then claiming that there is a ground (or grounds) of all things considered as a totality.[37] Moreover, it is evident that only the stronger claim has any chance of leading to an affirmation of the existence of an *ens realissimum*.

It is also evident that if it is to have any hope of success, the argument must rule out the possibility that nothing exists, since in that case nothing would be possible. Kant's argument for this is exceedingly cryptic and appears to turn on an analysis of the expression "absolute impossibility," which he claims to be synonymous with "that by means of which all possibility is cancelled" (EMB 2: 79_{3-4}; 124). As Kant points out, whatever is self-contradictory fits this description; but so does whatever cancels

---

[37] For justification for taking it in the latter sense, see EMB 2: 79_{20-2}; 124.

the material condition of all possibility. And since possibility presupposes existence as its material condition, it follows that it is absolutely impossible that nothing at all should exist (EMB 2: 79_{14-15}; 124).

Assuming the absolute impossibility of nothing existing, Kant attempts to explain the connection between the necessarily presupposed actual existent (or existents) and the possible. He claims that there are two alternatives: "*All possibility is given in something actual [Wirklichem] either as a determination existing within it or as a consequence arising from it*" (EMB 2: 279_{16-18}; 124).[38] Kant admits that his account is not a model of clarity and the source of the difficulty seems to lie primarily in the fact that these alternatives refer to the relation between possibilities and the central conception of an *ens realissimum*, which he is not yet prepared to introduce. Instead, Kant simply stipulates that the actual existent (or existents), through which the internal possibility (conceivability) of other actual existents is given, is to be characterized as "the first real ground of this absolute possibility," just as the principle of contradiction is its first logical ground (EMB 2: 79_{31-4}; 125).

Although Kant had earlier introduced the conception of an absolute *impossibility*, this is the first mention of an absolute *possibility* and he leaves it unexplained. But inasmuch as he has told us that by the former he understands that by which all possibility is cancelled, it seems reasonable to assume that Kant understands by the latter that by means of which all possibility is sustained, which is to say that it is the first real ground referred to previously.[39] In view of this, one would expect Kant to specify the nature of this real ground; but rather than doing so he states that he will endeavor to shed further light on the supposedly "almost unanalyzable" concept of existence. And to this end, he mounts a regress from a concept that everyone would accept as possible: that of a fiery body, to the conditions of its possibility.

Kant notes that there is no need to assume that a fiery body exists in order to recognize that the concept is internally possible, since all that is required is the recognition that there is no logical incompatibility between being fiery and being a body. Moreover, the same applies to the concept of body, since one can find no internal contradiction between the predicates extension, impenetrability, force, etc. The point, however, is that this process cannot proceed indefinitely, since one soon reaches a concept that cannot be further analyzed into its component marks, at least not sufficiently to establish its possibility. And at this point the question becomes how to account for the possibility of this concept and Kant's answer is that it can only be done by appealing to an existent (*ein Dasein*) (EMB 2: $80_{15}-1_{11}$; 125-6).

---

[38] In addition to the obscurity in Kant's own account, the problem is exacerbated by Walford's translation, which fails to distinguish consistently between "*Wirklich*" and "*Real*," both of which can be rendered in English as "real." Since the former is a modal term, it should be rendered as "actual." By "reality" Kant did not mean an entity's existence or actuality but its positive nature, that which defines its "whatness" (*quidditas* or *essentia*) or "thinghood." For my discussion of this, see Allison (2004), 399.

[39] In the *Critique* Kant defines "absolute possibility" as that which is possible in all respects (A232/ B284-5). For my account of this, see Allison (2004), 507, note 5.

Having argued that something (or somethings) must be assumed to exist as the material condition of possibility, Kant turns in the third reflection to the concept of absolutely necessary existence. The argument moves from an analysis of the concept of such an existence to the proposition that an absolutely necessary being exists and by means of some intermediate propositions, to the conclusion that such a being includes all reality, which is to say that it is the *ens realissimum*. Given this, the fourth reflection is devoted to the identification of the *ens realissimum* with God.

Kant's first step is to provide a nominal definition of an absolutely necessary existence; viz., "that of which the opposite is impossible" (EMB 2: 81_{20-1}; 126), while also noting that what is needed is a real definition, i.e., one that shows that such an existence is really possible. But rather than providing such a definition, which would not accord with the analytic method, Kant offers what amounts to an argument by elimination. He states that there are only two conceivable grounds on the basis of which it might be claimed that something exists with absolute necessity, both of which supposedly fit the nominal definition: either the denial of its existence is self-contradictory or it entails the elimination of the material element of possibility. And inasmuch as the former, which is the line of thought taken by proponents of the classical version of the ontological argument, turns on the erroneous assumption that "existence" is a real predicate or property, Kant concludes that this leaves only the latter. In other words, something has absolutely necessary existence if and only if its non-being "is at the same time the negation of all of the data of all that can be thought" (EMB 2: 82_{32-3}; 127). By this means Kant endeavors to preserve the conclusion of the traditional ontological argument (the existence of an absolutely necessary being), while rejecting its essential premise (that "existence" is a real predicate).

Since Kant recognizes that this result is compatible with the possibility that the concept of absolutely necessary existence is fictitious, he sets himself the task of removing this possibility by demonstrating that "*there exists an absolutely necessary being*" (EMB 2: 83_3; 127). The argument consists of three steps. The first, which is simply a reminder of what has already been argued, claims that all possibility presupposes something actual as its material condition, from which it follows that its cancellation would at the same time cancel all internal (logical) possibility. The second and pivotal step asserts that a being, the cancellation of the existence of which would negate all possibility, is absolutely necessary. Finally, Kant concludes from this that "it is apparent that the existence of one or more things lies at the foundation of all possibility, and that this existence is absolutely necessary in itself" (EMG 2: 83_{8-10}; 127).

Kant further argues that this necessarily existing being must be regarded as the *ens realissimum*, from which he concludes that it has the properties traditionally attributed to the Deity. Our concern, however, is only with the first step of the argument; viz., the move to the existence of a necessarily existent being as the ground of possibility. What is particularly notable about this move is that it involves a modal fallacy. Specifically, it argues from the necessity that something (or some things) exists as the ultimate material ground of possibility, which is a *de dicto* necessity, to the conclusion that this ground (whatever it may turn out to be) has an absolutely necessary existence, which is a *de re* necessity. Simply put, it is one thing to claim that it is necessary that something exists as the ground or material condition of possibility, and quite another to claim that this entity has itself an absolutely necessary existence.

In later formulations of the argument Kant avoids this particular fallacy by arguing first that the concept of the *ens realissimum* is the only suitable candidate for the ultimate material ground of possibility and second that its existence must be conceived to be absolutely necessary.[40] But Kant also came to realize that the crucial problem lies in the very concept of an absolutely necessary being, which he characterizes as the "true abyss of human reason" (A613/B641). What makes it an abyss is that, while, on the one hand, reason requires the assumption of something that exists with absolute necessity, on the other hand, it will not allow anything, including the *ens realissimum*, to exist in that manner. The former is the case because reason is constrained to posit something that exists in this manner as the ultimate ground of the contingent (A584/B612) and the latter because, even if the subject of a judgment is the *ens realissimum*, one can always deny without contradiction the existence of the subject together with its predicates, since there would then be nothing to contradict (A594/B622).[41]

The latter is decisive and points to both the continuity and difference between Kant's views on the topic in the 1760s and in the "critical" period. In addition to the denial that "existence" is a real predicate, the continuity consists in the view that contradiction has a material as well as a formal condition; the difference is in the way in which this is understood. For the younger Kant this meant an extension of the concept of contradiction to encompass not only the ordinary variety in which a predicate contradicts the concept of the subject in a judgment, but also the special case in which one attempts to deny that anything is actual, with this being considered "absolutely impossible." By contrast, while retaining a vestige of this distinction, the "critical" Kant draws a diametrically opposed conclusion from it, namely, that if one denies the subject of a judgment (the material of possibility) together with its predicate, there is nothing left to contradict, and therefore no contradiction. And by this means Kant effectively abandoned his earlier conception of the absolutely impossible, the correlate of which is the absolutely necessary.

After noting that all the examples of absolute necessity cited by defenders of the conception of an absolutely necessary existence, e.g., "a triangle necessarily has three angles," concern judgments rather than things, the "critical" Kant points out that "The unconditioned necessity of judgments . . . is not an absolute necessity of things" (A593–4/B621–2). And since the conflation of these two kinds of necessity is precisely the modal fallacy of which the younger Kant was guilty in his attribution of an absolutely necessary existence to the *ens realissimum*, whether or not Kant

---

[40] See A584–7/B612–15.   [41] See also RP 28: 1032.

intended it as such, this amounts to a criticism of his own earlier argument that holds even if the error of trying to derive this necessity directly from the concept of the *ens realissimum* is avoided.

Moreover, the "critical" Kant explicitly links his rejection of the notion that some entity could enjoy an absolutely necessary existence with the analytic-synthetic distinction. Indeed, he puts it in the form of a question: "[I]s the proposition, **This or that thing** (which I have conceded to you as possible, whatever it may be) **exists**— is this proposition . . . an analytic or synthetic proposition?" (A597/B625). If one opts for the former, Kant points out, by asserting existence you add nothing to your concept of the thing, then either you are identifying the thought of the thing with the thing or you have presupposed existence as belonging to its possibility, which is a tautology. But if you concede, as Kant thinks one must, "that every existential proposition is synthetic, then how can you assert that the predicate of existence may not be cancelled without contradiction?—since this privilege pertains only to analytic propositions, as resting on their very character" (A598/B626). In light of this, it seems reasonable to maintain that at least part of the reason why the younger Kant found the argument from the material condition of possibility to the existence of something that exists with absolute necessity compelling is that he had not yet drawn the analytic-synthetic distinction. For if Kant had posed the question that he did in the *Critique*, he presumably would have seen that all existential judgments, including those affirming absolutely necessary existence, are synthetic. And in that event, Kant presumably would also have recognized that there are no grounds for claiming that an entity has an absolutely necessary existence, because, as is the case with all synthetic judgments, the denial of an existence claim does not involve a contradiction.

Finally, if the preceding account is correct, it leaves us with a puzzle regarding the young Kant's denial that "existence" is a predicate. Simply put, the puzzle is: if, as the "critical" Kant suggests, this denial is closely related to the recognition of the synthetic nature of existential judgments, and therefore to the analytic-synthetic distinction, how could the younger Kant, who supposedly lacked this distinction, nevertheless recognize that "existence" is not a real predicate? Indeed, might not the fact that he did recognize this be taken as supporting the view of those who claim that he was already in possession of the distinction?

The short answer is that while the analytic-synthetic distinction provides a sufficient reason for the denial that "existence" is a real predicate, it is not a necessary condition of doing so.[42] The distinction does seem to be required, however, to

[42] This is evident from the fact that the point was made before Kant by critics of the ontological argument such as Gassendi, who in his objections to Descartes' version of the argument in the *Meditations* denied that "existence" is a perfection, which is equivalent to being a real predicate equivalent to being a real predicate in Kant's terminology. See Gassendi (1984), 224. Moreover, closer to home, the point was also clearly recognized by Hume in a non-theological context. See Hume (2007), 65–6. For my analysis of Hume's view on this issue see Allison (2008), 162–7. But since Hume's account is in the *Treatise* rather than the *Enquiry* it is not likely that it exerted a direct influence on Kant.

recognize the fallacy involved in the notion of an absolute positing, on which Kant's argument for an *ens realissimum* as the first real ground of possibility turns. For lacking that distinction one would not be in a position to recognize that *any* positing, even the putatively absolute variety, is a synthetic judgment, which, as such, can be denied without contradiction.[43] Accordingly, it seems possible to mount a provisional defense of Kant's procedure in the *Beweisgrund* in the sense that, within the framework of the analytic model of cognition, Kant offered not only a devastating critique of the traditional ontological argument, but an intriguing alternative, which avoided treating "existence" as a real predicate. Nevertheless, this defense is merely provisional, since we shall see that other considerations, most notably the concept of a real ground, led Kant to abandon this framework.

II

A) *Kant's announcement of his metaphysics lectures*: Kant's next publication concerning theoretical philosophy was an announcement of his course of lectures for the winter semester of 1765–66, one of which was on metaphysics.[44] Although brief and sketchy, Kant's account of his proposed lectures is far more informative than a present-day "course description" and worthy of note because of what it tells us about his views at the time. In particular, Kant makes it clear that he still considered the proper procedure for metaphysics to be the analytic method laid out in the *Prize Essay*. In fact, he expresses the hope that he will soon be able to use a textbook of his own based on this method, but until then he will continue to use as his text Baumgarten's *Metaphysica* (N 2: 308_{16-34}; 294–5).[45]

Kant also makes it clear, however, that he does not intend slavishly to follow Baumgarten, who, like Wolff, was a staunch advocate of the synthetic method. Rather, he suggests that he will adopt what is useful in Baumgarten's text to his own way of thinking (N 2: $308_{31}-9_1$; 294–5).[46] Kant notes that he will begin with

[43] In his *Lectures on the Philosophical Doctrine of Religion* Kant characterizes the necessity of assuming an original being as the ground of possibility as subjective on the grounds that "my reason makes it absolutely necessary for me to assume a being which is the ground of everything possible, because otherwise I would be unable to know what in general the possibility of something consists in" (RP $28:1034_{18-20}$; 375). In this way the "critical" Kant preserved his earlier view of the importance of the conception of a material ground of possibility, while denying that it can provide the basis of a genuine demonstration of existence.

[44] The other courses of lectures described in the announcement dealt with logic and ethics.

[45] Since Kant never wrote this textbook, perhaps because he soon abandoned the idea of a metaphysics constructed on the basis of the analytic method, he continued to use Baumgarten's text throughout his teaching career.

[46] The German, which is quite idiomatic, reads: "*Bis dahin aber kann ich sehr wohl durch eine kleine Biegung den Verfasser, dessen Lesebuch ich vornehmlich um des Reichtums und der Präcision seiner Lehrart Willen gewählt habe, den A. G. Baumgarten, in denselben Weg* lenken." Walford renders this as "I can easily, by applying gentle pressure, induce" Baumgarten (295), which does not seem to me quite right. Noting the unusual and idiomatic nature of Kant's language, in private correspondence Oliver Sensen has

empirical psychology, which he describes as "the metaphysical science of *man* based on experience," with the term 'man' (*Menschen*) chosen because it is not yet permitted at this stage to assert that man has a soul.[47] This will be followed by cosmology, which treats the material world as a whole, including both inorganic and organic phenomena. He will then turn to ontology, considered as the science concerned with the most general properties of all things, the conclusion of which will contain the distinction between material and immaterial things, as well as the separation and connection of these two types of being, which is the subject matter of rational psychology. Although Kant does not state it explicitly, the clear implication is that this science, in contrast to empirical psychology, regards the soul as an immaterial being and considers it in the two relations in which it stands: to the body and to other souls (N 2: 309_{1-17}; 295).[48]

This organization involves a significant modification of the order of topics in Baumgarten, who, like Wolff, began with ontology. Kant justifies this reordering on both philosophical and pedagogical grounds. Philosophically, it is justified by the fact that it reflects the analytic method, which moves from the concrete and particular to the abstract and general. Pedagogically, it is justified on the grounds that moving from the relatively concrete to the more abstract, rather than the reverse, makes an intrinsically difficult course of study easier to follow, which Kant seems to have thought was particularly important for retaining the attention of the "spirited and volatile" (*muntern und unbeständigen*) youth, who constituted his audience (N 2: 309_{29-31}; 295).

Kant's most notable discussion of pedagogy in the *Announcement*, however, occurs in its introductory portion, where he remarks that the proper method of instruction in philosophy is "*zetetic*" (*zetetisch*), which he also characterizes as the method of enquiry and which consists in enabling the student to think for himself (N 2: 307_{20-3}; 293). This clearly reflects the influence of Rousseau's *Émile*, the initial appearance of which in 1762 is said to have kept Kant from his customary afternoon stroll. But it also accords nicely with the analytic method and contrasts with the synthetic and dogmatic procedure of the Wolffians, who derive their conclusions deductively from definitions that are accepted as real.[49]

---

suggested as a possible English rendering something like: "Until that point I can indeed turn the author . . . — with a slight adjustment—onto the same path."

[47] It becomes evident when Kant turns to rational psychology that this is because the soul is conceived as an immaterial being and he did not think that the concept of an immaterial being is empirical. In his later treatments of the topic, Kant equates empirical psychology with anthropology, though due to his continued reliance of Baumgarten's text, he includes the subject in his metaphysical lectures.

[48] Kant does indicate that his lectures will conclude with a discussion of the relation between God and the world (N 2: 309_{25-6}; 295); but contrary to what a reader of the *Beweisgrund* might expect, this reference to theology here seems to be almost an afterthought.

[49] It should be noted, however, that this view of philosophy and of philosophical pedagogy long outlasted Kant's attachment to the analytic method; for in the *Critique* he famously remarked, specifically against Wolff 's deductive procedure from definitions, that "Among all rational sciences (*a priori*) . . . only mathematics can be learned, never philosophy (except historically); rather, as far as reason is concerned, we can at best learn only **to philosophize**" (A837/B865).

B) *Dreams of a Spirit-Seer, Illustrated by Dreams of Metaphysics*: This is undoubtedly Kant's most curious and perplexing work. Ostensibly, it takes the form of a harsh review of the Swedish visionary Emanuel Swedenborg's eight-volume *Celestial Mysteries* (*Arcana coelestia*) and it appeared without Kant's name in early 1766. It is divided into two parts. The first part, which Kant characterizes as "dogmatic," consists of four chapters dealing from a variety of points of view with metaphysical questions regarding the nature of spirits and the "spirit world," which are supposedly suggested by Swedenborg's work. The second part, which is called "historical," is composed of two chapters. The first relates in a sober matter-of-fact manner the main episodes in which Swedenborg supposedly demonstrated his extraordinary psychic powers, reports of which apparently were the occasion for Kant's initial interest first in the man and then in his work.[50] The second contains Kant's account of the work itself, which he states is "completely empty and contains not a single drop of reason" (T 2: 360$_{3-4}$; 346).[51]

The puzzling nature of *Dreams* was already noted by Mendelssohn in his brief and frosty review and this puzzlement has been reiterated by subsequent commentators.[52] The central interpretive issue was posed by Cassirer, who characterized the work as a "paradoxical mixture of jest and earnestness" and raised the question of which of these was the decisive factor.[53] But inasmuch as the element of jest was acknowledged by Kant in his response to a lost letter from Mendelssohn and it can hardly be doubted that any work of Kant has a fundamentally earnest intent, the interpretive questions can be more narrowly defined as: (1) Why did Kant concern himself with Swedenborg's work at all, given that he had such a negative view of it? (2) How are we to characterize the element of earnestness and why does Kant mix it with jest?[54] As a first step in attempting to deal with these questions, I shall consider two letters of Kant that shed light on both his intent in *Dreams* and his attitude toward metaphysics at the time.

The first is a letter to Lambert dated December 31, 1765. Although Kant does not refer to *Dreams*, which was then "in press," he expresses confidence in his recent insights regarding metaphysical method. Thus, he writes that "unless I deceive myself

---

[50] Kant expressed interest in (or at least curiosity about) Swedenborg in a lengthy letter to Charlotte von Knoblach, which is dated August 10, 1763 (Br 10: 43–8; 70–4). At this point Kant had not actually read any of Swedenborg's writings, but had become intrigued by reports of his spiritualist exploits. Although the work was published anonymously, Kant made no secret regarding its authorship.

[51] In my view, the richest and most insightful discussion of this work is by Laywine (1993), 55–100. Although some of what she says is certainly controversial, she provides an informed, original, and plausible reading of the work as a whole, encompassing its intent as well as its complex rhetorical strategy, which has no close counterpart in any of Kant's other writings.

[52] Mendelssohn's brief review of *Dreams* is cited by Schönfeld (2000), 181. For a useful critical taxonomy of the various interpretive camps, see Laywine (1993), 15–24.

[53] Cassirer (1981), 78–9.

[54] Presumably, the lost letter was a reply to Kant's initial letter of February 7, 1766, in connection with which Kant sent Mendelssohn a copy of the work, together with several other copies, which he requested be given to several dignitaries in Berlin, including Lambert.

I think I have finally reached some conclusions I can trust" (B10: 55_{21-3}; 81); and a few lines later he states that he has finally reached the point where he feels confident about the method that must be followed, if one is to arrive at secure results (B10: 55_{33}–6_2; 81–2). The key, he informs Lambert, is that "I always look to see what it is I have to know in order to solve a particular problem, and what degree of knowledge is possible for a given question" (B10: 56_{3-5}; 82).

The second is the above-mentioned letter to Mendelssohn of April 8, 1766. In addition to admitting an element of jest, which he characterizes as self-mockery (B10: 70_3; 90) and a lack of clarity in the expression of his intent, which he blames on the fact that the book was printed one page at a time (B10: 71_{24-5}; 91), Kant emphasizes the seriousness of his intent, which is to rescue metaphysics, not from visionaries such as Swedenborg, but from the inflated arrogance and pseudo-insights of would-be metaphysicians. Enunciating a central theme of the work, he suggests near the end of the letter that the means for this rescue might well lie in recognizing that there may be "boundaries imposed upon us by the limitations of our reason, or rather, the limitations of experience that contains the data for our reason" (Br 10: 72_{33-5}; 92). It is clear from this that Swedenborg was not Kant's main target, but merely a vehicle that he uses as a rhetorical weapon against metaphysicians, perhaps including Kant himself, who formulate metaphysical hypotheses without reflecting upon the ability of human reason to ground them. Moreover, Kant claims to have applied this lesson to a specific problem: explaining "*how the soul is present in the world, both in material and in non-material things*" (B10: 71_{29-31}; 91). Kant evidently viewed this as the fundamental issue in rational psychology or "*pneumatology*," and, as he indicates in the letter and makes clear in *Dreams*, he regarded it as insoluble, since the requisite data for solving it are lacking.[55]

Both letters indicate not only that Kant viewed *Dreams* as at bottom a serious work, but that its true concern is with metaphysical method, particularly as applied to the domain of rational psychology as specified in the announcement of his meta-physical lectures. Moreover, despite the negative conclusions regarding the claims of this branch of metaphysics expressed in his letter to Mendelssohn, the overall tone of both letters is positive, since Kant indicates that he thinks that he has made consid-erable progress in his ongoing methodological ruminations.[56] But, as the tenor of the

---

[55] In *Dreams* Kant speaks of pneumatology and pneumatic laws, which to modern ears may seem like a joke, but in Kant's time was taken seriously. For example, Crusius entitled the last book of his major metaphysical work *Die Pneumatologie, oder Lehre von dem nothwendigen Wesen der Geister* (1964, 819). The point is noted by Schönfeld (2000), 240.

[56] For this reason I question the claim of Schönfeld that *Dreams* marks "The Reductio and Collapse of the Precritical Project", Schönfeld (2000), 229. As I shall argue below, it is not that this thesis is radically wrong-headed, but simply that it goes too far; for Kant's abandonment of a significant portion of his project (his doctrine of the soul or rational psychology) should not be equated with his abandonment of the project as a whole, particularly since, as I emphasize, Kant continues to affirm the core of his analytic method. Moreover, we shall see that Kant's disenchantment with rational psychology was temporary and evidently based on a recognition of the incompatibility of its fundamental claims with the analytic method;

letter to Lambert and his remarks about the lack of data in the letter to Mendelssohn indicate, Kant had not abandoned the Newton-inspired analytic method, which he had confidently made use of in the writings considered in the first part of this chapter; rather, it appears that he thought that he had somehow improved it in an important way.

In order to understand why Kant believed this to be the case, we must turn to the text of *Dreams*, which indicates a significant change in Kant's understanding of the nature and task, though not the method, of metaphysics. Whereas in the *Prize Essay* Kant had defined metaphysics as "the philosophy of the fundamental principles of our cognition" (U 2: 283_{13-14}; 256), in *Dreams* he defines it as "a science of the *boundaries [Grenzen] of human reason*" (T 2: 368_{1-2}; 354).[57] Moreover, he suggests that, so conceived, metaphysics, with which he confesses having fallen in love (T 2: 367_{21-2}; 354), has two advantages. The first is that "it can solve the problems thrown up by the enquiring mind when it uses reason to spy after the more hidden properties of things" (T 2: 367_{23-5}; 354), to which Kant adds that "hope is here all too often disappointed by the outcome" and suggests that this includes the present occasion (T 2: 367_{25-7}; 354). The second advantage of metaphysics "consists both in knowing whether the task has been determined by reference to what one can know, and in knowing what relation the question has to the empirical concepts, upon which all our judgments must at all times be based" (T $367_{31}-8_1$; 354).

Since Kant clearly emphasizes the second advantage, it has been thought that already in 1766 he had arrived at the fundamental idea of a critique of pure reason as the essential philosophical task.[58] But while there is a kernel of truth in this view, it is deeply misleading because Kant had not yet formulated the problem for which the *Critique* proposed the solution: the possibility of synthetic a priori judgments. Obviously, the recognition of this problem presupposes the distinction between analytic and synthetic judgments, which I have argued Kant had not yet drawn and which is incompatible with the analytic model of cognition to which he still adhered. Accordingly, I believe that the most that can be plausibly claimed is that the methodological advance to which Kant alludes in his letters to Lambert and Mendelssohn consists in supplementing his analytic procedure by adding the cautionary note that before relying on its results one must be sure that the data for the analysis are at hand, that is to say, an assurance that what one is analyzing is a

---

for the available texts from the 1770s indicate that Kant had rehabilitated this discipline and included it in his radically revised metaphysical project. Indeed, we shall see that it was the last remnant of dogmatism to be discarded by Kant on his path to the *Critique*.

[57] In view of the importance that the "critical" Kant gives to the distinction between *Grenzen* (bounds or boundaries) and *Schranken* (limits), see Pro. 4: 352; 142, I am changing Walford's rendering from "limits" to "bounds."

[58] This view can be traced back to Kant's former student and biographer, L. E. Borowski, who in a portion of his biography that was approved by Kant said of it that "generally the attentive reader found already here the seeds of the *Critique of Pure Reason* and of that which Kant gave us later" Borowski (1968). The citation was noted by Werkmeister (1980), 45.

genuine concept rather than a product of the imagination. And since Kant at this point had not yet affirmed the existence of a priori or "pure" concepts grounded in the nature of the understanding, this means that the concept to be analyzed must be seen to have an experiential ground.[59]

There is also a serious question regarding the interpretation of the first alleged advantage of metaphysics. Kant's remark that "hope is here all too often disappointed by the outcome" indicates that he thought this advantage to be less than he had previously assumed in the optimistic program of the *Prize Essay*. But depending on how one interprets the phrase "all too often," it seems possible to take this remark in two quite different ways. One is to read Kant as suggesting that this first advantage turns out to be null, in which case he is seen as expressing a radical skepticism toward the possibility of metaphysics, not only as traditionally understood, but also, as he had understood it in the works considered in the first part of this chapter.[60] The other is that he is suggesting an important limitation of the scope of metaphysics, which excludes rational psychology, but leaves in place a major piece of his metaphysical program; viz., the metaphysics of the corporeal world.[61] In what follows, I shall attempt to argue for the second alternative.

To begin with, it is important to keep in mind Kant's previously discussed letters to Lambert and Mendelssohn. As far as the former is concerned, it should be noted that, in addition to the generally positive account of his work, Kant alludes to the imminent publication of two works: "The Metaphysical Foundations of Natural Philosophy" and "The Metaphysical Foundations of Practical Philosophy" (B10: 56_{24-7}; 82). To be sure, this is one of many instances of Kant's overly optimistic estimates of the state of his projects, since the apparent successors of these works (*Metaphysical Foundations of Natural Science* and *Groundwork for the Metaphysics of Morals*) were only published some twenty years later, but the very fact that Kant had expected to be able to publish the former work provides a strong indication that he had not given up on that part of his project.

Although virtually everything that he has to say positively about metaphysics in his letter to Mendelssohn pertains to its second advantage, the fact that this letter is essentially a defense against Mendelssohn's objections to both the tone and substance of *Dreams*, which is to say his critique of rational psychology, leaves it unclear how Kant viewed the remainder of his metaphysical project, in which Mendelssohn would

---

[59] As already indicated, however, this does not make Kant into an empiricist, at least not of the usual sort, since the experience to which he refers supposedly yields an intuitive certainty which provides the basis for sound deductive inferences.

[60] This view is clearly enunciated by Schönfeld, who cites a passage from Virgil that Kant attached to his statement of the first advantage as evidence that Kant discounts this advantage completely, indicating thereby a total despair over metaphysics as previously practiced (including by Kant himself). See Schönfeld (2000), 241.

[61] The third part of this program is rational theology; but we have seen that Kant only refers to this in passing in his announcement of his metaphysics lectures and it is touched upon only incidentally in Dreams.

presumably have been less interested than Lambert. Nevertheless, it is clear that the view Kant expresses in this letter is compatible with the preservation of a metaphysics of the corporeal world, since it may be assumed that in this case the requisite data are available.

Kant's continued commitment to this part of his metaphysical program is also evident in *Dreams*. The key idea, which Kant first developed in the *Physical Monadology* of 1756 and reiterated in the *Prize Essay*, is that the simple parts of bodies occupy a space through a repulsive force of impenetrability rather than through a plurality of their substantial parts (U 2: $286_{25}-7_{35}$).[62] In the first two chapters of the first part of *Dreams*, Kant's persona, who is a dogmatic pneumatologist, assumes this account of body as a given and uses it as the basis of a futile attempt to argue for two central tenets of pneumatology; viz., that despite being immaterial substances, souls stand in a real connection (physical influx) with material substances and in a real (spiritual) community with other souls.[63]

Kant's persona begins by posing the problem of how to conceive of a spirit or immaterial substance by contrasting it with the presumably sufficiently, if not completely understood concept of body. At this point, however, the concern is not with the notion of a spirit per se, but with one that is embodied. Such a substance, it is hypothesized, must in some way occupy space (since it is embodied) and have the capacity to influence (and be influenced by) the body, since, in contrast to the systems of occasionalism and pre-established harmony, the theory assumes a real interaction or physical influx. The problem is that this requires that the soul exerts a force of its own on the body and be receptive to the force exercised by the body on it, without itself being of a material nature. Moreover, it is argued that this cannot be a repulsive force, because, *ex hypothesi*, the soul is immaterial, which means that it lacks impenetrability and therefore cannot fill a space. In short, the soul must somehow occupy space without filling it and exert a force on body that is distinct from the force that is essential to body. And while this requires Kant's persona to admit that such a substance and its interaction with a body are strictly speaking inconceivable, he nonetheless insists that they are not for that reason impossible, since hypothesizing their existence does not involve a contradiction (T 2: 318_6-28_{33}).

In so doing, the persona purports to have created a conceptual space for the notion of a spiritual substance, which operates according to pneumatic rather than mechanistic laws, and in the second chapter he endeavors to fill this space by sketching a full-scale metaphysics of the spirit-world. This metaphysics is based on a presumptive analogy between corporeal beings in the physical world, which are governed

---

[62] For an account of Kant's conception of body at the time, see Friedman (1992a), 23–4.

[63] The fact that Kant is not here speaking in his own voice does not prevent him from putting aspects of his own views into the mouth of his persona. Indeed, this is precisely the means through which his critique of dogmatic pneumatology incorporates a self-critique.

by mechanistic laws, and putative immaterial denizens of a spirit-world, which supposedly constitute a community governed by pneumatic laws and which, anticipating Kant's later language, is referred to as a "*mundus intelligibilis*" (T 2: 329$_{34}$; 317).

Since Kant himself admits in his letter to Mendelssohn that at least one of the analogies that he uses, namely, that between a real moral influx by spiritual beings and the force of universal gravitation, is to not be taken seriously, there is no need for a detailed exposition and analysis of what is largely a fanciful and satirical account. The crucial point is simply that it proceeds on the basis of a presumed analogy between something of which we have experience; viz., bodies or material substances and their mutual relations, and something of which we do not; viz., souls or immaterial substances and their mutual relations.

That Kant's criticism of this procedure is at least in part a self-criticism is evident from even a cursory consideration of *Negative Magnitudes*. We have seen that Kant was there eager to suggest that the truths that he had discovered by his analytic method regarding negative magnitudes and real opposition were not limited to corporeal nature, but had the universal scope that one would expect of metaphysical principles. Thus, though he did not deal explicitly with the soul-body relation, Kant continually juxtaposed propositions regarding matter with those that apply to the psychological and moral domains and insisted that the twin concepts of a real ground and a real repugnancy were universally applicable, even though their application to the soul or to inner experience is more difficult to comprehend. For example, we have seen that Kant there insisted upon a strict isomorphism between the laws concerning coming into being and passing away in the physical and the mental domains. As he put it in a previously cited passage: "The difference here only relates to the different laws governing the two types of being; for the state of matter can only ever be changed by means of an *external cause*, whereas the state of the mind can also be changed by means of an *internal cause*" (NG 2: 191$_{29-24}$; 229).

Similarly, in *Dreams* Kant's persona appeals to psychological factors such as a conflict between the forces of egoism and altruism (T 2: 334$_{3-24}$; 321) and between "the strong law of obligation and the weaker law of benevolence" (T 2: 335$_{4-5}$; 322), in an effort to provide analogies that would give metaphysical respectability to the enterprise. The difference is that in the first case Kant apparently took these analogies fully seriously, while he here considered them as fanciful and as intended to support a polemical point regarding the flexibility of metaphysical propositions, which his persona admits can, with a little ingenuity, be made to accord with virtually any state of affairs short of those involving a self-contradiction (T 2: 341$_{6-15}$; 328).

Nevertheless, it is evident from his account of the proof of the immateriality of the soul in the *Prize Essay* that Kant did not regard the analogy between material bodies and souls as entirely arbitrary, which would effectively deprive the pneumatological project of even the appearance of plausibility. In fact, the problem, as Kant there saw it, does not lie in the proof itself, which is the familiar and at the time widely accepted argument to the effect that a thinking being must be a simple substance because a thought cannot be divided between distinct entities.[64] It lies rather in the attempt to derive a strong immaterialist conclusion from this simplicity, which is a problem because for Kant matter is likewise composed of simple substances (physical monads).[65] Accordingly, Kant objects that one cannot infer from the proposition that the soul is not matter (because of its simplicity), "that it is not a simple substance of the kind which could be an element of matter" (U 2: 293$_{9-10}$; 266).[66] The latter, he insists, requires a separate proof, actually two proofs, which would show (1) that a thinking being does not exist in space in the way in which a corporeal element does, i.e., in virtue of its impenetrability, and (2) that this thinking being could not, when combined with other thinking beings, constitute something extended (U 2: 293$_{12-15}$; 267). Kant notes that no such proof has yet been provided and he adds that, if perchance one could be found, it would indicate the incomprehensibility of the way in which a spirit is present in space.

The striking feature of this account is Kant's suggestion that if such a full proof of the immateriality of the soul were forthcoming, the result would not, as one might assume, be a major addition to his analytical metaphysical project, but the seemingly unsettling conclusion that the way in which spirit is present in space is incomprehensible. This result would seem unsettling because it appears to undermine the attempt to account for mind–body interaction or physical influx. Moreover, to make things worse, Kant's persona provides just such a proof and draws from it the proper conclusion; viz., the incomprehensibility of the mind–body relation. Thus, after presenting the argument from the simplicity of the thinking subject, the persona continues, "But this proof still leaves the question unresolved whether the soul is one of those substances which, when they are united together in space, form an extended and impenetrable whole and is thus material, or whether it is immaterial and therefore a spirit, or, indeed, whether a being of this type is even possible" (T 2: 322$_{10-13}$; 310). Inasmuch as this line of argument seems genuinely Kantian, it might be thought to call into question the operative hermeneutical assumption that Kant is not here speaking in his own voice. This conclusion should

---

[64] Kant presents this argument in syllogistic form in *False Subtlety* (FS 2: 52 16–18). In *Dreams* it appears twice: first in the metaphysical argument of chapter 1 of part 1 (T 2: 322$_{3-8}$), and second in a note attached to the second chapter of the first part (T 328$_{30-3}$). The argument in the context of *Dreams* is discussed by Ameriks (1982), 29–30.

[65] I am here adopting the view of Laywine, who, in discussing this passage, points out that what makes the analogy between souls and material elements both tempting and problematic is precisely that they share the property of simplicity. See Laywine (1993), 95.

[66] Underlying this objection is Kant's conception of matter as composed of physical monads, i.e., entities that are both simple because non-extended and physical because they possess repulsive and attractive force and which constitute extended things by conglomeration. Simply put, the problem is that the argument from the simplicity of the thinking "I" does not rule out the possibility that the latter (the soul) is a physical monad.

be rejected, however, for where Kant's persona differs from Kant and reveals his dogmatic colors is in his refusal to regard this result as ending the discussion. Rather, the persona clings to the slender reed of non-contradiction in order to construct a communal spirit-world as a possible scenario. In fact, the conclusion that he draws from this lack of contradiction is that, "We may...accept the possibility of immaterial beings without any fear that we shall be refuted, though there is no hope either of our ever being able to establish their possibility by means of rational argument" (T 2: 323_{10-12}; 311).

It is in light of this that we must understand the severe restrictions that Kant places on metaphysics in *Dreams*, restrictions, which, while giving this work a quite different tone than his earlier writings, do not result in the total abandonment of the metaphysical enterprise conducted along the lines laid out in the *Prize Essay*. The key to Kant's position is supplied in the letter to Mendelssohn, where we have seen he remarks that "everything depends on our seeking out data for the problem, *how is the soul present in the world, both in material and in non-material things*." The upshot of the matter is that there are no data regarding this problem and the moral is that metaphysicians should cease the futile effort to explain this presence. As Kant puts it in the work itself,

> Although I have not precisely determined this boundary [of human reason], I have nonetheless indicated it sufficiently to enable the reader ... to establish that he can spare himself the trouble of all futile research into a question, the answering of which demands data which are to be found in a world other than the one in which he exists as a conscious being.
>
> (T 2: 368_{7-11}; 354)

Implicit in this is the assumption that the requisite data are available in the physical domain where, as Michael Friedman puts it, "one could begin with the most certain and uncontroversial experience, that is, with *phenomena*—and ascend from there by means of evident mathematical reasoning to a knowledge of the first principles of natural bodies."[67] Granted, even here our knowledge is limited, since the question remains, "How am I to understand the **fact that, because something is, something else is?**" (NG 2: 202_{20-1}). But even though we have seen that Kant's attempt to answer this question is both tentative and murky, it seems clear that he did not regard this as the source of an insuperable difficulty for his analytic metaphysics. Presumably, this is because he thought that, despite such conceptual difficulties, there was ample experiential support for the law of universal gravitation and other fundamental principles of Newtonian physics, which warranted the attribution of repulsive and attractive forces to bodies, despite their ultimate inexplicability.

Accordingly, where *Dreams* differs from the *Prize Essay* and *Negative Magnitudes* is in its refusal to extend this line of reason to the immaterial domain, understood as a

---

[67] Friedman (1992a), 15.

mundus intelligibilis. To be sure, there are some data available regarding the mind–body relation. Thus, Kant admits that we know that thinking and willing move our body, but he continues, "That my will moves my arm is no more intelligible to me than someone's claiming that my will could halt the moon in its orbit" (T 2: 370_{26-8}; 356). In short, we know the fact of mind–body interaction but lack the capacity to explain it, because experience does not provide the requisite materials to form the concepts of immaterial forces. More precisely, it presents the would-be pneumatologist with a dilemma from which there appears to be no escape: either appeal to the known physical forces of attraction and repulsion, or some analogues thereof, which leads inevitably to the materialization of the soul, or posit distinct psychic forces and relations for which no epistemic support other than non-contradiction is available. Kant's solution is to draw a firm line at which the business of philosophy ends, namely, when one arrives at relations that are fundamental and therefore not reducible to anything more basic that can be derived from experience (T 2: 370_{9-13}; 356). In short, Kant specifies the limits of analysis and equates these with the limits of philosophy.

Save for one significant detail Kant's account here is quite similar to the one that he will provide fifteen years later in his discussion of hypotheses in the Transcendental Doctrine of Method in the *Critique*. As he there put it:

If the imagination is not simply to **enthuse** but is, under the strict oversight of reason, to **invent** [*dichten*], something must always first be fully certain and not invented [*erdichtet*], or a mere opinion, and that is the **possibility** of the object itself. In that case it is permissible to take refuge in opinion concerning the actuality of the object, which opinion, however, in order not to be groundless, must be connected as a ground of explanation with that which is actually given and consequently certain, and is then called an **hypothesis**.   (A770/B798)

As in *Dreams*, Kant here distinguishes between a genuine hypothesis and a mere invention or product of the imagination. Although he does not refer to them, it is evident that a paradigm case of the former would be the Newtonian law of universal gravitation and of the latter the "pneumatological laws" proposed by the dogmatic metaphysician of *Dreams*. The difference is that, whereas in *Dreams* Kant insists that the object that provides the original data for the formulation of an hypothesis must itself be given in experience, the "critical" Kant maintains that it is the *possibility* of the object being given that is required, where possibility does not mean merely logical but real possibility, understood as conformity to the conditions of a possible experience. And since the latter is determined by a priori conditions, this interjects an a priori element into the story that is lacking in *Dreams*.

The aim of the next two chapters is to trace the path through which this a priori element was introduced into Kant's developing views. As already suggested in the Introduction, two key steps on this path are the formulations of two distinctions that lie at the heart of Kant's "critical" thought: between analytic and synthetic judgments and between sensibility and understanding as distinct cognitive powers, each with its own set of a priori principles.[68] The latter, which was apparently first realized through Kant's "great light" of 1769 and developed in his *Inaugural Dissertation* of 1770, will be the central concern of Chapter 2.

---

[68] One substantive point on which I differ from Laywine is that she seems to import Kant's sensibility-understanding distinction into his self-criticism in *Dreams*. For example, at one point, she remarks that "Precisely because Kant himself subjects immaterial things to the conditions of sensibility, his early metaphysics has more than enough room for prophets and *Phantasten*" (1993), 77. Although this is clearly true, I do not think that it was a criticism (either of his own views or those of others) that Kant was in a position to raise in 1766, since the sensibility-understanding distinction that it presupposes was only drawn in 1769. Rather, I think that it was this distinction that led to Kant's break with the analytic model of cognition to which he still adhered in *Dreams*.

2

Kant's Inaugural Dissertation and Its Context

In view of its significance for understanding Kant's philosophical development, it is important to keep in mind that the *Inaugural Dissertation*: *On the Form and Principles of the Sensible and the Intelligible World* (1770) is not a work that Kant had planned to write. Rather, it owes its existence to his promotion that year to the professorship of logic and metaphysics in Königsberg, which required that he present and defend a Latin dissertation.[1] As such, it is best seen as a statement of Kant's thought at a time in which his views were in considerable flux.[2] Moreover, this suggests that the work must be considered not only in light of Kant's writings of the early sixties, but also in relation to his thought subsequent to *Dreams*, i.e., the period from 1767–69. And setting aside *Reflexionen*, which cannot be dated with any certainty, this essentially means two texts. One is the brief essay: *Concerning the Ultimate Ground of the Differentiation of Directions in Space* (1768), which was Kant's only publication during this period. The other is an oft cited *Reflexion*, the date of the composition of which is not important, since in it Kant notes that "The year '69 gave me a great light" (R 5037 18: 69).[3] Although the *Reflexion* does not tell us what Kant thought this "great light" to be, since the centerpiece of the *Dissertation* is the distinction between sensibility and understanding as two cognitive faculties, it is commonly assumed that it involves this distinction. Accordingly, the present chapter will be divided into two parts: the first considers briefly the essay of 1768 and the subsequent "great light;" while the second, which constitutes the bulk of the chapter, is devoted to an analysis of the *Dissertation*.

I

A) *The Differentiation of Directions in Space*: Kant begins this essay by referring to Leibniz's idea of an *analysis situs*, or what is today termed topology, which is

---

[1] For the history of this appointment, which Kant had been seeking since 1755, and its connection with the *Dissertation* see Kuehn (2001), 188–90.

[2] This point is illustrated by Beck, who provides the outlines of a very different conjectural dissertation that Kant might have written in 1768 had he been promoted to the professorship at that time (1969a), 455–6.

[3] Adickes locates its composition between 1776 and 1778.

concerned with the fundamental formal properties of space. Although he expresses some uncertainty regarding the nature of Leibniz's project, Kant suggests that he is concerned to determine the conditions of its possibility.[4] But Kant's main point is the necessity of distinguishing between the concepts of position (*Lagen*) and direction (*Gegend*).[5] The former refers to the relation of one spatial entity to others; whereas the latter refers to the system of these positions, which is itself defined with reference to "the absolute space of the universe" (G 2: 377_{26}; 365). The latter brought Kant into direct conflict with Leibniz, who having in his correspondence with Clarke defined space as "an order of coexistences, as time is an order of successions,"[6] dismissed the notion of an absolute space that is either ontologically or epistemologically prior to the ordered phenomena as a "merely ideal thing."[7] Kant's target is this Leibnizian thesis. As he succinctly puts it,

My purpose in this treatise is to see whether there is not to be found in the intuitive judgments about extension, such as are to be found in geometry, clear proof that: *Absolute space, independently of the existence of all matter and as itself the ultimate foundation of the possibility of the compound character of matter, has a reality of its own.*   (G 2: 378_{6-11}; 366)

By "intuitive judgments about extension" Kant meant not only those of solid geometry, but also the application of geometrical concepts and principles to the physical world. While he expresses general agreement with Euler on this issue, he also gently criticizes him for "not quite achieving his purpose" (G 2: 378_{20}; 366).[8] Behind this mild rebuke lies a distinction between two sets of difficulties with which a proponent of absolute space must cope. One, with which Euler dealt successfully in Kant's view, is to provide an a posteriori grounding for the conception of absolute space, thereby avoiding the metaphysical thicket in which Clarke became entangled in his dispute with Leibniz. Euler did this by affirming the necessity of presupposing absolute space as a framework for the conception of Newton's laws of motion. The other difficulty, with which Kant thought that Euler failed to deal satisfactorily, concerns the application of these laws to particular cases *in concreto* using the concept of absolute space (G 2: 378_{24-7}; 366).

Although Kant did not specify exactly what he had in mind by this, it seems from what he says later that the problem stems from the fact that absolute space cannot be

---

[4] As Walford notes, Kant seems to have been confused on this point, since he suggests that Leibniz's proposed branch of mathematics involves determining magnitudes mathematically, whereas Leibniz's *analysis situs* is not concerned with quantities or magnitudes, but with formal properties of space. See (1992), 459, note 7. Walford also suggests that Kant's argument may be seen as a demonstration of the impossibility of the Leibnizian *analysis situs* (Walford (1992), 459, note 6). Although this may be correct, it appears that Kant did not see it in this way, perhaps because of his less-than-clear understanding of the Leibnizian project.

[5] I am here following Walford in translating "*Gegend*" as "direction rather than the customary 'region.'" For the justification for this, see Walford (1992), 456–7.

[6] Leibniz (1956), 25.   [7] Ibid., 49.

[8] Kant is here referring to Leonard Euler's *Reflexions sur l'espace et le temps* (1748).

perceived or, as he puts it, it "is not an object of outer sensation" (G 2: 383_{19}; 371), which implies that one cannot apply the Newtonian laws simply by appealing to absolute space, as if it were a pre-given object in relation to which the motion of bodies could be determined. Since a Leibnizian could point to this as a fatal flaw in the absolutist account, it is a problem that must be dealt with.[9] Kant's solution is to claim that, rather than being an object, space is "a fundamental concept which first of all makes possible all such outer sensation" (G 2: 383_{20}; 371).

Kant's argument is structured around two interrelated points: the three dimensionality of physical space and the human body as the point of orientation on the basis of which one distinguishes between directions in space. In view of its three dimensions, Kant suggests that physical space can be regarded as having three planes that intersect each other at right angles; and he further suggests that the ultimate ground on which we form our concept of directions derives from the relation between these intersecting planes and one's body. Specifically, in relation to one's body these intersecting planes determine three pairs of directions: above and below, left and right, front and back. Accordingly, it is with respect to these that one orients oneself and determines the location of objects in three-dimensional physical space.

To illustrate this thesis Kant appeals to several examples, the most important of which are the ability to read a compass or map and to navigate by reference to the stars.[10] His point is that in each case the determination of direction is based ultimately on the relation of the objects in question to the sides of one's body. Apart from this relation, all we would have is the relative position of the various items, e.g., the points of a compass, the places on the map, and the position of the stars relative to each other, which would not suffice to orient oneself with respect to them. While one may define the position of x as to the right or left of y, the question remains: on what basis do we distinguish between right and left?

Kant's answer is that we do so with reference to the right and left sides of one's body. Accordingly, the perceived relation of objects to one's body serves as a surrogate for their unperceived relation to absolute space. Presumably, that is why Kant claims that the relation between bodies (or the parts of a body) depends on their relation to "universal absolute space, as it is conceived by the geometers," rather than simply on their relation to each other, even though the former relation "cannot itself be *immediately* [my emphasis] perceived" (G 2: 381_{15-20}; 369).

---

[9] In his dispute with Clarke, Leibniz did this largely by appealing to the principle of identity of indiscernibles. Stripped of the theological context in terms of which he often framed his replies, Leibniz's point is that no part of empty space has any feature that distinguishes it from others and could therefore serve to determine the direction of the motion of bodies.

[10] Kant also appeals in somewhat less convincing fashion to certain natural phenomena, such as the fact that hops wind around their poles from left to right, whereas beans wind in the opposite direction, and that the shells of almost all species of snails coil from left to right. He claims that these directional features, which are invariant (or nearly invariant) in a species, are rooted in the seeds and often serve to distinguish species of similar plants or animals from each other. He even suggests that right-handedness is the normal condition of human beings; though he admits that there are a few exceptions. See (G 2: 380_2-1_{14}; 368-9).

The centerpiece of Kant's argument is his analysis of incongruent counterparts or enantiamorphs. These are pairs of three-dimensional objects, including both geometrical objects, such as spherical triangles, and physical objects, such as left and right hands, which, while being "counterparts" in the sense that they are identical with respect to properties such as size, proportion, and relative situation of parts, are nevertheless "incongruent" in the sense that they cannot be superimposed on one another, i.e., made identical by a continuous motion of one of them in space.[11] Kant took the existence of enantiamorphs as decisive against a purely relational view of space and from this he concludes that,

Our considerations . . . make it clear that differences, and true differences at that, can be found in the constitution of bodies; these differences relate exclusively to *absolute* and *original* space, for it is only in virtue of absolute and original space that the relation of physical things to each other is possible.   (G 2: 383_{13-18}; 371).

Although Kant did not conclude from the epistemic function he assigned to the concept of space that space is merely a form of human sensibility, as he would two years later in the Dissertation and in his later treatment of incongruent counterparts during the "critical" period, it would be wrong to assume that he here granted to space the absolute reality assigned to it by Newton and Clarke.[12] Rather, Kant's argument moves at the empirical and mathematical levels and does not draw any conclusions regarding the ontological status of this absolute space. Indeed, Kant was not in a position to do this prior to drawing the distinction between sensibility and understanding, which made possible the view of space as a form of sensibility. Nevertheless, by characterizing absolute space as a fundamental concept and assigning it the epistemic function that he did, Kant prepared the ground for this move.

B) *The "great light" of 1769 and the distinction between sensibility and understanding*: According to Kant's "critical" view, sensibility and understanding are two distinct cognitive faculties, each with its own set of "forms" or a priori conditions, but which yield cognition only when working together. Through the former objects or, more precisely, the data for cognizing objects, are given in intuition, through the

---

[11] For a useful analysis of Kant's account of incongruent counterparts or enantiamorphs and the contemporary literature dealing with the issue see Buroker (1981). Buroker emphasizes that the problem of these counterparts rests at least in part on the fact that they are three-dimensional objects, since two-dimensional counterparts could not be incongruent. She further notes that the incongruence reveals itself when one endeavors to rotate one of the objects in a three-dimensional space.

[12] In addition to discussing incongruent counterparts in the *Dissertation* (ID 2: 403_{2-10}; 396), Kant also refers to them as part of his argument for the transcendental ideality of space in Pro 4: $284_{20}-5_{15}$; 80 and MAN 4: $483_{34}-4_{19}196-7$. Interestingly, Kant does not refer to them in the *Critique*, where he offers his fullest argument for the transcendental ideality of space. Despite this, Buroker has claimed that the appeal to incongruent counterparts provides the key to Kant's idealism (1981), esp. 3–4, 82–3, 113–18. Although I am in general agreement with Buroker's analysis of incongruent counterparts, particularly their anti-Leibnizian thrust, I have argued against the latter claim in Allison (1983), 99–102 and (1984), 169–75.

latter objects are thought by bringing these data under concepts. As Kant famously put it, "Thoughts without content are empty, intuitions without concepts are blind. It is thus just as necessary to make the mind's sensible concepts (i.e., to add an object to them in intuition) as to make its intuitions understandable (i.e., to bring them under)" (A51/B75). I have termed this the "discursivity thesis," and it was used by the "critical" Kant as a weapon against both rationalism, as represented by Leibniz, who allegedly **intellectualized** appearances, and empiricism, as represented by Locke, who "**sensitivized** the concepts of the understanding" (A271/B327).[13] In essence, Kant saw each of these approaches as guilty of the same fundamental error: the failure to recognize that human cognition requires the cooperation of two distinct faculties (sensibility and understanding).[14] The difference between rationalism and empiricism on this score concerns only the identification of the faculty that is viewed as the ultimate cognitive power to which the other is reducible.

Kant initially used this distinction against both Leibniz and his Wolffian followers and certain anti-Leibnizian metaphysicians such as Crusius and Clarke. With regard to the former, it is not that the Leibnizians rejected *any* distinction between the sensible and the intellectual. On the contrary, like all forms of rationalism, they viewed this distinction as central to their epistemology. It is rather that they considered it as one of degree rather than kind, which means that they differentiated intellectual from sensible cognition solely in terms of its clarity and distinctness rather than its content. For Kant, by contrast, mathematics, which for the Leibnizians is the paradigm of clarity and distinctness, is connected with sensibility, whereas metaphysics, which Kant regarded as a tissue of confusions, is concerned largely with the non-sensible.

Kant's break with the Leibnizian position on this issue turns on his view that the representations of space and time are essentially connected with sensible intuition. Combined with the recognition that space and time cannot be regarded simply as networks of relations, since these relations presuppose the representations of space and time from which the latter are supposedly derived, this led Kant to the view that space and time are a priori forms of human sensibility and that our representations thereof are pure intuitions, where "pure" means not containing any element derived from sensation. An important advantage of this view, which Kant continued to emphasize in the "critical" period, is that it explains the necessary conformity of nature to the principles of mathematics, something which Kant claimed the Leibnizian view was unable to accomplish.

Although perhaps not as evident as its anti-Leibnizian thrust, the sensibility-understanding distinction also provided Kant with a way to avoid an unacceptable consequence of the views of anti-Leibnizian metaphysicians such as Crusius; viz., that everything is somewhere and somewhen. This view was unacceptable to Kant

---

[13] For my discussion of the discursivity thesis, see Allison (2004), esp.12–16, 27–8.
[14] For an account of this distinction as Kant's main weapon in two-front war, see Beck (1969b).

because it entails that God and the human soul are in space and time and, as such, subject to spatiotemporal conditions. But while for the "critical" Kant this was rejected primarily on the grounds that it undermines the possibility of freedom, it is evident from our consideration of *Dreams* that his main concern at the time was its implications for the doctrine of the soul. In particular, it supports the view, which underlies the negative conclusion of that work concerning the prospects of rational psychology or pneumatology, that any account of the soul's relation either to the body or to other souls must be conceived in terms of a physicalistic model, according to which the *mundus intelligibilis* postulated by Kant's dogmatic persona is conceived as either a pale copy or inverted image of the physical world.

Inasmuch as this distinction is not present in the essay on space of 1768, but constitutes the centerpiece of the *Dissertation*, it is commonly assumed that this was at least part of what Kant had in mind when he wrote in the above-mentioned *Reflexion*:

If I only achieve as much as being convincing that one must suspend the treatment of this science until this point has been settled, then this text will achieve its purpose.

Initially I saw this doctrine as if in twilight. I tried quite earnestly to prove propositions and their opposite, not in order to establish a skeptical doctrine, but rather because I suspected I could discover in what an illusion of the understanding was hiding. The year '69 gave me a great light.   (R 5037 18: 69$_{15-22}$; 207)

Apart from the facts that the science to which Kant is referring is metaphysics and the text is a future critique of pure reason, as he conceived it at the time of the composition of this *Reflexion*, the interpretation of the first paragraph is impeded by the difficulty of determining what Kant meant by the point that must be settled before the text will be able to achieve its purpose, which is presumably to put metaphysics on a scientific basis.[15] In addition, the relation between the two paragraphs is rendered problematic by the fact that, whereas Adickes, the editor of the *Akademie Ausgabe*, treats them as two parts of a single text, Erdmann, in his earlier edition of Kant's *Reflexionen*, saw them as entirely distinct.[16] Given this unsettled state of affairs, I shall confine my remarks to the second paragraph, which, in any event, is the portion of the text that is of interest at this point.

While there is general agreement that Kant's great light involved the recognition of the sensibility-understanding distinction, there is a controversy regarding the question of whether this is the whole story.[17] At the root of this controversy is the second sentence, in which Kant refers to his attempt to prove certain propositions and their

[15] Erdmann suggests two possibilities: the bounds of our cognitive capacities and the problem of a priori cognition in general (1882), 18. Both are plausible, but lacking further context I fail to see how it is possible to decide between them and perhaps other possibilities as well.

[16] Erdmann numbers the first passage 55 and the second 4. See (1882), 4 and 18.

[17] See, for example, Beck (1969a), 457–60; Brandt (1992), 100–11; Cassirer (1981), 92–115; Gotz (2001), 19–26; Kuehn (2001), 186–7; and Tonelli (1963) 369–73.

opposite in order to locate an illusion of the understanding. Since this calls to mind Kant's discovery of the antinomial nature of reason, which is clearly related to the sensibility and understanding distinction, it has led some commentators to claim that this discovery likewise resulted directly from the "great light."[18]

This is a complex issue, which is further complicated by the fact that it has been argued that Hume had an important role in leading Kant to his discovery of the Antinomy in 1769.[19] Accordingly, in order to stay within the bounds of a commentary on the Transcendental Deduction, I shall simply note that, quite apart from the role of Hume, if Kant had come to a clear recognition of an antinomial problem in 1769, it is reasonable to assume that it would have played a prominent role in the *Dissertation* written in the following year. But we shall see that, though the work contains a discussion of the issues involved in the antinomial conflict of reason with itself articulated in the *Critique*, there is no clear statement of an antinomy. And, in light of this, I think it reasonable to conclude that, though in 1769 Kant was in possession of the key to the recognition of the antinomial nature of reason, he did not yet realize this. Otherwise expressed, the sensibility-understanding distinction was the starting point of the path that led to the discovery of the antinomial nature of reason in its speculative use, but it did not itself constitute that discovery.[20]

II

Rather than a direct contribution to metaphysics, Kant regarded the *Dissertation* as a specimen of a propaedeutic discipline that would help to lay the foundation for it.[21] Although Kant later said much the same thing regarding the *Critique*, there is a considerable difference in the nature of the metaphysics for which the two works supposedly provide the foundation. Whereas Kant maintained that the *Critique* laid the foundation for a two-fold metaphysics of nature and morals (A841/B869) and the *Dissertation* is likewise concerned with a metaphysics of morals, instead of a metaphysics of nature, which for the "critical" Kant encompassed a system of synthetic a

---

[18] See, for example, Erdmann (1882), xlv–vi, and de Vleeschauwer (1934), 148–9.

[19] Such a reading has been advocated by Kreimendahl and Gawlick (1987) and again by Kreimendahl (1991). It has, however, been subject to considerable criticism. See, for example, Brandt's lengthy review of Kreimendahl's book (1992), 99–111. For a fuller account of the literature on the subject, see Kuehn (2001), 472–3, note 42. Kuehn himself has argued that there is a kind of antinomy in Hume's *Treatise* and he emphasizes the importance for Kant of Hamann's translation of T 1. 4. 6 (1983a), 175–93 and (1983b), 24–5. But in the same note Kuehn emphatically disassociates himself from the Kreimendahl–Gawlick view, denying that Kant could have discovered *the* Antinomy of Pure Reason as it is found in the first *Critique* on the grounds that he had not yet drawn the sharp distinction between understanding and reason that underlies Kant's "critical" conception of an antinomy, see Kuehn (1983b), 473.

[20] It will be argued below that the possibility of a Kantian antinomy presupposes the discursivity thesis. Following Kuehn (see preceding note), one might add to this the distinction between understanding and reason, to which Kant appears to allude in passing (ID 2: 389$_2$;379), but which is otherwise absent from the *Dissertation*.

[21] See ID 2: 395$_{17-19}$; 387, 419$_7$; 415.

priori propositions regarding the phenomenal world, the theoretical metaphysics for which the *Dissertation* was intended to provide a foundation is concerned exclusively with intelligible objects or noumena. This foundation is provided by the sensibility-understanding distinction, which is correlated with the distinction between a sensible and an intelligible world.

The work is composed of five sections: (1) an analysis of the concept of a world in general; (2) the distinction between sensible and intelligible things in general; (3) an account of space and time as principles of the form of the sensible world; (4) a complementary account of the principles of the form of the intelligible world; and (5) a discussion of the method of metaphysics regarding what is sensible in our cognition and what pertains to the understanding or intellect. In a letter that he sent to Lambert together with a copy of this work, Kant suggests that he could simply skim the first and fourth sections, but that, despite some imperfections, the other three are worthy of a more extensive consideration (Br 10: 98_{10-14}; 98).[22] Inasmuch as it is in these sections that Kant distinguishes between sensibility and understanding and their respective objects, gives his account of space and time as forms of sensible cognition, and exposes the metaphysical fallacies grounded in subreption, he was certainly correct in drawing Lambert's attention to them. But since sections one and four are also integral parts of the work, it will be necessary to consider them as well. Accordingly, the discussion will be divided into five parts, corresponding to the five sections of the text.

A) *The concept of a world*: Kant defines a world as a whole which is not itself a part (of a larger whole) and its correlate, the simple, as a part which is not itself a whole (ID 2: 387_{3-5}; 377). This definition allows for the possibility of there being more than one world, with the proviso that these worlds are not related as parts to the whole.[23] In fact, Kant will refer to two "worlds" that fit this definition (a sensible and an intelligible world). But before he could be in a position to do so, it was necessary to introduce the distinction between the sensible and the intelligible, which is drawn in section 2. In reality, however, Kant already made use of this distinction in section 1 by contrasting two fundamentally different ways in which the relation between such a whole (a world) and its ultimate components (simple parts) can be conceived. Or, more precisely, since each manner of cognizing the part–whole relation can proceed in two directions, namely, from whole to part and from part to whole, which Kant

---

[22] In the same letter, Kant refers to the propaedeutic science, a sample of which is offered in the *Dissertation* as "*phaenomolgia generalis*" (Br. 10: 98_{18}; 7). Lambert himself had used the term "*Phänome-nologie*" to characterize the doctrine of appearance, which constitutes the fourth and final part of his *Neues Organon* (1764), 3–4.

[23] This is to be compared with the definition provided by Wolff for whom a world is defined as a whole, the parts of which are either simultaneous or succeed one another (1751), 333. This differs from Kant's definition in that it includes the spatiotemporal relations of its parts, which for Kant would pertain only to the sensible world, not to the concept of a world as such. For this reason (among others) Wolff asserts that only one world can be actual (1751), 585–7, which again differs from Kant's view.

refers to respectively as analysis and synthesis, there are four distinct ways of conceiving this relation.[24] Two of these proceed intellectually, appealing to the abstract concept of composition, which entails the concept of the simple; while the other two aim at an intuitive cognition of the relation, which is subject to the conditions of time.

The distinguishing feature of the concrete (intuitive) representation of either a composite or its parts is that it must be conceived as the product of a cognitive process that does not simply occur in time (that could be said of an intellectual analysis and synthesis as well), but that is governed by normative constraints stemming from the conditions of representation in time. Specifically, the intuitive representation of either a whole or its simple elements is only attainable if the process of composition (synthesis) or resolution (analysis) can be carried out in a finite time (ID 2: 388_{4-5}; 378).

Kant points out that this constraint raises problems for the intuitive representation of either a continuous or an infinite magnitude. In the case of the former, the regression from the whole to its parts and in the latter the progression from the parts to the whole has no end point (*termino*), which is to say that it can never be completed (ID 2: 388_{6-11}; 378). But inasmuch as it is only through these cognitive processes that such magnitudes can be represented intuitively, this means that they can never be represented in that manner. And, given the common view that the unrepresentable and the impossible are identical, Kant suggests that this explains why the continuous and the infinite are frequently rejected (ID 2: 388_{6-13}; 378).

Although he claims that his concern is not to defend these notions, Kant insists that their rejection on these grounds is erroneous. Moreover, in explaining this error, he introduces what amounts to the central claim of the work; viz., that the conditions and laws of intuitive cognition are not to be equated with the conditions of all cognition and therefore of what is really possible. As Kant puts it, "[W]hatever *conflicts with* the laws of understanding and the laws of reason [*legibus intellectus et rationis*] is undoubtedly impossible. But that which being an object of pure reason simply *does not come under* the laws of intuitive cognition, is not in the same position" (ID 2: 389_{2-4}; 379). Thus, Kant grants an unqualified normative superiority to the laws of understanding and reason, which, though he does not specify what he understands by these laws, clearly includes the principle of contradiction. And he concludes from this that, whereas whatever violates this law is known to be

---

[24] In a note Kant points out that the words "analysis" and "synthesis" are commonly given a double meaning. Thus, synthesis is either qualitative or quantitative. The former consists in a progression through a series of things which are subordinate to one another, i.e., from ground to grounded, the latter in a progression through a series of things that are coordinate with one another. Correlatively, analysis, considered qualitatively, is a regress from grounded to ground and quantitatively as a regress from a whole to its constituent parts. Kant also notes that he is here using these terms in the second (quantitative) sense (ID 2: 388_{17-23}; 378).

impossible, lack of conformity to the laws of intuitive cognition, which he likewise does not here specify, constitutes merely a "*subjective* resistance," which is mistakenly taken as a constraint on what is objectively possible (ID 2: 389_{8-9}; 378).

In addition to the nature of these laws, this gives rise to the question of how we can determine what is objectively possible. Kant's answer turns on the contrast between what is cognizable by *our* understanding, which involves sensible intuition as a condition, and what is cognizable by *any* understanding, including one that is more than human. And he suggests that the latter understanding, to which he later attributes a capacity for an intellectual intuition (ID 2: 396_{28}; 389), "might apprehend a multiplicity at a single glance, without the successive application of a measure" (ID 2: 388_{38-9}; 379n). Kant later puts the point in more general terms, stating that "*whatever cannot be cognized by any intuition at all is simply not thinkable*, and is, thus, impossible" (ID 2: 413_{10-11}; 409). The obvious problem with such a criterion of real possibility is that, lacking the requisite intellectual intuition, we seem to have no way of applying it. We shall return to this issue in the next section in connection with Kant's account of the distinction between intuitive and symbolic cognition; but it is first necessary to say a word about how this relates to the previously noted lack of a genuine antinomial conflict in the *Dissertation* and to complete the analysis of the argument of section 1.

To begin with, Kant here provides the basic ingredients of the mathematical antinomies of the *Critique*, without pointing to or even hinting at the presence of anything like an antinomial conflict. Instead, he presents the elements of what will become the theses of these antinomies in the guise of propositions to the effect that the synthesis of spatiotemporal magnitudes must be assigned a first beginning or limit and that the composite of substances that compose the world must consist of simple parts, as well as their antitheses that both the synthesis through which the size of these magnitudes is determined and the analysis through which the elements of their composition is attained have no terminating point. But rather than claiming, as he does in the *Critique*, that these lead to what appear to be contradictory propositions and that the contradiction can be removed only by realizing that both the thesis and antithesis in each pair are false, since each says more than it is entitled to claim, Kant assigns what will later become the theses to the laws of intellectual cognition and the antitheses to the laws of intuitive cognition.

Inasmuch as this suggests that both sets of propositions may be true, the situation might be thought to resemble what Kant later claims to hold for the theses and antitheses of the dynamical antinomies. This ignores, however, the fact that underlying the antinomial conflict in the *Critique* is the discursivity thesis, which as we have seen maintains that cognition requires the cooperation of sensibility and understanding. By contrast, in the *Dissertation*, in virtue of the legitimating function assigned to the notion of an intuitive intellect, these two sets of laws operate on parallel tracks. Accordingly, the task is to prevent the laws of sensible cognition from leaving their proper path and treading on the domain of the intellect, which precludes the possibility of an antinomial conflict such as Kant envisaged in the *Critique*.[25]

Kant devotes the remainder of the first section to the specification of the moments (*momenta*) of the concept of a world as previously defined. The claim is that anything that is to count as a world must possess a matter and a form and constitute an absolute totality (*universitas*). The matter of a world is its parts and, in agreement with the Wolffian view, Kant claims that these parts must be substances. The main thrust of Kant's argument is anti-Spinozistic or, more generally, anti-monistic. Inasmuch as these parts can be characterized neither as accidents, since these are rather its states or determinations, nor as modifications, since these are not parts of a subject, Kant concludes that they must themselves be substances (ID 2: 389_{22-35}; 380).

Correlatively, the form of a world is the relation of its constituent substances, which Kant claims must be one of coordination rather than subordination. This is because coordinates are related to one another as parts to a whole; whereas subordinates are related as ground and consequent. Kant further claims that this coordination must be regarded as real and objective and that this requires a possible influence of the component substances upon one another. The former is because only the assumption of a real relation is capable of yielding the *representation of a whole*, as contrasted with a *whole of representation* (ID 2: 390_{14-15}; 381). The latter is because it is precisely this possibility that provides the real unity requisite for a world.[26]

Kant's discussion of the third moment in the general concept of a world; viz., its universality or absolute totality, focuses mainly on the question of the succession of its states. He assumes without argument that the successive states of the world must extend infinitely and therefore can never be completed (ID 2: 391_{18-21}; 382). Accordingly, the problem is to understand how this is compatible with the absolute totality condition, which is built into the concept of a world and which seems to presuppose completion. Kant suggests that the problem cannot be avoided by dropping the concept of succession and conceiving all of the elements of the world (the substances and their states) as existing simultaneously. This is because canvassing the parts of a simultaneous infinite would itself require a never-ending successive synthesis, from which Kant concludes that if a simultaneous infinite were admitted, it would be necessary to admit a successive infinite as well (ID 2: 391_{33-4}; 382).

We again see from this that Kant presents the kernel of what will later be viewed as the First Antinomy. But rather than pointing to an antinomial conflict, he presents the inability to represent either a successive or a simultaneous infinite as a totality as

---

[25] It is largely for this reason that I reject Kreimendahl's thesis that in 1769 Kant had already recognized and resolved the antinomial problem as it was later formulated in the *Critique* and that the presentation of this solution is the central theme of the *Dissertation*. See Kreimendahl (1991), esp. 187–252.

[26] Kant notes that it is the *possible* influence of its constituent substances that constitutes a world, because actual influences pertain to the state rather than the essence of a world (ID 2: 390_{20-1}; 381).

something of a conundrum or "thorny question" (*spinosa quaestione*), which, since the concepts of succession and simultaneity have reference to time, is best dealt with by distinguishing between them and the concept of a whole, which is derived from the understanding (ID 2: 392$_{2-7}$; 382). In fact, in contrast to the *Critique*, where Kant distinguishes sharply between the elements of the composite being given (*gegeben*) and set as a task (*aufgegeben*) (A498/B526), he is here content to suggest that the coordinates (whether simultaneous or successive) should be given in some way and that should all be thought as constituting a unity (ID 2: 392$_{8-9}$; 383).

B) *The sensible and the intelligible*: Although the title that Kant gives to section 2 ("*On the distinction between sensible and intelligible things in general*") suggests an ontological concern, his initial focus is on the cognitive faculties through which these two types of entity (or aspects of entities) are represented. These are sensibility (*sensualitas*) and intelligence or understanding (*intelligentia*).[27] Kant defines sensibility as a receptivity of the subject and notes that it is in virtue of this receptivity that "it is possible for the subject's representative state to be affected in a definite way by the presence of some object" (ID 2: 392$_{13-14}$; 384). Correlatively, intelligence (or understanding) is defined as "the power to represent things which cannot by their own quality come before the senses of the subject" (ID 2: 392$_{13-16}$; 384).[28] The object of sensibility is the sensible (*sensibile*) and of intelligence is the intelligible (*intelligibile*). In addition, Kant points out that for the ancients an object of the former kind was termed a *phenomenon* and of the latter a *noumenon*. And, finally, introducing the notion of cognitive laws, Kant states that cognition, insofar as it is subject to the laws of sensibility, is *sensible* and, insofar as it is subject to the laws of the intellect, is *intellectual* or rational (ID 2: 392$_{18-21}$; 384).

Kant concludes from this that "things which are thought sensitively are representations of things *as they appear* (*esse rerum representations, uti apparent*), while things which are intellectual are representations of things *as they are* (*sicuti sunt*)" (ID 2: 392$_{27-9}$; 384). Kant's language here already reflects the tensions that have led to the ongoing dispute between the so-called "two-world" or "two-object" and "two-aspects" or "standpoints" readings of the transcendental distinction between appearances and things in themselves drawn in the *Critique*. Indeed, Kant's account provides support for both readings. On the one hand, the contrast between things

[27] In Kant's Latin terminology "*sensualitas*" (sensibility) designates the cognitive faculty; "*sensibile*" (the sensible) refers to the objects cognized through this faculty, which are also called phenomena; and "*sensitiva*" (sensitive) refers to the kind of cognition attainable through sensibility. But in the interest of simplicity and agreement with the usual English renderings of the German terminology of the *Critique* and related texts, except when it is a matter of direct translation I shall use the English "sensible" for each of these Latin terms. Correlatively, "*intelligentia*" (intelligence or understanding) designates the faculty; "*intelligibile*" refers to its objects, which are also termed noumena, and *intellectualis or rationalis* (intellectual or rational) characterizes that kind of cognition it provides. It must be kept in mind, however, that, while Kant at one point alludes to it (see note 19), he does not draw a sharp distinction between the understanding and reason (*Verstand* and *Vernunft*) in the *Dissertation* as he will in the *Critique*.

[28] See A19/B33.

as they are and as they appear to us because of the nature of our sensibility, as well as the above-cited definition of intelligence, as a "power to represent things which cannot by their own quality come before the senses of the subject," strongly suggest that at the time of the *Dissertation* Kant held the view that the very same things that appear to us in virtue of affecting us also exist in themselves (in their "own quality" that does not appear to the senses) and, so considered, are presumably parts of the intelligible world; while, on the other hand, Kant here clearly understands by the "intelligible world" a distinct world with its own unifying laws rather than merely a distinct standpoint with respect to what is ontologically speaking a single world.[29] In this respect at least, the Kant of 1770 is definitely a "two-worlder."

Our present concern, however, is not with these worlds but with sensibility and intellect as the faculties through which they are supposedly cognized. Inasmuch as the conception of space and time as forms of human sensibility is only introduced in the third section, Kant's argument for the connection between sensibility and phenomenality cannot appeal to it. In fact, it is only after first showing that receptivity or sensibility *as such* entails the phenomenality of its object that Kant will be in position to move from sensibility as such or in general (*generatim* or *überhaupt*) to *human* sensibility. And since all that Kant has provided to substantiate this conclusion is the definition of sensibility cited above, it must be assumed that he thought that the phenomenality thesis follows from it. Moreover, it seems clear that the essential element in this definition is the proviso that sensibility requires not merely that the mind be affected by an object, but that it "be affected in a definite way (*certo modo afficiator*)." This reflects Kant's view that sensibility is a cognitive faculty, which, as such, must not only present sensible data, but present them in such a way as to make their cognition possible.

In the *Critique*, where the discursivity thesis is in place and Kant's primary interest lies in the function of the understanding in structuring experience, he characterizes the role of sensibility in a somewhat muted fashion, indicating that cognition requires that sensations be received by the mind in a way that "allows the manifold of appearance to be intuited as ordered in certain relations," and he identifies this orderability with the "**form** of appearance" (A20/B34). Implicit in this is a critique of sensationalist epistemology, i.e., the view that cognition is built up entirely from sensations or sense data, which provide the unfiltered raw material of cognition. In sharp contrast to any such view, Kant notes that "that within which the sensations can alone be ordered and placed in a certain form cannot be in turn sensation" (A20/B34).

By contrast, in the *Dissertation*, Kant assigns a more robust role to sensibility with respect to phenomena. Rather than merely presenting the sensibly given data in a

---

[29] Although the issue is highly controversial, I believe that the latter reflects Kant's "critical" conception of the intelligible world. See Gr 4: 458$_{19-22}$; 104. For my most recent discussions of this topic, see Allison (2011), esp. 316–30 and (2012), 87–98.

way that *allows for* their being ordered by the understanding, i.e., a framework in and with respect to which they are ordered, which is the view of the *Critique*, Kant here apparently attributes an actual ordering function to its not yet specified forms. This is implicit in the way in which he distinguishes between the matter and the form of a sensible representation. The matter is straightforwardly identified with sensation and the form is described as that "aspect [*species*] of sensible things which arises according as the various things which affect the senses are co-ordinated by a certain law of the mind" (ID 2: 392_{31-2}; 384). In short, the function of the law of the mind connected with the form of sensibility is to co-ordinate what is sensibly given.

In claiming that the form of appearances arises from the co-ordination of what is given through a law of the mind, Kant also indicates that this form is acquired rather than innate.[30] What is innate is the "natural law of the mind," which functions as the principle of coordination. The crucial point, however, is that such a law is needed because "objects do not strike the senses in virtue of their form or aspect [*speciem*]" (ID 2: 393_{7-8}). As Kant notes, this is a problem because, in addition to the sensible data, cognition requires, that these data "coalesce into some representational whole [*totum aliquod repraesentationis coalescant*]," which, in turn, requires an internal principle of the mind (ID 2: 393_{9-10}; 385). Accordingly, it seems that in the *Dissertation* Kant attributes this coalescing function to the forms of sensibility; whereas in the *Critique* he will see it as the work of the understanding and/or imagination under the direction of the unity of apperception.[31]

Having analyzed sensibility as such and arguing that it has both a matter and form, Kant turns to the intellect, which he describes as the "superior faculty of the soul" (ID 2: 393_{17-18}; 385). But rather than introducing a parallel distinction between the matter and form of the intellect, Kant distinguishes between its two uses: real and logical.[32] By the former he understands that through which the concepts themselves, whether of things or relations, *are given* (*datur*), and by the latter that through which concepts, no matter how they are given, are subordinated and compared to one another in accordance with the principle of contradiction (ID 2: 393_{19-22}; 385). Although Kant's account of the real use of the intellect and the nature and genesis

---

[30] With respect to the representations of time and space the denial of innateness is implicit. We shall see, however, that Kant explicitly denies innateness with respect to the pure concepts of the intellect and it seems reasonable to assume that the same reasoning applies, *mutatis mutandis*, to the other species of a priori representations. Moreover, in his reply to Eberhard Kant states that "The *Critique* admits absolutely no implanted or innate *representations*. One and all, whether they belong to intuition or to concepts of the understanding, it considers them as *acquired*. But there is also an original acquisition ... and thus of that which previously did not yet exist at all, and so did not belong to anything prior to this act" (UE 8: 221; 312). Although this expresses Kant's "critical" view, I see no reason to deny that it was already in place in 1770.

[31] We shall also see, however, that in the *Critique*, particularly the B-Deduction, Kant maintains that space and time as a priori forms of sensibility impose conditions to which the unity of apperception must conform, if it is to issue in cognition rather than empty thought. This will be a central theme in Chapter 9.

[32] We shall see below that Kant does introduce such a distinction in section 4.

of its concepts are the central concerns of this section, before turning to it a word is in order regarding its logical use.

Unlike the real use, whose special provenance is metaphysics, the logical use is common to all the sciences (ID 2: 393_{23-4}; 385). As its initial characterization indicates, its basic function is to subordinate and compare (with respect to identity and difference) given representations, no matter what their genesis, such that inferences between them are possible. Kant emphasizes that, insofar as this subordination and comparison concerns sensible concepts, as it does in all the empirical sciences, the cognitions arrived at are always sensible, since the nature of a cognition is a function of its origin, not the logical process by which it is attained (ID 393_{29-32}; 385). Kant further claims that the use of the understanding with respect to experience is merely logical and that the path from appearances to experience is by reflection in accordance with the logical use of the understanding (ID 2: 394_{5-7}; 386).

Inasmuch as the concepts involved in the real use of the understanding are supposedly given by its very nature, Kant refers to them as concepts of the understanding. He also notes that, in contrast to the concepts involved in sensible cognition, these do not originate through a process of abstraction from the content of what is sensibly given and he endeavors to clarify this by disambiguating the troublesome term "abstract." According to Kant, this can mean either abstracting *from some things* or *abstracting something*. The former indicates that in entertaining a certain concept we do not attend to the other things that are in some way connected with it, while the latter suggests that the concept itself is only given concretely, i.e., in a particular experience, and is made general by separating it from that with which it is conjoined in experience (ID 2: 394_{15-22}; 386). In light of this, Kant claims that a concept of the understanding *abstracts* from everything sensible (in the sense of setting it aside), but it is *not abstracted* from what is sensible. And, in an attempt at further clarification, he suggests that such concepts might better be termed "*abstracting* [*abstrahens*] rather than abstract (or abstracted) [*abstractus*]" (ID 2: 394_{25-8}; 386).

Although he is silent on the point, it seems reasonable to assume that by the latter Kant understood the Lockean view, according to which "*Ideas* become general, by separating from them the circumstances of Time, and Place, and any other *Ideas*, that may determine them to this or that particular Existence."[33] On this view, we are to conceive of abstraction as a kind of extraction, whereby an idea is lifted, as it were, whole cloth from the other ideas with which it is conjoined in experience and thereby becomes capable of representing a sort. Kant had previously rejected such a view on the grounds that it is incapable of accounting for the universality that is the form of *every* concept (pure or empirical).[34] In the present context, however, he is not

---

[33] Locke (1975), 411.

[34] It is clear from Kant's *Lectures on Logic* and *Reflexionen* that he regarded abstraction in the sense of abstracting *from* something as a moment in the formation of all concepts (whether sensible or intellectual). In these texts, some of which date from around the time of the *Dissertation*, Kant distinguishes between the

concerned with a general theory of abstraction or concept formation, but with the special case of the formation or acquisition of what are claimed to be concepts that pertain to the very nature of the understanding. Thus, the question becomes: assuming that these concepts arise through an abstraction from *something*, from what exactly are they abstracted?

Kant's answer is that they are abstracted from the laws inherent in the mind and that this result is obtained "by attending to its actions on the occasion of experience," from which he concludes that they are acquired rather than innate, though their acquisition is not empirical (ID 2: 395_{21-3}; 387–88). In other words, the mind acquires its stock of inherent concepts by reflecting on its operations, i.e., its modes of conceptualization involved in various experiences, abstracting from (in the sense of setting aside or bracketing) the specific contents of these experiences.[35] As examples of such concepts, Kant cites "possibility, existence, necessity, substance cause, *etc.* together with their opposites or correlates" (ID 2: 395_{34-6}; 388).

The puzzling feature of this account is the claim that these concepts are acquired by attending to the actions of the mind "on the occasion of experience." This is puzzling because it appears to conflict with both the little that Kant says about experience and the real use of the understanding involving these concepts. With regard to the first point, as was noted above, Kant explicitly maintains that experience requires merely a logical rather than a real use of the understanding, from which it seemingly follows either that these concepts are involved in the logical (as well as the real) use of the understanding or that they cannot be acquired in the manner Kant indicates. And since Kant fails to discuss the former possibility, the question of their acquisition remains mysterious.

With regard to the second point, it is clear that, given the project of the *Dissertation*, Kant's failure to assign to the concepts of the understanding an experiential role, which might help to explain why experience is a condition of their acquisition, is not a mere oversight. Rather, as we shall see in more detail below, it is a reflection of Kant's systematic effort to preserve the purity of these concepts from any "contagion" by sensibility, which giving them an experiential function would presumably

---

matter and form of a concept and claims that the latter, which for all concepts is universality, is attained through the logical acts of comparison, reflection, and abstraction. Although there are differences in formulation, the basic idea is that in forming a concept (Kant's example is usually that of a tree) the comparison of intuitive representations (of different trees) yields the recognition of differences, reflection makes one aware of what these different representations have in common, and through abstraction one sets aside these differences, thereby producing a concept. Thus, abstraction is always *from* something in the sense that it consists in ignoring the differences that hold between the items falling under the concept. See, for example, LB 24: 137; LP 24: 566–7; DWL 24: LBu 24: 654; 753–4; WL 24: 907–8; JL 9: 4–5; R2862–84 16: 549–58.

[35] I take it that Kant must be committed to some such view, if his account of the acquisition of these concepts is to be made compatible with his general account of concept formation or acquisition. On the latter point, see the preceding note.

involve. In short, there is an unresolved tension between Kant's account of the acquisition of the concepts of the understanding and his view of their function.[36]

If this is correct, it invites the question: why did Kant opt for this account of the genesis of these concepts? I believe that it is because, under the influence of Leibniz's account in the *New Essays*, he saw it as the only viable non-empirical alternative to the traditional doctrine of innateness criticized by Locke. In an oft cited passage from this work, Leibniz replies to Locke's appeal to the scholastic dictum that "*Nihil est in intellectu quod non fuerit in sensu*," with the retort: "*excipe: nisi ipse intellectus.*"[37] In other words, the intellect has a reflective access to itself and this provides it with ideas that express its inherent nature rather than anything provided by experience. As examples of these ideas, Leibniz lists "substance, one, same, cause, perception, reasoning, and many other notions which the senses cannot provide."[38]

For present purposes, the essential feature of Leibniz's account is his claim that, though these concepts are grounded in the very nature of the intellect, our awareness of them is occasioned by experience.[39] By this means Leibniz attempted to do justice to the moment of truth in Lockean empiricism; viz., that experience is a necessary condition of these (indeed of any) concepts, while insisting that certain concepts are grounded in the nature of the intellect. Accordingly, the suggestion is that Kant accepted both Locke's critique of the theory of innate ideas as traditionally understood, according to which the mind is equipped from birth with determinate ideas and principles, which were presumably implanted by God, and Leibniz's alternative account of innateness together with the latter's Platonic view of the role of experience as a necessary occasion for the acquisition of determinate concepts such as cause and substance.[40]

As already noted, however, Kant parts company with Leibniz regarding the relation between the sensible and the intellectual components of human cognition. In fact, he grounds this rejection in the previously given characterization of the sensible as dependent on the special character of the subject. Given this, one cannot claim that the sensible is what is cognized confusedly and the intellectual what is cognized distinctly. And, in light of this, Kant chastises Wolff for further confusing matters with his misguided view that the distinction between the sensible and intellectual components of cognition is merely logical, which Kant suggests has led to the abolition of "the noblest of the enterprises of antiquity, the discussion of the character of phenomena and noumena, and has turned men's minds away from that enquiry to things which are often only logical minutiae" (ID 2: 395$_{11-14}$; 387).

---

[36] This tension is overcome in the *Critique*, particularly in the second edition, by connecting the concepts of the understanding with the logical forms of judgment.

[37] Leibniz (1981), 110.   [38] Ibid.

[39] Leibniz makes this point in several places in the Preface to the *New Essays* as well as in Book One, which deals explicitly with the topic of innate ideas.

[40] This is essentially the view expressed by Herz (1990), 34–5, whom it should be kept in mind was not only Kant's former student but also a respondent to the *Dissertation*.

There is a certain irony here, since Kant is in effect using Leibniz against Wolff. Moreover, in so doing, he is appealing to a Platonism, which was explicitly acknowledged by Leibniz and which appears to contrast strongly with the skeptical and seemingly anti-metaphysical empiricism of *Dreams*.[41] This Platonism is evident in Kant's account of the real use of the intellect to which he assigns two functions: elenctic and dogmatic. The elenctic function, which is at work in section 5, is merely negative: keeping what is sensibly conceived distinct from noumena. Although this does not purport to yield any advance in metaphysical knowledge, we shall see that it serves an essential limitative function by preserving the understanding in its pursuit of such knowledge from "the contagion of error" (ID 2: 395_{29-31}; 388).[42]

By contrast, the dogmatic function of the intellect is based on general principles of the pure understanding, such as are exemplified in ontology, rational psychology, and theology, and it leads to a paradigm (*exemplar*) of noumenal perfection (*Perfectio Noumenon*), by which Kant understands a maximal perfection (ID 2: $395_{31}-6_{12}$; 388). As was common in the Platonic tradition, Kant identifies perfection with reality, which means that the maximal perfection consists in the maximal or greatest reality. Considered as an entity, this maximal perfection is the *ens realissimum* of the *Beweisgrund*, which became the ideal of pure reason in the *Critique*.[43]

Ontological perfection is, however, only one of the two species of noumenal perfection recognized by Kant. The other is moral perfection, which he viewed as the source of the first principles of moral judgment (*principia diiudicandi*) (ID 2: 396_5; 388).[44] Moreover, Kant's account of the former has an epistemic thrust, since he initially characterizes God, the ideal of perfection, as "the principle of cognizing" (*principium cognoscendi*); though he notes that considered as really existing, God is also the principle of the coming into existence of all perfection whatsoever (ID 2: 396_{16-17}; 388). In other words, Kant seems to view God not only as the ground of being, which is the doctrine of the *Beweisgrund*, but also as the source of epistemic

---

[41] At the very beginning of the Preface to the *New Essays* Leibniz suggests that his views are closer to those of Plato and Locke's to those of Aristotle (1981), 47. The importance of Kant's reading of Plato and, more generally, Greek philosophy at the time for the *Dissertation* has been emphasized by Wundt (1924), 153–78.

[42] Setting aside the sensibility-understanding distinction, which Kant had not yet drawn in 1766, the elenctic function of the intellect is quite close to what Kant had characterized as the second and main advantage of metaphysics in *Dreams*. Similarly, the greatly diminished first advantage of metaphysics in *Dreams* appears to have been transformed into the considerably more positive dogmatic function of the intellect in the *Dissertation*.

[43] Anticipating the language of the *Critique*, Kant notes in passing that the maximum of perfection was at this time referred to as the ideal (ID 2: 396 12; 388).

[44] Kant's attribution of the first principles of moral judgment to the intellect marks a major shift from his view in the *Prize Essay*, where he noted that it is as yet undecided whether it is the cognitive faculty or feeling that is the source of the first principles of morality (U 2: 298–300). Moreover, in his announcement of his lectures on ethics for the winter of 1765–1766, Kant states that, though their accounts are "incomplete and defective," Shaftesbury, Hutcheson, and Hume "have nonetheless penetrated furthest in the search for the fundamental principles of all morality (N 2: 311_{25-8}; 298).

norms, at least as far as the cognition of noumena is concerned. We shall revisit the latter point below.

Our immediate concern, however, is with a significant restriction that Kant places on the dogmatic use of the intellect; viz., that there is no intuitive, but only a "*symbolic cognition*" of noumena or what belongs to the understanding (*Intellectualium*) (ID 2: 396_{19-20}; 388). Given the conceptual framework that Kant provides, it is clear that we can have no intuitive cognition of noumena, whether we understand by intuition either the sensible or the intellectual variety. By its very nature, sensible intuition cannot provide such cognition and, though the intellectual variety could, this is of little use to us, since we lack such a capacity. But since a dogmatic use of the intellect presupposes that *some* cognition of noumena is possible, and since Kant appears to assume that the only alternative to an intuitive is a symbolic cognition, the operative questions become: (1) what does Kant understand by "symbolic cognition" and (2) how is it supposed to yield cognition of the noumenal or intelligible world?

With regard to the first question, it is useful to consider the senses assigned to the terms "intuitive" and "symbolic" by those who, before Kant, distinguished between them as species of cognition. Once again the key figure is Leibniz, who drew this distinction in his seminal essay: "Meditations on Knowledge, Truth, and Ideas" (1684).[45] According to Leibniz's taxonomy, cognitions are either clear or obscure (depending upon whether they suffice for the recognition of their object); while a clear cognition is either distinct or confused (depending upon whether or not one can delineate the marks distinguishing its object from others); and distinct cognitions are either adequate or inadequate (depending upon whether everything that enters into such a cognition is itself distinctly known). Finally, adequate cognitions are either intuitiva or symbolic, which means that for Leibniz intuitive and symbolic cognitions are the two species of adequate cognition and as such, are sources of *scientia* or knowledge in the pre-eminent sense.[46]

Although Leibniz regarded symbolic cognition as a source of *scientia*, he granted epistemic supremacy to the intuitive variety. For Leibniz the defining feature of intuitive cognition and the basis of its primacy is its immediacy, which renders it both direct and non-inferential. Moreover, given Leibniz's view of the relation between the sensible and the intellectual, the intuition involved is intellectual. As adequate, symbolic cognition is likewise intellectual in Leibniz's sense, but it lacks the immediacy and directness of intuitive cognition. Rather than yielding a direct

---

[45] The distinction was apparently rooted in that drawn by Scotus and Ockham between *cognitio intuitiva* and *cognitio abstractive* and is also to be found in the writings of the German philosophers with whom Kant was most concerned at the time such as Wolff (2005), 173–83, Meier (1924), 814–15, and Crusius (1964), 171–3. For useful overviews of the history of this distinction and its predecessors, see Kobusch (1976), 524–40, and Oeser (1998), 710–23. Although there are interesting differences between these formulations, for present purposes they can be ignored, since the German thinkers mentioned all provide variations of the Leibnizian account, which is also the basis for Kant's.

[46] Leibniz (1989), 24.

apprehension of its object as it is in itself, such cognition relies on signs or symbols. The latter are usually but not always linguistic, e.g., numerals in arithmetic and lines or figures in geometry. In view of its lack of immediacy or direct access to its object, Leibniz also characterizes symbolic cognition as "blind."[47] But, despite its blindness, he insisted on the legitimacy of symbolic cognition insofar as it is based on the proper formal procedures or rules.

From a Kantian perspective, the most important feature of the Leibnizian view is the connection between intuitive and divine cognition. Although Leibniz did not maintain that human beings are totally incapable of intuitive cognition, he sharply limited its scope to primitive notions or truths, which being incapable of resolution by further analysis, if they are to be cognized at all, must be cognized intuitively.[48] Accordingly, the great bulk of human cognition can never be more than symbolic, since it relies on words, non-verbal signs, and formal principles of reasoning. By contrast, divine cognition is by its very nature intuitive and with respect to actual things consists in a "*scientia visionis*."[49] The latter is epitomized in Leibniz's conception of the complete concept of an individual substance. Since, *ex hypothesi*, such a concept involves everything that will ever happen to an individual, and since this involves a connection with the universe as a whole, it follows that such a concept involves infinity. As such, adequate cognition would seem to require an infinite analysis, which Leibniz recognized as impossible, not only for finite rational beings but even for God. Nevertheless, he maintained that God possesses such cognition by an intuition through which he "traverses the infinite series in one stroke of mind."[50]

Since this is precisely the idea to which Kant appeals in his claim that our inability to grasp the infinite indicates merely a subjective limitation rather than any incoherence in the concept, it seems reasonable to assume that Kant's conception of an intuitive intellect in the *Dissertation* is essentially Leibnizian.[51] Moreover, basically the same may be said regarding symbolic cognition.[52] The main difference is one of emphasis: whereas Leibniz emphasizes the indispensable role of words as signs or symbols for the inaccessible signified, Kant's account focuses on the conceptual or

[47] Ibid., 25.

[48] In "Meditations on Knowledge, Truth, and Ideas" Leibniz characterizes what can be known intuitively by humans as "distinct primitive notions" (*notionis distinctae primativae*) (1989), 25 and in the *New Essays* as "primary truths" (*verités primitives*) (1981), 361. In the latter he states that these encompass both truths of reason and truths of fact.

[49] Leibniz distinguishes between God's knowledge of actual and possible things, both of which are immediate. The former is termed "*scientia visionis*" and the latter "*scientia simplicis intelligentiae*." See, for example, Leibniz (1989), 99.

[50] Leibniz (1989), 28.

[51] For a very similar account, see also ND 1: 391_{26-30}; 10.

[52] This applies only to Kant's account in the *Dissertation*. In the third *Critique* he denied that there is a sharp distinction between intuitive and symbolic cognition, maintaining that the symbolic is merely a species of the intuitive and in light of this criticizes (unnamed) recent logicians for a distorted and incorrect use of the term "symbolic" (KU 5: 351_{33-5}; 226). A similar claim is also to be found in A 7: 191; 299 and in VSgE 20: 362_{15-20}, where Kant explicitly denies that cognition involving language is symbolic.

discursive nature of symbolic cognition. His main point is that thinking or intellection "is only possible for us by means of general concepts in the abstract, not by means of a singular concept in the concrete" (ID 2: 396$_{19-21}$; 397). Nevertheless, assuming that the use of concepts requires language and vice versa, this is compatible with the main thrust of the Leibnizian view.[53]

Accordingly, the answer to our first question is that symbolic cognition for Kant (at least outside of mathematics) is conceptual or discursive. It is essential, however, to keep in mind that this does not amount to the affirmation of the discursivity thesis. As has been emphasized throughout, the latter maintains not only that cognition by finite rational beings involves the use of concepts, but also that it requires the relation of these concepts to sensible intuition. But it is precisely the lack of any such relation that is the defining feature of symbolic cognition, so understood. Moreover, this gives added urgency to our second question: how can symbolic cognition yield knowledge of a *mundus intelligibilis*? Since both direct access through intellectual intuition and an appeal to innate ideas are precluded, the answer must be through conceptual analysis. There is simply no other alternative. But while this seems relatively clear, it leads to a third and more perplexing question; viz., on what basis did Kant assume that the products of conceptual analysis yield metaphysical truths about a *mundus intelligibilis*, rather than fanciful products of the imagination, such as those of Swedenborg or Kant's persona in *Dreams*? Although one of the major lacunae of the *Dissertation* is its failure explicitly to address this seemingly obvious question, I believe it possible to locate three factors that help to explain this failure.

The first is the purity of these cognitions. Unlike the visions of Swedenborg or the metaphysical dreams of Kant's persona, the claims in the *Dissertation* are not contaminated by any ingredients stemming from sensibility. As we shall see below, in the *Dissertation* Kant saw the threat to metaphysical reasoning as lying solely in the contamination of the intellectual by the sensible and thus failed to consider the possibility of a contamination that proceeded in the opposite direction.[54] Although this neglect may be understandable insofar as Kant's concern is with the non-sensible

---

[53] The non-linguistic side of Leibniz's view of symbolic cognition largely involves mathematics (and logic). Kant does not deal with (pure) mathematics in the *Dissertation*, but in the *Critique* he refers to a "symbolic construction" in algebra, which is the counterpart of the ostensive construction operative in geometry (A717/B745). While I have no wish to deny the radical difference between Leibniz's deductivist view of mathematics and Kant's constructivist conception, I do think that this shows that Kant recognized a non-linguistic or non-conceptual role for symbols. The same could also be said of his account of aesthetic ideas and of beauty as a symbol of the morally good in the third *Critique*, but pursuing these topics is well beyond the scope of the present work. For those who may be interested in my views on the latter, see Allison (2001), 236–67.

[54] Kant does, however, suggest the possibility of such a contamination in two *Reflexionen*. In one, he juxtaposes a "*petitio phaenomenorum*" which corresponds to a subreption in the sense of the *Dissertation*, with a "*petitio noumeni*," which involves using real concepts (*realbegriffe*) in connection with phenomena in such a way that this is taken to yield knowledge of the thing itself (R 4644 17: 623). In the other, he distinguishes between types of *axiomata aequivoca*: one in which the subject is sensible and the predicate intellectual and the other where the reverse is the case (R 4650 17: 625).

objects of rational psychology and theology (the soul and God), it becomes problematic when the concern is with ontology.[55]

The second factor is the converse of Kant's principle that *"whatever cannot be cognized by any intuition at all is simply not thinkable,* and is, thus, impossible" (ID 2: 413_{10-11}; 409); viz., that whatever can be cognized by *some* intuition (even a nonsensible one) is thinkable and therefore possible. In our initial consideration of this principle, we saw that Kant appealed to it in defending the possibility of an infinite magnitude on the grounds that our inability to intuit one signified only a "subjective resistance" rather than an objective impossibility, since it would be intuitable for an intellect (such as God's) that could intuit a multiplicity at a "single glance." The present suggestion is that the *lack* of any "objective resistance," i.e., logical or conceptual obstacles, may have led Kant to assume that what a finite intellect cognizes symbolically (by conceptual analysis) coincides with what would be grasped intuitively by an infinite one.[56]

The third and most important factor in Kant's apparently uncritical acceptance of the results of conceptual analysis is that in 1770 he had not yet drawn the distinction between analytic and synthetic judgments, which would have immediately led him to recognize that these results were merely a set of analytic judgments. Accordingly, it is likely that Kant had his own earlier view in mind, as well as those of the Leibnizians and others, when, as an entrée to his formulation of the analytic-synthetic distinction in the introduction to the *Critique*, he remarks:

A great part, perhaps the greatest part, of the business of our reason consists in *analyses* of the concepts that we already have of objects. This affords us a multitude of cognitions that, although they are nothing more than illuminations or clarifications of that which is already thought in our concepts (though still in a confused way), are, at least as far as their form is concerned, treasured as if they were new insights, though they do not extend the concepts that we have in either matter or content... Now since this procedure does yield a real *a priori* cognition... reason, without itself noticing it, under these pretenses surreptitiously makes assertions of quite another sort, in which reason adds something entirely alien to given concepts and indeed does so *a priori*, without one knowing how it was able to do this and without such a question even being allowed to come to mind.   (A5–6/B9–10)

Since the "critical" Kant acknowledged that the analysis of concepts that we already have yields "a real [*wirkliche*] *a priori* cognition," it is understandable how an earlier Kant, who had not yet formulated the analytic-synthetic distinction, not to mention uncovered the problem of the synthetic a priori, could succumb to the

---

[55] This problem was raised by Lambert, who in his letter to Kant of October 13, 1770 regarding the *Dissertation*, notes that in ontology it useful to take up concepts borrowed from appearance (*Schein*), "since *the theory must finally be applied to phenomena again*" (Br 10: 108_{28-9}; 117).

[56] This accords with the previously noted view of Leibniz that symbolic cognition is adequate despite its blindness. Moreover, it should also be noted that Crusius insisted that it would be an error not to regard symbolic cognition as sufficient for certainty (1965), 360.

thought that the purity of the concepts being analyzed, combined with valid reasoning, would suffice to ground the symbolic cognition of a *mundus intelligibilis*.[57] Otherwise expressed, in 1770 Kant was not yet in a position to claim, as he reportedly did in a metaphysics lecture, which stems from the "critical" period but which refers back to the *Dissertation*, that "Little is presented of the intelligible world [*mundo intelligibili*] since we can cognize little more of it through the understanding than what follows from the definition" (Met M 29: 850_{13-15}; 207).[58]

The path from the position of the *Dissertation* to this view is precisely the path to the "critical" standpoint, with which we shall be concerned in Chapter 3. In the meantime, however, we are still concerned with the *Dissertation* and our immediate subject matter is the concluding portion of section 2 (§11 and §12), where Kant all too briefly discusses two important epistemological topics: the nature and legitimacy of our knowledge of phenomena and the sphere of pure sensible cognition. Indeed, the brevity of his consideration of these topics, treating them essentially as side issues or perhaps as items on a checklist, is a reflection of the rushed nature and sketchiness of the work as a whole, as well as the distance between the essentially Platonic standpoint of the *Dissertation*, with its focus on the possibility of a metaphysics of the intelligible world, from both his analytic metaphysics of the early 1760s and his eventual "critical" position.

§11 begins with the claim that, "[A]lthough phenomena, properly speaking, are aspects of things [*rerum species*] and not ideas, and although they do not express the internal and absolute quality of objects, nonetheless cognition of them is in the highest degree true" (ID 2: 397_{6-8}; 389). Although this is presented as a single claim, for the purpose of analysis it can be broken down into two parts. The first consists in an attempt to show that the conception of the sensible world as composed of phenomena, which was initially affirmed in §3, does not amount to idealism. Accordingly, despite Kant's explicit rejection of the latter, his account is not so much a refutation of idealism, such as we find in the *Critique*, as it is an attempt to disassociate his own position from that presumably disreputable view.[59] The second is to show that this conception, unlike idealism, allows for the possibility of genuine empirical cognition of the sensible, i.e., corporeal, world. As such, it might be considered Kant's initial attempt to ground what in the *Critique* will be referred to as "empirical realism."

---

[57] Kant makes the point more clearly in his Logic by distinguishing between a formal and a material extension of knowledge. See JL 9: 111; 606–7. Analytic judgments extend our knowledge in the former sense and synthetic judgment in the latter. I discuss this in Allison (2004), 91–3.

[58] In the same context, Kant refers to a foreigner (*Auswärtiger*) (presumably an unnamed reviewer) who had suggested that to speak of an intelligible world was "*Schwärmerei*," to which Kant responded that it is just the opposite, "for one understands by it not another world, but rather this world as I think it through the understanding" (MM 29: 850_{16-20}; 207).

[59] That it is to be seen as such a refutation is argued by Guyer (1987), 11–24, esp. 21–2. Although he criticizes Guyer's account this view is also shared by Caranti (2007), 23–7.

Kant does not here specify exactly what he meant by idealism, but from other texts stemming from the "pre-critical" period it seems evident that he understood it as the metaphysical thesis that there are only thinking beings or spirits, i.e., immaterial substances. Although this is associated primarily with Berkeley, for Kant it also included Leibniz.[60] Broadly speaking, it corresponds to what the "critical" Kant referred to as "dogmatic idealism" as contrasted with the "problematic idealism" of Descartes, which is essentially an epistemological thesis. Kant points to what distinguishes this idealism from his own position, which, despite his doctrine of the subjectivity of space and time (to be discussed below), he does not yet characterize as a form of idealism, in the first sentence of §11, where he claims that, even though they do not express the internal and absolute quality of objects, i.e., their true inner nature or as they are in themselves, his phenomena are not ideas. Otherwise expressed, the objects to which Kant is referring are not appearances, understood as a distinct set of mental entities, which would constitute idealism, but things that exist in themselves as they appear to us in virtue of our forms of receptivity. Moreover, Kant expands on this in the subsequent sentence, where he states that "insofar as they [phenomena] are sensory concepts or apprehensions, they are, as things caused, witnesses to the presence of an object, and this is opposed to idealism" (ID 2: 397_{8-10}; 389). Since Berkeley likewise maintained that our ideas are caused, albeit by God rather than by independently existing material objects, it seems likely that Kant had specifically in mind the Leibnizian form of idealism, which in view of the pre-established harmony denied any real interaction or causal influx between substances.[61] But, quite apart from the question of Kant's possible target, it seems reasonably clear that he is here affirming the real existence of entities distinct from the human mind, the intrinsic nature of which remain inaccessible to us.[62]

---

[60] This corresponds to the definition of idealism in Baumgarten (1926), 111 and 117; (2013), 175–6 and 183. Kant's earliest published discussion of idealism is in ND 1: 411–12; 39 (1755), where he rejects it on the grounds that things external to the soul must be posited to account for its inner changes. As such, it is part of a polemic against the Leibnizian pre-established harmony and its denial of real influence or interaction between substances. Somewhat later, in Herder's transcript of Kant's *Metaphysics Lectures* from the early 1760s (MH 28: 42–3; 4–6), he treats egoism and idealism together, linking the latter to Berkeley's views as contained in *Siris*, and apparently regarding both as posing serious philosophical challenges, going so far as to claim that the latter cannot be refuted logically. For a discussion of these texts and the relation between them see Caranti (2007), 11–20. Finally, in ML_1 28: 206–8; 29–30 Kant presents a more nuanced account of both idealism and egoism, distinguishing (as he will do in the *Critique*) between dogmatic and problematic versions of both, and finding the latter philosophically valuable as a "skeptical trial." He also refers to dogmatic idealism as both mystical and Platonic and associates it with Leibniz as well as Berkeley.

[61] This is clearly the case in Kant's earliest published discussion of idealism in ND and Leibniz is paired with Berkeley as an idealist in ML1. See preceding note.

[62] On this point I am in agreement with Guyer (1987), 20–4, who claims that at this time Kant was committed to an ontological realism. As will become clear in subsequent chapters, I reject his claim that in the *Critique* this is replaced by a subjective idealism that Kant (mistakenly) thought was necessary in order to account for the possibility of a priori knowledge.

Having supposedly shown by this appeal to causation that our sensible representations bear witness to the existence of objects that are ontologically distinct from these representations, Kant's next step is to affirm the genuineness of our empirical, i.e., sensible, cognition of phenomena that is based upon these representations. Once again, his account is exceedingly cryptic. It is supported by two premises. The first is that judgments concerning phenomena conform to the truth conditions of judgment, which Kant here characterizes as the agreement of the predicate with the given subject (ID 2: 397_{12-13}; 389). The second is that both the predicate and the subject of such judgments are sensible (ID 2: 397_{14-15}; 389). Since this is at most a necessary and not a sufficient cognition of the truth of such cognition, it appears that Kant's reason for appealing to it is to differentiate such propositions (as possible candidates for truth) from those in which a sensible predicate is connected with a non-sensible, i.e., intellectual subject, which Kant will later designate as the prime source of metaphysical error. In fact, Kant does not claim that the sensible nature of subject and predicate is a sufficient condition of their agreement but merely that this provides a "foot hold" or "handle" (*anseam praedere*) "for cognition which is in the highest degree true" (ID 2: 397_{16-17}; 389). The most significant aspect of Kant's account, however, is his characterization of truth in terms of the agreement of the predicate with the concept of the subject, since it suggests that he is still appealing to the analytic model of cognition at work in the writings of the 1760s, which we have seen antedates the analytic-synthetic distinction.

After supposedly accounting for the possibility of empirical sensible cognition in §11, Kant turns in §12 to the question of a pure sensible cognition. This anticipates the account of space and time in section 3 as forms of sensible intuition and as themselves pure intuitions. Kant's intent is to show not simply that sensible cognition yields truth, but that it yields a priori truth, even though it does not involve a real use of the intellect.[63] As he puts it, "[T]*here is a science of sensory things*, although since they are phenomena, the use of the understanding is not real but only logical" (ID 2: 398_{3-5}; 390). In fact, it turns out that for Kant there are three such sciences or, more precisely, two that are pure and one of mixed heritage. The former are mathematics, by which Kant means geometry, which deals with space, and mechanics, which deals with time. This leaves arithmetic as the "mixed," science of sensory things, which Kant regards as such because, while the concept of number is intellectual, its concrete application, i.e., enumeration, "requires the auxiliary notions of time and space" (ID 2: 397_{30-1}; 390).

C) *The sensible world*: The third section of the *Dissertation* is entitled "On the principles of the form of the sensible world" and its subject is the nature of space and time. Since it covers basically the same ground and contains many of the same

---

[63] Although Kant does not use the term "*a priori*" in this context, it is clear that this is what he had in mind. See note 67.

arguments as the Transcendental Aesthetic of the *Critique* and I have discussed these arguments extensively elsewhere, I shall not consider them in the detail that their intrinsic importance warrants.[64] Instead, while not neglecting these arguments, I shall also consider their relation to the overall project of the *Dissertation* and to the views espoused in Kant's earlier works.

In order to understand Kant's position in this section of the *Dissertation*, it is necessary to consider it in light of the view of space that he articulated in his 1768 paper discussed in the first section of this chapter. We saw that Kant there broke with the Leibnizian relational view that he had advocated in his earlier writings and instead championed the Newtonian conception of an absolute space, which has a reality that is prior to and independent of the relation of things that are experienced therein and, as Euler had argued, is presupposed by the Newtonian laws of motion. It was also noted, however, that Kant did not affirm the Newtonian view regarding the ontology of space, which had been severely criticized by Leibniz in his correspondence with Clarke, and that he introduced an important consideration that had been overlooked by Euler; viz., that rather than being an object of outer sensation, space is "a fundamental concept which first of all makes possible all such outer sensation" (G 2: 383_{20}; 371).

Although clearly an advance over Kant's earlier views, the account given in this paper is inadequate in two respects. First, it leaves the ontological question unresolved. If absolute space does not have the ontological status Newton assigned to it, what sort of status does it have? Second, if space is a fundamental concept rather than an object of outer sense, what kind of concept is it and how does it make outer sensation possible? Kant's answer to these questions awaited the distinction between sensibility and understanding as cognitive faculties with their own forms and principles, which resulted from the "great light" of 1769. It was this that made possible the connection of space and time with sensibility, which was first affirmed in the *Dissertation* and which determined the subsequent shape of Kant's theoretical philosophy.

Kant assumes his conception of space and time as formal conditions of the sensible world in the first two sections of the *Dissertation*, but it is only in the third that he actually argues for it. Having provided an analysis of the concept of a world as such, which features the distinction between its matter (substances) and its form (coordination) in the first section, and of the distinction between the sensible and intelligible in the second, Kant turns in the third to the concept of a sensible world and the principle of its form. As the concept of a kind (or species) of world, that of a sensible world must conform to the condition of a world as such; viz., completeness or totality; its form must consist in a certain manner of coordination of the substances that constitute its matter; and the principle of this form would be whatever grounds the coordination of the substances that constitute its matter.

---

[64] For my more detailed treatment of Kant's arguments in their later form, see Allison (2004), 97–132.

Given these constraints, Kant's aim is to show that time and space are the principles of the form of the *human* sensible world (2: 398_{28-9}; 391). Kant proceeds in his usual analytic fashion by considering the differentia introduced into the concept of a world through the assumption that this world is cognizable through the senses. Appealing to the argument of section 2, he contends that, whereas the principle of the form of the intelligible world would be objective, i.e., "some cause in virtue of which there is a combining together of the things which exist in themselves" (ID 2: 398_{16}; 391), that of a sensible world must be subjective, which Kant characterizes as a "fixed law of the mind, in virtue of which it is necessary that all of the things which can be objects of the senses...are seen as *necessarily* belonging to the same whole" (ID 2: 398_{19-21}; 391).

This characterization of the principle of the form of a sensible world as such focuses on its two essential features: subjectivity and necessity. The former stems from its status as a "fixed law of the *mind*," specifically, of sensibility, the "lower" cognitive faculty, which, as a result of the "great light," was granted an independent status. As subjective, Kant notes that its scope is limited to objects of the senses, and therefore excludes immaterial substances, which he states are by definition excluded from the "outer senses," and the cause of the world, which due to its preeminence as cause of the mind, cannot be an object of the senses (ID 2: 398_{23-7}; 391).[65] Conversely, its necessity is grounded in its status as a *fixed law* of the mind, which means that whatever is deemed capable of "*falling under the senses*" (being an object of a possible perception) necessarily conforms to it. By way of underscoring the inelimin-able function of such principles, Kant adds that "These formal principles of the *phenomenal universe* are absolutely primary and universal; they are so to speak, the schemata and condition of everything sensible in human cognition," and he concludes by stipulating that these principles are time and space (ID 2: 398_{27-9}; 391).

The shift from talking about a principle of the form of a sensible world to talking about principles (in the plural) and the characterization of these principles as time and space marks Kant's abrupt transition from an analysis of the concept of a sensible world as such, which remains within the domain of conceptual analysis, to what amounts to a factual claim about *our* world; viz., that time and space happen to be the forms of human sensibility. Inasmuch as Kant regarded other forms of sensibility as at least logically possible, this has the status of a brute factual claim

---

[65] Kant's exclusion of immaterial substances from the sensible world on the grounds that they are not objects of the *outer* senses is an indication of the unsettled nature of his conception of inner sense at the time. In fact, the only reference to inner sense in the *Dissertation* is a passing one in which the phenomena of inner sense are said to provide the subject matter of empirical psychology (ID 2: 397_{23-4}; 390). Moreover, whereas both here and in the *Critique* space is connected specifically with outer sense, Kant does not, as he will in the *Critique*, connect time with inner sense. Instead, we shall see that he treats it as a general condition of sensibility. In R 4070 17: 403, which evidently stems from the period of the *Dissertation*, Kant states that time, unlike space, extends to outer as well as inner sensations, but there is no suggestion that the latter is its original domain.

for which no explanation is forthcoming.[66] Nevertheless, Kant thought that it could be justified by demonstrating that time and space actually function in this way in human experience. The remainder of the third section of the *Dissertation* is devoted to this demonstration: first for time and then for space.

Time: Kant's account of time in the *Dissertation* contains seven propositions:

1. "The idea of time does not arise from but is presupposed by the senses" (2: 398_{32-3}; 391).
2. "The idea of time is singular and not general" (2: 399_8; 392).
3. "The idea of time is an intuition," more precisely, a pure intuition (2: $399;_{18-20}$; 392).
4. "Time is a continuous magnitude" (2: 399_{21-2}; 392).
5. "Time is not something objective and real" (2: 400_1; 393).
6. "Although time, posited in itself and absolutely, would be an imaginary being," as belonging to the "immutable law of sensible things as such, it is in the highest degree true" (2: 401_{19-21}; 395).
7. Time is an "absolutely first formal principle of the sensible world" (2: 402_{8-9}; 395).

The first three propositions, which concern the idea (or representation) of time, correspond to what in the second edition of the *Critique* became the Metaphysical Exposition of the concept. The last four deal with the nature of time (what is represented or thought through the idea) and correspond to the Transcendental Exposition and the conclusions from drawn from them. Since the argument as a whole moves from a consideration of the nature of the representation of time to the nature of time itself, qua represented, the discussion will be divided into these two segments.

Although in contrast to the *Critique* Kant does not use the term, it is evident that the point of the first proposition is to show that the representation of time is a priori.[67] It is assumed that any viable empirical account of the genesis of this representation would have to show that it is derivable from the experience of successive and/or simultaneous phenomena and the argument contends that this is futile, since the experience of either already presupposes, and therefore cannot account for the possession of this representation (ID 2: $398_{32}-9_2$; 392).

The second and third propositions conjointly argue that the idea of time is a pure intuition. But since its purity is simply asserted, presumably on the basis of what has

---

[66] In the *Critique* Kant acknowledges the inexplicability of the fact that "space and time are the sole forms of our possible intuition" at B147.

[67] Since Kant was obviously familiar with the classical distinction between the a priori and the a posteriori, I assume that his failure to introduce it at this point is due to the fact that he had not yet arrived at the view that the notion is applicable to concepts (or intuitions) as well as propositions. See A2 and B5. In the *Dissertation* the term "*a priori*" appears twice and in both times merely in passing. See ID 2: 417_{15} and 418_{37}.

been shown in the first proposition, the brunt of the argument is that it is an intuition rather than a general idea. In support of this thesis Kant makes three points. The first consists in an appeal to the singleness of time. As he puts it, "no time is thought of except as part of the same boundless time" (ID 2: 399_{9-10}; 392). Thus, any period of time must stand in a determinable relation to all others in a single temporal framework. Implicit in this is the premise that an intuition is a singular representation and a concept (or idea) a general one. Second, in what constitutes the temporal counterpart of the appeal to incongruent counterparts, Kant notes that the relation of earlier and later among different times cannot, without vicious circularity, be determined by any characteristic marks which could be conceived by the understanding" (ID 2: 399_{12-16}; 392). In other words, *earlier* and *later* (like left and right) are primitive two-place predicates, which, as such, must be grounded in an intuition. Third, we conceive all actual things as located *in* time, and not as contained *under* a general concept of time, as under a common mark (ID 2: 399_{16-17}; 392).

The fourth proposition maintains that time is a continuous magnitude. Although this proposition does not appear in the Aesthetic, its basic point, namely, that time (like space) is infinitely divisible, is part of Kant's "critical" view. In the *Dissertation* Kant's interest in this proposition lies in its connection with the metaphysical law of continuity, which affirms the continuity of change and which is one Leibnizian thesis that Kant defends (ID 2: 399_{21}–440_{20}; 393). Moreover, this property of time provides a response to a possible objection to Kant's intuition thesis, at least insofar as it is based on the singleness of the idea of time; viz., that the idea of the world is likewise singular, but one would not therefore claim that it is an intuition. The response, suggested by the present claim, is that the parts of the world (substances) do not relate to the world as the parts of time do to time. In the former case, the parts logically precede the whole, just as the parts of a concept (the partial representations that compose it) precede it; whereas the "parts" of time, that is, particular times, presuppose the whole and are only conceivable as limitations or specific determinations of it.[68]

The fifth proposition concerns the ontological status of time. Kant's claim contains both a negative and a positive portion. The former consists in the denial that time is something objective and real on the grounds that it is neither substance, nor accident, nor relation, which are the three ontological alternatives.[69] The latter affirms, as a direct consequence of this, that "Time is rather the subjective condition which is necessary, in virtue of the nature of the human mind, for the co-ordinating of all

---

[68] See ID 2: 399_{21-32}; 392. Although Kant does not here refer to the concept of a world or relate his discussion specifically to the issue regarding the intuitive nature of the representation of time, he presents all the materials necessary for dealing with this issue. I discuss this issue with respect to Kant's treatment of space in the *Critique* in Allison (2004), 109–10.

[69] In the *Critique* Kant lists these three possibilities for both space and time and adds a fourth, namely, "relations that only attach to the form of intuition alone" (A23/B37), which is the view that Kant defends. For my discussion of this issue, see Allison (2004, 98–8 and 120–2).

sensible things in accordance with a fixed law." On this basis, Kant reiterates the claim that time is a *pure intuition.*" (ID 2: 400_{21-4}; 393).

Kant's argument for the thesis that time is a subjective condition consists of two parts. The first offers reasons for holding this view and the second affirms the untenability of the contrary thesis that time possesses objective reality. Appealing to the above-mentioned ontological alternatives, Kant argues that, since it is only through the concept of time, as a principle of form, that we coordinate substances and accidents (presumably by relating them to each other in terms of simultaneity and succession) this concept is (epistemically) prior to the concepts of substance and relation (ID 2: 400_{24-7}; 393). Inasmuch as Kant regards the concept of substance as a concept of the understanding and the concept of accident presupposes that of substance, this priority claim is hard to square with his sharp separation between sensibility and understanding. But assuming that Kant is talking about phenomena, the argument is more promising; for all that is needed to establish that time is a principle of the form of sensible cognition is to show that it is presupposed as a condition of the apprehension of the relation between phenomena as successive or simultaneous, which is what Kant does in the next sentence in connection with his discussion of relations (ID 2: 400_{27-30}; 393).

Kant considers two versions of the contrary thesis that time possesses objective reality, which, not surprisingly, are those of the Newtonians and the Leibnizians. The former, which regards time as a continuous flux within existence, which is independent of any existing thing, is summarily dismissed as an "absurd fabrication" (ID 2: 400_{31-4}; 394). Kant devotes more attention to the latter, according to which time is "conceived as something real which has been abstracted from the succession of internal states" (ID 2: 400_{34-5}; 394). Although he dismisses this view on the grounds that its derivation of the idea of time from the awareness of successive phenomena is circular and that it ignores simultaneity, Kant's real quarrel with the Leibnizian view concerns its implication for the Newtonian laws of motion. Just as he had done in the case of space in the 1768 paper, Kant argues that these laws presuppose a pre-given temporal framework and that the latter therefore cannot be derived from the observation of moving things without undermining their certainty (ID 2: 401_{4-13}; 394). Moreover, again applying the line of argument used in this paper with respect to space, Kant counters the anticipated objection that the measurement of the quantity of time can be based only on the measure of motion by in effect noting that this is because (absolute) time cannot be perceived, which is supposedly explained by the fact that, rather than being an innate intuition, the concept of time rests on an internal law of the mind (ID 2: 401_{7-12}; 394).

In the final two paragraphs of his discussion of time, Kant affirms what in the *Critique* will become the dual thesis that time is empirically real and transcendentally ideal. In the *Dissertation*, the ideality claim is expressed by the proposition that "posited in itself and absolutely" time "would be an imaginary being" and the correlative empirical realism by the proposition that, "insofar as it belongs to the immutable law of sensible things as such, it [time] is in the highest degree true" (ID 2: 401_{19-21}; 395). Finally, in support of the status of time as a fundamental principle of sensible cognition, and therefore of the sensible world, Kant affirms the main point of what will later become the transcendental exposition of the concept of time; viz., that time, so conceived, is the source of certain "axioms of time," of which he cites as an example the continuity of time discussed previously (ID 2: $401_{27}-2_1$; 395).[70]

Space: Kant's account of space closely tracks that of time, though he divides it into five rather than seven propositions.

1. "The concept of space is not abstracted from outer sensations" (2: 402_{16}; 395).[71]
2. "The concept of space is a singular representation embracing all things within itself" (2: 402_{16}; 395).
3. "The concept of space is a pure intuition" (2: 402_{28}; 396).
4. "Space is not something objective and real" (2: 403_{23}; 397).
5. "Although the concept of space as some objective and real being or property be imaginary, nonetheless, relatively to all sensible things whatsoever, it is not only a concept which is in the highest degree true, it is also the foundation of all truth in outer sensibility" (2:40_{21-4}; 398).

In denying that the concept of space is abstracted from outer intuitions, Kant is reiterating the claim regarding time and asserting in effect that the concept is a priori. In fact, Kant provides the very argument that he will use in the *Critique* in the first of his two arguments for the apriority thesis, namely, that the concept cannot be derived from an experience of objects as external to one another and to oneself because such experience already presupposes the concept of space (ID 2: 402_{16-19}; 395).[72]

Similarly, Kant derives the intuitive character of the concept of space from its singularity. But once again the deeper point is the difference between space and particular spaces, on the one hand, and a general concept and the items that constitute its extension, on the other. Whereas the extension of the latter consists of the items that fall *under* it, the parts of space or places fall *within* the same boundless space in which their relative position is determined. Kant concludes from this that the representation of space is a pure intuition and on this basis he provides what later became the Transcendental Exposition of the concept. The basic point, which he illustrates through a reprise of the appeal to incongruent counterparts, is that certain fundamental propositions about space, including but not limited to the axioms of geometry, cannot be derived from a general concept of

---

[70] Kant also refers to axioms of time at A31/B47, where he cites as examples the propositions that time has only one dimension and that different times are not simultaneous but successive. But in the *Critique*, unlike the *Dissertation*, Kant refers to these axioms as synthetic a priori.

[71] In the *Dissertation* Kant refers to the concept (*conceptus*) of space and the idea (*idea*) of time; but it is not clear what (if any) significance is to be attached to this.

[72] See A23/B38. For my analysis of this argument see Allison (2004, 100–4).

space, but "can only be *apprehended* concretely, so to speak, in space itself" (ID 2: 402_{35}–3_1; 396).[73]

Kant's last two propositions regarding space correspond to the conclusions later drawn in the *Critique*. As he had done in the case of time, Kant denies that space is something objective and real on the grounds that it does not fit any of the traditional ontological categories (substance, accident, and relation), from which he concludes that it is subjective and that "it issues from the nature of the mind in accordance with a stable law as a schema ... for co-ordinating everything which is sensed externally" (ID 2: $403_{23–6}$; 397). Moreover, in light of this, Kant criticizes the Newtonians and the Leibnizians for affirming the reality of space. The former are said to conceive of space as "an *absolute* and *boundless* receptacle of possible things" (ID 2: $403_{26–7}$; 397) and the latter as "the relation itself which obtains between existing things, and which vanishes entirely when these things are taken away" (ID 2: 403_{28}–4_1; 397). Once again, it is the latter who come in for the harshest criticism. Whereas the former are chided for their metaphysical excess, producing "an empty fabrication of reason," which "belongs to the world of fable" (ID 2: $404_{2–4}$; 397), the latter are charged with the more serious error of being in conflict with the phenomena and with geometry, "the most faithful interpreter of all phenomena" (ID 2: $404_{9–10}$; 397). Kant is here raising the same objection regarding geometry as he did in his account of time regarding the laws of motion and that he had initially raised regarding both in the 1768 paper. In all three cases the charge is that the Leibnizian view reduces geometry and physics to merely empirical sciences, which, as such, lack genuine universality and necessity.

Kant concludes his discussion of space by affirming what in the language of the *Critique* is its empirical reality and maintaining that this view safeguards the use of geometry in natural science. This follows from the proposition that the concept of space is a law of the mind governing all phenomena that can appear to the external senses and that the axioms of geometry are expressions of this law. It is noteworthy that Kant is here concerned not with pure geometry, which is grounded in a pure intuition, but with applied geometry or more precisely, with geometry as it is operative in Newton's mathematical principles of natural philosophy.

Section 3 concludes with a corollary, which considers space and time together and in which Kant makes three points. The first is a reiteration of the intuitive nature of both representations as principles of sensible cognition by contrasting them with representations stemming from the understanding. Although a new feature of the account is the reference to the infinite nature of both space and time, which anticipates the arguments of the *Critique*, the basic point is once again that, in contrast to the laws of reason, according to which the parts of a compound are

---

[73] If, as I have argued, Kant had not yet drawn the analytic-synthetic distinction at this time, this suggests that he held that the apodictic certainty of geometry is grounded in a pure intuition before he was in a position to claim that its propositions are synthetic.

logically prior to the whole, in the case of space and time the converse holds and the ground of each part presupposes the infinite whole of which it is a finite determination.[74]

Kant's second and most interesting claim in the corollary is that, despite the fact that the laws and fundamental properties of space and time lie beyond the laws of reason in the sense that they are inexplicable by purely conceptual means, "these concepts [of space and time] constitute *the underlying foundations upon which the understanding rests,* when, in accordance with the laws of logic and with the greatest possible certainty, it draws conclusions from the primary data of intuition" (ID 2: 405_{24-6}; 399). Viewed in light of the doctrine of the *Critique,* Kant is effectively maintaining that intuitions without concepts are *not blind,* but, rather, are the source of whatever light is attained by the understanding with respect to phenomena. Moreover, in saying that the understanding draws certain conclusions from intuition in accordance with the laws of logic, Kant is reiterating the point made in section 2 that the use of the intellect in connection with sensible data is merely logical.

Finally, Kant reiterates his denial that the intuitions of space and time are innate. Echoing Locke, he rejects the innateness thesis as the sign of a lazy philosophy, which endeavors to make things easy for itself by claiming innateness for whatever concepts or principles appear to resist explanation. Instead, he insists that these intuitions are acquired from the action of the mind in coordinating what is sensed in accordance with permanent laws (ID 2: 406_{15-19}; 400).

D) *The principle of the form of the intelligible world*: Although section 4 serves as the counterpart to section 3, doing for the intelligible world what the latter did for the sensible world, it is also a continuation of the argument of section 1. Moreover, together with the latter, it points backwards to Kant's earlier metaphysical forays, which is perhaps why Kant suggested to Lambert that he might simply skim these sections.

The central issue of the section is the condition under which a number of distinct substances constitute a world. Despite what he had said in section 3, Kant insists that location in the same space and time is not sufficient. For one thing, space is merely a form of sensible cognition, which means that it cannot be regarded as constituting the form of a world as such; for another, even assuming the absolute reality of space (time having apparently dropped out of the picture), "it would still only signify the intuitively given possibility of universal co-ordination" (ID 2: 407_{4-5}; 401). In other words, location in the same space would be a necessary condition of intuiting the coordination of the substances contained therein, but it would not be sufficient to explain how they form a unity that constitutes a world. The latter necessitates providing the principle of the form of the intelligible world.

---

[74] Kant evidently understood the infinitude of space and time to consist in their unboundedness, not in their containing an infinite number of parts. For my discussion of this point and the arguments from their infinitude to their intuitive nature in the *Critique,* see Allison (2004, 110–12).

Since Kant assumes that this requires the mutual interaction of the substances, his task is to explain "how it is possible *that a plurality of substances should be in mutual interaction with each other*, and in this way belong to the same whole, which is called a world" (2: 407$_{9-11}$; 401). Kant states that this is a problem that can only be resolved by the understanding, which presumably means that it is a genuinely metaphysical problem, not one that can be resolved by natural science. Moreover, the problem is completely general, being concerned with *any* conceivable world, not merely with some discrete *mundus intelligibilis*, such as Kant described in fanciful terms in *Dreams*.[75]

The remainder of the section is devoted to the determination of this principle. Kant's first step is to rule out existence. The claim is that the co-existence of a plurality of substances is not sufficient for them to constitute a world because it is conceivable that these substances would not stand in the requisite reciprocal relation. Kant adds that even if one were to assume a causal relation between these substances, this would still not suffice, because causation involves dependence rather than interaction (*commercium*) and it is the latter that is required (ID 2: 408$_{19-21}$; 403).[76]

After dismissing a simple appeal to existence as sufficient to solve the problem, Kant next insists that a world consisting of necessarily existing substances would be impossible, because, *ex hypothesi*, such substances would not depend on anything outside of themselves for their existence. And since what does not exist necessarily has a merely contingent existence, it follows that the world must consist of contingent substances. Finally, it follows from their contingency that these substances depend upon another being, which, since they are assumed to interact, must be the same being, from which Kant concludes that "[T]he UNITY *in the conjunction of substances in the universe is a corollary of the dependence of all substances on one being*" (ID 2: 408$_{16-17}$; 403). In support of the thesis of a single first cause, Kant argues that if (*per impossibile*) there were a number of necessary beings, their products would constitute distinct worlds, which is contrary to the hypothesis; and, on this basis, he rejects the Wolffian claim that the existence of a number of actual worlds existing outside one another is self-contradictory.[77] Rather, Kant counters, a plurality of worlds is impossible only in virtue of the impossibility of more than one absolutely necessary being (ID 2: 408$_{26-9}$; 403).

Kant's intent, however, was not to prove that a single world entails a single necessary being as its creator, but, rather, to establish the converse thesis that a single

---

[75] As such, it is a problem in ontology rather than special metaphysics. Kant makes this point by distinguishing between the form and matter of the intelligible world, with the latter being a function of the nature of the substances thought to compose it. Since the principle concerns the form, it must explain the unity whether these substances are material or immaterial (ID 2: 407$_{12-13}$; 401).

[76] Although "interaction" is used by both Walford and Beck to render "*commercium*" it is misleading, since it suggests a physical relation, which is incompatible with Kant's claim that he is arguing at a perfectly general level, which abstracts from the nature of the substances involved. Accordingly, I believe that "reciprocity," "reciprocal connection," or even "mutual influence" would be better.

[77] See Wolff (2005), 585–7.

necessary being entails a single world. Although Kant recognized that this does not follow from the proceeding argument, he evidently found this line of reasoning compelling because it enabled him to arrive at the desired result; viz., that the connection of substances is necessary rather than contingent, since (on this assumption) all of the substances would be sustained by a common principle and be governed by common laws (ID 2: 409_{7-8}; 404). Kant termed such a state of affairs a "*generally established harmony*" and he contrasted it with an "*individually established harmony*," according to which God coordinates the actions of the substances composing the world on what amounts to an ad hoc basis. Kant notes that on the former hypothesis the harmony would be real and physical, while on the latter, of which Kant distinguishes two forms: the pre-established harmony of the Leibnizians and the occasionalism of the Cartesians, it would be merely ideal and sympathetic (ID 2: 409_{10-20}; 404).

Although this result enabled Kant to re-affirm his cherished doctrine of physical influx or real interaction, the reasoning behind it is deeply flawed and could not have long satisfied him. The main problem, which was pointed out by Schultz in his review of the *Dissertation*, is that its fundamental assumption that the connection of substances into a whole follows from their dependence on a single necessary being is ungrounded.[78] As noted above, Kant himself acknowledged this, but he nonetheless insisted, without providing further explanation, that there are ample reasons for accepting its consequent: the existence of real interaction (ID 2: 409_{25-6}; 404).

Finally, there are further problems with Kant's account, which involve its compatibility with his sharp separation between the sensible and intelligible worlds. One of the advantages, which Kant thought that he had gained through this distinction, was to save the conception of real interaction, particularly insofar as it concerned the soul and body, from the difficulties that were made manifest in *Dreams*. As relocated in the intelligible world, this interaction is supposedly immunized against contamination from the conditions of sensible cognition. Indeed, we have seen that Kant notes at the beginning of section 4 that, by determining the principle of the form of the intelligible world, we are able to understand "how it is possible that a plurality of substances should be in mutual interaction with each other" (ID 2: 407_{9-10}; 401).[79] But while some kind of interaction between noumenal beings may be conceivable, interaction involving change, such as is involved in the theory of physical influx, clearly is not. For, as Lambert reminded Kant in his letter of October 13, 1770, change involves time and time has been relegated by Kant to the phenomenal or sensible world.[80] Moreover, since bodies belong to the sensible and souls to the intelligible

---

[78] See Schultz (1995b), 169–70.

[79] The point is noted by Laywine (1993), 121. The remarks in this paragraph are greatly indebted to her account.

[80] In this important letter to which we have already referred (see note 55) and will revisit in Chapter 3, Lambert criticizes Kant's assertion of the subjectivity (or ideality) of time on the grounds that since change is real and time a condition of change, time must likewise be real (Br 10: 107_{8-10}; 116). Similar criticisms

world, the possibility of mind–body interaction requires an interplay between these two worlds that has no basis in Kant's theory. In short, far from resolving the problem posed by his earlier writings, the distinction between the sensible and intelligible worlds seems to have created new difficulties.

E) *Metaphysical Method*: Inasmuch as Kant's goal in the *Dissertation* was to provide a propaedeutic to metaphysics rather than a direct contribution to this science, its fifth section (*On method in metaphysics concerning what is sensitive and what belongs to the understanding*) is the culmination of the work. Kant begins by noting that there is no need to search for a method in mathematics and natural science because this is evident from their success. The case is different with metaphysics, however, since it has not established itself as a science and the possibility of it ever doing so requires the adoption of an agreed-upon method.

In juxtaposing metaphysics to natural science, Kant made a sharp break with the analytic method of the *Prize Essay*. Clearly, he could no longer consider the latter a live option, since it is incompatible with the distinction between sensibility and understanding. But rather than attempting to lay out a complete new method for metaphysics, Kant limits himself to the relatively modest task of exposing one major source of metaphysical error: *the contamination of intellectual cognition by the sensitive* (ID 2: 411_{23-4}; 407).[81]

Kant's focus on avoiding the contamination of the intellectual by the sensible leads him to issue a prescription to all would-be metaphysicians to take care to ensure that the principles that pertain to sensible cognition do not transgress their proper bounds and affect what belongs to the understanding (ID 2: 411_{29-31}; 407). As Kant presents this prescription, it involves a constraint on predication, the violation of which amounts to a kind of category mistake. Although it seems that a similar mistake could occur in the other direction, i.e., the predication of an intellectual concept of something sensible, we have seen that in the *Dissertation* Kant is concerned only with the former. He terms the fallacy it commits the "*metaphysical fallacy of subreption*" (ID 2: 412_7; 408) and any axiom guilty of this fallacy a "subreptic axiom" (ID 2: 412_{11}; 408).

Before spelling out the main subreptic axioms, Kant offers a formula for uncovering them, which he terms "THE PRINCIPLE OF REDUCTION." It states: "*If of any*

were also raised by Schultz in his review (1995b), 168–9 and Mendelssohn in his letter to Kant of December 25, 1770 (Br 10: 115–16). Since Kant discusses these criticisms in his letter to Herz of February 21, 1772, I shall reserve a consideration of his response for Chapter 3. For the present, however, it is worth noting that, though he did not focus on the problem of interaction, Lambert offered a possible Kantian solution to it by suggesting that there must exist a counterpart (*Simulachrum*) of space (and time) in the intelligible world (Lambert (1995), 108_{13-16}; 116). In so doing, he was perhaps the first to have raised the notorious problem of the "neglected alternative," albeit more in the spirit of a friendly amendment than an objection. For my discussion of this classical objection and the possible Kantian response, see Allison (2004), 138–2.

[81] Kant's actual text states the reverse; viz., that what must be prevented is the contamination of sensible cognition by intellectual (*sensitivae cognitionis cum intellectuali contagium*); but it is clear that this is an error, since Kant is concerned entirely with the contagion of the intellectual (or "pure") by the sensible.

concept of the understanding whatsoever there is predicated generally anything which belongs to the relations of SPACE AND TIME, *it must not be asserted objectively; it only denotes the condition in the absence of which a given concept would not be sensitively cognizable*" (ID 2: 412_{21}–13_1; 408). As Kant's explanation makes clear, by "objective" is meant what holds of every *conceivable* object, considered apart from the sensible conditions through which it is cognized; whereas what holds of objects only in virtue of the latter may be asserted only subjectively. Accordingly, the "reduction" consists in demoting subreptic principles to a merely subjective status, which nonetheless leaves in place their status as principles of sensible cognition.

In explaining the prevalence of subreptic principles, Kant again cites the rule that what cannot be cognized through any intuition at all is not conceivable and therefore impossible (ID 2: 413_{10-11}; 409). As was noted when first considering this rule, the phrase "any intuition at all" is intended to include the intellectual variety or, as Kant here terms it, "a pure intuition of the understanding," which he connects with a divine intuition and a Platonic idea (ID 2: 413_{15-16}; 409). According to Kant's diagnosis, the source of the problem lies in the mistaken assumption that whatever cannot be intuited by means of *our* sensible intuition cannot be intuited at all, from which it is then erroneously inferred that it is impossible. But we saw that this leaves unresolved the question: how, given the fact that we lack a capacity for intellectual intuition, not to mention other forms of sensible intuition, could we ever decide that something is not intuitable at all?

Ignoring this problem, Kant proceeds directly to the task of cataloguing the major subreptic axioms. He breaks them down into three species, which he evidently regarded as exhaustive:

1. The same sensitive condition, under which alone the *intuition* of an object is possible, is a condition of the *possibility* itself of the *object*.
2. The same sensitive condition, under which alone it is *possible to compare what is given so as to form a concept of the understanding of the object*, is also a condition of the possibility itself of the object.
3. The same sensitive condition, under which alone some *object* met with can be *subsumed under a given concept of the understanding*, is also a condition of the possibility of the object itself (ID 2: 413_{22-9}; 409).[82]

Kant's example of the first species of subreptic axiom is the previously noted: "*Whatever is, is somewhere and somewhen*" (ID 2: 413_{30-1}; 409) and he finds its pernicious influence at work in speculation about both the soul and God. With

---

[82] Considered in terms of the *Critique*, each of these species of subreption constitutes an illicit extension of conditions of sensible cognition to things in general and in themselves. The difference is that whereas the "critical" Kant, armed with the discursivity thesis, infers from the illegitimacy of such an extension the denial of the possibility of things in themselves or noumena, the Kant of 1770, who did not yet recognize this thesis, appeals to the same illegitimacy to create conceptual space for the symbolic cognition of noumena.

regard to the former, it leads to idle questions about the place in the corporeal universe of immaterial substances and their interactions with material substances and each other. Presumably, these questions, which are among those with which Kant was tormented in *Dreams*, are "idle" because, while lent a spurious legitimacy by the subreptic axiom, they are beyond the scope of the human understanding. With regard to the latter, the pseudo-problems suggested by the axiom concern the presence of God in the world, the time of creation, which was a central issue in the Leibniz–Clarke debate, and the possibility of divine foreknowledge. Kant says of the last two problems that they "vanish like smoke, once the concept of time has been rightly understood" (ID 2: 415_{4-5}; 411), and he presumably would have said the same regarding space and the problem of God's presence.

Kant's account of the second species of subreptic axioms or, as he also terms them, "prejudices" (*praeieudicia*), is more complex because the fallacies are more deeply hidden. Rather than resulting from a simple extension of sensible concepts beyond their legitimate sphere, they stem from the fact that sensible conditions are intimately involved in our endeavor to grasp certain intellectual concepts and that this supposedly leads to a conflation of what is possible according to the conditions of sensible cognition and what is conceivable by the pure understanding. Kant cites two examples of such conflation, one concerning the cognition of quantity, the other of quality. "The first is: *every actual multiplicity can be given numerically*, and thus every magnitude is finite. The second is: *whatever is impossible, contradicts itself*" (ID 2: 415_{11-13}; 411).

Although Kant's account of the first of these prejudices occurs on terrain closely related to that of the mathematical antinomies, he once again does not present the issue in antinomial terms. His interest lies rather in the difference in the conditions required for the formation of a sensible and an intellectual concept of quantity and the conflation of the former with the latter. According to the conditions of sensible cognition, the distinct cognition of every quantum or series of coordinates is attained through a successive coordination or synthesis, which entails that it can only attain completeness if the synthesis can be completed in a finite time. But since the latter is not possible in the case of an infinite series, it follows that the distinct cognition of such a series is itself impossible. Kant further claims that the impossibility of such cognition is due to the limitations of our intellect, which is erroneously inflated into the impossibility of the series itself (ID 2: 415_{18-22}; 411).[83] In other words, a merely subjective impossibility is taken to be objective, which constitutes the subreption.

[83] This is to be contrasted with the argument for the thesis of the First Antinomy, where Kant argues that the proposition that an infinitely elapsed world series is impossible (A426/B454), rather than merely that it cannot be distinctly cognized. The basic difference, which accounts for the presence of the antinomial conflict in the *Critique* and its absence from the *Dissertation*, is that in the *Critique* Kant viewed the idea of the world as inherently dialectical because it purports to be at once empirical and rational, whereas this thought is lacking in the *Dissertation* with its undialectical division of labor between the laws of sensible and intellectual cognition and their respective objects.

Up to this point Kant's account seems relatively clear. Things become more confusing, however, when we consider his analysis of the cause of this subreption, which supposedly results from conflating the law of sensible cognition with a corresponding law of the understanding. By the former Kant understands the principle that "any series of co-ordinates has its own specifiable beginning" (ID 2: 415_{27-8}; 411), which is presumably derived from the above-mentioned impossibility of acquiring a distinct cognition of an infinite series (understood as one without a specifiable beginning). By the latter, he understands the proposition that "any series of caused things has its own *principle*; that is to say, in a series of caused things there is no regress which is without a limit" (ID 2: 415_{25-7}; 411).

Kant suggests that, while these principles may seem equivalent, since each in some way involves a denial of an infinite series, they are really saying something quite different. Whereas the law of sensible cognition concerns the *measurement* of a series (it must have a specifiable starting point), the law of understanding concerns the *dependence* of the whole on a first cause (ID 2: 415_{28-30}; 411). Although Kant is far from clear on the matter, his point seems to be that one should not conclude that the understanding's requirement of a first cause as the explanatory ground of a series of occurrences rules out the possibility of the conception of an infinite series of subsequent events, as would be the case if the conditions of intuitive cognition were given pride of place.[84]

If this is Kant's point, it is certainly correct; but it remains puzzling why anyone should make such a conflation, much less why there should be something like a propensity to do so. As is evident from Kant's account, the two principles are concerned with quite distinct conceptions of a series. The sensible series consists of *coordinate* elements and their synthesis, that is to say, of successive occurrences in time or successively counted entities in space, the extent of which supposedly has a determinate magnitude. By contrast, the series with which the pure understanding is concerned is a *causal* chain of successive dependencies. Accordingly, if one conflates these two principles, it would seem that one must conflate these two series and it is not clear who Kant thought was guilty of that.

Kant's second example of a subreption involving quantity is somewhat more revealing, since it suggests a line of reasoning to which Kant himself adhered in his *Physical Monadology*.[85] Here the subreption stems from the fact that the "argument of the understanding," which maintains that a composite of substances is composed of simples, has added to it the rule of sensible cognition that in such a compound there is no infinite regress in the composition of parts, which is to say that there is a definite number of parts in a compound (ID 2: 415_{30-5}; 411). Thus, rather than an antinomial conflict with respect to the composition of the continuum, which Kant will formulate in the *Critique*, we have here what seems like an agreement regarding a

---

[84] I am here following a suggestion of Laywine (1993), 118–19.
[85] This is also noted by Laywine (1993), 119.

consistently finitistic position. Once again, however, Kant's point is that this appear-ance of agreement is deceptive because the claims of sensible and intellectual cognition are not equivalent. Moreover, the fault does not lie with the intellect, which validly asserts that a substantial compound is composed of simple parts, but with the illicit extension of this principle, supposedly under the corrupting influence of the laws of sensible cognition, to yield conclusions such as that the universe is mathematically finite in size and duration and that everybody is composed of a finite number of simples (ID 2: 416_{4-6}; 412).

The subreption involving quality concerns the principle of contradiction and turns on a "rash conversion" of this principle stemming from its connection with the concept of time. The conversion is from the unconditionally valid "*whatever simul-taneously is and is not is impossible*" to its converse: "*everything impossible simul-taneously is and is not.*" As with all the subreptic axioms, Kant does not claim that this conversion yields an outright falsity; it is rather that it results in a proposition that is only subjectively valid because it appeals to the conditions of sensible cognition (ID 2: 416_{10-23}; 412). Thus, while our understanding may only be able to recognize impossibility when it can see that it involves the simultaneous assertion of opposites about the same thing, this should not be taken as an (objectively) necessary condition of impossibility. Moreover, the absence of *impossibility*, so construed, should not be taken as a sign of *real possibility*, which is what those who invent forces on the basis of their lack of a perceived impossibility supposedly do (ID 2: $416_{23}-17_3$; 412–13). As we have seen, the dogmatic metaphysician in *Dreams* was ridiculed for committing precisely the same fallacy.

The third species of subreptic axioms results from the fact that it is only through what is sensibly given that a concept of the understanding can be applied to a case given in experience. The subreption consists in the assumption that the sensible condition of subsuming an object under a concept of the understanding, which in the *Critique* Kant will term the schema of that concept, is also a condition of the possibility of the object.[86] Kant's example of this type of subreptic principle is the proposition, which he attributes to certain (unnamed) schools, that, "[W]*hatever exists contingently, at sometime did not exist*" (ID 2: 417_{11-12}; 413). Once again, Kant does not claim that this principle is false, but, rather, that it is a merely subjectively valid principle, which is erroneously taken to be objective. It is subjectively valid because it expresses a sufficient condition of contingency (whatever did not exist at some time may be said to be contingent) and a necessary condition for the *sensible*

---

[86] Beck (1969a), 463 suggests that this is not a surreptitious axiom, but "the starting point of a new revolution just as profound as the one of 1769." Beck, however fails to state the axiom fully, taking it to claim merely that "it is only by the aid of the sensibly given that an intellectual concept can be applied." Although this is a proposition that the Kant of 1770 would not accept in an unqualified form, since it rules out the real use of the intellect with regard to noumena, it is not the focal point of the subreption. The latter is rather the assumption that a condition of the application of a concept is likewise a condition of the possibility of the object to which that concept is applied.

determination of contingency. But it is *only* subjectively valid because it does not express a necessary condition of contingent existence; since there is no contradiction in the thought of something existing contingently and throughout all time. Kant's example is the world, which has a merely contingent existence (since it was created) and yet is supposedly sempiternal (ID 2: 417_{27-30}; 413–14). Accordingly, in order to avoid this confusion, Kant suggests that the principle should be reformulated to express the negative and somewhat cumbersome but genuine subjective law: "*if there be no evidence that there was a time when a certain thing did not exist, the common intelligence [communem intelligentiam] does not supply sufficient marks [for us] to infer its contingency*" (ID 2: 417_{24-5}; 413).[87] Presumably, by the "common intelligence" Kant means the human, sensibly conditioned understanding and his point, once again, is that this should not be taken to determine what must be the case for any conceivable understanding and therefore holds of reality itself.

The final paragraph of section 5 functions as an appendix to both this section and the *Dissertation* as a whole and introduces a topic that anticipates the more thorough treatment of the matter in the Appendix to the Transcendental Dialectic in the *Critique*. It presents a set of principles possessing a hybrid status: on the one hand, they differ from the previously considered subreptic principles in that they stem entirely from the intellect, without any contagion from the sensible side of the mind, while, on the other hand, like the actual subreptic principles, they are deceptive in presenting themselves in such a way as to lead one to believe that they hold objectively. The source of this deception lies in their epistemic indispensability, which stems from the fact that they make possible the use of the understanding in judgment. Kant indicates this by remarking that, "*if we abandoned them, our understanding would scarcely be able to make any judgment about a given object at all*" (ID 2:418_{11-12}; 414).

Kant terms these "principles of convenience" (or harmony) (*principia covenientiae*) (ID 2: 418_8; 414; 414) and he cites three examples, which are presented as selected from a longer list: (1) "*all things in the universe take place in accordance with the order of nature*" (ID 2: 418_{12}; 414); (2) "*principles are not to be multiplied beyond what is absolutely necessary*" (ID 2: 418_{8-29}; 415); and (3) "*Nothing material at all comes into being or passes away*" (ID 2: 418_{33}; 415). Seen from the vantage point of the *Critique*, it is evident that Kant is giving these principles a regulative function, which, as in the *Critique*, is to direct the understanding in its empirical use to strive for maximal unity among its cognitions. And, again as in the *Critique*, this unity is a projected one, which reason necessarily presupposes in its investigation of nature, rather than one which we have grounds to assume is there to be found.

---

[87] I have here substituted Beck's rendering of this sentence because, though less literal than Walford's, I believe that it provides a clearer statement of Kant's point. In Walford's translation it reads: "*if it is not established that there was a time when a certain thing did not exist*, the *sufficient mark of its contingency will not be given by a common concept of the understanding*."

Although the principles of convenience in the *Dissertation* anticipate Kant's later conception of the regulative function of reason, there are also significant differences, which point to the extent to which Kant's overall position in 1770 differs from his fully "critical" view. With regard to his treatment of these principles, the most fundamental difference stems from the fact that in 1770 Kant lacked a developed account of either the understanding or reason. Rather, as has been already noted, what later became distinct, though intimately related, faculties are here lumped together under the notion of intellect (*intellectus*) and contrasted solely with sensibility rather than also with each other. This is evident from the fact that of these three principles, only (2), which is commonly referred to as "Ockham's razor," is clearly a principle of *reason* in the sense of the *Critique*.[88] Moreover, lacking a theory of reason, Kant also lacked what is undoubtedly the essential feature of his later theory; viz., its connection with a natural and unavoidable illusion (transcendental illusion), which is inseparable from the use of reason, but can be deprived of power to deceive by a transcendental critique. To be sure, Kant gestures towards this doctrine in the *Dissertation* with the idea that the subjective principles of convenience deceptively present themselves as objective; but this here remains a curious and inexplicable fact, which Kant was apparently unable to integrate into his account.

This, then, completes our consideration of the *Dissertation*. Structured around the freshly drawn distinction between sensibility and understanding, regarded as principles of a sensible and an intelligible world, we have seen that it is, on the one hand, an attempt, on the basis of this distinction, to rehabilitate as much as possible of Kant's earlier metaphysics in response to the difficulties noted in *Dreams*; while, on the other, with its conception of concepts stemming from the nature of the intellect and account of space and time as forms of sensible cognition, a major way station on the path to the *Critique*. Chapter 3 will attempt to trace the remainder of this path on the basis of the fragmentary materials available from Kant's "Silent Decade."

---

[88] Of these, (1) is asserted by Walford (1992), 466, note 71 to be an appeal to what later became the Second Analogy. But I do not think that this is correct, since the latter is concerned with every event taken individually as an object of possible experience, whereas this principle, which Kant identifies with Epicurus (ID 2: 418_{14}; 414), concerns nature as a whole and essentially amounts to a proscription against seeking any explanation that transcends the bounds of nature. Moreover, as such, it would seem to qualify as a principle of reason in Kant's sense. By contrast (3) does seem to amount to an assertion of the central thesis of the First Analogy and as such pertains to the understanding rather than to reason.

3

The "Silent Decade"

Apparently because the decimal system does not yield a convenient term for an eleven-year period, the time between the publication of the *Inaugural Dissertation* (1770) and the first edition of the *Critique of Pure Reason* (1781), during which Kant published only three minor pieces, has been termed the "Silent Decade."[1] But though Kant may have been relatively silent during this period he was not idle. To the contrary, numerous *Reflexionen*, as well as other materials from his *Nachlass*, show that he was hard at work on the line of thought that would eventually lead to the *Critique*. Since their publication and attempted dating by Adickes, these *Reflexionen* have been a focal point of scholarly attention; but due to their ambiguous nature and the difficulty of constructing a reliable chronology, they have not yielded anything like a consensus regarding the development of Kant's thought.

The ambiguity stems largely from a combination of the fragmentary nature of these *Reflexionen*, which include many items that are crossed out as well as later additions, and Kant's own manner of working. With regard to the latter, Kant remarks to Herz in a letter dated June 7, 1771, that,

Long experience has taught me that one cannot compel or precipitate insight by force in matters of the sort we are considering; rather, it takes quite a long time to gain insight, since one looks at one and the same concept intermittently and regards its possibility in all its relations and contexts, and furthermore, because one must above all awaken the skeptical spirit within, to examine one's conclusions against the strongest possible doubt and see whether they can stand the test. (Br 10: 122$_{20-7}$, 126–7)

I believe that Kant's *Reflexionen* are best read as illustrations of this procedure and that this should give one pause before making any definitive pronouncement on their evidence alone about what views Kant actually held at the time of their composition.

The problem of establishing a reliable chronology is due to the difficulty of dating the individual *Reflexionen*. Adickes made a heroic attempt by dividing them into

---

[1] These works are: *Recension von Moscatis Schrift: Von dem körperlichen wesentlichen Unterschiede zwischen der Structur der Thiere und Menschen* (17781) ("Review of Moscati's Work: Of the Corporeal Essential Differences between the Structure of Animals and Humans"); *Von den verschiedenen Racen der Menschen* (1775) (Of the Different Races of Human Beings"); and *Aufsätze, das Philantropin betreffend* (1776–77) ("Essays Regarding the Philanthropinum").

thirty-three phases of which eleven cover the Silent Decade.[2] But since he was forced
to rely mainly on incidental factors such as the kind of pen and the color of ink that
Kant used rather than their contents and was indecisive about the dating of a number
of the most important *Reflexionen*, it has proven impossible to base an account of the
development of Kant's thought primarily on his dating.[3]

Nevertheless, there are some firm signposts that have provided the bases for the
various reconstructions of Kant's thought during the period. The two most important of these are Kant's letter to Herz of February 21, 1772 and the so-called "*Duisburg
Nachlass*," which consists of a set of related *Reflexionen* that are datable because one
of them was written on the back of a letter to Kant dated May 20, 1775. In addition,
on the back of another letter written to Kant by the rector of the university dated
January 20, 1780 there is a sketch of a transcendental deduction that is closely related
to the A-Deduction. It has been titled "*Loses Blatt* B 12" and Wolfgang Carl has
labeled it the "third draft" of Kant's deduction.[4] Since this contains features that are
not found in the texts composing the *Duisburg Nachlass* it suggests a further stage in
the development of Kant's thought immediately prior to the appearance of the
Critique. Accordingly, the present chapter is divided into three parts: the first focuses
on the letter to Herz and its context; the second is devoted to the *Duisburg Nachlass*;
and the third considers B 12 and related texts from the period just prior to the
publication of the *Critique*.

I

Like many "pre-critical" texts, Kant's letter to Herz of February 21, 1772 is Janus-
faced. On the one hand, it looks back to the *Dissertation*; while, on the other, it
appears to point forward to the properly "critical" problem of the possibility of a
priori cognition by means of pure (non-empirical) concepts. Not surprisingly, then,
the dispute that has arisen in recent years regarding the interpretation of this letter
turns on the question of whether the forward- or the backward-looking aspect
predominates. The major advocate of the forward-looking reading is Wolfgang
Carl, who sees in it a radical break with the standpoint of the *Dissertation* and an
anticipation of what will become the central problem of the Transcendental Deduction; viz., how pure concepts of the understanding relate to what is given through
sensibility. By contrast, Lewis White Beck has claimed that Kant's letter should be
seen as a last and futile attempt to answer some questions regarding the cognition of
noumena that he should have raised in the *Dissertation* but did not yet see cannot be

---

[2] See Adickes, KGS 14 XXXVI–XLIV.
[3] For a discussion of the problem of dating the *Reflexionen*, which was first attempted by Benno
Erdmann (1882) on the basis of their content and then by Adickes on the basis of extrinsic factors, see
de Vleeschauwer (1934), 43–9.
[4] Carl (1989a), 4.

answered.[5] More recently, the main lines of Beck's approach have been taken up and developed by Laywine.[6]

The view to be argued for here lies somewhere between these, though it is closer to the Beck-Laywine reading in that, unlike Carl's, it recognizes significant continuities between Kant's views in his letter to Herz and the *Dissertation*. The discussion is divided into three parts. The first investigates the lay of the land during the period between the appearance of the *Dissertation* and the letter to Herz. The second deals with the letter itself and some of its competing interpretations. The third considers R 4634, which contains not only what Carl regards as the first draft of the deduction but also the fullest account that we have of Kant's understanding of the analytic-synthetic distinction during this period.

A) *Kant's views in the immediate aftermath of the Dissertation*: Through Herz Kant sent copies of the *Dissertation* to Sulzer, Mendelssohn, and Lambert; and while the responses of the first two were perfunctory, as Beck and Laywine have pointed out, Lambert's response proved to be of considerable importance for the development of Kant's subsequent thought.[7] In his letter, which is dated October 13, 1770, Lambert offered three criticisms of Kant's argument in the *Dissertation*. The first and for present purposes most important of these concerns Kant's sharp separation of sensibility and understanding as two totally heterogeneous sources of cognition.[8] While not objecting to the distinction as such and agreeing with Kant that the propositions of geometry and chronometry are sensible, Lambert worried that Kant has separated the sensible and the intellectual so thoroughly that they could never come together (Br 10: 105_{27-9}; 115). And he further suggested that this was a serious problem because in ontology it is useful to take up concepts borrowed from appearances, "since *the theory must finally be applied to phenomena again*." Lambert illustrates this with an example from astronomy, noting that the astronomer derives his construction of the world from the phenomena, which he then applies to the phenomena and their predictions (Br 10: 108_{26-32}; 117).

Viewed from Kant's point of view, Lambert's complaint consists in the charge that in his zeal to protect metaphysics from contagion he had in effect undermined any attempt to apply intellectual concepts to the sensible world and that this application is necessary not only for ontology but also for science.[9] At one level this need not

---

[5] Beck (1989), 22.   [6] Laywine (2001).

[7] See Beck (1969a), 463–7 and (1978), 101–10; and Laywine (2001), 1–48.

[8] The other two criticisms are the well-known one regarding the ideality of time, to which Kant responded in his letter to Herz and again in the *Critique*, and Kant's treatment in section 5 of the *Dissertation* of allegedly subreptive axioms involving space and time.

[9] This is particularly evident from the third species of subreptic axioms introduced by Kant, which, as we saw in Chapter 2, lies in the assumption that the sensible condition of subsuming an object under a concept is also a condition of the possibility of the object. We also saw that Kant's example of such a subreptic axiom was that "[W]hatever exists contingently at some time did not exist." And we further saw that, as with the other species of subreptic axioms Kant does not claim that it is actually false, but merely that it is only subjectively valid, with the mistake consisting in the assumption that it is objectively valid.

have greatly bothered Kant, since his fundamental concern in the *Dissertation* was with special metaphysics (especially rational theology and pneumatology) rather than ontology. In fact, it was argued in Chapter 2 that the reason why Kant denied any experiential role for the real use of the intellect and its indigenous concepts was to avoid any hint of contagion of the intellectual by the sensible. Moreover, he could easily have raised the subreption charge against some of Lambert's pronouncements regarding fundamental concepts in physics, such as force and inertia, which Lambert characterized as "transcendent."[10]

At a deeper level, however, there are at least two reasons why this line of objection could have struck a nerve for Kant. First, although Kant's main goal in the *Dissertation* was to carve out a space for the special metaphysics of God and the soul, his proposed propaedeutic science was intended to provide the basis for metaphysics as a whole, including ontology, which, as *metaphysica generalis*, would apply to the sensible as well as the intelligible world. Indeed, for Kant at that time, as for the Wolffians, ontology provides the indispensable foundation for special metaphysics, since the concepts that apply to being as such are presupposed by those that apply to particular beings (including God and the soul). Moreover, Kant's own commitment to a foundational role for ontology is evident from the previously designated concepts of the understanding to which he refers in the *Dissertation*, namely, "existence," "necessity," "substance," "cause," which are all transcendent in Lambert's sense.[11]

Second, and perhaps even more to the point, these same concepts, particularly "substance" and "cause," are also essential to physical science. Consequently, to deny their application to the sensible world would undermine not only the metaphysical project for which the *Dissertation* was intended to lay the foundation, but the Newtonian science of nature, which was the centerpiece of Kant's project in the 1760s. We have seen that in his writings of that period Kant endeavored to preserve the key relational concept of ground and consequence from Hume's critique by anchoring it in the Newtonian conception of force, thereby giving it an experiential backing. Thus, even though Hume was right in claiming that there is no logical connection between a cause and its presumed effect, the objectivity of the causal relation is preserved by its impeccable empirical credentials. But for the Kant of 1770 this move might well have seemed problematic in view of its apparent incompatibility with the decontagion project of the *Dissertation*, a point that Lambert's remark about ontology might well have called to his attention.

The problem here is two-fold: (1) if the ground–consequence, i.e., causal, relation is grounded in experience by way of the concept of force, then Kant should not have

---

[10] On this point see Laywine (2001), 12–13. As she points out, "transcendent" for Lambert had the same sense as "transcendental" for Kant, i.e., applicable to things in general and therefore to both the sensible and the intelligible. She further notes that in his *Architektonik* Lambert claimed this status for the concept of force and in the *Organon* for both force and inertia.

[11] See preceding note.

included it in his list of concepts derived from the nature of the intellect; and (2) in that event any purported metaphysical use of it would be ruled out, not only on Humean grounds, but also because it would involve a fallacy of subreption. In short, Kant's procedure in the *Dissertation* presented him with a dilemma that is epitomized in his struggles with the ground–consequence relation: either abandon his worries about subreption, which would effectively undermine the main principle of his proposed propaedeutic science, or abandon the project of a special metaphysics, which would be to reject that for which the propaedeutic science is intended as a propaedeutic.[12]

A possible recourse, which has been noted by Laywine, would have been for Kant to regard this relation as one of the *principia covenientiae*.[13] As she points out, this would have granted it a subjective necessity, which might be regarded as a necessary condition of Newton's discovery of universal gravitation, presumably without undermining its purity. And, as she also notes, there is some textual basis for this move, since the first of these principles that Kant cites, namely, that "*all things in the universe take place in accordance with the order of nature*" (ID 2: 418_{14}; 414), is arguably closely related to the concept of ground and consequence.[14] Nevertheless, it is highly unlikely that the Kant of 1770 would have endorsed such a move. First, since Kant only introduces the *principia covenientiae* as an afterthought, which he fails to integrate into his account, it would amount to a case of the tail wagging the dog. Second, it is doubtful that Kant was in a position to make such a move, since it rests upon a "critical" conception of the merely regulative use of reason, which presupposes the not-yet-drawn distinction between reason and understanding.

Nevertheless, there are a number of *Reflexionen*, some of which also contain what appear to be Kant's earliest explicit formulations of the analytic-synthetic distinction, which suggest that, at least for a time, he entertained the idea that not only the ground–consequence relation, but all the principles of pure reason are only subjectively valid. For example, with respect to the former, Kant writes that, "[A]ll real grounds and even their possibility are cognizable only *a posteriori*; this reveals a constant accompaniment, but no universality of connection, hence the concept of a

---

[12] The analysis of this and the preceding paragraph is indebted to the excellent discussion of Laywine (2001), esp. 14–18. Her reconstruction of Kant's thought process circa 1770, with which I am in fundamental agreement, is based on the assumptions that Kant was primarily concerned with grounding special metaphysics; that this essentially involved avoiding subreption; and that he was familiar with and troubled by Lambert's discussion of ontology in his *Neue Organon* (if not in other texts). For a discussion of some points on which I disagree with Laywine's account, see notes 7 and 19.

[13] See Laywine (2001), 30–2. This would be at best a partial remedy because it does not seem possible to treat all of Kant's intellectual concepts in this manner, particularly the modal concepts. Nevertheless, one could go beyond Laywine and suggest that the concept of substance is capable of a similar treatment, since we have seen that the third of these principles that Kant cites, namely, that "*Nothing material at all comes into being or passes away, and all changes which take place in the world concern its form alone*" (ID 2: 418_{24-5}) is logically equivalent to the principle of the First Analogy in the *Critique*.

[14] The relation is even closer, however, between Kant's third principle and the concept of substance. See the preceding note.

ground is not objective" (R 3972 17: $370_{28}-1_2$; 107).[15] Kant here seems to have taken to heart Hume's account of the causal relation, denying it objectivity on the grounds that it is only cognizable a posteriori and therefore lacks the strict universality (and presumably necessity) that supposedly pertains to concepts stemming from the intellect.[16] At the same time, however, he retains the element of necessity that was called into question by Hume, interpreting it as a subjective necessity, albeit one that is grounded in the nature of reason rather than custom or habit as it is for Hume. In other words, as Laywine suggests, the necessity that Kant grants to the ground–consequence relation in its empirical use is akin to that which he attributed to the principles of convenience in the *Dissertation*.

Moreover, elsewhere Kant generalizes from this, going so far as to maintain that "[A]ll rational synthetic propositions are subjective and conversely only the analytic are objective" (R 3935 17: 354_{16-17}). And, apparently in an attempt to explain this denial of objectivity to principles of reason or rational synthetic propositions, he notes in another *Reflexion* that,

In addition to those determinations without which objects cannot exist, there are in our reason further conditions, without which we cannot conceive certain objects through reason, even though these conditions are not determinations of the objects themselves. These *conditiones* are therefore subjective, and their concepts do not signify anything in the object. All synthetic judgments of pure reason are accordingly subjective, and the concepts of them signify actions of reason toward itself.   (R 3938 17: 355_{15-22}; 99)

Since the subjective conditions to which Kant here refers presumably include the relational concepts of ground–consequence and substance–accident, this *Reflexion* calls to mind the question that Kant will later pose in the introductory portion of the Transcendental Deduction with respect to all of the categories, namely, "how **subjective conditions of thinking** should have **objective validity**" (A89–90/B122). But whereas the answer proposed in the *Critique* is that this validity stems from the function of the categories as necessary conditions of possible experience, Kant here affirms a quite different view, denying that they have such validity; though also suggesting that they have a subjective validity with regard to the internal operations of reason. Moreover, the same set of *Reflexionen* also contains others where the subjectivity of the judgments and principles of pure reason is applied to metaphysics. Thus, contrasting logic and metaphysics, Kant writes that "Logic treats the objective laws of reason, that is, how it should proceed. Metaphysics the subjective [laws] of pure reason, how it proceeds" (R 3939 17: 356_{1-3}). In addition, evidently anticipating

---

[15] A similar thought is expressed in R 3942 17: 357; R 3971 17: 370 and R 3977 17: 373.

[16] Evidently, Kant here had in mind Hume's understanding of the causal principle as articulated in the *Enquiry*, which concerns the necessity of particular causal relations, i.e., the principle that particular causes are necessarily followed by particular effects, rather than the general principle that every beginning of existence necessarily has some cause, which is the principle that Hume investigates in the *Treatise*. For my analysis of this issue, see Allison (2008), 93–134.

the problem of the antinomy, we find Kant noting in another *Reflexion* that "If subjective principles are considered as objective they contradict themselves" (R 3936 17: 355$_{3-4}$), which casts further light on Kant's claim that the concepts involved in synthetic judgment of pure reason involve "actions of reason toward itself" rather than toward objects.[17]

For present purposes, however, perhaps the most salient of these *Reflexionen* is one in which Kant contrasts metaphysical concepts with the concept of space, with the latter rather than the former being claimed to be objective. In the relevant portion of the *Reflexion* Kant writes:

A cognition is true which is in agreement with the constitution of the object. Since the representation of external objects is only possible by means of the idea of space, all of the axioms of space and what can be derived from them agree with the object, likewise all relations of concepts in accordance with the rule of identity. For the ideas agree among themselves. But since the metaphysical concepts of ground, substance, etc, are not properly speaking representations of the objects, while even the most perfect sense cannot have a sensation of these in anything and things can be represented on the whole [*ingesammt*] without these relations, although not by means of our reason, thus these concepts are not objective; therefore in the axioms of them everything is subjective.   (R 3942 17: 357$_{7-17}$; 100)[18]

At least with respect to synthetic a posteriori propositions, Kant here seems to appeal to the familiar correspondence theory of truth, wherein truth consists in the agreement of a cognition with its object. By contrast, in the case of the "relations of concepts in accordance with the rule of identity," i.e., analytic propositions, the agreement concerns the relation of the constitutive representations with each other, which appears to be a holdover from the analytic model of cognition of the 1760s that preceded the "great light." And, in light of this conception of truth or, more properly, objectivity, Kant proceeds to deny that metaphysical concepts, such as ground and substance, lack objectivity because they do not agree with an object or, as Kant puts it, "they are not, properly speaking, representations of the objects." Although it is not terribly clear why Kant claims this, his denial appears to be rooted in the Humean view that we cannot sense, i.e., have impressions, of relations. But, as already noted, though agreeing with Hume, that these concepts are not objective, Kant here insists, contrary to Hume, that these concepts are essential for the use of reason, which is to say that they possess a subjective necessity that is quite distinct from Hume's custom or habit.

What is particularly striking here is the difference between what Kant claims in this *Reflexion* and in the *Dissertation*. Whereas in the latter the representation of space was deemed subjective because of its origin in the nature of human sensibility, it is now claimed to be objective on the grounds that it is a condition of the

---

[17] See also R 3942 17: 357$_{23-4}$; 100.
[18] See also R 3952 17: 362$_{24-25}$; 103; R 3959 17: 367$_{3-5}$; and R 3970 17: 370$_{13-15}$; 107.

representation of external objects. Expressed in the language of the *Critique*, this amounts to the claim that space is empirically real, with the question of its transcendental ideality bracketed. And whereas in the *Dissertation* Kant held that the concepts of ground, substance, and the like, as grounded in the very nature of the intellect, are objective and serve as the vehicles for the symbolic (conceptual) cognition of an intelligible world, they are now demoted to a merely subjective status because their presumed necessity concerns only the use of reason with respect to its own needs, without any purchase on reality. Thus, whereas in the *Dissertation* Kant attributed a subjective status merely to the principles of convenience, in contrast to the dogmatic principles of the intellect involved in the symbolic cognition of noumena, he now regards *all* the principles of reason as merely subjective.[19]

The scantiness and fragmentary nature of the evidence makes any attempt to account for this sudden shift hazardous. But if, as suggested above, Kant was led to question central tenets of the *Dissertation* by Lambert's remarks about ontology, then this view of the concepts and principles of reason might be considered an initial response on Kant's part to the difficulties to which Lambert, at least indirectly, called attention, perhaps in connection with a renewed study of Hume. On this reading, these difficulties led Kant to entertain the possibility of preserving both the rational basis and application to experience of the intellectual concepts at the price of their objectivity. Instead of being concepts whose true provenance is the intelligible world of the *Dissertation*, Kant now follows Lambert in holding that metaphysical concepts and principles must apply to both worlds; though in a reduced role as subjectively necessary principles of reason, which presumably enabled Kant to avoid the subreption against which the *Dissertation* warned, while preserving for them a role with respect to the cognition of the sensible world.

Admittedly, in addition to its conjectural nature there is a potentially fatal objection to this interpretive hypothesis; viz., that the *Reflexionen* on which it is based belong to the group that Adickes classifies as phase k, which he claims stem from 1769. In other words, if Adickes' dating is correct, these *Reflexionen* were all written

---

[19] According to Laywine, Kant's focus at this time was almost exclusively on the concept of ground and consequence, which under the influence of Hume he came to regard as "peculiarly subjective," since it came under the suspicion that it might be a product of the imagination rather than reason. Moreover, on her account it was only after Kant became convinced that Hume was wrong and that the concept was a product of the understanding rather than the imagination that he extended his concern about the objectivity of this concept to all the others and posed the general question: "how can any pure concept of the understanding relate *a priori* to *any* object at all." See Laywine (2001, 3 and notes 42, 47–8). Although I agree with Laywine that, for largely Humean reasons, Kant was particularly interested in the concept of ground and consequence, I reject her contention that he regarded it as "peculiarly subjective," since we have seen that he treats the concept of substance in precisely the same way. And I likewise reject the idea that it was only after Kant came to realize the rational credentials of the concept of ground and consequence that he extended the objectivity worry to the other pure concepts. On the contrary, I think that for the Kant of 1770 the recognition that the concept of ground and consequence is derived from the very nature of the understanding would have been sufficient reason to abandon the worry that it was merely subjective and that the global statement of subjectivity that we find in these *Reflexionen* reflects a later position.

prior to the *Dissertation* and therefore cannot be viewed as containing Kant's second thoughts about it. But while it would be rash to reject Adickes' dating *tout court*, particularly since much of what Kant says in this large and diverse set of *Reflexionen* can be read as anticipating elements of the *Dissertation*, this does not preclude the possibility that *some* of them, specifically those referred to above and others containing similar claims, were written at a later time.[20] Indeed, if these *Reflexionen* were in fact written in 1769 or earlier, we are confronted with the problem of explaining how Kant could have moved so quickly from the view that the concepts and principles of metaphysics are subjective in the sense designated above to the express teaching of the *Dissertation* that the intellect, disconnected from any connection with sensibility, represents things as they are.

Moreover, according to Adickes' dating there are later *Reflexionen* that make basically the same point regarding the subjectivity of metaphysical concepts and principles. These are located in phases λ, μ, and γ, which together supposedly cover the period from the end of 1769 through 1771. For example, in phase λ we find Kant writing: "That ontology is nothing other than a transcendental logic (subjective), applied metaphysics [special metaphysics], however, is merely negative, and nothing but morality remains, whose *data* are given by the human will, and the *principia formalia* are analytic" (R 4152 17: 436_{2-5}; 116). And "One cannot represent to oneself a subject other than through its predicates and predicates not other than as in their subject. Accordingly, the necessity of representing to oneself substances is more a subjective necessity of the laws of the understanding than an objective one" (R 4158 17: 438_{8-12}).[21] Similarly, among the *Reflexionen* assigned to phase μ we find Kant writing: "*Analysis* of reason. *Principium contradictionis, identitatis*; yields objectively valid propositions. Synthesis of reason: various laws (*axiomata subreptitia*), [yields] subjectively valid propositions" (R 4275 17: 491_{18-22}).[22] And, finally, in phase γ, which according to Adickes definitely post-dates the *Dissertation*, Kant writes: "The

---

[20] Laywine likewise expresses doubts about Adickes' dating of these *Reflexionen* (2001, 44–5 note 34); though she suggests that they probably stem from between 1766 and 1770, which would mean that they predate the *Dissertation*.

[21] See also R 4146 17: 433. Phase λ, however, also contains *Reflexionen* that affirm a dogmatic role for metaphysics, similar to that which is assigned to it in the *Dissertation*. See, for example, R 4148 17: 434; R 4150 17: 434–5; and R 4168 17: 42.

[22] The parenthetical reference to "*axiomata subreptitia*" indicates that by "subjectively valid" Kant here means valid with respect to appearances rather than things in general. In another noteworthy *Reflexion* from phase m Kant poses a progressive series of questions that one may ask of a principle: "(1) Is it synthetic or analytic? (2) If it is the former, is it derived from universal experience or *a priori*? (3) Is it a principle of sensibility or reason? (4) Is it a ground of the possibility of appearances or of real concepts, *principium constitutivum*? (5) If it is the last: is it a *principium subjectivum* or *objectivum*? (6) Is it the first, then one asks, if it is a *principium covenientiae* or a *principium concipiendi per se*?" (R 4283 17: $494_{24}-5_7$). In addition to the fact that it seems to express Kant's developed view of the analytic-synthetic distinction, which allows for synthetic judgments that are known a priori, the interesting features of this *Reflexion* are the suggestions that a constitutive principle might be subjective and that this could be understood in two ways: either as a *principium covenientiae* or as a *principium concipiendi per se* (principle of conceiving something by itself). Unfortunately, it remains unclear what Kant understood by the latter.

question is whether metaphysics deals with objects that can be cognized through pure reason, or with the subject, namely, the principles and laws in the use of pure reason. Since we can cognize all objects through our subject, especially those that do not affect us, it is subjective" (R 4369 17: 521₂₁–2₂; 131).

Even if these *Reflexionen* do not show that Kant was fully committed to the views they espouse, they indicate that he was at least considering a position according to which the concepts and principles of both ontology and special (applied) metaphysics are denied any objective status and the real use of the intellect is limited to its elenctic function (in the sense of the *Dissertation*) and morality or practical reason. Moreover, the fact that Kant was entertaining the possibility of adopting such a position in the period shortly after the *Dissertation* finds confirmation in a firmly dated document; viz., Kant's letter to Herz of June 7, 1771.

Although it has received much less attention than its better-known counterpart, which was written some eight months later, this letter deserves consideration in any account of the development of Kant's thought because it provides a bridge between the *Dissertation* and the later letter. In addition to Kant's previously noted account of his manner of working, two features of this earlier letter are particularly germane. The first is Kant's remark on the importance of distinguishing "with certainty and clarity that which depends on the subjective principles of human mental powers (not only sensibility but *also the understanding* [my emphasis]) and that which pertains directly to objects" (Br 10: 122₃₁₋₄; 127). The second is Kant's remark that he is currently busy on a work called "The Bounds of Sensibility and of Reason," which will "work out in some detail the foundational principles and laws that determine the sensible world together with an outline of what is essential to the Doctrine of Taste, of Metaphysics, and of Moral Philosophy." Kant further informs Herz that during the past winter (1770–71) he had done much of the work on this project and has recently found a way to organize it (Br 10: 123₁₋₉; 127).

Given the breadth of the project that Kant describes and the fact that there were only a few months between the completion of the *Dissertation* and the winter of 1770–71, it is highly unlikely that this represents a wholly new enterprise that Kant first conceived after completing the *Dissertation*. In fact, in the letter of September 2, 1770, which he sent to Lambert along with a copy of the *Dissertation*, Kant informed him that he hopes to finish in the coming winter his work on "pure moral philosophy, in which no empirical principles are to be found, as it were the Metaphysics of Morals" (Br 10: 97₂₉₋₃₁; 108). And when we recall that the *Dissertation* owed its existence to the exigencies of his new academic position, it becomes evident that rather than being an independent work, it should be seen as extracted for the occasion from the larger and ongoing project to which Kant refers in this letter to Herz.

At the same time, however, this letter gives evidence of Kant's second thoughts regarding his account of the real use of the intellect.[23] Inasmuch as Kant says merely

[23] Near the end of this letter Kant expresses ambivalence regarding the *Dissertation*. On the one hand, he notes that in his next book (presumably "The Bounds of Sensibility and of Reason") he will say more

that it is necessary to distinguish what is subjective from what is objective in the use of reason it cannot be taken as showing that he had abandoned these doctrines and replaced them with the anti-metaphysical view noted above. Indeed, the fact that Kant assigns a prominent place to metaphysics in his projected work and indicates to Herz that it is pretty far along strongly suggest that Kant thought at the time that he had resolved whatever qualms he may have had regarding the status of metaphysical claims and had determined the proper bounds of reason. Nevertheless, the very fact that he regarded the latter task as necessary indicates a certain distancing from the standpoint of the *Dissertation*, where the only threat to metaphysics stemmed from the contamination of the intellectual by the sensible, which is clearly a form of Platonism to which Kant could no longer subscribe.

B) *Kant's letter to Herz of February 21, 1772*: In reporting his intellectual activities since his previous letter, Kant once again refers to his projected work ("The Bounds of Sensibility and of Reason") which he reminds Herz was to consist of a theoretical and a practical part. The theoretical part contains two sections: general phenomenology and metaphysics, with the latter being limited to questions of its nature and method.[24] This corresponds to the subject matter of the *Dissertation*, where Kant's account of the form and principles of the sensible world constitutes a general phenomenology and the propaedeutic science of the intellectual world deals with the nature and method of metaphysics. The second part is likewise divided into two sections: one is concerned with the universal principles of taste and sensuous desire, the other with the first principles of morality. Although Kant here goes into somewhat more detail, this accords with his earlier description of the project. But whereas in his previous letter Kant had given the impression that his initial difficulties with the metaphysical portion, which concerned the need to distinguish between the subjective and the objective aspects of reason, had been resolved, he now remarks that this project had been brought to a halt by the recognition that something essential was lacking in the theoretical part, namely, an account of the relation between representation and objects, which Kant characterizes as "the key to the whole secret of metaphysics" (Br 10: 130_{5-6}; 133).

Although it is clear that Kant's concern is with the intellectual concepts of the *Dissertation*, he initially formulates the issue in completely general terms, asking: "What is the ground of the relation of that in us which we call 'representation' to the object?" (Br 10 130_{7-8}; 133). But by systematically excluding other types of representation Kant quickly narrows the issue down to intellectual concepts. He begins by

---

about the ideas expressed in it and claims to be depressed by his expectation that it will soon fade into oblivion; while, on the other, he remarks that in view of all of its errors it does not seem worthy of reprinting (Br 10: $123_{32}-4_2$; 128).

[24] By "general phenomenology" (*Phaenomenologia generalis*) Kant evidently meant a priori knowledge of the sensible world. See R 4163 17: 440 and Kant's letter to Lambert of September 11, 1770, Br 10: 98_{18}; 108.

noting that sensible representations have an "understandable relation to objects" and the principles derived from them an "understandable validity" for objects of the senses (Br 10: 130_{12-16}; 133). Kant further notes that if we had either an archetypal or a purely ectypal intellect, the relation between representation and object would be non-problematic.[25] In the first case this is because the intellect would, *ex hypothesi*, be the creator of its object as well as its representation; whereas in the second it is because the object is the cause of its representation.[26] But since we possess certain pure concepts of the understanding our intellect is not purely ectypal, while, apart from the capacity to create its object in the domain of practice, it is also not archetypal, the problem of the relation between representation and object arises with regard to our intellectual representations.

Inasmuch as Kant assumes that the mind is equipped with intellectual representations, his problem is a legacy of the "great light" and was already present in the *Dissertation*. Kant acknowledges the latter, but confesses to Herz that he there treated it only negatively by asserting that intellectual representations were "not modifications of the soul brought about by the object" and that he "silently passed over the further question of how a representation that refers to an object without being in any way affected by it can be possible" (Br 10 $130_{33}-3_1$; 133). In so doing, however, Kant partially misdescribes what he had actually said and in the process collapses two distinct questions into one.

The first question concerns the source of intellectual representations, which Kant did not merely answer negatively in the *Dissertation* with the trivial claim that they were *not* produced by the object. Rather, he maintained that their source is the intellect and that they are acquired through reflection upon and abstraction from its logical use. Nevertheless, he did gloss over the question of reference or representation, stating, as he now puts it, that "The sensible representations represent things as they appear, the intellectual representations as they are" (Br 10: 131_{1-3}; 133).

The second question, which Kant now recognizes needs to be addressed, concerns the possibility of the latter mode of representation, wherein agreement with the object is not a function of any encounter with it. Kant notes that this problem does not arise in the case of mathematics because its objects are quantities and as such are constructed. But since it does arise in the case of qualitative relations, which presumably are those thought through the pure concepts, in their case we must ask:

---

[25] Kant offers a similar characterization of the problem in the *Critique* at A192/B 124–5.

[26] Although Kant glosses over the matter, it should be noted that in both of these scenarios the epistemic relation between representation and object is understood in terms of the causal relation. But while it does seem true that if we conceive of a divine intellect creating its object through an intellectual intuition, there is no room for the idea of a lack of conformity, the familiar distinction between primary and secondary qualities demonstrates that this is hardly the case for an ectypal intellect, whose data all derive from affection by its objects. In fact, in the *Prolegomena* Kant notes in passing a similar problem regarding the idea that there could be an empirical intuition of objects as they are in themselves, "since its properties cannot migrate over into my power of representation" (Pro 4: 282_{17-20}; 78).

[How] my understanding may, completely *a priori*, form for itself concepts of things with which concepts the things [*Sachen*] should necessarily agree, and as to how my understanding may formulate real principles concerning the possibility of such concepts, with which principles experience must be in exact agreement and which nevertheless are independent of experience-this question of how the faculty of the understanding achieves this conformity with the things themselves [*den Dingen selbst*] is still left in a state of obscurity.

(Br 10: 131$_{16-22}$; 134)^{27}

Viewed in light of the *Dissertation*, the surprising feature of this passage is its identification of the objects with which the pure concepts supposedly agree as objects of experience, i.e., phenomena.^{28} Although one might argue that by grounding the intellectual concepts in the logical use of the intellect in the *Dissertation*, Kant acknowledged that they had a *logical* use with respect to phenomena, he specifically denied that they had a *real* use, which would seem to entail that they could not be the source of "real [*reale*] principles" to which phenomena must conform. Since this claim is one of the two most puzzling features of the letter it calls for careful attention. But before turning to it we must consider the other puzzling feature; viz., Kant's proposed solution to the problem that he poses: the relation between the intellectual concepts and their objects.

Kant begins by summarily dismissing three attempts to deal with this issue: that of Plato, with his conception of a previous intuition of the divinity as the source of our intellectual concepts; of Malebranche, which Kant describes as "a continuous permanent intuiting of this primary being;" and of Crusius, who maintained that certain innate rules of judgment and concepts were implanted in the human soul in order to harmonize with things. Unfortunately, Kant is not terribly clear on the matter, since he appears to collapse the first two into versions of what he terms the "Hyper Influx Theory [*influxum hyperphysicum*]," while characterizing the third as the "Pre-established Intellectual Harmony Theory [*harmonium praestabilitam intellectualem*]." Moreover, the only one that he explicitly criticizes is the last, which he refers to as the "*deus ex machina*," stating that it is "the greatest absurdity one could hit upon in the determination of the origin and validity of our cognitions" (Br 10: 131$_{23-36}$; 134).

After rejecting these views, one might expect Kant to offer his own alternative, much as he will do in the *Critique*.^{29} But instead he seems to change the subject, informing Herz that,

As I was searching in such ways for the sources of intellectual knowledge, without which one cannot determine the nature and bounds of metaphysics, I divided this science into essentially

---

^{27} Kant also provides similar formulations of the problem in R 4473 17: 564; 138–9 and R 4633 17:615–16; 149. Unlike this passage, however, they formulate the problem in general terms rather than with specific reference to a priori propositions that apply to objects given in experience. This will prove to be of significance below when we consider Carl's interpretation of the letter.

^{28} We should not be misled by Kant's terminology in the above passage. Clearly, by "*den Dingen selbst*" he does not mean *Dingen an sich selbst* (things in themselves).

^{29} See A92–3/B125–6; B166–8.

distinct parts and I sought to reduce transcendental philosophy, namely all the concepts of a completely pure reason, to a certain number of categories, but not like Aristotle, who, in his ten predicaments, placed them side by side as he found them in a purely chance juxtaposition; rather, I arranged them according to the way in which they divide themselves into classes through a few fundamental laws of the understanding...I can say that as far as my essential purpose is concerned, I have succeeded and that now I am in a position to bring out a critique of pure reason that will deal with the nature of theoretical as well as practical knowledge, insofar as it is purely intellectual. Of this, I will first work out the first part, which will deal with the sources of metaphysics, its method and bounds...With respect to the first part, I should be in a position to publish it within three months.   (Br 10: 131_{37}–2_{30}; 134–5)

It is striking that a project that Kant estimated would take about three months to complete required approximately nine years; though this becomes understandable once it is realized that he soon came to see that his problem was much more complex than he had initially thought. Nevertheless, assuming that by his "essential purpose" Kant meant explaining how intellectual concepts can relate to objects, it remains perplexing why he apparently thought that providing a list and division of these concepts, a topic which he had treated causally in the *Dissertation*, could suffice to resolve *that* problem. But, rather than addressing this question directly, I shall first consider the first of the fore-mentioned puzzles (the identification of the objects with which the pure concepts supposedly agree with phenomena), in the hope that its resolution will shed light on this one as well.

Although he does not regard it as a puzzle, the importance of this identification has been emphasized by Carl, who takes it both as an indication of a decisive break with the standpoint of the *Dissertation* and as Kant's earliest statement of the problematic of the Transcendental Deduction. Carl breaks down Kant's account of "the key to the whole secret of metaphysics" into three steps. The first is to limit the problem to the class of representations that stand in a non-causal relation to their objects. The second is to limit the cases of this relation to the subset in which there is supposedly a necessary agreement between a priori concepts formed by the understanding and things. The third and for Carl decisive limitation is "that Kant considers only representations of things that affect us in some way or other, that are accessible only by way of experience;" to which he adds that "the intellectual representations of the *Dissertation* are explicitly excluded."[30]

Carl's analysis has come under criticism. The critique was initiated by Beck, who argues for the diametrically opposed view that in his letter to Herz Kant is making a last-ditch effort to plug a perceived gap in the argument of the *Dissertation* rather than embarking on a radically new project. The gap, as Beck sees it, concerns the need for an explanation of the possibility of a priori knowledge of *intelligibilia*, given our lack of intellectual intuition.[31] In support of this, Beck states his belief that Kant's

---

[30] See Carl (1989a), 5–6 and 8–10.   [31] Beck (1989), 22.

use of the words "intellectual representations" (*intellectuale Vorstellungen*) in the letter, which corresponds to the *intellectualia* of the *Dissertation*, indicates that he was still thinking that there can be pure conceptual knowledge of noumena. Indeed, Beck suggests that, pace Carl, Kant held at the time of the letter that intellectual concepts *do not apply to phenomena*, which coincides with what he said in §5 of the *Dissertation*, where "he denied that there is a real use (*usus realis*) of reason in our observational knowledge."[32]

Both Predrag Cicovacki and Laywine concur with Beck's denial of Carl's thesis that in his letter to Herz Kant was excluding the applicability of intellectual representations to noumena. According to Cicovacki, while Carl is correct to call attention to the passage in which Kant relates the intellectual representations to phenomena, he has no textual basis for his claim that Kant excluded them from noumena.[33] Similarly, Laywine contends that, while Carl is correct in noting that the problem that Kant poses in the letter concerns the agreement between intellectual concepts and things accessible through experience, he is incorrect in denying that it also concerns their agreement with things in themselves.[34]

At the same time, however, both Cicovacki and Laywine reject Beck's denial that in the letter to Herz Kant contends that intellectual concepts also apply to phenomena. In fact, Cicovacki calls attention to the major lacuna in Beck's account; viz., that it fails to give an adequate analysis of the passage on which Carl places the entire weight of his interpretation. It is not that Beck ignores this passage, but, rather, that his suggestion that Kant held in the *Dissertation* that intellectual concepts do not apply to phenomena is ill-founded.[35] Accordingly, both Cicovacki and Laywine advocate a third alternative in which Kant is concerned with the perfectly general question: "how there can be any application of intellectual representations to any objects whatsoever" or, alternatively, "how to explain the agreement of pure concepts with their objects, no matter what the nature of objects is."[36]

While Cicovacki and Laywine are correct regarding the generality of Kant's concern, I believe it possible to take the analysis a step further by noting that the discipline that has been traditionally construed as concerned with "any objects whatsoever" and of the agreement of concepts with their objects, "no matter what the nature of objects is" is ontology. The point is that it is only by applying to objects qua objects that concepts can apply to objects regardless of their specific nature, and

---

[32] Ibid., 23.   [33] Cicovacki (1991), 354–5.   [34] Laywine (2001), 44, note 27.

[35] See Cicovacki (1991), 356–7. As he points out, Beck bases his claim on Kant's denial that empirical knowledge involves a real use of the intellect and he notes that this does not imply that intellectual concepts do not apply directly to objects of experience. As an example of such application, he cites the note to §24 in which Kant states that "whatever is somewhere exists" (the conversion of the surreptitious axiom: "*whatever exists is somewhere*") is "in the highest degree true" (ID 2: 412_{35-6}; 408). Cicovacki fails to note, however, that this proposition is a tautology.

[36] See Cicovacki (1991), 357. Following Nicolai Hartmann, Cicovacki refers to this question as the "aporia of *a priori* knowledge." For her concurrence, see Laywine (2001), 44, note 27 and 47, note 42.

therefore to both phenomena and noumena.[37] Indeed, if the preceding analysis of the problem posed for Kant by Lambert's remarks about ontology is correct, this is precisely the issue with which we should expect Kant to have been concerned.

Moreover, this provides the basis for a possible answer to the second of the two fore-mentioned puzzles; viz., why Kant might (erroneously) have thought that determining the intellectual concepts in a systematic manner would be essential to the resolution of the problem of how such concepts relate to objects. The key point is that if the intellectual concepts are concepts of an object as such, it would follow that everything that can be thought as an object (whether phenomenal or noumenal) must conform to them as a condition of being thought. And, if this were the case, it would also be necessary to arrive at the complete list of such concepts, a task that Kant did not seem to regard as urgent in the *Dissertation*.

Although admittedly speculative, this proposed reconstruction of Kant's line of reasoning circa February 1772 not only explains why he seems to suggest at various points in this letter that the intellectual concepts apply to both phenomena and noumena, but also why the three months that Kant thought would be required to complete the theoretical portion of his proposed "critique of pure reason" became approximately nine years and the work that eventually emerged is quite different from the one that he envisioned at the time. Clearly, part of the problem was that the determination of the list of concepts turned out to be a much more complex endeavor than Kant had estimated at the time.[38] The main reason, however, is that, though the "critical" Kant would have recognized the fallacious nature of the line of reason that I have attributed to him in the letter to Herz, he was not in a position to recognize this at the time. In fact, if something like this were Kant's view, he had at least two more crucial lessons to learn before arriving at his fully "critical" position.

Expressed in terms of the *Critique*, the first lesson is that "neither concepts without intuition corresponding to them in some way nor intuition without a concept can yield a cognition" (A50/B74), which is to say the discursivity thesis. Given this thesis, it is not only the case that whatever is sensibly given necessarily conforms to the conditions under which something can be given (this part of the "critical" position was already in place in the *Dissertation*), but also that in order for a thought to yield cognition it must relate to a corresponding intuition. Accordingly, while conformity to the conditions under which an object can be thought is a necessary condition of

---

[37] Admittedly, there is an ambiguity in the question posed by Cicovacki, since "any objects whatsoever" might be taken to mean either simply any object at all, which appears to be how Laywine takes it or any and every object. Although Cicovacki's first characterization of the problem in terms of "any objects whatsoever" suggests the former, his second, which emphasizes that the applicability of the concepts is not a function of the specific nature of the objects, suggests the second. But regardless of how either Cicovacki or Laywine understand the problem, my view is that the second best defines the issue that confronted Kant at the time.

[38] Kant provides accounts of the lengthy process through which he arrived at his final table of pure concepts or categories in R 5015 18: 60 and Pro 4: 322–4. For a discussion of this process see de Vleeschauwer (1934), 217–33.

cognition, it is not also a sufficient condition; for this requires that something be given in intuition corresponding to the thought.

The second lesson is more subtle and can be learned only after the first is fully grasped. It is that, in addition to showing the necessity of whatever is sensibly given conforming to the conditions of sensibility and what is thought relating to a corresponding intuition in order to yield cognition, it must also be shown that what is sensibly given necessarily conforms to the conditions of the understanding. This is necessary because the radical separation of sensibility and understanding makes it evident that it cannot simply be assumed that whatever conforms to the former conforms to the latter as well. We shall see in Chapter 4 that in the first section of the A-Deduction Kant notes that it is precisely this point that makes a transcendental deduction of the categories so difficult.

If the interpretation of the letter to Herz presented here is correct, Kant had not yet fully learned the first of these lessons in February 1772. And since the second lesson presupposes the first, he could not have learned that one either. It will be argued in the next section, however, that Kant had mastered the first lesson but not the second in R4634, which suggests that it must have been written after the letter to Herz.[39] And since Carl sees in this text both the answer to the problem that he takes Kant to have posed in this letter (the applicability of the categories to experience) and as the first draft of the Transcendental Deduction, the discussion will involve a further engagement with his views.

C) *R 4634*: The first three paragraphs of this lengthy *Reflexion* contain an illuminating account of the distinction between analytic and synthetic judgments and the problem of the synthetic a priori, which in all essentials is the view that Kant held in the *Critique*. Kant begins by noting that we can know (*kennen*) an object only through the predicates that we apply to it and that prior to this predication "whatever representations [presumably intuitions] we find in us are to be regarded only as materials for cognition but not as cognition," from which he concludes that "an object is only a something in general that we think through certain predicates that constitute its concept" (R 4634 17: 616_{20-4}; 149).

The first part of this claim speaks to the conceptual nature of human cognition. At least from the time of the *Dissertation* this had been a central part of Kant's position and we have seen that he endeavored to underscore its significance by contrasting it with a hypothetical intuitive intellect, which grasps its object directly without the need for any conceptual mediation. The second part spells out the implication of this for the conception of the object to which the concepts are applied as predicates in a

---

[39] Adickes tentatively dates R4634 at sometime in 1772 or 1773. My reason for dating it after the letter to Herz is that I am unable to see why Kant would have posed the problem of the relation between the intellectual concepts and objects in the way in which he does in the letter, if he had then been in possession of the analytic-synthetic distinction and the conception of propositions that are both synthetic and cognized a priori, as he clearly is in this *Reflexion*.

judgment. Since, *ex hypothesi*, the descriptive content of an object is supplied entirely by these predicates, when considered apart from them it can be characterized only as "a something in general," which Kant sometimes refers to as a "something in general $= x$," or simply as "x." We shall see that this conception of an object will play a central role in both versions of the Transcendental Deduction in the *Critique*.

The novel nature of the account of cognition and judgment that Kant sketches in the *Reflexion* becomes evident when it is compared with an earlier one to which it bears a superficial similarity. For example, in a *Reflexion* which Adickes dates from 1769, Kant writes:

> In all judgments of the understanding things are like this. (If anything x can be cognized by means of a representation a, then a is a mark of something x; but the cognition of x by means of a is a concept. Thus extension, motion, ignorance, etc., is a mark of something x.) If anything x, which is cognized by means of the representation a, is compared with another concept b, as either including or excluding this concept, then this relation is in the judgment. This judgment is thus either the cognition of the agreement or of opposition, so that in the thing x, which I know [*kenne*] by means of the concept a, either b is contained as a partial concept and thus x, which is cognized by means of a, can also be cognized by means of b, or x negates the concept of b.   (R 3920 17: 344_{19}–5_6; 94).

Although Kant here already assumes the conceptual nature of human cognition and refers to the undetermined object of such cognition simply as "x," it is clear that his account antedates the analytic-synthetic distinction because it considers the relation between the predicates a and b solely in terms of their agreement with or opposition to each other, which presumably would be determined by either the principle of identity or contradiction. Accordingly, when viewed from the standpoint of Kant's later accounts of judgment, all judgments to which this schema applies would be analytic, which we have seen was characteristic of Kant's position in the writings of the 1760s.[40] By contrast, in R 4634 Kant provides a generic schema that fits *both*

---

[40] The same can be said about R 3921 17: 345; though Kant here exempts the I from the principle that a subject cannot be represented apart from its predicates. By contrast, R 3928 17: 350–1 seems to represent an interesting transitional stage. Here Kant distinguishes between analytic and synthetic judgments, but seems to do so in terms of the analytic model. Thus, he states that the principles of the form of analytic judgments are identity and contradiction and the identity (agreement) or opposition of the predicate with the subject is demonstrated by means of an analysis of the "**given** concept." But he also states that the principles of the form of synthetic judgments are that: "whatever is always combined with a known part of the possible concept of a thing also belongs as a part to this concept, etc." (R 3928 17: 350_{6-8}; 96), which suggests that the predicate in an affirmative synthetic judgment is also thought as part of the concept of the subject, albeit one that cannot be demonstrated to be such through an analysis of the concept. Moreover, after providing as an example of an analytic judgment: "every body is impenetrable" and of a synthetic judgment: "every body is inert," Kant reflects: "If one had the whole concept of which the notions of subject and predicate are *compartes* [partially equated], synthetic judgments would be transformed into analytic ones. One wonders to what extent there is something arbitrary here" (R 3928 17: 350_{18-20}). Since this anticipates an objection that has often been raised against Kant's account of the analytic-synthetic distinction in the *Critique*, it shows how far Kant was at this point from the "critical" view, for which the distinction is not arbitrary because it is grounded in what Beck calls the "fixity of a concept." For Beck's

analytic *and* synthetic judgments and that provides the basis for distinguishing between them. As Kant puts it:

In every judgment ... there are two predicates that we compare with one another, of which one, which comprises the given cognition of the object, is the logical subject, and the other, which is to be compared with the first, is called the logical predicate. If I say: a body is divisible, this means the same as: Something x, which I cognize under the predicates that together comprise the concept of a body, I also think through the predicate of divisibility. x @ is identical with x b. Now a as well as b belongs to x. Only in a different way: either b lies in that which constitutes the concept a, and thus can be found through the analysis of that, or belongs to x without being contained or comprised in a. In the first case the judgment is analytic, in the second synthetic.

(R 4634 17: 616_{24} -17_7; 149–50)

Strictly speaking, Kant cannot claim that every judgment contains two predicates, since hypothetical and disjunctive judgments can have more. But inasmuch as it does apply to categorical judgments, which is the type that Kant almost always appeals to when discussing his general theory of judgment, he could say that every judgment has *at least* two predicates.[41] Moreover, in addition to being implicit in Kant's account of the discursive nature of human cognition, the multi-predicate schema makes it easy to see why the genus judgment is naturally divided into two species: the analytic and the synthetic. This is because, in contrast to the earlier schema, it makes it clear that the act of judgment involves not merely the relation of the predicates to each other, which can be understood in logical terms (agreement or (logical) opposition), but also their relation to an identical object = x, which is what is asserted in the judgment. Indeed, it is the latter relation that is fundamental to the act of judgment and the former must be understood in light of it. In other words, the "comparison" of the subject and predicate concepts that is made in the judgment does not simply concern the relation of the concepts to each other (as it does in the earlier schema), but their relation to an identical object = x. Thus, considered from this point of view, the inclusion of the predicate in the subject concept (b being contained or comprised in a) is merely one of two distinct ways in which the relation of both a and b to x can be determined.

Kant notes that his example of a judgment ("a body is divisible") is analytic, but the crucial point is that in being used as an illustration of what pertains to judgment as such it is not considered qua analytic. Kant clarifies the point by providing an example of a synthetic judgment, "Every body is heavy", which falls under the same schema. In the latter case, he remarks, there is "a *synthesis*; the one predicate is not involved in the subject, but is added to it" (R 4634 17: 617_{8-9}; 150). Here, the "synthesis" is the act through which b is predicated of the object = x; and it is by being predicated of x that b is related to a in the judgment.

account of this issue, which refers to this *Reflexion*, see his (1965a), 74–91. I discuss the issue, albeit without reference to this *Reflexion*, in Allison (1973a), 65–7.

[41] Kant evidently thought that this was justified by the fact that hypothetical and disjunctive judgments consist in combinations of categorical ones. See JL 9: 106–7; 602–3.

After explicating the distinction between analytic and synthetic judgments, Kant turns to the question of apriority. He notes in agreement with his earliest formulations of the distinction, that "We can have insight into all analytic judgments *a priori*, and what can only be cognized *a posteriori* is synthetic. Hence properly empirical judgments are synthetic" (R 4634 17: 617_{9-13}; 150). But whereas Kant previously had also affirmed the converse of the latter; viz., that all synthetic judgments are empirical, he now claims that "there are judgments whose validity seems to be established *a priori*, but which are nonetheless synthetic, e.g., everything that is alterable has a cause," which gives rise to the question: "whence does one arrive at these judgments? On what basis do we associate one concept with another of the same object when no observation and experience indicates that[?]" (R 4634 17: 617_{15-17}; 150). And, after reaffirming that such judgments cannot be based upon experience because they claim strict universality and necessity and include concepts that cannot be derived from experience, Kant further queries: "These concepts may lie in us where they will: whence do we derive their connection[?] Are they revelations, prejudices, etc.[?]" (R 4634 17 6171_{31-3}; 150).

By suggesting that the problem concerns the connection of the concepts involved in synthetic a priori cognitions and that this is distinct from the question of the origin of these concepts ("they may lie in us where they will"), Kant appears to have broken decisively with his position in the letter to Herz, where he held that the key to understanding how pure concepts relate to objects lay in understanding how they are grounded in the nature of the intellect. Rather, Kant's focus is now explicitly on the function of these concepts as conditions of the possibility of experience. The gist of his position is contained in a paragraph that Carl claims contains the first draft of the Transcendental Deduction. In view of its importance, I shall cite it in full and then comment on its component parts, numbering its four sentences for ease of reference:

1. If certain concepts do not contain anything other than that by means of which all experiences are possible on our part, then they can be asserted *a priori* prior to experience and yet with complete validity for everything that may ever come before us (*alles, was uns jemals vorkommen mag*).
2. In that case, to be sure, they are not valid of things in general, but yet of everything that can ever be given to us through experience, because they contain the conditions by means of which these experiences are possible.
3. Such propositions would therefore contain the condition of the possibility not of things but of experience.
4. However, things that cannot be given to us through any experience are nothing to us; hence we can very well treat such propositions as universal from a practical point of view, only not as principles of speculation about objects in general.

(R 4634 17: 618_{1-12}; 150)

The first sentence sets the stage for the argument by formulating the issue in hypothetical terms. It claims that *if* there are concepts that express the necessary conditions of a possible experience, then all possible objects of experience or, as Kant here puts it, "everything that may ever come before us," must fall under them. It is not that Kant had any doubts about the existence of such concepts, but merely that he does not attempt (at least in the above-cited paragraph) to argue for it. Accordingly, it seems too strong to say with Carl that Kant here provides a first draft of the Transcendental Deduction; rather, he stipulates what any such deduction must accomplish.

The second sentence does two things, albeit in reverse order. One is to explain why such concepts would be valid (they contain conditions of the possibility of experience). The other is to introduce a crucial restriction; viz., that their validity would be limited to what is given in experience and not extended to things in general. Accordingly, it distinguishes between things in general and whatever can be given in experience, with the latter presumably constituting a subset of the former.

The third sentence clarifies the conclusion reached in the first two by introducing the distinction between conditions of the possibility of things and of the experience of them. Since by "experience" Kant understands empirical cognition, a condition of experience is an epistemic condition; whereas a condition of the possibility of things is ontological in the sense that it is a condition apart from which a thing cannot be conceived to exist.[42] These two kinds of condition can but need not coincide; for a concept might be a condition of the possibility of the cognition of a certain species of thing or of things under a certain description (e.g., considered as spatiotemporal) rather than of things as such, in which case it would be an epistemic but not an ontological condition. Moreover, this is precisely the position that Kant adopts, when he claims that the concepts in question would be conditions of the possibility "not of things but of experience."

The fourth sentence spells out the implications of both the positive result (these concepts would be epistemic conditions) and the restriction (they would not be ontological conditions) that have supposedly been established up to this point. It is noteworthy, however, that in so doing Kant makes use of variants of two expressions that are characteristic of his "critical" position. One is "nothing to us" (*vor uns nichts*), which corresponds to the "nothing for me" (*für mich nichts sein*) that Kant uses in the Transcendental Deduction to refer to representations that do not conform to the conditions of apperception. Since at the time of the composition of this *Reflexion* Kant had not yet developed his doctrine of apperception, he obviously did not use it in that sense. Instead, it seems likely that he had in mind objects that cannot be given in a possible experience, e.g., the noumena of the *Dissertation*. The other expression is "from a practical point of view" (*in praktischer Absicht*). Whereas

---

[42] For my discussion of the difference between epistemic and ontological conditions, which I consider central to Kant's transcendental idealism, see Allison (2004), 11–13, 25, 37, and 45–7.

during the "critical" period Kant used this primarily with reference to God and freedom, indicating that we have a warrant to assume their reality only from a (morally) practical point of view, he here apparently uses it to note the irrelevance for (epistemic) practice of the fact that the validity of the concepts at issue does not extend to all things but only to those that are objects of a possible experience.

In interpreting this paragraph, it is also essential not to be misled by Kant's use of the term "concepts." In particular, one should avoid assuming that he is here concerned exclusively, or even primarily, with the pure concepts of the understanding or categories. While it may be the most natural reading of the text, it is clear from the context that Kant is here using the term in the broad sense to include *both* concepts of the understanding *and* space and time (as pure intuitions).[43] In fact, the line of argument that Kant proposes assumes a strict isomorphism in the status of these two sets of epistemic conditions. As he puts it in the next paragraph,

In every experience there is something through which an object is given and something through which it is thought. If we take the conditions that lie in the activities of the mind by means of which alone it can be given, then we can cognize something of the object *a priori*. If we take that through which alone it can be thought then we can also cognize something *a priori* about all possible objects. For by that means alone does something become an object for us or a cognition of it. (R 4634$_{17}$: 618$_{18-24}$; 150-1)

Kant develops this thought in the final two paragraphs, first with respect to the conditions of sensibility, through which objects are given as appearances, and then with respect to the intellectual conditions, under which they are cognized as objects. In both cases, the aim is to show how these conditions make possible a certain body of a priori knowledge. Inasmuch as Kant's account of sensibility closely tracks the treatment of the topic in the *Dissertation*, there is no need to consider the paragraph devoted to it in any detail. Suffice it to note that it turns on the distinction between the matter and form of sensibility, with the former consisting of sensations (or impressions) and the latter in a subjective ground through which these data are ordered by an activity of the mind. Kant points out that nothing can be known a priori regarding the former but such knowledge is possible regarding the latter (R 4634 17: 618$_{25}$-19$_7$; 151).

It is only in the final paragraph that Kant explicitly discusses the contribution of the understanding to the a priori cognition of appearances. He writes:

(If we place [*setzen*] something in space and time, we act; if we place it next to and after another, we connect [*Verknüpfen*]. These actions are only means to bring about each position; but one can take them separately; if we take the same kind of thing several times or posit it in the one action and at the same time another [*einerlei etliche mal oder in der einen Handlung zugleich die andere setzen*], this is a kind of action, through which we posit something in

---

[43] This accords with Kant's use of the term in both the *Dissertation* and the Transcendental Aesthetic in the *Critique*. See ID 2: 398-9; 402 and A26/B42 and A32/49.

accordance with the rule of appearances, where this positing must have its special rules, which are distinct from the condition of the form with regard to which they are to be located in appearance). (R 4634 17: 619$_{7-15}$; 151)[44]

Despite its overall obscurity two things are relatively clear about this passage. First, Kant is asserting the need for a second set of a priori rules governing the relation of appearances, beyond those provided by space and time as forms of sensibility. Second, the rules are connected with an act of mind that is distinct from the one that sets appearances in space and time. To a reader of the *Critique* the connection of sensibility with an "act of mind" might seem strange; but it must be kept in mind that in the *Dissertation* Kant maintained that appearances attain their spatiotemporal form as the result of being "co-ordinated by a certain natural law of the mind" (ID 2: 392$_{31-2}$; 384). In other words, the view of sensibility with which Kant is here working is that of the *Dissertation* rather than the more nuanced view of the *Critique*. Accordingly, experience, as Kant here conceives it, involves two distinct acts of mind: one through which appearances are placed in space and time and another through which they are connected with each other in the same space and time.

The most obscure part of this passage is Kant's account of the nature and function of the second set of rules. The most plausible reading seems to be that the rule to which Kant is appealing to illustrate his general thesis is that of cause and effect. But even if this is the case, there is no sign in this passage that Kant had arrived at the set of pure concepts of the understanding to which he alluded in his letter to Herz and no indication that he took himself to have provided an answer to the problem he posed in that letter regarding the relation of these concepts to objects as such. To the contrary, if the interpretation of this letter sketched in the preceding section is correct, Kant abandoned in R 4634 his last-ditch effort to ground ontology in an analysis of the nature of the understanding and by connecting these rules, i.e., concepts, to the sensibly given took a decisive step in the direction of the view of the *Critique*.

If we are to understand the development of Kant's thought in the remainder of the "Silent Decade," however, it is also necessary to become clear about the ways in which his position in this *Reflexion* differ from his eventual "critical" view. It was previously suggested that, starting with the standpoint of the letter to Herz, there were two fundamental lessons that Kant needed to learn before the problematic of the Transcendental Deduction could become fully evident to him. The first is that pure concepts of the understanding can only yield cognition of objects insofar as they are related to sensible intuition, which effectively restricts cognition to objects of possible experience. Regardless of how one reads this letter, it is apparent that this

---

[44] I have here made several modifications of Guyer's translation of this passage. In so doing, I have been influenced by (though I have not strictly followed) the looser, less literal rendering by Werkmeister (1979), 87, which suggests that Kant is here attempting to contrast a causal relation between phenomena with a mere juxtaposition of phenomena in space or succession in time.

lesson was learned in R 4634 and that it is inseparable from Kant's account of the possibility of the synthetic a priori.[45]

The second lesson is that it does not follow from the fact that whatever is given in intuition necessarily accords with the a priori forms of intuition that it also conforms to the conditions of the understanding and that a further argument is needed in order to establish this result. Indeed, we have seen that this is precisely the issue that Kant poses as crucial in the introductory portion of both versions of the Transcendental Deduction, where the great worry is that, despite conforming to the formal conditions of sensibility, "appearances could be…so constituted that the understanding would not find them in accord with the conditions of its unity" (A90/B123). As Carl points out, however, inasmuch as Kant's entire focus is on the claim that the concepts make experience possible, it seems that in R 4634 he failed to consider the possibility that appearances might not conform to the conditions required for experience, which effectively means that he had not yet learned the second lesson.[46] In order to ensure this conformity a further constraint upon appearances is required, and as Kant will argue in these series of *Reflexionen* known as the *Duisburg Nachlass* this is provided by the unity of apperception. Accordingly, it is to this document, which is generally regarded as the most important text from the "Silent Decade," that we now turn.

II

The *Duisburg Nachlass* is the title given to a set of Kant's notes by their second editor (Theodor Haering) because they had been in the possession of a family in Duisburg. Although their significance stems mainly from the fact that they contain the most detailed picture that we have of Kant's wrestling during the "Silent Decade" with the issues that will become the central concerns of the Transcendental Analytic in the *Critique*, their relative datability, one of them (R 4675) was written on the back of the envelope of a letter that Kant received that was dated May 20, 1775, gives them a unique value for the reconstruction of Kant's thought during this period.[47] Assuming that Kant wrote this note shortly after receiving the letter and that the other notes, which, with one significant exception, deal with the same issues in a similar fashion, were written at around that time, we can with some confidence date their composition as sometime in or around 1775, which is roughly the mid-point of the "Silent Decade."[48]

---

[45] It may not have been completely learned, however, since we shall see in the next section that Kant continued to adhere to certain theses of rational psychology, understood as synthetic a priori principles regarding the soul.

[46] See Carl (1989a), esp. 8–10, and (1989b), 55–73.

[47] The letter was from a gentleman named Johann Friedrich Bertram and is of absolutely no philosophical import, consisting merely of a brief note inviting Kant to visit Bertram's brother's estate. See Br 10 23: 102.

[48] The significant exception is the second page of R 4684 17: 672–3, which is written in Latin and contains a brief sketch of the central topics in rational psychology.

Since the eleven *Reflexionen* of which the text is composed cover much the same ground from slightly different points of view, I shall not attempt to analyze them individually. Instead, I shall endeavor to sketch the basic line of argument that Kant appears to be working out in the set as a whole, noting the most significant terminological variations and apparent problems. Generally speaking, this line of argument may be seen as a continuation and development of that of R 4634. The main differences are that the contribution of the understanding to empirical cognition, which in R 4634 was only discussed in the final paragraph, now occupies center stage and that Kant introduces a whole new dimension into his analysis with the conception of apperception and its necessary unity.

The essential continuity between R 4634 and the *Duisburg Nachlass* is evident from the latter's characterization of the analytic-synthetic distinction and the role that it plays in the overall argument, which takes the form of an extended reflection on the conditions of the possibility and the restriction of the scope of synthetic judgments involving pure concepts of the understanding as predicates. Kant not only appeals to the same conception of judgment, he also uses the same set of symbols (a, b, x) to formulate the contrast. At one point Kant writes:

> The principle of identity and contradiction contains the comparison of two predicates a and b with x, but only in such a way that the concept a of x is compared with b (*substantive*), thus the x is idle [*unnütze*]. It is a principle of form, not of content, thus merely logical. A principle of analysis, from which nothing *objective* can be cognized. It can be cognized in categorical, hypothetical, and disjunctive form. If I refer both predicates to the x and thereby to one another, then it is synthetic: no x who is learned is lacking in science, for there it needs the restriction of time, namely: at the same time. The lack of science contradicts learnedness ... but not the person who is learned, except insofar as he is learned. Thus the contradiction is directed either to the concept a that I have of x or to the x to which this concept does not necessarily apply. The synthetic validity of b and *non* b with regard to x, which can be thought through the concept a or *non* a, is called alteration. (R 4676 17: 653_{12}–4_{14}; 165)[49]

Kant once again provides a schematic account of judgment as involving two concepts (a and b) that are predicated of an object x. As before, this holds of judgment as such, quite apart from the subsequent question of whether the judgment is analytic or synthetic.[50] The latter turns entirely on whether the relation between a and b

---

[49] For similar accounts of the analytic-synthetic distinction in the *Duisburg Nachlass*, see R 4674 17: 645_{16}–64; 159; R 4678 17: 662_{13}–19; 170; and R 4684 17: 671_{3}–15; 176.

[50] It is noteworthy that in the above-cited passage Kant suggests that analytic judgments can assume the hypothetical and disjunctive as well as the categorical form. This is important because it has frequently been objected by critics, who base their understanding of Kant's analytic-synthetic distinction solely on the misleading formulation in the introduction to the *Critique*, that according to Kant's formulation the distinction is applicable only to categorical judgments. To be sure, Kant does not here explain why he rejects this charge; but it can easily be seen in light of his view that the hypothetical and disjunctive judgments are composed of combinations of categorical ones and his insistence in the *Prolegomena* that the distinction between analytic and synthetic judgments concerns their content rather than their logical form (Pro 4: 266_{15}–23; 62). Kant also makes the point in R 4674 17: 645_{21}–3; 159.

expressed in the judgment is mediated by their common relation to x. In the case of analytic judgments it is not, since the truth (or falsity) of the judgment is determined by directly comparing the predicates with each other according to the principle of identity and contradiction (here considered a single principle), rather than by endeavoring to determine whether they are both applicable to x. Accordingly, in their case "x is idle" or, as Kant also puts it, "the x drops out completely, because a taken substantively already stands in a determinate identical relation with b" (R 4678 17: 662_{12-13}; 170).

By contrast, in the case of synthetic judgments everything turns on the relation of a and b to x. As Kant puts it at one point, "[I]n synthetic propositions the x is that in which a is determined and b is determined through the condition of a" (R 4678 17: 662_{14-15}; 170). To say that x is "that in which a is determined" is to say that the nature of x (its inherent properties, molecular structure, or the like) provides the ground for taking it under the predicate a, which implies that x is a condition of a; and since no other elements besides a, b, and x are under consideration, this implies that x is also the condition of b. Consider, for example, the synthetic proposition "Gold is soluble in *aqua regia*." The properties of x; viz., being a malleable yellow metal, etc., provide the condition of the application of both predicates: the one-place predicate "gold," which functions as the grammatical or logical subject, and the two-place relational predicate "being soluble in *aqua regia*," which serves as the grammatical or logical predicate.

The obvious question suggested by this account is its applicability to synthetic cognition a priori. Does it suffice to say that in such cognitions the nature of x is determinable a priori or is the issue more complex? If the former is the case, it might appear that Kant had already provided the key to the resolution of the problem in the *Dissertation* with his account of sensibility as having its a priori formal conditions in space and time. Assuming, as Kant now does, that x must be given in sensible intuition, the fact that x is subject to a priori conditions of its form provides a basis for explaining the possibility of a priori cognition with respect to x. It is, however, clear that in the *Duisburg Nachlass* Kant does not adhere to such a view; for while he maintains that a priori forms of intuition constitute a necessary condition of synthetic a priori cognition, he denies that they are sufficient. Expressed in terms of Kant's notation, this requires a consideration of the nature and function of b as well as x.

Kant points to the nature of the problem in R 4674. After noting that the status of space as a subjective condition of the representation of objects is a condition of a priori cognitions of these objects and that synthetic judgments of experience are cognized a posteriori "because they are immediately directed to given objects," he remarks in a tantalizingly incomplete thought that "But now if anything were to be cognized [*erkannt*] about things not merely with regard to the form of their appearance, but with regard to the rest of their nature [*Beschaffenheit*] etc." (17: 645_{13-15}; 159). Although Kant does not indicate what he understands by the "rest of their nature," it is not difficult to fill in the gap. Since, *ex hypothesi*, it cannot be the form (that being provided by space and time), and since it also cannot be the matter of appearance (that being provided by sensation), there remains only the relations in which these objects stand to one another. Moreover, this accords with the overall argument of the *Duisburg Nachlass*, one of the central premises of which is that "This object [*x* taken under *a*] can be represented only in accordance with its relations" (R 4674 17: 646_{10-11}; 160); or, as Kant elsewhere puts it, "Determinate predicates (relational predicates) which are real pertain only to relations" (R 4676 17: 65_{12-13}; 167).

Admittedly, the identification of the relations in question with those in which objects stand to one another amounts to a radical oversimplification of Kant's view, since an essential strand of the argument attempts to link the representation of objects with the unity of apperception. Nevertheless, for analytic purposes it is useful to separate the two strands. Accordingly, the ensuing discussion is divided into two parts. The first considers Kant's endeavor to show that the three categories of relation are necessary conditions of the cognition of an objective temporal order. The second analyzes his attempt to ground the normative status of these categories in their connection with the unity of apperception. The former will be referred to as the "objectivity argument" and the latter as the "argument from the unity apperception." But the essential point is that they are considered two strands in a single argument rather than as two distinct lines of argument.[51]

1) *The objectivity argument*: The underlying premise of this line of argument is that, despite their status as a priori forms of sensibility, space and time are insufficient to account for the cognition of an objective spatiotemporal order of appearances and a contribution of the understanding, which provides the a priori laws or principles through which this order can alone be experienced, is also required. In short, these laws or principles are, like space and time, necessary conditions of the possibility of experience, which accounts for both their objective validity and the restriction of their scope to objects of possible experience. We have seen that the seeds of this line of argument are already to be found in R 4634. But we also saw that Kant there did little more than hint at how such an argument might proceed and he glossed over the crucial issue of the inter-relation of the two sets of a priori conditions.

In dealing with the latter issue in the *Duisburg Nachlass*, Kant was led to an even more radical break with the position of the *Dissertation* regarding the experiential function of the understanding than is to be found in R4634. Common to all three texts is the distinction between mere perception and experience and the assignment of a role to the understanding in making possible the move from the one to the other. We saw that in the *Dissertation* the real use of the intellect is reserved for the

---

[51] In this respect my reading differs fundamentally from Guyer's, for whom these strands represent two independent and incompatible lines of argument and are thus supposedly indicative of Kant's "fundamental ambivalence" regarding his argumentative strategy. See Guyer (1987), esp. 39–46. It also differs, though less drastically, from Carl's interpretation, which turns on the distinction between an objective and a subjective deduction in Kant. See Carl (1989a), 11–20; (1989b), 74–102.

cognition of noumena and it is only its logical use that is required for experience. We further saw that in R 4634 Kant affirmed the need for a real experiential use of the understanding (indeed this was already foreshadowed in the 1772 letter to Herz), but he there seemingly viewed it as functioning in a way that was somehow parallel to the forms of sensibility, which left its actual role mysterious. The point is clarified in the *Duisburg Nachlass*, where Kant writes, "One can, to be sure, see much but under-stand nothing that appears unless it is brought under concepts of the understanding and by means of these into relation to a rule; this is the presumption [*Annahmen*] through the understanding" (R 4681 17: 66_{10-12}; 174). This conceptualizing function of the understanding is primarily exercised with respect to time, considered as the form of inner sense. Kant claims that it is necessary because "If I were not able to determine every relation in time through a universal condition of relation in time, I would not be able to assign any appearance to its place" (R 4683 17: 669_{3-5}; 175). Moreover, he continues, "The concepts of substance, ground, and whole, serve only to assign every reality in appearance to its place, insofar as each represents a function or dimension of time in which the object that is perceived is to be determined and experience to be made from appearance" (R 4682 17: 669_{6-10}; 175). What makes the appeal to these concepts necessary is that the temporal location of an entity or event cannot be determined simply by reference to time. As Kant here puts it, anticipating the central thesis of the Analogies that time cannot be perceived, "since a time in which something happens is not to be distinguished from another, the succession can only be determined through a rule of time" (R 4684 17: 670_{15-16}; 176). In other words, the relation of appearances *to time* (their duration) and to other things *in time* (their coexistence and succession) can be determined only by means of rules con-necting these things and their states necessarily with one another. Moreover, this cannot be accomplished by sensibility alone, since all that it provides is a series of appearances succeeding one another in inner sense, from which it follows that the task must be assigned to the understanding.

Kant also indicates that the need for a contribution of the understanding is a consequence of our lack of intellectual intuition. Although this is implicit throughout the argument, Kant makes it explicit when he notes:

If we intuited intellectually, then no title of apprehension would be needed to represent to oneself an object. In that case the object would not even appear. Now the appearance must be subordinated to a function by means of which the mind disposes over it, and indeed to a universal condition of this [disposition], because otherwise nothing universal would be found therein.   (R 4677 17: 658_{19-24}; 167–8)[52]

---

[52] This passage is cited by Laywine (2006), 106, who notes its importance. Elsewhere, she states that "Kant's story about the objectivity of our representations stands or falls with his conception of a finite intellect" (2005), 19. While I am in general agreement with Laywine on this point, I view Kant's appeal to the finitude of the intellect and consequent denial of intellectual intuition as a consequence of his adoption of the discursivity thesis; whereas she considers it in terms of Kant's endeavor to preserve as much of his early metaphysical project as possible by whatever means are available.

Setting aside for the present a consideration of the fresh terminology contained in this passage, such as "title of apprehension," "function," and "disposition," its central point is that the lack of intellectual intuition entails not only that cognition requires that data must be given to the mind before cognition is possible, but also that this is not sufficient to yield cognition, because this requires that the data be brought under concepts before they can be related to an object in an act of judgment. While the latter would not be necessary for a being with a capacity for intellectual intuition, since, *ex hypothesi*, such intuition would, of itself, generate determinate objects, it is necessary for any finite intellect, since sensibility provides merely the material for cognition.

Nevertheless, simply bringing perceptions under a concept is not sufficient to refer these perceptions to an actual object; otherwise, the most fanciful conceptualization of a set of perceptions would have to be regarded as "objective." This requires that the perceptions be unified in a way that holds not merely for a given subject under certain conditions, for example, one who happens to perceive an oar in a body of water as bent because the light is distorted by the water, but in accordance with a rule that makes a normative demand on the judgment of every perceiver. Kant expresses this fundamental point in a number of ways at various places in the *Duisburg Nachlass*, but in the most succinct of these he writes: "Only because the relation that is posited in accordance with the conditions of intuition is assumed to be determinable in accordance with a rule is the appearance related to an object; otherwise it is merely an inner affection of the mind" (R 4677 17: 657_{25-8}; 167).[53] I call the necessity expressed in this rule normative because it imposes a conceptual constraint on how the human understanding must unify the data provided by the senses in accordance with its forms of sensibility, if it is to relate them to an object, thereby converting mere perceptions into experience through the "exposition of appearances."[54]

Kant provides his clearest account of what he understands by such exposition in the following passage:

The principles of appearance (in general) are merely those of form, namely time.

The *principium* of the exposition of appearances is the ground of the exposition in general of that which was given. The exposition of that which is thought depends solely on consciousness, but the exposition of that which is given, if one regards the matter as undetermined, depends on the ground of all relation and of the concatenation of representations (sensations). The concatenation is grounded (like the appearance, not on mere sensation, rather in inner principles of form) not on the mere appearance, rather it is a representation of the inner

---

[53] See also R 4675 17: 650_{11-13}; 163; R 4677 17: 657_{25-8}; 167, 659 $_{20-1}$; 168; R 4678 17: 661_{6-7}; 169; R 4681 666_{15}–7_{13}; 173–4.

[54] See R 4674 17: 643_{7-22}; 158; R 4677 17: 658_{27}; 167; R 4678 660_{17}; 169. By an "exposition" (*Exposition*) Kant generally understands the clarification of a concept; but by an exposition of *appearances* he evidently understands not a clarification of the concept of an appearance, but of what is required for relating given appearances to an object. For a discussion of this, see Carl (1989b), 75–82.

action of the mind in connecting representations, not merely for placing them next to one another in intuition, but for constituting a whole as regards its matter. Thus there is here a unity not by means of that wherein but rather by means of that through which the manifold is brought into one, hence universal validity. Hence it is not forms but rather functions on which rest the *relationes* of appearances depend. The exposition of appearances is thus the determination of the ground on which the interconnection of the sensations in them depends.

(R 4674 17: 643$_{5-22}$; 157–8)

In this dense bit of text, Kant manages both to introduce some additional terminology and to encapsulate many of the central tenets of the *Duisburg Nachlass*. Accordingly, its explication should take us a long way towards the interpretation and evaluation of text as a whole. It will not take us all the way, however, since in addition to some essential details, which I shall attempt to fill in on the basis of the schema that this passage provides, we shall still be missing a discussion of the nature and function of apperception, which requires a separate treatment.

Kant's intent is to articulate the role of the understanding in empirical cognition. He attempts to do this by presenting a five-step contrast between the respective roles of sensibility and the understanding in such cognition. The first is between principles of appearance and the principle of the *exposition* of appearances. Since it is clear that by the former Kant understood the forms of sensibility, the focus is on the latter and how its role differs from the former, which was precisely the question left open in R 4634. This obviously requires an explication of what is understood by "exposition," which Kant defined in the *Critique* as "the distinct (even if not complete) representation of what belongs to a concept" (B38).[55] Here, however, he introduces a second contrast between two kinds of exposition: of that which is thought and of that which is given. Kant says of the former that it rests "merely on consciousness." Since for discursive cognizers what is thought is done so through concepts, the consciousness involved must concern the content of a given concept. Likewise, since what is given are appearances, the second kind of exposition must concern appearances. This appears to be equivalent to what Kant will later refer to in a more illuminating way as the "spelling out appearances according to synthetic unity in order to be able to read them as experience" (A314/B370–1). An example of such an exposition or "spelling out" is the cognition of an occurrence, for example, water changing from a liquid to a solid state when its temperature is decreased to 0 degrees Celsius. The "reading" consists in taking this occurrence as the change of state under a certain condition (the change of temperature) of some matter or stuff that is assumed to endure throughout the process.

The concern is to uncover the ground or principle of such an exposition, which would also be a principle of the possibility of experience. To this end Kant introduces a third contrast: between merely placing appearances next to one another in intuition

---

[55] Kant here uses the term "*Erörterung*" rather than "*Exposition*"; but since he equates it with the Latin "*expositio*," it is evident that he regards these terms as synonymous. See A728–9/B757–8.

and linking them in a more substantive way such that they constitute a whole. Although Kant does not spell it out, the clear implication is that the former task is accomplished by sensibility in virtue of its a priori forms and the latter by the understanding through an "inner action of the mind." In developing this thought, Kant draws his fourth contrast, which is between two kinds of unity. One kind is grounded in that *in which* the manifold of appearance is contained; the other in that *through which* it is unified. The former is the unity that appearances possess in virtue of being located in a single space and a single time. Kant's fundamental point, which indicates the distance he has traveled from the *Dissertation*, is that while necessary, this unity is insufficient to account for the cognition or experience of appearances as connected in a single spatiotemporal world. Once again, this requires the linking of these appearances by a rule-governed act of mind, which provides the basis for their exposition. Kant goes significantly beyond what has been said up to this point, however, by introducing in connection with the latter unity the normative notion of "universal validity." The point, which Kant does not here explain, is that the unity produced by the rule-governed act is taken to be not merely one that holds for a given perceiver under contingent conditions, but one that possesses normative force because it is claimed to hold for any discursive cognizer (hence its universal validity).

Kant's final contrast is between forms and functions. The former are attributed to sensibility and the latter to the understanding. Although Kant could easily have drawn the same contrast by distinguishing, as he did in the *Dissertation*, between two types of form, he evidently found the term "function" preferable because it brings out both the active nature of the understanding and the fact that there must be something (what is given in sensibility) on which this function is exercised.[56] Moreover, Kant continued to use the term "function" in this sense in the *Critique*, characterizing the function of thinking, i.e., judging, as "the unity of the action of bringing different representations under a common one" (A68/B93), whereby "the unity of the action" is its unifying rule. In fact, it seems that all that separates Kant's account of the functions of the understanding in the *Duisburg Nachlass* from that of the *Critique* is that he had not yet arrived at his definitive view of the forms of judgment. Instead, he identifies the functions of the understanding with the three categories of relation: substance–accident, ground–consequence, and reciprocal action or whole (part) and equates their functions with the determination of time. Accordingly, the bulk of the *Duisburg Nachlass* may be characterized as a series of attempts, from slightly different points of view, to demonstrate that these categories are the necessary (intellectual) conditions of empirical cognition.

---

[56] We shall see that besides "analogies" and "functions" Kant uses several other expressions to refer to these functions. These include: "titles of self-perception "R 4678 17: 658_{4-5}; 167; "titles of apprehension" R 4677 17: 658_{19-21}; 167; "titles of thinking" R 4678 17: 661_{27-9}; 170; "titles of the understanding" R 4679 17: $664_{2-4, 18-19}$; 171-2; "titles of apperception" R 4679 17 $664_{22-4, 29-30}$; 172; "titles of appearances" R4684 17 667_{4-7}; 174; and "presumptions of experience" R 4681 17: 667_{23}; 174.

With its focus on time-determination, the *Duisburg Nachlass* also touches upon issues dealt with in the *Critique* in connection with the Schematism as well as the Analytic of Principles. The point is not that Kant had already arrived at his doctrine of the Schematism of the understanding in 1775; inasmuch as the latter turns on the attribution of a transcendental function to the imagination, Kant was hardly in a position to entertain any such view at the time. It is rather that in these *Reflexionen* Kant addresses the fundamental problem with which the Schematism will deal; viz., the sensible conditions of the application of the categories to appearances. This problem did not exist for Kant in the *Dissertation*, since his concern there was to keep the concepts of the intellect free from contagion by the sensible. But, given the radical separation of sensibility and understanding, which resulted from the "great light," it assumed central importance once Kant recognized (perhaps with the help of Lambert and/or Hume) that his main problem concerned understanding how (and under what conditions) these concepts could apply to appearances, as they supposedly do in the synthetic a priori cognitions involved in the exposition of appearances. And, in view of the fact that in his various accounts of synthetic judgments Kant assigns to the ubiquitous and multi-faceted x the function of grounding the synthesis of the concept of the subject (a) and the predicate (b), the suggestion is that in such judgments x assumes the function that Kant will assign to the transcendental schemata in the *Critique*.[57]

Consider the following passage, which contains a succinct expression of the main elements of Kant's complex position:

If x, which is the objective condition of a, is at the same time the subjective condition of b, there then arises a synthetic proposition, which is only true *restrictive* [*restrictiv*]. E.g. all existence belongs to a substance; everything that happens is a member of a series [i.e., as a member of a causal chain];[58] everything that is simultaneous is a whole whose parts determine each other reciprocally. x, the time wherein it is determined what happens, is the subjective condition of what in the concept of the understanding is thought of only as the consequence of a ground. The subjective condition signifies the condition of the specification of the concept of the understanding corresponding to this relation.   (R 4675 17: 652$_{1-10}$; 164)

Four features of this passage call for comment. The first is that Kant claims that in a synthetic judgment x is at once an objective and a subjective condition. Specifically, it is an objective condition of a and a subjective condition of b. Although the point of Kant's contrast between objective and subjective conditions in these *Reflexionen* is frequently far from clear, by claiming that x is the objective condition of a, which, in Kant's notation, signifies the concept serving as the logical subject of a proposition,

---

[57] Although he does not suggest any connection with the Schematism in the *Critique*, Haering (1910), 38 underscores the complexity of the role given to x in different contexts in the *Duisburg Nachlass* and notes that the most important one is to ground the synthesis between a and b in synthetic judgments.

[58] This gloss is suggested by Haering (1910), 112. I have added it because it seems necessary to make the passage coherent.

he presumably means that it is the sensible or intuitive datum through which a is exhibited in experience. Correlatively, it is the subjective condition of b or, as Kant puts it later in the passage, of "the specification of the concept of the understanding corresponding to this relation" (which is likewise b). But since Kant's use of the notion of "specification" (*Specification*) is itself one the features of this passage calling for comment, I shall set that aside for the moment and consider merely the initial claim that x is the subjective condition of b, where b is a concept of the understanding used in the exposition of appearances. Since "subjective" here presumably means "sensible," the claim is that x is the subjective condition of the application of b to appearances, which, in the case of synthetic judgments involving the concepts of the understanding, is precisely the function that Kant assigns to the schemata of the categories in the *Critique*. As Kant there put it in a well-known passage, "Without schemata ... the categories are only functions of the understanding for concepts, but do not represent any object. This significance comes to them from sensibility, which realizes the understanding at the same time that it restricts it" (A147/B187).

The second relevant feature of this passage is also an anticipation of the above-cited passage from the Schematism; in this case its second sentence. It is the claim that the synthetic a priori propositions to which Kant refers and which correspond to the Analogies in the *Critique* are only "true *restrictive*." I take this to mean that these propositions are valid only for appearances or objects of experience rather than for things in general.[59] Assuming that this restriction is a consequence of the fact that x is the subjective, i.e., sensible, condition of b, it once again follows that x has a function (limiting the scope of the pure concepts of the understanding) that will later be assigned to the schemata of the categories.

The third noteworthy feature is closely related to the first two. It is the identification of x, as subjective condition, with time, rather than, as is the case with empirical propositions, with the determinate object thought under a, or in mathematical propositions with an object constructed in pure intuition under the rule thought in the concept (a), e.g., the concept of a triangle. Kant evidently regarded this identification as necessary in order to account for the synthetic a priori character of the propositions through which appearances are "exposited." In fact, at one point Kant poses for himself the question: "Is x the form of inner sensibility or that which is real in apprehension?" (R 4676 17: 657_{21-2}; 167). Kant does not explicitly answer the question and it is perhaps not even clear whether he intended it rhetorically or as indicating a genuine indecision on his part; but I believe that the proper answer is both, depending on the nature of b. When b is an empirical concept predicated of an object in a synthetic a posteriori proposition, x refers to the real in apprehension (or perception), that is, a determinate object with its specific qualities; whereas when b is one of the three pure relational concepts x is the form of inner sensibility, i.e., time.

---

[59] See also R4678 17: 661_{14-16}; R4683 17: 669_{14-17}; 175. This reading of Kant's claim as a scope restriction is to be contrasted with that of Guyer (1987), 53–4. I discuss his view in the Conclusion.

Nevertheless, this identification of x with time, or the form of inner sensibility, cannot be made without qualification, since this form as such is empty and therefore could not function to determine anything. Accordingly, by "time" must here be understood the relations of appearances in time, i.e., their relative, rule-governed positions or, what amounts to the same thing, the relation of things qua temporal, in virtue of which they are subsumed under the relational concepts and their corresponding principles or "expositions."[60] In the *Critique* Kant refers to these relations as "transcendental determinations of time" and identifies them with the schemata of the categories.[61] The basic idea is that these determinations constitute the application conditions of the categories and their corresponding principles to appearances, which, in turn, explains why they both realize the categories and restrict their use.[62]

The fourth significant feature of this passage is the previously noted reference to specification in the final sentence. Kant there states that x (the "subjective condition") "signifies the condition of the specification of the concept of the understanding corresponding to this relation." Again, this corresponds to an essential function assigned to the transcendental schemata in the *Critique*. What is "specified" by x are the temporal relations in which an appearance must stand, if a particular relational concept is to be applicable to it. Consider the ground–consequence relation. The question is: what is the temporal condition of the specification of an appearance as falling under this relation or, as Kant here puts it, of what can be thought only as the consequence of a ground? Although the text is none too clear, Kant seems to suggest that such an appearance must be regarded as an occurrence, which involves a temporal succession of appearances, e.g., water in a liquid state at t_1 and a solid state at t_2.[63] But we have already seen that constant succession is not sufficient to warrant the application of the notion of being a consequence to the latest member of the series of appearances. Rather, the succession must be conceived as necessary in the sense of being grounded in a rule, e.g., water freezes at 0 degrees Celsius, which is, in turn, dependent on the function or exponent of that rule, namely, the ground–consequence relation. Accordingly, a rule-governed or necessary temporal succession (x) is the application condition or condition of the specification of the ground–consequence relation, which is essentially equivalent to what in the *Critique* is characterized as the schema of the concept of cause (A144/B183). And, as the passage indicates, similar claims are made for the two other pure concepts of relation.

---

[60]   See, for example, R 4675 17: $644_{27}-5_5$; R 4676 17: $654_{29}-5_{21}$; 165–6.

[61]   See A138–9/B178–9 and A145/B184.

[62]   More precisely, the fact that schemata provide the application conditions explains how the schemata can realize the categories; while the fact that this application is limited to appearances in virtue of their relation to time explains how they restrict them. For my discussion of this topic, see Allison (2004), 210–28.

[63]   The point is not that the later state of the object must be viewed as the causal consequence of its earlier state, but that the succession of its states must be attributed to a cause. For my discussion of this and related issues in connection with the Second Analogy, see Allison (2004), 247–9, 258–9.

Moreover, this is not the only place in the *Duisburg Nachlass* where there are anticipations of the Schematism.[64] In addition to passages paralleling the one just considered, we find Kant at one point writing: "All synthetic propositions possess homogeneity, although it seems that one concept is intellectual, the other is empirical. In the exposition they are homogenous. One merely takes its specification instead of the concept" (R 4683 17: 669_{26-9}; 175). Kant is here referring to the very problem to which the Schematism in the *Critique* is officially devoted: the need for homogeneity between the (intellectual) pure concepts of the understanding and (sensible) appearances, if the latter are to be subsumed under the former.[65]

Assuming that a specification of a pure concept is the functional equivalent of what he will later call its schema, Kant is here also pointing to the solution that he will provide in the *Critique*, which, in essence, is that in the application of the categories to appearances (what he here refers to as "the exposition") "we set its schema in its place as the key to its use, or rather set the latter alongside the former as its restricting condition, under the name of its formula" (A181/B224). For the "critical" Kant this resolves the problem of homogeneity because, as the sensible expression or, better, the translation into temporal terms of what is thought in the pure (non-temporalized) category, the schema is homogenous with both the category and appearances. Granted, Kant does not here offer anything approaching an argument for this thesis (and not much more of one in the *Critique*), but it does support the point that has been emphasized throughout the entire discussion of the *Duisburg Nachlass* up to this point; viz., that by 1775 Kant had arrived at the basic elements of his "critical" view regarding both the Principles of Pure Understanding (at least the Analogies of Experience) and the Schematism.

2) *The argument from the unity of apperception*: Despite the detail in which the consideration of the *Duisburg Nachlass* has enmeshed us, a central feature of it, namely, the role of apperception and its unity, has been left out of the story up to this point. As already indicated, this omission is deliberate, motivated by the conviction that the argument contains two strands, which, though not distinguished clearly by Kant, are best analyzed separately. To recapitulate, the first strand endeavors to show that the three pure concepts or relational categories are necessary conditions of the cognition of an objective temporal order. The second attempts to ground these concepts in the unity of apperception.[66]

---

[64] See R 4674 $643_{23}-4_{18}$; 158; R 4678 17: 662_{23-4}; 170; R4679 17: 664_{18-21}; $31-4$; 172; R 4680 17: 665_{1-12}; 173; and R 4684 17: $670_{13}-1_2$; 176.

[65] The point is noted by Guyer (2005), 564, note 17.

[66] Although when viewed retrospectively from the standpoint of the *Critique* Kant's discussion of apperception in the *Duisburg Nachlass* is obviously the point of central interest, it plays a somewhat muted, albeit still highly significant role in the actual text of these notes. According to a topical index compiled by Jay Reuscher, whom I wish to thank for supplying me with a typescript of his unpublished translation together with a digest and topical index of the *Duisburg Nachlass*, it is mentioned only at $646_{29}-7_3$; 647_{8-21}; $650_{25}-1_8$; 651_{13-17}; 656_{2-7}, $18-23$; 658_{1-5}; $10-12$; 659_{7-20}; 662_{27-30}; 664_{29-34}. Moreover, as should become

In the effort to spell out this grounding argument, we must first determine how Kant understood apperception in the *Duisburg Nachlass* and why and in what sense he considered its unity necessary.[67] A quick survey reveals that he characterizes apperception in a number of ways, including as "the perception of oneself as a thinking subject as such" (R 4674 17: 647_{14-15}); "the consciousness of thinking, i.e., of the representations as they are posited in the mind" (R 4674 17: 647_{16-17}; 160); as "the intuition of our self... that pertains to all cognitions, even those of understanding and reason" (R 4675 17: 651_{6-8}; 163); as "self-perception" (R 4677 17: 658_{1-2}; 167); and as "self-sensation" (R 4677 17: 658_{11}; 167). To a student of the *Critique* the most striking feature of these formulations is their reference to the intuition, perception, and even sensation of the self; for this suggests the equation of apperception and inner sense, which is something that Kant explicitly warns against in the B-Deduction.

Kant's characterization of apperception in these terms becomes comprehensible, however, if we consider it in light of the cognitive function that he attributed to inner sense in his 1762 essay on the syllogism. As we saw in Chapter 1, Kant there defined inner sense as the "faculty of making one's own representations the object of one's thought" (FS 2: 60_{13-15}; 104) and suggested tentatively that it is the "mysterious power" that makes judging possible and therefore provides the key to differentiating between the cognitive capacities of rational and non-rational beings.[68] Although in the interim Kant had abandoned the analytical model of cognition operative in this essay and the other writings of the early 1760s considered in Chapter 1, both of these

clear below, these scattered discussions indicate that at this time Kant is by no means completely clear about the nature and status of this conception.

[67] As is well known, "apperception" was introduced into philosophy as a technical term by Leibniz as a contrast to "perception." Whereas Leibniz attributed the latter activity to all monads in virtue of his central metaphysical thesis that every monad represents or expresses the universe from a particular point of view, albeit in most cases without consciousness, "apperception" is reserved for conscious representation. There is, however, an ongoing interpretive dispute among Leibniz scholars regarding the question of whether "apperception" should be understood broadly to encompass all conscious perception, in which case subhuman minds can apperceive, or whether it is to be understood as a form of reflective consciousness or self-consciousness, which is limited to rational minds, in virtue of which they have the capacity to grasp necessary truths, which lie innate in the structure of the mind. Since most of Leibniz's best-known discussions of apperception stress the latter view (e.g., *Principles of Nature and Grace* §4 (Leibniz (1989), 208); *Monadology* §30 (Leibniz (1989), 30); *New Essays* (Leibniz (1981), 51), this has become the standard interpretation; but there are also important texts pointing in the other direction. For a useful analysis of both the Leibnizian texts and the secondary literature, see Kulstad (1991). Beginning with Wolff, the term in either its Latin or German form ("*apperceptio,*" "*Apperzeption*") was incorporated into the psychological and epistemological theories of many eighteenth-century German thinkers before Kant, where it was generally taken to refer to a reflective awareness of the contents of one's mind, which for the Wolffians was equated with the possession of a clear (*klar*) as contrasted with an obscure (*dunkel*) representation. See Janke (1975), 448–50, and Wunderlich (2005). Although the earliest use of the term and its cognates in the Kantian *Nachlass* is to be found in the *Duisburg Nachlass*, the centrality of the thought of the I and the connection between the capacity to say I and rationality and personality are already expressed in Kant's anthropology lectures of the early and mid-1770s. See AP 25: 245 and AF 25: 473.

[68] We also saw that in the Prize Essay (1763) Kant used the "inner experience" in essentially the same manner, effectively treating it as a synonym for "inner sense."

features can be ascribed to apperception as construed in the *Duisburg Nachlass*. Accordingly, despite the radical difference in the view of cognition brought about with the introduction of the discursivity thesis, which will eventually lead Kant to insist upon a sharp separation of apperception and inner sense, it is not surprising to find him trying to assimilate them in his initial attempts to formulate his conception of apperception. Simply put, it is a matter of pouring new wine into old bottles.

Setting that issue aside for the present, Kant appears to have understood apperception in the *Duisburg Nachlass* as a form of self-consciousness, specifically, a consciousness of oneself qua thinker, that encompasses a consciousness of the act of thinking, of the contents of this act, and of oneself as a subject that thinks, i.e., as a thinking thing or *res cogitans*. The fundamental feature of apperception in these *Reflexionen* on which Kant focuses and which is involved in each of these aspects is its unity. In his most explicit account of this topic Kant writes: "The condition of all apperception is the unity of the thinking subject. From this [*daraus*] flows the connection of the manifold in accordance with a rule and in a whole, since the unity of function must suffice for subordination as well as coordination" (R 4675 17: 651_{13-16}; 163).

According to Carl, the passage admits of two interpretations, which depend on the referent of "*daraus*" and which yield what he terms respectively the "epistemological" and the "ontological" foundations of the rule-governed connection of the manifold. On the former interpretation, the term is taken as referring back to the whole of the preceding sentence and Kant's claim is (roughly) that "the consciousness of an identical self [apperception] implies the connection of representations according to a rule." On the latter interpretation, the term refers simply to the phrase "the unity of the thinking subject," in which case Kant's point is that the rule-governed connection of the manifold is grounded in this unity.[69] Accordingly, on the epistemological reading, the move is from the self's consciousness (or knowledge) of its own identity to the rule-governedness of its representations; whereas on the ontological reading it is from the unity of the subject (as substance) to the rule-governedness of its representations.

An important consideration underlying Carl's ontological interpretation of the unity of apperception in the *Duisburg Nachlass* is the fact that at the time Kant was still committed to the legitimacy of rational psychology as a branch of metaphysics. Carl does not maintain that Kant's commitment to rational psychology, which purports to derive fundamental tenets regarding the nature of the soul, e.g., its immateriality, simplicity, and freedom, by an analysis of its concept, proves the correctness of the ontological interpretation, since it is clearly not entailed by it. Instead, he emphasizes the fact that it fits nicely with it and that this conception could

---

[69] See Carl (1989a), 13–14, (1989b), 90–1.

not survive Kant's belated recognition of the paralogistic nature of the principles of rational psychology.[70]

In analyzing Carl's proposal it is noteworthy that, while he connects the onto-logical interpretation, which he favors, with the *unity* of apperception, he links the epistemological interpretation, which he rejects, with its *identity* or, more precisely, with the consciousness of an identical self. Although as Patricia Kitcher points out, Kant does not refer to the latter in the *Duisburg Nachlass*, we shall see in subsequent chapters that the difference and relation between these two conceptions plays a major role in both versions of the Transcendental Deduction in the *Critique*.[71] To antici-pate, Kant there generally understands by the unity of apperception (or conscious-ness) what he refers to as its "synthetic unity." This is a unity in sense of a many in one and it consists in the unifiedness of its representational content produced by an act of synthesis. By contrast, the identity of apperception is what he sometimes refers to as an "analytic unity," i.e., a one in a many, and it consists in the sameness or numerical identity of the I with respect to the manifoldness of its representational content.[72]

Considered in light of this distinction, it seems that Kant's failure to refer to the identity of apperception in the *Duisburg Nachlass* can be taken in one of two ways: either he had not yet arrived at this conception of identity (or analytic unity) and recognized only the (synthetic) unity of apperception, or he had arrived at the distinction between these two conceptions, but had not yet developed the termin-ology in which to express it, with the result that his formulations in these *Reflexionen* appeal to an ambiguous notion of unity. On the first assumption, the ontological interpretation is the only viable option, since the epistemological alternative, at least as formulated by Carl, requires an appeal to the identity as well as the unity of apperception. If, however, one concedes the possibility that Kant's use of "unity" in this context is ambiguous, then one must also concede the possibility that the epistemological interpretation is applicable to Kant's account in the *Duisburg Nachlass*.

Accordingly, we must consider Carl's argument for the ontological interpretation in terms of his analysis of the text of the *Duisburg Nachlass*. He finds decisive support for his reading in Kant's account of the three "functions of apperception, which are met with in the thought of our own state in general and under which all appearance must on that account fit" (R 4674 17: 646_{29}–7_1; 160). Citing another passage (R 4674 17: 647_{16-19}; 160–1), Carl identifies these functions with (1) the relation to a subject; (2) the relation of consequences under one another (subordination); and (3) com-position (coordination) and he notes that they coincide with the categories of relation. His central point is that Kant characterizes these functions as ways of

---

[70] On the latter point see Carl (1989b), 173.   [71] Kitcher (2011), 75.

[72] At MM 29: 89; 257 Kant defines a synthetic unity as the unity of many in one and an analytic unity as the unity of a one in a many.

conceiving the relation between representations and oneself (qua *res cogitans*). Assuming that being connected by these is the same as being taken up into the functions of apperception, Carl contends that this favors the ontological interpretation, since it indicates that it is the unity of the thinking subject, rather than the consciousness of one's own identity, that grounds the connection of the manifold by means of these functions.[73]

Further consideration of these functions, however, suggests that the situation is not so clear cut. To begin with, only the first (relation to the subject) appears to support the ontological reading, since the other two concern the relation between appearances, which is supposedly the function exercised by the relational categories. Moreover, it should be kept in mind that in the *Duisburg Nachlass* (and elsewhere) Kant frequently uses the term "subject" to refer to the object in the sense of the subject judged about, that is, the *x*, instead of the cognizing subject. Indeed, we have seen that this is the case with regard to the deeply misleading expression "transcendental subject."[74] And if the first function is taken in this way, then all three functions of apperception are concerned with the relation of appearances to each other, which is just what the objectivity argument leads one to expect.

Against this it might be objected that this reading ignores Kant's claim that these functions are "met with in the thought of our own state [*Zustandes*] in general." Indeed, if we take "our own state" to mean our nature as a thinking substance, then Kant is read as claiming that it is by reflecting on this "state," i.e., our substantial nature qua *res cogitans*, that we "meet with," i.e., become aware of, these functions of apperception or relational categories, which leads us to the ontological interpretation. But even within the interpretive options specified by Carl, it is not clear why this claim could not be brought under the epistemological interpretation, in which case what is met with in the thought (consciousness) of one's own state is an identical rather than a substantial I and this identity implies the connection of representations according to a rule. On this reading, then, by one's "state" (condition, or situation) is understood one's identity as the same thinking subject with respect to a manifold of representations.

Moreover, following Haering, Carl notes that on the ontological interpretation Kant's central argument for the relational categories is guilty of a serious error that evidently does not occur on the epistemological alternative and is not repeated in the *Critique*, namely, that,

[O]ne takes a unity that consists in representations belonging to a unitary subject to be a unity possessed by the representations themselves. Whereas the first unity is based on the unity of the thinking subject, the second unity concerns the representations' interconnectedness, which

---

[73] Carl (1989a), 13–14; (1989b), 91–3. In the passage to which Carl refers Kant characterizes these relations as "exponents" rather than "functions;" but I believe that he is correct in viewing these as synonymous.

[74] See also R4674 17: 644$_{24}$; 159; R469 17: 649$_{21}$; 162; R4679 17: 663$_{17}$; 171; R4683 17: 670$_{9}$; 176.

must be specified not by reference to the subject but to the content of the representations. The first kind of unity can be realized without the second one.[75]

Carl is correct in noting that the ontological interpretation has the untoward consequence he indicates. The fact that I am a single-thinking being does not entail that my representations have any unity beyond the one that they trivially possess as belonging to the same thinking being. Moreover, even assuming that these representations possess such unity and that it stems from the categories of relation, we are left with the problem of explaining how this unity, which supposedly justifies the applications of these categories to the *self*, is transferable to the *objects* of these representations, which is presumably what Kant wants to show.[76] And while this does not preclude the ontological interpretation, since it cannot be claimed that Kant was incapable of such an error, particularly in a private jotting, it at least gives one reason to consider seriously whether the text of the *Duisburg Nachlass* can support an interpretation of apperception that is roughly along the lines of the one rejected by Carl.[77]

Before we are in a position to do this, however, we must consider the subtle and complex reading of the text proposed by Laywine, who endorses Carl's ontological interpretation, albeit on somewhat different grounds. Whereas Carl sees Kant's appeal to the unity of apperception as his "first draft" of a "subjective deduction," which is intended to remove a possibility left open by the "objective deduction" of the categories from the conditions of the possibility of experience; viz., that we have no experience because there are no objects to which the categories apply, Laywine maintains that Kant's concern with the thinking subject as *res cogitans* is to be understood in terms of his effort to preserve as much as possible of his earlier metaphysics and that he was not concerned with the problematic of a deduction as Carl conceived it.[78] Moreover, whereas Carl begins by addressing the question of the relation between the two previously cited sentences, Laywine initially focuses on the first sentence: "The condition of all apperception is the unity of the thinking subject."

---

[75] Carl (1989a), 17. See also Carl (1989b), 100.

[76] A similar objection was raised by Guyer (1987), 53.

[77] Carl's ontological reading has been challenged by Klemme (1996), 127–37. Although Klemme acknowledges that Kant at the time of the *Duisburg Nachlass* held the dogmatic view that the categories applied to the soul qua *res cogitans*, he denies that this dogmatism carries over into Kant's account of the categories as conditions of experience. This has been challenged in turn by Laywine, who in defense of Carl's reading states that "the evidence indicates on balance that the thinking subject can do what it does to get experience and empirical thought off the ground precisely because it has the metaphysical properties of a thinking substance." She further notes that Klemme gives no evidence for his reading beyond his discussion of Kant's views in the *Pölitz* lectures on metaphysics (ML₁) and suggests that even if everything that Klemme claims about the latter be granted it does not decide anything regarding the *Duisburg Nachlass*, since this would require a close analysis of the text, which Klemme does not provide (Laywine (2006)) note 71,100–1. Laywine is correct to point out that Klemme does not provide such an analysis and much of what I say below may be seen as an attempt to fill this gap.

[78] See Carl (1989a), 11–20; (1989b) 74–102, and Laywine (2005), esp. 23, note 9, and (2006), esp. 98–101.

Since this sentence claims that the unity of the thinking subject is in some sense the condition of apperception, understood as the consciousness that the subject has of its own thoughts, Laywine quite reasonably asks what kind of condition it is supposed to be. Like Carl, she acknowledges two possible readings. One, which she claims to be the most natural, is that the thinking subject is a condition of apperception in virtue of possessing an "inner unity," which she takes to mean that it must be something single and simple, and that this unity is a necessary condition of the subject's consciousness of its representations. The other is that the unity of the subject is a condition of apperception in the sense of being its necessary concomitant, by which is understood that the thinking subject cannot be conscious of its thoughts without *also* being conscious of its unity, i.e., of being the identical thinker of the various thoughts that it has.

In addition to following Carl in appealing to the notion of identity in character-izing the second alternative, the key point is that, while the former has metaphysical import, the latter need not. Laywine notes that it would have such import, if it is assumed that being a simple thinking thing is a necessary condition of the conscious-ness of this unity; but it would not, if it is taken as claiming that "consciousness of having unity [in the sense of identity] *only* depends on being conscious of producing unity in the manifold."[79] She further notes correctly that the latter (non-metaphys-ical) conception is equivalent to the position that Kant took in the *Critique*, where he claimed that, "[T]he mind could not think of the identity of itself in the manifoldness of its representations, and indeed think this *a priori*, if it did not have before its eyes the identity of its action, which subjects all synthesis of apprehension … to a tran-scendental unity, and first makes possible their connection in accordance with *a priori* rules" (A108).

Laywine constructs her interpretation largely on the basis of two passages. In the first Kant claims that, "This object [identified with something real] can only be represented in accordance with its relations and is nothing other than the subjective representation (of the subject) itself, but made general, for I am the original of all objects" (R 4674 17: 646_{10-14}; 160). According to Laywine, this passage contains two major claims. The first is that objects can be cognized only in accordance with their relations and not in terms of their own inherent natures. Since this has already been examined, it requires no further comment at this point. The second, expressed in Laywine's terms, is that "representing the object essentially involves representing the self."[80] While there is certainly a sense in which this is true, since it is a consequence of Kant's view of the inherently self-conscious or apperceptive nature of thought, this formulation is ambiguous because it can be understood in terms of either of the proposed interpretations of apperception. Taken in the former sense, it means that the source of a cognizer's conceptual representation of objects is its representation of

[79] Laywine (2006), 98.   [80] Laywine (2005), 9.

itself as substance, cause, etc. Taken in the latter sense, it means merely that the conceptual representation of objects is dependent upon certain subjective functions or categories (functions of apperception), which are grounded in the nature of the understanding and through which one brings representations to the unity of apperception, thereby representing to oneself an object. But rejecting the latter alternative, which, as she notes, is the view of the *Critique*, Laywine takes Kant to be claiming that the only genuine subject to which the mind has access is itself and that our judgments about empirical objects as enduring entities or substances presuppose the transfer of the cognizer's conception of itself as subject to the mind-independent objects it represents to itself. And she finds this expressed in the claim that I (as thinking substance) am "the original of all objects," which she takes literally as meaning that the cognizer's thought of itself as subject is the prototype of its thought of objects.[81]

While this may be the most natural reading of this passage, it is not the only viable one. The main issue is the interpretation of the proposition that "the object...is nothing other than the subjective representation (of the subject) itself, but made general." To begin with, inasmuch as Kant's concern is to explain how a cognizer's representations acquire relation to an object or objective validity, it is perfectly appropriate for him to characterize these representations as "subjective." Accordingly, the problematic feature of the proposition is the parenthetical expression "of the subject." On the ontological interpretation it is taken as referring to the thinking subject, as *res cogitans*, whose (subjective) representation *of itself*, when made general, is the object. And on this interpretation, which is held by both Carl and Laywine, the conclusion that Kant draws from this is that the I or mind is literally the original or model of the representation of objects because its representation of objects is a projection of its representation of itself. By contrast, on the alternative interpretation the parenthetical phrase "of the subject" refers not to the thinking subject but to the logical subject of a judgment of which the relational categories are predicated, i.e., the *x* of Kant's schematic account of judgment.

Having already suggested this possibility in connection with the discussion of Carl's interpretation, I can see no need to consider the matter further here. Suffice it to say that the reading of a number of passages in the *Duisburg Nachlass* turns on how one takes Kant's reference to "the subject" in such contexts. Assuming that this reading is correct, however, a word is in order regarding Kant's identification of the object with the cognitive subject's (subjective) representation of the logical subject of the judgment "*made general*" (my emphasis). My proposal is that this should be understood in terms of the previously considered analysis of objectivity as grounded in a rule or function of apperception through which the unification of representations in the thought of a single cognizer is "made general" in the sense of being claimed to

---

[81] Laywine (2005), 7–10.

hold for all cognizers and is thereby deemed objectively valid.[82] This not only accords with the analysis of objectivity as grounded in rules that is contained in the *Duisburg Nachlass* but also with the account in the *Prolegomena* according to which "Objective validity and necessary universal validity (for everyone) are interchangeable concepts" (Pro 4: 298₂₈₋₉; 93).[83] And since I shall argue that the latter is equivalent to the account of objectivity in both versions of the Transcendental Deduction in the *Critique*, it accords with what we may characterize as the "critical" view of objectivity and its subjective grounds.

In a second passage highlighted by Laywine, Kant claims that "the mind is ... itself the archetype [*Urbild*] of just such synthesis through original and not derived thinking" (R 4674 17: 647₃₋₅; 160).[84] This comes at the end of a dense paragraph dealing with the synthesis through which experience is constituted. Its central contention is that this synthesis is based on the three functions of apperception, "which are met with in the thought of our state in general [*Zustandes überhaupt*] and under which all appearance must on that account fit, because in it there would lie no synthesis in itself if the mind did not add it or make it out of the *datis* of appearance" (R 4674 17: 646₂₉₋₇₃; 160). Eschewing details, this amounts to the by-now familiar thesis that the activity of the mind (synthesis) is the source of the unity of appearances and that the relational categories are the principles governing this synthesis. The proposition that the mind (or understanding) is the "archetype" of this synthesis, which Laywine takes as equivalent to the previous claim regarding the I as the original of all objects, is the conclusion from this statement.

Whereas in the preceding passage the problematic feature was the phrase "of the subject," it is here the claim that the functions of apperception are "met with in the thought of our state in general." This thought of our state in general (or as such) can be taken to refer either to our status as a *res cogitans*, whose thoughts are its accidents or states, or to our cognitive state, i.e., the relations between our representations considered as thoughts held together in consciousness by a single thinking subject. In the former case the relation in question is an ontological (or ontic) one between a peculiar kind of thing (one that thinks) and its properties (thoughts); while in the latter it is a logical or conceptual relation between the thoughts themselves, considered not with respect to their relation to the thinker, *qua res cogitans*, but their

---

[82] It is crucial to keep in mind here that becoming objective or, what amounts to the same thing, acquiring objective validity is not equivalent to being true. As we shall see in the analysis of the B-Deduction, in these contexts "objective validity" is to be understood as having a truth value, i.e., the capacity to be either true or false, which pertains to a judgment qua judgment. In other words, being subsumed under a function of apperception generates a normative claim on the agreement of others, but does not ensure that the claim is true. In the case of empirical propositions this is determined empirically; though this determination is guided by a priori principles such as causality.

[83] This will be discussed in Chapter 7.

[84] Laywine ignores Kant's final qualifying cause, citing him as saying simply that "the mind is itself the model of all synthesis" (2005), 13.

logical relation to each other, which Kant frequently refers to in the *Duisburg Nachlass* and elsewhere as subordination and coordination.

Although Laywine opts for the former, her gloss on the passage as referring to "the relations among the mind's representations and between these representations and the mind that has them"[85] preserves the ambiguity of the text. Relations among the mind's representations and between the mind and its representations are of quite different natures and cannot simply be lumped together as Laywine here seems to do. She further contends that these relations provide the "pattern" that the mind uses "to inform its empirical concepts with the needed relational component." And, in light of this, she suggests that when we use ordinary empirical concepts in a judgment, the relations "are somehow transferred from one level of thought to another."[86] In other words, the relation between representations in and to the mind is reconceived by analogy as a relation between the objects represented. But the phrase can also be taken to refer to a cognizer's epistemic state of consciousness as containing a rule-governed unification of representations that is produced by the exercise of the functions of apperception. On this reading, these functions are "met with in the thought of our state in general" because they provide the rules through which this state (of synthetic unity) is brought about. And for the same reason they also supply the above-mentioned "pattern."

Accordingly, the issue is in which of the two ways distinguished above the relation between representations in the mind is to be taken in Kant's account of cognition in the *Duisburg Nachlass*. Otherwise expressed, how are we to understand what, in Laywine's terms, is transferred from one level of thought to another? On the ontological interpretation it is the relation between the mind and its representations; while on the alternative view it is the relation between the representations themselves as thoughts. In the *Critique* the latter are the logical forms or functions of judgment, which become categories when applied to a sensible content. Although we have seen that Kant does not seem to have been in possession of either the full set of categories or the corresponding table of judgments contained in the *Critique* at the time of the *Duisburg Nachlass*, it seems plausible to assume that he had arrived at the idea of the correlation of the relational forms of judgment and the objective relations thought in terms of the three relational categories on which he here focuses.[87]

Moreover, at least two considerations speak in favor of regarding the "functions of apperception," depicted in the *Duisburg Nachlass*, as the ways in which representations are subordinated or coordinated with one another in thought rather than, as the ontological interpretation would have it, ways in which the mind, qua *res cogitans*, is related to its representations. First and foremost is the fact that it makes better sense of the transfer from one level of thought to another of which Laywine speaks. While the reasoning that she attributes to Kant is not as manifestly fallacious as that

---

[85] Ibid., 14.   [86] Ibid.   [87] See, for example, R4676 17: 657$_{12-16}$; 167.

assumed by Carl (a completely unwarranted jump from one form of unity to another), it is nonetheless deeply problematic in its own right. For why, one might ask, should Kant have thought it warranted to assume that the rules (or functions) governing the relation between a particular kind of substance (the mind) and its accidents or states (representations) should be transferable to appearances, thereby transforming mere perception into experience? To be sure, the proposed alternative is likewise problematic, since one might also ask on what grounds it can be assumed that the logical functions by means of which representations are brought to the unity of apperception can also have an objectivating function. But we shall see that this is precisely the question that the Transcendental Deduction in the *Critique* is designed to answer, when, in introducing the problematic of the Deduction, Kant asks "how **subjective conditions of thinking** [which is precisely what the functions of apperception are] should have **objective validity**" (A89/B122).

Second, this reading also makes better sense of what Laywine refers to as the "analogy" between the (subjective) functions of apperception and the (objective) rules governing the exposition of appearances. On her (ontological) reading, the presumed analogy, which underlies and justifies the transfer, is between the concept of substance and its relation to its accidents and states derived from the relation of the mind as *res cogitans* to appearances, in which there is found merely relations but nothing genuinely substantial. As she puts it at one point, "It is precisely the idea of the mind as a thinking substance that teaches us to think of a piece of gold as sufficiently substance-like that we can predicate of it the relevant properties in a judgment."[88] But why should this idea of the mind be said to "teach us" rather than, say, seduce us, as Kant evidently thought that it did after the discovery of the Paralogisms?[89] As Laywine points out, such a move is Leibnizian in its inspiration; but in attributing it to Kant she adds the important caveat that he managed to avoid the fundamental metaphysical error into which Leibniz was led by this bit of analogical reasoning; viz., the erection of a universal monadology of intelligible beings or noumena. In contrast to Leibniz, she notes that Kant's theory of sensibility led him to restrict this analogical predication to appearances.[90] But though from the "critical" standpoint this no doubt counts as an improvement, it leaves in place the fundamental question: what justifies applying this analogy to appearances, since, *ex hypothesi*, the latter consist merely of relations and contain nothing substantial? To say that it makes possible empirical thought, the exposition of appearances, or the transformation of perception into experience begs the question.[91]

---

[88] Laywine (2005), 12.

[89] There the "seduction" or, as Kant termed it, "illusion" concerns the mind's idea of itself as substance not the substantial nature of external objects.

[90] Laywine (2005), 12–13.

[91] Laywine maintains that accounting for the possibility of empirical thought is the central concern of the *Duisburg Nachlass*. Presumably, however, it must be valid, i.e., warranted, thought, with the warrant provided by something like a transcendental deduction. But I fail to see why one should think that

Although, once again, it cannot be said that the critical interpretation of apperception provides an easy and persuasive answer to the question, it does make it possible to find in the *Duisburg Nachlass* an anticipation of the answer that Kant will offer in the *Critique*. On this reading, the analogy (although Kant does not call it that) is between the logical and the real use of the understanding. Kant does not use the term in this context because it is really a matter of identity not analogy or similarity; the point being that it is one and the same understanding that is operating at two levels. At one level, that of general logic, it relates thoughts in judgments according to the functions of relation, through which these thoughts are subordinated or coordinated with each other; at another level, that of transcendental logic, these same functions serve as rules for the exposition or determination of appearances.[92] As before, it is assumed that, while Kant had not at the time formulated his corresponding tables of judgment forms and categories, which will be discussed in Chapter 4, he did make use of a preliminary and partial version of this conception involving the relational functions and categories. And if it is one and the same understanding that is operative at two levels, then there is no longer a question of why the functions operative in one domain are also operative in another. Rather, the problem, as it is in the *Critique*, is demonstrating that the understanding has the real use that is claimed for it with respect to experience, which in the *Duisburg Nachlass* is presumably the task of what has here been termed the "objectivity argument."

Admittedly, this reading is speculative and I cannot claim that the considerations offered in support of it are decisive. As has been emphasized throughout, the texts of the *Duisburg Nachlass* are ambiguous and subject to widely different interpretations. Moreover, on any interpretation, they yield a Kant in *medias res*, who is moving from the views of the *Dissertation* to those of the *Critique*. Accordingly, differences in interpretation are in large part due to judgments regarding what elements of Kant's earlier views are retained and what features of his "critical" position are already in place. Nevertheless, I maintain that, all things considered, including Kant's seemingly anomalous commitment to rational psychology, this reading is more plausible than the ontological interpretation, which appears to be its only serious alternative. In the next section of this chapter we shall consider Kant's latest texts from the "Silent Decade," which constitute a further important step on the road to the Transcendental Deduction as it will appear in the first edition of the *Critique*.

considering appearances as standing in relations to each other that are analogous to the relations that the mind's representations stand to it should provide such a warrant or, more precisely, why Kant might have thought this circa 1775. The fact that he had not yet discovered the Paralogisms and therefore viewed the mind as an immaterial substance may be a necessary condition of attributing such a view to him, but it does not explain it.

[92] Although Kant does not provide a systematic discussion of the relation between general and transcendental logic in the *Duisburg Nachlass* such as he does in the *Critique*, he does refer to both in ways that suggest that he already had the "critical" view in mind. See (R4675 17: 6 $_{9-11}$; 163); (R4676 17: 656$_{26}$–67$_1$; 166); and (R4676 17: 656$_{15-16}$; 167).

III

The final stage in the development of Kant's thought in the "Silent Decade" is the period between the composition of the *Duisburg Nachlass* (circa 1775) and the publication of the first edition of the *Critique* in 1781. Its distinctiveness stems from the fact that it introduces a psychological dimension into Kant's account of cognition, specifically the attribution of a central role to the imagination, which is not found in the texts previously considered and anticipates the "subjective deduction" of the first edition. Perhaps even more so than for the "Silent Decade" as a whole, however, the problem of reconstructing Kant's thought during this period is exacerbated by the paucity of materials with which to work. The discussion will focus on three texts: B 12, Kant's account of empirical psychology in ML_1, and R 5636 (also called E 67), which bear directly on the problematic of the Deduction.

A) *B 12*: This note is the major source for Kant's views regarding topics pertaining to the subjective deduction prior to the publication of the *Critique*. Given the importance of this text, I shall cite it in full (numbering each paragraph for ease of reference). But since it reads more like a list of assertions or "talking points" than an argument, I shall not attempt to supply anything resembling a running commentary. Rather, I shall discuss what I take to be its salient points, noting significant differences from the account in the *Duisburg Nachlass* and their relations to the Transcendental Deductions in the *Critique*.

1. The unity of apperception in relation to the faculty of imagination is the understanding. Rules.
2. In relation to the reproductive faculty the unity is analytic, in relation to the productive, synthetic. The synthetic unity of apperception in relation to the transcendental faculty of imagination is the pure understanding. This transcendental faculty is that which universally determines all appearances in general with regard to time in accordance with rules that are valid a priori.
3. The three first faculties are not to be explained.
4. The transcendental synthesis of the imagination lies at the basis of all the concepts of our understanding.
5. The empirical use of the imagination rests on the synthesis of apprehension of empirical intuition which can then also be reproduced or made into another in accordance with the analogy therewith. In the latter case it is the productive imagination.
6. The productive imagination is either pure or empirical. The pure one.
7. The imagination is a synthesis, in part productive, in part reproductive. The former makes the latter possible, for if we have not previously brought it together through synthesis then we could not also connect with others in our subsequent state.
8. The productive imagination is (1) empirical in apprehension, (2) pure but sensible with regard to an object of pure sensible intuition, (3) transcendental

with regard to an object in general. The first presupposes the second, and the second presupposes the third.

9. The pure synthesis of the imagination is the ground of the possibility of the empirical synthesis in apprehension, thus also of perception. It is possible a priori and produces nothing but shapes. The transcendental synthesis of imagination pertains only to the unity of apperception in the synthesis of the manifold in general through the imagination. Through that a concept of the object in general is conceived in accordance with the different kinds of transcendental synthesis. The synthesis happens in time.

10. All appearances concern me not insomuch as they are in the senses but as they can at least be encountered in apperception. In this, however, they can only be encountered by means of the synthesis of apprehension, i.e., of imagination, but this must agree with the absolute unity of apperception, thus all appearances are only elements of a possible cognition insofar as they stand under the transcendental unity of the synthesis of imagination. Now the categories are nothing other than the representations of something (appearance) in general so far as it is represented through the transcendental synthesis of imagination, thus all appearances as elements of a possible cognition (experience) stand under the categories.

11. All intuitions are nothing for us if they cannot be taken up into consciousness. Thus their relation to possible cognition is nothing other than their relation to consciousness. But all connection of the manifold of intuition is nothing if it is not taken up in the unity of apperception, thus every cognition that is possible in itself belongs to a possible cognition insofar as it belongs with all other possible cognitions in relation to a single apperception.

12. The manifold, however, cannot thoroughly belong to one apperception except by means of a thoroughgoing synthesis of imagination and its functions in one consciousness. This transcendental unity in the synthesis of imagination is thus an a priori unity under which all appearances must stand. Those [sic] however, are the categories, thus the categories express the necessary unity of apperception under which all appearances belong insofar as they belong to a cognition a priori and necessarily.

13. It is no wonder that the understanding can prescribe to experience a priori laws that contain the conditions of all empirical ones. For through this understanding that unity is alone possible which appearance must primordially have in apperceptions and through which it conjoins into one experience.

14. The understanding as the ground of all analytical unity in judgments is therefore also the ground of rules and the source of them.

15. The suspension of the restriction seems to be an amplification. Something and nothing, Being and non-entity. Paralogism of the power of judgment.

16. Sensibility, imagination, and apperception cannot be further explained.

17. **Summary concept** of the faculty of pure understanding with regard to objects.

18. If the objects that are given to us were things in themselves and not mere appearances then we could not have any a priori cognition of them at all. For if we took it from the objects, then the cognition would be empirical and not a priori, but if we would form concepts of them independently from them then this would have no relation at all to any object, thus it would be concepts without content; from this one sees that there must be appearances. Now as representations these belong to one and the same apperception and as [breaks off].   (B12 23: 183–2015; 258–60)

The two most striking features of the eighteen paragraphs constituting B 12 are the prominence given to the imagination and the seemingly diminished status allotted to the understanding. Although at one point Kant assigns to the latter the familiar function of prescribing a priori laws to experience (13), and at another makes a passing reference to the relation between the understanding and judgment (14), rather than being considered one of the primary cognitive faculties, which are initially unnamed but later identified as sense, imagination, and apperception (3 and 16), the understanding is defined in terms of the relation between apperception (or the unity thereof) and the faculty of imagination (1and 2).

Similarly, the categories are themselves closely connected to the imagination. Thus, at one point Kant states that "The transcendental synthesis of the imagination lies at the basis of all the concepts of our understanding" (4); while at another he characterizes them as "nothing other than the representations of something (appearance) in general so far as it is represented through the transcendental synthesis of imagination" (10). This likewise accords with what Kant will say in the A-Deduction and it implies that the categories are effectively, if not in so many words, identified with their schemata. At the same time, however, Kant also stipulates that the categories "express the necessary unity of apperception under which all appearances belong insofar as they belong to a cognition *a priori* and necessarily" (12).

By connecting the categories directly to the transcendental synthesis of the imagination, Kant addresses the previously cited need to account for their necessary relation to appearances. Since the empirical synthesis of the imagination is directed immediately upon appearances in their apprehension and this is grounded in the transcendental synthesis (9), the postulated connection of the categories with the latter entails that everything that is apprehended, not simply everything that is judged an object of experience, is subject to the categories. And since whatever is *not* apprehended or apperceived is "nothing for us" (11), this means that whatever is something for us (cognitively speaking), i.e., everything that appears before the mind or is apprehended, necessarily conforms to the categories, which is what Kant needs to show.[93]

---

[93] The qualification "cognitively speaking" is necessary because we shall see that in his accounts of apperception in the *Critique* Kant does not deny the possibility of (unconscious) representations that may be something to us in a non-cognitive sense, e.g., affect our behavior.

Although it consists in sheer assertion rather than argument, we shall see that this line of thought contains all the elements of Kant's subjective deduction of 1781.[94] Its centerpiece is the correlation between the unity of apperception and the transcendental synthesis of the imagination. On the one hand, this synthesis is the act through which the (synthetic) unity of apperception is produced, which presumably accounts for its transcendental status; while, on the other hand, this synthesis is itself subject to the condition of the (analytic) unity of apperception, since it must conform to the "absolute unity" of the latter (10). Otherwise expressed, there is a reciprocity or bi-conditionality between the synthesis of the imagination and the unity of apperception. We shall see in future chapters how this reciprocity is articulated in the A-Deduction, only to be replaced in the B-Deduction by a reciprocity between the unity of consciousness and the consciousness of unity and a distinction between two transcendental syntheses: an intellectual synthesis governed by the pure concepts and a figurative or imaginative synthesis (*synthesis speciosa*) governed by their schematized counterparts.

A further complicating feature of B 12 is the sheer number of distinctions that Kant introduces in rapid order with little or no attempt at explanation. While Kant cannot be faulted for not providing explanations for these distinctions, since he is writing a note to himself rather than attempting to explain his views to others, it is nonetheless frustrating to those who endeavor to reconstruct the development of his thought. But since we shall encounter many of these distinctions in the A-Deduction, I shall forego an attempt to analyze them at this juncture, and instead simply provide a sketch of the taxonomy of mental faculties and functions that Kant provides in this text.

a. *The cognitive faculties*: Kant distinguishes three fundamental (irreducible and non-definable) cognitive faculties: sense, imagination, and apperception (with the understanding defined in terms of the relation between the latter two) (1and 2).

b. *The unity of apperception*: Kant here distinguishes between the analytic and synthetic unities of apperception (2), which we have seen that he failed to do, at least explicitly, in the *Duisburg Nachlass*. But, apart from hinting at a connection of the former with the reproductive and the latter with the productive imagination, he does not tell us how he then understood the distinction and

---

[94] Carl finds in B 12 a deduction, which he divides into the following six steps: (1) All appearances that concern me can be met with in apperception. (2) Everything that is met with in apperception is connected through the imagination. (3) The synthesis of the imagination agrees with the unity of apperception. (4) All appearances, which are elements of a possible cognition, stand under the transcendental unity of apperception. (5) The categories are representations of appearances, which are represented in accordance with the synthesis of the imagination. (6) Therefore, all appearances, which are elements of a possible cognition, stand under the categories. See Carl (1989b), 139. This roughly corresponds to what in the A-Deduction is referred to as the "argument from above" (from pure apperception) (A116–19). It seems equally possible, however, to construct on the basis of the materials contained in B 12 what Kant himself characterized as the argument "from below" (from the empirical) (A118–26). But given the nature of the text, I think it more accurate to say that B 12 contains the materials for a deduction rather than an actual deduction.

whether he considered it a break with his earlier views. In addition, Kant also refers to the absolute unity of apperception (10), which, though absent from the Transcendental Deduction, is found in his first edition account of the Paralogisms (A402), where it appears to designate the unity that is illicitly inflated into the unity of a substantial self in the paralogistic inferences of rational psychology.

c. *The faculty of imagination*: Kant introduces in short order a complex and interconnected set of distinctions: (i) between a productive and a reproductive faculty, the former, as noted above, is linked with the synthetic and the latter with the analytic unity of apperception (2 and 5); (ii) between a transcendental or pure and an empirical function of the productive faculty (6); (iii) a three-fold distinction with respect to the function of the productive faculty between: (a) empirical, (b) pure, i.e., a priori but sensible with respect to an object of "pure sensible intuition" (a mathematical object) and (c) transcendental with respect to an object in general (an empirical object as such or qua object) (8). In addition, he suggests that the imaginative synthesis is partly productive and partly reproductive, though the former is a condition of the latter (7). Finally, Kant asserts, again without explanation, a presuppositional relationship between these three functions of the productive faculty, which indicates that the transcendental synthesis is the condition of the other two (8).

Before leaving B 12, there is one further topic that stands apart from the central line of argument but merits discussion; viz., Kant's claim that "The suspension [*Aufhebung*] of the restriction seems to be an amplification. Something and nothing, Being and non-entity. Paralogism of the power of judgment" (15). The main interest of this obscure and ungrammatical passage lies in its reference to a "Paralogism of the power of judgment." Setting aside for the moment the perplexing connection of a paralogism with the power of judgment rather than reason, this seems to support Carl's view that the difference between Kant's account of the unity of apperception here and in the *Duisburg Nachlass* is the result of his discovery of the paralogistic nature of the inferences of rational psychology, which led him to abandon his earlier view that this unity was grounded ontologically in the unity of a *res cogitans*. Although Carl does not insist that this is the sense of "paralogism" to which Kant is here appealing, he appears to think that it quite likely is and he suggests that other texts from the same period demonstrate that by the time of the composition of B 12 Kant had formulated the critique of rational psychology that is contained in the Paralogism chapter in the *Critique*.[95]

Carl is likely correct that the discovery of the Paralogisms was a late (if not last-minute) addition to the argument of the *Critique* and we shall see below that its absence is evident in the treatment of rational psychology in ML_1. And he is certainly

[95] Carl (1989b), 119.

correct in locating the earliest known statement of the "critical" view of the Paralogisms in R 5553, where Kant provides a sketch of the overall structure of the Transcendental Dialectic as it is found in the *Critique*.[96] Nevertheless, a further consideration of paragraph 15 of B 12 and R 5552 (to be discussed below) suggests that the situation is somewhat more complex than the scenario that Carl provides.

To begin with, Kant's reference to a "Paralogism of the faculty of judgment" must be understood in the context of paragraph 15 as a whole. As the first sentence indicates, Kant's central point is that, while the suspension of the restriction on the limitation of cognition to appearances may *seem* to lead to the amplification or extension of cognition, it actually does not. Accordingly, what require further explanation are the juxtaposition of the paralogisms with the something–nothing contrast, which calls to mind Kant's discussion of these concepts in the Amphiboly of the Concepts of Reflection (A292/B348–9), and the connection of the paralogism with the faculty of judgment.

It is at here that R 5552 becomes relevant. This *Reflexion* has the heading "Concepts of Reflexion (their Amphiboly)" to which Kant originally added but later crossed out the clause "which lead to paralogisms." The heading is immediately followed by the definition of a paralogism as "a syllogistic inference that is false as far as its form is concerned, although so far as its matter (the major premise) is concerned it is correct;" to which Kant adds that "It arises when the middle concept is taken in different senses in the two premises—when, namely, the logical relation (in thinking) in one of the premises is taken as a real one (of the objects of intuition) in the other" (R 5552 18: 218_{5-12}; 236–7). While this is similar to the definition of a logical paralogism as a formal fallacy that Kant provides at A397, his account of a paralogism here differs from that of the *Critique* in that he links it to an amphiboly rather than to the inferences of rational psychology in which the substantiality, immateriality, and identity of the I are inferred from the unity of apperception.

This indicates that at one point (before he erased the phrase "which leads to paralogisms") Kant connected the notion of a paralogism with the "Amphiboly of Concepts of Reflection" rather than with the inferences of rational psychology and this provides the most natural explanation of their juxtaposition in B 12. This may also explain why Kant attributed the paralogism that he here had in mind to the faculty of judgment rather than to reason. According to the account in the *Critique*, this amphiboly consists in "the confusion of the empirical use of the understanding with the transcendental" (A260/B316). As such, it is best described as a misuse of the understanding. But Kant also attributes this misuse to a failure to engage in transcendental reflection, the function of which is to locate the cognitive faculty to which

---

[96] Carl (1989b), 119 and 173. Adickes is unsure about the dating of this vitally important *Reflexion*, suggesting that it was composed sometime between 1778 and 1783. But the fact that it provides an overview of the Transcendental Dialectic as a whole renders it unlikely that it was written after the publication of the *Critique*.

the representations compared in a judgment belong (A261/B317); and since this failure is ascribed to judgment, it does not appear to be too much of a stretch to attribute the paralogism, so construed, to that faculty.[97]

In any event, Kant's explicit connection between paralogism and amphiboly in both R 5552 and B 12 provides a strong indication that at the time of their composition he had not yet connected the notion of a paralogism with what he later identified as the underlying fallacy of rational psychology. Granted, the fact that Kant later crossed out the statement in R 5552 that the amphiboly leads to a paralogism might be taken as evidence that it was shortly after the original composition of the *Reflexion*, and perhaps B 12 as well, that Kant formulated his "critical" view of the Paralogisms. As already noted, the latter is in place in R 5553, which appears to stem from roughly the same period of time (perhaps sometime in late 1779 or 1780).[98] Nevertheless, whatever the precise dating of these texts, the fact remains that the parallelism with R 5552 gives us good reason to assume that the reference to a paralogism of the faculty of judgment in B 12 *does not* refer to the Paralogisms as Kant understood them in the *Critique*.[99]

B) *Ml₁*: This is the label given to the only transcript of Kant's metaphysics lectures from the "Silent Decade" that we possess. Its dating has long been a matter of controversy, but I believe that the fact that in these lectures Kant still affirms the legitimacy of rational psychology and that his analysis of the imagination strongly suggests the influence of Tetens' supports Carl's proposed dating as sometime between the winter semesters 1777–78 and 1779–80.[100] Although these lectures are of considerable importance for the understanding of Kant's views at the time on a number of issues, including apperception and freedom of the will, the present discussion is limited to his account of the imagination in the section on empirical psychology. This account, like that in B 12, is formulated in terms of a faculty psychology and is divided into two parts. The first, which is included in a discussion of the sensible faculty of cognition (*sinnlichen Erkenntnissvermögen*), considers the

---

[97] Kant states that "all judgments, indeed all comparisons, require a **reflection**, i.e., a distinction of the cognitive power to which the given concepts belong" (A261/B317).

[98] Adickes is also uncertain about the dating of these *Reflexionen*, suggesting only that they likely both stem from 1778–79 and possibly from 1780–83. It seems clear, however, that at least R 5552 was written before the publication of the *Critique*.

[99] I do not wish to make too much of this point. In particular, I do not take it as showing that Kant had not arrived at his critique of rational psychology at the time of the composition of B 12, but merely that he had not yet connected this critique with the notion of a paralogism. It could be argued in support of the stronger claim that in what appears to be the earliest expression that we have of this critique; viz., R 5553, it takes the form of a demonstration of a set of paralogisms (see 18: 224₁₋₇; 240); but while this gives some credence to the view that Kant had not arrived at his critique of rational psychology, it is not decisive. Moreover, I do not place as much weight on this issue as do Carl and Laywine, since for the reasons already given, I do not subscribe to their ontological reading of Kant's account of apperception in the *Duisburg Nachlass*. And if this is rejected there is no need to view Kant's quite different (non-metaphysical) account of the unity of apperception in B 12 as a consequence of his discovery of the Paralogisms.

[100] See Carl (1989b), 118.

"formative power" (*bildende Kraft*) in its empirical function. This power corresponds to the imagination in a broad sense. As a subdivision of the sensible faculty (the other being the senses themselves), the formative power is considered as part of sensibility. It differs from the senses themselves in that the representations stemming from the latter are purely passive (since they depend upon being affected by objects), whereas those stemming from the formative power or imagination involve an activity of the mind, albeit one that is based on what is passively received.

Kant divides the formative power into several subpowers, the most germane for our purposes being the illustrative power (*abbildende Vermögen*) and the imitative power (*Vermögen der Nachbildung*).[101] These seem to correspond to what in B 12 are characterized as the productive and reproductive imagination in their empirical functions. The latter consists in the capacity to form an image of something that one has previously perceived. The former is more complex, since Kant includes two distinct activities under it. One is the formation of a single image out of a manifold of distinct impressions. Kant's examples are of a city, a room piled high with items, and St. Peter's. His point is that the formation of an image of such an object requires that one "run through" (*durchgeht*) the manifold of impressions connected with the object (ML_1 28: 235_{32}–6_{12}; 54). The second is the formation of an image of something that one has not actually perceived (ML_1 28: 236_{20-2}; 54). We shall see that the first of these, under the title "synthesis of apprehension," plays a major role in Kant's account of the three-fold synthesis in the *Critique*; while the second is crucial for understanding the connection between the transcendental synthesis of the imagination and the representation of time.

Confining ourselves to Kant's account of the imagination or formative power in ML_1, the key point is that, in addition to the discussion of its sensibly conditioned empirical function examined above, Kant also discusses its connection with the higher faculty of cognition, i.e., the understanding, which is defined at once as the faculty of concepts, the faculty of judgment, and the faculty of rules (ML_1 28: 240_{6-8}; 57).[102] In fact, Kant equates the formative power "considered *in abstracto*," with the understanding and the conditions and actions of this power, likewise considered *in abstracto*, with the pure concepts of the understanding (ML_1 28: 239_{16-19}; 57). Kant illustrates this thesis with respect to the concept of substance by noting that this power must have something permanent underlying its operation besides the manifold; for otherwise it could not represent anything as changing.[103]

---

[101] The others are the faculty of anticipation (*Vermögen der Vorbildung*), the faculty of imagination (*Vermögen der Einbildung*), the faculty of correlation or characterization (*Vermögen der Gegenbildung*), and the faculty of cultivation (*Vermögen der Ausbildung*). Kant notes that the main divisions within the formative power concern time, but the last three of the above-mentioned faculties involve imagistic capacities that are not related to time. See ML_1 23: 236_1–7_{28}.

[102] For a similar account, which also connects the understanding with spontaneity, see A126.

[103] What the text literally says is that without the permanent the formative power could change nothing ("*denn ware nichts zum Fundament der bildenden Kraft, so könnte sie auch nichts wechseln*"). But since the imagination cannot actually change things in the world and Kant is here talking about it as a representative

While it is not totally clear what Kant intended by considering the formative power or imagination "*in abstracto*," the context suggests that he meant considering it in abstraction from its relation to the understanding, regarded as a distinct faculty. In other words, the formative power, so construed, functions as an autonomous cognitive power, structuring experience in much the same way as the transcendental synthesis of the imagination does in the *Critique*. Accordingly, as Carl has noted, and as we have already seen to be the case in B 12, at this juncture in his philosophical development Kant appears to have let the imagination virtually usurp the function elsewhere given to the understanding.[104]

C) *R 5636 (E 67)*: Apart from one discordant element to be discussed below, this fragment, which apparently stems from 1780, seems to be closely related to B 12.[105] Although Kant does not use the term "deduction," he distinguishes between the *quaestio facti* and the *quaestio juris* in essentially the same manner as he will in the *Critique*. The former is described as concerned with the manner in which one first comes into possession of a concept and the latter with the question of the right of its possession and use. And Kant further claims that the universality and necessity in the use of the pure concepts reveals their non-empirical origin (R 5636 18: 267_{6-12}; 260). Accordingly, as in the *Critique*, Kant draws a sharp distinction between the questions of the origin and the manner of acquisition of concepts.

As in B 12, Kant distinguishes between sensibility, the power of imagination, and apperception; but he is more explicit in locating an a priori ground of the possibility of empirical cognition and the synthesis according to concepts that has objective reality in the pure aspect of each power (R 5636 18: 267_{13-16}).[106] The above-mentioned seemingly discordant note occurs when, after claiming that they (presumably, the pure exercise of the three powers) pertain only to appearances, which are themselves contingent and lack unity, Kant suggests that it follows from this that "one properly cognizes only oneself as the thinking subject, but everything else as in this one thing [*diesem Einen*]. Heautognosy [*heautognossee*]" (R 5636 18: 267_{16-19}; 260). This seems discordant because Kant's language suggests that it supposedly follows from the fact that our cognition is limited to appearances that what we properly cognize is only ourselves ("Heautognosy") and that other objects are cognized only as in the thinking subject ("this one thing"). At first glance, this

---

power, I take it that what he meant to say was that with the permanent the imagination could represent something as changing, which apart from the reference to the imagination is the thesis of the First Analogy in the *Critique*.

[104] Carl (1989b), 134.

[105] Adickes dates it as stemming from sometime between 1780 and 1783, but since it contains the same language as the *Critique* it is difficult to see why Kant would have written it after the publication of that work.

[106] The use of the singular form of the verb (*hat*) indicates that objective *reality* pertains to the (objectifying) synthesis, not to the concepts. Although Kant does not make the point here, it may be assumed that he would ascribe objective *validity* to the concepts in question.

sounds like a combination of the ontological conception of apperception, which has been attributed to Kant circa 1775 by Carl and Laywine, and a radical form of subjective idealism (appearances are cognized as in the thinking subject). But inasmuch as both Carl and Laywine would presumably agree that by the time of the composition of this note Kant no longer maintained that view (if, indeed, he ever had) and he had never subscribed to a subjective idealism of this sort, it appears unlikely that this is the view that he was trying to express.[107] Instead, I think that Kant is best read as claiming in an extremely clumsy way that, since our cognition is grounded in subjective conditions through which we represent objects to ourselves, these objects are "in us," in the transcendental, but not the empirical sense.[108] Otherwise expressed, the "objecthood" (or objectivity) of these objects is grounded in transcendental conditions stemming from the nature of the human understanding.

Beyond this, there are two other noteworthy features of this *Reflexion*. One is the prominence given to inner sense and its connection with a three-fold synthesis, which is described in essentially the same terms as it will be in the A-Deduction. Kant writes: "All representations, wherever they might come from, are in the end as representations modifications of the inner sense, and it is from this viewpoint that their unity must be regarded. To their receptivity there corresponds a spontaneity of *synthesis*. Either of apprehension as sensations or of reproduction as images or of recognition as concepts" (R 5636 18: 267_{20}–8_3; 260). Kant does not refer to inner sense in B 12, but he makes it clear in the *Critique* that the fact that all our representations are modifications of inner sense and, as such, are necessarily subject to time, the formal condition of inner sense is a fundamental premise underlying the subjective side of the Transcendental Deduction (A99). The point, which will be further explored in subsequent chapters, is that it is because all our representations are subject to the conditions of time, which is to say that they are given successively, that a synthesis is required in order to bring them to the unity of consciousness. Correlatively, this synthesis has three aspects, depending on whether it is regarded as exercised upon sensations in apprehension, upon images in reproduction, or results in bringing the representations under concepts (recognition). While Kant's language here suggests that he regards these as alternatives, it is clear from the *Critique* that he viewed all three as required for cognition. Moreover, the fact that Kant did not

---

[107] My own view is that Kant was never a subjective idealist of any stripe. But since this remains a controversial issue, with some interpreters maintaining that Kant's idealism is similar to Berkeley's, with the gratuitous addition of things in themselves, I am at present denying merely that Kant ever maintained the view that we cognize appearances *as in us*, which is also something that to my knowledge Berkeley never maintained. For my discussion of the relation between Kant's transcendental idealism and Berkeley, see Allison (1973b) and (2004), 22–6 and passim.

[108] I discuss Kant's distinction between an empirical and a transcendental sense of objects being "*in uns*" and "*ausser uns*" in Allison (1983), 6–7, 17, and 83.

explicitly connect the activity of the imagination with inner sense in B 12 does not mean that the present text marks a development in Kant's thought. It is rather that R 5636 makes explicit a point that remained implicit in B 12 and in that respect deepens our understanding of Kant's views at the time.

Similar considerations apply to the other noteworthy feature of R 5636; viz., its inclusion of a reference to what in the *Critique* Kant characterizes as the mathematical principles of the understanding and distinguishes from the dynamical principles (A162/B201). The former are called the "Axioms of Intuition" and the "Anticipations of Perception," and they are concerned respectively with extensive and intensive magnitudes. The latter are the three "Analogies of Experience."[109] Up to this point we have seen that Kant's focus has been virtually entirely on the latter or, more precisely, on the three relational categories that underlie the Analogies. But now Kant writes: "(Transcendental principles of mathematics (not mathematical principles), namely that all intuitions and sensations are magnitudes and that the mathematical propositions about magnitude have reality, although only as of appearances)" (R 5636 18: 268_{4-7}; 260). Although this passage does not bear directly on the Transcendental Deduction, it is important because it indicates that Kant had arrived at the view of the *Critique* regarding the necessity of distinguishing between two sets of transcendental principles: one concerned with the content of intuition and the other with what must be thought, if what is intuited is to be transformed into experience. And here the distinction between mathematical principles and transcendental principles of mathematics is of particular significance; for previously, even in B 12, Kant had distinguished between mathematical and transcendental principles, but did not introduce the conception of transcendental principles of mathematics, which function as a priori conditions of the application of mathematics to nature. Moreover, this has at least an indirect bearing on the Transcendental Deduction, since it entails that the latter must establish the validity of all of the categories, or at least those falling under the headings of quantity and quality, as well as the relational categories, which we have seen were the sole concern of the *Duisburg Nachlass*.[110] But while this indicates a clear advance in Kant's thought from his views circa 1775, for the reasons noted above, we cannot assume this to be the case with respect to B 12.

This, then, completes our survey of Kant's thought during the "Silent Decade" insofar as it bears on the Transcendental Deduction. We have seen that with the

---

[109] Kant also includes the "Postulates of Empirical Thought," which are concerned with the modal categories, under the dynamical principles, but this seems to be motivated by an interest of attaining a systematic organization rather than by the nature of the principles themselves.

[110] Once again, the modal categories constitute a special case due to the special nature of modality with respect to judgment. For my account of that issue, see Allison (2004), esp. 138–9. The question of whether the Transcendental Deduction applies also to these categories (and if so, how) will be taken up in Chapter 9.

inclusion of a central role for the imagination in his transcendental account Kant had arrived at all the elements of his "critical" view. But before turning to the texts of Kant's actual deduction in the first two editions of the *Critique*, we must consider the relation between his views and those of Johann Nicolaus Tetens, a thinker with whom Kant was very much concerned at the time and who arguably exerted a significant influence on both the texts discussed in this section and the subjective side of the Transcendental Deduction in the first edition of the *Critique*.

Appendix to Chapter 3
Kant and Tetens

Assuming that the evolution of Kant's thought from the standpoint of the *Duisburg Nachlass*, in which the analytic-synthetic distinction, the ideality of space and time, and the "critical" conception of objectivity are firmly in place, to the views expressed in the latest texts from the "Silent Decade" considered in the last portion of Chapter 3 and given their definitive formulation in the first edition of the *Critique*, is not purely the result of an internal development but was occasioned, at least in part by external influence, the single most important such influence is undoubtedly Johann Nicolaus Tetens. Indeed, the eminent Kant scholar Herman Jan de Vleeschauwer claimed that evidence of Kant's debt to Tetens for the innovations in his thought during this period is "so striking that it does not seem possible to give an account of the constitution of the Critical philosophy without explicitly referring to the contribution of Tetens."[1] Moreover, he is not alone in this assessment, since the importance of Tetens for understanding Kant has become increasingly recognized in the recent literature. Accordingly, this appendix to Chapter 3 on the "Silent Decade" will be devoted to an exploration of the relation between the two thinkers and is divided into three parts: (1) a discussion of Kant's reaction to Tetens' work as it is contained in his correspondence and *Nachlass*; (2) a comparison of their treatments of some common themes, which do not necessarily indicate any direct influence; and (3) a consideration for the case of the actual influence of Tetens on Kant with respect to two of the chief issues with which Kant was concerned in the last years of the "Silent Decade;" viz., the role of the imagination in empirical cognition and Kant's belated rejection of rational psychology.

I

Tetens' magnum opus, *Philosophische Versuche über die menschliche Natur und ihre Entwickelung* (*Philosophical Essays on Human Nature and Its Development*) was published in 1777, which was roughly at the mid-point between the composition of the notes that constitute the *Duisburg Nachlass* and the publication of the first edition

---

[1] de Vleeschauwer (1962), 88.

of the *Critique*.[2] Moreover, Kant's keen interest in this work was noted by Hamann, who, in a letter to Herder dated May 17, 1779, remarked that Kant constantly had it in front of him.[3] And first-hand evidence of Kant's engagement with Tetens' work during this period is provided by his own correspondence. The earliest example is a letter to Herz from April 1778, in which, while noting that Tetens has made some "penetrating points," Kant complains about the undo prolixity of his work, with particular reference to the lengthy and inconclusive discussion of freedom in its second volume, and he effectively accuses Tetens of failing to exercise sufficient editorial constraint, the need for which, Kant suggests, is delaying the completion of his own work (Br 10: 232; 167). In another letter to Herz, dated after May 11, 1781, Kant thanks Herz for distributing the copies of the just-published *Critique*, which he had sent to him in Berlin, and remarks that Tetens, along with Herz and Mendelssohn, are the three thinkers on whom he most heavily relies to explain the *Critique* to the world (Br 10: 270; 181). Kant later expresses much the same sentiment in a letter to Christian Garve dated August 7, 1783, substituting Garve for Herz (Br 10: 341; 199). Finally, he reiterates this thought in a letter to Mendelssohn, dated August 16, 1783, in which he laments that "Mendelssohn, Garve, and Tetens have apparently declined to occupy themselves with this sort of business," and asks rhetorically, "where else can any one of sufficient talent and good will be found?" (Br 10: 346_{26-9}; 203).

Nevertheless, turning from what Kant said about Tetens in his correspondence to the remarks in his *Nachlass*, we find only six brief references, none of which indicate that Tetens' work played a major role in the development of Kant's thought. Of these, two are marginal comments in Kant's own copy of the first volume of Tetens' work. The first is on page 19 and contains only the name "Tucker" (R 4847 18: 5_6). It is directed to Tetens' discussion of Charles Bonnet and Edward Search, whom he viewed as researchers who believed that the brain contains material traces of ideas.[4] The second is on page 131 and consists in the comment that "the omission of all determinations of an action can make a general representation without comparison" (R 4848 18: 5_{10-11}). It refers to Tetens' essentially Lockean account of the formation of a general image and suggests a certain sympathy with this view.

---

[2] Tetens had published another important work, *Über die allgemeine speculativische Philosophie* (*On Universal Speculative Philosophy*) (1775), which was intended to prepare the public for the later and more systematic work. As the title suggests, however, it also has a more explicitly metaphysical focus, its aim being to show, against the Scottish commonsense philosophers, the compatibility of metaphysics or "transcendent philosophy" and common sense. Since I have no evidence that Kant was familiar with this work, I shall not discuss it here; but it is important to keep in mind that this metaphysical concern underlies Tetens' cognitive psychology. For a discussion of this work and its relation to the better known *Philosophical Essays*, see Uebele (1912), esp. 69–111, and Beck (1969a), 413–15.

[3] Hamann (1959), 81.

[4] Inasmuch as Edward Search was the pseudonym used by Abraham Tucker in connection with the publication in 1765 of the first four volumes of his seven-volume work, *The Light of Nature Pursued*, it is evident that he is the Tucker to whom Kant was referring in his marginal note. This also indicates that Kant was aware, as Tetens evidently was not, that Search really was Tucker.

Two other references are contained in Kant's *Vorabeit zu den Prolegomena*. The first is in a draft of Kant's response to the notorious Garve-Feder review. Kant is discussing the failure of the reviewer, at that time unknown to him, to understand the nature of his project in the *Critique*, with particular emphasis on the problem of the possibility of synthetic cognition a priori. In this context, he refers to Tetens, whom Kant suggests might have given the reviewer reason to recognize the importance of the issue for metaphysics (23: 57_{18-20}), which indicates that Kant thought that Tetens, though not actually formulating the problem, had at least indicated some awareness of it.[5] The second is a remark that appears to charge Tetens with enthusiasm (*Schwärmerei*). Loosely translated, it reads: "Healthy reason as a principle gives rise to enthusiasm, for example Tetens, specifically, the kind that aims at raging quite in accordance with reason, which is the only way in which it can become fashionable in an age of philosophy" (23: 59_{9-11}).[6] Although given Tetens' cautious empiricism, charging him with enthusiasm might seem bizarre, it becomes comprehensible when one considers that Kant did the same for Locke.[7] Given this, as well as some of Tetens' own metaphysical proclivities, it is not difficult to envision Kant as accusing Tetens of a Lockean sort of enthusiasm, which he suggests is the only kind of enthusiasm that is fashionable in "an age of philosophy."[8]

The final two references to Tetens are more substantive and provide us with an understanding of how Kant considered the relation between Tetens' project and his own. They consist in the following two *Reflexionen*:

I concern myself not with the evolution of concepts, like Tetens (all actions by means of which concepts are produced), nor with their analysis, like Lambert, but solely with their objective validity. I am not in competition with these men.   (R 4900 18: 23_{12-15})

Tetens investigates the concepts of pure reason merely subjectively (human nature), I investigate them objectively. The former analysis is empirical, the latter transcendental.

(R 4901 18: 23_{16-18})

These remarks suggest that Kant viewed Tetens' project as essentially that of Locke; viz., providing a genetic account ("evolution of concepts") of how the human mind

[5] It seems clear that Kant did not wish to credit Tetens with anticipating him in the formulation of the problem, since he credited himself with this, as well as the analytic-synthetic distinction. See B19. For my discussion of Kant's claim to originality in this regard see Allison (1985), 15–38. In discussing this text, Alexi Krouglov speculates as to why Kant failed to mention Tetens in the published version of the *Prolegomena* and suggests two possible reasons: that Kant was disappointed by Tetens failure to review the *Critique* and that Kant considered Tetens as essentially a Lockean rather than an independent thinker. See Krouglov (2013), 85–6.

[6] The English rendering is loose because the passage is ungrammatical and ambiguous. The German text reads: "*Gesunder Verstand als princip bringt schwärmerei hervor Tetens nämlich die es es sich vorsetzt recht mit Vernunft zu rasen, die einzige die in einem Zeitalter der Philosophie Mode werden kan.*" I wish to thank Manfred Kuehn and Oliver Sensen for their helpful comments regarding this passage.

[7] See B128.

[8] One possibility, which has been suggested to me by Manfred Kuehn, is that Kant is referring to Tetens' *On Universal Speculative Philosophy*. Although this is a possibility, I think that the passage is equally explicable in terms of the reference to Locke.

arrives at its conception of a public, objective, law-governed world of things and events.[9] And they further indicate that Kant wished to distinguish sharply between this and his own project, which is concerned with the objective validity of the concepts that are conditions of the possibility of the experience of such a world. In the language that Kant introduced in R 5636 and made famous in the *Critique*, whereas Tetens, like Locke, is concerned with the *quaestio facti*, he (Kant) is concerned with the *quaestio juris*. Kant sharpens the point in the second *Reflexion*, where he contrasts Tetens' subjective-empirical with his own objective-transcendental analysis. As is clear from the context, Kant understands the term "transcendental" in the way in which he does in his initial definition in the *Critique*, where he writes "I call all cognition **transcendental** that is occupied not so much with objects but rather with our *a priori* concepts of objects in general" (A11–12).[10]

Despite this fundamental difference in orientation, even a cursory examination of the *Versuch* indicates a host of theses and conceptions that would have both intrigued and exasperated Kant. In addition to the attribution of an essential cognitive function to the imagination (to be discussed below), these include the claim that there are three cognitive faculties: sensation (*Empfindung*) or feeling (*Gefühl*), the power of representation (*Vorstellungskraft*), and the power of thought (*Denkungskraft*);[11] a complex and nuanced account of consciousness, of which apperception (*Gewahrnehmen*) constitutes only one part, the other being feeling;[12] the active, relational nature of thinking as contrasted with sensing;[13] the identification of thinking and judging;[14] the distinction between the form and matter of cognition;[15] the assertion of a set of fundamental concepts that pertain to the nature of the understanding;[16] an analysis of the problem of objectivity that focuses on its subjective conditions;[17] critiques of Hume's accounts of the idea of the self and the causal principle in the *Treatise*, which may have introduced these aspects of Hume's views to Kant;[18] an emphasis on the spontaneity of the mind, encompassing cognition as well as volition;[19] and the distinction between reason and understanding.[20]

---

[9] At least partly because of this, Tetens is often referred to in the literature as "the German Locke." It has also been pointed out, however, that this characterization is a gross over-simplification, since his complex position embodies many non-Lockean components, particularly, but not exclusively, Leibnizian ones. On this point, see, for example, de Vleeschauwer (1934), 299; Kuehn (1989), 368, and Krouglov (2013), 486–7.

[10] In the second edition, this is changed to read: "I call all cognition transcendental that is occupied not so much with objects but rather with our mode of cognition of objects insofar as this is to be possible *a priori*" (B25).

[11] See Tetens (1777a), 590, 611. Although he does not assert it to be the case, Tetens also speculates regarding the likelihood that these are different expressions of a single fundamental faculty (*Grundvermögen*). See Tetens (1777a), 611–17.

[12] Tetens (1777a), 262–94. Tetens usually uses the term "*Gewahrnehmen*," which he regards as synonymous with "*Apperzeption*." It can be translated as "awareness." See Watkins (2009), 361 and passim.

[13] Tetens (1777a), 273–80; 295–372.   [14] Tetens (1777a), 353–72.

[15] Tetens (1777a), 336–45.   [16] Tetens (1777a), 388–95.   [17] Tetens (1777a), 470–569.

[18] For the former, see Tetens (1777a), 392–4; for the latter, 312–27.

[19] Tetens' many discussions of the spontaneity of the mind are scattered throughout a number of essays. For a discussion of Tetens' views on spontaneity and their relation to Kant, see Dyck (2014b).

[20] Tetens (1777a), 426–529. Since Kant had already drawn this distinction in the *Duisburg Nachlass*, it cannot be said that he took it over from Tetens. But de Vleeschauwer (1934), 323–6, argues that Tetens'

Since the concern of this appendix is to assess the relevance of Kant's reading of Tetens' work for the development of his thought in the last segment of the "Silent Decade," it is not possible to provide a comparison of the views of the two thinkers on the full range of these (and other possible) topics.[21] But in an endeavor to convey a sense of both the affinities and divergences of their positions, I shall briefly compare and contrast their views on two of the above-mentioned topics: the assertion of a set of fundamental concepts, which underlie any use of the understanding, and the analysis of objectivity in terms of its subjective conditions.

II

1) *Fundamental concepts of the understanding*: We have seen that at least since the *Dissertation* Kant had recognized a set of concepts, which as inherent in the nature of the intellect or understanding, are conditions of its real use, first with respect to the intelligible world and later with respect to the sensible world, and were the ancestors of the pure concepts of the understanding or categories in the *Critique*. Accordingly, it must have intrigued Kant to learn that an empiricist such as Tetens recognized a set of privileged concepts, which he refers to as "fundamental concepts of the understanding" (*Grundbegriffe des Verstandes*) and claims to be required for judgments regarding the existence of things.[22] Moreover, there is considerable overlap in their lists of these concepts. While Kant's focus during the "Silent Decade" was largely on the relational categories, which he had not yet connected with the nature of judgment, the canonical list in the *Critique*, which is derived from the table of judgments, consists of unity, plurality, and totality (under quantity), reality, negation, and limitation (under quality), substance and accident, cause and effect, and community or reciprocity (under relation), and possibility-impossibility, existence-non-existence, and necessity-contingency (under modality) (A80/B106).[23] For Tetens, by contrast, the fundamental concepts include that of a subject and its properties, the I, object, being or actuality, substance, causation, and space and time. Although Tetens' account is presumably based on observation, he suggests that it is taken largely from Locke and Leibniz.[24]

Comparing Tetens' list to Kant's, the most notable differences are that Tetens' lacks Kant's categories of quantity and quality, the third relational category, and two

lengthy discussion of the matter likely influenced Kant during the time in which he was giving the *Critique* its final form.

[21] The fullest and most informative discussion of this topic with which I am familiar is that of de Vleeschauwer (1934), 299–326. The list of topics noted above corresponds partly, but not completely, with his.

[22] See Tetens (1777a), 388.

[23] There are also many lists to be found in various *Reflexionen* stemming from different periods in Kant's thought and they contain both different categories and organizing principles. For a useful listing of some of these, see Guyer and Wood (1998), 724, note 12.

[24] Guyer and Wood (1998).

of Kant's modal categories. Correlatively, and most significantly, Kant's list lacks the I, which the "critical" Kant did not consider a concept in the ordinary sense,[25] and space and time, which he assigns to sensibility rather than to the understanding. From Kant's point of view, however, the crucial difference concerns their respective accounts of the origin of these concepts. Tetens' account is intended to show how, like all general ideas or concepts, their content stems from sensation, from which they are produced by acts of abstraction from what is sensibly given. Thus, despite their supposedly foundational nature, they are a posteriori rather than a priori and as such cannot function as necessary conditions of the possibility of experience, as Kant understood it.

As Kant indicates, Tetens was interested in the evolution of these concepts, while his concern is with their objective validity. Had Tetens been aware of Kant's views in the *Critique*, he might well have replied that he, too, was concerned with the question of validity, though he approached it in a different way. He might also have pointed to Kant's claim in the *Dissertation* that concepts, which pertain to the intellect, as well as those of space and time, are acquired by abstraction rather than being innate, as indicating a basic agreement on this issue.[26] Nevertheless, Kant would no doubt have countered that, whereas for Tetens these concepts are abstracted from sensation (at least as far as their content is concerned), for him they are abstracted from the laws inherent in the mind, to which he does attribute innateness. Moreover, though they are acquired, it is by reflecting upon the operations of the mind on the occasion of experience which accounts for their apriority, rather than upon the content of experience, as Tetens maintained.

2) *Transcendental internalism*: In present-day parlance, both Tetens and Kant are epistemic internalists, which is to say that they analyze and attempt to justify cognition in terms that are internal to the cognizing subject. They differ in that Tetens may be viewed as a psychological internalist in the sense that he is concerned with the mental processes through which a cognizer constructs for itself representations of objects that are assumed to have a real existence independently of these representations; whereas Kant may be considered a transcendental internalist, since he is concerned with the a priori conditions through which a cognizer grounds the objectivity of its judgments. Since we have already seen Kant's "critical" analysis of objectivity in terms of the unification of representations through a priori rules (functions of apperception) at work in the *Duisburg Nachlass* and will examine it in considerable detail in the coming chapters in the form that it will take in the *Critique*, it is not necessary to spell it out further at this point. Instead the focus will be on the contrasting account provided by Tetens. But since Tetens' account is itself

---

[25] At A341/B399 Kant refers to the I of the "I think" as the "vehicle of all concepts."

[26] Although at the time of the composition of his work Tetens did not, of course, have access to the *Critique*, he did discuss favorably Kant's account of space and time in the *Inaugural Dissertation*. He credits Kant with recognizing that space and time are relational concepts and that they are examples of relations that can precede the ideas of their relata. See Tetens (1777a), 356–60. Tetens ignores, however, Kant's connection of space and time with sensibility and his sharp distinction between the sensible and the intellectual, presumably because these run counter to his view.

quite complex and involves materials from a number of different essays, it will only be possible to sketch its basic features.

Tetens frames his account in terms of the contrast between a subjective and an objective necessity. But whereas Hume begins with the putative objective necessity of the causal relation and reduces it to a merely subjective necessity based on custom or habit, Tetens begins with subjective necessity and attempts to show how the concept of an objective necessity arises from it. By a subjective necessity Tetens understands the necessity of thinking or judging in a certain manner, e.g., thinking that a thing is identical with itself; that everything that comes into existence has a cause; or that two plus two equals four. To say that these ways of thinking are subjectively necessary is to say that they are grounded in natural laws of the power of thought. Inasmuch as these laws are causal laws, subjective necessity is a species of *causal* necessity, which, as such, is without any normative import.[27]

As this suggests, Tetens' account of subjective necessity is more nuanced than Hume's. Rather than reducing subjective necessity to custom, Tetens cites four kinds of such necessity in addition to custom, which he regards as the least important kind and relegates to an appendix.[28] The first of these are judgments that are necessary in virtue of their form, which includes tautologies and the three classical laws of thought. He characterizes the necessity of such judgments as subjective because they concern the causal incapacity of the power of thought to form judgments that violate them; e.g., it is incapable of representing to itself something with contradictory predicates, say a circle with four sides.[29] Tetens' second category of subjectively necessary judgments encompasses those regarding the immediate objects of consciousness. These are first-person reports, which are traditionally viewed as immune to doubt. As examples Tetens cites: "I hear," "I see," "I feel pain," "I think," and the like; and he notes that even Hume and Berkeley, whom he presents as arch-skeptics, recognized judgments of this type as fundamental truths.[30] Once again, Tetens views the necessity of such judgments in causal terms as the incapacity of the power of thought to deny them. Tetens' third category consists of deductive inferences, under which he includes geometrical demonstrations. He claims that when the truth of the premises is presupposed and the proper rules of inference followed it is not possible to doubt the conclusion, where impossibility is again understood in a causal sense.[31]

Tetens' fourth category of subjectively necessary judgments is composed of causal judgments of which he distinguishes two types. The first is the causal principle or axiom "**Nothing comes from nothing**," which affirms the necessity of ascribing a cause to everything that comes to be.[32] It is presumably intended to correspond to

---

[27] See Tetens (1777a), 513. Tetens there provides a clear statement of his position, when he draws an analogy between the natural laws of the power of thought, to which the understanding qua understanding is subject, and the laws of reflection and refraction governing vision.

[28] Tetens (1777a), 512–19.   [29] Tetens (1777a), 513.   [30] Tetens (1777a), 491–2.

[31] Tetens (1777a), 492–3.   [32] Tetens (1777a), 495.

Hume's causal principle as affirmed in the *Treatise*: "[W]hatever begins to exist must have a cause of existence."[33] The second is composed of particular causal judgments such as "My volition to move my arm is the cause of its motion" and "Daylight is the effect of the sun," which seem to the untutored understanding to be immediately certain, without any need to appeal to general laws of nature.[34] Assuming that such occurrences must have *some* cause, since the antecedents are obvious, he contends that it is subjectively necessary to view these relations as causal, and therefore as involving a necessary connection. In justification for this contention, Tetens appeals to the natural law of the power of thought: "that it accepts or can accept nothing as an actually existing thing, without either sensing it or finding a ground for it in other thoughts."[35]

Tetens also notes, however, that the subjective necessity of particular causal judgments is merely conditioned rather than absolute because of the possibility of introducing additional considerations, which could lead one to abandon the original judgment without changing the initial thoughts that led to it.[36] But this is not for the reason that one might expect; viz., the presence of some hidden natural cause that was not initially taken into account. Rather, as is evident from his reference to views such as occasionalism and the Leibnizian pre-established harmony, Tetens' assignment of a merely conditioned subjective necessity to such judgments was motivated by metaphysical considerations. His intent is not to advocate or defend some such view, but to note that their mere subjective possibility (they were sincerely believed by important philosophers) is sufficient to render the belief in genuine transient causation in nature merely conditionally necessary.

As has been noted, Tetens' lengthy account of subjective necessity is intended, not for its own sake, but as a propaedeutic to an analysis of objective necessity and, more generally, objectivity. It is not, however, a matter of simply equating the two forms of necessity, since what is subjectively necessary need not be objectively necessary or, indeed, even objective at all. It is rather that subjective necessity is a necessary condition of objectivity or, alternatively, that objectivity must be grounded in a certain kind of subjective necessity. Accordingly, the question is what warrants the attribution of objectivity in certain cases of subjective necessity and its denial in others.

Tetens' problematic results from the combination of his psychological internalism and a commitment to the traditional correspondence theory of truth, which he claims is affirmed both by the ordinary understanding and philosophers.[37] Since his internalism precludes the possibility of standing outside one's representation in order to compare them with the things represented (the so-called "veil of perception"), the human understanding must determine this correspondence on the basis of immanent criteria; while the psychological nature of this internalism leaves as the

[33] Hume (2007), 56.   [34] Tetens (1777a).   [35] Tetens (1777a).
[36] Tetens (1777a), 496.   [37] Tetens (1777a), 533.

only viable candidate the subjective necessity of the judgment, which is something that must be felt before it can be thought.

Tetens' application of this criterion consists of three steps. He begins by noting that even the ordinary understanding distinguishes relations between representations that hold under particular conditions from relations that hold constantly and attributes objective reality only to the latter. This yields the formula, which Tetens attributes to some philosophers, that "**A constant appearance** [*Schein*] **is for us reality.**"[38] Although Tetens acknowledges that there is a moment of truth in this formula he points out that it misses an essential element in our conception of objectivity; viz., its inter-subjective dimension, which is also emphasized by Kant. In claiming that the manner in which I relate my representations in a judgment is objectively valid, I am, in effect, claiming that every other cognizer in similar circumstances and with a similar power of thought should relate them in the same manner.[39] Moreover, Tetens states that, while this is as far as an analysis of objectivity can proceed, it is sufficient to defeat a radical subjectivism, since it amounts to nothing more than the non-problematic claim that all truth is subjective in the sense that it is dependent on a power of thought that is receptive to it.[40] In short, since the same power of thought is shared by all human beings, what is subjectively necessary in the appropriate sense for one cognizer can be generalized to all.

Tetens realizes, however, that this does not suffice to quell the subjectivist's challenge. Thus, despite claiming that this is as far as one can go, he actually takes the analysis a step further by addressing a new worry concerning the possibility of cognizers who are equipped not simply with a different sensory apparatus, but with different powers of thought, which might relate their representations in radically different ways than ours, e.g., God and the angels.[41] Expressed in present-day terms, this is the worry that beings with different conceptual schemes or sets of categories would effectively relativize our common way of thinking, thereby undermining its claim to objective necessity. Tetens proposes what amounts to a two-pronged solution to this problem. He first dilutes its significance by pointing out that this possibility is of no import to us, since we can form no concept of such a power of thought. But apparently feeling that this still does not suffice, since there is nothing inherently absurd in the thought, he proposes a terminological shift; viz., replacing "the words **objective** and **subjective** with the words **unchangeably subjective** and **changeably subjective.**"[42] As Tetens sees it, this is more than a merely verbal ploy, since it clarifies what we actually mean when we pose the question of objectivity; viz., what is objective *for us*, which is just what is unchangeable as long as we remain

[38] Tetens (1777a), 536.   [39] Tetens (1777a), 538.
[40] Tetens (1777a), 538–9.   [41] Tetens (1777a), 539.
[42] Tetens (1777a), 540. Tetens later reiterates the point by claiming that the **objective** is "the **unalterable** and **necessary** in the **subjective**" (see Tetens (1777a), 560).

thinking beings, however much "the corporeal tools of our thinking" may have altered.[43]

Tetens devotes the remainder of his analysis of objectivity to spelling out the implications of this line of thought. Two aspects of his account are worthy of note. The first concerns the laws of thought. Tetens asks whether these laws are themselves merely subjectively necessary laws of *our* understanding or laws of the power of thought as such, i.e., laws for *any* understanding. As a test case, he considers the law of contradiction, for which he offers three possible interpretations. The first, expressed schematically, is that one simply cannot think the thought "A is not A." Tetens characterizes this as an empirical proposition, presumably because this incapacity is viewed as psychological in nature. The second is that the proposition "A is not A," is absolutely unthinkable, meaning that it cannot be thought by *any* understanding. So construed, Tetens notes, the principle is neither an empirical proposition nor a conclusion, but an accepted axiom. The third is that such a contradictory thing, e.g., a four-sided circle, is not a real object. Tetens notes that, so-construed, the law of non-contradiction is a metaphysical principle, but he suggests that it is likewise an accepted axiom.[44]

Although Tetens apparently accepts all three interpretations, he places greater weight on the last two. But his basic point is that the appeal to a different understanding, including God's, which would supposedly be capable of thinking what for us are contradictions, can be rejected on the grounds that the very thought of such an understanding is itself self-contradictory. According to Tetens, this is because in order actually to think of such an understanding (one that thinks both A and not-A), it would be necessary to think that contradictory thought oneself, which is impossible.[45] In short, if we cannot think a thought because it involves a contradiction, then neither can we conceive of an understanding that can think it.[46]

Finally Tetens distinguishes between necessary and contingent truths. This is a special problem for him because his attempt to ground all objectivity in a subjective necessity forces him to distinguish between what is objectively necessary and objectively contingent within the domain of the subjectively necessary. Otherwise expressed, his task is to explain how a judgment can be subjectively necessary and objectively contingent. As examples of the latter, Tetens cites propositions such as "I exist," "I have a body," and "the sun lights the earth." Although we *necessarily believe* such propositions to be true, we do not believe them to be *necessarily true*. His explanation turns on the equation of necessary truths with propositions, the truth of which is independent of the actual existence of the object and depends only on the

---

[43] Tetens (1777a).   [44] Tetens (1777a), 541.   [45] Tetens (1777a), 542.

[46] Tetens raises a similar objection, *mutatis mutandis*, against the account of the physiologically oriented thinker J. C. Lossius, who attempted to explain our inability to think contradictions in terms of the structure of the brain, implying that it might be possible for a being with a different brain. See Tetens (1777a), 543–4.

relation between the subject and predicate concepts.[47] Since this is not the case with the examples cited above, they are contingent truths despite their subjective necessity and apodicticity.

Despite his internalism and recognition of the inter-subjective nature of objectivity, it seems evident that Kant would not have been impressed by Tetens' analysis of objectivity. Simply put, it is the wrong sort of internalism, since it appeals to the wrong sort of necessity and presupposes an erroneous, transcendentally realistic conception of an object. As Kant had learned from Hume, a merely subjective necessity concerning belief cannot be transmuted into an objective necessity regarding knowledge; while if one understands the purported object of cognition in a transcendentally realistic manner, i.e., as existing in its determinate nature independently of the conditions of our cognition of it, we could never understand how these conditions ("subjective conditions of thinking") could have the normative status of objective validity. The latter requires that the object be reconceived as subject to the conditions of our cognition of it (epistemic conditions), which is just Kant's so-called "Copernican revolution."[48]

III

It appears, however, that these fundamental disagreements did not prevent Kant from being influenced by Tetens' account on important topics in the period immediately prior to the appearance of the *Critique*. I shall here consider two of these: the epistemic function of the imagination and the rejection of rational psychology.[49]

A) *The imagination*: It was argued that the seeds of Kant's recognition of the need for an inclusion of the imagination in his developing transcendental project lay in his efforts, which were already evident in the *Duisburg Nachlass*, to overcome the sharp

---

[47] Tetens (1777a), 565–6. In his account of the general character of contingent judgments, Tetens had earlier provided a somewhat different but presumably equivalent answer to this question in terms of revisability. His claim was that contingent judgments are those that could be revised through experience and reflection, even if the representations related in the judgment (its "matter") remain the same and retain the same level of clarity and distinctness. This would occur, for example, when the judger came to realize that the initial judgment, say that the sun and the moon are of nearly equal size, was based upon misleading factors such as the visual images and associations of ideas, but it presumably would also include any empirical generalization made on the basis of the best available evidence. Conversely, judgments expressing necessary truths are not revisable (Tetens (1777a), 486).

[48] For a similar assessment of Tetens' project expressed in different terms see Beck (1969a), 423–4.

[49] An additional topic on which a direct influence of Tetens has been claimed is inner sense. This view was advanced by T. D. Weldon, who argued (albeit tentatively) that Tetens' view of inner sense served as a model for Kant's, because it provides an explanation of the representational character of inner sense by maintaining that the act of thinking modifies the ideas in the mind and by showing that an awareness and the awareness of that awareness are necessarily successive occurrences, which supposedly accounts for the temporal nature of inner sense. See Weldon (1958), 261–3. Although this is an intriguing suggestion, particularly given the notorious obscurity of Kant's account, I believe that the fact that Kant first articulated his conception of inner sense in the second edition of the *Critique* and therefore some years after his engagement with Tetens' work, makes it somewhat dubious.

duality between sensibility and understanding. The claim was that in these *Reflex-ionen* Kant recognized the need for *some* mediating element or faculty, which would play the role later assigned in the *Critique* to the transcendental schemata, which are themselves characterized as (among other things) "transcendental products of the imagination." What I now wish to consider is the thesis that it was Tetens' account of the imagination that led Kant to recognize its suitability for this role. The basis for this view is a number of oft-noted similarities between Kant's accounts of the imagination in texts such as B12, R 5636 (E67), and ML_1, all of which have been dated with various degrees of reliability as having been composed after the appearance of Tetens' work and reappear with some modifications in the first edition of the *Critique*.

Unlike Kant, at least the Kant of the last years of the "Silent Decade" and the first edition of the *Critique*, Tetens did not regard the imagination as a separate cognitive power.[50] Instead, he treated it in the context of his analysis of the *Vorstellungskraft*. And the situation is complicated by the fact that he distinguished three different cognitive functions falling under this power to which he assigned distinct names, but which Kant subsumed under the imagination in various guises. These functions are: perception (*Perception*), imagination proper (*Einbildungskraft*), and fancy or the formative power (*Dichtkraft*), which Tetens viewed as operating at successive stages or levels of representation.[51]

The most basic of these is perception, which for Tetens is directly related to sensation. Its function consists in the retention of the content of sensation in the form of after-images (*Nachbildungen*), which makes possible subsequently to take the latter as designating an object. The function that Tetens assigns to the imagination proper is to relate distinct after-images to each other on the basis of their past relations by means of the law of the association of ideas. Accordingly, the imagination in this sense is a reproductive power, which corresponds to what Kant called the "reproductive imagination." By contrast, as its name suggests, the function of the *Dichtkraft* is to produce new images by combining after-images in ways that are not determined by past associations. Thus, it is here that spontaneity enters the story for Tetens and to that extent at least corresponds to the productive power of the imagination, which Kant distinguished from the reproductive power in B 12, ML_1, R 5636, and later in the *Critique*.

This suggests an affinity between Tetens' account of these functions of the *Vorstellungskraft* and Kant's three-fold synthesis (apprehension, reproduction, and recognition), which is the centerpiece of the A-Deduction. The correspondence is far from exact, however; for while Kant's apprehension and reproduction correlate fairly closely with Tetens' perception and imagination, Kant's recognition (*Recognition*) cannot be similarly aligned with Tetens' *Dichtkraft*. Rather, as de Vleeschauwer has

---

[50] We shall see that in the B-Deduction Kant no longer regarded the imagination, at least in its transcendental function, as a distinct cognitive power but as a manifestation of the understanding.

[51] Tetens (1777a), 104–7.

pointed out, the counterpart to this in Tetens is *Auskennung*; and though this can also be translated as "recognition," it has a quite different sense than the Kantian notion.[52] Again following de Vleeschauwer, whereas for Kant recognition concerns the identity of what is apprehended and what is reproduced, for Tetens it produces a clear and distinct grasp of the object (recall his "clear feeling" of the I).[53] Accordingly, one might say that whereas recognition for Kant is *in a concept*, for Tetens it is best described as *under* one.

The main issue, however, is the relation between Tetens' *Dichtkraft* and Kant's productive imagination. Since both are claimed to be spontaneous and to produce something new, as contrasted with a merely reproductive imagination, it is evident that there is a certain family resemblance between them; but the question is whether this resemblance is close enough to support the claim that Tetens' conception was taken over by Kant and forms the basis of his view of the function of the productive imagination. And, unlike many such situations, we have a clear statement of Kant that bears directly on the matter. It is found in an important note in the A-Deduction, where Kant writes:

No psychologist has yet thought that the imagination is a necessary ingredient in perception itself. This is so partly because this faculty has been limited to reproduction, and partly because it has been believed that the senses do not merely afford us impressions but also put them together, and produce images of objects, for which without doubt something more than the receptivity of impressions is required, namely a function of the synthesis of them.

(A120, note)

Given Kant's familiarity with Tetens' work, his claim that *no* psychologist had recognized that the imagination is a necessary ingredient in perception is surprising; for though, unlike Kant, Tetens did not regard the imagination as a distinct fundamental faculty, treating it instead as an aspect of the truly fundamental *Vorstellungskraft*, he certainly paved the way for the subjective side of Kant's Deduction by emphasizing its indispensable role in cognition. But while Kant may be charged with ignoring the importance of Tetens' contribution to the subject in this note, the reasons that he provides give at least partial support for his claim of originality. First, Kant is technically correct in not recognizing Tetens as a predecessor in assigning a role in perception to the imagination. As we have seen, Tetens construed the imagination (proper) (*Einbildungskraft*) in a much narrower sense than Kant, distinguishing between it and perception as distinct aspects of his generic *Vorstellungskraft* and identifying the former with the capacity to form after-images (*Nachbildungen*), which corresponds to the reproductive capacity of the imagination for Kant. Second, Tetens was among those who held that the senses do not merely afford us impressions, but also put them together and produce images of objects, which is a task that Kant assigns to the imagination. Third, it cannot be maintained that Tetens

[52] de Vleeschauwer (1992), 86.   [53] Ibid.

assigned such a function to his *Dichtkraft*, which is the analogue of the productive imagination in Kant; for, as de Vleeschauwer points out, "The object of *Dichtkraft* ... is the image which has no perceptual correlate and is in consequence a free creation."[54] Moreover, this is borne out by Tetens' own characterization of the *Dichtkraft*, which he explicitly equates with genius, rather than with anything as prosaic as sense perception.[55]

de Vleeschauwer goes beyond this, however, maintaining that Tetens had "no idea of the specifically Kantian synthetic function attributed to productive imagination, which consists in an operation on the *a priori* spatio-temporal intuitions."[56] In other words, de Vleeschauwer, who considered it a virtual certainty that Tetens was a major influence on Kant, particularly with regard to the imagination, nonetheless denied not only that the former's *Dichtkraft* anticipated the use to which Kant assigned to the productive imagination in perception (empirical synthesis), but also the function that Kant assigned to it with respect to the a priori representations of space and time (pure synthesis).

The latter part of this conclusion has been questioned by Cory Dyck, who, while not claiming that Tetens anticipated Kant with respect to the role of imagination in sense perception, nevertheless maintains that the role he assigns to the *Dichtkraft* in the representation of particular spaces and times provides the model for Kant's own thought on the topic. And what adds to the interest of Dyck's account is that it is based on a portion of the text to which we can be assured that Kant paid close attention, namely, Tetens' discussion of Kant's account of the genesis of the representations of space and time in the *Inaugural Dissertation*. With particular focus on this discussion, which evidently was overlooked by de Vleeschauwer, Dyck claims that,

[I]n spite of important differences in their treatments (for instance Tetens discusses the unification of a manifold of obscure representations rather than of pure intuition), it seems quite likely that Tetens' treatment of the *Dichtkraft* would have served as a model even for Kant's distinctive account in the KrV of the productive imagination and its activity in unifying the pure manifolds of space and time."[57]

Since Dyck's disagreement with de Vleeschauwer is based largely on a particular bit of text in Tetens, its adjudication obviously requires an examination of it. The larger context is the relational nature of thought and Tetens' view that relations can be felt or obscurely represented prior to the conceptual grasp of them. Apparently in support of this larger thesis, Tetens considers Kant's claim in the *Inaugural Dissertation* that the representations of space and time are neither innate nor acquired by abstraction from sensations, but are acquired from the action of the mind in coordinating what is sensed in accordance with permanent laws (2: 406_{15-19}; 400).

---

[54] Ibid., 86. See Carl (1992), 215, note 37.   [55] Tetens (1777a), 107.
[56] de Vleeschauwer (1992), 86.   [57] Dyck (2014b), 24.

Although evidently impressed by what he regarded as Kant's attempt to find a third way between deriving these representations directly from sensation and resorting to the discredited innateness thesis, Tetens amends Kant's proposed alternative, replacing his law-governed action with the effect of that action, which for Tetens meant the product of the operation of the *Dichtkraft*.[58] The process, as he described it, consists of two steps. In the case of space, starting with a set of sensations or feelings of co-existing things, the first step consists in the production by the *Dichtkraft* of the representation of a particular space, e.g., the distance between the Earth and the moon or a figure with a circular shape by uniting them into a whole.[59] The second step is the move from the representation of particular spaces that have been constructed by the unifying activity of the *Dichtkraft* to the formation of the idea of space itself (from the idea of spaces to the idea of space). Viewing the matter in Lockean fashion as a move from particulars idea to a general one, Tetens grounds it in an act of abstraction. As he succinctly puts it with reference to both space and time, "From the ideas of individual spaces and times originate the common concepts [*Gemeinbegriffe*] of space and time; and then the concepts of a **Single total** [*Einem ganzen*] all inclusive **infinite space**, and of an **infinite time**."[60]

On the basis of this account, Dyck claims that the unifying activity that Kant attributed to the *Dichtkraft* closely corresponds to what the "critical" Kant assigned to the productive imagination, and that Tetens was therefore the inspiration for this core feature of Kant's position in the *Critique*. But while the similarities between these two unifying acts are sufficient to indicate the likelihood of an influence, I believe that the differences are great enough to rule out the stronger claim that Kant modeled his account on Tetens'. In fact, to read Kant in this way is to ignore what is most distinctive in his view; viz., his conception of the representations of space and time as pure intuitions. Although Dyck explicitly acknowledges this difference, he does not appear to give it the weight it requires.

That Tetens ignored this aspect of Kant's position is evident from his underlying assumption that the representations of space and time are general ideas of relation (of co-existing and successive things), which is just the Leibnizian view.[61] In fact, this assumption, which Kant had explicitly challenged, not only underlies Tetens' entire analysis, since he sees the problem of explaining how, starting with co-existing and successive sensations or feelings, we arrive at the general ideas of space and time as such, but also his view of what Kant was attempting to show. In other words, Tetens evidently considered Kant to be engaged in something like his own project and offered his introduction of the unifying function of the *Dichtkraft* as a friendly amendment that provides a key step in the process that Kant (in Tetens' view) overlooked. But rather than providing something that Kant overlooked, it turns out that Tetens overlooked what was essential to Kant's account already in the

---

[58] See Tetens (1777a), 359–60.   [59] Tetens (1777a), 359.
[60] Tetens (1777a), 360.   [61] Tetens (1777a), 359.

Inaugural Dissertation; viz., that space and time are not general ideas of relation but pure intuitions, which means that they are both subjective forms of receptivity and singular representations: there is only a single space and a single time of which all particular spaces and times are delimited portions.

More to the present point, this results in a fundamental difference between the functions that Tetens assigns to his *Dichtkraft* and Kant to his productive imagination with respect to the representation of space and time. Although considering the details of this difference would require an examination of Kant's own evolving account of the function of the imagination, which will be a major concern of the chapters dealing with the Transcendental Deduction, I believe that the main point can be sufficiently illustrated for present purposes by noting that the difference concerns the nature of the manifolds that are supposedly unified by these powers and how this unification is understood. Confining ourselves to outer intuition: for Tetens the manifold consists of a number of co-existing visual and tactile sensations and feelings, which through the combinatory action of the *Dichtkraft* are taken as constituting a determinate spatial figure or distance; for Kant the manifold is given through outer sense *as spatial*, apart from any activity of the mind, and the function of synthesis is to make possible its representation as a particular determination of a single, all-embracing space, which requires the productive activity of the imagination because this space is not given as such. In short, for Kant the imaginative synthesis, which in the B-Deduction he will call the "figurative synthesis," or "*synthesis speciosa*," presupposes the pure intuition of space as the form in which the matter of outer sense is perceived and with respect to which the manifold given under this form is determined; and the same applies, *mutatis mutandis*, with respect to time and the manifold of inner sense.

Finally, it follows from this that de Vleeschauwer was correct, at least with respect to the guarded way in which he posed the issue. Tetens could have had "no idea of the specifically Kantian synthetic function attributed to productive imagination, which consists in an operation on the *a priori* spatio-temporal intuitions," because he lacked the requisite concept of an a priori intuition, to which it should be added that he also lacked the a priori concepts that serve as the rules governing the conceptual determination of such intuitions. Accordingly, though it seems highly likely that Tetens' account of the unifying activity of the *Dichtkraft* was an important influence on Kant in the final period of the "Silent Decade," it cannot be said that he modeled his view of the productive function of the imagination on it.

B) *The rejection of rational psychology*: Whereas there appears to be a consensus that Kant's reading of Tetens played a crucial role in his account of the imagination and more generally the subjective side of the Transcendental Deduction, as it is sketched in the *Nachlass* circa 1778–80 and formulated in the first edition of the *Critique*, Tetens' role in Kant's discovery of the Paralogisms and consequent rejection of rational psychology is more controversial. Although there are a number of considerations that appear to support the view that here, too, Tetens exerted significant influence on Kant (to be discussed below), this has been challenged by Carl on two grounds. One of these is chronological. On his view, while a first look at this chronology seems to be at least compatible with this view, since this discovery clearly occurred after the appearance of Tetens' work (1777), a closer examination suggests a more complicated story. For Carl, the key text with regard to this question is the set of lectures referred to as ML_1, which he contends could not have been delivered before the winter semester of 1777–78 or after the winter semester of 1779–80.[62] Carl bases both his dating of these lectures and their import for determining the role of Tetens in Kant's discovery of the Paralogisms on the fact that their account of the cognitive faculties in the section of empirical psychology strongly suggests the influence of Tetens, while the positive view of rational psychology in the section devoted to that topic indicates that he had not yet discovered the Paralogisms. Simply put, Carl's reasoning seems to be that, since Kant's reading of Tetens did influence his account of the cognitive faculties, if it had also led to the discovery of the Paralogisms the section on rational psychology in these lectures would have taken a very different course.

As far as Carl's dating is concerned, the former determines the earliest possible date, since if Tetens did influence Kant's views on the cognitive faculties in these lectures, they obviously could not have been delivered before the appearance of Tetens' book (1777); while the latter determines the latest possible date, since Carl believes that they must have preceded B-12, which we have seen was written on the back of a letter dated January 20, 1780. But the reason why Carl thinks that this constitutes the latest possible date is not that B-12 contains a clear indication of Kant's recognition of the paralogistic nature of the inferences of rational psychology; it is rather that he there distinguishes between the analytic and synthetic unity of apperception, which Carl regards as decisive evidence that Kant had finally abandoned the conception of apperception as the consciousness of a substantial self to which (according to Carl) he had adhered since the *Duisburg Nachlass* and which the discovery of the Paralogisms forced him to abandon.[63]

Carl's second ground for rejecting the thesis that Tetens played a significant role in Kant's discovery of the Paralogisms is more substantive. It concerns the nature of Tetens' project and Kant's own understanding of it. While Carl is willing to acknowledge that in his role as a cognitive scientist Tetens could have influenced Kant's views on the cognitive faculties and the importance of the imagination, he seems to think that the story is somewhat different with regard to purely conceptual issues

[62] See Carl (1989b), 118–19.

[63] Carl (1989b), 175. Since, as noted in Chapter 3, I do not accept Carl's account of Kant's conception of apperception in the *Duisburg Nachlass*, I am not impressed by this line of reasoning. Nevertheless, I agree that the lectures could not have been delivered after the winter semester of 1779–80, since the next possible date would be the winter semester of 1780–81, which would make their delivery virtually coincide with the publication of the *Critique* in May 1781.

such as the paralogistic nature of the inferences of rational psychology, where Tetens' essentially Lockean form of empiricism would seem to have little to contribute to the matter.[64] In fact, rather than being a critic of rational psychology, Tetens was a moderate defender of some of its tenets, as is evident from his critique of Hume's bundle theory of the I, which would seem to cast further doubt on the attempt to credit Tetens with a major influence in this matter.

Nevertheless, Carl's negative assessment of this claim has been challenged by both Patricia Kitcher and Corey Dyck. Kitcher questions the chronological portion of Carl's argument on the grounds that it assumes that if Tetens had in fact influenced Kant's views on both the cognitive faculties and rational psychology, the influence in both domains would have been felt at once, which would preclude him from expressing both his new theory of the cognitive faculties and his long-held views in rational psychology in the same set of lectures. Against this, she notes that this assumes that if Kant were influenced by Tetens in this regard, which she understands as coming to the realization that there is no intuition of a self, it must have had the form of a "Eureka" experience; but it could well have been instead a lengthy process.[65] I believe that her point is well taken and that it is all that need be said about the chronological part of Carl's argument.

Carl's second reason for rejecting the proposition that Tetens influenced Kant's belated rejection of rational psychology calls for a fuller consideration, however, since it concerns Kant's view of that discipline. Both Kitcher and Dyck address this part of Carl's case (the latter in considerable detail) by calling attention to the fact that the rational psychology to which Kant adhered during the "Silent Decade" prior to the discovery of the Paralogisms was itself supposedly based on experience.[66] As Dyck points out, this empirical starting point can be traced back to Wolff and was retained by all proponents of rational psychology in the Wolffian tradition up to and including Kant.[67] In fact, Kant is quite explicit on the matter, stating that, "The concept of the soul in itself is a concept of experience. But in rational psychology we take nothing more from experience than the mere concept of the soul, *that* we have a soul. The rest must be cognized from pure reason" (ML$_1$ 28: 263$_{10-13}$; 276).[68] In other words, though the procedure of rational psychology is based on conceptual analysis

---

[64] Although Carl does say this in so many words, I take this to be the main point of his assessment of Tetens and his relation to Kant. See Carl (1989b), 119–26.

[65] Kitcher (2011), 37.

[66] See Kitcher (2011), 35–8, where she uses this to argue against Carl that Kant could have learned a good deal from Tetens on the subject of rational psychology, particularly the crucial point that we have intuition of the I. Dyck's more recent treatment of the topic, which is indebted to Kitcher's, will be discussed below.

[67] Dyck (2014a), 19–49, 60–9.

[68] It should also be noted that the empirical basis of the claims of rational psychology is retained in the *Critique*. For example, in the A-Paralogisms the minor premise in each of the Paralogisms purports to be empirical; while in the B-version Kant insists that "I think" or "I exist thinking" is an empirical proposition (B420 and B422).

("cognition from pure reason"), the concept that it analyzes (the soul) is itself empirical. And, as both Kitcher and Dyck point out, this is precisely why Tetens' genetic-empirical account of the idea of the I (self or soul) is directly germane to Kant's views on the subject. In support of this thesis, I shall briefly sketch Tetens' account of self-consciousness, which is episodic, being spread over several essays, rather than located in a single place.

The main features of Tetens' account are the inseparability of consciousness of self from the consciousness of an object and the connection of both with feeling. Tetens maintains that a consciousness of oneself is built into the consciousness of an object, since the latter necessarily involves the distinction from oneself, and that this self-consciousness initially assumes the form of a feeling.[69] He further maintains that this consciousness of self, like the corresponding consciousness of an object, has a temporal thickness, which distinguishes it from a momentary awareness. Moreover, though self- consciousness, like all consciousness for Tetens, is in part a feeling, he insists that it is capable of becoming a *clear* feeling through the exercise of the power of thought. As he puts it, "[T]he robust feeling of the self is no longer a mere feeling, but a **clear** feeling, a **sensation**, a **consciousness of our self**. For it [the power of thought] combines itself with the feeling of the distinction between the felt modification and the feeling subject, and of the relation of that modification to the subject in which it is."[70] Accordingly, for Tetens the concept of the self that provides the foundation for the claims of rational psychology is based upon a conceptually clarified feeling rather than an a priori concept.[71] But instead of turning directly to an examination of the claims of rational psychology on the basis of this analysis, Tetens uses it to mount a critique of Hume's analysis of the self in the *Treatise*. In characterizing Hume's position he writes:

Hume, as the author of the famous work on **human nature**, explicated the idea that we have of our I, or our soul, as a collection of a number of particular sensations, which follow one another, but are single as well as separate and scattered, and from the combination of which in the imagination has been made the idea of **One** whole, which is a subject that supports particular sensations as qualities of it. He concluded from this that we can justifiably say no more about the soul than that it is an aggregate of qualities and alterations, which, since they are immediately felt, really exist; but not that it [the soul] is an **Identical Object [Ein Ding]**, a **whole**, or an actual thing. And in this consists what his opponents have charged him with, namely, that he even reasoned away the **existence** of the **soul** and admitted *the reality of only his thoughts and* **alterations**. Certainly, this was the outermost bounds of a reasoned skepticism.[72]

---

[69] See Tetens (1777a), 263. My account of Tetens on self-consciousness is based heavily on that of Wunderlich (2005), 77–81.

[70] Tetens (1777a), 298–9.

[71] Recall, however, that for Tetens the I was one of the fundamental concepts.

[72] Tetens (1777a), 392–3.

Tetens notes further that the critique of Hume's account by Reid and Beattie, who were presumably the opponents to whom he alludes, is "not incorrect but unphilosophical."[73] As his subsequent account indicates, he meant by this not that Hume's account was simply wrongheaded or contrary to reason, as Reid and Beattie had claimed, but rather that it neglected a crucial point. In fact, Tetens expresses a general agreement with Hume's procedure, particularly his refusal to admit anything into his account of the self that is not warranted by the evidence. He criticizes Hume, however, for failing to consider a crucial bit of such evidence.[74] In short, Hume is charged with not being a sufficiently good empiricist regarding the self.[75]

According to Tetens, the fault lies with Hume's atomistic view of sensation, the idea that our sensations are given as discrete, isolated entities. Against this he insists that particular sensations are always given against a background of self-feeling, which is the crucial point that Hume supposedly ignores. Moreover, Tetens claims not only that this background feeling remains the same throughout the alteration of sensations, but also that the concept of an identical self is derived from it in precisely the same manner as the concept of an enduring thing with distinct qualities is derived from outer sensation. And from this he concludes that,

[T]he idea or representation of my **I** is no **bundle** [*Sammlung*] of single representations, which the imagination has made into a whole, just as it unifies the individual representations of soldiers into the representation of a regiment. That unification lies in the **sensation** itself, in nature, not in a self-made combination. Thereby originates a representation of **one** subject with **different** properties, that is to say, the **representation** that arises immediately from the **sensation** must be so **thought**, and be made into an **idea** such that the common human understanding actually makes.[76]

Although it seems safe to assume that Kant would not have been impressed by Tetens' attempt to ground the idea of the self in a feeling and his application of it to Hume, it does not appear to be far-fetched to surmise that Tetens' account made Kant aware of the problematic nature of his own view at the time that the self's representation of itself provides a basis for the construction of a rational psychology. Moreover, when Tetens returns to the topic in the second volume of his essays, he considers some of the possible metaphysical implications of his account, particularly with regard to the materialist view of the self, thereby addressing directly one of the central concerns of rational psychology. Echoing the Leibnizian view, which was also shared by Kant, Tetens argues that the unity required for thought makes it impossible to provide a plausible account of the thinking self in materialist terms, since the latter requires assuming it to consist in a collection of distinct parts. Against this, he claims

---

[73] Tetens (1777a), 393.   [74] Tetens (1777a).

[75] Largely because of this, Manfred Kuehn has questioned the radicality of Tetens' critique, suggesting that it concerned only a matter of detail. See Kuehn (1989), 366–7. This has been challenged, however, by Wunderlich (2005), 79, note 297.

[76] Tetens (1777a), 394.

that "My I is a unity [*ein Eins*] not a heap [*Haufen*] of several things."[77] But, in opposition to the rational psychologists, Tetens refused to conclude from this that the soul is an immaterial substance, citing Locke's thesis that it would not be impossible for God to create matter that can think. Instead, he insists that, though the immaterialist view is far more plausible, the issue is ultimately undecidable.[78]

Once again, it seems evident that Kant would have rejected the Lockean terms in which Tetens posed the issue; but the fact remains that the gap that Tetens posits between the necessary unity of the I and the metaphysical conclusions regarding the nature of the I drawn by rational psychology from this unity lies at the heart of Kant's position in the Paralogisms. Accordingly, though there is certainly much more to the story, I believe that there is a strong case for the thesis that Kant's reading of Tetens played a significant role in the reasoning that led him from an adherence to a dogmatic rational psychology based on an analysis of the concept of the I or self to the Paralogisms in the first edition of the *Critique*. Moreover, the plausibility of this claim is increased if one factors in the frequently neglected fact that for both the Wolffian rational psychologists and Kant the concept of the I from which the propositions of that branch of metaphysics are supposedly derived is assumed to be empirical. And seen in this light, the lesson that Kant learned from Tetens' unsuccessful attempt to answer Hume's critique of the notion of an enduring I on empirical grounds is that experience cannot provide the basis for a concept of the I that is suitable for the aims of rational psychology, not to mention cognition as such. While this might seem to be obvious, it becomes less so if we keep in mind Kant's own commitment to the empirical foundations of rational psychology.

---

[77] Tetens (1777b), 178.   [78] Tetens (1777b), 180.

4

Setting the Stage

Our first task is to locate the Transcendental Deduction in the complex architecture of the *Critique*. As its title indicates, Kant envisaged the work as a whole as containing a critical examination of the faculty of pure reason with respect to its capacity for a priori cognition (Axii).[1] Co-opting the term "transcendental" to signify cognition "that is occupied not so much with objects but rather with our *a priori* concepts of objects in general" (A11–12), Kant also characterized the *Critique* as an essay in transcendental philosophy (A13–14/B27–8).[2] Its most fundamental division is between a Doctrine of Elements and a Doctrine of Method (A15/B29). By "elements" Kant understood the cognitive powers that provide the bases for such cognition; viz., sensibility and understanding. Accordingly, the Doctrine of Elements is divided into a Transcendental Aesthetic and a Transcendental Logic. The former deals with the a priori contribution of sensibility and the latter of the understanding. This division is the legacy of the "great light" and is the organizing principle of Kant's theoretical philosophy from the *Inaugural Dissertation* on.

Kant's Transcendental Logic is both modeled on and contrasted with general logic.[3] By the latter Kant understood an analysis of the "mere form of thinking," which abstracts from "all the contents of the cognition of the understanding and of

---

[1] Kant uses "reason" (*Vernunft*) in both a broad sense in which it encompasses the capacity for a priori cognition through concepts (in contrast to mathematics, which attains such cognition through the construction of concepts), and a narrow sense in which it is the faculty of inferences. Accordingly, a critique of pure reason is concerned with reason in the broad sense, which includes the narrow sense within it. Kant's use of the term "pure" is also ambiguous. Sometimes he simply equates it with "*a priori*"; whereas at others times he distinguishes between the a priori and the *pure* a priori, with the latter indicating that the cognition does not contain any empirical element (see B3). In the passage cited above "absolutely pure" seems to be equivalent to what Kant later referred to as "pure *a priori*." The situation is complicated, however, by the fact that Kant also distinguishes between the comparatively and the absolutely or completely a priori with the mark of the latter being necessity and strict universality (see A2/B3).

[2] Rather than simply equating the *Critique* with transcendental philosophy, Kant characterizes it as the *idea* of such a philosophy on the grounds that it lacks the completeness of analysis requisite for the latter (A13–14/B27–8). Kant's endeavor to define what he understands by "critique" and its relation to transcendental philosophy as an "organon," a "system," and a "canon of pure reason," are, however, by no means clear. For a discussion of the textual difficulties, see Kemp Smith (1962), 71–3.

[3] As I have done with "Transcendental Deduction," I shall capitalize "Transcendental Logic" when referring to the portion of the *Critique* bearing that title and small letters when referring to the project of a transcendental logic.

the difference in its objects" (A54/B78). By contrast, transcendental logic assumes the distinction between pure and empirical intuition established in the Transcendental Aesthetic and draws a parallel distinction between pure and empirical thinking of objects. Since transcendental logic contains the rules for the pure, i.e., non-empirical or a priori thinking of objects, Kant claims that it does not abstract from *all* content of cognition (A76–7/B102). But since by the "form of thinking" Kant means discursive thinking, i.e., judging, general logic is broader than "formal logic" in the modern sense.[4]

Transcendental Logic is divided into an Analytic and a Dialectic. Kant characterizes the former as a "logic of truth" because it determines the conditions under which an object can alone be thought (A62/B87). The latter provides an analysis and critique of the dialectical illusion that is built into the very nature of human reason.[5] The Transcendental Analytic is concerned with the elements of a priori cognition stemming from the understanding and is divided into an Analytic of Concepts and an Analytic of Principles. The Transcendental Deduction constitutes the second of two parts of the Analytic of Concepts. The first part, which Kant named "On the Clue to the Discovery of all Pure Concepts of the Understanding" (A70/B95) (henceforth to be referred to as "the Clue") is, as the heading indicates, concerned with providing a complete inventory of the concepts that are indigenous to the understanding. The Transcendental Deduction is assigned the dual task of establishing the objective validity of these concepts and determining the limits of their applicability.

In the first edition, the Transcendental Deduction is divided into three sections: an introductory discussion that is intended to explain to the reader the nature and purpose of a transcendental deduction in general and of the pure concepts of the understanding in particular, together with a sketch of the method of its execution; a preliminary discussion of the central issues and concepts involved in the deduction, which Kant says is intended to prepare rather than instruct the reader (A99); and a systematic statement of the argument, which Kant presents in two forms. Of these, only the first section is retained, albeit with some modifications, in the second edition of the *Critique*. The present chapter, which is the first of three devoted to the A-Deduction, is itself divided into two parts: the first dealing with "the Clue" and the second with the first section of the Deduction.

---

[4] The formal aspect of Kant's logic is, however, much narrower than modern logic, consisting essentially of syllogistics and immediate inferences such as *modus ponens* and *modus tollens*.

[5] Kant's initial characterization of the Transcendental Dialectic in his discussion of the division of Transcendental Logic is misleading, since he there describes the illusion as resulting from the attempt to judge synthetically about objects by the pure understanding alone (A62–3/B87–8). As becomes clear from his actual discussion of transcendental illusion in the Dialectic, it is to be sharply distinguished from the error of attempting to judge about objects in general by the understanding alone. The latter involves a transcendental use of the understanding and the former a transcendent use of reason (see A295–6/B351–2). For a discussion of this issue, see Grier (2001), 117–30 and Allison (2004), 322–2.

I

We have seen that the determination of a set of pure concepts of the understanding or categories is an issue with which Kant had been concerned at least since 1770, when, under the influence of Leibniz's *New Essays*, he specified in the *Dissertation* a number of concepts stemming from the nature of the intellect, albeit without any apparent attempt to be systematic or complete.[6] We also saw that, in his 1772 letter to Herz, Kant acknowledged the importance of providing a systematic account of these concepts for his metaphysical project and suggested that he was making progress with this endeavor and hoped to complete the portion dealing with the sources, method, and bounds of metaphysics within about three months. But we further saw that in the *Duisburg Nachlass* Kant seems to have dropped, or at least suspended, his interest in a systematic list of pure concepts or categories and focused instead on the function of what later became the relational categories in the determination of an objective temporal order.

Considered in this light, "the Clue" may be seen as a much-delayed redemption of the promissory note that Kant had issued to Herz some nine years earlier. Kant describes his task in two ways. According to his official account, it is to discover all the pure concepts of the understanding, which is a matter of taking an inventory, thereby assuring the completeness of the list and the exclusion of any inappropriate members, e.g., those pertaining to sensibility rather than to the pure understanding (A65–7/B90–2). But in the passage in the B-Deduction, where Kant characterizes this project as the "Metaphysical Deduction," he describes it as establishing "the *a priori* origin of the categories...through their complete agreement with the universal logical functions of thinking" (B159).

Although establishing the a priori origin of the categories might seem to differ from ensuring the completeness of their list, it is precisely by locating their origin in the understanding that their completeness is ensured through their correlation with the logical functions of judgment, the completeness of which is supposedly ensured within general logic.[7] Presumably, the latter formulation reflects Kant's intent to suggest a parallel between the Metaphysical and the Transcendental Deductions and the Metaphysical and Transcendental Expositions of the concepts of space and time in the Transcendental Aesthetic, which were likewise added in the second edition.[8]

I take the main point, however, to be that, inasmuch as the categories are defined (nominally) as "concepts of an object as such [*überhaupt*]" (B128), it would make no sense to claim to have identified one or more of such concepts, unless one could

---

[6] To reiterate, as examples of such concepts, Kant cites "possibility, existence, necessity, substance cause, *etc.* together with their opposites or correlates" (ID 2: 395$_{34–6}$; 388).

[7] I am grateful to Till Hoeppner for pointing out to me the essential equivalence of Kant's two formulations of his task in his comments on an earlier version of this chapter. For my analysis of the completeness of the logical functions see Allison (2004), 135–46.

[8] On this point see Horstmann (1981).

derive them all from the nature of the understanding, in which case one would have a complete inventory. As Kant puts it, "They [these concepts] spring pure and unmixed from the understanding, as absolute unity, and must therefore be connected among themselves in accordance with a concept or idea" (A67/B92), which for Kant is that they are concepts of an object as such. And since judgment for Kant is the act through which representations are related to an object, it is natural to seek them in the forms of judgment, which are the distinct ways in which this relation can be thought by a discursive understanding.

"The Clue" is divided into three sections. The first contains a brief sketch of the conception of judgment underlying the argument of the Transcendental Analytic as a whole (A67–9/B92–4). In the second section, Kant presents his table of "the logical functions of the understanding in judgments," which purports to contain an exhaustive inventory of the forms of judgment distinguished in general logic (A70–6/B92–101). The table is composed of twelve "moments" or functions falling under four "titles": quantity, quality, relation, and modality, which Kant supplements by an explanation of some of the seemingly problematic features of this table and some reflections on the peculiarity of the functions of modality. In the third section, Kant attempts to establish a one-to-one correspondence between these logical functions and the pure concepts or categories, thereby putting the determination of the latter on a systematic footing that was lacking in Aristotle and subsequent treatments of the topic (A76–83/B102–16). It is here that our main interest lies.

A) *The nature of judgment*: As one might expect, underlying Kant's account of judgment is the discursivity thesis as it was articulated in the conception of judgment discussed in Chapter 3 in connection with R 4634, the *Duisburg Nachlass*, and other texts from the "Silent Decade." Once again, the fundamental point is the identification of thinking with judging, which follows from the combination of the view of thinking as a conceptual activity and the fact that the only use that the understanding can make of concepts is to judge by means of them (A68/B93). In light of this, Kant contends that "[w]e can . . . trace all actions of the understanding back to judgments, so that the **understanding** in general can be represented as a **faculty for judging** [*Vermögen zu urteilen*]" (A69/B94), from which he concludes that "The functions of the understanding can therefore all be found together if one can exhaustively exhibit the functions of unity in judgments" (A69/B94).

Although Kant's account rests on his conception of judgment, the fact that the view of judgment sketched in this passage is essentially the same as the one contained in R 4634 and the *Duisburg Nachlass* renders a detailed treatment of it here redundant. The present account is based on the characterization of judgment as the "mediate cognition of an object," which Kant glosses as "a representation of a representation of it" (A68/B93). The basic idea is that discursive cognition, which occurs in and through acts of judgment, yields a representation of an object only under a certain description (concept), which, as such, is also applicable to other objects, and which in order to link up with a determinate object (or set thereof) must ultimately be related to a representation that is in immediate relation to an object, i.e., an intuition. Thus, in the judgment "All bodies are divisible," "divisibility," which serves as the logical predicate and occupies the place of b in Kant's notation, is the broader concept (in addition to bodies, it is also applicable to one- and two-dimensional figures, numbers, and perhaps other things as well); whereas "body" as subject concept, occupies the logical place of a and, as such, provides the description under which the objects (the set of xs of which the concepts are predicated in the judgment) are initially taken. Accordingly, the relation of "divisibility" to bodies is mediated by its relation to "body," while the relation of the latter to bodies is mediated by its relation to the sensible intuition (x) that is brought under the concept "body."

B) *The logical forms and functions of judgment*: Given this generic account of judgment, one would expect that the main concern of the second section of "the Clue" is to connect judgment with what Kant refers to as the "functions of the understanding," or, as he also terms them, the "functions of unity in judgments" (A69/B94). But apart from Kant's opening statement that, "If we abstract from all content of a judgment in general, and attend only to the mere form of the understanding in it, we find that the function of thinking in that can be brought under four titles, each of which contains under itself three moments" (A70/B95), for which he offers no explanation, all that we find in the second section is the forementioned table and a terse supplemental account of certain of the moments. Accordingly, if we are to reconstruct Kant's thinking on the matter, it is necessary to return to aspects of the account of judgment in the first section that were initially passed over.

The most important of these is Kant's use of the term "function." We have already seen that Kant made heavy use of it in the *Duisburg Nachlass*, where "functions of the understanding" was one of the expressions used to characterize the relational categories. In the present context, Kant claims that, whereas intuitions, as sensible, "rest on affections," by which he means that they result from being affected by objects, concepts, as products of the spontaneity of the understanding, rest on functions. And Kant stipulates that by a function he understands "the unity of the action of ordering different representations under a common one" (A68/B93). The "action" to which Kant refers is judgment and its "unity" is the unifying principle or rule that determines the manner in which the constituent representations are related to an object by being combined with each other in a judgment.

The situation is complicated, however, by the fact that Kant here uses the term "function" in two senses.[9] One is the biological or physiological sense in which it refers to the characteristic activity of an organ, e.g., the function of the heart is to

---

[9] On Kant's use of the term "function" in the *Critique*, see Schulthess (1981), 219–33; Wolff (1995), 65f, and Longuenesse (1998b), 140–3.

pump blood. Kant co-opts this sense of the term and applies it to the understanding, when he claims that its function is to judge, i.e., to combine representations in such a way as to relate them to an object. The second is the mathematically inspired sense in which a function is a unifying act through which the relation to an object is attained. This is clearly the main sense in which Kant uses the term and it is the sense that is expressed in the above stipulative definition. So construed, the functions of the understanding are the ways in which representations are unified in a judgment such that they relate to an object. Accordingly, in order to uncover these functions, it is necessary to determine their connection with the forms of judgment specified in the table of judgment forms.

Whereas in the *Duisburg Nachlass* Kant contrasted form and function, relating the former to sensibility and the latter to the understanding, he now introduces this distinction within the understanding itself, regarded as the "faculty for judging." Moreover, he does so in such a way that, rather than being sharply distinguished, forms and functions of the understanding are intimately related, constituting, as it were, two sides of the same coin, which accounts for the fact that Kant sometimes appears to treat them as interchangeable.[10] Nevertheless, for analytic purposes it is essential to distinguish them; and, following the suggestion of Longuenesse, I believe that this can best be done by considering them respectively as product and process.[11] In other words, the logical forms of judgment, which characterize the various ways in which judgment types are classified in general logic, are the products of the unification of representations in accordance with the various "functions of unity in judgment."

Consider again Kant's own example: "All bodies are divisible." Setting aside the question of modality, which raises separate considerations that cannot be dealt with here, this judgment contains a universally quantified subject, an affirmatively qualified copula, and a relation between the predicate and the subject.[12] And, again leaving aside the question of modality, this indicates that, given a determinate quantity, quality, and relation, we have a well-formed judgment; while lacking any one of these we do not.[13] Accordingly, each of these characteristic properties, as well as the three "moments" falling under each of them, are "forms" or structural features of judgment in the sense of being individually necessary and jointly sufficient formal conditions of a judgment as such, whatever its particular content may be.

Kant also maintains that a judgment acquires each of these forms as the result of its constituent concepts being unified in a certain way, with these ways or forms of unification being the logical functions of judgment. Although I believe it possible to demonstrate this with regard to each of the functions, for present purposes it should suffice to illustrate the point through brief examinations of the categorical and

---

[10] This is noted by Longuenesse (1998b), 143.   [11] Ibid., 143.
[12] For my analysis of modality as a judgment form see Allison (2001), 76–7 and (2004), 138–9.
[13] My initial discussion of this point in Allison (2001) was based on that of Brandt (1995).

hypothetical forms, which are arguably the two most important, and their corresponding functions.[14]

1) *The categorical judgment*: Since a judgment of this form predicates properties of a subject, it presupposes the concept of the relation between a subject and its properties. Accordingly, the subject of a categorical judgment (the object judged about) is necessarily conceived *within the judgment* as a bearer of properties and that which is predicated of it is likewise necessarily conceived as its property. Returning to Kant's example, "All bodies are divisible," the quantified subject (all bodies) is conceived as the bearer of a property (divisibility), which requires the conceptual capacity to distinguish between and relate a subject and its properties. Without the concept of the relation of properties to a subject one could not form a categorical judgment, and since the other forms of judgment (hypothetical and disjunctive) are composed of categorical judgments, one could not judge at all.

This does not mean, however, that in order to make judgments of the categorical form we must apply the pure concept or category of substance to the subject. In his table of categories Kant equates the category with the relation of inherence and subsistence (or substance and accident) (A80/B106) and in the B-Deduction he describes it more perspicaciously as the concept of something that can be conceived only as subject, and never as predicate of anything else (B129).[15] As such, "substance" is the concept of something that not only *can* serve as the subject and bearer of properties in a particular judgment, but that *must always* be conceived in that manner within any judgment, i.e., is necessarily taken substantively. And it is obvious that *this concept* is not required to form categorical judgments; since we can make perfectly good categorical judgments about properties and abstract objects, which lay no claim to being substances. Jonathan Bennett's "His amiability cloys" is an oft-cited case in point.[16] Accordingly, in order to understand Kant's view it is necessary to distinguish between the logical and ontological senses of this relational concept. Whereas the former applies to whatever serves as the subject or bearer of properties in a categorical judgment, the latter designates whatever must necessarily be assigned this place in every judgment in which it appears.[17]

---

[14] What follows is a condensed restatement of the account of the connection between these judgment forms and their corresponding function, which I initially offered in Allison (2004), 148–51. I also there discussed the connection between the disjunctive form and the pure concept of community; but this raises difficulties that need not be considered here.

[15] Both of these definitions are merely nominal, however, since Kant denies the possibility of a real definition of the pure concepts (apart from their schemata). On this point, see A240–1/B300–1.

[16] Bennett (1966), 183. While acknowledging that Kant was aware of this point, Bennett nevertheless criticizes him for "disrupting the simple relationship which is supposed to hold between the categories and the table of judgments." Although Kant affirms an isomorphism between the two tables, we shall see below that their relationship is not simple, since it turns on the isomorphism between general and transcendental logic.

[17] To understand Kant on this point it is necessary to keep in mind that he regarded action or force, which are predicables of cause (A82/B109), as empirical criteria of substance (A204–5/B249–50). This issue will be revisited in Chapter 7.

2) *The hypothetical judgment*: Since this judgment form connects two propositions rather than two concepts in a single proposition, its analysis requires a somewhat different treatment. Nevertheless it yields a similar conclusion; viz., the need to distinguish between the logical function embedded in the hypothetical judgment form and the pure concept or category of the relation of cause and effect. To begin with, this form should not be construed in truth-functional terms as the material conditional.[18] Rather, the hypothetical judgment, as Kant understands it, asserts a connection between two propositions, such that the assumption of the truth of one justifies the inference to the other. Accordingly, each of the two propositions, taken individually, is merely problematic and the judgment asserts only the dependence relation between them. As Kant puts it in connection with his own example of a hypothetical judgment ("If there is perfect justice, then obstinate evil will be punished"), "[i]t is only the implication [*Konsequenz*] that is thought by means of this judgment" (A73/B98).

It follows from this that a hypothetical judgment presupposes an "ordering rule" for the sequence of propositions connected in the judgment. And here again the hypothetical differs from the categorical function; for whereas the latter in its merely logical employment is indifferent to which of the terms is placed in the subject and which in the predicate position (B128–9), for the former everything depends on which of the constituent propositions is considered as ground and which as consequent. Nevertheless, just as the categorical function in its logical employment does not appeal to the category of substance, so the hypothetical function does not appeal to the category of causality. Indeed, though Kant does not call attention to it, this is nicely illustrated by his above-cited example of a hypothetical judgment; since the dependence of the punishment of obstinate evil on perfect justice is not a causal one.[19]

C) *From the logical functions to the categories or the metaphysical deduction (proper)*:[20] Whereas the second section of "the Clue" dealt with the logical functions of judgment, the third is concerned with the relation between these functions and the

---

[18] This is pointed out by Melnick (1973), 39.

[19] I take it that this is because the reason why we assume that the obstinately wicked would be punished in a world in which there is perfect justice is not that we presuppose that the latter contains some causal mechanism to bring about this result, but simply that such punishment constitutes part of the concept of a world in which there is perfect justice (at least it constitutes part of Kant's concept of such a world). In short, the hypothetical judgment is analytic, with the concept of such a world providing a logical but not a real ground of the punishment of the obstinately wicked.

[20] I have added the qualifier "proper" because Kant does not specify precisely where he locates the Metaphysical Deduction to which he refers at B159. The two viable candidates are "the Clue" chapter as a whole and its third section (§10 in B). My own view is that, in the strict or proper sense, it is located in the latter; but inasmuch as the account in this section rests upon the previous two sections, if taken in a broad sense, it can be assigned to the chapter as a whole. The question of the locus of the Metaphysical Deduction is taken up by Horstmann (1981), esp. 234, who situates it in §10, albeit without considering the possibility of locating it in the chapter as a whole.

categories. As we shall see, the underlying idea is the isomorphism between the logical functions of judgment specified in the table of judgment forms and the categories listed in the table of categories. More precisely, it is that the same concepts, which when considered in relation to the table of judgment forms in general logic, serve as logical functions of judgment, i.e., forms of conceptualization through which judgments of the corresponding form are produced, also function as categories in connection with the unification of the manifold of sensible intuition. Kant's account is contained in the first seven paragraphs of the third section of "the Clue" (A76–80/ B102–5). Of these, the first five contain an anticipatory sketch (to be further developed in the Transcendental Deduction) of the real use of the understanding in connection with the manifold of sensibility; while the last two conclude from this that it is the same understanding, through the same activity (unification or synthesis), that is operative in both its logical and its real uses. In what follows, I shall comment upon each paragraph in turn, concluding with some general reflections on the import of the argument as a whole.

Paragraph 1 (A76–7/B102): Kant begins by contrasting general and transcendental logic. The fundamental difference is that, whereas general logic abstracts from all the content of cognition, assuming that its representations will be somehow given to it from elsewhere, thereby enabling it to transform these into concepts by means of analysis, transcendental logic has "a manifold of sensibility that lies before it *a priori*." In other words, unlike general logic, transcendental logic has a particular content that pertains to it. The understanding is not the source of this content, however, since it is provided by sensibility in virtue of its a priori forms (space and time), which contain an a priori or pure, yet sensible manifold.

An additional significant feature of this paragraph is the introduction of the contrast between analysis and synthesis, which underlies Kant's whole account and due to the multitude of ways in which Kant construes these terms in various contexts, is a major source of confusion and misunderstanding. For example, this is sometimes taken as indicating that Kant is contrasting the activity of the understanding in forming analytic judgments, which is supposedly the concern of general logic, with its activity in forming synthetic judgments a priori, which is thought to be the business of transcendental logic.[21] Such a reading is, however, not warranted by the text. First, since Kant here explicitly links analysis with concept formation, it is clear that the analysis is not of already-determined concepts, as it is in analytic judgments, but of the data on the basis of which concepts are formed by the understanding in its logical use.[22] Second, synthesis, as Kant here understands it, has nothing specifically to do with synthetic judgments, since it is introduced as a condition of *all* cognition, which includes analytic judgments. Rather, Kant links it with the spontaneity of thought and defines it stipulatively as the action through

---

[21] See, for example, Kemp Smith (1962), esp. 176–80, and Wolff (1963), 68–77.
[22] Longuenesse (1998b), 150.

which this manifold is "gone through, taken up, and combined in a certain way in order for a cognition to be made of it."[23] And, finally, general logic for Kant is not concerned specifically with analytic judgments, but with judgment as such, which encompasses both forms.

Paragraph 2 (A77–8/B103): Building on the conception of synthesis that was introduced at the end of the first paragraph, Kant devotes the second paragraph to its further articulation. He begins with a definition of the term, which is likewise stipulative, since it specifies how he understands the term in its "most extended sense" (*der allgemeinsten Bedeutung*), namely, as "the action of putting different representations together with each other and comprehending their manifoldness in one cognition." This suggests that Kant understands synthesis as not only involving the combing or putting together of different representations, but as grasping the combined representations as in some sense constituting a unity. And, referring to one species of this generic conception, Kant states that "[s]uch a synthesis is **pure** if the manifold is not given empirically but *a priori* (as is that of space and time)." Although he does not refer explicitly to the other species of synthesis; viz., the empirical variety, he does suggest in passing that the distinction turns on how the manifold to be synthesized is given. In other words, if the manifold is given a priori, as is the manifold of space and time, the synthesis is pure; if it is given empirically, which applies to the sensible content given in space and time, it is empirical.

A second important topic taken up in this paragraph is the relation between synthesis, so construed, and analysis. Once again, Kant understands by "analysis" the act of concept of formation, which he elsewhere describes as consisting in the "logical acts" of comparison, reflection, and abstraction (JL 9: 94–5; 592). But he adds significantly to the little that was said about it in the first paragraph by remarking that "Prior to all analysis of our representations these must be given, and no concepts can arise analytically as far as **the content is concerned**." Since analysis is assigned the task of forming concepts, but is denied the capacity to form the content of concepts, this being provided by sensibility, it must be responsible for their form. And since universality is the form of all concepts for Kant, it follows that analysis must be the source of the universality that pertains to every concept, qua concept, regardless of its content. Moreover, analysis, so conceived, presupposes synthesis, since it is synthesis that actually "collects the elements for cognitions and unifies them into a certain content," which can then be clarified through analysis. Accordingly, Kant contends

---

[23] Since Kant explicitly connects synthesis with "this manifold" (*dieses Mannigfaltige*), he is presumably referring to the pure manifold, which he had previously attributed to space and time as a priori forms of sensibility. But since it is clear from what follows that this involves what Kant terms a "pure synthesis" and that he does not maintain that all synthesis is pure, i.e., a priori, it is evident that this restriction cannot be regarded as his considered view. Indeed, when we consider Kant's account of the three-fold synthesis in the A-Deduction to which this stipulative definition evidently alludes, it will become clear that he views it as having both an a priori or pure and an empirical dimension.

that synthesis is "the first thing to which we have to attend if we wish to judge about the first origin of our cognition."

Paragraph 3 (A78/B103): In this brief paragraph, Kant contrasts synthesis as such (*überhaupt*) with bringing this synthesis to concepts. These are depicted as distinct acts, each of which plays an indispensable role in cognition. As far as the depiction of synthesis is concerned, three aspects call for comment. The first is the connection between synthesis "in the most extended sense," which was the concern of the preceding paragraph, and synthesis "as such," which is Kant's current topic. Neither the Kemp Smith nor the Guyer-Wood translations help to clarify matters with their rendering of the two characterizations as "synthesis in the most general sense" and synthesis "in general," since it is unclear what this contrast amounts to.[24] The mystery disappears, however, if we keep in mind that in the preceding paragraph Kant distinguishes between two aspects of synthesis "in the most extended sense:" the act of combining representations and the logically subsequent act of grasping what is combined in one cognition. Presumably, then, it is this distinction to which Kant refers in the third paragraph in terms of the distinction between synthesis and bringing the synthesis to concepts. In other words, by "synthesis as such" or, perhaps better, "synthesis qua synthesis," Kant understands the first aspect of "synthesis in the most extended sense;" whereas the second aspect is now more precisely characterized as "bringing this synthesis to concepts."[25]

The most important feature of this paragraph is its assignment of "synthesis as such" to the imagination rather than to the understanding. As Kant famously puts it, synthesis, so construed, is "the mere effect of the imagination, a blind though indispensable function of the soul, without which we would have no cognition at all, but of which we are seldom even conscious." Since Kant suggests that this will subsequently be shown to be the case, it is clear that he is here issuing a promissory note rather than making a claim for which the ground has been prepared. But, in light of the preceding chapter, we can see that he is also articulating the view that he had sketched in B 12 and other texts from the last period of the "Silent Decade," which point to the influence of Tetens. And by characterizing the imagination as not only cognitively indispensable but as "blind," Kant is presumably linking it to sensibility, since he had previously claimed that intuitions (which are always sensible for Kant) without concepts are likewise blind (A51/B75).

Nevertheless, this characterization of the imagination is puzzling, since it is not immediately apparent how it is to be reconciled with Kant's initial characterization of synthesis in terms of the spontaneity of thought (A77/B102). But a frequently cited

---

[24] Here the Pluhar translation is much superior, rendering the contrast as between "synthesis in the most general sense of the term" and "synthesis as such." See Pluhar (1996), 130.

[25] We shall see that the same ambiguity is present in Kant's account of the three-fold synthesis in the A-Deduction, where the third aspect is characterized as "the synthesis of recognition in the concept" (A103–10).

emendation of the text that Kant made in his own copy of the first edition of the *Critique*, yet strangely failed to include among the many related changes made in the second edition, indicates that he was at least aware of the problem. It consists in replacing "function of the soul" with "function of the understanding" (E 24 23: 45), which suggests that what Kant intended to say, at least upon further reflection, was that rather than being considered a distinct faculty, as it was in B 12 and as we shall see he regarded it in the A-Deduction, the imagination is really a function of the understanding. But while this may enable us to see how the imaginative synthesis could be an expression of the spontaneity of thought and perhaps be "pure," it also makes its alleged blindness and the fact that we are seldom conscious of it even more mysterious. How could a function of the *understanding* for Kant be blind and, at least for the most part, unconscious?

A fuller discussion of this question must await an analysis of the B-Deduction, where Kant rethinks the relation between the understanding and the imagination in light of the point expressed in the above-cited emendation. Our immediate concern is rather with the question of what Kant had intended in 1781 in the unemended text of the first edition. And here I take the main point to lie in the previously noted contrast between "synthesis as such" and "bringing this synthesis to concepts," which are the two aspects of "synthesis in the most extended sense." It is only the first aspect that is attributed to the imagination; the second being an action of the understanding. Accordingly, only this aspect of synthesis might be characterized as blind, since this obviously could not apply to the act of bringing this synthesis to concepts, which is the proper work of the understanding. Moreover, I take it that Kant's reference to blindness is intended to underscore the contrast between the two aspects of "synthesis in the most extended sense;" the idea being that, though an indispensable precondition of cognition, "synthesis as such" does not of itself yield "cognition properly so-called" because the latter is conceptual in nature.

Paragraph 4 (A78/B104): Kant here returns to the notion of a pure synthesis, which was initially introduced in the second paragraph under the description of a synthesis that operates upon a manifold that is given a priori rather than empirically. Here, however, he approaches it from the other side, stipulating that by a "**pure synthesis generally represented**" he understands one that "yields the pure concept of the understanding." And he further characterizes this synthesis as one "which rests on a ground of synthetic unity *a priori*." This suggests that by the pure concept of the understanding, which presumably governs a pure synthesis, Kant understands a concept that provides an a priori ground of the unity of such a synthesis. In other words, a pure synthesis requires both a pure manifold to unify and a pure concept to do the unifying. Inasmuch as Kant refers to "the pure concept of the understanding" in the singular rather than to the pure concepts of the understanding or categories, he is best read as introducing the concept of a pure concept by characterizing its function rather than as referring obliquely to the specific categories.

Kant introduces an element of possible confusion, however, by attempting to illustrate this function through a simple mathematical example (the act of counting), rather than one involving a pure concept of the understanding or category. He notes that the presence of a synthesis in accordance with concepts is especially noticeable (not that it is only required) when counting larger numbers and the concept to which he appeals is that of the decad, which serves as a "common ground of unity," thereby rendering the synthesis of the manifold (the units counted) necessary. In other words, the concept of the decad serves as a rule or organizing principle governing the counting of units and it presumably renders the synthesis necessary by determining the location of each unit counted. As such, it can be taken as a functional analogue rather than a token of a pure concept. It differs from the latter in that there are alternative ways in which the synthesis of the units (counting) can be structured leading to an equivalent result, e.g., according to the binary system, which is presumably not the case with the categories.

Paragraph 5 (A78–9/B104): This is the last of the introductory paragraphs and it recapitulates the claims of the preceding four. After again contrasting general and transcendental logic, the former being concerned with the act of bringing different representations under one concept, and the latter with bringing under concepts not representations but the pure synthesis of representations, Kant cites three a priori factors that are required for the cognition of objects: (1) the manifold of pure intuition; (2) the synthesis of this manifold by the imagination; and (3) the concepts that give unity to this synthesis, which Kant states consist solely in "the representation of this necessary synthetic unity."

Since the concepts to which Kant refers as the third a priori condition of cognition are the pure concepts of the understanding or categories, our immediate concern is to attain clarity regarding the notion of the representation of the necessary synthetic unity of the imaginative synthesis. This can best be done by considering a concrete example: the cognition of an event, for which it will be convenient to return once again to the example frequently cited in Chapter 3: water changing its state from liquid to solid form, when the temperature is lowered to 0 degrees Celsius. This example furnishes us with all three of the conditions that Kant claims to be requisite for empirical cognition. First, we have a succession of states, which presupposes the pure intuition of time with its a priori manifold. Second, we have an imaginative synthesis of these states, which places them in a certain temporal order (liquid at t_1 – solid at t_2). This is the dimension of Kant's account that was missing in the *Duisburg Nachlass*, since at the time he apparently assigned this placing to sensibility alone, not recognizing any role for the imagination. But for present purposes the crucial point is that without being directed by the understanding, the imagination is free to place these states in either of the two possible temporal orders. Third, the understanding determines this order by fixing the sequence of states as necessary, which is what Kant means by a "representation of this necessary synthetic unity." And the representation through which this synthetic unity is rendered necessary is the relation of cause and effect.

Paragraph 6 (A79–80/B104–5): Kant here attempts to link the conclusions arrived at in the preceding five paragraphs with his previous account of the logical functions of judgment. To this end he writes:

> The same function that gives unity to the different representations **in a judgment** also gives unity to the mere synthesis of different representations **in an intuition**, which, expressed generally, is called the pure concept of understanding. The same understanding, therefore, and indeed by means of the very same actions through which it brings the logical form of a judgment into concepts by means of the analytical unity, also brings a transcendental content into its representations by means of the synthetic unity of the manifold of intuition in general, on account of which they are called pure concepts of the understanding that pertain to objects *a priori*; this can never be accomplished by general logic.

The paragraph is composed of two sentences, the second of which might be considered as either an elucidation of or a conclusion from the first.[26] Kant begins by talking about the "same function," by which he apparently means the unification of representations by bringing them under a concept, which is the generic work of the understanding. The claim is that this unifying function produces two results, which are differentiated by what is unified: (1) where the unification is of concepts and consists in bringing them under a further concept it results in a judgment; and (2) where what is unified is the manifold of a sensible intuition the result is the conceptual determination of this manifold through which it is related to an object. In the second sentence, Kant concludes that both unifications must be attributed to the same understanding and brought about through the same activity. These results are more fully described as bringing "the logical form of a judgment into concepts by means of the analytical unity" and introducing a transcendental content into its representations by means of the "synthetic unity of the manifold of intuition in general."[27]

Assuming that by the "logical form of a judgment" Kant means a judgment with a particular logical form and that he regards concepts as analytical unities, the first part of his claim consists in the assertion that by unifying representations under a concept the understanding produces judgments with the logical forms specified in the table of

---

[26] The first alternative was suggested to me by Till Hoeppner in his comments on an earlier version of this chapter. I am not sure, however, what if anything turns on this point.

[27] Kant's use of the expression "intuition in general" or, better, "intuition as such," is noteworthy because it suggests that the transcendental or objectifying function of the understanding is independent of the particular nature of the manifold of intuition; all that is required is that it be sensible. Although this important point does not enter explicitly into the argument of the A-Deduction, it is entailed by Kant's separation of sensibility and understanding and, as we shall see, it plays a central role in the B-Deduction, where it underlies the division of the argument into two distinct parts: one which relates the categories to intuition as such; the other which connects them first with the forms and then the content of human sensibility, i.e., empirical intuition.

logical functions. The interpretation of the second part of Kant's claim turns on the meaning assigned to the expression "transcendental content." Given the fact that the contrast with which Kant is here operating is between the logical and the real use of the understanding, I take it to mean simply relation to an object or objective validity. In other words, to bring a transcendental content into one's representations just is to relate them to an object given in intuition, which is precisely what the understanding in its merely logical function cannot do. And, as Kant had already maintained in the *Duisburg Nachlass*, this is accomplished by producing in these representations a synthetic unity under the direction of a concept understood as a unifying rule, which is essentially what Kant is here claiming as well.

One might still wonder what justifies Kant's seemingly unsupported claim that it is the *same* understanding through the exercise of the *same* functions that achieves these disparate results.[28] The simple answer is that it must be the same understanding because the results are achieved through the same activity; viz., the production of a synthetic unity in a manifold. But this seems only to push the question back one step; for one might then ask whether, given the disparate nature of the results, Kant has in fact shown that the unifying activities are really the same rather than being merely similar or analogous, which would not be sufficient to warrant the claim of a one-to-one correspondence between the logical forms of judgment and the categories. And since the Metaphysical Deduction stands or falls with the demonstration of this claim, it is far from clear that Kant has succeeded. On the contrary, it might seem that he has simply helped himself to the desired result, thereby begging the main question at issue.

Although Kant may be faulted for the dogmatic way in which he presents his conclusion, suggesting that the demonstration of the sameness of the understanding and its activity in the two domains is a fait accompli, which invites the objection suggested above, his actual view is more nuanced. What this objection neglects is the anticipatory, conditional nature of his claim, which we have seen Kant himself notes. Specifically, what is anticipated is that the understanding actually has a real use or transcendental function, which can only be anticipated at this point, since establishing it is the task of the Transcendental Deduction. Moreover, so understood, the claim seems far more plausible, since Kant can point out that the logical use of the understanding has been already established in his account of judgment in the first part of "the Clue" and the question is only whether *this* understanding and *its* unifying activity *also* functions at the transcendental level in connection with the manifold of intuition in general. In other words, by formulating the issue in this way it becomes possible to assume the sameness condition rather than having to argue for it; though at the potentially high cost of leaving it an open question whether there is anything at the transcendental level corresponding to the logical function of the understanding.

---

[28] This is essentially the line of objection advanced by Kemp Smith and R. P. Wolff. See note 25.

Paragraph 7 (A79–80/B105): Kant here infers from the isomorphism between the logical and the real uses of the understanding the existence of an isomorphism between the logical functions of judgment and the pure concepts of the understanding or categories, which enables him to construct a table of the latter based on the former, thereby attaining the goal which had eluded Aristotle. He writes:

In such a way there arise exactly as many pure concepts of the understanding, which apply to objects of intuition in general *a priori*, as there were logical functions of all possible judgments in the previous table: for the understanding is completely exhausted and its capacity entirely measured by these functions. Following Aristotle we will call these concepts categories, for our aim is basically identical with his although very distant from it in execution.

This conclusion rests on two presuppositions, which cannot be further considered here: (1) the completeness of the table of logical functions and (2) the claim that the understanding has a real use and its pure concepts categoreal status, which was noted above. But setting these aside, it should be noted that Kant has here created for himself a narrow conceptual space between two unacceptable alternatives. One is a strict identification of logical function and category. This is unacceptable because it would reduce the latter to the former; thereby obviating the need for anything like a metaphysical deduction. The other is the denial of any significant connection between them, which would be unacceptable because it undermines the possibility of such a deduction. Kant's solution, which is adumbrated in the above-cited passage, is to affirm what might be termed their "quasi-identification," by which I understand their substantive identity and functional difference.[29] In other words, rather than two sets of concepts, one involved in the unification of representations in a judgment, the other in the relation of concepts to intuitions, there is a single set of concepts belonging to a single understanding, which exercises two distinct and irreducible functions: the unification of concepts in a judgment and the determination of the manifold of an intuition.

Although Kant did not express himself in precisely this way in the first edition of the *Critique*, he did so often enough elsewhere to remove any doubt that this is his considered view. For example, at a key point in the B-Deduction he states that "the categories are nothing other than these very functions for judging [the logical functions of judgment], insofar as the manifold of given intuition is determined with regard to them" (B143).[30] And returning again to Kant's exemplary "All bodies are divisible," at one point he notes that as far as its logical form or syntactic structure is concerned, either concept can occupy the subject position; but by bringing the concept of body under the category of substance, one is claiming that in its empirical intuition in experience a body must always be considered as subject and never as

[29] See Allison (2004), 155–6.
[30] Other places in which Kant makes this claim, listed in chronological order, include: Pro 4: 324; 116; Man 4: 474; 189; B128–9; and Fort 20: 272; 363.

mere predicate, which he extends to all the other categories (B128–9).[31] In other words, one is fixing the relation of subordination in which the two concepts must be thought, if their connection is to yield empirical cognition. Similarly, in the case of the judgment "water freezes at 0 degrees Celsius" the concept of cause fixes the temporal order of the two states of the water on the condition of the requisite change of temperature.

Finally, this shows the misguided nature of the critique of Kant's project advanced by Strawson, Guyer, and others; viz., that he is arguing for the untenable view that the necessity of each category is supposed to be derived from its indispensability in making judgments of the corresponding logical form, e.g., to judge hypothetically one must be able to apply the category of causality.[32] These critics are correct in insisting that such a view is untenable, since it is easy to produce counter examples; but they err in attributing it to Kant. If the interpretation sketched here is correct, Kant's view is rather the obverse of this, namely, that we can be in possession of a given category only because we are capable of judging under the corresponding form. Of course, as has been emphasized throughout, this result is conditional, since it assumes that the understanding has an extra-logical function through which it introduces a "transcendental content" into its representations; and demonstrating this is the task of the Transcendental Deduction to which we now turn.

II

Although the Transcendental Deduction as a whole has a well-deserved reputation for being one of the more obscure portions of the *Critique*, if not the entire philosophical canon, its introductory section, which remained largely unchanged in the second edition, is comparatively clear. It consists of two parts entitled "On the principles of a transcendental deduction in general" and "Transition to the transcendental deduction of the categories," which in the second edition are numbered §13 and §14 respectively. In the first part, which consists of eight paragraphs, Kant introduces the concept of a transcendental deduction, which involves the application of the juridical conception of a deduction as the grounding of a right or claim of legitimate possession, to the case of concepts, particularly a priori concepts. He argues that because of their purported universality and necessity the deduction of such concepts cannot be empirical; affirms the absolute necessity of providing such a deduction for the pure concepts of the understanding; claims that this renders necessary a deduction of the other species of a priori concepts (space and time) as well; and explains the peculiar difficulties involved in a deduction of the former.

---

[31] For Kant's statements of a similar view in the 1770s, see R 4285 17: 496; R4629 17: 617; and R 4672 17: 635–6.

[32] See, for example, Strawson (1966), 81–2; Guyer (1987), 98–9.

In the first edition, the second part of the section consists of three paragraphs, the last of which was replaced in the second edition by three new paragraphs. Of the two common paragraphs, the first spells out the basic strategy for a deduction of the categories; viz., it must show that they are a priori conditions of a possible experience; while the second elevates this into a methodological principle governing the deduction of all a priori concepts (space and time as well as the categories). The third paragraph in the first edition recalls B 12 and foreshadows the upcoming subjective deduction by referring to sense, imagination, and apperception as fundamental cognitive faculties, each of which has both an empirical and a transcendental function. Like Kant's text, the analysis is divided into two parts.

A) *The principles of a transcendental deduction in general* (A84–92/B116–24):

1) *The nature and aim of a transcendental deduction, its difference from an empirical deduction, and the unsuitability of the latter for a priori concepts* (A84–7/B116–19): Since Kant had coined the term "transcendental deduction" to characterize his project, he begins by explaining what he intends by it, which would have appeared puzzling to his contemporaries, as it still does to uninitiated present-day readers for whom a deduction is understood as an argument in which a conclusion is supposed to follow from its premises with logical necessity. As was noted in the Introduction, Kant does this by alluding to the juridical sense of "deduction" as the determination of a legal right or claim to possession of some property, as opposed to the fact of possession and how it was acquired. The former addresses the quid juris and the latter the quid facti (A84/B116).[33] Kant's terminological innovation consists in the application of the conception of a deduction as justification or legitimation to concepts, which for this purpose he divides into three classes.

The first is the large class of empirical concepts to which we take ourselves as justified in attributing a sense (*Sinn*) and signification (*Bedeutung*) without any deduction because their objective reality is evidenced by experience. Given the juridical sense that Kant attaches to the term, his claim that we accept empirical concepts "*without any deduction*" (my emphasis) is misleading, since it would seem that the appeal to experience just is their deduction, i.e., validation. But Kant evidently shies away from making this perfectly obvious point, instead characterizing an empirical deduction as concerned with "how a concept is acquired through experience and reflection on it, and therefore concerns not the lawfulness but the fact from which the possession has arisen" (85/B117). In other words, he considers an empirical deduction as addressing the *quid facti*, even though he had just claimed that a deduction, as such, is concerned with the *quid juris*.[34] Nevertheless, this unfortunate formulation is clearly attributable to a sloppiness on Kant's part rather

---

[33] The distinction is also to be found in R 5636 18: 277; 260, which is dated by Adickes as composed between 1780 and 1783, but seems to be closely related to this section of the Transcendental Deduction.

[34] See also A87/B119.

than to any deep confusion. The trouble stems from the fact that Kant is concerned to introduce two distinctions: (1) between the *quid juris* and the *quid facti* and (2) between a transcendental and an empirical deduction; but he fails to do so with sufficient precision, suggesting instead that they are co-extensive. Moreover, once this is pointed out, there is nothing to prevent Kant from acknowledging that, in the case of empirical concepts, an account of their acquisition, i.e., of the conditions under which they are formed, constitutes their deduction in the juridical sense.[35]

The second class of concepts to which Kant refers are what he terms "usurped concepts" (*usurpirte Begriffe*), as examples of which he cites fortune and fate. At issue is not whether a particular use of such concepts is warranted, but whether it is *ever* legitimate to use them. Kant notes that, though such concepts are in common use, generally without any question of their legitimacy, when the *quid juris* is raised with respect to them no answer is forthcoming from either experience or reason (A84–5/ B117).[36]

Kant's concern, however, is neither with genuine empirical nor usurped or pseudo-concepts, but with those "destined for pure use *a priori* (completely independent of experience)." He claims that the right to use such concepts always requires a deduction, "since proofs from experience are not sufficient for the lawfulness [*Rechtmässigkeit*] of such use, and yet one must know how these concepts can relate to objects that they do not derive [*hernehmen*] from any experience" (A85/B117). Here, again, Kant seems to misspeak. Since he is not yet ready to argue for the necessity of a deduction at all, what he should have said, and presumably meant to say, is that *if* a deduction of these concepts is necessary, it must be transcendental rather than empirical.

By the "lawfulness" of the use of such concepts Kant means their warrant, which in their case cannot be provided by experience. Although Kant does not here specify why this is the case, we know from the Introduction to the *Critique* that it is because such concepts and the propositions in which they are used make a claim for strict universality and necessity, which cannot be justified empirically. The question that Kant raises, namely, how these concepts can relate to objects that they do not derive from any experience, does, however, call for some comment. First, it suggests that, at least in the case of a priori concepts, addressing the *quid juris* involves a how-question, which concerns their relation to objects. Moreover, this question seems to contain an ambiguity between "how" in the sense of "by what means" and in the sense of "on what grounds." But since this distinction between two senses of "how"

---

[35] On this point see Paton (1936a), 316.

[36] In *Dreams* Kant provides an analogous account of what he there describes as "surreptitious concepts" (*erschlichene Begriffe*), of which he offers as an example the concept of spirit (*Geist*). He does not claim outright that it is a spurious concept, as he does with regard to fortune and fate in the *Critique*, but merely that, given the way it is commonly used, it cannot be considered an empirical concept derived by abstraction from experience. Nevertheless, Kant's point is that it has a deeply problematic status, which accords with the skeptical orientation of that work. See T 2: 321n; 308.

correlates with Kant's distinction between the subjective and the objective sides of the Transcendental Deduction as he presents it in the first edition, it is likely that he intended both. Nevertheless, at this juncture, Kant's focus is clearly on the latter, which calls to mind the question that he posed rhetorically to Herz: "What is the ground of the relation of that in us which we call 'representation' to the object?" As we saw, Kant initially posed this question in general terms, concerning *any* representation, but then narrowed its scope to intellectual representations, which are included in, but not co-extensive with, the a priori concepts with which he is presently concerned.

A second aspect of Kant's question that requires further explanation concerns the statement that the concepts in need of a transcendental deduction "relate to objects that they do not derive from any experience." This formulation likewise contains an ambiguity, since these could be either non-sensible objects (noumena) or sensible objects, (phenomena); though in the latter case, it is *the relation to the objects*, rather than the objects themselves, that is not derived from experience because it involves strict universality and necessity. And, here again, it is likely that Kant had both in mind, as well perhaps as the ontological concept of an object as such, which was his concern in the 1772 letter to Herz.

After spelling out the nature of a transcendental deduction in the first two paragraphs, Kant turns in the third to a consideration of the a priori concepts that are its intended recipients. He distinguishes two sorts of concepts that are purported to relate to objects in a way that only a transcendental deduction can account for: space and time, as forms of sensibility, and the categories, as pure concepts of the understanding. In both cases, Kant points out that "they are related to their objects without having borrowed anything from experience for their representation," which amounts to a not particularly elegant way of saying that the determination of their relation to objects, which Kant equates with their objective reality, cannot be based upon an appeal to experience. And he concludes from this, again in light of the contrast between a transcendental and an empirical deduction, that "if a deduction of them is necessary, it must always be transcendental" (A85–6/B118).

Since he has not yet argued that any deduction is required, this is the appropriate conclusion for Kant to draw at this point and it helps set the stage for the argument for the indispensability of a transcendental one. But before proceeding to this, Kant interjects a paragraph devoted to the rejection of what might seem to many philosophers a viable alternative to a transcendental deduction; viz., a Lockean account of the empirical acquisition of these concepts, which Kant refers to as their "physiological derivation." Kant acknowledges both the possibility and the value of such a derivation, while denying that it can be viewed as a substitute for a transcendental deduction on the grounds that it addresses the *quid facti* rather than the *quid juris*. As he puts it in a passage that could readily be directed at Tetens as well as Locke, "[A] **deduction** of the pure *a priori* concepts can never be achieved in this way ... for in regard to their future use, which should be entirely independent of experience, an entirely different birth certificate than that of an ancestry from experiences must be produced" (A86/B119).

2) *The indispensability of a transcendental deduction of all* a priori *concepts as a precondition of metaphysics* (A87–8/B119–21): After dismissing the empiricist alternative to a transcendental deduction, Kant devotes the lengthy fifth paragraph to making the case for the unavoidable necessity of the latter as a pre-condition for entering "the field of pure reason," i.e., metaphysics. Although this is hardly unexpected, given Kant's metametaphysical concern, it is somewhat surprising to find him insisting on the need for such a deduction for the concepts of space and time as well as the categories and further insisting that the need for a deduction of the former is a direct consequence of the necessity of a deduction for the latter. Kant does not, however, propose to provide a deduction of the concepts of space and time, since he claims that this was already accomplished in the Aesthetic. Instead, he endeavors to explain why, at least in the case of the concept of space, such a deduction does not at first appear to be necessary, but is rendered such (for the concept of time as well as space) by the necessity of one for the categories.[37]

Kant illustrates the apparent lack of a need for a deduction of the concept of space by the example of geometry. He notes that the geometer can proceed confidently in his demonstrations without having to turn to philosophy for the justification of the concept of space and he offers two reasons for this, neither of which applies to the metaphysician, whose conceptual tools are the categories. The first is the status of space as the form of outer sense, which limits its scope to objects of outer sense, thereby avoiding any worries about its relation to a non-sensible reality, which is the traditional concern of the metaphysician. The second concerns the nature of geometrical cognition, which has immediate evidence "because it is grounded on intuition *a priori* and the objects are given through the cognition itself *a priori* in intuition (as far as their form is concerned)" (A87–8/B119). This recalls Kant's account of the synthetic procedure of mathematics and the kind of certainty it was deemed capable of attaining in the *Prize Essay*. While Kant no longer assigned to philosophy the analytic method as described in that work and used in the other writings from the early and mid-1760s, he retained the view that mathematical cognition made of use of a synthetic method that was not available to philosophy, since it cannot construct its objects in intuition. Accordingly, the lack of intuitive evidence creates ample conceptual space for a skepticism regarding metaphysical cognition (cognition through pure reason), which does not naturally arise in the case of mathematics.

---

[37] Although Kant here claims the necessity of a deduction merely for the concept of space, his earlier inclusion of time as among those a priori concepts for which any deduction must be transcendental indicates that he intended it as well.

Nevertheless, for the "critical" Kant the intuitive certainty of geometry does not obviate the need for a transcendental deduction of the concepts of space and time. This is not because of anything inherently problematic in these concepts, but because of the effect that the categories have on the way in which they are regarded by the metaphysician. As Kant puts it in a difficult but crucially important passage dealing with the two species of a priori concepts,

> [S]ince they [the categories] speak of objects not through predicates of intuition and sensibility but through those of pure *a priori* thinking, they relate to objects generally [*allgemein*] without any conditions of sensibility; and since they are not grounded in experience and cannot exhibit any object in *a priori* intuition on which to ground their synthesis prior to any experience, they not only arouse suspicion about the objective validity and limits of their use but also make the **concept of space** ambiguous by inclining us to use it beyond the conditions of sensible intuition, on which account a transcendental deduction of it was also needed above.
>
> (A88/B120–1)

Kant here claims that it is the peculiar nature of the categories, as pure concepts of the understanding, that not only renders their need for a deduction evident, but makes it necessary to provide one for the concept of space (and time) as well. The peculiar nature of these concepts stems from the fact that they concern pure a priori thinking, which abstracts from any relation to sensibility. Accordingly, they are concepts through which we think objects in general or as such, i.e., simply qua objects, which is also the defining feature of the concepts of traditional ontology. This pretence to an absolutely universal scope is what differentiates them from mathematical concepts, which are likewise a priori, as well as from empirical concepts, for which no such scope can be claimed, and it is this difference that initially indicates the need for a deduction.

Although Kant suggests that this claim generates a worry about the objective validity, as well as the scope of these concepts, the present argument for the necessity of a transcendental deduction turns more on the latter than the former. In other words, the worry calling for such a deduction, as Kant here characterizes it, does not concern the applicability of these concepts to empirical objects (that will come later), but their seemingly unrestricted scope as concepts of objects as such. The scope restriction of the categories to objects of possible experience is not an innovation of the *Critique*, since it was operative already in the *Duisburg Nachlass*, if not earlier. What is new is the claim that the failure to acknowledge this restriction gives rise to an ambiguity in the use of the concepts of space and time, which makes it necessary to provide a transcendental deduction of them as well.

Since the latter deduction was provided in the Transcendental Aesthetic through the twin claims that space and time are empirically real (have objective reality) and transcendentally ideal (have a restricted scope), Kant here regards it as a fait accompli. But the fact that, save from some remarks added in the second edition, he was largely silent on the necessity for and implications of this restriction, has helped to fuel the objection that Kant unjustifiably denied the possibility that things as they are in themselves are in space and time (or some noumenal simulacrum thereof).[38] We can now see, however, that this relative silence was necessitated by the architecture of the *Critique*, which required Kant to treat sensibility and its forms prior to and independently of the understanding and its pure concepts. But the main point is that the mere fact that the understanding possesses concepts that purport to relate to objects qua objects tends to lead the unwary metaphysician, who has not been illuminated by the great light, to recognize the distinction in kind between sensible and intellectual representation, to assume that the concepts of space and time have a similar scope, as, for example, Crusius did when he proclaimed that everything is somewhere and somewhen.

In this respect, Kant's position recalls his view in the *Dissertation*, where he likewise considered it essential to limit the scope of spatial and temporal predicates to the sensible world. The difference is that, whereas in 1770 Kant saw this restriction as necessary to preserve the intellectual concepts from contamination by the sensible, in the *Critique*, where he restricts the understanding to the conditions of sensibility, curbing the pretension of sensibility is now considered necessary to restrict the understanding as well. In other words, if one considers spatial and temporal predicates to be applicable to things or objects in general, rather than merely to phenomena, then, even with the doctrine of the restriction of the categories to sensible conditions, it would follow that these categories would not merely be rules for the *thought* of objects in general, but would yield genuine *cognition* of them. And since whatever may be claimed to hold of things in general *eo ipso* holds also of things as they are in themselves, this would mean that the human understanding could cognize things as they are in themselves.[39] Kant does not introduce these added complexities at this point; but he does in both the chapter on the distinction between phenomena and noumena, where he returns to the issue of the need to limit sensibility as a means to limit the understanding as well (see A255–6/B311–12), and in the Amphiboly. In the latter he writes:

The understanding accordingly bounds sensibility without thereby expanding its own field, and in warning sensibility not to presume to reach for things in themselves but solely for appearances it thinks of an object in itself, but only as a transcendental object, which is the

---

[38] The materials added to the Transcendental Aesthetic in the second edition pertaining to the scope restriction of space and time are located at B66–72. For my views on the non-spatiality and temporality of things in themselves see Allison (2004), 128–32.

[39] An important but frequently neglected distinction underlying the whole discussion of the mutual limitation of sensibility and understanding in the *Critique* is between things or objects in general and things in themselves. Although the focus of most critical discussion of Kant concerns his understanding of things in themselves (or as they are in themselves) and his denial of the possibility of any cognition thereof, it usually goes unnoticed that Kant generally bases this denial on the inability of human understanding to cognize objects in general. The point is that if the human understanding could cognize objects as such or qua objects they could also cognize them as they are in themselves. For my fullest discussion of this issue, see Allison (2006).

cause of appearance (thus not itself appearance) and cannot be thought of either as magnitude or as reality or as substance, etc...If we want to call this object a noumenon because the representation of it is nothing sensible, we are free to do so. But since we cannot apply any of our concepts of the understanding to it, this representation still remains empty for us, and serves for nothing but to designate the boundaries of our sensible cognition and leave open a space that we can fill up neither through possible experience nor through the pure under-standing.   (A288-9/B344-5)[40]

3) *The peculiar difficulty of a transcendental deduction of the categories* (A89–92/ B121–4): Although Kant concludes from his analysis in the preceding paragraph the necessity of a transcendental deduction for both the categories and the concepts of space and time, we have seen that the argument turns on the need to restrict the scope rather than to establish the validity of these concepts. In paragraphs six through eight, however, Kant shifts to the question of their validity and notes a difficulty in establishing this that does not arise in the case of the concepts of space and time. The problem, which was already noted in Chapter 3, is that, unlike space and time, the categories are not conditions under which objects are given in intuition, from which it seems to follow that "objects can [*können*]...appear to us without necessarily having to be related to functions of the understanding, and therefore without the understanding containing their *a priori* conditions" (A89/B122). And from this Kant concludes that a problem arises that was not encountered in the case of space and time, namely, "how **subjective conditions of thinking** should have **objective validity**, i.e., yield conditions of the possibility of all cognition of objects" (A89/B122). As the contrast with the deduction of space and time indicates, the problem is not how subjective conditions as such could have objective validity, since in their case this has already been shown, but merely how subjective conditions of *thinking* could have such validity.[41]

---

[40] There is an at least apparent contradiction in this passage between the claim that the transcendental object is to be thought as the cause of appearances and the denial that any of the categories (presumably including causality are applicable to the object so considered. As such, it is also one of the many passages that underlie Jacobi's famous remark that "without the presupposition [of the thing in itself] I cannot enter the system [of the *Critique*], and with that presupposition I cannot remain in it." See Jacobi (1968), 304. Since the present concern is solely with the notion that in curbing sensibility the understanding is also restricting itself, this classical and complex issue cannot be considered here; but I do attempt to address it in Allison (2004), 64–73.

[41] The question of what Kant means by "objective validity" is not as straightforward as it might appear, since he uses the term with respect to both concepts and judgments and, as we have already seen, it cannot simply be equated with truth. Moreover, the situation is further complicated by the need to distinguish it from "objective reality," which Kant also uses frequently in connection with the categories. While I cannot purport to resolve all the textual issues involved, since this would require a consideration of the multiple uses of these terms in the Dialectic and the Doctrine of Method as well as the Deduction and the remainder of the Analytic, I believe it possible to clarify how they are to be understood and the relation between them insofar as it bares on the categories. To begin with, the avowed goal of the Transcendental Deduction is to demonstrate the objective validity of the categories, by which is understood their warranted use. Accordingly, if successful, the Deduction would provide such a warrant, not for any particular use (since a category can be misapplied), but for the general claim that they have a legitimate use within the domain of possible experience. Correlatively, to provide this

In a not altogether successful attempt to illustrate the problem, Kant cites the example of the concept of cause, which he maintains "signifies a certain kind of synthesis, in which given something *A* something entirely different *B* is posited according to a rule" (A90/B122). The problem stems from the rule-governed, and therefore necessary, nature of this succession. Since this can be explained neither by the nature of sensibility alone nor warranted by experience, Kant remarks that it "is therefore *a priori* doubtful whether such a concept is perhaps entirely empty and finds no object anywhere among the appearances" (A90/B122). But while we can readily understand Kant's use of the concept of cause to illustrate the point, his failure to distinguish between two quite different kinds of necessity that are involved in his account is a potential source of confusion. One is causal necessity, which is built into the concept of a cause; the other is the putative necessity that appearances conform to *all* of the categories, which I call the "non-contingency thesis" and shall examine in subsequent chapters. Although Kant's concern is clearly with the latter, the example explicitly appeals only to the former, thereby obfuscating the broader point, which is that the latter likewise cannot be accounted for by an appeal to the forms of human sensibility. This is because:

[T]hat objects of sensible intuition must accord with the formal conditions of sensibility that lie in the mind *a priori* is clear from the fact that otherwise they would not be objects for us; but that they must also accord with the conditions that the understanding requires for the synthetic unity of thinking is a conclusion that is not so easily seen. For appearances could [*könnten*][42] after all be so constituted that the understanding would not find them in accord with the conditions of its unity, and everything would then lie in such confusion that, e.g., in the succession of appearances nothing would offer itself that would furnish a rule of synthesis and thus correspond to the concept of cause and effect, so that this concept would therefore be entirely empty, nugatory, and without significance. Appearances would nonetheless offer objects to our intuition, for intuition by no means requires the functions of thinking.

(A90–1/B123).

warrant is to address the *quid juris*. By contrast, a concept has objective reality just in case the object to which it refers is really, as opposed to merely logically, possible (see, for example, A155–7/B194–6, A217/B264, B291, A235/B288, A254/B310, A279/B335, A310/B367, B412, A510/B538, and A596/B624 note). Kant argues in the Transcendental Deduction that the only way to establish this warrant for the categories is to demonstrate that they are necessary conditions (from the side of thought) of a possible experience, in which case they would also have objective reality as conditions of the real possibility of objects of experience. In other words, their objective reality is conditioned by their objective validity. In the case of empirical concepts, however, the situation is reversed. Since the warrant for the use of an empirical concept is provided by establishing its experiential credentials and this is equivalent to establishing its objective reality, the objective validity of such concepts follows directly from their objective reality, which is why they can be given an empirical deduction. For further discussion of these points and some of the broader issues involved in the objective validity-objective reality distinction, see Meerbote (1972) and Zöller (1984), esp. 132–4.

[42] Kant's use of the subjunctive (*könnten*) in this context as contrasted with the indicative (*können*) in the parallel passage at A89/B122 is noted by Paton (1936a, 324, note 3). The difference points to the possibility of a tension in Kant's thought between the view that objects can (actually) appear without conforming to the conditions of thought and the view that this is a provisional supposition that is the aim of the Transcendental Deduction to lay to rest. This issue will be discussed below.

This passage, which was initially cited in the Introduction, and others like it, have been the occasion of considerable controversy and have sometimes been thought to point to a deep contradiction, the resolution of which requires the drastic remedy of the so-called "patchwork thesis," which effectively undermines all hope of finding in the Transcendental Deduction anything approaching a coherent line of argument.[43] Although the issues are complex, the basic problem concerns the understanding of the term "object," as Kant uses it in this passage, and its compatibility with the "critical" conception of object for which he argues in the body of the Deduction.[44] While the latter maintains that objects of a possible experience are to be considered as the intentional correlates of a rule-governed unification of sensible data by the understanding, Kant here appears to assume that objects are given in intuition as appearances without any contribution of the understanding, which is viewed as a

[43] "Patchwork thesis" is the label attached to the view that, rather than containing a single, coherent line of argument, the Transcendental Deduction in the first edition of the *Critique* is a mosaic of different and inconsistent strands, stemming from different stages in Kant's philosophical development, which he supposedly stitched together at the last moment. Although it has predecessors, most notably Adickes, the canonical formulation of this view is by Vaihinger (1967), who maintained that the A-Deduction can be deconstructed into four strata or layers of argument, which are datable and differentiated in terms of their diverse accounts of "the subjective sources of knowledge," i.e., Kant's accounts of the cognitive faculties (the subjective side of the deduction). These are: (1) the layer of the transcendental object, but without the categories; (2) the layer of the categories, but without the productive imagination; (3) the layer of the productive imagination, but without the three-fold synthesis; (4) the layer of the three-fold synthesis (Vaihinger (1967), 61). According to Vaihinger, the section with which we are currently concerned (A84–92) is located in the first layer; but since it includes a discussion of the categories (though not of the transcendental object), it is considered a transitional stage between (1) and (2). It is also claimed to be early or "pre-critical" on the dual grounds that the categories still appear to be applicable to "the transcendent world" (noumena) and are not yet viewed as conditions under which objects are given in intuition (Vaihinger (1967), 45–6). In Anglophone Kant scholarship, Vaihinger's reading was taken over virtually whole cloth by Kemp Smith, who describes it as "an excellent example of detective genius in the field of scholarship" (1962), 202. This reading was, however, subjected to a detailed and devastating critique by Paton (1967). But in the more recent literature a patchwork reading in a modified form (without the claim to date the various strands of argumentation) has made something of a comeback in the accounts of Robert Wolff (1963), esp. 81–4, and Guyer (1987), 73 and 432 note 1, both of whom view the Deduction (though in the case of Wolff only its subjective side) as a collection of distinct and incompatible lines of argument, which are only artificially linked together. In subsequent chapters I shall endeavor to counter this reading; but for present purposes my concern is merely to show that the argument of A84–92, which was retained in the second edition, does not have the aberrant nature attributed to it by Vaihinger and Kemp Smith.

[44] Although he does not refer to this particular passage, the charge that there is a fundamental contradiction between the "critical" conception of an object as the product of the activity of the understanding and that of the object as given in sensibility in accordance with its a priori forms, apart from any contribution of the understanding, was raised by Schopenhauer (1958), esp. 437–51. But while the same alleged contradiction is appealed to by Vaihinger and Kemp Smith in their reading of this passage (see the preceding note), they draw diametrically opposed conclusions from it. For whereas they considered the conception of objects as apprehended independently of the contribution of the understanding (the view that they attribute to Kant in A90–1) as a remnant of the long-discarded doctrine of the *Dissertation*, Schopenhauer regarded the "critical" conception of an object as the culprit, seeing it (and with it the whole of the Analytic) as an unwarranted abandonment of the for him estimable doctrine of the Aesthetic.

contradiction.[45] Moreover, if this is the case, it seems that the problem that Kant suggests makes a deduction of the categories so difficult is one that the "critical" Kant, as opposed to the Kant of 1772, would not have recognized as a problem at all, which is grist for the mill of patchwork theorists.

There are two main retorts to this line of objection in the literature. One points to the progressive, dialectical nature of Kant's argument.[46] So construed, there is no contradiction because Kant is not actually claiming that it is possible to be aware of objects that do not conform to the requirements of the understanding, i.e., the unity of apperception. The claim is rather that from all that we have learned so far, which means essentially from the Transcendental Aesthetic, which abstracts from the role of the understanding, this possibility has not been precluded.

The second retort focuses on the ambiguity of the term "object." The alleged contradiction in the claim that "objects can appear to us without having to be related to functions of the understanding" depends entirely on the assumption that Kant is here using the term in the specifically "critical" sense designated above. Given this assumption, the charge is clearly warranted; for it would be contradictory to claim that objects, so defined, could appear independently of their relation to these functions. The problem, however, is that this is neither a natural nor even a plausible reading of the text. First, despite his "critical" conception, Kant frequently uses the term in a commonsensical, non-technical way to refer to what we ordinarily think of as physical objects. Moreover, there is no contradiction in the thought that objects, so understood, and considered merely as they appear, i.e., as they are sensibly given, might not conform to these functions.[47] Second, since Kant had not yet introduced his "critical" conception, of an object he would hardly have expected his readers to have taken the passage in this way. Accordingly, the most that Kant can reasonably be accused of at this point is a certain terminological looseness, which might be attributed to the impossibility of saying everything at once.

Although the first response contains a kernel of truth (Kant's account is progressive, if not dialectical in the sense designated above) and the second essentially correct as far as it goes, they do not tell the whole story. What is omitted is a consideration of Kant's emphasis on the peculiar difficulty in a deduction of the

---

[45] A similar worry, albeit without accusing Kant of a contradiction, was raised by J. S. Beck in his letters to Kant of November 11, 1791 (Br. 11: 311; 396) and May 31, 1792 (Br. 11: 338–9; 414). Kant's only extant response to this is a marginal note attached to Beck's initial letter in which he wrote: "The fashioning of a concept, by means of intuition, into a cognition is the work of judgment; but the reference of intuition to an object in general is not. For the latter is merely the logical use of representation insofar as a representation is thought to belong to cognition" (Br 11: 311; 396–7). In other words, Kant is claiming that his characterization of an intuition as an immediate representation of an object is a matter of logical classification, which distinguishes it from feelings and gives intuition an epistemic function. I discuss the issue in Allison (2004), 80–2.

[46] Versions of this response, some directed against Schopenhauer and others against Vaihinger and Kemp Smith, are to be found in Cohen (1885), 360–1; Cassirer (1911), 700–1; de Vleeschauwer (1936), 177–8; and Paton (1936a), 329.

[47] The point is nicely developed by Paton (1936a), 324–6.

categories *vis à vis* one of the concepts of space and time. If we take this difficulty seriously, then, rather than viewing it as a pseudo-problem, which was initially posed only to be later dismissed as such, we must admit that appearances might indeed "be so constituted that the understanding would not find them in accord with the conditions of its unity." In fact, this scenario is precisely what is characterized in the Introduction as the specter that the Transcendental Deduction must exorcize if it is to establish the necessary conformity of appearances to the categories, which is itself required if it is to show that they are necessary conditions of the possibility of experience. And it was further pointed out that the (logical) possibility of such a scenario is a direct consequence of the radical separateness of the cognitive faculties, which underlies the entire problematic of the Deduction. Thus, unless one wishes to argue that this is merely a provisional hypothesis that is abandoned in the actual Deduction, we must regard the Transcendental Deduction as an attempt to demonstrate the necessary applicability of the categories to appearances *in spite of the radical separateness of the sensible and the intellectual conditions of cognition.* For better or worse, this is the framework in which the problematic of a justification of pure concepts of the understanding arose for Kant and in which he endeavored to resolve it.

In the final paragraph of the first part of the initial section of the Transcendental Deduction, Kant attempts to underscore the indispensability of such a deduction by dismissing the empiricist alternative. Speaking again specifically of the concept of cause, Kant reminds us that it cannot be justified by appealing to instances of regular succession, from which it could be derived by abstraction, thereby obviating any need for a transcendental deduction. In an argument apparently directed against Locke and Tetens rather than Hume, Kant points out that this concept cannot arise in this way, "but must either be grounded in the understanding completely *a priori* or else be entirely surrendered as a mere fantasy of the brain [*Hirngespinst*]. For this concept always requires that something A be of such a kind that something else B follows from it **necessarily** and **in accordance with an absolutely universal rule**" (A91/B124). Once again, however, the problem is that, even if one accepts Kant's account of the nature of the causal relation as involving necessary connection, it is not clear how this bears on the deduction of the categories, since that involves a normative rather than a causal necessity.

B) *Transition to the transcendental deduction of the categories* (A92–5/B124–9): As its heading suggests, this section is intended to provide a transition from the analysis of the nature and need for a transcendental deduction of all a priori concepts and of the peculiar difficulties in providing one for the categories to the actual deduction of the latter. As such, it contains an account of how such a deduction must proceed, given the nature of the categories and the radical separation of sensibility and understanding. In the first edition the section is composed of three paragraphs and in the second the last of these is replaced by two new paragraphs.

1) *The transition in the first edition* (A92–5): Kant begins by contrasting the two possible ways in which "synthetic representation and its objects can come together, necessarily relate to each other, and, as it were meet each other: Either if the object alone makes the representation, or if the representation alone makes the object possible" (A92). Since Kant usually uses "synthetic" to characterize either a judgment, a method, or a kind of unity, the expression "synthetic representation" (*synthetische Vorstellung*) seems odd; but the fact that he uses "representation" in the singular and "objects" in the plural suggests that Kant may have meant a synthetic *representing*, i.e., a judgment, rather than a representation, which would help to explain the presence of the adjective.[48] Apart from this complication, however, Kant's main point is relatively clear. Assuming that there are a priori representings, the first way of understanding their relation to objects is a non-starter; since it entails that all representings would presuppose an encounter with their object; while the problem with the second alternative is that it is only in the practical domain (volition) that the representing can literally make its object possible. Accordingly, it seems that the only hope for explaining the possibility of such a relation, and therefore of synthetic a priori cognition, is to find some non-causal sense in which a representing can be said to make its object possible.

This formulation of the problem calls to mind once again the 1772 letter to Herz, where, with primarily the intellectual concepts of the *Dissertation* in mind, Kant posed the issue of the relation between representations and objects in terms of the contrast between an ectypal and an archetypal intellect. As we saw, Kant noted that if we had either a purely ectypal or a purely archetypal intellect the general problem would not arise. In the former case, this is because all our representations would be derived from a prior acquaintance with their objects; while in the latter case, the representation would be the ground of the existence of its object. We also saw, however, that Kant ruled out the former possibility on the controversial grounds that we have intellectual representations (this would be rejected by an empiricist), and the latter on the incontrovertible grounds that our intellect is not archetypal, at least not in the literal sense that is traditionally attributed to the divine intellect. Assuming that the human intellect is equipped with concepts derived from its own nature rather than abstracted from experience, this led to the conclusion that it is neither purely ectypal nor purely archetypal; but it left intact Kant's worry regarding how to understand the relation between intellectual representations and their objects. And we further saw that, apart from rejecting three metaphysically based attempts to

---

[48] According to Erdmann, however, "*Vorstellung*" should be pluralized, which would seem to preclude this reading. Moreover, he is followed by Kemp Smith in his translation. Correlatively, according to de Vleeschauwer (1936), 183, note 4, Vaihinger suggested deleting "synthetic" on the grounds that Kant's use of it in this context was inadvertent. But de Vleeschauwer himself defends Kant's use of the term, claiming that it refers to an a priori representation formed by the understanding through an act of synthesis (de Vleeschauwer (1936), 183–4).

account for this relation, Kant seems to have set aside this problem in the remainder of the letter.

We have also seen, however, that in the *Duisburg Nachlass* and elsewhere Kant developed a non-causal view of how the human intellect can make an object possible, through his accounts of synthesis, spontaneity, and apperception, thereby also effectively showing how such an intellect could be regarded as an analogue of the genuinely archetypal divine intellect.[49] And now, in his transition to the Transcendental Deduction, Kant gives succinct expression to this view with the claim that, though it "does not produce its object as far as its **existence** is concerned, the representation is still determinant of the object *a priori* if it is possible through it alone to **cognize something as an object**" (A92/B125). Otherwise expressed, a representation may be said to make its object possible, if it can be regarded as an epistemic (rather than a causal) condition of the object.

Kant notes that there are two such conditions under which alone the cognition of an object is possible: intuitions and concepts. Through the first an object is given, though only as appearance, and through the second it is thought as corresponding to its intuition. With regard to the latter he asks: "whether *a priori* concepts do not also precede, as conditions under which alone something can be, if not intuited, nevertheless thought as an object, for then all empirical cognition of objects is necessarily in accord with such concepts, since without their presupposition nothing is possible as **object of experience**" (A93/B125–6). And Kant proceeds, without further ado, to answer this rhetorical question by claiming that,

[A]ll experience contains in addition to the intuition of the senses, through which something is given, a **concept** of an object that is given in intuition or appears; hence concepts of objects in general lie at the ground of all experiential cognition as *a priori* conditions; consequently the objective validity of the categories, as *a priori* concepts, rests on the fact that through them alone is experience possible (as far as the form of thinking is concerned). For they then are related necessarily and *a priori* to objects of experience, since only by means of them can any object of experience be thought at all.   (A93/B126)

The second of the above-cited passages contains the gist of what Kant refers to in the A-Preface as the "objective deduction" (Axvii). Although as presented in the text it is more assertion than argument, it does point to a line of argument that underlies the Deduction as a whole. Its basic claim is that empirical concepts (though necessary) do not suffice to account for the possibility of experience and that pure concepts are also necessary. Since a more detailed consideration of this line of argument must await the examination of the Deduction itself, for the present it should suffice to note that it turns on the conception of the categories as concepts of an object as such or,

---

[49] In this context Kant's remark in the *Duisburg Nachlass* that "the mind is…itself the archetype [*Urbild*] of just such synthesis through original and not derived thinking" (R 4674 17: 647_{3-5}; 160), which was discussed in Chapter 3, takes on added salience.

what amounts to the same thing, as rules for the thought of an object simply qua object. As we shall see, such concepts are necessary because empirical concepts are rules for the thought of an object as of a certain kind and, as such, presuppose that what they are applied in a judgment is already thought as an object, understood as something that stands over and against the representation of it (*ein Gegen-stand*). Accordingly, in addition to the empirical concepts that determine an object as falling under a certain description, judgment, i.e., discursive cognition, presupposes concepts that function to relate the empirical representations to an object in the first place. These concepts are the categories and what enables them to relate representations to objects is just that they are concepts of an object as such.

The final paragraph of the section contains a list of the subjective sources (cognitive faculties), which Kant claims condition the possibility of experience. As in B 12, Kant designates these as **sense**, **imagination**, and **apperception**, and claims that they are respectively responsible for a **synopsis** of the manifold a priori through sense, its **synthesis** through the imagination, and the **unity** of this synthesis through original apperception. And, also like B 12, Kant contends that, in addition to their empirical use, the faculties have a transcendental use, which is a priori and is concerned with the form of experience (A94). But since what Kant says here is sheer assertion, with no attempt at explanation, I shall reserve further discussion of these important topics for subsequent chapters.

2) *Material added in the second edition* (B127–9): Among the substantive changes that Kant made in the structure of the B-Deduction is the replacement of the paragraph dealing with the subjective sources of cognition with three new paragraphs. In the first of these he contrasts his views regarding the categories with those of Locke and Hume; and while he criticizes both philosophers, he does so in a way that clearly favors Hume. Kant charges Locke with two fundamental mistakes and Hume with only one. According to Kant, Locke's first mistake consisted in a misguided endeavor to derive the categories from experience, which he then compounded by attempting to apply these same concepts beyond experience. By contrast, Hume correctly recognized that, in order to use the concepts in the manner that Locke proposed, it would be necessary to show that they have an a priori origin and his error consisted only in the failure to consider the possibility that "the understanding itself, by means of these concepts, could be the originator of the experience in which its objects are encountered" (B127). Instead, Kant suggests that "driven by necessity [Hume] derived them from experience (namely from a subjective necessity arisen from frequent association in experience, which is subsequently falsely held to be objective, i.e., **custom**)." Unlike Locke, however, Hume subsequently proceeded consistently, "declaring it to be impossible to go beyond the boundary of experience with these concepts and the principles that they occasion" (B127). But despite the relative superiority he attributes to Hume's position, Kant notes that the **empirical** derivation of concepts and principles, which both philosophers affirm, "cannot be

reconciled with the reality of the scientific cognition *a priori* that we possess, that namely of **pure mathematics** and **general natural science**, and is therefore refuted by the fact [*das Factum*]" (B128).

Two points in this paragraph are of particular interest. One is an invocation of the analytic procedure of the *Prolegomena* in the final sentence, where Kant considers the existence of a priori knowledge in mathematics and general or pure natural science as a fact that is beyond dispute.[50] With respect to the latter at least, this is noteworthy because in both editions of the *Critique* Kant treats the transcendental principles of the understanding, and especially the Analogies, which presumably constitute the content of general or pure natural science, as standing in need of a transcendental proof rather than as unquestionable fact. The second point of interest is the reason that Kant offers for regarding Hume as a more consistent empiricist than Locke; viz., his recognition of the impossibility of deriving the categories from experience, because a non-categoreally structured experience could yield nothing more than a merely subjective, custom-based necessity.[51] In short, Kant considers Hume to be fundamentally correct in his characterization of what experience would be like, if one were to reject his alternative; whereas Locke (and Kant would presumably say the same of Tetens and Hume's "commonsense" critics) naively assumes that the understanding could conduct business as usual with merely empirical materials.

In the second added paragraph, Kant continues his contrast between Locke and Hume, this time linking the former with enthusiasm (*Schwärmerei*) and the latter with skepticism. Although there is nothing odd in referring to Hume as a skeptic, it might seem surprising to find him connecting Locke with enthusiasm, particularly given the latter's attack on enthusiasm.[52] But we have seen that Kant also did this with Tetens, whom he viewed as a follower of Locke. Moreover, Kant does not actually accuse Locke of being a *Schwärmer* or enthusiast; rather, he claims merely that he "opened the gates wide" to the latter, "since reason, once it has authority on its side, will not be kept within limits by indeterminate recommendations of moderation" (B128). In other words, Kant's charge against Locke is basically the same as the one noted above; viz., that, though supposedly deriving all of the materials of cognition

---

[50] In the *Prolegomena*, Kant refers to "pure natural science," meaning thereby its a priori component as manifested in the Principles of Pure Understanding in the *Critique*. See especially §14 and §15 (Pro. 4: 294–5; 89–90). By contrast, in the *Metaphysical Foundations of Natural Science* Kant distinguishes between a general and a special metaphysics of natural science (MAN 4: 470; 185), where the former contains the transcendental principles of the *Critique*, which therefore corresponds to the pure natural science of the *Prolegomena*.

[51] Although he does not call attention to it here, in the *Prolegomena* Kant specifies the consequence of Hume's view with regard to the connection of cause and effect, namely, that "reason completely and fully deceives herself with this concept, falsely taking it for her own child, when it is really nothing but a bastard of the imagination, which is impregnated by experience" (Pro. 4: 257–8; 55).

[52] For his attack on enthusiasm, see Locke (1975), 697–706. Nevertheless, Locke meant by "enthusiasm" something quite different than Kant meant by *Schwärmerei*, namely, a specifically religious form of fanaticism, in which a believer relies on a personal rather than a Scriptural revelation, such as the Quaker's "inner light."

from experience, he surreptitiously extended them beyond experience without sub-jecting his procedure to a critique.[53] Kant concludes the paragraph by characterizing his own project in the Transcendental Deduction as an attempt to "steer human reason between the two cliffs, assign its determinate boundaries, and still keep open the entire field of its purposive activity" (B128). Since Kant typically describes his task as finding a "critical" path between dogmatism and skepticism (not enthusiasm and skepticism), this way of putting the matter is unusual; but it suggests that Locke and Hume were the two thinkers most on Kant's mind when formulating his revised version of the Deduction.[54]

  In the final paragraph added in the second edition, Kant provides the previously cited explanation (*Erklärung*) of the categories as "concepts of an object as such, by means of which its intuition is regarded as **determined** with regard to one of the **logical functions** for judgments" (B128). Having already noted the importance of this "explanation," which could also be regarded as a nominal definition of the categories, there is nothing further to say about it at present, except to note that the lack of a similar statement in the A-Deduction leaves the connection between Kant's conception of the judgment and the categories largely unexplained, a defect which he will remedy in the B-Deduction.

---

[53] As we saw in the Appendix to Chapter 3, Kant raised precisely the same objection against Tetens in his preparatory notes for the *Prolegomena*.

[54] Kant also uses the metaphor of two cliffs between which criticism must steer but characterizes them as dogmatism and skepticism in R 5645 18: 276.

5

The A-Deduction

Section 2

It was noted in Chapter 4 that Kant divides the A-Deduction into three sections, the first of which was there analyzed. The present chapter will be concerned with the second section, which contains a preliminary discussion of the central issues and concepts involved in the Deduction and which Kant points out is intended to prepare rather than to instruct. But since in the A-Preface, Kant suggests a different, thematic division of the Deduction into an objective and a subjective deduction, which he also, and more appropriately, describes as the objective and subjective sides of a single deduction, this division must also be considered. Accordingly, the present chapter will be divided into two parts: the first discusses the objective–subjective division and some of the issues it raises and the second analyzes the text of section 2.

I

After noting in the Preface to the first edition that the section entitled "**Deduction of the Pure Concepts of the Understanding**" cost him the most effort, Kant writes:

This enquiry, which goes rather deep, has two sides. One side refers to the objects of the pure understanding, and is supposed to demonstrate and make comprehensible the objective validity of its concepts *a priori*; thus it belongs essentially to my ends. The other side deals with the pure understanding itself, concerning its possibility and the powers of cognition on which it itself rests; thus it considers it in a subjective relation, and although this exposition is of great importance in respect of my chief end, it does not belong essentially to it; because the chief question always remains: "What and how much can understanding and reason cognize free of all experience?" and not: "How is the **faculty of thinking** itself possible?" (Axvi–xvii)

Kant here appears unequivocal with regard to the primacy of the objective side of the Deduction. Indeed, in the remainder of the paragraph he goes so far as to advise the reader "that even in case my subjective deduction does not produce the complete conviction that I expect, the objective deduction that is my primary concern would come into its full strength, on which what is said at pages 92–93 should even be sufficient by itself" (AXVII). By contrast, he says of the subjective deduction that it is something like the search for a cause for a given effect, and is therefore something like a hypothesis (although, as I will elsewhere take the opportunity to show, this is not in fact how matters stand), it appears as if I am taking the liberty in this case of expressing an **opinion**, and that the reader might therefore be free to hold another **opinion**.   (Axvii)

It is difficult to avoid concluding from this that Kant was trying to have it both ways regarding the import as well as the status of the subjective side of the Deduction. With regard to the former, he insists upon the supremacy and apparently also the sufficiency of the objective side, while also suggesting that the subjective side is itself very important, albeit without explaining why this is the case. With regard to the latter, he acknowledges, on the one hand, that the subjective side is something like (*gleichsam*) the search for a cause of a given effect and, as such, is similar to a hypothesis, which, in turn, seems to suggest that it is a matter of opinion, which makes no normative demands upon the reader, while, on the other hand, insisting that this is not really the case.

Inasmuch as Kant refers to a worry about whether the subjective side of the Deduction will produce "the complete conviction" he hopes for, he is best read as concerned with the rhetorical force of his argument rather than its cogency, which he does not appear to doubt. Moreover, this concern with his argument's power to convince is certainly warranted, given its obscurity and complexity, which has led many critics to dismiss the subjective side of the Deduction, if not the Deduction as a whole, as incoherent or as "part of the imaginary subject of transcendental psychology."[1]

Setting that large issue aside for the present, we are left with the question of the systematic import of the subjective side, which boils down to the question of whether Kant is entitled to claim that the objective side suffices of itself. But in order to answer this question, we must ask a further one, namely, suffices for what? And though the obvious answer would seem to be to establish the objective validity of the categories, which Kant suggests "belongs essentially" to his ends, if we keep in mind that the preface is to the *Critique* as a whole, of which the Transcendental Deduction is only a part, albeit a vitally important one, the issue turns out to be more complicated than it initially appears.

The complication becomes evident when one considers the context in which the above-cited passages are contained. In the immediately preceding discussion, Kant is concerned with the issue of the certainty that is to be attributed to the tenets of the *Critique*, and he insists that in such an endeavor there is no place for hypotheses or opinions. With this in mind, Kant in effect pleads with the reader not to be dissuaded by portions of the work that may initially seem to lack the requisite certainty, but are only incidental to its chief end (Axv–i). As the ensuing remarks indicate, the portion that Kant has in mind is the subjective side of the Deduction, which also explains why he suggests that it is something like an hypothesis and something about which one

---

[1] Strawson (1966), 32.

may have an opinion; though he makes sure to add that it is not really such. Clearly, Kant could not say that it is merely a hypothesis or a matter of opinion, since by his own criteria that would preclude its presence in the *Critique*.

Despite initial impressions, the contextualization of Kant's remarks regarding the subjective side of the Deduction indicates that his focus is on its place within the total architecture of the *Critique* rather than its role in the proof-structure of the Deduction. Moreover, this places a different light on his ambiguous comments about the relation between the two sides of the Deduction. Consider the expressions "chief end" (*Hauptzwecks*) and "chief question" (*Hauptfrage*). Kant describes the latter as "What and how much can understanding and reason cognize free of all experience?" And he contrasts this with the question "How is the faculty of thinking itself possible?" Since the latter is the question with which the subjective side of the Deduction supposedly deals, Kant is usually read as maintaining that the chief question is that which is dealt with by the objective side of the deduction; viz., the objective validity of the categories, and that the subjective side is not essential to answering *that* question, which leaves its very presence in the *Critique* something of a puzzle.

Nevertheless, the issue is rendered moot by a more careful consideration of what Kant actually describes as the chief question, which, as the reference to reason as well as understanding suggests, is more appropriately viewed as the chief question of the *Critique* as a whole rather than of the Deduction. Moreover, it is evident that the issue dealt with in the subjective side of the Deduction, however germane it may be to the Deduction, is not directly relevant to *that* question; whereas the issue posed in the objective side, though, likewise, not equivalent to the chief question of the *Critique*, clearly belongs essentially to it, since it addresses the question of the possibility and bounds of a priori cognition through the understanding.[2] Indeed, we have already seen that from the perspective of the *Critique* as a whole the latter question is given equal prominence with the former. And this implies that when Kant claims that the objective side would be "sufficient by itself" he should be taken to mean sufficient for the chief end of the *Critique* rather than for the deduction of the categories.

This implies that in the Preface Kant does not even address, much less specify, the role of the subjective side of the Deduction in its overall argument. Instead, keenly aware of its obscurity and seeming arbitrariness, and fearful that this may detract from the larger message of the *Critique*, Kant goes out of his way to minimize the relevance of this side of the Deduction to the latter, thereby glossing over the lesser, but still vitally important question of its role in the Deduction. Our present concern, however, is with the latter question and the central contention is that the subjective side of the Deduction is an indispensable complement to its objective side, since both are required to attain its goal. And though making this case will be the main task of

---

[2] This point is noted by Carl (1992), 45.

the remainder of the present and the next chapter, I shall here attempt to lay the foundation for this endeavor by considering three fundamental questions that must be dealt with by any serious interpretation of the text: (1) What is the overall goal of the Deduction? (2) What is contained in its subjective side? (3) How does the latter contribute to this goal?

1) *The goal of the Deduction*: This goal can be described in two complementary ways. The first and most obvious is that it is to demonstrate the objective validity of the categories specified in "the Clue" as a priori conditions of the possibility of experience, thereby both resolving the *quid juris* and limiting the scope of the categories to objects of possible experience. The second, less obvious but equally important way, is that it endeavors to exorcize the previously noted specter that "appearances could ... be so constituted that the understanding would not find them in accord with the conditions of its unity" (A90/B123). We saw that this specter is both the source of the peculiar difficulty confronting a transcendental deduction of the categories, as contrasted with one of the concepts of space and time, and that it arose as a direct consequence of Kant's radical separation of sensibility and under-standing brought about by the "great light."

   To recapitulate, the problem is that this separation leaves open the possibility that what is given in sensibility might not conform to the requirements of the understand-ing, which would leave the categories without a purchase on the world. What makes this both a serious problem for the prospects of a transcendental deduction and its resolution equivalent to the attainment of its goal under the first description is that the mere possibility of such a lack of cognitive fit seems sufficient to derail at least the positive side of the project. This is because the latter requires not merely a *de facto* conformity of the sensible with the intellectual, which might be established by an appeal to the regularity of experience, but a *necessary* one, which can only be estab-lished a priori and which precludes the real possibility of the scenario described by the specter. Accordingly, exorcizing this specter is both a necessary and sufficient condi-tion of establishing the a priori validity of the categories with regard to objects of possible experience and, as such, deserves equal billing as the goal of the Deduction.

2) *The contents of the subjective side of the Deduction*: We have seen that in the Preface Kant states that this side of the Deduction deals with the seemingly arcane and tangential question of how the faculty of thinking is possible; but he gives a more informative account of the matter in the introductory portion of section 2 of the A-Deduction, where he writes:

Now these concepts, which contain *a priori* the pure thinking in every experience, we find in the categories, and it is already a sufficient deduction of them and justification of their objective validity if we can prove that by means of them alone an object can be thought. But since in such a thought there is more at work than the single faculty of thinking, namely the understanding, and the understanding itself, as a faculty of cognition that is to be related to objects also requires an elucidation of the possibility of this relation, we must first assess not the empirical but the transcendental constitution of the subjective sources that comprise the *a priori* foundations for the possibility of experience.   (A96–7)

Combining these passages, we arrive at the idea that the subjective side of the Deduction is concerned with the question of how the understanding is itself possible and that this is to be determined by investigating the "transcendental constitution of the subjective sources" that underlie the exercise of this faculty and function as a priori conditions of the possibility of experience. Although Kant does not here specify these sources, this was not necessary, since he had already done so at A94. As we saw in Chapter 4, these sources are said to be the faculties of sense, imagination, and apperception, which Kant claimed are responsible respectively for a synopsis of the manifold a priori through sense, its synthesis through the imagination, and the unity of this synthesis through original apperception.[3]

In discussing this topic in Chapter 3 in connection with B 12, where this list of sources or cognitive powers initially appears, it was noted that the understanding was not included among them, being characterized instead as "the unity of apperception in relation to the faculty of imagination" (LB 23: 18_{3-4}; 258). This seems to suggest that Kant assigned to it a merely secondary or dependent status, which is difficult to reconcile with the grandiose claim in the *Critique* that the human understanding is the "lawgiver to nature" (A126). Nevertheless, the reappearance of this characterization in virtually the same terms in the *Critique* at A119 indicates that, rather than being merely a passing thought entertained in a private jotting, it represents Kant's considered view at the time.

We shall see why this is the case in addressing our third question; but before leaving the second it is necessary to consider Kant's contention that it is the *transcendental* rather than the empirical constitution of the subjective sources of cognition with which the subjective side of the Deduction is concerned. This claim, which Kant clearly intended to distance his views from the superficially similar views of Tetens and perhaps other empiricists, has met with a peculiar fate in the literature. At one extreme is Strawson's previously noted delegation of this part of Kant's project to "the imaginary subject of transcendental psychology." This dismissive view, which has many echoes in contemporary analytic Kant interpretation, evidently regards the so-called "transcendental turn" as an illicit speculative venture into the noumenal, which is totally at variance with "critical" principles. By contrast, at the other extreme are those older Kant interpreters, who apparently ignored Kant's claim and regarded the subjective side of Deduction as an ill-considered lapse into an

---

[3] Kant obviously does not understand "synopsis" in its contemporary sense; viz., as the summary of a plot or abstract of an argument. Rather, he evidently takes it in its original Greek sense (*syn-horan*) as a seeing together or at once. But since he connects it with the senses, and therefore regards it as passive, it must be contrasted with seeing a multiplicity of items as in some sense belonging or fitting together to constitute a whole of some sort, which for Kant requires a synthesis.

empirical psychology.[4] And, finally, occupying a middle position are some more recent commentators, who likewise ignore this claim, but see in Kant's account of our cognitive capacities a welcome engagement on his part in the naturalistic project of a broadly empirical cognitive psychology or cognitive science.[5]

An examination of the text indicates that none of these views reflects a genuine understanding of the nature of Kant's project. In order to appreciate this, however, it is necessary to recognize what Kant understands by "transcendental" in this context. Although he uses the term in a variety of ways in the *Critique* and elsewhere, what is most germane for present purposes is his initial stipulative definition of it as a species of cognition, which was cited at the beginning of Chapter 4.[6] As we saw, Kant states that he calls "all cognition transcendental that is occupied not so much with objects but rather with our *a priori* concepts of objects in general" (A11–12), for which he substituted in the second edition "cognition...that is occupied not so much with objects but rather with our mode of cognition of objects insofar as this is possible *a priori*" (B25).[7] Setting aside the subtle differences between these formulations, the essential point is that transcendental cognition, which is the kind of cognition operative in the subjective side of the Deduction, is a second-order cognition of the a priori conditions of first-order empirical cognition, which, as such, are also conditions of the possibility of experience.[8] Accordingly, it is neither a cognition of mysterious noumenal capacities or activities, as the Strawsonian view assumes, nor a descriptive psychological account of the actual operations of our cognitive powers, as the two other views distinguished above maintain, albeit in quite different ways. Rather, it is an attempt to show how the powers of sense, imagination, and apperception, which were investigated in their empirical functioning by Tetens, also have a transcendental function as sources of a priori conditions of empirical cognition.

3) *The place of the subjective side of the Deduction in the Deduction as a whole*: We have seen that in the Preface to the first edition of the *Critique* Kant suggests that the subjective side of the Deduction is concerned with the question: "How is the faculty of thinking [*das Vermögen zu denken*] possible"? (Axvii), which seems at first glance

---

[4] For a clear statement of the non-psychological nature of Kant's claims in the "subjective side" of the Transcendental Deduction and critique of some of the older commentators who read Kant in this way, specifically Erdmann and de Vleeschauwer, see Carl (1992), 52.

[5] The contemporary commentators whom I have in mind prominently include Kitcher (1990 and 2011) and Brook (1994). For my discussion of Kitcher's view in her earlier work see Allison (1996), 53–66.

[6] Among the variety of ways in which Kant uses the term "transcendental" two stand out as fundamental. One is the "critical" or epistemological sense, as in the definitions considered above, in which it refers to a second-order investigation. The other is the traditional sense, discussed in earlier chapters, in which it refers to a consideration of things or objects in general or as such, in which case transcendental philosophy is ontology or *metaphysica generalis*. I discuss these two senses of the term with respect to the contrast between transcendental idealism and transcendental realism in Allison (2012), 67–83.

[7] See also A56–7/B80–1.

[8] The difference between these formulations and their implications for understanding the shift in Kant's views between the first and second editions of the *Critique* has been analyzed at length by Pinder (1986). I discuss Pinder's account in Allison (2012), 70, note 6.

to be peripheral to the goal of the Deduction under either of the descriptions of this goal formulated above. Nevertheless, a closer consideration of the matter indicates that this is not the case. The essential text is a previously cited passage from the introduction to section 2 of the A-Deduction (A96–7), where, after stating that it would be sufficient for a deduction of the categories to show that it is only by means of them that an object can be thought, and identifying the faculty of thinking with the understanding, Kant goes on to note that "in such a thought," by which he evidently meant the thought of an object, more is at work than the understanding and that the explanation of the possibility of its relation to objects requires an examination of the "transcendental constitution of the subjective sources that comprise the *a priori* foundations of the very possibility of experience."

In order to grasp what Kant was getting at here, it is essential to recognize what he meant by an "object." Although in a broad sense, every thought, simply qua thought, is the thought of an (intentional) object, including, for example, that of a figure enclosed by two straight lines, it seems that Kant must here be taken to mean the thought of a *really* (as opposed to merely logically) possible object; for only an object in this sense could count as an object of possible experience and, outside of mathematics, only such an object requires more than merely the understanding for its conception. Otherwise expressed, Kant is concerned with the conditions of the real rather than the merely logical use of the understanding, since only the former requires the categories, as contrasted with the logical functions of judgment. And it follows from this that if the Deduction is to show that and how the categories make possible the cognition of empirical objects, it is necessary to explain how a real use of the understanding is possible, which, in turn, requires explaining the relation of the understanding to the above-mentioned subjective sources or powers of the mind.

This leads us directly to the previously noted characterization of the understanding in terms of the relation between apperception and the imagination. On the one hand, this reflects Kant's view, which can be traced back at least to the *Duisburg Nachlass*, that apperception, understood as the power of self-consciousness, which can also be regarded as the capacity to represent something to oneself, is a necessary condition of *any* use of the understanding, and therefore of its real use; while, on the other hand, it is not a sufficient condition of the latter. This is because the real use of the understanding is also dependent upon the imagination, a view which, with respect to the categories, finds its definitive expression in the Schematism. Moreover, the reason for this is not hard to find. As we have already seen, the essential point is that for the "critical" Kant the real use of the understanding depends upon its relation to sensibility and that during the last portion of the "Silent Decade," likely under the influence of Tetens, Kant came to think that this mediation was made possible by the imagination because it had one foot in each camp.

Finally, it should be clear from this that a demonstration of the real use of the understanding is just what is required to exorcize the specter that appearances might not conform to the conditions of thought. For such a scenario might well be characterized as one in which the understanding would have a logical use (if we could speak of the understanding at all in such circumstances), since such a use is independent of its relation to sensibility, but not a real one, since, *ex hypothesi*, the categories, which as conditions of possible experience are conditions of its empirical use, would have no application. And, once again, it must be kept in mind that this real use cannot be limited to *some* appearances, i.e., those which through the application of the categories become experience in the technical Kantian sense, but must extend to everything that could become an object of conscious awareness. In short, the real use of the understanding must extend to perception. Accordingly, our present task is to examine the multi-faceted argument of the A-Deduction, in order to determine how and if it establishes this result.

II

As Kant's "preliminary reminder" that his concern is to prepare rather than to instruct indicates, he was acutely conscious that the concepts and arguments he introduces in section 2 would seem obscure and perplexing to his readers, who had not followed him on his novel philosophical path and whose philosophical orientations were likely either Wolffian rationalism, one of the various forms of empiricism, or perhaps the practically oriented eclecticism characteristic of the Berlin *Aufklärung*.[9] In addition to this reminder, the section is composed of five prefatory paragraphs and four "numbers," the first three of which spell out the various aspects of a "three-fold synthesis" and the fourth contains a provisional or preliminary explanation of the possibility of the categories. I shall discuss each of these in turn, while attempting to show that together they constitute a regressive or analytic account that moves from a view of experience with which Kant could assume all parties would agree, or at least recognize as familiar, to a set of propositions concerning the conditions of empirical cognition, which would likely meet resistance and puzzlement.

A) *Kant's prefatory remarks* (A95–8): Kant begins with a reflection on what might be called the concept of an a priori concept or, more precisely, the concept of a pure concept of the understanding.[10] Assuming the principle that concepts without a corresponding intuition are empty or, as he here puts it, "would be only the logical form of a concept, but not the concept itself through which something could be thought," Kant argues that it would be impossible for a concept to both be generated a priori and relate to an object, unless it either belonged itself within the concept of a possible experience or consisted of elements of a possible experience (A95). Although

---

[9] This may help to explain Kant's keenness in gaining the support for the *Critique* of Mendelssohn, Tetens, and Garve, who were arguably the leading representatives of these orientations in Germany.

[10] Although Kant initially suggests that his characterization holds of any a priori concept, his failure to mention mathematical concepts and his account of the conditions that such a concept must meet indicate that he is here interested merely in pure concepts of the understanding.

it is not clear what Kant had in mind with this distinction, it is evident that this claim constitutes a challenge to both empiricism and rationalism. The challenge to the former consists in the assertion of the possibility that a concept could be generated a priori, yet still relate to an object. The challenge to the latter consists in the restriction placed on a priori concepts; viz., that they can only contain conditions of a possible experience and the objects falling under them must be objects of a possible experience.

Kant admits that, once possessed of such concepts, it is possible to conceive objects that cannot be given in a possible experience, either by omitting something that necessarily belongs to the conditions of a possible experience (e.g., the concept of a spirit) or by extending it further than experience can encompass (e.g., the concept of God).[11] But he also insists that the "**elements** of a priori cognitions," including "arbitrary and absurd fantasies," must always contain "the pure a priori conditions of a possible experience and of an object of it;" for otherwise nothing would be thought through them (A96).

In a previously discussed passage, Kant identifies these concepts with the categories and contends that it would constitute a sufficient deduction of them, "if we can prove that by means of them an object can be thought" (A97). Although this might seem to make the task of the Deduction rather easy, since an object can be thought through any concept that does not contain a contradiction, we have seen that what Kant really meant was not simply thought, but thought as a really possible object. And since Kant notes that in such a thought more than merely the understanding is involved, it is also necessary to investigate the conditions of the possibility of this faculty's relation to objects, which, in turn, necessitates an examination of the "transcendental constitution of the subjective sources that comprise the a priori foundations of the very possibility of experience" (A97).

Underlying this examination is the principle that cognition requires both receptivity and spontaneity, which Kant here connects with the contrast between a synopsis, through which a manifold is given in intuition, and a synthesis, through which it is unified.[12] While it is clear that Kant had in mind a single act of synthesis, he indicates that it is "three-fold" (dreifachen), meaning that it has three aspects or levels, which he characterizes as "the **apprehension** of representations, as modifications of the mind, in intuition; of the reproduction of them in the imagination (der Einbildung); and of their **recognition** in the concept" (A97). And since the three layers of this synthesis correspond to three stages in the development of an empirical

---

[11] We saw in Chapter 2 that in Dreams Kant equated the concept of spirit with that of an immaterial substance, which indicates that what it omits is materiality, which for the "critical" Kant is a necessary condition of the real use of the concept of substance. And the concept of God is transcendent in the technical sense that it requires us to go beyond the bounds of a possible experience.

[12] For what Kant understands by a synopsis see note 3.

cognition: as intuition, as image, and as concept, this suggests that the three-fold synthesis is to be taken as the process through which such cognition is generated.

Although the terminology is different, Kant's position here is substantially the same as that contained in "the Clue," where he distinguished between synthesis, which is attributed to the imagination, and bringing this synthesis to concepts, which is assigned to the understanding. In analyzing that distinction in Chapter 4, the focus was on the contrast that Kant there drew between two conceptions of synthesis: "synthesis as such," which is the combining of representations that is attributed to the imagination, and "synthesis in the most extended sense," which encompasses both this act of combination and the conceptual act of bringing the former to concepts. Relating this to the three-fold synthesis, apprehension and reproduction can be regarded as two aspects of the "synthesis as such" of "the Clue"; whereas "recognition in a concept" pertains to synthesis in "the most extended sense."

A further point in Kant's prefatory account that merits attention is his remark that immediately precedes his discussion of synthesis and provides the framework in terms of which the latter is to be understood. He writes: "If every individual representation were entirely foreign to the other, as it were isolated and separated from it, then there could never arise anything like [*so etwas*] cognition, which is a whole of compared and connected representations" (A97). This conception of cognition as a unified whole is central to Kantian epistemology, since it is presupposed by his account of synthesis and the need for the categories. Of equal import for the Deduction, however, is the phrase "anything like;" for this implies that not merely what Kant referred to in "the Clue" as "cognition in the proper sense" (A78), but also that its precondition; viz., perception, presupposes such a whole. And we shall see that this is precisely what Kant attempts to show.

B) *The synthesis of apprehension in intuition*: Kant begins his account of the three-fold synthesis with what he characterizes as a general remark that is applicable to everything that follows:

Wherever our representations may arise, whether through the influence of external things or as the effect of inner causes, whether they have originated *a priori* or empirically as appearances— as modifications of the mind they nevertheless belong to inner sense, and as such all of our cognitions are in the end subjected to the formal condition of inner sense, namely time, as that in which they must all be ordered, connected and brought into relations.   (A98-9)

Kant here affirms that the temporal nature of consciousness is the starting point of his account of cognition, which gives to the A-Deduction a phenomenological dimension that is largely lacking in its second edition counterpart. The essential point is that because all our representations, as modifications of inner sense are given in time, i.e., successively, they must be unified in order to constitute a whole such as is required for cognition. Accordingly, time is both the source of the necessity for this unification and the medium in which it occurs.

This general point is then illustrated by an analysis of apprehension, which is the most basic mental act for Kant because it is exercised directly upon intuition. He writes:

Every intuition contains a manifold in itself, which however would not be represented as such if the mind did not distinguish the time in the succession of impressions on one another; for **as contained in one moment** [*Augenblick*] no representation can be anything other than absolute unity. Now in order for **unity** of intuition to come from this manifold ... it is necessary first to run through [*das Durchlaufen*] and then to take together [*die Zusammenehmung*] this manifoldness, which action I call the **synthesis of apprehension**, since it is aimed directly at the intuition, which to be sure provides a manifold but can never effect this as such, and indeed as contained in one representation, without the occurrence of such a synthesis.   (A99)

This paragraph contains at least four distinct claims, three of which are packed into the first sentence. The first is that every intuition, qua intuition, contains a manifold in itself.[13] This means that, even though Kant defines an intuition as the representation of an individual, it is not regarded as something simple, e.g., a Humean simple impression; rather, it involves a multiplicity of items (impressions) received together, i.e., a synopsis.

The second claim is that it is necessary to distinguish between being presented with a manifold and representing it *as* a manifold. The point here is that, while a multiplicity of impressions is given through sensibility, it is not *given as a multiplicity*. The latter requires *taking* it as such, which, in turn, means taking the impressions as in some sense belonging together, i.e., as constituting a synthetic unity (a many in one).

The third claim is that, since impressions, qua modifications of inner sense, are given successively, it is a necessary condition for representing a manifold of impressions as a manifold that the mind distinguish the time in the succession of these impressions, which presumably means being aware of them as successive. And the reason given for this is that "**as contained in one moment** (*Augenblick*) no representation can be anything other than absolute unity." In other words, an awareness of a temporal succession is a necessary condition of the representation of the manifoldness of the impressions contained in an intuition.

The fourth claim, which occupies the second sentence and supposedly follows from the first three, is that the production of the unity required for the representation of the manifold given in an intuition as a manifold, and therefore for the representation of an intuition as an intuition (the representation of an individual), presupposes a synthesis through which the successively given items are run through and taken together. Kant terms this act of canvassing and unifying the "synthesis of apprehension." By "apprehension" Kant means the awareness, empirical consciousness, or perception

---

[13] At A120 Kant claims that every appearance contains a manifold; but since by "appearance" Kant understands the "undetermined object of an empirical intuition," these are equivalent.

(these here being taken as equivalent) of a determinate object, e.g., the apple lying on my table.[14] To be sure, I do not apprehend it as an apple, since that would require its recognition in a concept (the third layer of the three-fold synthesis); but, limiting ourselves to visual qualities, I do apprehend it as a red and roundish something.

The problematic nature of Kant's account of apprehension is located mainly in its third claim, which is subject to at least two lines of objection: that it turns on a conflation and that it involves a contradiction. The alleged conflation is of what is actually given in an intuition and what is involved in its processing by the mind. The former, it might be argued, can contain a succession, as in the perception of a sequence of states, e.g., of water in a liquid and a solid state; but it can also contain a multiplicity of co-existing items. Consider, for example, the perception of a house. Its perception encompasses a multiplicity of items, e.g., windows, roof, door, and, depending on the angle of vision, perhaps two of its sides, all of which could be said to be taken in at a glance. More generally, every outer intuition for Kant comprises a multiplicity of sensory data arranged in space, which is presumably apprehended with one glance. Accordingly, so the objection goes, it seems that either Kant himself or the interpreter who attributes the patently false view to him that the awareness of a multiplicity requires an awareness of the succession in one's representations is guilty of conflating what is actually given at one time with the act through which the given is processed, i.e., run through and taken together by the mind, which does require a certain period of time.[15]

The problem with this line of objection is that it ignores the premise that the given with which Kant is here concerned is not the given as such, which need not be successive, but the given qua modification of inner sense. And since time is the form of inner sense, this means (1) that what is given in inner sense is necessarily given successively and (2) that because of this the awareness of its manifoldness requires that it be run through and held together by the mind, which, as noted, is a temporal process. In short, we need to distinguish between a manifold being given successively and being given as successive. Although the latter does not apply to the manifold of inner sense, the former does, which, as we shall see below, is precisely why Kant insists that apprehension requires reproduction.

The alleged contradiction concerns two of Kant's major claims: that every intuition contains a manifold and that "[A]s **contained in one moment** no representation can be anything other than absolute unity." Assuming that by "absolute unity" is meant one that is not relative, i.e., a synthetic unity or a unity of a plurality of items, an intuition contained in a single moment would not contain any manifoldness,

[14] See, for example, A120, B160, A161/B202, and A167/B209. We saw that apprehension was already a central topic in the *Duisburg Nachlass*.

[15] A version of this objection was directed against my interpretation by an anonymous reader for Oxford University Press. de Vleeschauwer (1934), 243, notes 3 and 4 refers to K. Burkhard and Laas as raising similar objections against Kant.

thereby apparently generating a contradiction.[16] Simply put, the objection is that one cannot claim both that every intuition contains a manifold and that some intuitions; viz., those contained in a single moment, do not.

This objection has recently been posed in stark terms by Lorne Falkenstein, who, while acknowledging the importance for Kant of the proposition that every intuition, qua intuition, contains a manifold, insists that it is contradicted by the claim that, insofar as it is contained in a single moment, an intuition is an absolute unity.[17] Falkenstein's preferred remedy for this situation is radical surgery, which takes the form of a denial that the latter claim has "canonical" status, and therefore need not be taken seriously. In justification for this proposal, he points out that the troublesome claim is surrounded by passages in which Kant either explicitly states or implies the opposite, and that it is absent from the B-Deduction, which he takes as indicating that Kant had belatedly recognized its erroneous nature.[18] But apparently realizing that these reasons for dismissing Kant's claim as an aberration are not decisive, Falkenstein proposes an alternative interpretation, which avoids saddling Kant with a contradiction. On his proposed alternative, in the passage in question Kant takes "representation" to refer to "*representations of intuitions*" rather than to "*intuitive representations*," from which it supposedly follows that what constitutes an "absolute unity" are not the intuitions themselves, qua given, but qua conceptualized or brought under the unity of apperception.[19]

Although Falkenstein's proposal avoids the contradiction, it does so at the high cost of foisting a totally implausible reading upon the text. First, we cannot take Kant as appealing to the unity of apperception at this juncture, since the chief purpose of his account of the three-fold synthesis is to lead the reader to the point at which the necessity of this conception emerges. Second, since intuitions are themselves representations, a representation of an intuition would be a representation of a representation. And while this is itself a perfectly coherent notion, indeed, Kant affirms a version of it with his judgments of inner sense, it has no place in the present context because, again, conceptualization has not yet entered the story. Third, and most important, Kant held that bringing representations under the unity of apperception imposes an *objective* unity upon them and this has nothing to do with the "absolute unity" with which we are presently concerned.

Moreover, there is a simpler and more effective way of avoiding this apparent contradiction, namely, by considering what Kant understands by a "moment" or "instant" (*Augenblick*). While Kant does not explain this crucial point in the passage currently under consideration, he does elsewhere. In what is his fullest statement of his view of the matter in the *Critique* he writes:

The property of magnitudes on account of which no part of them is the smallest (no part is simple) is called their continuity. Space and time are *quanta continua*, because no part of them

[16] On the meaning of "absolute unity" see de Vleeschauwer (1934), 245.
[17] Falkenstein (1995), 75.   [18] Ibid., 75–6.   [19] Ibid., 76–7.

can be given except as enclosed between boundaries (points and instants [*Augenblicke*]), thus only in such a way that this part is again a space or a time. Space therefore consists only of spaces, time of times. Points and instants are only boundaries, i.e., mere places of their limitation; but places always presuppose those intuitions that limit or determine them, and from mere places, as components that could be given prior to space and time, neither space nor time can be composed.   (A169–70/B211)

For present purposes, the crucial point is that an instant or moment (*ein Augenblick*) is a boundary or limit rather than a part of time, just as a point is a boundary or limit rather than a part of space.[20] Thus, pace Falkenstein, there is no contradiction for the simple reason that since, *ex hypothesi*, an instant or moment is not a part of time *nothing* is intuited in it, including an absolute unity. Moreover, it is clear from this that time for Kant is not composed of successive atomic moments, which need to be unified by a synthesis in order to generate the manifoldness that pertains to an intuition. Applying this to the passage in question, it follows that Kant should not be read as maintaining that in a moment we intuit only a miniscule portion of time that constitutes an "absolute unity," a temporal analogue of Berkeley's *minimum visibile*. His point is rather that, if we (mistakenly) ignore the successive way in which the manifold is given and focus instead on what might conceivably be contained in a single moment, we would never have the manifoldness that requires a synthesis in order to be represented *as a manifold*. Not only does this reading not contradict the proposition that every intuition contains a manifold, it presupposes it. In fact, Kant makes this very point in a *Reflexion* that is closely related to the argument of A99, where he writes:

All appearances stand as representations in time and are determined in time. As a part of an entire appearance it cannot be determined (genetically apprehended) in a moment [*Augenblick*], but only in a part of time. A part of time lies between two limits and therefore two moments; it is therefore itself [determinable in the] one time, therefore every part of appearance is exhibitable [*exponibel*] in time; therefore, like time itself, it does not consist of simple parts.   (R5390 18: 169–70)

This not only resolves the apparent contradiction noted by Falkenstein, but sheds light on a broader issue concerning the interpretation of the subjective side of the Transcendental Deduction as a whole; viz., whether Kant's argument is based on an atomistic view of perception, in which the "given" is regarded in terms of the model of isolated Humean simple impressions and the task of the imagination and/or understanding is to unify them. Despite its unattractiveness on phenomenological grounds and its manifest incompatibility with central aspects of Kant's thought (including the proposition that every intuition contains a manifold) this is the sort

---

[20] See Paton (1936a), 358.

of view to which interpreters who ignore what Kant says about the continuity of time and focus instead on the notion that what is given in a moment must have absolute unity are led to attribute to him.

One who does this grudgingly is Robert Paul Wolff, who laments the fact that "Kant appears to think that at any moment in time I can only perceive one simple sensation and nothing more."[21] And while he regards this as not only incorrect but at variance with Kant's view in the *Critique* as a whole (in which respect he is quite correct), he takes Kant as having meant to say that "[W]e could never *know* a representation as diverse in a single moment. In order to know a diversity of representations, even if they are given as simultaneous, the mind must run over them *one after another*."[22] Although this is likewise correct, it is beside the point, since in the passage in question Kant is discussing the successive nature of the manifold of an intuition as given, not the process through which it is represented as a manifold.

By contrast, a noteworthy example of a non-grudging atomistic reading of Kant's claim that insofar as a representation is contained in a single moment it "can never be anything but absolute unity" is provided by Guyer. Rather than viewing it as an error and incompatible with Kant's view, Guyer maintains that "this premise... will ultimately provide the key to the objective validity of the categories."[23] And, somewhat later, he explains what he means by this when he remarks that "this statement [the above-mentioned premise]... implies that at any given time *my representation of a manifold of representation* is not itself a manifold of representations but rather a *single representation* which must be *interpreted* or *judged* to *represent* a diversity or manifold of representations."[24] This claim evidently reflects Guyer's view that Kant's best argument for the validity of the categories is not to be found in the Transcendental Deduction in either edition but in a late formulation of the Refutation of Idealism. Quite apart from that, however, it is clear that Guyer holds that the given according to Kant consists of single, atomic representations, which are subsequently "interpreted" as belonging to collections of other such representations.

Guyer's atomistic reading commits the opposite of Wolff's error. Whereas Wolff, in an endeavor to preserve Kant's claim that every intuition contains a manifold, erroneously considered this as contradicted by the claim that all that could be represented in a moment would be an absolute unity, Guyer, taking the latter as the starting point of Kant's account, appears to gloss over the claim that every intuition contains a manifold.[25] But their opposite conclusions stem from a common

---

[21] Wolff (1963), 152.   [22] Ibid., 152–3.   [23] Guyer (1987), 122.   [24] Ibid., 148.

[25] An indication of this is to be found in a later account by Guyer in which he equates "a manifold of intuition" with "several intuitions of an object" Guyer (2006), 83, thereby either ignoring or denying Kant's claim that every intuition contains a manifold.

mistake: the view that by "*ein Augenblick*" Kant understood a minimal extent of time rather than a limit that is not, properly speaking, a part of time at all.[26]

Kant concludes his discussion of the first layer of the three-fold synthesis by interjecting the element of apriority. He writes:

Now this synthesis of apprehension must also be exercised *a priori*, i.e., in regard to representations that are not empirical. For without it we could have *a priori* neither the representations of space nor of time, since these can be generated only through the synthesis of the manifold that sensibility in its original receptivity provides. We therefore have a **pure** synthesis of apprehension.   (A99–100)

Although Kant's language might suggest that he is distinguishing between two syntheses of apprehension, one of which is "exercised *a priori*" and is "pure," while the other is exercised a posteriori (whatever that could mean) and is empirical, further consideration indicates that he is really referring to a single synthesis that is exercised upon two kinds of representations: empirical and pure intuitions. Accordingly, the important point added in this paragraph is that, since we have learned from the Transcendental Aesthetic that the pure intuitions of space and time each contain a manifold (of spaces and times), the representation of them as containing these manifolds likewise presupposes a synthesis, which is termed "*a priori*" or "pure" because of the nature of the material that is synthesized. Moreover, insofar as pure intuition for Kant is the form of empirical intuition, it also seems plausible to take the pure syntheses of space and time as not only necessary for the cognition of space and time but as the formal conditions of every empirical synthesis of apprehension.[27]

C) *The synthesis of reproduction in an imaginative representation (Einbildung)* (A100–2): This constitutes the second layer of Kant's account of the three-fold synthesis and its three paragraphs provide the first glimpse of a line of thought that will play a central role in the Deduction. Kant begins by articulating a proposition with which he can count upon the agreement of his readers: the principle or "law" of the association of ideas. He writes:

It is, to be sure, a merely empirical law in accordance with which representations that have often followed or accompanied one another are finally associated with each other and thereby placed in a connection in accordance with which, even without the presence of the object, one of these representations brings about a transition of the mind to the other in accordance with a constant rule.   (A100)

While this account of association is reminiscent of Hume and was likely formulated with Hume in mind, Kant is actually expressing a view with wide currency in the psychology textbooks of the time; indeed, one that would be shared by rationalists as

---

[26] Kant is not completely consistent on this score, however, since he sometimes uses "Augenblick" in the colloquial sense to mean a very short period of time. See A103.

[27] See Paton (1936a), 360.

well as empiricists.[28] Moreover, except perhaps for quibbles about terminology, few would quarrel with Kant's immediately following claim that,

This law of reproduction, however, presupposes that the appearances themselves are actually subject to such a rule, and that in the manifold of their representations an accompaniment or succession takes place according to certain rules; for without that our empirical imagination would never get to do anything suitable to its capacity, and would thus remain hidden in the interior of the mind, like a dead and to us unknown faculty.   (A100)

Whether framed in terms of association or reproduction, the essential point is that unless appearances were obliging enough to exhibit sufficient regularity, the imagination would never have occasion to exhibit its associative capacity—a view to which Hume gave classical expression with his ironic reference to "a kind of pre-established harmony between the course of nature and the succession of our ideas."[29] And to bring home the point, Kant devotes the remainder of the initial paragraph to a series of graphic examples, which are intended to illustrate the dependence of the operation of the human mind upon an assumed regularity in the course of nature. In the first and best known of these, Kant notes that, "If cinnabar were now red, now black, now light, now heavy ... then my empirical imagination would never even get the opportunity to think of heavy cinnabar on the occasion of the representation of the color red" (A100). Although Kant poses the issue in terms of the empirical functioning of the imagination, the stakes are much higher; for the real point, which Kant is not yet ready to introduce, is that without the regularity according to which objects perceived to possess certain properties can be assumed to possess certain others, the understanding would be unable either to form or to apply empirical concepts, in which case empirical cognition would be impossible.

   This is also a conclusion that would likely be endorsed by readers of all philosophical persuasions, including the skeptic, who might well conclude from this: "Well, so much the worse for empirical cognition!" In the next paragraph, however, Kant takes the matter in a new and more problematic direction, claiming in seemingly dogmatic fashion that, "There must therefore be something that itself makes possible this reproduction of appearances by being the *a priori* ground of a necessary synthetic unity of them" (A101). This suggests that Kant is here not simply making the non-controversial point that the regularity of appearances is a necessary condition of their reproducibility or associability by the imagination and, going one step further, of the formation of empirical concepts, but the much stronger claim that this reproducibility is itself necessary a priori. And, as Guyer is quick (perhaps too quick) to point out, such reasoning appears to involve a crude modal fallacy; viz., the move

---

[28] We have seen that this conception of association and its relation to the reproductive power of the imagination was a central topic in Tetens. In addition to Hume and Tetens, Longuenesse points out that it was affirmed by Wolff (*Psychologia empirica* §104) and Baumgarten (*Metaphysica* §561). See Longuenesse (1998a), 39 and note 11.

[29] Hume (1999), 129.

from a *hypothetical* or *conditional* necessity to an unconditional one. The former, which is a legitimate inference from the above, maintains: necessarily, if we are to find our way about amongst appearances, i.e., form reliable associations and empirical concepts, appearances must be reproducible; whereas the latter maintains that appearances necessarily are reproducible and that this can be known a priori.[30]

This line of objection poses a fundamental challenge to Kant's procedure in the A-Deduction, which is best dealt with through a consideration of the argument as a whole. But, not yet possessing such a synoptic view, our immediate concern is with the lesser question of whether it is reasonable to accuse Kant of such a fallacy in the text currently under consideration. And I maintain that a consideration of these three paragraphs strongly suggests that Kant is not here guilty of the crude fallacy of which Guyer accuses him, since the argument, such as it is, is quite different than the one that Guyer attributes to him.

To begin with, only a modicum of charity is required in order to take Kant's claim that "There must therefore be something that itself makes possible this reproduction of appearances by being the *a priori* ground of a necessary synthetic union of them" as the expression of a desideratum rather than a statement of a fait accompli. The existence of such an a priori or transcendental ground is certainly a desideratum for Kant, since the fate of the Deduction turns on it. Nevertheless, it would take an exceedingly literally minded and uncharitable interpreter to charge Kant with mounting an argument from the need for a transcendental ground for the reproducibility of appearances to its necessary existence.

Moreover, as already noted, the argument to which Kant at least gestures in his discussion of the synthesis of reproduction takes a quite different course. Reflecting on the need for a transcendental ground, he begins by suggesting that, "One soon comes upon this [something] if one recalls that appearances are not things in themselves, but rather the mere play of our representations, which in the end come down to determinations of inner sense" (A101). Kant here seems to be suggesting that, if we recognize that appearances are not things in themselves, but mere modifications of inner sense, i.e., if we accept transcendental idealism, we can account for the necessary synthetic unity in question; whereas if we view the matter from a transcendentally realistic standpoint, according to which the necessary synthetic unity would pertain to things in themselves, we cannot do so.

Clearly, this is not to claim that transcendental idealism is of itself sufficient to provide the a priori ground of the synthetic unity in question, since that would imply that the task had already been essentially accomplished in the Aesthetic, effectively

---

[30] See Guyer (1987), 122–3. Although Guyer formulates the issue in terms of whether "I am to experience an object" rather than, as I have here done, in terms of the modal status of the assumption that appearances involve regularity, I believe that the point remains the same. Moreover, we shall see that this gets to the heart of Guyer's critique of Kant's overall argument in the Transcendental Deduction, which turns on the charge that Kant conflates a merely conditional with an unconditional necessity.

making the Transcendental Deduction redundant.[31] But it does indicate that Kant regarded transcendental idealism as a necessary condition of locating such a ground, which is of itself sufficient to lead many commentators to reject the argument out of hand.

Nevertheless, transcendental idealism is *only* a necessary condition of a transcendental deduction and not itself either a sufficient condition or the sought-for transcendental ground. We shall see in the sequel that the latter is provided by the unity of apperception, the appeal to which as transcendental ground of the necessary synthetic unity, reproducibility, or affinity of appearances (these being here regarded as equivalent) presupposes transcendental idealism, but which Kant is not yet in a position to introduce. Thus, rather than appealing to a conception for which he has not yet prepared the reader, Kant continues:

[I]f we can demonstrate that even our purest *a priori* intuitions provide no cognition except insofar as they contain the sort of combination of the manifold that makes possible a thoroughgoing synthesis of reproduction, then this synthesis of the imagination would be grounded even prior to all experience on *a priori* principles, and one must assume a pure transcendental synthesis of this power, which grounds even the possibility of all experience (as that which the reproducibility of the appearances necessarily presupposes).   (A101–2)

It is noteworthy that, instead of attempting to provide a demonstration of the proposition to which he refers, Kant here presents a program for a future demonstration.[32] Moreover, rather than arguing directly from the presupposed reproducibility or regularity of appearances to its purported a priori condition or transcendental ground, this proposed demonstration will turn on the thesis that the cognition of space and time likewise presuppose a reproductive synthesis. And, in support of the latter point, Kant continues:

[I]t is obvious that if I draw a line in thought, or think of the time from one noon to the next, or even want to represent a certain number to myself, I must necessarily first grasp one of these manifold representations after another in my thoughts. But if I were always to lose the preceding representations (the first parts of the line, the preceding parts of time, or the successively represented units) from my thoughts and not reproduce them when I proceed to the following ones, then no whole representation and none of the previously mentioned thoughts, not even the purest and fundamental representations of space and time, could ever arise.   (A102)

As Kant himself notes, the point he is making here is obvious. Simply put, it boils down to the non-controversial proposition that in order to think a whole as such, whether it be a determinate portion of space (represented by a line), a stretch of time, or a number, it is necessary to think together all its constituent parts and, insofar as

---

[31] As Bird (2006), 287, puts the point, Kant is here specifying an enabling condition rather than providing a guarantee.

[32] The point is emphasized by Longuenesse (1998a), 40.

the representations of these parts are given successively, this means that it is necessary that the thought of the earlier ones be preserved while apprehending the later ones. What is not obvious, however, is the bearing that this is supposed to have on the point at issue; viz., the necessity of a transcendental ground of the reproducibility or regularity of appearances, such that this can be cognized a priori.

Presumably, the examples of a line, a stretch of time, and a number were chosen by Kant because, as a priori intuitive representations, the synthesis required for their representation must itself be a priori. And since space (which is represented by the concept of a line) and time are forms of appearances, the a priori syntheses required for their reproduction, like that of their apprehension, are arguably forms or conditions of the empirical syntheses of the appearances apprehended and reproduced in space and time. Nevertheless, it hardly follows that appearances are necessarily reproducible with respect to their *empirical content*, e.g., the physical properties that are thought to pertain to cinnabar, the representations of which constitute its concept, which is supposedly what Kant was trying to account for. Although Kant's argument on this interpretation is not guilty of a crude modal fallacy, it seems that it can be charged with the equally heinous offense of a gross non-sequitur.

This conclusion assumes, however, that Kant is here attempting to provide a relatively self-contained argument for his thesis regarding reproducibility of appearances, which, though requiring further articulation, will be retained in the definitive formulation of the Deduction in section 3. But, in addition to Kant's reminder that his concern in section 2 is to prepare rather than to instruct, the structure of his account (ascending from intuition, to imaginative representation, to concept) makes it implausible to assume that he would attempt to provide any such argument at this juncture. Instead, what one should expect to find is the introduction of an indispensable building block of such an argument, which, since we have already been told that it aims at demonstrating that the categories are necessary conditions of the possibility of experience, must also include an essential role for conceptualization.[33] Moreover, this is precisely what is provided by the claim that apart from the reproductive synthesis "not even the purest and fundamental representations of space and time, could ever arise."

This reading is confirmed by the final paragraph, where Kant concludes that,

The synthesis of apprehension is therefore inseparably combined with the synthesis of reproduction. And since the former constitutes the transcendental ground of the possibility of all cognition in general (not only of empirical cognition, but also of pure *a priori* cognition), the reproductive synthesis of the imagination belongs among the transcendental actions of the mind, and with respect to this we will also call this faculty the transcendental faculty of the imagination.   (A102)

---

[33] A similar conclusion is arrived at, albeit by a somewhat different route, by Longuenesse (1998a), 43–4.

The import of this paragraph is two-fold. First, it assigns a transcendental status to the reproductive synthesis, which, as was the case with apprehension, is due to its role in determining the representations of space and time. This synthesis is required because, while sensibility provides a pure manifold, it cannot account for the representation of it as a manifold. Second, it makes it clear that the synthesis of reproduction is not to be regarded as subsequent to, or as supervening upon, the synthesis of apprehension, but as inseparably connected with it. In fact, it can be regarded as a condition of apprehension, since the apprehension of the successively given items of a manifold that failed to keep in mind what has been previously apprehended would not yield the apprehension of it as a manifold.

D) *The synthesis of recognition in the concept* (A103–10): This is the third and final layer of the three-fold synthesis. As the heading indicates, it is also the point at which the understanding, qua faculty of concepts, first enters the story. It corresponds to what in "the Clue," Kant termed "bringing the synthesis to concepts," thereby first producing cognition in the "proper sense" (A78/B103). This segment consists of eleven paragraphs and can be divided into four parts. The first (paragraphs one and two) deals with the nature of concepts and their role in the recognition of a manifold as a manifold. The second (paragraphs three through six) contains an analysis of the expression "object of representations" and of what is involved in relating the synthesized manifold to an object. The third (paragraphs seven through ten) contends that the unity of apperception is the transcendental ground of the representation of an object. The fourth (paragraph eleven) introduces the concept of the transcendental object.

1) *Consciousness and concepts*: Kant begins by noting that,

Without consciousness that that which we think is the very same as what we thought a moment before, all reproduction in the series of representations would be in vain. For it would be a new representation in our current state, which would not belong at all to the act through which it had been gradually generated, and its manifold would never constitute a whole, since it would lack the unity that only consciousness can obtain for it.   (A103)

Kant here claims that without the above-mentioned form of consciousness reproduction would be in vain, not that it would be impossible. In fact, from what Kant says elsewhere it may be surmised that he would be willing to attribute something very much like a capacity to apprehend and reproduce previous representations to infants and higher animals, insofar as they have the ability to detect similarities and difference in a non-conceptual manner.[34] Moreover, if this is the case, it further

---

[34] Kant distinguishes between being acquainted with something (*etwas kennen*), which involves a capacity to represent it in comparison with other things, and to cognize (*erkennen*) something, which consists in a capacity to recognize something as an instance of a kind, and he attributes the former but not the latter capacity to animals. See JL 9: 64–5; 569–70. Similarly, in his 1762 essay on the syllogism Kant remarks that, "The dog differentiates the roast from the loaf, and it does so because

suggests that such capacities would be "in vain" only in the narrow sense that their exercise would not lead to cognition in the "proper sense," which Kant is about to argue requires concepts and ultimately the categories, not that it would play no cognitive role whatsoever.

Making sense of Kant's claim, however, requires a closer look at the notion of reproduction and the meaning of the phrase "the very same as," which is supposedly essential to the consciousness of the reproduced representation and the one presently before the mind as constituting a whole. Inasmuch as Kant here explicitly links reproduction to the *series of representations*, he seems to understand by it the preservation in the imagination of the previously apprehended series of representations in the thought of its continuation rather than simply its last member.[35] And if this is what Kant means, it follows that "the very same as" must refer to the same series that has been generated through a reproductive synthesis. Kant illustrates this by revisiting the concept of number, which was already used in connection with the analysis of the reproductive synthesis. He writes:

> If, in counting, I forgot that the units that now hover [*schweben*] before my senses were successively added to each other by me, then I would not cognize the generation of the multitude [*Menge*] through this successive addition of the one to the other, and consequently I would not cognize the number; for this concept consists solely in the consciousness of the unity of the synthesis.   (A103)

Inasmuch as this and the other examples of reproduction that Kant provides (drawing a line and a stretch of time) are geared towards mathematical cognitions, one might wonder how his account of the reproductive synthesis applies to empirical cognitions, where being "the very same as" supposedly refers to a generic identity, i.e., being the same kind of thing, rather than to being the member of the same

---

the way it is affected by the roast is different from the way in which it is affected by the loaf" (FS 2:60; 140). Although Kant there explains this capacity to differentiate in terms of sensory stimuli rather than in terms of the possession of images of the roast and the loaf constructed through a reproductive synthesis based on past associations, he also emphasizes the distinction between differentiating things from one another and *recognizing* the difference, which is presumably what a dog cannot do, and he attributes the latter to judgment, which is a capacity possessed only by rational beings (FS 2: 59; 140). Moreover, in the segment on empirical psychology in his *Lectures on Metaphysics* dated from either 1782 or 1783, Kant remarks that, though they have no concepts, "animals indeed compare representations with one another, but they are not conscious of where the harmony or disharmony between them lies" (MM 29: 888; 257). And, finally, in his important discussion of reflection, which involves comparison and the basis of concept formation, in the First Introduction to the *Critique of the Power of Judgment*, Kant states that, "even animals reflect, though only instinctively, that is, not in reference to acquiring a concept, but rather for determining an inclination" (FI 20: 211; 400).

[35] Kant's connection of reproduction with a series is noted by Carl (1992), 163. We saw in Chapter 3, however, that in his discussion of empirical psychology in ML_1 Kant referred to a *Vermögen der Nachbildung*, by which (presumably under the influence of Tetens) he understood a capacity to retain an image of something that one has previously perceived.

spatial, temporal, or numerical series.[36] Assume, for example, that one has an imagistic representation (e.g., a Humean complex idea) of something that is yellow, metallic, malleable, and soluble in *aqua regia*. In such cases reproduction is presumably to be understood as the transference of these properties to other instances in which a similar collection of properties is encountered, such that, given the presence of the first three, one would have a reason to assume the presence of the fourth.

This assumption presupposes that these representations collectively constitute a token of a single type of thing (gold), which is to say that they are joined together in a rule-governed way that justifies the projection from a token of this type to others; much as the rule-governed unification of the parts of a line makes them parts of the same line and warrants the conception of additional parts falling under the same rule as an extension of the "very same" line. Although he does not distinguish clearly between them, Kant here seems to be making two important points. One is that the difference between this kind of unity or wholeness and one produced by a reproduction based merely on past association is that the former allows for a projection and the latter does not. The other, which is what Kant emphasizes, is that the former is imposed by consciousness through the unification of the representations in accordance with a rule, which he identifies with a concept. Accordingly, the consciousness of such a projectable unity is what Kant understands by "recognition in a concept" and it corresponds to what he refers to in "the Clue" as "bringing the synthesis to concepts," which is the work of the understanding and first produces cognition in the "proper sense." We shall see below that for Kant even empirical concepts, understood as rules, have normative force in this sense and express a certain kind of necessity.

In the second paragraph Kant suggests that this idea is suggested by the term "concept." As he puts it:

The word "concept" [*Begriff*] itself could already lead us to this remark. For it is this **one** consciousness that unifies the manifold that has been successively intuited and then also reproduced, into one representation. This consciousness may often only be faint [*schwach*],[37] so that we connect it with the generation of the representation only in the effect, but not in the act itself, i.e., immediately; but regardless of these differences one consciousness must always be found, even if it lacks conspicuous clarity, and without that concepts, and with them cognition of objects, would be entirely impossible.   (A103–4)

As Longuenesse points out, in this paragraph Kant is appealing to two distinct but related conceptions of a concept.[38] The first is a concept as a rule for the unification

---

[36] Alternatively, one might take "the very same as" to refer to the same individual thing, e.g., piece of gold, which would point to Hume's skeptical analysis of identity. I believe, however, that the context indicates that Kant is concerned with the issue of concept-application, which requires a generic identity as the same kind of thing.

[37] I am following Kemp Smith and Pluhar in translating "*schwach*" as "faint" rather than as "weak," which is the rendering of Guyer and Wood.

[38] See Longuenesse (1998a), 47.

of sensible data. This is also the conception that is operative in the first paragraph of the segment, where we have seen that Kant maintains that it is by bringing the manifold of representations under a concept that consciousness becomes capable of representing to itself, i.e., recognizing, the unity of this manifold. Moreover, it is this sense of "concept" that Kant points out is suggested by the German verb "*begreifen*," which includes in its connotation the notion of grasping and from which the noun "*Begriff*" is derived.[39]

The second conception of a concept is the more familiar one of a general representation, i.e., the representation of a kind or sort, which can function as a predicate in a judgment. Kant refers to this conception of a concept in passing near the end of the paragraph, when he remarks that without the requisite one consciousness "concepts, and with them cognition of objects, would be entirely impossible." Since, as Longuenesse further notes, Kant had already identified the "one consciousness" with a concept in the sense of a rule, unless we take this second reference to concepts in this second sense, Kant's claim reduces to the tautology that concepts are required in order to have concepts.[40] Given this distinction, however, Kant can be read as making the non-trivial point that concepts qua unifying rules are necessary conditions of the formation of concepts qua general representations, since the latter are formed by reflection on the synthetic unity produced by such rules.[41]

This distinction between two conceptions of a concept is also essential to the interpretation of Kant's claim in the second sentence that, though it may be faint, such consciousness must be present as a necessary condition of the cognition of objects. In order to make sense of this claim it is necessary to take the one consciousness, which however faint, must always be found if cognition is to be possible, as a concept in the sense of a rule. The point is nicely illustrated by Kant's example of counting. Clearly, in order to able to count or perform basic arithmetical operations, one need not possess a clear concept of number, which could only be attained by a complex process of reflection and analysis and which few, apart from mathematicians and logicians, likely possess. But since counting is a rule-governed procedure, in order to perform it one must be aware of such a rule, even if one is unable clearly to articulate it.

---

[39] I am here following Longuenesse (1998a), 46. An alternative etymology is suggested by Pluhar (1996), 156, who claims that it connotes comprising or bringing together rather than grasping. I am not sure, however, how much turns on this philological point.

[40] Longuenesse (1998a), 47.

[41] Kant's view is that all concepts, including the categories, qua general representations, are formed by acts of reflection. We have seen that in the *Dissertation* he maintained that the intellectual concepts (the ancestors of the categories of the *Critique*) were formed by a reflection on the logical use of the intellect and that this provided the basis for Kant's claim that they are acquired rather than innate. The importance of reflection with regard to both the categories and empirical concepts and of reflective judgment is a central theme in Longuenesse (1998a). I discuss Kant's conceptions of reflection and reflective judgment, including the kind of reflection involved in the formation of empirical concepts, in Allison (2001), esp. 14–42, where I take issue with some aspects of Longuenesse's account.

2) *The concept of an object*: Kant next poses the question of what is meant by the expression "an object of representations" (A104). Although patchwork theorists contend that with this question Kant is embarking on an entirely new line of thought that is essentially unrelated to what preceded it, it seems more reasonable to take it as the natural continuation of the analysis contained in the preceding two paragraphs.[42] For since he had just claimed that without concepts cognition of objects would be entirely impossible, it certainly behooved Kant to explain what he understands by such an object, which is precisely what he proceeds to do.

Kant begins by pointing out that what makes this question particularly problematic is the fact that the previous discussion had assumed that the objects at issue were appearances, which he now acknowledges are "nothing but sensible representations, which must not be regarded in themselves, in the same way, as objects (outside the power of representation)." And given this, Kant recognizes that he owes the reader an explanation of what could then be meant by "an object corresponding to and therefore also distinct from the cognition," which is how one would naturally characterize the object of cognition (A104).

Kant's preliminary answer, which calls to mind the formulations of the *Duisburg Nachlass*, is that "this object must be thought of only as something in general $= X$, since outside of our cognition we have nothing that we could set over against this cognition as corresponding to it" (A104). This characterization, however, is not so much a solution to the problem as a reformulation of it. Specifically, it amounts to a radical internalization of the problem of knowledge, where rather than worrying about whether our cognition corresponds to an inaccessible *an sich* reality, the issue becomes the grounds on the basis of which the mind may attribute objectivity to its synthesis of representations or, alternatively, distinguish between what pertains to the object and what holds merely for the subject. And, recalling the *Duisburg Nachlass* as well as other texts from the "Silent Decade," Kant once again claims that the decisive factor constitutive of objectivity is necessity. He writes:

> We find, however, that our thought of the relation of all cognition to its object carries something of necessity with it, since…the latter is regarded as that which is opposed to our cognitions being determined at pleasure or arbitrarily rather than being determined *a priori*, since insofar as they are to relate to an object our cognitions must necessarily agree with each other in relation to it, i.e., they must have that unity that constitutes the concept of an object.   (A104)

The difficulty in interpreting this single-sentence paragraph largely concerns the sense of "necessity" to which Kant appeals. Although the depiction of the object as

---

[42] According to Vaihinger (1967), 40–5 and Kemp Smith (1962), 2004–22, A104–10 the final eight paragraphs of The Synthesis of Recognition in the Concept belong to the earliest stage of the Transcendental Deduction and are marked by a focus on the concept of the transcendental object and the lack of reference to the categories. As Paton (1967), 79–80, points out, however, these paragraphs are most naturally read as a continuation of the analysis in the paragraphs that precede them.

that which "is opposed to" (in the sense of preventing) our cognitions being determined in an arbitrary manner suggests a causal necessity, such as is found in causal theories of perception or cognition, this is precluded by Kant's radical internalization of cognition. And since the claim that in the cognition of an object the relation between representations is "determined *a priori*" can only mean determined by an a priori rule, it indicates that he had in mind a normative necessity, such as is imposed by a rule. Moreover, this is further reinforced by Kant's closing remark that, insofar as our cognitions relate to an object, "they must have that unity that constitutes the concept of an object," where the necessity concerns the unity that pertains to the *concept* of an object and "must" clearly has a normative sense.

Accordingly, we should expect Kant in the next paragraph to provide an account from the side of the cognizing subject of the nature and ground of "that unity that constitutes the concept of an object." And this is precisely what we find. Kant begins by stating that,

It is clear ... that since we have to do only with the manifold of our representations, and that X which corresponds to them (the object), because it should be something distinct from all of our representations, is nothing for us, the unity that the object makes necessary can be nothing other than the formal unity of the consciousness in the synthesis of the manifold of the representations.   (A105)

Kant here relocates this unity from the side of the object to that of the subject on the grounds that the object, considered as an X that is ontologically distinct from our representations of it, is "nothing to us," because we have no cognitive access to it, from which it follows that we have no alternative but to locate the requisite unity in the cognizing consciousness. Kant does not explain why this unity of consciousness is "formal"; but the answer presumably lies in the fact that it is determined by the form or manner in which the representations are unified rather than the content of the representations that are unified.

Since Kant's formulation of the problem assumes that the cognizer is at once both the determiner of what counts as objective and the arbiter of its own determinations, it is essential for him to spell out the criterion of a successful determination or, equivalently, for the objective validity of its claims. Kant turns to this task in the next two sentences of the paragraph, where he writes:

Hence we say that we cognize the object if we have effected synthetic unity in the manifold of intuition. But this is impossible if the intuition could not have been produced through a function of synthesis in accordance with a rule that makes the reproduction of the manifold necessary *a priori* and a concept in which this manifold is united possible.   (A105)

Inasmuch as Kant's formulation of the criterion has the form of a stipulation ("we say"), it might leave the impression that his account is question-begging; but this is not objectionable, if one keeps in mind the goal of preparing rather than instructing the reader. In other words, at this point Kant is not so much mounting an argument as he is putting his cards on the table. Nevertheless, one might still object that by equating cognizing an object with producing a synthetic unity in the manifold of intuition Kant has characterized cognition in far too liberal a manner, or at best given merely a not very informative necessary condition of such cognition. For even though only a synthetic unity of representations is a viable candidate for the ascription of objectivity, this cannot be ascribed to every conceivable synthetic unity, since one can readily imagine any number of such unities to which it does not apply, e.g., the proverbial golden mountain. On a more charitable reading, however, Kant is not speaking of a synthetic unity as such, but of a specific kind of synthetic unity; viz., one "that makes the reproduction of the manifold necessary *a priori* and a concept in which this manifold is united possible."

In addition to the awkward use of a double negative ("impossible...could not have been"), a striking feature of Kant's formulation is its complex modality. Rather than stating that the synthetic unity in question must have been produced in the manner described, he claims merely that it is necessary that it *could have been* brought forth (*hervorgebracht werden können*) in this way. In other words, Kant is affirming the necessity of a possibility, much as we shall see that he later does with respect to the "I think" and its accompaniment of one's representations. Specifically, the possibility that must be preserved by a rule-governed synthesis contains two components: that it makes the reproduction of the manifold necessary a priori and that it makes possible a concept in which the manifold of intuition is united.

The requirement that the synthesis be governed by a rule that makes the reproduction of the manifold of intuition necessary a priori is to be understood in light of the analysis of the reproductive synthesis and the postulated connection between objectivity and necessity. Since the necessity stems from the rule governing the unification of an intuited manifold and concerns the reproducibility of the elements of this manifold in subsequent intuitions of the "very same [kind of] thing" it is normative or, nomological; but since it only applies if the unity is objective, the necessity in question is also conditional.[43] And since the rule that governs this unification is itself a concept, the claim that this unification makes possible a concept in which the manifold of intuition is united must be understood in light of the previously noted distinction between two senses of "concept": as unifying rule and as reflected general representation, which is produced by a reflection on the result of this unification. Kant devotes the remainder of this segment of his account to the further clarification and illustration of this view through two examples: one of a mathematical and the other of an empirical concept. With respect to the former he claims:

Thus we think of a triangle as an object by being conscious of the composition of three straight lines in accordance with a rule according to which such an intuition can always be exhibited.

---

[43] The conditional and nomological nature of this necessity is emphasized by Thöle (1991), 230.

Now this **unity of rule** determines every manifold, and limits it to conditions that make the unity of apperception possible, and the concept of this unity is the representation of the object = X, which I think through those predicates of a triangle.   (A105)

The new element here is the unity of apperception, which Kant suggests is what must be preserved by an objectifying synthesis. Accordingly, when viewed in connection with the preceding portion of the paragraph, Kant appears to be suggesting an equivalence between a synthetic unity that is brought about in such a way as to make "the reproduction of the manifold necessary *a priori* and a concept in which this manifold is united possible" and one that makes possible the unity of apperception. But inasmuch as Kant only explicates his conception of apperception and its role in the grounding of the "critical" conception of objectivity later (paragraphs seven through eleven), we shall set this aside for the present and consider only the triangle example, which does not *directly* depend upon it.[44] And here the main point is simply that it is the unity of the rule, which just is the concept of a triangle, considered as a rule for thinking as object, i.e., constructing in intuition a triangular figure, which necessitates that the predicates contained in the concept of a triangle as a reflected general representation, e.g., the equality of the sum of its three interior angles to two right angles, will necessarily attach to every figure that is constructed in accordance with this rule.

Kant's second illustration, the concept of body, which serves as an example of an empirical concept, is introduced in support of the principle that all cognition requires a concept, which however imperfect or obscure it may be, "is always something general, and that serves as a rule" (A106). Kant's account is complicated, however, by the fact that he speaks of the concept of body as a rule in a two-fold sense: (1) "as the rule for our cognition of outer appearances by means of the unity of the manifold that is thought through it;" and (2) as "a rule of intuitions" insofar as "it represents the necessary reproduction of the manifold of given intuitions, hence the synthetic unity in the consciousness of them" (A106).

Kant is here referring to two roles that an empirical concept can play when construed as a rule.[45] The first is as a token of the rule through which representations are related to an object qua something in general = X, in which case X is determined as an object of outer experience. Otherwise expressed, unifying representations in accordance with the concept of body is one way of producing the formal unity of consciousness, which has already been characterized as the unity that the object makes necessary. What makes this confusing is that one tends to assume that for

---

[44] I say not directly because for Kant even mathematics depends indirectly upon the unity of apperception as the condition of all thought; but that is not germane to the point that Kant is trying to make with regard to the concept of a triangle.

[45] The following analysis is based largely on the accounts of Carl (1992), 175–6 and Longuenesse (1998a), 49–50. The distinction between two kinds of rule will be revisited in Chapter 6 in connection with an analysis of the relation between concepts and their schemata.

Kant this objectifying function is supposed to be exercised by the categories rather than by empirical concepts, even those with as broad an extension as the concept of body. Indeed, if empirical concepts can do this, one might wonder why we need the categories. But before jumping to this conclusion, it is important to keep in mind that, even though Kant had already introduced the categories in "the Clue" and the first section of the Deduction, they have not yet made their appearance in section 2, which up to this point reads like Hamlet without the prince. And once this is recognized, the present discussion can be seen as part of Kant's elaborate preparation for the eventual appearance of the categories, at which point we shall supposedly see that, as second-order concepts, the categories make possible the application of first-order concepts such as that of body and that it is by doing this that they function as necessary conditions of the possibility of experience.

The second role that Kant assigns to empirical concepts is already familiar from the preceding analysis; viz., their function as rules for the recognition of some intuited object = X as a determinate thing of a certain sort, to which specific predicates can be assigned. Kant makes this clear when, in explicating how the concept of body can function as a rule for intuitions, he notes that "[I]n the case of the perception of something outside of us the concept of body makes necessary the representation of extension, and with it that of impenetrability, of shape, etc." (A106). Simply put, it fills in the blank or, if you will, solves the equation. Once again, Kant is alluding to the necessity stemming from the rule, which requires us to conceive anything regarded as a body as extended, impenetrable, having a certain shape, as well as various other unspecified properties that are considered essential to bodies of every sort.

Inasmuch as the proposition that bodies are extended for Kant is analytic and that their possession of a certain shape (and other properties such as divisibility) is entailed by their extendedness, it might seem that the necessity to which he here is appealing is logical rather than merely normative or nomological. And if this is the case, it might further seem that Kant is dangerously close to equating objective validity with logical necessity, which would threaten to undermine the analytic-synthetic distinction that is central to the whole "critical" project. The problem, however, lies in Kant's misleading presentation of his example (though he does include impenetrability, which presumably does not follow analytically from the concept of body, as well as the additional unspecified properties indicated by the "etc."), rather than in the view that he is attempting to articulate. In order to see this we need only fill in the "etc." with the properties of weight (or heaviness) and attraction, since he elsewhere uses these as examples of properties that are necessarily connected with bodies in experience, though not contained in the concept of body.[46] The point is that this amended list would still function as the rule through which the

---

[46] See, for example, A7/B11 and JL 9: 111; 607.

manifold of an empirical intuition must be unified in order to be brought under the concept of body, and this rule, formulated propositionally, states that "All bodies are extended, impenetrable, have weight and attractive force (or mass), etc." And since this claim is synthetic, it follows that the necessity at issue is not logical, at least not in the objectionable sense that the denial of the rule would yield a logical contradiction.

Accordingly, the issue becomes the grounds of the rule and the justification for attributing a certain kind of necessity to it, even when it concerns an empirical concept such as body rather than a mathematical concept such as a triangle, the constitutive properties of which are determinable a priori. This is a fundamental question that will soon lead us to the transcendental unity of apperception and through this to the categories. But before turning to these it may prove useful to compare briefly Kant's approach to it to those of Hume and Tetens, since they appear to be the thinkers with respect to whom Kant framed his account. For Hume, of course, the only necessity involved is the subjective, custom-based necessity to expect similar concatenations (synthetic unities) of perceptions in the future to those that were encountered in the past. It was noted in the Appendix to Chapter 3 that Tetens, building on Hume's account, attempted to interject objectivity into the story by appealing to a more robust and variegated account of "subjective necessity," which he did by defining the objective as the "unchangeably subjective." It was also pointed out, however, that since Tetens understood this subjective necessity in a naturalistic, causal sense, it lacked a normative dimension. Seen in this context, Kant can be read as responding to these accounts and introducing normativity into the conception of a subjective necessity by considering it as stemming from a rule.[47]

3) *Transcendental apperception as transcendental ground*: After annunciating the general principle that "Every necessity has a transcendental condition as its ground," Kant concludes that,

A transcendental ground must therefore be found for the unity of the consciousness in the synthesis of the manifold of all our intuitions, hence also of the concepts of objects in general, consequently also of all objects of experience, without which it would be impossible to think of any object for our intuitions; for the latter is nothing more than the something for which the concept expresses such a necessity of synthesis. (A106)

Kant here lists in rapid succession three items for which a transcendental ground must be sought: (1) "the unity of the consciousness in the synthesis of the manifold of all our intuitions," (2) "the concepts of objects in general" (or as such); and (3) "all objects of possible experience." Moreover, it is clear that Kant did not consider these merely as three distinct items on a longer list; for it is suggested that they are related in such a way that the first implies the second and the second the third. The first is

---

[47] Since we have seen that Kant had already appealed to a rule theory of objectivity in the *Duisburg Nachlass*, he cannot be said to have developed it in response to Tetens. Nevertheless, I think it plausible to suggest that Tetens' account was likely on Kant's mind when composing the A-Deduction.

fundamental because without it, it would be impossible to think of an object corresponding to our intuition. And since by the concept of an object as such is meant the concept of just such an object, it follows that this unity of consciousness is also the ground of this concept. In other words, assuming the transitivity of the ground–consequent relation, whatever grounds the unity of consciousness will also ground the concept of an object as such. The third point involves the move from conditions of our representation of objects to conditions of the objects represented, and therefore interjects an ontological dimension that was previously lacking. But inasmuch as Kant first deals with this explicitly in the fourth "number," its consideration will be reserved for the analysis of that segment of section 2.

Kant's first step is to identify the transcendental ground with transcendental apperception. When we first encountered Kant's conception of apperception in the *Duisburg Nachlass*, we saw that he characterized it in a number of ways, including as "the consciousness of thinking, i.e., of the representations as they are posited in the mind;" as "the intuition of our self…that pertains to all cognitions;" as "self-perception" and even as "self-sensation." Here, and in most other treatments of the topic, however, Kant is careful to distinguish apperception, as the consciousness of self-qua thinker, from the consciousness of self obtained through inner sense. Kant points out that the latter, "is "forever variable;" whereas "That which should **necessarily** be represented as numerically identical cannot be thought as such through empirical data. There must be a condition that precedes all experience and makes the latter itself possible, which should make such a transcendental presupposition valid" (A107). Hume would undoubtedly agree with Kant's claims that inner perception does not yield an awareness of an abiding self and that something that must necessarily be regarded as numerically identical cannot be thought as such on the basis of empirical data. But, for that very reason, he would question the justification for postulating a numerically identical self and wonder how such a "transcendental presupposition" could function as a necessary condition of the possibility of experience.

Kant begins to address these questions in the next paragraph, where he claims that,

[N]o cognitions can occur in us, no connection and unity among them, without that unity of consciousness that precedes all data of the intuitions, and in relation to which all representation of objects is alone possible. This pure, original, unchanging consciousness, I will now name **transcendental apperception**. That it deserves this name is already obvious from this, that even the purest objective unity, namely that of the *a priori* concepts (space and time) is possible only through the relation of the intuitions to it. The numerical unity of this apperception therefore grounds all concepts *a priori*, just as the manifoldness of space and time grounds the intuitions of sensibility.   (A107)

A complicating factor is that Kant here refers to two distinct conceptions of unity, one of which is said to be in need of the transcendental ground that is provided by the other. The unity that supposedly requires a transcendental ground is the unity of representations produced by bringing them under a concept through which they are related to an object. Clearly, it is the relation to an object that needs a transcendental ground, since according to Kant a merely empirical grounding would not suffice. It is also a synthetic unity (a unity of many in one). By contrast, the unity that serves as transcendental ground of the former is the unity of the consciousness of a cognizing subject. As such, it is a unity in the sense of being a single consciousness and can be regarded as an analytic unity (a one in many), which understood diachronically is an identity.[48] It is the latter that precedes all the data of intuition in that it is that unity for which the data are regarded as data; whereas the former unity presupposes these data because it is the product of their unification by the cognizing subject.

In the passage before us, Kant claims that transcendental status is assigned to the latter unity (the unity of apperception) because it is the ground (necessary condition) of the former unity or, more precisely, of the unifying act through which representations are related to an object; and it is this dependence-relation that is supposedly illustrated by the concepts of space and time. The argument underlying this claim is not, however, immediately apparent. The problem does not concern the notion that space and time are here referred to as a priori concepts rather than as a priori intuitions, since already in the Aesthetic Kant indicates that we have such concepts, the point being only that they presuppose an intuition.[49] It concerns rather why Kant thought it obvious that the (objective) unity of these concepts is grounded in the unity of apperception and how he could conclude from this that this same unity grounds *all* concepts a priori.

Since Kant could hardly maintain that the claim that the unity of the concepts of space and time is grounded in the unity of apperception is self-evident, he must be taken to mean that he has already shown this to be the case. And since it is clear that no such claim could be made for the Aesthetic, the most plausible place to look for such an argument is Kant's account of the three-fold synthesis. We have seen that Kant claimed that without a synthesis of apprehension, "we could have *a priori* neither the representations of space nor of time, since these can be generated only through the synthesis of the manifold that sensibility in its original receptivity provides" (A99–100), and that without a reproductive synthesis "not even the purist and most fundamental representations of space and time, could ever arise" (A102). Assuming that by "the representations of space and time" Kant meant the concepts of them as objects of which certain properties, e.g., infinite divisibility and either one dimensionality (in the case of time) or three dimensionality (in the case of space) can be predicated a priori in synthetic judgments, and that these concepts are produced by the unification of the manifold given in intuition (the pure manifold) through the syntheses of apprehension and reproduction, it follows that these concepts are to be

---

[48] In the B-Deduction Kant will refer to these respectively as the analytic and the synthetic unity of apperception. See B134–6.

[49] For further discussion of this point see Allison (2004), 112–16.

viewed as products of a reflective grasp (recognition in a concept) of the unification brought about by the syntheses of apprehension and reproduction, and therefore by the three-fold synthesis. And, if this is the case, by adding the seemingly non-problematic premise that recognition in a concept presupposes a single recognizer, we have at least a rough sketch of an argument linking the concepts of space and time with the unity of apperception as their transcendental ground.

This still leaves us, however, with the question of how Kant could conclude from this that the unity of apperception is the a priori ground of *all* concepts, not simply those of space and time.[50] The answer lies in the relation between the concepts of space and time and other concepts. As far as empirical concepts are concerned, if the unity of apperception is a condition of the a priori concepts of space and time, it is also a necessary condition of all empirical concepts, since the Aesthetic has shown these are subject to the conditions of space and time. And since, apart from the categories the only concepts that yield a priori cognition of objects for Kant are mathematical concepts and these presuppose the concepts of space and time, it holds for these as well.

Having claimed that the transcendental unity of apperception is the a priori ground of all concepts, Kant's next step is to argue that the same unity "makes out of all possible appearances that can ever come together in one experience a connection of all of these representations in accordance with laws." And this, he suggests, is because:

[T]his unity of consciousness would be impossible if in the cognition of the manifold the mind could not become conscious of the identity of the function by means of which this manifold is synthetically combined into one cognition. Thus the original and necessary consciousness of the identity of oneself is at the same time a consciousness of an equally necessary unity of the synthesis of all appearances in accordance with concepts, i.e., in accordance with rules that not only make them necessarily reproducible, but also thereby determine an object for their intuition, i.e., the concept of something in which they are necessarily connected; for the mind could not possibly think of the identity of itself in the manifoldness of its representations, and indeed think this *a priori*, if it did not have before its eyes the identity of its action, which subjects all synthesis of apprehension (which is empirical) to a transcendental unity, and first makes possible their connection in accordance with *a priori* rules.   (A108)

---

[50] Strictly speaking, the claim should be understood as applying to all concepts save the categories. But since Kant has not yet introduced the categories in section 2, they cannot be considered as falling within the scope of the present argument. In support of the thesis that this segment of the A-Deduction reflects the earliest stage of Kant's thought because of its failure to mention the categories, Vaihinger (1967), 44–5, offers as "decisive proof" that space and time are the only a priori concepts which interested Kant at the time and that "he had not yet considered *a priori* concepts other than space and time, at least for the world of sensuous phenomena, which is the only thing of concern in this context." By reading the passage in this way Vaihinger totally ignores even the possibility that Kant is deliberately preparing the way for the introduction of the categories, which, like Paton, I believe to be the most natural and plausible way to interpret Kant's account.

Kant here moves beyond the claims of the preceding paragraph in two crucial and interconnected ways. First, as already noted, he extends his analysis of the transcendental function of the unity of apperception from being a condition of the formation of concepts to being the ground of the subjection of all appearances to a priori laws. Second, in arguing for this claim, Kant now asserts not merely that the unity of apperception is the transcendental ground of the synthetic unity of appearances, but also that the possibility of the former is itself dependent upon the production of the latter. Applying the terms in which Kant explained the relationship between freedom and the moral law in the second *Critique*, one might say that the unity of apperception is the *ratio essendi* of the consciousness of unity, i.e., of the synthetic unity of appearances, and the latter is the *ratio cognoscendi* of the unity of apperception.[51] The crucial point, however, is that, whereas Kant initially affirmed only a one-way dependence (that of the consciousness of unity upon the unity of apperception) he now affirms a co-dependence or reciprocity between the two unities.

Here, as well as in subsequent treatments of the topic, Kant's account of the reciprocity between the unity of consciousness and the consciousness of unity turns crucially on the dependence of both on the consciousness of a rule-governed act of unification. Assuming that by "function" is understood a rule-governed synthesis through which a synthetic unity is produced in the manifold of representations, Kant is claiming that a cognizer's consciousness of itself as cognizer is dependent upon the possibility of becoming conscious of the identity of this action, which encompasses the dual awareness of it as its action and of its governing rule. As he graphically puts it later in the passage, the cognizer must "have before its eyes the identity of its action," which involves not only an awareness of it as its unifying action but also of its underlying rule.

Moreover, since appearances, qua representations, can be nothing to us qua cognizers apart from the possibility of bringing them to the unity of apperception, it follows that all appearances must stand in a *possible* synthetic unity in order to be apperceivable, which is to say that an appearance that could not be brought into a synthetic unity with other appearances, a cognitive outlier, as it were, would be "nothing to us," cognitively speaking. And inasmuch as a synthetic unity presupposes rules through which its particular unification is constituted, it also follows that, as a condition of their apperceivability, all appearances necessarily stand under rules, which is to say that the rule-governedness of appearances is an a priori truth.

Since this does not entail that appearances stand under rules that are themselves necessary, and therefore a priori, which is what Kant wants to claim, it might be thought to give rise to the worry that the latter is unfounded; perhaps the product of a conflation of the proposition that it can be determined a priori that some rules are necessary as conditions of the unity of apperception with the quite different claim

---

[51] See KpV 5: 4 note; 140.

that special a priori rules are necessary. This worry can be assuaged, however, if not completely eliminated, by extending the preceding argument a step further.

This step consists in distinguishing between the concept of an empirical object of a particular kind, e.g., the concept of a body, and the concept of an empirical object or, equivalently, an object of possible experience considered merely as such. The underlying assumption is that it is a necessary condition of the representation of something as an empirical object of a certain kind that this something also be recognized as an empirical object *tout court*. And just as the representation of something as a body necessarily requires rules, say that whatever falls under this concept must be extended in three dimensions, have a determinate magnitude, a shape, be impenetrable, etc., so the representation or recognition of something simply as an empirical object also requires rules for the representation of such an object considered merely as such. But inasmuch as the representation of an object as such or qua object (an "object in general"), *ex hypothesi*, cannot be based on its conformity with any *empirical* rules, it must be based on a priori ones. Consequently, the consciousness of unity, and therefore the unity of apperception, presupposes the conformity of what is represented through them and therefore all appearances, insofar as they are represented as such, to a priori rules.

Presented in summary form, the argument as a whole, which I take to be implicit in section 2 of the A-Deduction, can be broken down into the following six steps:

a. The unity of consciousness and the consciousness of unity reciprocally imply one another. Hence, whatever is a necessary condition of the consciousness of unity is also a necessary condition of the unity of consciousness and vice versa.

b. The consciousness of unity at issue concerns the unity required for the consciousness of an object distinct from one's representation of it.

c. By the rule-theory of objectivity, this requires that the manifold of representations united in the concept of an object be governed by rules.

d. Insofar as it is a matter of the representation of an object of a particular kind, these rules are merely empirical.

e. But a necessary condition of representing something as an object of a particular kind is that one also represents it as an object *tout court*, which by the rule-theory of objectivity also presupposes rules.

f. But inasmuch as the rules required for the representation of an object as such or simply qua object, cannot be based on anything required for the representation of an object of a particular sort, they cannot be merely empirical and must therefore be a priori.

Therefore, whatever is brought to the unity of consciousness necessarily conforms to a priori rules.

4) *The transcendental object*: It is at this point that Kant introduces the concept of the transcendental object = X as the concept of an object considered merely as such,

which is needed to account for the subjection of appearances to a priori rules. In support of the claim that the action "which subjects all synthesis of apprehension... to a transcendental unity... first makes possible their connection in accordance with *a priori* rules," Kant continues:

Further, we are now also able to determine our concept of an **object** as such more precisely.[52] All representations, as representations, have their object, and can themselves be objects of other representations in turn. Appearances are the only objects that can be given to us immediately, and that in them which is immediately related to the object is called intuition. However these appearances are not things in themselves, but themselves only representations, which in turn have their object, which therefore cannot be further intuited by us, and that may therefore be called the non-empirical, i.e., transcendental object=X.   (A108–9)

Kant here suggests that the line of thought leading to the introduction of the concept of the transcendental object = X is essentially a clarification of the previous analysis of the concept of an object as such, which at A104 was characterized as "something in general=X." And since the two main points that we have learned in the interim are that the relation of representations to an object also involves their relation to the unity of apperception and that the rules through which representations must be unified to be brought to the unity of apperception and related to an object are a priori, it may be expected that these points will underlie this further clarification. More specifically, we might expect Kant to point out that the concept of a transcendental object is not the concept of a special sort of object, but of what is common to every empirical object considered merely as such, which consists precisely in being an empirical object. In other words, it is a second-order or "meta-concept," which encompasses what might be termed the "objectivity of an object," i.e., the characteristics in virtue of which a representation of an object is deemed as such. Indeed, it would have been better if Kant had referred to it as the *transcendental concept* of an object rather than the concept of a transcendental object, since, despite Kant's evident intensions, the latter does suggest a special sort of object. Unlike its counterpart in traditional ontology, however, Kant's transcendental object is not a concept of a set of properties that may be attributed to every object, but a set of a priori rules through which representations are related to an empirical object, regardless of its specific nature.

An indication that this reflects Kant's intent is provided by his fuller analysis of the concept of the transcendental object = X and its epistemic function in the next paragraph. As he there puts it,

The pure concept of this transcendental object (which in all of our cognitions is really always one and the same=X) is that which in all of our empirical concepts in general can provide

---

[52]   I am here following Adickes, Kemp Smith, and Pluhar in reading "*Begriff*" rather than "*Begriffe*," as it is in the *Akademie Ausgabe*; Pluhar rather than Kemp Smith and Guyer and Wood in rendering "*überhaupt*" as "as such" rather than "in general;" and rendering "*richtiger*" as "more precisely" rather than "more correctly" as it is in Guyer and Wood.

relation to an object, i.e., objective reality. Now this concept cannot contain any determinate intuition at all, and therefore concerns nothing but that unity which must be encountered in a manifold of cognition insofar as it stands in relation to an object. This relation, however, is nothing other than the necessary unity of consciousness, thus also of the synthesis of the manifold through a common function of the mind for combining it in one representation. Now since this unity must be regarded as necessary *a priori* (since the cognition would otherwise be without an object), the relation to a transcendental object, i.e., the objective reality of our empirical cognition, rests on the transcendental law that all appearances, insofar as objects are to be given to us through them, must stand under *a priori* rules of their synthetic unity, in accordance with which their relation in empirical intuition is alone possible, i.e., that in experience they must stand under conditions of the necessary unity of apperception just as in mere intuition they must stand under the formal conditions of space and time; indeed, it is through those conditions that every cognition is first made possible.   (A109–10)

This paragraph contains several claims that speak to the nature and significance of the concept of a transcendental object = X. The first is that in all our cognitions it is "really always one and the same=X." Clearly, this must be the case, if it is the concept of an object as such; since there could no more be more than one object as such than there could be more than a single most perfect being. This would not be true, however, if this object were identified with the *Ding an sich*; since there would then be as many transcendental objects as there are such things.

The second claim, viz., that this concept "is that which in all of our empirical concepts in general can provide relation to an object, i.e., objective reality," addresses the objectivating function of this concept. One might wonder why Kant limits this to *empirical* concepts, since, again setting aside the categories, he maintains that mathematical concepts also have objective reality. The answer lies in the distinctive nature of mathematical cognition; viz., the fact that there the actual object is constructed in intuition. Thus, rather than a vacuous "something in general=X," we have an exhibition of triangularity or circularity *in concreto*. By contrast, in the case of empirical cognition what is "constructed" is not the object itself, but merely its representation.[53] And since in this case the correspondence of representation and object cannot be determined by comparison because the object itself is always something represented, it must be done by means of immanent criteria, i.e., rules for the representation of an object as such, which are contained in the concept of a transcendental object, considered as the transcendental concept of an object.

The third claim connects the concept of the transcendental object = X with "that unity which must be encountered in a manifold of cognition insofar as it stands in relation to an object," i.e., the objective unity of consciousness, and through this with the unity of apperception ("the necessary unity of consciousness"). Again, given the

---

[53] We saw in Chapter 3 that in the *Duisburg Nachlass* Kant remarks that in non-mathematical synthetic a priori cognition, "We represent to ourselves the object through the analogue of a construction, namely that it can be constructed in inner sense" (R 4684 17: 670_{20-2}; 172).

reciprocity between the consciousness of unity and the unity of consciousness, this is precisely what one would expect Kant to say at this point. Moreover, Kant is even more explicit on the latter point in a subsequent discussion of the concept of the transcendental object = X, stating that this concept "can serve only as a correlate of the unity of apperception for the unity of a manifold in sensible intuition, by means of which the understanding unifies that in the concept of an object" (A250).

Finally, the fourth claim affirms the a priori nature of the rules involved in the unification through which representations are related to an object as such, and thereby gain objective reality. As was argued above, rules for the thought of an object as such must be a priori because they abstract from all features that could serve to classify an object as being of a certain sort. And since this is precisely what is provided by the concept of the transcendental object = X, all that remains in order for Kant to complete his preliminary present of the elements of the Transcendental Deduction is to identify these rules with the categories.[54]

E) *Provisional explanation of the possibility of the categories as* a priori *cognitions*: This is the heading for the last of the four numbers into which Kant divides section 2 of the A-Deduction. As the heading indicates, it is also the place in which Kant introduces the categories; though we shall see that even here their appearance is belated. He begins the process of setting the stage for their appearance by claiming that, just as there is only space and one time of which all particular spaces and times

---

[54] Although a detailed discussion of the topic would take us well beyond the scope of this study, it should be noted that the term "transcendental object (*Objekt* or *Gegenstand*)" occurs (with and without the "=X") in many different contexts in the first edition of the *Critique* and plays a variety of roles in addition to the one assigned to it above. Prominent among these are as the noumenon qua limiting concept (A287–9/B343–5); the ground or cause of appearances (A288/B3445, A379–80, A393–4, A538–9/B566–7, A544–5/B572–3, A494/B522, A565–6/B593–4, A613/B641; the thing in itself (A366); the merely intelligible object of a transcendental idea (A566–7/B593–4); and the transcendental object of the ideal, i.e., God (A679/B707). Moreover, while Kant excised all references to it in those portions of the *Critique* that he either completely or significantly revised for the second edition; viz., the Transcendental Deduction, the Phenomena-Noumena chapter, and the Paralogisms, the above citations indicate that many other occurrences remain in the portions that he did not revise. But while a quick glance at these might give the impression that Kant had no clear conception of what he meant by the term, further consideration indicates not only the existence of a common core of meaning, but also that this accords with the understanding of it sketched above, namely, that it designates the concept of an object considered simply as such. The diversity and seeming incompatibility between the tasks assigned to it in the Deduction and in other portions of the *Critique* stems from the fact that this concept is Janus-faced. One face is turned towards the positive role of the categories as a priori conditions of empirical cognition; the other is turned towards the proposition that the pure categories, apart from their schemata, are mere forms of discursive thinking without a determinate object. The latter is the side on which Kant focuses in the vast majority of occurrences outside of the A-Deduction (the major exception being A350–1, which refers back to the Deduction). In these texts Kant is effectively maintaining that the object in question (one thought through either the pure categories or the transcendental ideas) is a "merely transcendental object," which is to deny that it is a genuine object of cognition. Accordingly, in these contexts the transcendental object functions as a limiting concept. Presumably, the confusion produced by this dual usage was at least one of the factors that led Kant to drop references to it in those places he revised for the second edition. For example, in the second edition version of the Phenomena-Noumena chapter, the transcendental object is replaced by "the noumenon in the negative sense" (B309).

are delimited portions, so "[t]here is only **one** experience, in which all perceptions are represented as in thoroughgoing and lawlike connection." Consequently, Kant continues, "If one speaks of different experiences, they are only so many perceptions insofar as they belong to one and the same universal experience. The thoroughgoing and synthetic unity of experience is precisely what constitutes the form of experience, and it is nothing other than the synthetic unity of the appearances in accordance with concepts" (A110). Kant is here suggesting an analogy between the relationship between particular experiences, which he also refers to as "so many perceptions," and a universal or global experience, on the one hand, and that which holds between particular spaces and times and space and time, on the other. In other words, just as the Aesthetic had shown that particular spaces and time must be considered as delimited portions of a single space and a single time, so the Deduction will show that particular experiences must be considered as presupposing and as only conceivable in relation to a single experience, the universal form of which is a synthetic unity of appearances governed by necessary laws.

The analogy is somewhat misleading, since space and time for Kant are intuitions, i.e., singular representations, in which particular spaces and times are contained; whereas universal experience is a concept, more precisely an idea, of the totality of experience, under which particular experiences fall as instances rather than as contained in it as parts. But setting that aside, the main point is that the objectivity of particular synthetic unities, which are thought in an empirical concept, are dependent upon the presence of a thoroughgoing or global synthetic unity, which is that of nature as a whole under universal laws.[55] Moreover, showing this is obviously essential to Kant's project in the Deduction; for without the assumption of the unity of experience in this sense, there would be no need for anything like his categories.

Kant further contends that a synthetic unity based merely on empirical concepts would not suffice to structure experience, so understood. This is likewise essential to his project, since if empirical concepts could do the job there would again be no need for the categories. And in support of this thesis he argues that,

Unity of synthesis in accordance with empirical concepts would be entirely contingent, and, were it not grounded on a transcendental ground of unity, it would be possible for a swarm of appearances to fill up our soul without experience ever being able to arise from it. But in that

---

[55] Kant may be read here as affirming a form of coherentism, broadly construed, in which the locus of normativity is placed in the unity of experience as a whole. It differs from more familiar forms of coherentism in two respects. First, it is concerned with the conditions of the formation and application of empirical concepts (understood as rules) rather than the justification of particular beliefs. Second, and most important, rather than arguing directly from coherence with experience as a whole as a presupposed norm, Kant endeavors to provide the unity of experience with a transcendental ground (the unity of apperception), which justifies the appeal to it. In this respect, Kant may be said to be arguing *to* coherentism rather than *from* it. For a sympathetic account of Kant as offering a coherentist form of transcendental argumentation see Stern (2000), 193–9.

case all relation of cognition to objects would also disappear, since the appearances would lack connection in accordance with universal and necessary laws, and would thus be intuition without thought, but never cognition, and would therefore be as good as nothing for us.

(A111)

Kant here spells out the implications of a thoroughgoing empiricism, which would deny any need for a transcendental ground of the synthetic unity required for a particular experience. His analysis proceeds in two steps. First, he points out that the unity of synthesis according to merely empirical concepts, which, *ex hypothesi*, is what we would be left with absent a transcendental ground, would be contingent. This is because, as based upon experience, the rules according to which such synthetic unities are produced by the understanding, e.g., the rule stipulating that solubility in *aqua regia* goes together with being a yellow, malleable metal etc., are themselves contingent; since, in contrast say to the rule requiring the sum of the three angles of a triangular figure to be equal to two right angles, it is readily conceivable that such rules might cease to hold. And given this, Kant further notes that if such contingency were acknowledged, it would be necessary to recognize the possibility of a state of affairs in which the kind of empirical cognition that the empiricist accepts as a matter of course would not itself be possible. In Kant's graphic terms, it would be one in which the "soul" was filled with "a swarm of appearances," i.e., an abundance of sensory data, "without experience ever being able to arise from it."

Although such a state of affairs would hardly be desirable, one wonders why Kant seems to have regarded it as impossible. Certainly it is not *logically* impossible, since there is no contradiction in its conception. Indeed, it seems to invite the response that Kant is requiring more than is necessary for coherent experience, since all that this requires is that nature does in fact exhibit the kind of regularity that Kant posits, not that it must necessarily do so, except in the conditional sense that without it genuine empirical cognition would not be possible. As the issue is sometimes put, why can we not simply regard the thoroughgoing synthetic unity of appearances or, what amounts to the same thing, the uniformity of nature, as a matter of good "epistemic luck?"[56]

---

[56] The notion of epistemic luck has gained some currency in contemporary analytic epistemology in connection with the classical analysis of knowledge as justified true belief and the well-known challenges to this analysis, e.g., Gettier counter-examples. The issue seems to reflect a clash of intuitions. On the one hand, there is the deeply entrenched view that, in virtue of the justification requirement, genuine knowledge, as contrasted with true opinion, precludes luck; while, on the other hand, the element of fallibility that pervades even fully justified beliefs (at least those concerning empirical matters) seems to require an acknowledgment of an element of luck. Moreover, the effort to avoid admitting this by requiring infallibility only plays into the hand of the skeptic by affirming for genuine knowledge that can seldom, if ever, be met. The most thorough discussion of the topic of which I am aware is by Pritchard (2005). Although the context in which Kant is here operating is obviously quite different from that of contemporary analytic epistemology, particularly since the element of luck appears to attach to the order of appearances rather than to the procedures of the cognizer, I think it appropriate to characterize the Humean scenario to which Kant is responding as one that affirms that our empirical cognition is at bottom a matter of epistemic luck. Moreover, I think it evident that Hume's rhetoric in both the *Enquiry* and *Treatise* indicates that he would be highly sympathetic to this characterization.

Since this raises a fundamental issue with which we shall be concerned throughout the remainder of this study and the account presently under consideration is preparatory in nature, we are not yet in a position to deal with all of the ramifications of the issue. But from what we have already seen, it is clear that Kant's response turns on two closely related points, both of which he had argued for previously in section 2. The first is the conception of concepts as rules, which was operative throughout the preceding discussion. The second is the previously analyzed proposition that "our thought of the relation of all cognition to its object carries something of necessity with it" (A104).

Kant's conception of concepts as rules is clearly at work here, since it underlies the connection between concepts and the unity of synthesis on which the analysis turns. Indeed, it seems safe to say that Kant's entire anti-empiricistic argument in the Deduction assumes that concepts are rules, a view that is alien to the forms of classical empiricism to which Kant was responding.[57] In fact, the worry over contingency with regard to the applicability of empirical concepts, at least in its Kantian form, only arises when these concepts are construed as unifying rules; for it entails that if the rules fail to hold the concepts in which they are reflected would lose their grip upon reality, which would, in turn, undermine the possibility of cognition. Kant gives clear expression to this worry when he notes that such contingency allows for the possibility of a chaotic scenario in which "all relation of cognition to objects would...disappear."

The conception of concepts as rules also underlies Kant's assertion of a place for necessity in empirical cognition and is the reason why he insists that the possibility of such cognition requires a transcendental, i. e., non-empirical, ground. We have seen that the necessity in question applies specifically to concepts qua rules and that it is normative rather than logical (or causal) in nature. The essential point is that as rules concepts are themselves normative in the sense that they involve a kind of epistemic right to expect that whatever objects fall under the rule contain the properties that are expressed in the concept-rule and to require that other cognizers, who possess the concept, will agree with one's judgment. Moreover, any such right requires a warrant or justifying ground, which, for good Humean reasons, cannot be provided by experience. Returning to our previous example, upon perceiving a bit of metal that is yellow and malleable, one has an expectation that it will also be soluble in *aqua regia*. As based on experience, any such expectation is defeasible, which is why the rule is contingent. But while Kant could readily acknowledge this, he would maintain that it does not touch the main point, which is that such conceptual breakdowns are

---

[57] The point is noted by Allais (2011), 102 note 15, 102 note 15, who remarks that the imagistic view of concepts held by classical empiricism is too soft a target and that to appreciate the force of Kant's argument and presumably its present-day relevance we should regard Kant's opponent as someone who acknowledges that concepts are rules, but insists that all that we need to account for the possibility of empirical cognition are empirical concepts/rules. I agree with this assessment and thereby interpret Kant as arguing, at least by implication, that empirical concepts/rules presuppose a priori ones.

only intelligible against the backdrop of a thoroughgoing rule-governed synthetic unity of appearances, which is reflected in the conception of a single experience of which all particular experiences are regarded as instances. Lacking that, any expectation would be nothing more than the product of an association based on past perceptions, which, as such, is without the normative force of a genuine concept. Accordingly, what is required is a warrant or justifying ground to assume such an overall synthetic unity, which is usually understood as the uniformity of nature and which Kant will refer to as affinity.

This argument may also be considered a reprís at a dialectically later stage of Kant's account of the reproductive synthesis. We saw that Kant there proceeded in a similar fashion, initially appealing to the seemingly non-controversial point that the capacity of the human imagination to connect its representations through association, such that it can subsequently reproduce them, is dependent upon the representations being associable; and we further saw that, after giving a number of examples, including the famous one concerning cinnabar, Kant made the highly controversial and seemingly unsupported claim that, "There must therefore be something that itself makes possible this reproduction of the appearances by being the *a priori* ground of a necessary synthetic unity of them" (A101).

In evaluating Kant's overall account in section 2, it is essential to keep in mind the difference as well as the intimate relation between these two arguments. The difference stems from the fact that they are concerned with conditions of the successful operation of distinct cognitive faculties: the imagination, as the faculty of imagistic representations and their association, on the one hand, and the understanding, as the faculty of concepts understood as rules, on the other. This is important because, while the activity of the understanding is governed by norms, that of the imagination is not, at least not directly. And this is why Kant can plausibly affirm the need to provide a transcendental ground for the normative necessity that is presupposed by the formation and application of empirical concepts, whereas a comparable claim in the case of reproduction initially seemed gratuitous.

Nevertheless, Kant's earlier argument for the necessity of a similar a priori grounding for the assumption of the reproducibility of appearances appears in a different light, if we view it in terms of the just-considered argument regarding concepts. This is because the reproductive activity of the imagination is *indirectly* governed by cognitive norms, indeed by the same norms as the understanding; for even though reproduction and cognition are distinct enterprises, unless appearances contained the synthetic unity required for association and reproduction, they could not be brought under concepts by the understanding. In other words, if we consider Kant's account of the reproductive function of the imagination in light of its contribution to cognition, the case can be made for the necessity of a transcendental ground that would ensure that appearances conform to universal and necessary laws.

It is only after completing his argument for the necessity of some transcendental ground for the uniformity of nature that Kant introduces the categories. He writes:

The *a priori* conditions of a possible experience in general are at the same time conditions of the possibility of the objects of experience. Now I assert that the **categories** that have just been adduced are nothing other than the **conditions of thinking in a possible experience**, just as **space** and **time** contain the **conditions of the intuition** for the very same thing. They are therefore also fundamental concepts for thinking objects in general for the appearances, and they therefore have *a priori* objective validity, which is just what we really wanted to know.   (A111)

The first sentence contains Kant's well-known dictum. Its importance is reflected in the fact that he repeats it in a slightly different form in the Analytic of Principles, where, in explaining the possibility of synthetic judgments a priori, he writes: "The conditions of the **possibility of experience** in general are at the same time conditions of the **possibility of the objects of experience**, and on this account have objective validity in synthetic judgments *a priori*" (A158/B197). It is evident that this dictum expresses the essence of Kant's so-called "Copernican revolution;" for to say that conditions of the possibility of experience are also conditions of the possibility of the objects of experience is to say that objects (of experience) necessarily conform to the conditions of the possibility of their cognition. And it is also evident that this conclusion follows directly from Kant's analysis of the conditions under which cognition can relate to an object, since these are grounded in the nature of the understanding, specifically its requirement of a thoroughgoing synthetic unity.

In the second sentence, Kant identifies these conditions, from the side of thought, with the categories and in the third asserts their objective validity. The problem is that this is presented as a sheer assertion, without a scintilla of argument in support of this crucial claim. In other words, even assuming that some a priori rules are required as conditions of empirical cognition and that all possible objects of experience must conform to them, which is the most that Kant can claim to have shown up to this point, one may still ask why these rules should be identified with the categories derived from an analysis of the logical functions of judgment in "the Clue." Moreover, since the issue is not addressed in section 3, it is only in the B-Deduction that we find a serious effort on Kant's part to link a general argument for the necessity of some categories as a priori conditions of a possible experience and the particular list of categories identified in what is there characterized as the "Metaphysical Deduction."

Having argued that the categories ground the possibility of experience by functioning as a priori rules through which particular experiences can be regarded as instances of a universal experience, Kant connects them to the unity of apperception by claiming that,

[T]he possibility, indeed even the necessity of these categories rests on the relation that the entire sensibility, and with it also all possible appearances, have to the original apperception, in which everything is necessarily in agreement with the conditions of the thoroughgoing unity of self-consciousness, i.e., must stand under universal functions of synthesis, namely of the synthesis in accordance with concepts, as that in which alone apperception can demonstrate *a priori* its thoroughgoing and necessary identity.   (A111–12)

Kant here indicates a shift in focus from the validity of the categories to their possibility and necessity. The juxtaposition of possibility and necessity is perplexing, since if the categories are necessary they must also be possible. And since it is presumably their necessity that Kant wants to clarify, why does he also refer to their possibility?[58] While the obscurity of the text makes any reading conjectural, it seems that Kant's inclusion of the two modalities is best understood in light of two claims that he distinguished in the preceding paragraph: that the categories are "conditions of thinking in a possible experience" and that they are "fundamental concepts for thinking objects in general for the appearances." In light of this, I take Kant to be stating that the necessity of the categories is based on their status as conditions of thinking in a possible experience and their possibility on their status as the fundamental concepts in such thinking, the idea being that the latter is the condition under which categories are possible.

Nevertheless, regardless of which claim or claims concerning the categories Kant is endeavoring to clarify, it is evident that he proposes to do so by showing that both their possibility and their necessity rests on the relation between "the entire sensibility, and with it also all appearances, . . . to original apperception."[59] In other words, in order to understand the nature and function of the categories it is necessary to comprehend their role linking appearances to the unity of apperception, an act which both relates appearances to objects and synthesizes them in such a way that they conform to the condition of the unity of apperception. Accordingly, while the unity of apperception, rather than the categories, is the sought-for transcendental ground of the thoroughgoing unity of appearances, the categories are the rules guiding the synthesis through which this unity is produced by and for consciousness. Kant illustrates this by appealing once again to the concept of cause. This concept, he writes, "is nothing other than a synthesis (of that which follows in the temporal series with other appearances) in **accordance with concepts**; and without that sort of unity, which has its rule *a priori*, and which subjects the appearances to itself, thoroughgoing and universal, hence necessary unity of consciousness would not be encountered in the manifold of perceptions" (A112). Whereas in his canonical account of causation in the Second Analogy Kant's emphasis is on the category's or, more precisely, its corresponding schema's, role in determining the cognition of an objective succession, he here focuses on its role in producing the unity of consciousness.[60] But this should not be surprising, since we have seen that these are really two sides of

---

[58] It should be noted that Kant's heading for number four is "Provisional explanation of the possibility of the categories as *a priori* cognitions" (A110).

[59] Kant also uses the expression "original [*ursprüngliche*] apperception" at A94, A107, A108, A122, and A123 in the A-Deduction. At A94 he also terms sense and imagination as "original" and indicates that he means by this that they are not derived from any other cognitive faculty.

[60] In his discussion of the Principles of Pure Understanding Kant says that, "[W]hile in the principle itself we make use of the category . . . in its execution (its application to appearances) we set the schema in its place" (A181/B224). I discuss the relation between the schemata of the categories and their corresponding principles in Allison (2004), 225–8.

the same coin; viz., the reciprocity between the unity of consciousness (apperception) and the consciousness of unity (cognition) on which Kant's whole account turns. In other words, what Kant must show is that the categories are necessary conditions for bringing the sensible manifold to the unity of apperception, on the one hand, and for relating this manifold to an object = X, on the other.

Another important feature of this paragraph, which must at least be noted at this point, is Kant's seemingly seamless move from the *unity* of apperception to its *identity*. Thus, in the first sentence we see that Kant glides from speaking of "the conditions of the thoroughgoing unity of self-consciousness" to the need for apperception to demonstrate its thoroughgoing and necessary identity." But since this is not the first time we have encountered this move and it will not be the last, further treatment of this topic will be reserved for Chapter 6, when we should be in a better position to consider its importance for the overall argument of the Deduction.[61]

The final important conception that Kant introduces is that of affinity (*Affinität*), which he initially defines as "[t]he ground of the possibility of the manifold, insofar as it lies in the object" (A113). Although this marks his initial use of the term, Kant had already appealed to the underlying conception in his account of the reproductive synthesis, where we have seen that he argued that the reproducibility of appearances presupposes their associability, which is equivalent to their affinity. But whereas he there appealed vaguely to the ideality of appearances (the fact that they are not things in themselves) as a condition of their associability, now, having introduced all of the elements of cognition, culminating in original or transcendental apperception, Kant maintains that the latter is the ground of this affinity, which assumes the form of the uniformity of nature. Again, at issue is not the fact of such uniformity or lawfulness, but its necessity and Kant contends that on his principles it is readily comprehensible, since "All possible appearances belong, as representations, to the whole possible self-consciousness. But from this, as transcendental representation, numerical identity is inseparable, and certain *a priori*, because nothing can come into cognition except by means of this original apperception" (A113).[62] And from this it is but a short step to the conclusion that, "All appearances…stand in a thoroughgoing connection according to necessary laws, and hence in a **transcendental affinity**, of which the **empirical affinity** is a mere consequence" (A113–14).

---

[61] Kant first makes this move at A108 and within section 2 he also refers to numerical identity at A113. In my initial discussion of the former passage I did not call attention to it, however, because the focus was on the correlation between the unity of consciousness and the consciousness of unity. The significance of the distinction between Kant's appeals to the unity and numerical identity of the I of apperception (the *res cogitans*) has been emphasized by Henrich (1989b and 1994), who maintains that they lead to two different strategies for demonstrating the validity of the categories (from the conditions of the cognition of the unity and from the conditions of the identity of the I), only the second of which holds out any prospects for success. A variation on this theme is also advocated by Guyer (1987). I shall discuss their views on this issue in Chapter 6.

[62] In concluding his discussion of affinity in section 2 Kant once again appeals to transcendental idealism, though this time as an explanation of why nature can be said to conform to the requirements of apperception (A114).

This distinction between a transcendental and a merely empirical affinity suggests that Kant's analysis operates at three levels. The first, which seems to be motivated strategically by an attempt to link it to Hume's treatment of the subject, concerns the association of representations, which involves merely the activity of the imagination rather than cognition in the "proper sense."[63] As Kant had already noted in the discussion of the reproductive synthesis, this presupposes their associability, i.e., reproducibility, which he now labels "empirical affinity," by which is understood the *de facto* uniformity of nature. This is the second level, with which Hume would concur, since he readily acknowledged a *de facto* uniformity of nature and questioned only the grounds of our reliance upon its continuation (that the future will resemble the past). The third level marks Kant's decisive break, not only with Hume, but with any empiricistic position. It consists in the claim that empirical affinity must be considered as the consequence of a transcendental affinity, which has its source in the human understanding and which interjects the missing ingredient of necessity. As such, it constitutes the central thesis of the A-Deduction; but for that reason I shall reserve further consideration of it for Chapter 6, where Kant's account of affinity in section 3 will be examined in more detail.

---

[63] In his explicit critique of Hume, Kant accuses him of deflating "a principle of affinity, which has its seat in the understanding and asserts a necessary connection, into a rule of association, which is found merely in the imitative imagination and which can present only contingent combinations, not objective ones at all" (A766–7/B794–5).

6

The A-Deduction

Section 3

After preparing his readers in section 2, Kant turns in section 3 to the task of instructing them, which involves presenting his argument in a systematic form. But rather than providing a single formulation of his argument, Kant presents it in two forms, which are commonly referred to as "the argument from above" and "the argument from below."[1] The former begins with pure apperception and proceeds to the conclusion that appearances stand in a necessary relation to the understanding, and therefore to the categories. The latter begins with appearances (the empirical) and proceeds to apperception and the categories as necessary conditions of their cognition, which are also necessary conditions of possible experience. Accordingly, the chapter will be divided into two parts, the first dealing with "the argument from above" and the second with "the argument from below"; though each part will also consider the other materials that Kant connects with these formulations.

I

Kant begins the section by referring to the three subjective sources of cognition or cognitive faculties: sense, imagination, and apperception. He claims that each of these can be considered empirically with respect to given appearances, but that "they are also elements or foundations *a priori* that make this empirical use itself possible" (A115). In other words, each of these faculties is assigned both an empirical and a transcendental function, with the latter being a necessary condition of the former.[2]

---

[1] Kant implies this division but does not quite state it as such. For though immediately upon completing the formulation of the argument that begins with apperception he states that "Now we will set the necessary connection of the understanding with the appearances by means of the categories by beginning from beneath [*von unten*], namely with what is empirical" (A119–20), he does not actually refer to the former as an "argument [or deduction] from above." Paton (1936a), 457–98, refers to them respectively as the "progressive" and "regressive exposition," which accurately reflects their logical structures.

[2] A striking feature of this list, which we initially encountered in B12 and was repeated in the first section of the A-Deduction at A94, is the lack of any reference to the understanding. The explanation for this omission lies in the characterization of the three faculties listed as "original," in the sense of not being derivable from any more basic cognitive powers. Despite the significance that Kant gives to the human understanding in the A-Deduction as the source of the laws of nature (A127), he regards its normative

According to Kant, "Sense represents the appearances empirically in **perception**, the **imagination** in association (and reproduction), and **apperception** in the empirical consciousness of the identity of these reproductive [*reproduktiven*] representations with the appearances through which they were given, hence in recognition" (A115).

The common features of the empirical function of these faculties or cognitive powers is that they are directed towards the representation of appearances. While Kant's characterization of the empirical function of the imagination does not require further comment at this point, since it essentially reiterates what was claimed in the account of its reproductive and associative functions in section 2, a word is in order regarding what Kant now says concerning the empirical functions of sense and apperception. With respect to the former, the obvious point of difference is that the attribution of a synopsis to sense, which we also encountered at A97, is dropped.[3] This is not because Kant no longer attributed a synopsis to sense, since we have seen that he meant by this merely that sensible intuition contains a manifold, which is surely something that he continued to maintain. Rather, it seems more likely that Kant's reason for dropping a reference to a synopsis was strategic, having to do with his desire to link perception with time as the form of inner intuition. As far as the empirical function of apperception is concerned, the main point is that it cannot be equated with empirical apperception, at least as Kant understood it in the A-Deduction, since we have seen that he equated the latter with inner sense (A107).[4] In fact, rather than being a form of self-consciousness, apperception in its empirical function is the capacity to form and apply empirical concepts through the recognition of relevant commonalities (identities) between empirical intuitions and reproduced representations.

In the second paragraph Kant deals with the transcendental or grounding functions of these faculties. He notes that, "[A]ll perceptions are grounded *a priori* in pure intuition (in time, the form of their inner intuition as representations), association in the pure synthesis of the imagination, and empirical consciousness in pure apperception, i.e., in the thoroughgoing identity of oneself in all possible representations" (A115–16).[5] By "perceptions" Kant evidently means conscious representations, i.e., perceivings, rather than objects perceived which is why he says that they are grounded a priori in time, as a form of inner sense. As such, they have already received their grounding in the Transcendental Aesthetic, allowing Kant to regard

---

force as derived from its relation to the unity of apperception, on the one hand, and the imagination on the other.

[3] For an explanation of what Kant means by "synopsis" see Chapter 5, note 3.

[4] Kant's view of empirical apperception in the B-Deduction is not entirely clear. At B132 he distinguishes it from pure or original apperception, but fails to explain what he understands by it; while at B140 he refers to the empirical unity of apperception, saying only that, unlike the transcendental unity, it is only subjectively valid and that it is derived from the latter "under given conditions *in concreto*." We shall revisit this issue in connection with the analysis of the B-Deduction.

[5] I have used, with some modifications, Kemp Smith's translation of this paragraph because I found it much clearer than the Guyer and Wood rendering.

this as a fait accompli for the purposes of the Deduction. But while Kant had introduced a pure, i.e., a priori, synthesis of the imagination and the conception of a pure, i.e., original or transcendental apperception in section 2, the claims that they ground respectively the empirical synthesis of the imagination and empirical consciousness, understood as the recognition of objects by means of empirical concepts, remain at this point largely promissory notes, which Kant needs to redeem in the remainder of section 3. Accordingly, in order to pursue these topics, we must turn to Kant's actual analysis, starting with "the argument from above."

He begins this line of argument by noting that,

[I]f we wish to follow the inner ground of this connection of representations up to that point in which they must all come together in order first to obtain unity of cognition for a possible experience, then we must begin with pure apperception. All intuitions are nothing for us and do not in the least concern us if they cannot be taken up into consciousness, whether they influence it directly or indirectly, and through this alone is cognition possible. We are conscious *a priori* of the thoroughgoing identity of ourselves with regard to all representations that can ever belong to our cognition, as a necessary condition of the possibility of all representations (since the latter represent something in me only insofar as they belong with all the others to one consciousness, hence they must be at least capable of being connected in it). This principle holds *a priori,* and can be called **the transcendental principle of the unity** of all the manifold of our representations (thus also in intuition). Now the unity of the manifold in a subject is synthetic; pure apperception therefore yields a principle of the synthetic unity of the manifold in all possible intuition.   (A116)

Inasmuch as Kant refers specifically to intuitions being "taken up into consciousness," he evidently means their being apprehended. Once again, the claim that, apart from being taken up, the intuition would be nothing "for us" or of no concern to us, refers to us considered qua cognizers. The suggestion that these intuitions could influence empirical consciousness indirectly is a new element, however, which is apparently intended to include intuitions, which, though not immediately apprehended, can be directly inferred from what is, e.g., the existence of fire from the perception of smoke.[6] Moreover, the possibility of the latter is obviously crucial because, as Hume had noted, the central task of any account of empirical cognition is to determine "the nature of that evidence, which assures us of any real existence and matter of fact beyond the present testimony of our senses, or the records of our memory."[7] In other words, what is required is an "inference ticket" (in Ryle's sense), which enables us to move beyond the immediate contents of consciousness. But whereas Hume located this ticket solely in the relation of cause and effect, which he grounded in custom, Kant extends it to all of the categories, or at least the relational categories, and attempts to provide it with a transcendental grounding in the unity of apperception.

[6] See Paton (1936a), 458.   [7] Hume (1999), 108.

Kant takes a major step in this direction in the second sentence, when he refers to "the thoroughgoing identity of ourselves with regard to all representations that can ever belong to our cognition." Following Henrich, I take this to refer to the "moderate identity" of the cognizing subject, which means that it is "the very same I" that is the subject of all the representations that enter into a cognition.[8] As Kant points out in the Third Paralogism, since this identity is ascribed merely to the I qua cognizing subject, which he there refers to as the "logical identity of the I" (A363), it has no implications for personal identity. To claim that this identity is "thoroughgoing" (*durchgängig*) is to claim that it extends to "all representations that can ever belong to our cognition," which, seen in connection with the preceding sentence, means that it extends to all those representations that can be taken up into consciousness indirectly.

The problem posed by this sentence concerns just what it is that we are supposed to be "conscious *a priori*." There seem to be two possibilities. One, which is suggested by the initial reference to consciousness, is that we are aware of our (moderate) numerical identity. So construed, the argument claims that a kind of Cartesian consciousness of one's identity with respect to all episodes of conscious representations, which supposedly entails that the unification of these representations by means of the categories, is a necessary condition of cognition. Moreover, the existence of such a consciousness and its entailment of a categoreal synthesis is precisely what Henrich claims to be the fundamental principle of the Deduction.[9] The other is suggested by the word "as." On this reading, rather than appealing to the existence of a Cartesian, i.e., indubitable, consciousness of our numerical identity, Kant is merely affirming the necessity of presupposing such a thoroughgoing identity as a necessary condition of cognition. Inasmuch as the claim that we actually possess such a consciousness, which involves a radical extension of the Cartesian *cogito* from any given episode of thought to the collective unity of thoughts (both actual and possible), is itself deeply problematic, the second reading appears to provide the more viable alternative.[10] On this interpretation, the task is merely to show that the *possibility* of a consciousness of the identity of the I is a necessary condition of cognition and that this possibility requires the unification of one's representations by means of the categories. In other words, what is at issue here (and in many other instances) is the necessity of a possibility.[11]

---

[8] See Henrich (1994), 178–80. Henrich distinguishes a strict conception of numerical identity, which he associates with Leibniz, and is termed strict because it precludes any change of state of a substance, and a moderate conception, which affirms identity throughout change. His claim, with which I concur, is that the identity attributed to the I is of the latter variety.

[9] Ibid., esp. 185–92.

[10] Henrich's claim regarding the existence of such a Cartesian consciousness has been criticized by Hossenfelder (1978), 132, and Guyer (1979), 62–3.

[11] This formulation is used by both Reich (1992), 27 and de Vleeschauwer (1937), 101.

Kant terms this proposition "**the transcendental principle of the unity** of all the manifold of our representations." And since it affirms a necessity (albeit of a possibility), he maintains that it holds a priori. Moreover, inasmuch as this unity is synthetic, Kant concludes that this principle, now characterized as "pure apperception," "yields a principle of the synthetic unity of the manifold in all possible intuition." But rather than explicating the latter point in the main text, Kant leaves this task to a lengthy note in which he advises the reader to attend carefully to this proposition, by which he evidently means the above-mentioned transcendental principle. In an endeavor to clarify this principle and its import Kant writes:

All representations have a necessary relation to a **possible** empirical consciousness; for if they did not have this, and if it were entirely impossible to become conscious of them, that would be as much as to say that they did not exist at all. All empirical consciousness, however, has a necessary relation to a transcendental consciousness (preceding all particular experience), namely the consciousness of myself, as original apperception. It is therefore absolutely necessary that in my cognition all consciousness belong to one consciousness (of myself). Now here is a synthetic unity of the manifold (of consciousness) that is cognized *a priori*, and that yields the ground for synthetic *a priori* propositions concerning pure thinking in exactly the way that space and time yield such propositions concerning the form of mere intuition. The synthetic proposition that every different **empirical consciousness** must be combined into a single self-consciousness is the absolutely first and synthetic principle of our thinking in general. But it should not go unnoticed that the mere representation I in relation to all others (the collective unity of which it makes possible) is the transcendental consciousness. Now it does not matter here whether this representation be clear (empirical consciousness) or obscure, even whether it be actual; but the possibility of the logical form of all cognition necessarily rests on the relationship to this apperception **as a faculty**.   (A117n)

The notion of the necessity of a possibility is clearly expressed in the first sentence, where Kant speaks of a necessary relation of representations to a *possible* empirical consciousness rather than to an actual one. Moreover, in this case the necessity is evident; for, as Kant notes, if it were not possible to become conscious of representations, they would not exist (for me), which is a variant on the familiar theme that they would be nothing to me (qua cognizer). Once again, this leaves open the possibility that these representations could influence me in a non-cognitive way, say by affecting my feelings and desires, thereby influencing my behavior in the manner of Leibnizian small perceptions.[12]

The key move occurs in the next sentence, where Kant claims that all empirical consciousness has a necessary relation to a transcendental consciousness, which he contends precedes all particular experience (presumably in a logical rather than a temporal sense). Although Kant's use of the expression "transcendental consciousness" is unique to this note, his equation of it with "original apperception" and "the

---

[12] Perhaps Kant's clearest statement of this view is in his letter to Herz regarding Maimon of May 26, 1789 (B 11: 52$_{6-17}$; 314).

mere representation I," indicates that the underlying conception is not; for these
terms are synonyms for transcendental apperception, understood as the capacity of
the I to become conscious of itself qua thinker. Kant concludes from this that "It
is...absolutely necessary that in my cognition all consciousness belongs to one
consciousness (of myself)," which he attempts to clarify by pointing out that "it
does not matter here whether this representation be clear (empirical consciousness)
or obscure, even whether it be actual." By denying that this transcendental consciousness requires an actual awareness of the "I think," much less a clear one, Kant
effectively undermines any effort to interpret his thesis in psychological terms. As his
closing remark that "the possibility of the logical form of all cognition necessarily
rests on the relationship to this apperception **as a faculty**" indicates, its thrust is
entirely epistemological.[13]

In order to understand this point, it is useful to contrast Kant's claim about a
transcendental consciousness with his prior claim about empirical consciousness.
Although Kant does not explicitly formulate the latter in these terms, he effectively
maintains that *if* a representation is to be something for me qua cognizer, it must be
related (either directly or indirectly) to a possible empirical consciousness. By
contrast, the new claim is that *all* my representations are necessarily ascribable to
an identical I (myself), which, as Kant proceeds to point out, entails that they
constitute a (thoroughgoing) synthetic unity, which can itself be cognized a priori.
In other words, whereas the first claim leaves open the possibility that a cognizer
could have many distinct episodes of empirical consciousness, i.e., apprehendings or
perceivings, which stand in no relationship to each other beyond being ascribable to
the same subject, this possibility is ruled out by the attribution of the variety of these
empirical consciousnesses to a single transcendental consciousness.

The significance of this step stems from the fact that it entails that all of a
cognizer's representations, or at least all those that can enter in any way into
empirical consciousness (either directly or indirectly), constitute a thoroughgoing
synthetic unity, which, since this synthetic unity is a necessary one, means that all of
these representations are connected according to a priori rules. This both paves the
way for the introduction of the categories as these rules and provides the transcendental ground for the necessary uniformity of nature under them, a uniformity
which, without such rules, would have, as it did for Hume, a merely contingent
status. Kant signals the importance that he assigns to this claim by noting that, "The
synthetic proposition that every different **empirical consciousness** must be combined into a single self-consciousness is the absolutely first and synthetic principle of
our thinking in general."

Inasmuch as Kant regards this proposition as synthetic a priori, it itself stands in
need of a deduction. The most direct path to this goal appears to be something like

---

[13] One of the most confusing features of Kant's treatment of apperception is that, though defining it as a
faculty or power, he also frequently speaks of it as an act. On this, see Paton (1936a), 397.

the proposition that the I has a Cartesian certainty regarding its numerical identity with respect to all the representations of which it can become conscious, which is evidently why Henrich sees it as the best strategy available to Kant for carrying out the Deduction. Indeed, if this claim were justified, Kant would be more than halfway home, needing only to connect the thoroughgoing synthetic unity of apperception with the categories in order to complete the argument. Unfortunately, however, we have seen that this move does not pass muster, either as an interpretation of Kant or as a justifiable proposition, which means that we must seek to find in the text of the A-Deduction a different foundation for Kant's first principle.

As an alternative proposal, I suggest that we consider more closely Kant's cryptic claim that "the possibility of the logical form of all cognition necessarily rests on the relationship to this apperception **as a faculty.**" Assuming that by the "logical form of cognition" Kant is referring to its discursive nature, rather than to anything like the present-day conception of logical form, what must be shown is that the very possibility of discursive cognition depends upon the truth of this principle. Moreover, a promising starting point for this enterprise is Kant's previously discussed thesis that "our thought of the relation of all cognition to its object carries something of necessity with it" (A104). In discussing this claim in Chapter 5 it was suggested that necessity was to be understood in a normative sense, meaning thereby that, while it is neither causally nor logically necessary to unify one's representations in such a way that they relate to an object, one must do so insofar as one takes them as so related. Since Kant made this claim in section 2, before introducing his conception of apperception, he did not connect it explicitly with the latter; though he did state that it involved a formal unity of consciousness. Accordingly our present task is to see whether it can be connected with transcendental apperception or, more precisely, with the principle that "every different **empirical consciousness** must be combined into a single self-consciousness."

Since Kant claims that this principle is synthetic, it is sometimes thought to contradict his insistence in the B-Deduction that the principle of the unity of apperception is analytic (B135 and 138). This issue will be dealt with in Chapter 8, where it will be argued that the principles that Kant here refers to as synthetic and there as analytic are not in fact the same. For the present, however, the salient point is that the price of denying this synthetic principle is the relinquishment of the possibility of attributing objective validity to our cognition. As Kant had already argued in section 2, this is because the merely *de facto* connection of representations in an empirical consciousness is a purely contingent matter, lacking the normative necessity built into a claim of objective validity.[14] The latter requires that the

---

[14] The difference is that in the earlier discussion Kant framed the issue in terms of the unity of experience, whereas he here does so in terms of the unity of consciousness. This is because in the earlier discussion Kant had argued for the necessary unity of experience prior to appealing to the necessary unity of apperception as its transcendental ground. Otherwise expressed, the argument of section 2 is not only preparatory but "from below;" whereas the present argument is both systematic and "from above."

unification of representations in a particular consciousness holds independently of
the cognitive state of the subject, which means that the rules on the basis of which a
cognizer produces this unification are deemed by the cognizer to hold for that
subject, even if it had been in a different cognitive state. Moreover, this is precisely
what the principle in question maintains. In other words, by the same "I think" is to
be understood not merely the numerically identical subject, but the same unification
of representations by that subject, i.e., not merely the same *I* but the same *I think*.

Although it may not be immediately evident that such a reading can be constructed on the basis of the texts considered up to this point, there are a number of
things to be said in its favor. First, it is at least a possible construal of Kant's first
principle, since it accounts for the status that he assigns to it. Second, it accords with
Kant's insistence that apperception be "pure," since this requires that it be independent of the subject's cognitive state at a particular time and the capacity to abstract
from the contingent features of that state (how things may appear in an empirical
consciousness under certain conditions).[15] Third, as we shall see in Chapter 7, it finds
strong confirmation in Kant's distinction in the *Prolegomena* between a unification of
representations in a particular consciousness and in "consciousness in general" and
the attribution of objective validity to the latter and a merely subjective validity to the
former.[16]

The remainder of the "argument from above" is exceedingly perfunctory, consisting of three paragraphs in which Kant moves quickly from the synthetic unity of
apperception to the imagination as the synthesizing agent and from this to the
understanding and its categories. And since, apart from some apparent modifications, it consists largely in a restatement in a skeletal but systematic form of views
already expressed in section 2, it does not require extensive analysis.

Kant begins by noting that the synthetic unity of the manifold, which was
connected with transcendental apperception in the preceding paragraph and its
appended note, "presupposes or includes [*einschliesst*] a synthesis," and he adds
that if the former is necessary a priori, the synthesis must also be a priori (A118).
That this unity presupposes a synthesis is clear, since all synthetic unities for Kant
presuppose one.[17] It is also clear that if this synthetic unity is necessary a priori, as it

---

[15]   The same can be said, *mutatis mutandis*, with regard to Kant's parallel emphasis on the apperception
in question being original, since this requires that the "I think" not be derived from a pre-given unity of
representations. We shall see that this feature of Kant's conception of apperception is more prominent in
the B-Deduction, with its greater emphasis on spontaneity.

[16]   See Pro 4: 304–5; 98.

[17]   Since it is also clear that for Kant a synthetic unity includes or contains (*einschliesst*) a synthesis, the
"or" must be understood as the "or of equivalence." And since presupposing and including or containing
do not appear to be equivalent, this raises a question about Kant's intent. For example, one might conclude
that he is simply being careless and that he meant to use "and" rather than "or." But while this is certainly
possible, I believe that the use of "or" becomes understandable, if we keep in mind that for Kant there is no
real distinction between synthetic unity and synthesis; for, as he had suggested at A108, consciousness of
the synthetic unity in question is inseparable from consciousness of the unifying function or rule through

must be, if, as Kant claims, it is a necessary condition of the unity of apperception, the synthesis must have an a priori status.[18] To deny this would be to make this necessary unity dependent upon something contingent, which is an obvious contradiction.

Kant then infers from this that "the transcendental unity of apperception is related to the pure synthesis of the imagination, as an *a priori* condition of the possibility of all composition of the manifold in a cognition" (A118). Since this is the first reference to the imagination in the current discussion, Kant could hardly have intended to suggest that it followed directly from the preceding claim regarding the relation between a necessary synthetic unity and a necessary synthesis. It does follow, however, if we take him to be alluding to the preparatory account in section 2, where he had argued that determinate spatiotemporal representations, e.g., of a line or a stretch of time, require an a priori exercise of the imagination. Nevertheless, Kant also appears to break with his earlier account, when he remarks emphatically that "only the **productive synthesis of the imagination** can take place *a priori*; for the reproductive synthesis rests on conditions of experience" (A118). Inasmuch as in his initial account of the reproductive synthesis Kant claimed that it is exercised a priori with regard to the pure intuitions of space and time, his present statement marks at least a terminological shift. A survey of Kant's use of the productive/reproductive contrast with respect to the imagination shows, however, that it is the formulation of section 2 rather than his present formulation that is non-standard, since he elsewhere characterizes the productive synthesis as a priori and the reproductive as empirical.[19]

Kant concludes the paragraph with a further inference from what has supposedly already been shown; viz., that "The principle of the necessary unity of the pure (productive) synthesis of the imagination prior to apperception is . . . the ground of the possibility of all cognition, especially that of experience" (A118). There are three points to note here. First, by the unity of the pure, i.e., a priori, synthesis of the imagination Kant understands its underlying rule, which, like all rules, is a product of the understanding. Second, Kant's claim that this synthesis (and its unifying rule) is "prior to [*vor*] apperception" is to be taken in a logical rather than a temporal sense and refers to the *act* of apperception (the thinking I's consciousness of itself as *res cogitans*) not to apperception as the faculty or capacity of thinking. Specifically, this

which it is brought about. This reading is suggested by de Vleeschauwer (1936), 335. See also Paton (1936a), 464, note 2, for a somewhat different reading.

[18] In an early paper, Guyer (1980) takes an extremely negative view of Kant's conception of a priori synthesis (at least outside the domain of mathematics), which is evidently an expression of his more general hostility to transcendental idealism. Specifically, he considers this conception as entailing a radical theory of metaphysical constitution, according to which the subject supposedly constructs the world a priori through such syntheses. But though some of Kant's language might suggest such a reading, particularly his claim that a synthesis can "take place" (*stattfinden*) a priori, I find little reason for taking this literally, and certainly not in the metaphysically objectionable sense insisted upon by Guyer. On my view, when Kant speaks of an a priori synthesis he is always referring to its normative rather than its metaphysical status.

[19] We have already seen that this is the view to which he adheres in B 12, which is closely related, both temporally and thematically, to the A-Deduction. See also A123, B152, and Anthro 7:167; 278.

priority consists in the fact that it is a necessary condition of the possibility of this self-consciousness, since it first provides a content to be thought or apperceived (a unified manifold). Third, Kant contends that, though this synthesis has a special relevance to experience, it is actually the ground of *all* cognition, including mathematics.

The next step in Kant's descent from apperception to appearances is to grant transcendental status, under certain conditions, to both the a priori synthesis of the imagination and its unity. He does this, however, through stipulation rather than argument. Kant writes: "[W]e call the synthesis of the manifold in imagination transcendental if, without distinction of the intuitions, it concerns nothing but the connection of the manifold *a priori* and the unity of this synthesis is called transcendental if it is represented as necessary *a priori* in relation to the original unity of apperception" (A118). As this passage indicates, the reason why this synthesis is deemed transcendental is that it is not concerned with the specific nature of the manifold of intuition being synthesized and is directed only at unifying the data in accordance with the conditions of the unity of apperception. Kant concludes from this that its unity, i.e., the unifying rule embedded in it, is "the pure form of all possible cognition, through which … all objects of possible cognition are represented" (A118). To claim that this rule is "the pure form of all possible cognition" is to elevate it to the status of space and time, which are likewise forms of all possible cognition; and since its source is the understanding, this becomes the means whereby Kant brings the understanding and its categories into the account. Thus, as in section 2, they not only make their initial appearance in the last act, but through the back door, as it were, of the transcendental synthesis of the imagination. Finally, given this conceptual framework, Kant completes this segment of the Deduction in four quick steps, which like most of this account, consists more of assertion than argument.

1. Kant concludes from this that the understanding contains "pure *a priori* cognitions that contain the necessary unity of the pure synthesis of the imagination in regard to all possible appearances" (A119). If there is such a thing as the pure understanding as Kant conceives it (the unity of apperception in relation to the transcendental synthesis of the imagination), this clearly follows.

2. Kant identifies these pure a priori cognitions with the categories. Unfortunately, this step, though obviously essential to the Deduction, is sheer assertion, since, unlike Kant's other claims, it cannot be justified by appeal to earlier portions of the argument, including the account of the categories in "the Clue." Accordingly, much as in section 2, the most that Kant can claim to have shown at this point is that *some* a priori concepts are required and that the categories identified in "the Clue" are the most likely, or perhaps even the only readily available candidates. What he cannot show is that they are the only *conceivable* candidates. Moreover, this is the direct result of Kant's chosen strategy to link the categories directly with the transcendental synthesis of the imagination;

bypassing their connection with judgment, a defect that he will rectify in the B-deduction.

3. Kant further concludes from this that the human understanding is "related to all objects of the senses ... and to their synthesis by means of imagination, under which ... all appearances as data for a possible experience stand" (A119). This enables Kant to affirm the universality of the scope of the understanding (and its categories) with respect to all appearances, simply qua appearances. In addition, it helps us to understand Kant's strategy in the A-Deduction of relating the understanding directly to the transcendental synthesis of the imagination; for it makes it possible for him to claim such universality for the pure understanding and categories, a claim that could not be directly derived from their connection with the logical functions of judgment. We shall see that Kant makes this claim in the second part of the B-Deduction, after connecting the categories with the logical functions in the first part.

4. Kant insists upon the necessity of the connection between appearances and possible experience, on the grounds that "without it [the relation to possible experience] we could not gain any cognition at all through them, and they would thus not concern us at all;" from which he infers that "the pure understanding, by means of the categories, is a formal and synthetic principle of all experiences, and that appearances have a **necessary relation to the understanding**" (A119). This last step is required because of Kant's abiding concern to preclude the possibility that the agreement of appearances with the categories is merely contingent, which would leave in place the dreaded specter. As we shall see in more detail below, this is the most problematic aspect of the Deduction, with the crucial issue being the kind of necessity involved.

II

Kant prefaces this exposition of the "argument from below" (A119–28) by indicating that it has the same goal as the one just considered, namely, showing that there is a necessary relation between the understanding and appearances by means of the categories. Once again, the emphasis is on the necessity of this connection, since a merely *de facto* or contingent agreement would fail to exorcize the specter that appearances might not conform to the conditions of the understanding. The difference is that it proceeds in the opposite direction, beginning with appearances and regressing to the conditions of their cognition. Kant further suggests that this manner of presentation makes the argument more intuitively evident, since it sets the necessary connection between appearances and the understanding "before our eyes" (*vor Augen legen*) (A119), a claim which he did not make and, indeed, could not make, for the argument from above.

A) *Imagination and perception*: Much as in the argument from above, Kant's discussion of the empirical function of the imagination is perfunctory, compared to the much richer account that he provided in section 2. Kant evidently assumed that the reader could turn to that account for the details, while he focused his attention on the more salient issue of the connection between the imagination and the categories. Nevertheless, he does call attention to a crucial point, which, though implicit in his initial account, could easily have been overlooked; viz., the role of the imagination in perception. And, as is often the case, Kant does this in a note rather than the main body of text. He writes:

No psychologist has yet thought that the imagination is a necessary ingredient in perception itself. This is partly because this faculty has been limited to reproduction, and partly because it has been believed that the senses do not merely afford us impressions but also put them together and produce images of objects, for which without doubt something more than the receptivity of impressions is required, namely a function of the synthesis of them.   (A120n)[20]

I had called attention to this note in the Appendix to Chapter 3 because it implies that Kant did not regard Tetens as having anticipated him in this regard. But we shall see that Kant's target here is not merely Tetens, but the general empiricist view of perception, particularly Hume's. Kant begins his account by characterizing a perception as an appearance combined with consciousness.[21] And, given this characterization, he notes parenthetically that "without the relation to an at least possible consciousness appearance could never become an object of cognition for us, and would therefore be nothing for us, and since it has no objective reality in itself and exists only in cognition it would be nothing at all" (A120).

The first question raised by this characterization is why Kant maintains that in order to be something an appearance need only stand in a relation to a *possible* consciousness rather than an actual one. Although Kant is here silent on the matter, the most likely explanation is that he had in mind his previously discussed claim that in order to be anything for us, cognitively speaking, an appearance must be taken up in consciousness either directly or indirectly. Presumably, at the level of perception, at least part of the role of the imagination is to make possible an indirect connection

---

[20] Although Kant appends this note to the opening paragraph of the exposition, which discusses apprehension, it clearly applies to the second paragraph as well, which discusses the essential role of reproduction in the formation of a perceptual image.

[21] At B207 Kant defines perception as "empirical consciousness, i.e., one in which there is at the same time sensation," and he characterizes appearances as "objects of perception." I take it that this is the relation between perception and appearance that he has in mind here. In his progressive taxonomy or *Stufenleiter* of the genus representation Kant defines "*perceptio*" as a "representation with consciousness" and states that "A perception that refers to the subject as a modification of its state is a **sensation** (*sensatio*); an objective perception is a **cognition** (*cognitio*)" (A320/B366–7). Elsewhere he equates perception with an intuition of which I am conscious and indicates that he takes "*Wahrnehmung*" and "*Perceptio*" as synonyms (Pro 4: 300; 94).

between an appearance and consciousness.[22] Moreover, this accords with the definition of the imagination provided in the second edition as "the faculty for representing an object even **without its presence in intuition**" (B151).[23] We shall consider below how this should be understood.

For the present, however, Kant's main point is that because an appearance contains a manifold it requires a synthesis in order to be apprehended. But whereas in his initial discussion of the synthesis of apprehension in section 2 Kant took great pains to emphasize that, as modifications of inner sense, appearances are given successively in time and that it is their mode of givenness that made necessary a synthesis in order to yield the representation of a manifold, it is here merely implicit. Rather than bringing in the element of time, Kant simply notes that the manifoldness inherent in an appearance entails the necessity of a synthesis, which, when exercised immediately upon perceptions, is termed "apprehension." And, by way of explanation, Kant adds that the task of the imagination is to bring the manifold of intuition into an **image (*Bild*)** and to this end "it must take up the impressions into its activity, i.e., apprehend them" (A120).

The identification of the activity of the imagination (*Einbildungskraft*) with the formation of an image (*Bild*) both reflects the etymology of the term and strongly suggests that the "psychologists" to whom Kant refers in the note and charges with failing to realize that the imagination is a necessary ingredient in perception, were the empiricists who viewed perception as consisting entirely in the reception of images and the activity of the mind (including the imagination) as consisting merely in combining or otherwise relating these images in various ways. In other words, rather than seeing the mind operative at the ground floor of cognition (in the guise of the productive imagination), they only acknowledge its activity at a later stage, which takes the form of combining these images (e.g., Humean impressions) according to principles of association.

Although this is an accurate depiction of the view that Kant opposed, it provides a misleading characterization of his own view; since it suggests that the fundamental activity of the imagination for Kant; viz., synthesis, consists in the production of images. But Kant's analysis of the synthesis of apprehension-cum-reproduction in section 2 gave no indication that the unification of the manifold of an empirical intuition, which is what this synthesis supposedly effects, need result in an image or mental picture. Indeed, this view is difficult to reconcile with Kant's claim in the note that it is the *productive*, not merely the reproductive function of the imagination that is operative in perception. While it was a standard view within the empiricist tradition that the imagination can produce new images, e.g., of a golden mountain,

---

[22] For a similar analysis, see Paton (1936a), 477–8. It should also be kept in mind that, given the regressive nature of exposition, Kant cannot offer such an explanation at this point; hence the vagueness of his account.

[23] See also Anthro 7: 167; 278.

by combining elements that had never actually been perceived together, this is obviously not applicable to *perception*, which leaves Kant's claim that the imagination is an essential ingredient in the latter mysterious. Finally, and most important, the view that the essential business of the imagination is the production of images appears to be incompatible with Kant's claim that the imagination is "a blind but indispensable function of the soul, without which we would have no cognition at all" (A78/B103), since it renders inexplicable its connection with the understanding as the faculty of concepts upon which Kant also insists in both versions of the Deduction. Simply put, it is difficult to see how Kant could maintain that "the function of the understanding is to bring the synthesis to concepts" (A78/B103), if the function of the synthesis is simply to produce an image. Thus, one naturally asks: what exactly is brought to concepts on this view? Or, alternatively, to what sort of concept could an image be brought? The answer suggested by Hume is a pale copy of itself; but this is obviously not Kant's view.

Assuming, then, that for Kant the product of the synthesis through which perception is constituted is not simply an image, yet, as a creation of the imagination must be something like an image, what is it? The short answer is that it is a schema or, more precisely, since a percept, like an image, is inherently particular, it is a schematic image. To flesh out and evaluate this answer we need to turn to the Schematism, where Kant discusses the relation between schemata and images. As he there puts it, "The schema is in itself always only a product of the imagination; but since the synthesis of the latter has as its aim no individual intuition but rather only the unity in the determination of sensibility, the schema is to be distinguished from the image" (A140/B179). Despite linking schematization to the imagination, this particular way of distinguishing between schema and image does not appear to be of much help in relating the former to perception, since Kant here seems to deny that a schema has anything to do with particulars, which are what is perceived. Moreover, Kant's initial illustration of the schema–image distinction also does not at first glance seem to facilitate understanding the role of a schema in perception. It concerns number, and Kant characterizes the image of the number five as five dots. Obviously, there is no schema for the number five or any particular number, just as there is no image of number in general or as such. There is, however, a schema for the latter, which Kant characterizes as "more the representation of a method for representing a multitude (e.g., a thousand) than the image itself [presumably a thousand dots], which in this case I could survey and compare with the concept only with difficulty" (A140/B179).[24] And, generalizing from this, Kant notes that by the schema for any concept he understands the "representation of a general procedure of the imagination for providing a concept

---

[24] The situation is complicated by the fact that Kant also characterizes number as the schema of the category of magnitude (A142/B182). Accordingly, number has a unique status for Kant, since it is both the schema of a pure concept of the understanding and a "pure sensible concept," i.e., an a priori sensible or mathematical concept, which, as such, itself requires a schema.

with its image" (A140/B179–80). Since a general procedure is a rule, this means that a schema is a rule for providing a concept with a corresponding image; and, as suggested, the product of this schematization may be dubbed a schematic image.

Nevertheless, this formulation, if taken as a characterization of a schema as such, is problematic. At the heart of the problem is the fact that Kant is attempting to accomplish two quite distinct things in the Schematism, between which he fails to distinguish clearly. The primary concern is to account for the possibility of the application of the pure concepts of the understanding to sensible appearances, which is posed by the utter heterogeneity of sensibility and the understanding. It was argued in Chapter 3 that Kant was already aware of the problem in the *Duisburg Nachlass*, but that he did not then have the tools for its solution, since that required the recognition of the role of the imagination. In the Schematism in the *Critique* Kant formulates the issue in terms of the need for a "third thing" to mediate between the understanding and sensibility, thereby making the application of the former to the latter possible (A138/B177). Kant calls this third thing a "transcendental schema," which is further identified as a "transcendental determination of time," and his basic claim is that it can accomplish this mediating function because, like the imagination itself, it is both sensible and intellectual (A138/B177).

All of this is familiar enough, albeit deeply controversial, and is perhaps the main reason why the Schematism vies with the Transcendental Deduction as the most obscure portion of the *Critique*. Our present concern, however, is with the other, less discussed task of the Schematism, which concerns the power of judgment (*Urteilskraft*), understood as the faculty responsible for the subsumption of particulars under concepts. By linking his discussion of the schematization of the categories to the more general issue of subsumption or concept-application, Kant indicated that, rather than being a problem unique to the categories in virtue of their "purity," the need for a schema arises for concepts of all types. Accordingly, corresponding to the three types of concepts (pure concepts of the understanding or categories, "pure sensible" or mathematical concepts, and empirical concepts), there are three types of schema, each of which functions as a rule. And while Kant states categorically that the schemata corresponding to the pure concepts of the understanding "can never be brought to an image at all" (A142/B181), he also indicates that, though distinct from images, the schemata of the other two types of concept are related to them.

The relation is clear in the case of pure sensible (mathematical) concepts, where Kant notes that,

No image of a triangle would ever be adequate to the concept of it. For it would not attain the generality of the concept, which makes this valid for all triangles, right or acute, etc., but would always be limited to one part of this sphere. The schema of the triangle can never exist anywhere except in thought, and signifies a rule of the synthesis of the imagination with regard to pure shapes in space.   (A141/B180)

It seems likely that Kant here had in mind Locke's notorious characterization of the general idea of a triangle as "neither Oblique, nor Rectangle, neither Equilateral, Equicrural, nor Scanelon; but all and none of these at once," which he also described as "something imperfect, that cannot exist."[25] But while Kant rejects the Lockean view because it assumes an imagistic conception of concepts, which fails to do justice to the discursive nature of human cognition, unlike Berkeley and Hume, he does not dismiss it as manifest nonsense. Instead, Kant attempts to preserve it in modified form by replacing the concept with its schema, understood as a rule governing the construction of an image of a triangle, thereby giving to both concept and schema a normative force. And rather than denying with Locke that the concept exists at all (as a kind of psychological impossibility), Kant affirms that the schema (as a rule) exists in thought.

A much-noted difficulty with Kant's account is that, since he regards concepts as rules, in characterizing the schema also as a rule, he seems to be caught in a dilemma. On the one hand, this threatens to undermine the distinction between concept and schema on which his whole account is based; while, on the other, it appears to violate Kant's dictum that we cannot posit rules for the application of rules, since that would lead to an infinite regress.[26] I have argued elsewhere that the solution lies in the distinction between two types of rule, which I characterize as discursive and perceptual.[27] As the term suggests, a discursive rule is a rule for determining what is thought in a given concept and is grounded in the conception of concepts (including empirical concepts) as not simply collections of marks (partial representations) associated together on the basis of past experience, but as synthetic unities in which the constitutive marks are bound together by a rule such that they are in a sense necessarily connected.[28] Returning to a passage cited in Chapter 5, "[T]he concept of body makes necessary the representation of extension, and with it that of impenetrability, of shape, etc." (A106). Accordingly, someone who did not realize that the term "body" signifies something with this set of properties could be said not to possess the concept of body.

In the case of most mathematical concepts and familiar empirical ones there seems to be little practical difference between these two sorts of rules, and *a fortiori* between concept and schema, since one who has the concept also has the capacity to recognize its instantiations, which seems to render the appeal to schemata with respect to such concepts redundant. Moreover, the problem is exacerbated by Kant's example; viz., the concept of a dog, which he characterizes as "a rule in accordance with which my imagination can specify the shape of a four-footed animal in general, without being

---

[25]   Locke (1975), 596.

[26]   See A133/B172. For my discussion of this issue, see Allison (2004), 2004–10.

[27]   See Allison (2004), 210. The term "discursive rule" is borrowed from Longuenesse.

[28]   This should not be considered incompatible with Kant's characterization of concepts as analytical unities, since they are both. A concept is an analytic unity with respect to its extension (the items falling under it); whereas it is a synthetic unity with respect to its intension (the concepts of which it is composed).

restricted to any single particular shape that experience offers me or any possible image that I can exhibit *in concreto*" (A141/B180). Since this characterization obviously refers to a schema, we must conclude either that Kant here simply misstates his view, referring to the concept when he really intended the schema, or that he is suggesting that in the case of empirical concepts such as that of a dog there is no real difference between concept and schema. The latter is ruled out, however, by Kant's claim, comparing mathematical and empirical concepts, that "Even less does an object of experience or an image of it ever reach the empirical concept, rather the latter is always related immediately to the schema of the imagination, as a rule for the determination of our intuition in accordance with a certain general concept" (A141/B180).

Although it might seem paradoxical to suggest that the gap between concept and image or object is wider in the case of empirical than of mathematical concepts, Kant's point is that, while mathematical concepts have only a limited number of possible forms, which are determinable a priori, e.g., the various kinds of triangle, in the case of empirical concepts the forms of possible instantiation, e.g., types of dog, are indeterminate. Simply put, while we can be certain that we shall never discover a new type of triangle (at least within the confines of Euclidean geometry), it remains quite possible that we shall encounter new breeds of dog, which points to the need for a schema to recognize them as such. Moreover, as Lauchlin Chipman has noted, the need for schemata for empirical concepts is more readily apparent with respect to less familiar ones such as those of a tadpole or bone marrow, because one might have these concepts in the sense of being able to talk intelligently about the generation, size, and behavior of tadpoles and the chemistry and medicinal powers of bone marrow without the ability to recognize a specimen of either.[29] And, of course, the same can be said, *mutatis mutandis*, of scientific concepts, such as those of sub-atomic particles.

This suggests that the schema of an empirical concept functions as a rule guiding the processing of sensory data by the imagination, in accordance with which these data (the manifold of intuition) are taken or interpreted in perception as belonging together in a determinate way, which leaves open the possibility of alternative readings of the same data. So considered, Kant's view has obvious affinities with Wittgenstein's well-known account of perception as a "seeing as."[30] Moreover, these affinities, if not always their basis in Kant's own position, have not gone unnoticed in the literature. A clear example of this is P. F. Strawson, who appealing explicitly to Wittgenstein, while ignoring Kant's account of the connection between empirical concepts and their schemata, focuses on perceptual recognition, by which he understands the immediate recognition of an object either as of a certain kind or as a particular instance of that kind. In the spirit of Wittgenstein, Strawson contends that

---

[29] Chipman (1972), 45–6.   [30] See Wittgenstein (1963), 193–229.

what makes such recognition possible is that "[T]he visual experience is *irradiated* by, or *infused* with, the concept; or it becomes *soaked* with the concept."[31] And he connects this with the imagination by suggesting that it is the source of the irradiating, infusing, or soaking with concepts, which enables the perceiver to recognize that "Non-actual perceptions are in a sense represented in, alive in, the present perception; just as they are represented, by images, in the image-producing activity of the imagination."[32]

Another important philosopher who has concerned himself with Kant's attribution of a significant role to the imagination in perception is Wilfrid Sellars, whose reading of Kant is both idiosyncratic, in that it reflects Sellars' own complex position, and deeply rooted in the Kantian texts. The imagination plays a prominent role in Sellars' reading because he takes it as built into intuitions qua representations of individuals.[33] In an essay entitled "The role of the Imagination in Kant's Theory of Experience," Sellars focuses on Kant's account of the imagination, noting approvingly that perception for Kant is already in a sense "theory laden," and suggesting that, according to Kant, it is because of the imagination's role in perception, which likewise relates to individuals, that intuition (as distinct from images and sensations) has a categorial form and even "embodies a proto-theory of a world."[34] This reflects Sellars' distinction between perceptual takings, which are attributed to the imagination and provide a perceiver with the subject terms for judgment, and judgment proper, which involves explicit predication.[35] In the same essay, he remarks in a phenomenological vein that the products of the imaginative synthesis, which he terms "image models," are perspectival or "point of viewish in nature."[36] And following the letter, as well as what he takes to be the spirit of Kant's account, Sellars identifies the rule operative in the interpretation with the schema of an empirical concept.[37]

More recently, Michael Young, while not referring to Sellars, has offered a similar interpretation of Kant's account of the imagination, though it differs from Sellars' in at least one essential respect. Like Sellars, Young insists that the Kantian imagination is an interpretive rather than merely an image-making faculty, where the interpretation concerns what is given in sensibility.[38] Also like Sellars, he recognizes that the attribution of an interpretive function to the imagination requires a careful distinction between its activity and that of the understanding. And much like Sellars, he notes that,

It is one thing merely to be able to construe or interpret something sensibly present as an *F* and to discriminate it from things of other types, which is a function of imagination. It is quite another thing to have the discursive representation of a thing of kind F, the *concept* of such a

---

[31] Strawson (1982), 93.   [32] Ibid., 89.   [33] See, for example, Sellars (2002), 67–8.
[34] Sellars (1978), 243.   [35] Ibid., 233.   [36] Ibid., 237–40.
[37] See Sellars (1978), 238. The point is also emphasized by Gibbons (1994), 76–7.
[38] Young (1992), 140–64.

thing, and to be able to *judge* that what is sensibly present is an F, both of which are functions of the understanding.[39]

Since both the interpretive activity of the imagination and the properly conceptual activity of the understanding are rule-governed, this leads Young, like Sellars, to attribute to Kant a distinction between two kinds of rule, one governing interpretation and the other predication, which corresponds to the previously noted distinction between a discursive and a perceptual rule, which Kant refers to as a "rule of apprehension."[40] Finally, Young agrees with Sellars (and Strawson) in emphasizing the perspectival nature of this interpretation, claiming that it involves "the taking or construing of that awareness as the awareness of something other, or something more than what immediately appears."[41] For example, in perceiving a house from a certain point of view, say a direct frontal perspective, I apprehend it as having sides and a back that are not contained in my visual field. For Young and Sellars this is the work of the imagination, specifically the productive imagination.[42]

The major difference between their interpretations concerns the conceptual nature (or lack thereof) of the imaginative synthesis, which in the B-Deduction Kant will refer to as the "figurative synthesis" or "*synthesis speciosa*." Although Sellars denies the fully conceptual nature of this synthesis, since it would effectively undermine the distinction between interpretation and predication, he also insists, for reasons having as much to do with his own philosophical position as his reading of Kant, that the imagination must be granted a minimal conceptual character in order to avoid reducing sensibility into a sheer receptivity, which could not contribute to cognition.[43] By contrast, Young, despite giving the imagination an interpretive function, insists upon its fully non-conceptual nature, going so far as to maintain that the kind of interpretation it involves is accomplished by animals, despite their lack of any conceptual capacity.

With respect to the latter point, neither of these views can pass muster as a reading of Kant. The problem with Sellars' account is that through his use of metaphors such as "theory laden" or embodying a "proto-theory of a world," like Strawson, he comes perilously close to over-intellectualizing the Kantian imagination. For if these descriptions are already applicable to the products of its synthesis, it becomes difficult

---

[39] Ibid., 149.

[40] See R 2880 16: 557. For my discussion of this and similar texts, which borrows heavily from Longuenesse, see Allison (2001), 24–30.

[41] Young (1988), 142.

[42] This also applies to Strawson; though he does not seem to have been concerned with the distinction between two types or functions of rules.

[43] Sellars (1968), esp. 1–30. In a particularly illuminating passage Sellars notes that "[I]t is only if Kant distinguishes the radically non-conceptual character of sense from the conceptual character of the synthesis of apprehension in intuition [which is, of course, to be distinguished from the conceptual synthesis of recognition in a concept, in which the concept occupies a predicative position] and, accordingly, the *receptivity* of sense from the *guidedness* of intuition that he can avoid the dialectic which leads from Hegel's *Phenomenology* to nineteenth-century idealism (Sellars (1968), 16).

to understand how the act of bringing this synthesis to concepts, which for Kant is the distinctive function of the understanding, can amount to anything more than a clarification, which would constitute a return to the Leibnizian view that Kant had abandoned with the "great light." To be sure, Sellars was acutely aware of the issue and attempted to deal with it by distinguishing between the minimally and the fully conceptual: the former being attributed to the product of the imagination and the latter to the product of judgment. But the problem is that being minimally conceptual seems to be a bit like being minimally pregnant.

Correlatively, by denying that the imaginative synthesis is *in any sense* conceptual, Young commits the opposite error. On his reading, it is possible for a being to have sensibility and imagination, understood as "the capacity to be sensibly aware of its surroundings, as well as the ability to interpret or construe that awareness—and yet *lack* understanding, the capacity for discursive representation, and hence for concepts and for judgment."[44] As an illustration of this, he cites the example of his cat, which he claims, not only has sensibility, which provides it with an awareness of sensible data, but also a capacity to construe or interpret these data in a certain way, e.g., as indicating the presence of a bird or perhaps something to be stalked.[45] As Young also points out, however, the cat lacks a capacity to reflect upon its interpretation with respect to its truth, which would be an act of judgment and require the application of concepts. On Young's account, one might also say that the cat does not understand what it is doing, since it cannot apperceive or represent to itself its act *as an interpretation* and thereby subject it to norms. In short, it lacks not only the concept of a bird or even of something to be stalked but also of its own activity.

There is little doubt that Young's cat is both sensibly aware of its surroundings in the manner that he indicates and that it lacks the capacity to understand, at least as Kant construed this power. At issue is whether it may be said to possess a capacity to "interpret" that is comparable to the capacity that Kant appears to attribute to the human imagination at A120n. In claiming that it does, Young suggests a picture of animal mentality in which the higher animals perform the first two parts of the three-fold synthesis in much the same way as humans, but are incapable of the third part, which is to say that they are capable of synthesis but not of bringing this synthesis to concepts.[46] And in support of the claim, Young relies heavily on the rule-governed nature of animal perceptual awareness, in virtue of which the latter can be regarded as a kind of interpretation.[47]

---

[44] Young (1992), 149.   [45] Ibid., 149–50.

[46] Although I claim that Young's account seems to suggest such a view, I do not believe that he actually held it, since his paper includes a sophisticated and informative account of the role of the imagination in arithmetic. My disagreement with Young concerns only his, in my view, overly facile and deeply misleading attempt to include the perception and imagination of animals in his account.

[47] See Young (1992), 153. In support of the rule-governed, yet non-conceptual nature of animal perception Young appeals to Kant's claim in the *Groundwork* that whereas everything in nature proceeds in accordance with law, rational beings proceed in accordance with the conception of law (4: 412). Unfortunately, however, this does little to support Young's view, since the laws in question are of quite

Although an adequate discussion of this topic would require a consideration of Kant's shifting and sketchily presented views on animal mentality, this is not necessary for present purposes.[48] The salient point is that granting both the correctness of Young's account of the latter and the freedom to use the term "interpretation" as he chooses, applying it to his cat is deeply misleading, if the intent is to interpret Kant's claim that the imagination plays an essential (interpretive) role in perception for human cognizers. While this point could be expressed in a number of ways, perhaps the simplest is to note that an interpretation of which one *could not become conscious* as an interpretation would not count as an interpretation in the relevant sense. This is not to claim that one must be conscious of one's interpretation of the sensory data in ordinary instances of perception, e.g., of a house or a dog, since that is both absurd in its own right and explicitly denied by Kant, when he characterized the imagination as "a blind though indispensable function of the soul [understanding], without which we would have no cognition at all, but of which we are seldom even conscious" (A78/B103). It is rather that one *must be able to become conscious of it as such* because this is a condition of its being brought to consciousness or recognized in a concept, through which it enters into cognition. And, as Young readily acknowledges, this is not a capacity possessed by his cat.

The upshot of the matter is that, if it is to play the indispensable role in cognition that Kant assigns to it, while not itself constituting cognition in the "proper sense," the "blind" synthesis of apprehension-cum-reproduction can be neither entirely non-conceptual, as Young insists, nor minimally conceptual, as Sellars contends. The former is ruled out because what is simply non-conceptual, such as an image, a sensation, or the instinct- and association-based "interpretations" attributed to Young's cat, cannot be brought to or recognized in a concept (which is not to be confused with being made the object of a judgment); whereas the latter is precluded because, as already noted, it reduces the for Kant decisive act of bringing a synthesis to concepts or recognizing it in a concept to the Leibniz-like process of clarification through analysis. Accordingly, we are left with the default position that the synthesis involved in perception is *proto*-conceptual, which enables us to see how it is capable

distinct natures: laws of nature in the former case, laws of freedom (or, more precisely, objective practical principles) in the latter. And while the latter, like the former, are objectively necessary, in the case of finite rational beings they are subjectively contingent, which means that it is possible for such agents to disobey them. For my analysis of this passage see Allison (2011), 151–7.

[48] The issue of Kant's view of the nature of animal mentality was touched upon in Chapter 5, note 35. Applying what was said there to Young's account, it seems that Kant would have been willing to attribute to animals such as Young's cat perceptual and imaginative capacities that are analogous but not equivalent to those possessed by humans. Since Kant himself does not explicitly appeal to the notion of interpretation in this context, it remains an open question whether he would attribute such a capacity to animals; but if he did I believe that for the reason given below it would have to be quite different from the kind attributed to the human imagination by Sellars and presumably Young. For a useful survey of Kant's views on the issue of animal mentality see Naragon (1990), 1–23.

of becoming conceptualized through being brought to or recognized in a concept, without itself being properly conceptual in even a minimal sense.

Although the distinction between being minimally conceptual, which is Sellars' view, and the present claim that the imaginative synthesis involved in perception is proto-conceptual may seem overly subtle and elusive, I regard it as essential for a correct understanding of Kant's position. The basic point, which is built into his account of the three-fold synthesis, is that the imagination has the task of unifying the perceived sensory data in a way that makes possible its subsequent conceptualization without itself being a mode of conceptualization.

Moreover, if the preceding account is correct, this is precisely the function that Kant gives to the schema of an empirical concept, as contrasted with both the concept itself and either an image or a particular instance falling under it. Consider Kant's own example, the schema of the concept of a dog, which might be characterized as the representation of "dogishness as such." Like the image or perception of a particular dog, "dogishness" is sensible rather than conceptual, since it is "seen" rather than conceived; but unlike these it is also indeterminate, which enables it function as a vehicle through which particular dogs are recognized, even if they belong to a breed that one had not previously encountered. And as a schema, "dogishness" is a product of the imagination, which leads us to the unexpected conclusion that the reason why previous psychologists had not realized the role of the imagination in sense perception is that they had also failed to recognize the schematism of the understanding, i.e., that "hidden art in the depths of the human soul, whose true operations [like the 'blind' operations of the imagination 'of which we are seldom even conscious'] we can divine from nature and lay unveiled before our eyes only with difficulty" (A141/B180–1).

B) *Affinity and apperception* (A121–3): The four paragraphs devoted to affinity in section 3 constitute both the heart and the most problematic feature of the A-Deduction. In his preliminary discussion of the topic in section 2, Kant had defined the term as "the ground of the possibility of the association of the manifold insofar as it lies in the object" (A113) and he had claimed that "all appearances ... stand in a thoroughgoing connection according to necessary laws, and hence in a **transcendental affinity**, of which the **empirical affinity** is the mere consequence (A113–14). Kant also defines "affinity" in the *Anthropology*, where he writes: "By *affinity* I understand the unity of the manifold in virtue of its derivation from one ground" (Anthro 7: 176–7; 286), which suggests that the use of the term in the *Critique* is to be seen as an application (to appearances) of this broader conception. Although the language of this definition is that of the *Critique*, the context in which it is offered in the *Anthropology* is a discussion of a subject that was of great interest to Kant; viz., casual social conversation of the sort that is typically conducted at a dinner party. The basic idea, which Kant also applied to "silent thinking," is that such conversation (or thought) requires, as a condition of its possibility, some kind of guiding thread or unifying theme, which takes the flow of conversation from one thought or topic to another in a natural and hopefully entertaining, but not necessarily logically compelling, way. Since it is not a matter of strict reasoning, Kant considers it as an associative rather than a purely ratiocinative process, in which the imagination and its rules of association play a central role. But he also insists that the understanding is involved as a limiting or restraining factor. Simply put, as a condition of its continuation, the conversational flow must at some level make sense and the same applies, *mutatis mutandis*, to the silent musings of an individual thinker, which Kant evidently understands in Platonic fashion as a dialogue of the soul with itself. Kant expresses the point in a highly evocative manner, noting that, "[T]he play of the power of sensibility here still follows the rules of sensibility, which provide the material whose association is achieved without consciousness of the rule, and this association is in *conformity with* the understanding although not derived *from* it" (Anthro 7: 177; 287).

In discussing Kant's account of affinity in Chapter 5 we saw that, prior to introducing the term, he had appealed to the underlying conception in connection with his analysis of the reproductive synthesis of the imagination, where he claimed that the reproduction of appearances by the imagination presupposed that the appearances themselves were reproducible, and therefore subject to a certain rule. As Kant famously put it, "If cinnabar were now red, now black, now light, now heavy, . . . then my empirical imagination would never even get the opportunity to think of heavy cinnabar on the occasion of the representation of the color red" (A100–1). And, in commenting on this claim, it was noted that the stakes were far higher than the requirements of the empirical imagination, since at issue was the possibility of forming and applying empirical concepts, which we have now seen depends upon a capacity to provide schemata for these concepts.

It was further noted that the issue raised by Kant's account concerns the kind of necessity that he claims for the affinity of appearances. Although Kant clearly intended to establish an absolute or unconditional necessity for it, which presupposes transcendental idealism, we saw that this was challenged by Guyer on the grounds that the most that his argument can support is a hypothetical or conditional one: necessarily, if appearances are to be reproducible by the empirical imagination in such a way as to allow for the possibility of forming empirical concepts, then they must stand in a thoroughgoing affinity; rather than that appearances necessarily stand in such a relation. In short, as he does in several different contexts, Guyer accuses Kant of an egregious modal fallacy, conflating a merely *de dicto* with a *de re* necessity, which, in the manner of Strawson, he uses as a means to separate what is viable in Kant from his discredited transcendental idealism.[49] But while the problematic nature of this move was noted, beyond pointing out that Kant there

---

[49] See Chapter 5, note 30.

viewed transcendental idealism as a necessary (though not sufficient) condition of a transcendental affinity, the case for this strong claim was not further analyzed. Instead, appealing to Kant's statement that his intent in this section was to prepare rather than to instruct, it was suggested that he be taken as laying the foundation for a subsequent argument to this end, rather than actually offering one. But since whatever preparation Kant was able to provide must now be assumed to be in place, this new account of affinity cannot be treated in this cavalier fashion. Whatever its inadequacies, this is Kant's definitive treatment of the matter and must be regarded as such.

As in his initial formulation, Kant links affinity directly to the reproductive synthesis, presenting it as a necessary condition of its functioning. He notes that,

> Since...if representations reproduced one another without distinction, just as they fell together, there would in turn be no determinate connection but merely unruly heaps of them, and no cognition at all would arise, their reproduction must thus have a rule in accordance with which a representation enters into combination in the imagination with one representation rather than with any others. This subjective and **empirical** ground of reproduction in accordance with rules is called **association** of representations. (A121)

This not only echoes Kant's initial formulation, but also the opening sentence of Hume's discussion of the association of ideas in the *Enquiry*, where he writes: "It is evident, that there is a principle of connexion between the different thoughts or ideas in the mind, and that in their appearance to the memory or imagination, they introduce each other with a certain degree of method and regularity."[50] Thus, at this point Kant occupies common ground with Hume; both insisting that the connection of representations (ideas for Hume) in the imagination must be rule-governed. Kant parts company with Hume, however, in insisting that these rules or principles of the imagination, which govern association and reproduction, are not sufficient to account for our cognition, since that presupposes objective rules or conditions. As Kant puts it,

> (1) [I]f this unity of association did not also have an objective ground, so that it would be impossible for appearances to be apprehended by the imagination otherwise than under the condition of a possible synthetic unity of this apprehension, then it would also be entirely contingent whether appearances fit into a connection of human cognitions. (2) For even though we had the faculty for associating perceptions, it would still remain in itself entirely undetermined and contingent whether they were also associable; and in case they were not, a multitude of perceptions and even an entire sensibility would be possible in which much empirical consciousness would be encountered in my mind, but separated, and without belonging to **one** consciousness of myself, which, however, is impossible. (3) For only because I ascribe all

---

[50] Hume (1999), 101. Hume makes essentially the same claim in the *Treatise*, where he draws the analogy with the Newtonian force of attraction (Hume (2007), 12–14); but I cite the *Enquiry* because, while it is certain that Kant was familiar with that work, there remains considerable controversy regarding the extent of his acquaintance with the *Treatise*.

perceptions to one consciousness (of original apperception) can I say of all perceptions that I am conscious to myself of them [*dass ich mir ihrer bewust sei*].[51] (4) There must therefore be an objective ground, i.e., one that can be understood *a priori* to all empirical laws of the imagination, on which rests the possibility, indeed even the necessity of a law extending through all appearances, a law, namely, for regarding them throughout as data of sense that are associable in themselves and subject to universal laws of a thoroughgoing connection in reproduction. (5) I call this objective ground of all association of appearances their **affinity**. (6) But we can never encounter this anywhere except in the principle of the unity of apperception with regard to all cognitions that are to belong to me. (7) In accordance with this principle all appearances whatever must come into the mind or be apprehended in such a way that they are in agreement with the unity of apperception, which would be impossible without synthetic unity in their connection, which is thus also objectively necessary.   (A121–2)

I have quoted this lengthy paragraph in its entirety because of its indispensability for understanding Kant's position; and, as has been done in similar circumstances, the sentences are numbered for ease of reference. An overview of its contents indicates that its seven sentences (the fifth of which simply stipulates what Kant here under-stands by "affinity") contain an argument that can be broken down into six steps.

1. Kant notes that, absent an objective ground, the associative unities produced by the imagination in its reproductive activity would be merely contingent (sentence one).
2. Kant points out the deleterious consequences of this contingency and claims that such a state of affairs is impossible (sentence two).
3. Kant appeals to the conception of original apperception to explain why it is impossible (sentence three).
4. Kant concludes from this impossibility the necessity of assuming an objective ground of the associative unity produced by the imagination (sentence four).
5. Kant locates this objective ground in the unity of apperception (sentence six).
6. Kant claims that it extends to all appearances, i.e., to everything that can be apprehended, and is therefore objectively necessary (sentence seven).

The introduction of a worry about the contingency of the associability (or repro-ducibility) of appearances (steps 1 and 2) is not a new element in Kant's account, and we have already encountered it in various contexts. Nevertheless, given its centrality to Kant's project in the Deduction, Guyer's modal fallacy charge, which is directed explicitly against Kant's effort to deny such contingency, calls for further consider-ation in this new context. To reprise the ground already covered, Kant's initial rejection of the contingency of the synthetic unity of appearances was in response to the empiricist thesis that all concepts are empirical, which he must refute in order

---

[51] Although the reflexive nature of Kant's claim is suppressed by Kemp Smith, Guyer and Wood, and Pluhar in their translations (all of whom ignore the inclusion of "*mir*"), in my view it is essential to the understanding of Kant's argument.

to make room for the categories and, more generally, the possibility of synthetic cognition a priori. Kant pointed out that this thesis entailed such contingency and it was suggested that his argument against it turned largely on his conception of concepts as rules, which, as such, possess a normative force. Specifically, it was argued that the application of concept-rules presupposes a kind of implicit epistemic right to assume that the objects falling under them contain the properties designated in them; otherwise there would be no grounds to attribute objective validity to the judgments in which they are predicated of these objects. In light of this, it was argued that the putative normative force that is built into even empirical concepts on Kant's view requires a warrant or justifying ground that cannot itself be merely empirical. Rather, it must be transcendental, since it calls for the *necessary synthetic* unity of appearances. Accordingly, the denial of the necessity of this synthetic unity, as well as the deflationary proposal that it is merely hypothetical or conditional, entails the denial of the possibility of empirical concepts, and therefore, empirical cognition, not to mention the a priori variety.

Although I regard this as sufficient to reject Guyer's charge of a modal fallacy on Kant's part and the consequent claim that he should have been content with the above-mentioned conditional necessity, it does not suffice to establish the (unconditionally) necessary synthetic unity of appearances on which Kant insists. Kant attempts to establish this by grounding the transcendental affinity, i.e., the necessary synthetic unity, of appearances in the unity of apperception, which also involves connecting it with transcendental idealism. This grounding did not enter into Kant's initial account in section 2 because he had not yet introduced the conception of apperception; though he did connect it with affinity later in the section. In making this appeal (step 3), Kant states that it is "only because I ascribe all perceptions to one consciousness (of original apperception) can I say of all perceptions that I am conscious to myself of them." In translating this sentence, I have included the reflexive element (conscious to myself), which is present in the German but suppressed in the standard English translations, because I consider it essential to understanding Kant's point.[52] As I have argued on similar occasions, for Kant it is a matter of representing to myself or, in this case, of being conscious to myself, i.e., of not being merely conscious but *self*-conscious.

This qualification is necessary in order to understand the nature of the impossibility to which Kant here refers; viz., that "a multitude of perceptions and even an entire sensibility . . . in which much empirical consciousness would be encountered in my mind, but separated, and without belonging to **one** consciousness of myself." Clearly this is not *logically* impossible, since it does not involve a contradiction. Moreover, we can easily envisage a mind for which such a scenario holds, e.g., that of Young's cat, assuming that it perceives and associates its perceptions as Young

---

[52] See note 51.

suggests. Indeed, I can imagine that it might even hold of my mind, perhaps as the result of some kind of severe brain damage. What is impossible is rather that such a scenario could hold *for me*, since it would preclude the possibility of my being aware of myself as the identical subject of these representations. In other words, it is not something that a cognizer could represent to itself as actual, which makes it a kind of performative impossibility, analogous to the impossibility of denying the Cartesian *cogito* on some interpretations.[53]

Kant's fourth step is to claim that this impossibility entails that there must be an a priori objective ground of the associability of appearances and, he adds, "on which rests the possibility, indeed even the necessity of a law extending through all appearances, a law, namely, for regarding them throughout as data of sense that are associable in themselves." There are three aspects of this claim that call for comment. First, we have seen that at the beginning of this paragraph Kant characterizes an "objective ground" as one that makes it impossible "for appearances to be apprehended otherwise than under a condition of a possible synthetic unity of this apprehension." In other words, such a ground governs the manner in which we apprehend or take up the sensible manifold, thereby guaranteeing that its apprehension conforms to the conditions of a possible synthetic unity. This is intended to rule out the possibility that what is apprehended constitutes an "unruly heap," which would be possible if the unifiability of what is apprehended were merely contingent. Second, Kant assigns to this objective ground a complex modality, in that it supposedly grounds both the possibility and the necessity of a synthetic unity of apprehension. This manner of expression is infelicitous, however, since an objective ground is not required for the possibility of a synthetic unity of representations. That requires merely that appearances be associable and the mind equipped with subjective principles of association; both of which were acknowledged by Hume. Rather, as noted above, an objective ground is needed to preclude the possibility that the synthetic unity is merely contingent. Third, despite Kant's claim of an objective ground, the law to which he here refers is subjective in the sense that it dictates how appearances are to be *regarded* (*ansusehen*); viz., "as associable in themselves and subject to universal laws of a thoroughgoing connection in reproduction." This is to be contrasted with a law stating straightaway that appearances themselves are necessarily subject to such laws, which would seem to be the ultimate goal of the Deduction. Although this is not completely clear in the Guyer and Wood translation, it is certainly suggested by it. It is fully explicit, however, in Kemp Smith's translation, which renders it somewhat loosely but accurately by having Kant say that this law "constrains us to regard all appearances as data of the senses that must be associable in themselves."[54]

---

[53] See Hintikka (1962), 3–22.

[54] See Kemp Smith (1958), 145. Similarly, Pluhar (1996), 169, characterizes the law as stipulating that "appearances throughout are to be regarded as data of the senses that are intrinsically associable and subject, in reproduction, to universal rules of a thoroughgoing connection."

After defining "affinity" as the objective ground of the associability of appearances, in the final two steps Kant concludes that the (transcendental) ground of affinity must be located in the principle of the unity of apperception and that the scope of this principle extends to all appearances, which entails that all appearances constitute an objectively necessary synthetic unity. Although it is formulated in terms of the transcendental affinity of appearances, which is equivalent to their necessary synthetic unity, it is important to realize that this conclusion does not introduce any radically new elements into the argument; for the key point remains the reciprocity between the unity of apperception and the synthetic unity of appearances, i.e., the unity of consciousness and the consciousness of unity. In other words, not only is the unity of apperception a necessary condition of the synthetic unity of appearances (as representations "in us"), but, conversely, the synthetic unity is a necessary condition of the unity of apperception, since apart from it, it would not be possible to become conscious of an identical "I think." Moreover, in stating that the synthetic unity of appearances is "also objectively necessary," which implies that it is likewise "subjectively necessary" (as a condition of apperception), Kant is effectively reiterating in different terms the core claim of the A-Deduction that "The *a priori* conditions of a possible experience in general are at the same time conditions of the possibility of the objects of experience" (A111).

The final two paragraphs dealing with affinity spell out some of the implications of this analysis. The first of these consists of a single sentence, in which Kant maintains that, "The objective unity of all (empirical) consciousness in one consciousness (of original apperception) is thus the necessary condition even of all possible perception, and the affinity of all appearances (near and remote) is a necessary consequence of a synthesis in the imagination that is grounded *a priori* on rules" (A123). This sentence contains two distinct claims. If the preceding analysis of perception is correct, the first of these; viz., that the objective, i.e., non-contingent, unity of all empirical consciousness in original apperception is the necessary condition of all possible perception, is incorrect as it stands. The problem is that it implies that apperception is a necessary condition of perception, which suggests that we must either attribute to Kant the highly implausible view that animals (and infants) cannot perceive at all or modify his claim to be that this unity is a necessary condition of *apperception*, which is all that Kant really needs to claim. This particular difficulty is avoided in Kant's second claim; for rather than stating *tout court* that all syntheses performed by the imagination entail the (transcendental) affinity of appearances, he limits this to those grounded in a priori rules. Nevertheless, one might wonder where exactly it is supposed to have been established that the imaginative synthesis is grounded in a priori rules. It might be claimed that Kant is appealing to his account in section 2, where he argued that the syntheses of apprehension and reproduction had a priori as well as empirical functions in virtue of their role in synthesizing the pure manifolds of space and time. But since that argument relies on the results of the Aesthetic and Kant has not yet appealed to these results in the present argument (from below), it is not clear that this is the best interpretive option. Instead, I think that we should take Kant as referring to the claim in the fourth step of the affinity argument, where he maintains that there must be an a priori ground, prior to all empirical laws of the imagination, which dictates that appearances are to be regarded as subject to "universal laws of a thoroughgoing connection in reproduction." Inasmuch as Kant assigns reproduction to the activity of the imagination, it seems reasonable to take this as implying that this synthesis is grounded in a priori rules governing the reproduction of appearances.

In the fourth and final paragraph of his discussion of affinity Kant attempts to clarify his account of the imagination. The claim is that, in addition to its empirical functions in apprehension and reproduction, the necessary affinity of appearances indicates that it must also be considered as a power of a priori synthesis, in virtue of which Kant names it the "productive imagination" (the contrasting reproductive power being merely empirical). Moreover, insofar as this a priori power is considered in relation to the unity of apperception, as the power through which the manifold of intuition is brought to this unity, it has a transcendental function as a necessary condition of the possibility of experience. In other words, the claim is not that there is a distinct transcendental imagination, which somehow either operates alongside of or supervenes upon the familiar empirical imagination; rather, it is that the analysis of affinity and the conditions of its possibility reveal that the human imagination has a transcendental function. Kant concludes the discussion with the following notable reflection on this function:

It is therefore certainly strange, yet from what has been said thus far obvious, that it is only by means of this transcendental function of the imagination that even the affinity of appearances, and with it the association and through the latter finally reproduction according to laws, and consequently experience itself, become possible; for without them no concepts of objects at all would converge into an experience.   (A123)

Although few would likely agree that the need to attribute a transcendental function to the imagination is as obvious as Kant suggests, it is difficult to quarrel with his contention that it is strange. Indeed, like Kant's closely related claim regarding a role for the imagination in perception, it is a thesis for which there appears to be no genuine historical precedent. Moreover, this is no accident, since the need for it presupposes the sharp distinction between sensibility and understanding, which, as Kant recognized at least from the time of the *Duisburg Nachlass*, calls for some mediating power. In other words, apart from this distinction, which was not drawn by his predecessors in the form in which Kant embraced it, there is no explanatory role for such a function, no matter how much weight is placed on the empirical function of this faculty.

C) *The imagination, cognition, and experience* (A123–5): Following his account of affinity, which was directly concerned with the relation between the productive imagination and appearances, Kant devotes three paragraphs to the relation between the imagination and the understanding, which once again leads to a belated and almost perfunctory introduction of the categories. In the first of these Kant writes:

For the standing and lasting I (of pure apperception) constitutes the correlate of all our representations, so far as it is merely possible to become conscious to ourselves of them [*sich ihrer bewust zu werden*],[55] and all consciousness belongs to an all-embracing pure apperception just as all sensible intuition as representation belongs to a pure inner intuition, namely that of time. It is this apperception that must be added to the pure imagination in order to make its function intellectual. For in itself the synthesis of the imagination, although exercised *a priori*, is nevertheless always sensible, for it combines the manifold only as it **appears** in intuition, e.g., the shape of a triangle. But while concepts, which belong to the understanding, are brought into play through relation of the manifold to the unity of apperception, it is only by means of the imagination that they can be brought into relation to sensible intuition.   (A123–4)[56]

The first sentence of this paragraph contains yet another instance of the unclarity that is a persistent feature of the Deduction, particularly in the segment currently being analyzed. Either Kant is saying that pure apperception is the correlate of *all* conscious representations, in which case he appears to conflate consciousness and self-consciousness, or the claim is that all representations, which *I can be aware of as mine* belong to a single, all-embracing self-consciousness, in which case the emphasis is on the *unity* of apperception, the numerical identity of the I.[57] Nevertheless, a consideration of the paragraph as a whole strongly supports the latter alternative. First, it is suggested by the analogy with the pure intuition of time: just as all sensible intuition is located in a single time, so all episodes of conscious representing, i.e., of taking *x* as *a*, must be attributable to a subject capable of becoming aware of its numerical identity with respect to all its cognitions. Second, it makes better sense of

[55] Once again, I have modified the Guyer and Wood translation to include the element of reflexivity, which they omit, and which I believe to be essential to the understanding of Kant's position. It should be noted that this time the reflexive element is also omitted by Kemp Smith and Pluhar, who more frequently include it. In the present case, this omission may be simply due to the fact that it is implicit, since Kant here speaks of becoming conscious, which is an act, rather than merely being conscious.

[56] I am citing Kemp Smith's translation of this sentence rather than Guyer and Wood's since I do not believe that theirs makes sense of it. The German text (Schmidt edition), which is itself none too clear, states: "*Durch das Verhältnis der Mannifaltigen aber zur Einheit der Apperzeption werden Begriffe, welche dem Verstande angehören, aber nur vermttelst der Einbildungskraft in Beziehung auf die sinnliche Anschauung zustande kommen können.*" In Guyer and Wood it reads: "Through the relation of the manifold to the unity of apperception, however, concepts that belong to the understanding can come about, but only by means of the imagination in relation to sensible intuition." As Kemp Smith points out, he is basing his reading on an emendation by Vaihinger, who interpolated "*werden Begriffe ins Spiel gebracht*" (concepts are brought into play). Moreover, this reading is also adopted by the French translation by Renaut (1997), 193), who renders the sentence: "*Or, á travers le rapport du divers á l'unite de la apperception, des concepts appartenant á l'entendement pourront etrê mis en oeuvre, mais uniquement, par l'intermédiare de l'imagination, en relation avec l'intuition sensible.*" The point is that Kant is making two quite distinct claims in the sentence: (1) that it is the relation of the manifold to the unity of apperception that brings the understanding and its concepts into the story; and (2) that these concepts only apply to the manifold of sensible intuition by means of their relation to the imagination. Kant will, of course, later characterize the relation of the concepts of the understanding to the imagination as their "schematization."

[57] The claim that Kant is guilty of this conflation is made by Guyer (1980), 209–10.

Kant's claim in the second sentence that apperception must be added to the pure imagination in order to make its function intellectual; for it does not seem that apperceiving in the sense of simply being aware of one's imaginative synthesis would suffice for this. That would also require a consciousness of the rule governing the synthesis, which relates all of the subject's representings to an identical "I think" or representer. Finally, the third sentence explicitly states that it is the relation of the sensible manifold to the *unity* of apperception, i.e., "the standing and lasting I," which gives rise to the concepts of the understanding; though Kant also insists that these concepts, which he has not yet identified with the categories, only apply to this manifold through their relation to the imagination.

Instead of proceeding directly from this result to the categories, Kant begins the next paragraph by noting that, "We therefore have a pure imagination, as a fundamental faculty of the human soul, that grounds all cognition *a priori*" (A124). Kant's language here reflects the view, which is characteristic of the A-Deduction, that it is the imagination, rather than the understanding, that is one of three original, i.e., underived, cognitive faculties (the others being sensibility and apperception). And Kant points out that the imagination's status stems from the fact that it makes possible the combination of the manifold of intuition and the unity of apperception, which, in turn, accounts for the possibility of experience. In short, the imagination not only has the empirical-perceptual function of converting a manifold of representations into the representation of a manifold, which is the aspect of the imagination that Kant emphasizes in his accounts of apprehension and reproduction, but also the a priori function of mediating between sensibility and understanding, which, as previously noted, was made necessary for Kant by his radical separation of the two faculties. Although Kant's most important account of the latter function is in the Schematism, it is noteworthy that he refers to it already in the Deduction.

Having completed his account of the imagination, Kant is finally ready to introduce the categories, which he does through a consideration of their relation to the imagination and through this to experience. Revisiting for a final time the three-fold synthesis, Kant notes that actual experience consists in the apprehension, association or reproduction, and recognition of appearances and contends that it

contains in the last of and highest of the merely empirical elements of experience [i.e., recognition] concepts that make possible the formal unity of experience and with it all objective validity (truth) of empirical cognition. These grounds of the recognition of the manifold, so far as they concern **merely the form of an experience in general** are now those **categories**. On them is grounded ... all formal unity in the synthesis of the imagination, and by means of the latter also all of its empirical use (in recognition, reproduction, association, and apprehension) down to the appearances; for only by means of these elements [the categories] can appearances belong to cognition, and to our consciousness as such, and hence to ourselves.   (A125)[58]

---

[58]   The last sentence of this passage is another of those difficult sentences in which the Guyer and Wood reading differs significantly from the other main translations. Except for retaining Kant's sentence

Kant here makes two claims regarding the categories, which together constitute the objective side of the Deduction. The first concerns what they do and the second how they do it. According to this account, what they do is to make possible "the formal unity of experience," by which Kant understands that unity of representations in consciousness through which experience is possible. One might also express the point by saying that, as the grounds of this unity, the categories bring appearances into the field of cognition or, if one prefers, the logical space of reasons, which is why Kant says that they are the source of the objective validity or truth of empirical cognition.[59] They supposedly do this by serving as grounds "of the recognition of the manifold, so far as they concern **merely the form of an experience in general.**" Simply put, they are the rules through which a manifold of representations is taken as the cognition of an empirical object as such. The crucial point is the explicit connection between the categories and recognition. Just as empirical concepts function as rules for the recognition of empirical objects as instances of a particular kind, the categories, as pure concepts of the understanding, are rules for the recognition of an object as such, or qua object, i.e., as a spatiotemporal somewhat, standing over and against our representations.

D) *The human understanding is the lawgiver to nature* (A125–8): Apart from a final paragraph, which provides an assessment of the correctness of the Deduction and specification of the condition of its possibility, which I shall consider separately, the last three paragraphs of section 3 are devoted to the formulation and explanation of this idealistic thesis. As Kant's formulation indicates, it is intended to serve not only as a conclusion to the argument from below, but to the A-Deduction as a whole.

structure, I have here followed the Pluhar translation. Similar renderings are provided by Kemp Smith and Renaut's French version. The German text reads: "*Auf ihnen gründet sich also alle formale Einheit in der Synthesis der Einbildungskraft, und vermittelst dieser auch alles empirischen Gebrauchs) derselben (in der Rekognition, Reproduktion, Assoziation, Apprehension) bis herunter zu den Erscheinungen, weil diese, nur vermittelst jener Elemente der Erkenntnis und überhaupt) unserem Bewusstsein, mithin uns selbst angehören können.*" In Guyer and Wood the sentence reads: "On them is grounded, therefore, all formal unity in the synthesis of the imagination, and by means of the latter also all of its empirical use (in recognition, reproduction, association, and apprehension) down to the appearances, since the latter belong to our consciousness at all and hence to ourselves only by means of these elements of cognition." The contentious portion is the final clause beginning with "since." At issue is whether Kant is claiming that it is only by means of these elements (the categories) that appearances belong to *our cognition*, and therefore to our consciousness as such and hence to ourselves or, as Guyer and Wood have it, that it is only by means of the categories that appearances *belong to our consciousness at all*. I believe that the first alternative makes better sense of the text, since Kant's point seems to be that the function of the categories is to bring appearances to cognition, and therefore to ourselves qua cognizers. By contrast, the Guyer and Wood reading seems to suggest that the categories are a necessary condition of consciousness, which brings us back to the previously discussed issue regarding the question of whether Kant conflates consciousness and self-consciousness, a charge which Guyer raises.

[59] This is one of the places where Kant apparently equates objective validity with truth. I have suggested that his considered view, according to which objective validity is a defining feature of judgment, is to equate it with the capacity to be either true or false, i.e., to have a truth value.

Kant begins by asserting, apparently as a conclusion that is supposed to follow seamlessly from the preceding argument, that "[W]e ourselves bring into the appearances that order and regularity in them that we call **nature**, and ... we would not be able to find it there if we, or the nature of our mind, had not originally put it there" (A125). In support of this bold, seemingly paradoxical claim Kant simply reminds us that, "[T]his unity of nature should be necessary, i.e., *a priori* certain unity of the connection of appearances." And, assuming this to be the case, he asks rhetorically:

But how should we be able to establish a synthetic unity *a priori* if subjective grounds of such a unity were not contained *a priori* among the original sources of cognition in our mind, and if these subjective conditions were not at the same time objectively valid, being the grounds of the possibility of cognizing any object of experience at all?   (A125–6)

Kant thus derives the mind-dependence of the unity of nature directly from its a priori status. And, given the core "critical" principle that "we can cognize of things a priori only what we ourselves have put into them" (Bxviii), this clearly follows. The crux of the matter, however, is the premise from which this conclusion is derived; viz., that the unity of nature, by which Kant understands its uniformity, i.e., order and regularity, is necessary, and therefore cognized a priori. This is, of course, Kant's ubiquitous non-contingency thesis, which we have seen underlies the entire problematic of the Deduction. But having ventured an analysis of it in connection with Kant's account of affinity, there is little to add to it at present, particularly since Kant appears to understand virtually the same thing by the (transcendental) affinity of appearances and the unity (or order and regularity) of nature.[60] Accordingly, for present purposes it must suffice to recall that Kant rejects the possibility that appearances do not "fit into a coherent whole of human cognition" on the grounds that such a state of affairs would not be apperceivable. In other words, unless appearances were unifiable in such a way as to constitute a common order of nature, they could not be thought together as constituting a whole by a single cognizer. And while this does not preclude the possibility of such a state of affairs—it is not, after all, claimed to be logically impossible—it arguably does show that it is *epistemically impossible*, since it would not be cognizable by beings such as ourselves, with a discursive understanding.[61]

---

[60] This is not to suggest, however, that the latter is redundant. It is, I believe significant that Kant refers to the affinity of *appearances* and the unity of *nature*; for this suggests that there is at least a dialectical distinction between them, the latter entering the discussion at a later stage. Moreover, this appears to be due to the fact that the discussion of affinity precedes and that of unity follows the introduction of the categories. Thus, one might say that the unity of nature is the affinity of appearances considered qua brought under the categories.

[61] It should be evident that, as I am using the phrase "epistemically impossible," it is not the negation of "epistemically possible," as the former is understood in current debates in contemporary analytic epistemology. As I understand the issue, in that context, to claim that something is epistemically possible, e.g., that it is possible that someone I know does not have cancer, is to say that as far as I know this is possible, though it is also possible that this person does have the disease. See DeRose (1991), 581–605. Within that framework, the negation of the claim that x is epistemically (for all that I can know) possible is that x is

As already noted, this line of argument should not be taken as providing a refutation of a radical, Cartesian-type skepticism regarding the reality or objectivity of experience, much less of its present-day "brain in the vat" versions. But it has also been maintained that it should not be judged in these terms, since Kant distinguished sharply between the two tasks and assigned the latter to the Refutation of Idealism. Rather, the Transcendental Deduction presupposes that we have experience of a public, objective world and is concerned with the conditions of its possibility. Accordingly, as I have tried to argue, its target is a form of empiricism, exemplified classically by Locke and often referred to as "concept empiricism," according to which we have genuine empirical cognition, even though all the materials of this cognition are derived from experience. And, as I have also tried to argue, Kant's main weapon against this form of empiricism is his non-contingency thesis.

Before leaving this paragraph, however, a further word is in order. It concerns Kant's claim that subjective conditions (the categories) are also objectively valid. We have seen that Kant initially posed the question: "how **subjective conditions of thinking** should have **objective validity**" in the first section of the Deduction (A89–90/B122) as a statement of what needs to be shown. Accordingly, Kant's return to this locution indicates that he here took himself to have here answered this question. And if the reading proposed here is correct, this answer can be succinctly expressed in the proposition that, apart from these subjective conditions, there could be no such thing as objective validity.

Although Kant claims to have shown that the human mind is the source of the uniformity of nature, he has not yet identified the understanding as the relevant faculty or power. Admittedly, having also claimed that the categories, which are by definition pure concepts of the understanding, are the vehicles of this uniformity, this lacuna might seem to be a mere detail, requiring no more than a brief mention. This neglects, however, the fact that, throughout the A-Deduction, Kant had regarded the understanding as the product of the relation between apperception and the imagination, thereby denying that it is an original (underived) faculty. Indeed, since he assigns a transcendental function to the imagination, he might well be taken as claiming that it (rather than the understanding) is the source of the uniformity of nature, which, to say the least, would give a quite different tenor to the Deduction.

While I cannot offer any proof (textual or otherwise), I strongly suspect that it was for this reason that Kant devotes the next paragraph (A126–7) specifically to the understanding, in what amounts to an attempt to clarify its cognitive import. He begins by referring to previously given explanations or descriptions of the

---

straightforwardly impossible, there being no room, as far as I can see, for a properly epistemic impossibility. For Kant, however, something can be epistemically *impossible* (in the sense that it is impossible to know that it is the case) even though it might actually be the case. Within the Kantian standpoint, this most obviously applies to claims about the noumenal, but I am suggesting that it also applies to the (logically) possible scenario in which the sensibly given could not be brought to the unity of apperception. As suggested above, this could also be regarded as a performative impossibility.

understanding, viz., as the spontaneity of cognition, as a faculty of thinking, as a faculty of concepts, and of judgments, suggesting that carefully considered, these amount to the same thing.[62] But then he adds a new characterization of it as "the **faculty of rules**," which he claims to be "more fruitful and closer to its essence" (A127). Since we have seen that concepts for Kant are themselves rules, this is not surprising; but its significance lies in the fact that it enables us to see why Kant regards the understanding as the law-giver to nature. As Kant notes, this is because laws are a species of rules. Although this clearly applies also to practical rules and laws, Kant is here concerned merely with the theoretical variety and he states that, "Rules, so far as they are objective (and thus necessarily pertain to the cognition of objects) are called laws." Moreover, we have seen that, though the imagination for Kant is governed by rules, as "blind" it cannot be considered the source of the rules (or laws) by which it is governed.

Two further steps are necessary before Kant is in a position to claim that the human understanding legislates to nature. The first is a distinction between levels of laws of nature. On the one hand, there is the multitude of empirical laws, which we learn from experience and cannot establish a priori. On the other hand, there are "higher laws," which are a priori and of which empirical laws are only "particular determinations," i.e., species of the genus law. Furthermore, inasmuch as Kant claims that the highest of these "higher" laws, under which all the others stand, stem from the understanding itself, and "provide the appearances with their lawfulness and by that very means make experience possible," it seems that these higher, i.e., a priori, laws come in various levels or gradations. Thus, Kant sketches a picture of a system of laws of nature as constituting a nested hierarchy, which he partly filled in in the *Metaphysical First Principles of Natural Science*, by deriving the Newtonian laws of motion from the Analogies in the *Critique*, through the addition of the empirical concept of matter, but never completed.[63] And since each level of law is nested or embedded in a higher one and the highest of these, i.e., the transcendental laws delineated in the Analytic of Principles, are supposedly derived from the understanding, the understanding may be said to be at least indirectly the source of all of the laws of nature, even though empirical laws are not deducible from the a priori ones.[64]

Kant's second step is to ground the understanding in the unity of apperception, thereby preserving its derived status, albeit in a manner that avoids any reference to

---

[62] In the architectonic structure of the *Critique*, the understanding is considered the faculty of concepts, which is why the Transcendental Deduction is located in the Analytic of Concepts.

[63] This completion was supposedly the task of Kant's so-called "*Opus Postumum*."

[64] The nesting metaphor is borrowed from Michael Friedman, who in my view provides the definitive account of Kant's view of the relation between the transcendental laws stemming from the pure understanding, the essentially Newtonian principles of the *Metaphysical Foundations*, and empirical laws. His basic claim is that genuine empirical laws for Kant have a more-than-inductive certainty, which is derived from the transcendental laws in which they are "nested," even though they cannot be deduced from these transcendental laws. For a succinct statement of his complex view, see Friedman (1992b), 161–99.

its relation with the imagination, which is now completely suppressed. The basic point is that "The unity of apperception is…the transcendental ground of the necessary lawfulness of all appearances in an experience" (A127). And since the unity of apperception functions as a rule, more precisely, a meta-rule, to unify the sensible manifold so as to render it apperceivable, and the understanding is the faculty of rules, Kant concludes that, "All appearances as possible experiences, therefore, lie *a priori* in the understanding, and receive their formal possibility from it, just as they lie in the sensibility as mere intuitions, and are only possible through the latter as far as their form is concerned" (A127). In the final two paragraphs Kant provides a brief overview of what he takes himself to have accomplished in the Deduction. In the first of these he affirms the correctness of his seemingly paradoxical thesis that the understanding is the source of the laws of nature, which entails that empirical laws, though, qua empirical, are not derivable from the a priori laws grounded in the understanding, yet, as particular determinations of these laws, nonetheless conform to them as norms. In the second and concluding paragraph he writes:

> The pure understanding is thus in the categories the law of the synthetic unity of all appearances, and thereby first and originally makes experience possible as far as its form is concerned. But we did not have to accomplish more in the transcendental deduction of the categories than to make comprehensible this relation of the understanding to sensibility and by means of the latter to all objects of experience, hence to make comprehensible the objective validity of its pure *a priori* concepts, and thereby determine their origin and truth.   (A128)

Kant here claims to have redeemed the promissory note issued in the first section of the Deduction by showing that the categories are necessary conditions of the possibility of experience, as he there put it, "so far as the form of thinking is concerned" (A93).[65] Since he asserts that he has thereby established the truth and origin of these categories, this is presumably what he means by making these comprehensible (*begreiflich*).[66] For present purposes, however, the most salient feature of this claim is Kant's account of how this was accomplished, namely, by making "comprehensible this relation of the understanding to sensibility and by means of the latter to all objects of experience."

The significance of this remark, which might well be dismissed as incidental, stems from the fact that it underscores the nature of the problematic underlying the Deduction. As has been emphasized throughout, this problematic must be viewed

---

[65] This qualification is necessary to leave room for the parallel claim that space and time, as forms of sensibility, are likewise necessary conditions of the possibility of experience, albeit with respect to intuition rather than thought.

[66] On the apparent identification of objective validity and truth, which Kant also makes on A125, see note 62. The suggestion that the Deduction also accounts for the origin of the categories (presumably in the pure understanding) is puzzling, however, since Kant claims that this was accomplished in the "Clue" or, the second edition, the Metaphysical Deduction.

in light of Kant's sharp distinction between sensibility and understanding. We have seen that Kant's initial response to this distinction was an attempt to account for the possibility of a priori cognition through the understanding (the real use of the intellect) in the *Inaugural Dissertation* of 1770 by separating it from any influence from the side of sensibility (a kind of decontamination project). But we further saw that, after arriving at the discursivity thesis and the analytic-synthetic distinction sometime in the early 1770s, the issue shifted to the question of their integration, particularly with respect to a priori cognition (the problem of the synthetic a priori). And, finally, we saw that it was this shift that gave birth to the problematic of a transcendental deduction of the concepts grounded in the nature of the understanding, with which Kant struggled from about the mid-1770s (the time of the *Duisburg Nachlass*) to the publication of the *Critique* in 1781.[67] Moreover, the lesson to be drawn from this is that for those who ignore or even downplay this distinctively Kantian feature of the Transcendental Deduction, which prominently include those who consider it primarily as an attempt (usually an unsuccessful one) to establish the reality of experience against a radical skeptical challenge, this Deduction and, indeed, the *Critique* as a whole, must remain a closed book.

E) *The transcendental deduction and transcendental idealism* (A128–9): In the final paragraph of section 3 Kant provides what he terms a "summary representation of the correctness and unique possibility of a transcendental deduction of the categories." His claim is that the procedure he has followed constitutes the only possible ground on which such a deduction could be successfully conducted. As such, it amounts to both a justification of the underlying presuppositions of the Transcendental Deduction and an affirmation of the correctness of its results. Despite a radical change in doctrine, Kant's procedure mirrors that of his 1763 work, *The Only Possible Basis [Beweisgrund] for a Demonstration of the Existence of God*. Just as Kant there maintained that his argument from the necessity for a real ground of possibility was the only possible (*einzig mögliche*) basis for a demonstration of the *ens realissimum*, so he here affirms the same status for the ground that he provides for the Transcendental Deduction of the categories.

Although Kant does not refer to it by name, it is clear that this ground is transcendental idealism. Accordingly, Kant is effectively claiming that a transcendental deduction of the categories is only possible if it proceeds on the basis of transcendental idealism, which is not to claim that the truth of transcendental idealism is sufficient to ground the possibility of such a deduction. This would only follow if these objects conformed to the categories simply in virtue of conforming to the conditions of sensibility. But that Kant did not think this was the case is evident

---

[67] Needless to say, I do not wish to suggest that Kant's struggles ended at this point, since we shall see in Chapter 7 that they continued at least until the publication of the second edition of the *Critique* in 1787, with its radically revised formulation of the Deduction.

from the fact that he had arrived at the "Critical" view of sensibility already in the *Inaugural Dissertation* in 1770, yet spent virtually the entirety of the "Silent Decade" wrestling with the problem of showing that and why the objects given through sensibility also necessarily conform to the quite different conditions of the understanding.

In support of the claim that transcendental idealism provides the required ground, Kant adopts his usual manner of arguing by elimination. The proposed alternatives are two ways of characterizing the objects of our cognition, as things in themselves or as appearances, which are surrogates for the two forms of transcendentalism: transcendental realism and transcendental idealism.[68] The first alternative is rejected because under it there could not be any a priori concepts at all and, *a fortiori*, no categoreal concepts. This is because on this view there are two possibilities, neither of which is acceptable. One is that these concepts would be derived directly from an encounter with the objects (as things in themselves). This would preclude their transcendental deduction because making them empirical would amount to denying their categoreal status as a priori concepts of objects in general. The other is that we take these concepts from ourselves, which is to say that they are innate. While this seemingly allows for the possibility of categories (as innate ideas), it does not allow for the possibility of demonstrating that objects (as things in themselves) necessarily conform to them, which is the task of a transcendental deduction. If, however, we take the objects to which the categories supposedly apply to be appearances, things look considerably more promising; for in that case, Kant notes, "it is not only possible but also necessary that certain *a priori* concepts precede the empirical cognition of objects," because, "[A]s appearances, they constitute an object that is merely in us [*in uns*], since a mere modification of our sensibility is not to be encountered outside us [*ausser uns*] at all" (A129).

Kant's complex claim has two parts, which need to be considered separately. The first is that it is possible that a priori concepts precede empirical cognition. As Kant here formulates this requirement it seems ambiguous, since it could be taken to mean either that it is possible that there are such concepts, i.e., categories, or that it is possible to know that objects necessarily conform to them. But inasmuch as the second presupposes the first and only the second depends upon transcendental idealism, I take it that Kant intended the latter. On this reading, then, the point is that, even assuming that things as they are in themselves might conform to the categories, this would not suffice for a transcendental deduction, since the *necessity* of their conformity could not be established. Moreover, Kant showed his awareness of the difficulty in the introductory section of the Transcendental Deduction, where he

---

[68] I have argued elsewhere that transcendental realism and transcendental idealism are to be regarded as mutually exclusive and all inclusive metaphilosophical alternatives, which are the theoretical analogues of heteronomy and autonomy in Kant's taxonomy of practical philosophies. See Allison (2004), 20–49 and 388–95.

contrasts the task of demonstrating the necessary relation of space and time to objects with that of doing so for the categories. As we saw in Chapter 4, Kant notes that the former is relatively easy, since, as forms of sensibility, conformity to them is a necessary condition of the appearance of objects; whereas "objects can indeed appear to us without necessarily having to be related to the functions of the understanding, and therefore without the understanding containing their *a priori* conditions" (A89/B122).

Since the argument of the Aesthetic, which supposedly suffices to establish the ideality of appearances, is not capable of grounding the necessity of the conformity of appearances to the categories, the questions become what more would be required and what is its connection with transcendental idealism. Kant addresses these issues in the remainder of the paragraph, where he writes:

Now even this representation—that all these appearances and thus all objects with which we can occupy ourselves are all in me [*in mir*], i.e., determinations of my identical self— expresses a thoroughgoing unity of them in one and the same apperception as necessary. The form of all cognition of objects (through which the manifold is thought as belonging to one object), however, also consists in this unity of possible consciousness. Thus the way in which the manifold of sensible representation (intuition) belongs to a consciousness pre- cedes all cognition of the object, as its intellectual form, and itself constitutes an *a priori* formal condition of all objects in general, insofar as they are thought (categories). Their synthesis through the pure imagination, the unity of all representations in relation to original apperception, precede all empirical cognition. Pure concepts of the understanding are therefore possible, indeed necessary *a priori* in relation to experience, only because our cognition has to do with nothing but appearances, whose possibility lies in ourselves, whose connection and unity (in the representation of an object) is encountered merely in us, and thus must precede all experience and first make it possible as far as its form is concerned. And from this ground, *the only possible one* [my emphasis] among all, our deduction of the categories has been conducted.   (A129–30)

It is clear from this that the additional factor (besides the necessary conformity of appearances to the forms of sensibility) that is required for a deduction of the categories is their necessary conformity with the conditions of apperception, which will be referred to as the apperceivability condition. It would seem, however, that a transcendental realist could acknowledge the necessity of the conformity of anything that is cognized with this condition, but insist that it is merely a conditional necessity, which can be met by things in themselves and does not entail idealism. One such Kantian anti-idealist is Guyer, who uses it as the basis for his critique of both Kant's idealism and his procedure in the Transcendental Deduction. As we have seen, Guyer's critique turns on the charge that Kant conflated a merely conditional, *de dicto* necessity that objects must conform to the subjective conditions of cognition, *if* we are able to cognize them, with an unconditional, *de re* necessity that objects *necessarily* conform to these conditions. In short, Guyer sees two alternatives for Kant. One is the "restriction" view, according to which the forms of sensibility and

categories function as gatekeepers, which prevent representations that do not conform to them from entering consciousness. The other is the "imposition" view,
according to which these forms and concepts are imposed upon the given, thereby
guaranteeing its conformity to them. And, once again, Guyer concludes from this
that the former is all that Kant is entitled (or, indeed, needs) to claim; while it is only
the latter that requires transcendental idealism.[69]

Another notable Kantian anti-idealist is Kenneth Westphal, whose views correspond to Guyer's in at least three essential respects. First, like Guyer, Westphal adopts
a strongly metaphysical and negative view of transcendental idealism, rejecting any
attempt, including my own, to interpret it in a sympathetic manner.[70] Second, also
like Guyer, Westphal's project is to construct on a presumably Kantian basis a
transcendental argument that not only does not rely on idealistic premises, but also
establishes a form of realism that is much stronger than the empirical realism
affirmed by Kant, which they both reject because of its connection with transcendental idealism. Westphal usually refers to this as "realism *sans phrase*," meaning
without the qualification "empirical" and sometimes as a transcendental realism.
Third, like Guyer, he contends that Kant's fundamental mistake consists in ignoring
the possibility that, rather than being imposed by the mind, Kant's epistemic
conditions are to be understood as conditions which outer objects, i.e., transcendentally real entities, must meet if we are to experience them and which, as such, are only
conditionally necessary. Accordingly, much like the well-known claim regarding
space, Kant is deemed guilty of neglecting an alternative, since he precipitously
assumed that if transcendental conditions of experience are possible at all, they
must be imposed by the mind.[71]

Despite this partial overlap with Guyer, Westphal's account calls for a separate
consideration because of his treatment of Kant's conception of transcendental
affinity, which was largely glossed over by Guyer. According to Westphal, the
principle of affinity has a unique status, being at once both a material and a formal
transcendental condition of experience, which on his view is the alternative neglected
by Kant. It is allegedly "material" because it must be a function of the characteristics
of the objects we experience," which Westphal equates with being a function of "the
matter of our sensations," but it is also "formal" because "it concerns the relations
among the material (qualitative) characteristics of the objects we experience."[72] And
he denies that the material component of this conception, and therefore the conception itself, can be accounted for in terms of Kant's transcendental idealism, "because
his idealism and the arguments for it are based on the thesis . . . , that sensation can

[69] I shall analyze Guyer's view in more detail in the Conclusion.

[70] See Westphal (2004), 56–61. Elsewhere (2001), 593–622, he accuses me of equivocation on the
methodological-metaphysical issue. Unfortunately, Westphal does not consider my more recent treatment
of this issue, particularly in Allison (2004); though he can hardly be faulted for this since that appeared in
the same year as his book.

[71] Westphal (2004), 77–8.   [72] Ibid., 91.

provide no connection among sensations, and relations among sensations are strictly and solely the product of our understanding."[73]

Indeed, Westphal's account of affinity is even more radically anti-idealistic and naturalistic than Guyer, since he contends that it is not only compatible with but actually presupposes transcendental realism. A key ingredient in Westphal's analysis is his "sensationism" (the term is borrowed from Rolf George), according to which "sensations are nonintentional mental states that do not, of themselves, present objects to the mind."[74] Given this conception, Westphal argues that affinity, so construed, is a transcendentally real property of sensations, i.e., one not produced by the synthesizing activity of the mind, but which nevertheless serves as a transcendental, yet material condition of experience in the sense that it is necessary for the possibility of a self-conscious experience. In fact, on the basis of this sensationism Westphal insists provocatively, if not paradoxically, that Kant is a "mental content externalist," and he also refers to him as "a staunch justificatory externalist *avant la lettre*."[75]

Since it is impossible here to deal with the complexities of Westphal's multi-pronged critique of transcendental idealism and of what purports to be a defense of a Kantian "realism *sans phrase*," I shall limit the discussion to his "sensationism" and his use of it to argue against transcendental idealism and for a transcendentally realistic Kant. The above definition of the term is not objectionable inasmuch as it accords with Kant's own definition of "sensation" (*Empfindung*) as "the effect of an object on the capacity of representation insofar as we are conscious of it" (A20/B34). Problems begin, however, when Westphal goes on to claim that "sensations have a basic kind of intentionality (roughly they carry information about a particular sensed object), though their intentionality is insufficient for them to be intentional."[76] This suggests that sensations have a non-intentional intentionality, which, if not oxymoronic, is certainly deeply problematic.

Moreover, in giving sensations a cognitive role at the ground floor, so to speak, and their affinity, i.e., associative relations, a transcendental status as a condition of the possibility of experience, Westphal is not merely, as he sometimes suggests, introducing an exception to Kant's formal apriorism in which epistemic conditions are located in the mind as subjective conditions of thinking (or intuiting), he is effectively denying the fundamental principle of the Analytic; viz., the spontaneity of the understanding. He is also well aware of this and uses this naturalistic turn, which he relates to recent work in the neurophysiology of perception, to undermine transcendental idealism. The basic point, which is entailed by his sensationism, is that the primitive intentionality of sensations, in virtue of which they "guide our empirical judgments," "entails that the role of the intellectual synthesis is only to *re*construct the order of nature that produces our sensations."[77] Accordingly, on

---

[73] Ibid., 87.   [74] Ibid., 44.   [75] Ibid., 9–10 and passim.
[76] Ibid., 45.   [77] Ibid., 89–90.

Westphal's reading, the human understanding does not legislate to nature but merely reconstructs in thought an order that is given in our sensations. And in light of this he claims:

I submit that Kant cannot have it both ways: if sensations are sufficiently structured to guide empirical judgments, then intellectual synthesis can only *reconstruct* but cannot construct *tout court*, the structure and order of nature; conversely, if intellectual synthesis alone constructs the order of nature, it must construct its particular order and content as well. Transcendental idealism is an unstable halfway house between realism and subjective idealism.[78]

Although like most philosophers Kant often wanted to have his cake and eat it too, I deny that he wished to have it both ways in the manner suggested by Westphal. Admittedly, if Kant had subscribed to anything like the sensationism attributed to him by Westphal, he would have to be regarded as a transcendental realist *malgré lui* and the interpretation offered here, which focuses on the discursivity thesis and the spontaneity of the understanding, where cognition consists in the rule-governed act of taking *x* as *F*, would have to be completely rejected. To be sure, this does not speak directly to the philosophical merits of the view that Westphal and others ascribe to Kant; but the present claim is merely that whatever these merits may be, the position that he describes is not Kant's and that imposing it upon the Kantian texts obfuscates rather than illuminates them.

Before concluding this discussion, however, we must consider a different challenge to the view that the Transcendental Deduction presupposes transcendental idealism. It has been mounted by Lucy Allais and it differs from those of Guyer, Westphal, and other anti-idealists in that it does not involve a rejection of transcendental idealism. In fact, Allais attributes to Kant and defends an ontological idealism of a moderate, i.e., non- Berkeleyan type, which is based on the analogy with the mind-dependence of secondary qualities such as color and is supposedly compatible with a direct realist view of perception.[79] Nevertheless, evidently motivated by a desire to make the argument of the Deduction as appealing as possible to die-hard realists and, more specifically, to present-day analytical philosophers, who tend to view Kant through the lens of the Strawsonian conception of a transcendental argument, she argues that much of the Deduction is independent of even this form of idealism, not to mention the more radical and disreputable forms that are usually attributed to Kant by critics.

A case in point is her analysis of Kant's claim that a priori concepts determine what counts as an object for us. Although she notes that this seems to be a clear expression "of a kind of idealism," Allais suggests that it might also be taken as the expression of "an epistemological point, which a realist could accept."[80] And the crux of the matter, as she construes it, is that the representation of an object, as expressed in an act of judgment, requires a "certain kind of unity" in which the properties of an object are represented as connected "with something like necessity," which cannot be

---

[78] Ibid., 90.   [79] Allais (2011), 92–3.   [80] Ibid., 104.

accounted for as the result of association, but must rather be grounded in the necessary unity of apperception.[81]

There are two points to be made in response to this suggestion. First, what she refers to as an epistemological point is, from Kant's point of view, more properly described as logical, since it is grounded in his characterization of judgment as "nothing other than the way to bring given cognitions to the **objective** unity of apperception. That is the aim of the copula is in them: to distinguish the objective unity of given representations from the subjective one" (B141–2).[82] Moreover, though this characterization of judgment is clearly not logical from a present-day point of view, it is arguably not epistemological either. Rather, it might best be regarded as semantic, since it concerns what is meant by the claim that a given unification of representations counts as a judgment, in contrast, say, to a mere association of representations that cannot be assigned a truth value. Second, quite apart from the question of how one should characterize the point to which Allais refers, her contention that it could be accepted by a realist is vitiated by a failure to consider Kant's distinction between an empirical and transcendental realism.

Insofar as Allais' intent is to make the claim under consideration plausible to present-day philosophers, who, having no use for transcendental idealism, would likewise have no use for the distinction between an empirical and a transcendental realism, particularly since it does not map onto the contrast between a direct (or naive) and an indirect (or representative) realism, her procedure is understandable, albeit somewhat too facile. But if, as also seems to be the case, she wishes to show that transcendental idealism is to be taken seriously in the present-day philosophical arena, then this distinction cannot be ignored because, together with the contrast between transcendental idealism and transcendental realism, with which it is joined at the hip, it is an integral component of this idealism.

In order to appreciate the relevance of this distinction between the two forms of realism to the point at issue it should suffice to note that empirical realism for Kant is not only compatible with but presupposes that the conditions of apperception are normative in the sense that they determine what counts as an object for beings such as ourselves, i.e., discursive cognizers.[83] It is clearly incompatible, however, with a

[81]   Ibid., 104–5.
[82]   In view of its contrast with the other definition of judgment that Kant offers in the *Critique* (A68/B93) and the *Jäsche Logic* (9:101; 597), I have argued elsewhere (Allison (2004), 83), that this definition is oriented toward transcendental rather than general logic. I now think, however, that this is misleading, since it is concerned with the meaning of judgment as such. Moreover, as I there noted, a similar definition of judgment as involving a claim of objective validity is to be found at WL 24: 928; 369. What makes this definition part of general logic in Kant's sense is that it is concerned with the nature of discursive thought as such, which, as we have seen, consists in judgment.
[83]   I am here appealing to the conception of empirical realism and its relation to transcendental idealism on the one hand and transcendental realism on the other for which I argued in Allison (2012), 67–83. My main point there was that empirical realism for Kant is not to be understood as an inferior, second-best

transcendental realism, since the latter appeals, at least implicitly, to a God's eye view of things as the normative standard governing cognition.[84] Accordingly, for a transcendental realist the question of what counts as an object or as objective *for us*, as contrasted with what is objective "sans phrase," as Westphal might put it, may be of interest as a matter of cognitive psychology, but it would be of no normative import. And it follows from this (assuming that transcendental idealism is the logical negation of transcendental realism) that if a transcendental deduction is possible, it could only be on the basis of transcendental idealism, which is at the same time an empirical realism. Once again, this is not to claim that a transcendental deduction is possible, or that transcendental idealism is its first premise. It is rather that transcendental idealism provides the logical space in which alone such a project is conceivable. Admittedly, this may be sufficient for many philosophers to dismiss this project as a fool's errand; but at least they would not be misled by false advertising.

---

form of realism, but as fundamentally involving a scope limitation or deflation of cognitive claims from objects in general to objects of possible experience. Accordingly, despite Kant's misleading phenomenalistic language, objects of the latter sort are fully real and our cognition of them genuinely objective. See also Chapter 5, note 6.

[84] For my explanation of this claim see Allison (2004), 27–34. My basic point is that the so-called "transcendental turn" or "Copernican revolution" is best understood as a shift from a theocentric to an anthropocentric model of cognition.

7

The Interlude

"The interlude" refers to the period between the publication of the first and second editions of the *Critique* (1781–87) and the concern of this chapter is with Kant's work in this period, insofar as it relates to the Transcendental Deduction.[1] Although in sharp contrast to the "Silent Decade" Kant published a good deal during these years, the discussion will focus on three texts: the *Prolegomena* (1783), particularly its second part, a note to the Preface of the *Metaphysical Foundations of Natural Science* (1786), in which Kant responds to a critique of his formulation of the Transcendental Deduction in the first edition, and a set of *Reflexionen* (5923–35), which apparently stem from this period and shows Kant in the process of reformulating the argument of the Deduction. Accordingly, the chapter will be divided into three parts.

I

Considered with respect to its explicit aims, the *Prolegomena* is both forward and backward looking. The former is indicated by its full title (*Prolegomena to any future metaphysics that will be able to come forward as science*), as well by the first sentence of the Preface, where Kant states that, "These prolegomena are not for the use of apprentices, but of future teachers, and indeed are not intended to help them to organize the presentation of an existing science, but to discover this science itself for the first time" (Pro 4: 255_{1-4}; 53). The latter is due to the fact that the work is intended to provide an overview of the contents of the already-published *Critique*. What unifies these two, seemingly opposed, directions are Kant's underlying assumptions that metaphysics does not yet exist in the form of a science, which he believed to be the only form in which it can properly exist, and that the *Critique of Pure Reason* provides the only basis on which such a project has any prospect of success.[2]

---

[1] In its broad outlines, though not in its details, the following analysis is indebted to the account of de Vleeschauwer (1936), 419–593.

[2] According to Kant metaphysics can properly exist only in the form of a science because it is concerned with pure reason, which is a self-contained domain, and therefore unlike other sciences cannot be augmented from without. In short, metaphysics, as Kant conceived, is an all or nothing affair. See Pro 4: 263; 99–100 and 365–6; 154–5.

The *Prolegomena* is also the product of a two-fold concern on Kant's part. On the one hand, it is intended to present the central tenets of the *Critique* in a more accessible form, an aim that is reflected in his characterization of it as containing "preparatory exercises" (Pro 4: 261$_{28}$; 58), where the preparation is for studying the text of the *Critique* itself. On the other hand, it has a clear polemical intent, where the targets are those who have avoided dealing seriously with the *Critique* because of its difficulty and those who (in Kant's judgment) had read it selectively and willfully distorted its content. The prime example of the latter is the notorious Garve-Feder review, which, in addition to its charge of undue obscurity, completely ignored the Transcendental Deduction and accused Kant of affirming Berkeleyen idealism, according to which the sensible world is transformed into an illusion.[3] Kant responds indignantly to the latter charge in three places in the *Prolegomena*: two lengthy notes to §13, where he appeals to the phenomenon of incongruent counterparts in support of his doctrine of the ideality of space and time (4: 288–94; 83–8) and, more explicitly, in the Appendix to the work as a whole (4: 372–80; 160–6). In the latter place, in an effort to obviate any misunderstandings that may have been occasioned by the characterization of his idealism in the first edition of the *Critique* as "transcendental," Kant states that in the future he wishes it to be called "formal, or better, critical, in order to distinguish it from the dogmatic idealism of Berkeley and the skeptical idealism of Descartes" (Pro 4: 375$_{23-6}$; 163).

In contrast to his unequivocal rejection of the objection that the idealism of the *Critique* entails the denial of the reality of the sensible world, Kant pleads guilty to the obscurity charge; though he claims extenuating circumstances by noting that this obscurity is the unavoidable concomitant of the inherent difficulty of the project of the *Critique* and states that he will attempt to address it in the body of the present work (4: 261$_{14-25}$; 58). Kant also states that his main tool for doing this is the analytic method rather than the synthetic method that was used in the *Critique* (Pro 4: 263$_{27-32}$; 60). As Kant here understands this method, however, it has nothing in common besides the name and the direction of inquiry (regressive rather than progressive) with the analytic method that he had adopted in his writings of the 1760s and contrasted with the synthetic method of mathematics.[4] Whereas we saw that for the earlier Kant the analytic method, at least as it was operative in metaphysics, was essentially a form of conceptual analysis, this method, as he now understands it, begins with a body of accepted truths and investigates the conditions of their possibility.[5] Accordingly, rather than asking *whether* these truths (synthetic a

---

[3] For English translations of both the published Garve-Feder (*Göttingen*) Review and Garve's original, unedited version, see Sassen (2000), 53–77.

[4] Kant also adopted the analytic or regressive method of exposition in the first two parts of the *Groundwork*. I discuss the relation between the analytic method in that work and in the *Prolegomena* in Allison (2011), 33–6.

[5] In a note added to §5 Kant goes to great pains to make clear that the distinction between the analytic and synthetic methods is not to be confused with that between analytic and synthetic judgments. See Pro 4: 276$_{24-37}$; 73.

priori propositions) are possible, Kant assumes that they are actual and attempts to determine what must be assumed in order to account for their possibility.

Although such a procedure is inadequate for a critique of pure reason, since the goal of the latter is to present a self-examination of pure reason with respect to its pretension to yield synthetic a priori cognitions, Kant evidently thought that it was appropriate for a work that merely attempted to provide an overview of the results of the *Critique*.[6] More precisely, he considered it appropriate for the first three of the four parts of the *Prolegomena*, which deal respectively with the conditions of the possibility of pure mathematics, pure natural science, and metaphysics in general, by which Kant understood metaphysics as a propensity of human reason to seek explanatory totality. But inasmuch as the fourth and final part deals with the question of how metaphysics is possible as a science and the central thesis of the work is that metaphysics did not yet exist in that form, and therefore did not really exist at all, Kant could not proceed in that fashion. Instead, he argues that a critique of pure reason is a necessary condition of the eventual actualization of such a science. Our present concern, however, is limited to the second part of the *Prolegomena*, which corresponds to the Transcendental Analytic in the *Critique*, and within this the primary focus will be on the portion corresponding to the Transcendental Deduction.

A) *How is pure natural science possible?*: Kant states that by "pure natural science" he understands "universal natural science in the strict sense" (Pro 4: 295_{13}; 90). Accordingly, before proceeding further, it is necessary to become clear about both its purity and its universality. To begin with, this formulation marks a shift in Kant's use of the term "pure," which is articulated here for the first time and is retained in the second edition of the *Critique* and in his later writings, albeit not consistently. Whereas in the first edition of the *Critique* Kant had used the term as a synonym for "*a priori*," in the second edition he takes it in a narrower sense to designate a subset of a priori cognitions; viz., those in which "nothing empirical is intermixed" (B3).[7] As Kant points out, this precludes from pure natural science a priori cognitions involving concepts with an empirical element. He further notes that these include concepts

---

[6] This is not to say, however, that a regressive procedure based on the weaker premise that we have experience, i.e., empirical knowledge, is inappropriate. In fact, this thesis has been argued forcefully by Ameriks (1978), 273–87. Moreover, we shall see that, despite the way in which Kant frames the issue in the second part of the *Prolegomena*, his actual argument turns on the assumption that we are capable of empirical knowledge (judgments of experience), not that we have synthetic a priori knowledge. It appears that Kant framed it in this way in order to underscore the parallel with the argument of the first part, which was concerned with the conditions of the synthetic a priori knowledge provided by mathematics; but this parallel is misleading.

[7] Since as an example of a proposition that is a priori but not pure Kant here gives "Every alteration has a cause," whereas at B5 he cites the same proposition as an instance of the pure a priori, he directly contradicts himself. This was pointed out in a review of the second edition to which Kant responded at the end of "On the Use of Teleological Principles in Philosophy" in which he acknowledged the contradiction, attributed it to mere carelessness and indicated that he had intended in the entire work to take the term "pure" in the sense given to it at B3. See GTP 8: 183_{31}–4_9; 218.

such as motion, impenetrability, and inertia, which will be central to the argument of the *Metaphysical Foundations of Natural Science*.

As Kant here uses the expression, the "strict universality" that he attributes to pure natural science stems from the fact that, unlike a universal physics, it encompasses objects of inner as well as outer sense. In other words, it refers to the scope of pure natural science rather than its a priori ground.[8] Moreover, Kant claims that there is in fact such a universal and pure science and as instances of it he cites the propositions "*that substance remains* and *persists*" and that "*everything that happens* always previously is *determined by a cause* according to constant laws, and so on" (Pro 4: 295_{18-21}; 90). These propositions are equivalent to the first two Analogies in the *Critique* and the addition of the "and so on" indicates that Kant regarded them as examples rather than as the complete list of the propositions belonging to pure natural science. Although it is unclear exactly what Kant had in mind here, it seems reasonable to assume that he intended it to include all of the Principles of Pure Understanding of the *Critique* rather than merely the Analogies.[9]

Kant further complicates the issue by distinguishing between two senses of "nature." According to his account, the term can be understood in either a formal or a material sense (*natura formaliter spectata* and *natura materialiter spectata*). Taken in the former sense, it is defined as "the existence of things, insofar as that existence is determined according to universal laws" (Pro 4: 294_{7-8}; 89); whereas taken in the latter sense it is defined as "*the sum total of all objects of experience*" (Pro 4: 295_{28-9}; 90). Kant also points out that the question at issue can be framed in two ways, depending upon the sense in which "nature" is understood. Assuming that the kind of cognition at issue is a priori, one can ask either: "How is it possible to cognize *a priori* the necessary conformity to law *of things* as objects of possible experience, or: How is it possible in general to cognize *a priori* the necessary conformity to law of experience itself with regard to all of its objects?" (Pro 4: 296_{18-21}; 91).

Although Kant notes that on either formulation the solution will be the same, viz., that the necessary conformity to law that is presupposed by a pure natural science or, more generally, by any a priori cognition of nature, must be grounded in the nature of the understanding, he states a preference for the first on the grounds that, "we can indeed, *a priori* and previous to any objects being given, have a cognition of those conditions under which alone an experience regarding objects is possible, but never of the laws to which objects may be subject in themselves without relation to a possible experience" (Pro 4: 297_{1-6}; 91). Kant's concern here seems to have been to

---

[8] Elsewhere, most notably at B4, Kant contrasts a strict with a merely empirical (inductively based) universality, understanding by the former one that has an a priori ground.

[9] The obvious problem with this conception of a universal pure science of nature (as contrasted with a universal pure physics), is the extension of these Principles (or even the Analogies) to objects of inner sense, which is to say the mind or soul. Not only does this conflict with Kant's explicit denial that psychology is a science (MAN 4: 471_{11-37}; 186), but it raises further questions, which Kant never really addresses, about the applicability of the categories to objects of inner sense.

prevent a possible misunderstanding of the scope that he attributes to the proposi-tions of pure natural science, i.e., that they might apply to things in themselves. And he evidently thought that this is blocked by the first formulation because it relegates the necessary lawfulness of experience to its form (*natura formaliter spectata*); though not by the second, since this appears to leave open the possibility that the objects of which nature is composed (*natura formaliter spectata*) are things in themselves.[10]

Nevertheless, one might still wonder why Kant makes this relatively straightfor-ward point in such a roundabout way, rather than simply noting, as he routinely did in the *Critique*, that the necessary conformity to law applies only to appearances. I believe that the answer lies in the strategic nature of Kant's account in the *Prolegomena*. Although he does not retract the doctrine that our cognition is limited to appearances, in his effort to respond to the charge of idealism, Kant seems to have endeavored, perhaps somewhat disingenuously, to present the issue in a way that detracts attention from the underlying idealistic commitment of his argument. This is accomplished by reformulating the restriction thesis in terms of objects of possible experience, thereby leaving open the question of the nature of these objects.

This is not to suggest, however, that Kant disavows his idealism completely in the *Prolegomena*. That he does not is clear from his return to the general question of the second part in a new form in §36, which has the heading: "How is nature itself possible?" (Pro 4: 318_2; 110). We have seen that in its original form the question concerned the possibility of a pure science of nature rather than of nature itself and the shift in formulation seems to reflect a broadening of Kant's concerns. This is suggested by the fact that, rather than insisting upon the essential equivalence between the formal and material conceptions of nature, as he had initially done, Kant now correlates the material sense with the first part of the *Prolegomena*, characterizing it as the sum-total of appearances, and, focusing on the spatiotemporal nature of these appearances, he grounds their possibility in the nature of human sensibility, which was the conclusion of the first part dealing with the conditions of the possibility of pure mathematics. Correlatively, Kant now connects nature in the formal sense with the concern of the second part, defining nature, so considered, as "the sum-total of rules to which all appearances must be subject if they are to be connected in one experience" (Pro 4: 318_{16-18}; 111), which indicates the idealistic thrust of his argument. And, after suggesting that the lawfulness of nature, so considered, lies in "necessary apperception" (Pro 4: 318_{30}; 111) and "the conditions of the necessary unification [of appearances] in one consciousness" (4: 319_{9-10}; 111), which echo the language of the Transcendental Deduction in the *Critique*, Kant concludes, as he had done in the Deduction, that, with respect to the universal laws of nature: "the understanding does not draw its (*a priori*) laws from nature, but prescribes them to it" (Pro 4: 320_{11-13}; 112).

---

[10] For a similar formulation see B164–5.

B) *The Transcendental Deduction in the Prolegomena*: Despite its use of the analytic method, which would seem to preclude a deduction comparable to that contained in the *Critique*, in the Appendix to the *Prolegomena* Kant expresses dissatisfaction with the Deduction and the Paralogisms as contained in the first edition of the *Critique* and requests that the examination of his views on the topics covered in these chapters be based instead on what he says in the *Prolegomena* (Pro 4: 381_{23-9}; 168). In the case of the Deduction, this means essentially §18–§20.[11] To be sure, Kant indicates that his dissatisfaction is based upon the prolixity of his argument rather than its lack of cogency; but it will become clear from the materials considered in the remainder of the chapter that Kant was deeply engaged in rethinking the strategy of the Deduction throughout the interlude between the first two editions of the *Critique*. The center-piece of this new deduction is the distinction between judgments of perception and judgments of experience as two species of empirical judgment. In introducing this distinction, Kant writes:

Empirical judgments, insofar as they have objective validity, are JUDGMENTS OF EXPERIENCE; those, however, that are *only subjectively* valid I call mere JUDGMENTS OF PERCEPTION. The latter do not require a pure concept of the understanding, but only the logical connection of perceptions in a thinking subject. But the former always demand, in addition to the representations of sensory intuition, special *concepts originally generated in the understanding*, which are precisely what makes the judgment of experience *objectively valid*.   (Pro 4: 298_{1-8})

It seems likely that Kant was led to this distinction by Georg Friedrich Meier's distinction between intuitive and discursive judgments. In his *Auszug aus der Vernunftlehre*, which Kant used as the textbook for his logic lectures, Meier characterized an intuitive judgment consisting merely of empirical concepts as an immediate experience, and as singular.[12] In the *Vernunftlehre* itself, however, he claimed that such judgments are composed merely of sensations and he gave as examples: "I think," "I am warm," "I am cold," and "This wine tastes sweet."[13] By discursive empirical judgments Meier understood those involving concepts that are not taken directly from sensation and which therefore lack the immediate certainty of intuitive judgments. As examples of such judgments he cites "There are spots on the sun" and "The air is heavy," which require observations and experiments to be validated.[14]

---

[11]   There is, however, some dispute in the literature regarding the precise location in the *Prolegomena* of its counterpart to the Transcendental Deduction. For example, according to de Vleeschauwer, Apel, locates it in §18–§22, whereas he confines it to §20. For a discussion of the issue, see de Vleeschauwer (1936), 443–9. Moreover, there is something to be said for each of these views, and since Kant himself is silent on the matter any attempt at a precise location of it is somewhat arbitrary. Nevertheless, the fact remains that §18–§20 constitute a coherent line of argument, while §21 corresponds to the Metaphysical Deduction in the *Critique*, which, interestingly, follows rather than precedes the Transcendental Deduction in the *Prolegomena*, and §22 contains a summary of the whole line of argument.

[12]   Meier §319 Ak 16: 674–5.   [13]   Meier (1752; 520); cited from Ak 16: 674–5.

[14]   Meier (1752; 520); cited from Ak 16: 674–5.

Apart from the terminology, Kant's account differs from Meier's in at least three respects. First, for Kant all judgments, simply qua judgments, are discursive. Thus, there could be no intuitive judgments in Meier's sense. Second, in contrast to Meier and, indeed, all pre-Kantian thinkers for whom intuition is the epistemic gold standard with respect to which all other modes of cognition are weighed, Kant attaches merely a subjective validity to judgments of perception, which presumably correspond to intuitive judgments in Meier's scheme. Third, and most important, for Kant judgments of experience require not merely concepts (since this is a condition of *all* judgments), but a special set of concepts, which stem from the nature of the understanding and are the source of their claim to objectivity. And since by "experience" Kant understands empirical cognition and all cognition is a matter of judgment, it follows that the conditions of the possibility of judgments of experience are, *eo ipso*, also conditions of the possibility of experience.

Kant's conception of judgments of perception will be considered below; but our immediate concern is with judgments of experience, since these are the vehicles through which Kant inserts the categories into his account of experience. Contrary to what one might expect, the target of Kant's appeal to such judgments is not the skeptic, who would question the very notion of objective validity; but, rather, a widely shared conception of empirical judgment as based solely on the comparison of perceptions or, more precisely, of empirical concepts, which are themselves based on perceptions. It is not that Kant entirely rejects this view since it is an integral part of his own account of empirical judgment. What he rejects is the underlying empiricist assumption that such judgments consist *merely* in such a comparison. According to Kant, such judgments also require a contribution of the understanding in the form of a category under which the perception-based concepts must be subsumed. And he claims that unless this is recognized all judgments would have to be considered as lacking in objective validity, and therefore as merely judgments of perception, which is contrary to the hypothesis that such judgments suffice for experience.

Kant introduces his account of the objective validity of empirical judgments in the context of the distinction between judgments of perception and judgments of experience. He writes:

All our judgments are at first mere judgments of perception; they hold only for us, i.e., for our subject, and only afterwards do we give them a new relation, namely to an object, and intend that the judgment should also be valid at all times for us and for everyone else; for if a judgment agrees with an object, then all judgments of the same object must agree with one another, and hence the objective validity of a judgment of experience signifies nothing other than its necessary universal validity.   (Pro 4: 298$_{9-16}$; 92)

Setting aside for the moment the claim that judgments of perception precede judgments of experience, our present concern is with Kant's characterization of the objective validity of the latter as consisting in its "necessary universal validity."

Since Kant is concerned explicitly with empirical judgments, it is evident that the necessity and universality to which he here refers are not to be equated with those that he presents in the *Critique* as the twin criteria of the a priori. Thus, it is essential to examine his view of each with some care, as well as the relation between them. I shall begin with their necessity, which is the most problematic feature, since it seems to have suggested to at least some commentators that Kant is committed to the paradoxical view that a posteriori judgments are really a priori.[15]

Kant addresses this issue in a note to §22, where he asks rhetorically: "[H]ow does this proposition: that judgments of experience are supposed to contain necessity in the synthesis of perceptions, square with my proposition ... that experience, as *a posteriori* cognition, can provide merely contingent judgments?" (Pro 4: 305_{23-6}; 99). In response he distinguishes between the perceptual content, which is acquired through experience and is contingent, and the a priori element (the pure concept of the understanding), through which this experience is first generated. Unfortunately, in illustrating this point Kant muddies the waters, as he frequently does, by choosing as his example of a judgment of experience the causal judgment that the illumination of a stone by the sun causes it to become warm. As he puts it, "That this warming follows necessarily from illumination by the sun is indeed contained in the judgment of experience (in virtue of the concept of cause), but I do not learn it from experience; rather, conversely, experience is first generated through this addition of a concept of the understanding (of cause) to the perception" (Pro 4: 305_{30-3}; 99). The problem here is that the causal necessity expressed in the judgment is conflated with the necessity in virtue of which the combination of perceptions constitutes an objectively valid judgment. For example, the categorical judgment "The stone is warm" would likewise be objectively valid, even though it merely predicates a property (warmth) of an entity (a stone), without any reference to the cause of the presence of this property.[16]

In dealing with this problem in connection with the A-Deduction, it was argued that the necessity that Kant attributes to empirical judgments is normative in nature and linked to the notion of concepts as rules. Despite the misleading nature of the account discussed above, which we shall also find in other passages, the normative nature of the necessity attached to judgments of experience is clearly operative in the *Prolegomena* as well. For example, Kant notes that in making such a judgment

[15] We shall see in the next part of this chapter that this worry was expressed by J. G. Schultz in his favorable review of a work that was critical of Kant. In recent times such a view has been affirmed by Guyer (1987), 114, who referring to the B-Deduction attributes to Kant the "shocking" view that "empirical judgments are a form of necessary truth," and later (1992), 148, makes the same claim with respect to judgments of experience in the *Prolegomena*.
[16] Although this judgment for Kant presupposes the principle of causality, since it is assumed that the warmth of the stone has a cause, unlike Kant's example, it does not assign a cause and therefore does not affirm a causal necessity. We shall see below, however, that the problem is complicated by the fact that in one of Kant's examples of a categorical judgment of experience he does assign the objectivating function to the concept of cause rather than substance.

one intends (*wollen*) that "the judgment should also be valid at all times for us and for everyone else," which he justifies on the grounds that "if a judgment agrees with an object, then all judgments of the same object must also agree with one another," from which he infers that objective validity consists in "necessary universality" (Pro 4: 298_{16}; 92).

Obviously, the mere fact that one intends to make an objectively valid judgment does not make it so; but Kant's point is that this necessity characterizes the formal structure of such judgments not their content. Kant clarifies the formal nature of his claim, when, rather than simply stating that the resulting judgment in fact agrees with its object, he remarks that under these conditions we must "deem it objective" (*müssen wir es auch für objectiv halten*), which he glosses as "expressing not merely a relation of a perception to a subject, but a property of an object." And he underscores the normative nature of the necessity at issue by pointing out that, "there would be no reason why other judgments necessarily would have to agree with mine, if there were not the unity of the object—an object to which they all refer, with which they all agree, and, for that reason, must also harmonize among themselves" (Pro 4: 298_{22-6}; 92).

This brings us, then, to the universality of judgments of experience or, more precisely, their "necessary universal validity." Inasmuch as judgments of experience can refer to one or some, as well as all of the objects falling under the extension of the subject-concept, the universality they involve cannot be understood as referring to their logical quantity. Instead, it must be a "subjective universality," which applies to the universe of judging subjects. Moreover, as is indicated by its connection with necessity, this universality cannot be regarded merely as a contingent circumstance, as if it just happens that everyone agrees regarding the matter; it is rather that in some sense everyone *must agree* because the judgment holds of the object, which suggests that the universality, like the necessity, is normative in nature.

We can see from this that, though quite distinct from the logical necessity and universality to which Kant appeals in the *Critique* as the twin criteria of a priori cognition, the necessity and subjective universality of judgments of experience are likewise inseparably connected. Moreover, Kant underscores this inseparability when he states that "Objective validity and necessary universal validity (for everyone) are interchangeable concepts," to which he adds that, "although we do not know the object in itself, nonetheless, if we regard the judgment as universally valid and hence necessary, objective validity is understood to be included" (Pro 4: 298_{28-31}; 93). In short, universal validity (understood as a subjective universality) and (normative) necessity reciprocally imply each other and jointly entail objective validity.

If, as I have argued, the necessity to which Kant appeals in the A-Deduction in connection with his analysis of objective validity is likewise normative, it follows, as suggested above, that the A-Deduction already assumes, though it does not mention, the notion of a subjective universality and the intersubjective or transpersonal account of objectivity that it entails. The problem, however, is that this seems difficult to reconcile with the Cartesian-like focus on the conditions of the I's consciousness of its unity and identity that constitutes what is commonly viewed as the core of its argument. In fact, in his review of Henrich's *Identität und Objektivität*, whose analysis of the structure of the Deduction his closely models, Guyer strongly rejects any such reading on the grounds that, despite what he says in the *Prolegomena*, "Kant clearly conceived of the problem of knowledge in terms of methodological solipsism."[17] And while it is seldom expressed so bluntly, this appears to be a fairly widely shared view of the Deduction.[18]

In addition to the many philosophical objections raised against the Deduction by the critics who read it in this manner and the previously noted fact that it conflates the task of the Deduction with that of the Refutation of Idealism, a further and seldom noticed difficulty with this reading is its inability to reconcile the account of objective validity and the role of the categories as necessary conditions thereof in the *Prolegomena* with that of the *Critique*. Rather than regarding the former as an attempt to provide a bare-bones sketch of the central argument of the objective side of the Deduction, which is evidently how Kant viewed it, this reading forces one to consider it as a total abandonment or radical distortion of the latter.

An essential ingredient in the *Prolegomena*'s version of the Transcendental Deduction is its correlation of the distinction between judgments of perception and judgments of experience with two ways in which perceptions can be connected in consciousness: in "a consciousness of my state" or in "a consciousness in general" (Pro 4: 300_9; 94). By the former Kant understands an awareness of the relations in which perceptions stand in one's own mind at a given time and under particular conditions, and the underlying claim is that, though involving an act of thought, and therefore a judgment, such a consciousness cannot lay claim to objectivity because of the contingency of these relations, which prevents their projection from the particular circumstances of the perceiver to all conceivable circumstances. By contrast, a connection of perceptions in consciousness in general allows for such a projection because it is governed by a priori rules in the form of pure concepts of the understanding, which hold independently of these circumstances.

The question, then, is what Kant understood by "consciousness in general" (*Bewusstsein überhaupt*), a phrase which appears three other times in the *Prolegomena* but on only five other occasions in the remainder of Kantian corpus.[19] Given the way in which Kant often uses the ubiquitous particle "*überhaupt*," one might expect

---

[17]   Guyer (1979), 161. In my view, the only thing that is clear about the matter is that Guyer bases his own reading of the Deduction on this assumption.

[18]   Although he does not refer to methodological solipsism, the view that the conclusions that Kant draws in the Transcendental Deduction are supposed to be derived from an analysis of the conditions of the consciousness of the unity or identity of the self has been characterized by Thöle (1991), 2, as the standard interpretation and his monograph contains a systematic critique of this reading. Moreover, other interpreters emphasize the inter-subjective or trans-personal dimension of Kant's account. Prominent among these are Walsh (1975), esp. 49–59, and Rohs (1978), 307–78.

[19]   The others are B143; KU 5: 484_{17}; 346; Br. 11: 376_{18}; 434; and R 5927 18: 389_6; 307. This list is taken from Amrhein (1909), 49–52.

that he would understand by it consciousness as such, considered in abstraction from all the features that differentiate particular consciousnesses, just as "*Ding*" or "*Gegenstand überhaupt*" refers to a thing or object considered as such, or qua thing or object. It is evident that this cannot be the correct rendering, however, since that would undermine the whole point of the distinction between a connection in the consciousness of one's state (or a particular consciousness) and in consciousness in general. This requires rendering the latter as "universal consciousness" (or some close variant thereof) and understanding it as referring to a norm shared by all members of the community of discursive cognizers, which stipulates the rules under which the projection or universalization of a connection of perceptions is warranted. These rules are the categories, and since for Kant this projection takes the form of a judgment, it occurs through the subsumption of the empirical concepts united in the judgment under them.

While it is obvious that in the *Prolegomena* Kant treats consciousness in general as the functional equivalent of transcendental apperception, since he assigns to it the objectifying role that he gives to the latter and its unity in the *Critique*, it is not so obvious that they can be considered equivalent in a more substantive sense. As already noted, the difference is that, while the unity of apperception refers to the unity of the I, qua thinking thing, consciousness in general appears to assume something like a "transcendental we." Closer consideration, however, indicates that these are actually two sides of the same coin and that the difference between them is one of emphasis rather than substance. In other words, though the Deduction in the *Critique* focuses on the unity (or identity) of consciousness and the *Prolegomena* on its universality, these two features, like universality and necessity, reciprocally imply each other, which makes it possible to regard the discussion in the *Prolegomena* as a simplified and more accessible surrogate for the Deduction in the *Critique* rather than as a radically distinct line of argument.

Although it is implicit rather than explicitly presented as such, this reciprocity is illustrated in the important note to A117 discussed in Chapter 6, where Kant appeals to the notion of a transcendental consciousness, which he contrasts with an empirical consciousness. We saw that Kant there characterizes the former as "the consciousness of myself as original apperception" and claims that all empirical consciousness has a necessary relation to it. It is this necessary relation between transcendental and empirical consciousness that is of interest to us here, because it precisely parallels the relation between the unification of representations in a particular consciousness or, equivalently, the consciousness of one's state (at a particular time and under given conditions) and in consciousness in general in the *Prolegomena*.

First, a unification of representations in the mental state of an individual at a particular time and under particular circumstances is what Kant means by an empirical consciousness. Its salient feature is the contingency of the relation between its perceptual contents, which in the language of the *Prolegomena* yields only a judgment of perception without a warranted claim to objectivity. Second, transcendental consciousness, like consciousness in general, grounds objectivity by providing a standpoint that is invariant with respect to the contingent contents of the various episodes of empirical consciousness. Once again, the apparent difference is that here the invariant factor is the I, which remains numerically identical (one and the same I) throughout all the episodes of empirical consciousness to which it can be attached. But precisely because it is empirical consciousness that furnishes this I with its representational content, this transcendental or pure consciousness is without any content of its own that could individuate it, which means that by default it is a universal consciousness, which makes it a true counterpart of the consciousness in general of the *Prolegomena*.

Finally, Kant's claim that when we relate our representations to an object in a judgment, we are presuming that the judgment is valid "at all times for us and for everyone else" involves two distinct but closely related points. First, to say that the judgment is "valid at all times for us" is to say that its validity is not a function of one's cognitive state at a particular time or, equivalently, of the relation of one's representations in empirical consciousness; but, rather, of their relation in consciousness in general, which remains numerically identical throughout changes in empirical consciousness and, as already noted, is the counterpart of the transcendental consciousness of the A-Deduction. Second, for the very same reason it is also valid "for everyone else," i.e., universally valid.

C) *Judgments of Perception*: Having analyzed Kant's conception of objective validity and its application to judgments of experience, we turn next to judgments of perception. The discussion will be divided into three parts: (1) an analysis of the discursive nature of such judgments, which is essential to seeing why Kant characterizes them as judgments; (2) an examination of the relation between judgments of perception and the categories; (3) a consideration of the roles that the conception of a judgment of perception plays in the *Prolegomena* and more broadly in Kant's account of empirical cognition.

1) *Judgments of perception as judgments*: Insofar as judgments of perception contain the logical connection of representations they are judgments in the sense of being products of discursive thought. The problem, however, is understanding how there could be such a thing as a *logical* connection of *perceptions*.[20] Clearly, any such connection must be in a thinking subject, since only for such a subject could there be anything like a logical connection; but this leaves unexplained how this connection could be *between perceptions*. Simply put, perceptions do not appear to be the sort of things that are capable of logical connections, as contrasted with mere associations.[21] Expressed in Sellarsian terms, the association of perceptions occurs in the logical space of causes rather than reasons. To which one might add that judgment, as both

---

[20] The problem is noted by Freudiger (1991), esp. 418–21.
[21] See R 3051 and R 3053 16: 633.

Kant and the tradition conceived it, involves the relation between *concepts* rather than perceptions.

This focus on perceptions reflects the fact that Kant is here concerned exclusively with empirical judgment rather than judgment in general. Empirical judgments involve perceptions in the sense of *perceivings*, since these constitute their matter. The difference between the two species of empirical judgment concerns the manner in which the relations between these perceivings are thought: either as holding only between them in the consciousness of my state or as holding for any observer in the relevant circumstances (consciousness in general), and therefore of the object.

Kant divides his examples of judgments of perception in the *Prolegomena* into two classes: those that can and those that cannot be transformed into judgments of experience by the addition of a category. As examples of the latter Kant lists: "the room is warm, the sugar sweet, the wormwood repugnant" (Pro 4: 299_{10-11}; 299). The examples of the former are: "the air is elastic" (Pro 4: 300_7; 94) and "If the sun shines on the stone, it becomes warm" (Pro 4: 301_{29}; 95). In the first example of a transformable judgment of perception, the corresponding judgment of experience has the same semantic form, which makes it impossible to determine its epistemic form (whether it is a judgment of perception or experience) by simply inspecting it. This is possible with the second example, however, where the corresponding judgment of experience is the straightforwardly causal judgment: "The sun warms the stone" (Pro 4: 301_{33-4}; 95). It is therefore evident in this case that the distinction is between a judgment that merely affirms a constant conjunction and one that affirms a causal connection between the same data. And it is also evident that the category responsible for the difference is that of cause.

The distinctive feature of judgments of perception is their irreducibly first-person nature. They express how things seem to a subject under certain conditions and, as such, make no claim to universalizability. In their categorical form they can be expressed schematically as "It seems to me that P." Although others could have similar perceptions under similar conditions, if the judgment concerns merely the relation between these perceptions in the subject's own conscious state it can make no demand on their agreement.

Underlying Kant's account is his identification of thinking and judging (Pro 4: 304_{31-2}; 98). As already noted, since judgments of perception involve acts of thinking, they are proper judgments with their own mode of validity. Accordingly, even though such judgments are based on nothing more than how perceivings are connected in the mental state of a particular subject, Kant needs to distinguish them from mere associations, e.g., touching the stone when the sun is shining on it and having a sensation of heat. While a sentient being lacking the capacity to think would likewise have a sensation of heat when touching the stone and modify its behavior accordingly, such a being could not be said to have recognized that there is an invariable connection between perceptions in its mental state, much less that there is a causal connection between the heat and the action of the sun on the stone.

Indeed, a merely sentient being could not even form judgments such as "sugar is sweet," since this requires a conceptual capacity.

This still leaves us, however, with the problem with which we began: how can perceptions stand in the logical relations necessary for being connected in judgment? Apart from providing a definition of perception as "an intuition of which I am conscious" (Pro 4: 300₅), which is basically equivalent to the one contained in the Critique (A320/B376), Kant has precious little to say on the topic in the Prolegomena. Nevertheless, it is clear that the fundamental point is that if perceptions are to be capable of logical as opposed to causal or merely associative connections they must contain a conceptual component. Moreover, Kant gives an indication of his under-lying position when he remarks that judgments of experience must add something "beyond the sensory intuition and its logical connection (in accordance with which the intuition has been rendered universal through comparison in a judgment)" (Pro 4: 304₁₇₋₁₈; 98). To say that the intuition has been "rendered universal" is to say that it has been brought under a concept; while saying that this universalization has been accomplished "by comparison in a judgment" refers to the logical activities of reflection, comparison, and abstraction through which concepts on Kant's view are formed.[22] Otherwise expressed, the perceivings, which Kant claims are connected according to their logical relations in judgments of perception, are to be considered not only as the products of a unification of a sensible manifold through the synthesis of apprehension-cum-reproduction, but also as recognized in an empirical concept. This is clearly the case in Kant's examples, where the items judged to be connected in the mental state of the subject are not raw perceptions, but conceptualized ones. Indeed, this must be the case if judgments of perception are to be considered judgments in contrast to mere associations.

2) *Judgments of perception and the categories*: We have seen that Kant claims that judgments of perceptions require the logical connection of perceptions in a thinking subject but not a category, and that the categories first enter the picture when a judgment of perception is transformed into a judgment of experience through subsumption under a category. The problem, however, is that this seems difficult to reconcile not only with what Kant maintains in both versions of the Transcen-dental Deduction in the Critique, but also with his own examples of judgments of perception and their transformation into judgments of experience in the Prolegom-ena. And we have also seen that the Prolegomena provides two examples of a transformable judgment of perception: (1) "The air is elastic," which with the subsumption of "air" under a category becomes a judgment of experience; and (2) "If the sun shines on the stone, it becomes warm," which with the subsumption of "sun" under a category becomes "The sun warms the stone." Even accepting what Kant says about these examples, the most that can be claimed is that the judgments of

---

[22] On the latter point see Longuenesse (1998), esp. 107–30.

perception do not involve the three categories of relation, which in the *Prolegomena* he refers to as substance, cause, and community (Pro 4: 303_{15-17}; 97).[23] And this leaves open the possibility that the other categories might also be involved in different ways.[24]

In fact, it has often been noted that Kant's judgments of perception involve at least the categories of quantity and quality.[25] For example, the warmth referred to in the judgment of perception that Kant cites in the *Prolegomena* obviously has a degree, and therefore an intensive magnitude, which presupposes the categories of quality; just as it can be said of the stone that it has a certain size and weight, and therefore an extensive magnitude. More generally, the problem is that because of his focus on the transformation of judgments of perception into judgments of experience, Kant left unmentioned another way in which categories are claimed to be necessary conditions of experience in both editions of the *Critique*; viz., as conditions of apprehension.

Moreover, the situation is even more problematic, since among the categories of relation the only one that Kant discusses in connection with his examples is causality. As already noted, the role of this concept in the second example is evident and does not call for further discussion at this point, since the judgment of experience "The sun warms the stone" is explicitly causal. But the same cannot be said about "The air is elastic." Since this judgment is in the categorical form and qua judgment of experience predicates a property (elasticity) of an entity (air), one would expect Kant to claim that the category at work is substance. What he actually claims, however, is that here too the judgment involves a subsumption under the category of cause on the grounds that this concept renders it (the air) "hypothetical with respect to expansion" (4: 301_3; 95). And in explanation of this Kant notes that,

This expansion is thereby represented not only as belonging merely to my perception of the air in my state of perception or in several of my states or in the state of others, but as *necessarily* belonging to it, and the judgment: the air is elastic, becomes universally valid and thereby for the first time a judgment of experience, because certain judgments beforehand, which subsume the intuition of the air under the concept of cause and effect, and thereby determine the perceptions not merely with respect to each other in my subject, but with respect to the form of judging in general (here, the hypothetical), and in this way makes the empirical judgment universally valid.   (Pro 4: 301_{3-13}; 95)

Following the illuminating analysis of this passage by Longuenesse, the salient points are that Kant regards elasticity as one of the two fundamental properties of matter, specifically, its expansive force, which is the property through which it fills space (MAN 4: 500; 212), and that it is derived by subsuming this concept of matter under the category of cause. Assuming that air is something material rather than mere

[23] In the *Critique* Kant provides a more detailed characterization of these categories, which emphasizes their relational nature. See A80/B106.
[24] The point is noted by Prauss (1971), 163.
[25] For a recent statement of this view, see Pollok (2012), 115, 120–1.

empty space, it follows that "The air is elastic" can be shown to be objectively valid, and therefore not merely a judgment of perception, since by directly subsuming it under the dynamical property of elasticity one is *eo ipso* also subsuming it indirectly under the category of cause. And in light of this Longuenesse explains Kant's claim that the category renders the judgment "hypothetical with respect to expansion" as an oblique reference to the fact that, due to its elasticity, air can be known to behave in different ways under different circumstances.[26]

Although Longuenesse does not present it as such, her analysis underscores what we have seen to be a pervasive problem with Kant's account; viz., his penchant for using causal judgments to illustrate a more general point regarding the objectifying role of the categories in *all* objectively valid empirical judgments. This is a problem because, as we have also seen, Kant links the latter with a normative necessity, understood as a demand for universal agreement, which is distinct from the necessary connection that is either affirmed or presupposed in causal judgments.

In sum, there are three problems posed by these examples of transformable judgments of perception and the role of the categories in their transformation. (1) Kant's analysis applies only to the categories of relation, which, since this is the only function that he assigns to the categories in the *Prolegomena*, means that he cannot plausibly claim to have provided a comprehensive deduction of them. (2) By neglecting the concept of substance, Kant's analysis of the judgment of experience regarding the elasticity of air, together with the lack of any example that might suggest a possible role for the category of community, suggests that of the relational categories only causality does any heavy lifting, thereby in effect further narrowing the scope of the deduction to that single category. (3) By appealing to examples featuring causality in an effort to illustrate the thesis that only a category can ground the necessity that pertains to every empirical judgment to which objective validity is ascribed, Kant focuses the reader's attention on the wrong kind of necessity, thereby obfuscating his central point regarding the equivalence of objective validity and a necessary (subjective) universality.

I think that Kant should be found guilty on all three counts, though with mitigating circumstances. While it is impossible here to explore the charges further, I shall say a word about their mitigation. Proceeding in reverse order, we have seen that Kant does provide an account of the normative necessity that applies to empirical judgment as such, not merely to causal judgments. Accordingly, the problem concerns Kant's somewhat careless use of examples rather than his underlying theory.

The account of "The air is elastic" and presumably other categorical judgments of experience as falling under the category of cause rather than substance must be considered in light of Kant's view of the relation between these categories. Although Kant held that they express two distinct relations (inherence and dependence), he

[26] Longuenesse (1998), 174–7.

also maintained in the *Critique* that action or force, which are predicables of cause (A82/B109), function as the empirical criteria of substance (A204–5/B249–50). Such criteria are necessary because substance itself is unperceivable and, as such, can be cognized only through the actions through which it expresses itself.[27] Moreover, while Kant does not provide an example of a judgment of experience involving the concept of community and its contrast with a corresponding judgment of perception, he arguably could have done so.[28]

Finally, in mitigation of Kant's failure to note that the mathematical categories are operative in judgments of perception, I shall note two points. First, doing so would have required him to introduce the issue of perceptual synthesis, which would have greatly complicated the story. Second, Kant does deal with the matter indirectly by distinguishing between the functions and the mode of proof of the various principles corresponding to the categories, and even uses the notion of warmth to illustrate the conception of an intensive magnitude. (Pro 4: 308–10; 101–3).[29]

3) *The role of judgments of perception in the deduction in the Prolegomena and in Kant's epistemology*: Considered from a purely strategic point of view, it is clear that Kant uses the conception of a judgment of perception didactically in the *Prolegomena* to illustrate what an empirical judgment would be like on the assumption that it consists merely in the comparison of empirical concepts, without the inclusion of any a priori elements.[30] The point is that on this view all empirical judgments would be merely judgments of perception, which, given the normative conception of experience assumed throughout, would mean that experience is impossible.

Although this appears to be an essential part of the story, the fact that it cannot be the whole story is evident from Kant's previously cited claim that "All our judgments are at first merely judgments of perception" (Pro 4: 298_9; 92). In our initial consideration of the passage that begins with this claim the focus was on Kant's characterization of the objective validity of a judgment as its necessary universal validity; but the claim that judgments of experience are to be regarded as the products of a transformation of judgments of perception indicates that Kant attributed to the latter

---

[27] Kant notes this in his discussion of the psychological ideas in the *Prolegomena*, which corresponds to the Paralogisms in the *Critique*. Moving from the self as substance to phenomenal substance as such, he there argues that our discursive understanding prevents us from thinking of anything that meets the condition of an absolute subject, from which it follows that "all real properties by which we cognize bodies are mere accidents—even impenetrability, which must always be conceived only as the effect of a force" (Pro 4: 333–4; 125).

[28] Kant provides such an example (or at least the materials for one) in the second edition version of the Third Analogy with his analysis of the cognition of the objective coexistence or simultaneity of the Earth and the Moon (B257–8) through the category of community or interaction. Presumably, the idea would be that the category converts what is initially merely a subjectively valid estimation of the coexistence of the phenomena (and therefore a judgment of perception) into an objective one (and therefore a judgment of experience). I analyze Kant's argument in Allison (2004), 260–74.

[29] Kant also appeals to the categories of quantity; though he illustrates this through their role in mathematics rather than empirical cognition. See Pro 4: 301_{20}–2_2.

[30] The classical formulation of this view is by Cassirer (1953), 245–6.

a positive function in his overall account of empirical cognition, if not of its transcendental conditions. Accordingly, it seems that in the *Prolegomena* Kant assigned to the concept of a judgment of perception two distinct roles, viewing it both as a didactic device for rejecting what he takes to be an inadequate view of judgment and as an integral part of his own account of empirical cognition.[31]

In order to comprehend this second role it is necessary to keep in mind Kant's equation of thinking with judging. Since what is subsumed under a category in a judgment of experience for Kant must already have been brought under a concept, it follows that such judgments presuppose a prior judgment in which this initial conceptualization is achieved. This is the epistemic function of judgments of perception. Moreover, the judgment of perception is not the only conception to which Kant assigns this preliminary function. Indeed, if we consider the Kantian corpus as a whole, this role is usually assigned to the "preliminary [or provisional] judgment" (*vorläufiges Urtheil*).[32]

Unfortunately, the task of providing a concise account of this conception is complicated by Kant's failure to offer a formal definition. Perhaps the closest thing to one that he supplies is the characterization of a preliminary judgment as one that precedes investigation (LD-W 24: 737_{10-11}; 472). And his examples include the judgment that a book that one has not yet read is good because of the repute of its author (PE 29: $24_{36}-5_1$); or, alternatively, because of its title (WL 24: 861_{28-9}); the judgment of a person's character on the basis of his appearance and bearing (WL 24: 861_{22-4}; 313); and the judgment that the sun rises and sets on the basis of what one perceives (ML₁ 28: 234_{16-17}; 52). Although these examples might suggest that Kant considers a preliminary judgment simply as one that is rash or precipitous, that this is not the case is evident from his distinction between a preliminary judgment and a prejudice. Thus, in one place Kant claims that prejudices are the exact opposite of preliminary judgments because, whereas preliminary judgments are based on reflection, which involves an appeal to reasons or objective grounds for holding something to be true, in prejudices one holds something to be true without any reflection (WL 24: 862; 314). Elsewhere, Kant maintains that "Prejudices are preliminary judgments *insofar as they are accepted as principles*" (JL 9: 75; 578). While this may suggest more

---

[31] My emphasis on the dual function of judgments of perception in the *Prolegomena* is one of two major respects in which my interpretation of such judgments differs from that of Longuenesse, who evidently denies that they play anything like the didactic role, which I (following Cassirer) attribute to them (Longuenesse (1998a), 167–97). The other is her denial that such judgments involve the categories as distinct from the logical functions. I discuss this aspect of her position, which extends also to the first part of the B-Deduction, in Allison (2012), 31–48. I am quite sympathetic, however, to her central claim that reflection according to the logical forms of judgment is essential to understanding such judgments, which she rightly claims to have been the first to have pointed out ((Longuenesse (1998a), 169, note 5). Although I express it in different terms, I believe that my account is compatible with this view.

[32] Michael Young has translated the term as "provisional judgments," but for reasons that should become apparent, I find "preliminary judgments" preferable.

commonality between them than the preceding, they really come to much the same thing; for an essential feature of a genuinely preliminary judgment is that it does not inflate its assessment into a principle, by which Kant presumably meant a judgment that is firmly established. And, as Kant also notes in this context, even though a prejudice can on occasion amount to a true preliminary judgment, it nonetheless involves a deception in that "subjective grounds are falsely held to be objective, *due to lack of reflection*" (JL 9: 76; 579).

Of greater interest is the distinction between preliminary and determinate judgments, since it provides a framework in terms of which we can understand the distinction between judgments of perception and judgments of experience. As already suggested, Kant understands by a preliminary judgment an initial assessment, which is subject to revision. Accordingly, its two defining features are primacy and revisability. Kant's main emphasis, however, is on the former, since he considered such judgments to be the indispensable starting point of any cognitive endeavor. As Kant put it at one point, "We do not attain complete certainty except by means of investigation; but any investigation must still be preceded by a preliminary judgment" (LB 24: 164; 129). By contrast, a determinate judgment is one that emerges as the result of this investigation in which the weight of the reasons for and against the initial assessment has been determined. Thus, they are considered respectively as the *terminos a quo* and the *terminos ad quem* of the cognitive process. And whereas a preliminary judgment is merely problematic, a determinate one purports to be assertoric in virtue of the process through which it has been determined.[33]

Although this points to a parallelism between the preliminary and determinate judgments and the judgments of perception and judgments of experience distinctions, the overlap is not complete. For one thing, it holds only for those judgments of perception that are transformable to judgments of experience, since the non-transformable ones are not viewed by Kant as the starting point of a cognitive process that could end in an objectively valid claim. For another, the distinction between preliminary and determinate judgments, as Kant characterizes it in the various versions of his logic lectures, is far broader than the distinction between judgments of perception and judgments of experience. Whereas judgments of perception are limited to empirical cognitions, Kant's examples of provisional judgments indicate that they encompass a broad array of judgments, including value judgments such as judgments of a person's character. But since preliminary judgments for Kant do include empirical judgments, such as that concerning the rising and setting of the sun, which might well be viewed as a judgment of perception, it does seem plausible to

---

[33] This does not mean, however, that a determinate judgment is non-revisable, since that would make it apodictic rather than merely assertoric. At least in the case of empirical determinate judgments, it is rather that they are to be regarded as well-confirmed hypotheses, which would require further contrary evidence to be overturned.

suggest that judgments of perception are a species of provisional judgments.[34] Indeed, such a relationship is strongly suggested by Kant's analysis of "The air is elastic," which though initially considered a mere judgment of perception, became a judgment of experience as the result of the air being subjected to certain tests, which showed that it retains this property under different conditions. Be that as it may, however, the crucial point is that Kant's account of empirical cognition requires something like judgments of perception to serve as the starting point of a cognitive process that culminates in judgments deemed objectively valid.[35]

II

Our next text is a note that Kant added to the Preface of his *Metaphysical Foundations of Natural Science* (1786) (henceforth referred to as "the Note") in which he responds to criticisms of his account of the Transcendental Deduction in both the first edition of the *Critique* and the *Prolegomena* (MAN 4: 474–6; 188–90). Although the work itself occupies an important place in Kant's theoretical philosophy, since it marks a return to his original project of a metaphysics of nature on a reduced scale, our concern here must be limited to this note.[36] But since in order to understand the Note it is necessary to be cognizant of the criticisms to which it responds, the discussion will be divided into two parts: an account of these criticisms and an analysis of Kant's response to them.

A) *The criticisms*: The Note was occasioned by a review by Johann Schultz of Johann August Heinrich Ulrich's *Institutiones Logicae et Metaphysicae* (1785). A somewhat heterodox Wolffian philosopher and professor at Jena, who was the first German

---

[34] While I am not sure that he would accept this characterization of the relation between preliminary judgments and judgments of perception, I am indebted to Svendsen (1999), 285–95 for his discussion of the former and of their relevance to the understanding of judgments of perception.

[35] Another analogue to the contrast between judgments of perception and judgments in experience in the Kantian corpus is the distinction between having an opinion (*Meinen*) and knowing (*Wissen*), which together with believing (*Glauben*) are three forms of taking something for true (*Fürwahrhalten*). Setting aside believing, which Kant links essentially with the practical, the distinction between having an opinion and knowing turns on the notions of subjective and objective sufficiency. Having an opinion with regard to a matter of fact, by which Kant apparently understands recognizing that it is *only* an opinion, involves the consciousness that one's grounds for taking a judgment to be true are neither subjectively nor objectively sufficient; whereas when the grounds of this judgment are recognized as both subjectively and objectively sufficient it is considered knowing. See A820–31/B848–59; JL 9: 66–7; 571–2; BL 24: 218–25; 173–8; LPö 24: 420–3; LD-W 24: 732–5; 467–70; WL 24: 850–6; 303–8; and R 2422–504; 16: 359–96. As was the case with the preliminary judgment, having an opinion cannot be simply identified with making a judgment of perception, since the former is the broader conception; but they appear to be closely related, particularly since Kant attributes a subjective validity to both.

[36] The reduction in scale is evident from the title of the work, since it indicates that rather than a full-scale metaphysics of nature, which Kant still envisaged as part of his complete system of metaphysics, its concern is only with the metaphysical first principles of natural science. As such its systematic function is analogous to the *Groundwork for the Metaphysics of Morals*, which was published one year earlier. The difference is that whereas Kant did eventually publish his *Metaphysics of Morals* (1796–97), he never did produce a metaphysics of nature; though his work in that direction is contained in his *Opus Postumum*.

professor to lecture on Kant, Ulrich attempted in this work to reconcile the main positive results of the *Critique* (e.g., the ideality of space and time and the validity of the Principles of Pure Understanding) with a Leibnizian metaphysics by arguing that, given its own premises, the *Critique* should not have limited cognition to objects of possible experience. But rather than considering the Transcendental Deduction, Ulrich focused his attention on the Analogies, arguing that the first two demonstrate, pace Kant, that the categories of causality and substance apply to noumena as well as phenomena, which in the case of substance is the I.[37]

What evidently disturbed Kant the most, however, was not Ulrich's book, which, though critical, was more favorable to Kant than many of the earlier discussions of the *Critique*, but the largely favorable review of that work by Schultz, who was both a close friend and disciple of Kant and who had authored the first commentary on the *Critique*.[38] Although the review was published anonymously, Kant was aware of its authorship and apparently considered it an act of apostasy on Schultz's part.

From Kant's standpoint, the basic problem with the review was what it said about the Transcendental Deduction. Instead of chastising Ulrich for ignoring it, as he might have expected from a trusted disciple, Schultz had sympathized with Ulrich's neglect of the Deduction on the grounds of its obscurity. Evidently deeply conflicted by the matter, after succinctly summarizing the main points of Ulrich's argument, Schultz, writing in his own voice, remarks:

The reviewer must admit that he found his own doubts reflected in many of the author's doubts. This agreement is, of course, not a presumption of their correctness, but perhaps only a mere consequence of a long familiar mode of thought. Nevertheless, it is at least certain that these doubts, which no impartial person can take as entirely insignificant, directly concern the main foundation of the entire Kantian doctrine and that the latter, no matter how much it contains of what is excellent, important, and indubitably certain, does not yet carry the sort of apodeictic conviction that would be necessary to an **unrestricted** acceptance of what is really its main purpose. At the same time, the doubts that I have mentioned do not have such a degree of evidence that one could take them to be a complete refutation of the Kantian system. Many, much deeper insights into the entire totality of the system would be necessary for that to occur. The main element of **Kant's** system, on which the true limitation of pure reason depends, rests primarily on the **deduction** of the pure concepts of the understanding... It is regrettable, therefore, that the author has not in the first instance examined it. But perhaps it was only its obscurity that prevented him from doing so, an obscurity that occurs primarily here, in this part of the *Critique* that should be the clearest, if the Kantian system is to afford complete conviction.[39]

Not content with the complaint of obscurity, which Kant readily acknowledged, Schultz provides a specific example of it, which threatens to undermine what he takes

---

[37] For a discussion of Ulrich's complex and shifting views of Kant and Kant's reaction see Beiser (1987), 203–10.

[38] See note 45.   [39] Landau (1991), 246–7; Sassen (2000), 212–13.

to be the central claim of the Deduction that the categories are necessary conditions of the possibility of experience. According to Schultz, Kant's argument for this thesis, which he formulates in the language of the *Prolegomena* rather than the *Critique*, turns on an equivocation and leads to a dilemma. The equivocation concerns Kant's use of the term "experience." Schultz claims that sometimes Kant uses it to mean simply judgments of perception and other times judgments of experience, which he notes gives two quite distinct aims for the Deduction: one in which the objective reality of the categories is a necessary condition of the possibility of judgments of perception; the other in which it is a necessary condition of the possibility of judgments of experience.[40]

Despite Kant's denial in the *Prolegomena* that judgments of perception involve a use of the categories, Schultz maintains that Kant does construe them this way in the *Critique*, particularly in the proofs of the Analogies. Focusing on Kant's claim that the manifold is always given successively, Schultz takes the point of these proofs to be to show that the categories are necessary for the determination of what is (object-ively) simultaneous and what is successive, which, appealing to the language of the *Prolegomena*, he regards as requiring merely a judgment of perception. Moreover, he claims that this thesis is false, since we can make such determinations, i.e., judge that *x* is either simultaneous with or succeeds *y*, without appealing to a category. And he expresses the main point of his objection in the form of a rhetorical question, which is intended as a *reductio* of this view:

[I]f I cannot perceive anything without first bringing my empirical representations under an objectively valid category, does this not say: in order to be able to judge **empirically**, I must first judge *a priori* and, more specifically, synthetically? For example, would I have to know that the sunlight is the cause of the warmth of the stone in order to be able to say: when the sun shines, the stone grows warm?[41]

The other possible interpretation of the aim of the Deduction; viz., demonstrating that the objective reality of categories is necessary for judgments of experience, which Schultz takes to be Kant's true intent, is likewise rejected, albeit on different grounds. The problem here is not that the claim is false, but that it is tautologous or trivial, which, he notes, had already been pointed out by Ulrich. As Schultz cautiously puts it,

[U]nless we are mistaken, the preceding proposition [that no judgment of experience is possible without the objective reality of the categories] says nothing more than the following: if the categories did not have a necessary relation to appearances, that is, if they did not have **objective** validity in them, then we would never be able to make *a priori*, that is, universally and **objectively valid** judgments about appearances. We would not be able to say, for example, that warmth follows always and **necessarily** upon sunshine.[42]

---

[40] Landau (1991), 247; Sassen (2000), 213.
[41] Landau (1991), 247; Sassen (2000), 213.
[42] Landau (1991), 248; Sassen (2000), 214.

Schultz thus finds Kant caught up in a dilemma, according to which the central claim of the Deduction is either false or trivial, depending upon the sense of "experience" for which the categories are supposed to supply the necessary conditions.[43] Moreover, he also proposes in the form of a conjecture "for further examination" a possible way to avoid this dilemma. The avoidance comes at a high cost, however, and it is not clear how seriously Schultz intended it. It consists in replacing Kant's thesis that the understanding prescribes laws to nature with the assumption of a pre-established harmony, grounded in the will of God, according to which "certain appearances (which are, after all, nothing other than representations in us or certain modifications of our consciousness) are always followed by certain other ones in the most orderly fashion, without there being the least **real** connection between them." As Schultz points out, on this scenario the categories of causality and reciprocity (he does not mention substance) would not be applicable to appearances and, rather than prescribing laws to nature, the understanding would only learn its merely apparent lawfulness from it a posteriori through perception.[44]

B) *Kant's response*: The Note is attached to a passage in which Kant claims that the schema for the completeness of a metaphysical system, whether of nature in general or, as in the present case, of corporeal nature, is provided by the table of categories (MAN 4: 473$_{35}$–4$_1$; 188). But though the Note begins with a reference to this table and emphasizes its importance for the "critical" project, the fact that it is not concerned (at least not directly) with the completeness issue makes it evident that the reference to the latter was used as a pretext for including the Note, which, in any event, does not stand in an organic relation to the text to which it is appended.

Kant indicates at the very beginning of the Note that his major concern is not with Ulrich's work, but with Schultz's review. What he specifically objects to are not doubts directed against the table itself, since both Ulrich and Schultz accept it as it stands. It is rather the doubts against the inferences drawn therefrom by Kant concerning "the determination of the limits [*Grenzbestimmung*] of the entire faculty of pure reason, and thus all metaphysics," which were expressed by both Ulrich in his book and Schultz in his review (MAN 4: 474$_{3–8}$; 188). And what particularly bothered Kant about these doubts is that he considered them as directed against the principle basis of his system, which therefore provide grounds "for thinking that this system, with respect to its principle aim, does not come close to carrying the apodictic conviction that is required for eliciting an unqualified acceptance" (MAN 4: 474$_{8–12}$; 188). Kant remarks that this principle basis is said to be the Transcendental Deduction, as expounded partly in the *Critique* and partly in the *Prolegomena*, "and, which, however, in the part of the *Critique* that ought to be precisely the most clear, is rather the most obscure, or even revolves in a circle, etc." (MAN 4: 474$_{12–15}$; 188–9).

---

[43] On this dilemma, see Thöle (1991), 279–80 and Pollok (2008), 327 and (2012), 118.
[44] Landau (1991), 248; Sassen (2000), 214.

It is evident from Kant's language that he is referring to Schultz's review, since it emphasized the centrality of the Deduction to the project of the *Critique* and lamented its obscurity, which, in Schultz's view, prevented it from attaining the apodictic conviction at which it aimed. To be sure, Schultz did not charge Kant's argument with circularity in so many words, but this objection is clearly implicit in the second horn of his proposed dilemma. What is most notable about Kant's response, however, is that rather than addressing the circularity charge and the other objections alluded to in his "etc.," he changes the subject by downplaying the significance of the Deduction. Kant writes:

I direct my reply to these objections only to their principle point, namely, the claim that *without an entirely clear and sufficient deduction of the categories* the system of the *Critique of Pure Reason* totters on its foundation. I assert, on the contrary, that the system of the *Critique* must carry apodictic certainty for whoever ascribes (as the reviewer does) to my propositions concerning the sensible character of all or intuition, and the adequacy of the table of categories, as determinations of our consciousness derived from the logical functions in judgments in general, because it is erected upon the proposition *that the entire speculative use of our reason never reaches further than to objects of possible experience*. For if we can prove **that** the categories which reason must use in all its cognition can have no other use at all, except solely in relation to objects of possible experience (insofar as they simply make possible the form of thought in such experience), then, although the answer to the question **how** the categories make such experience possible is important enough for *completing* the deduction where possible, with respect to the principle end of the system, namely, the determination of the limits of pure reason, it is in no way *compulsory*, but merely *meritorious*. For the deduction is already carried *far enough* for this purpose if it shows that categories of thought are nothing but mere forms of judgment insofar as they are applied to intuitions (which for us are always sensible), and that they thereby first of all obtain objects and become cognitions; because this already suffices to ground with complete certainty the entire system of *Critique* properly speaking.   (MAN 4: 474_{15-39}; 189)

Kant attempts to illuminate this complex claim by drawing an analogy between his system of the *Critique* and Newton's system of universal gravitation. His point is that just as the Newtonian system remains intact despite the inexplicability of action at a distance, so the fundamental basis of his system "stands firm, even without a complete deduction of the categories" (MAN 4: 474_{40-1}; 189). Moreover, Kant contends that this is because this basis follows from three propositions: (1) that the table of categories contains the complete set of pure concepts of the understanding; (2) that there must also be pure intuitions to which these categories can be applied; and (3) "that these pure intuitions can never be anything other than forms of the appearances of outer or of inner sense (space and time), and therefore of the *objects of possible experience* alone" (MAN 4: 475_{3-29}; 189–90).

Since each of these propositions is deeply problematic, one might wonder how Kant could have so nonchalantly helped himself to them. But this is easily understood in light of the dialectical context of the Note, which indicates that they were selected by Kant because they had not been questioned either by Ulrich, who had called into question only Kant's refusal to extend the scope of the Principles, specifically the Analogies, beyond possible experience, or by Schultz, whose concern was limited to the Deduction.[45]

A striking feature of this portion of the Note is the difference between what Kant says here about the Deduction and what he had said in 1781. We have seen that in the Preface to the *Critique*, Kant had proclaimed that he was "acquainted with no investigations more important for getting to the bottom of that faculty we call the understanding and at the same time for the determination of the rules and boundaries of its use, than those I have undertaken in the second chapter of the Transcendental Analytic, under the title **Deduction of the Pure Concepts of the Understanding**" (Axvi). Similarly, in the introductory section of the Deduction itself he had insisted that "the reader must be convinced of the unavoidable necessity of such a transcendental deduction before he has taken a single step in the field of pure reason" (A88/B121).

By contrast, Kant now seems to suggest that one can take many steps in this field without having to concern oneself with a transcendental deduction, or at least without having to complete it. Kant indicates that by completing the Deduction he understands demonstrating *how* the categories make experience possible and that he does not regard this as absolutely essential to the main goal of the *Critique*, which he here characterizes in negative terms as restricting "the speculative use of our reason," which is to say the categories and the principles based upon them, to objects of possible experience.[46] Moreover, though he contends that this task is accomplished in the Deduction, he further diminishes the importance of the latter by suggesting that it is not strictly necessary for this task, since the restriction could also be inferred from the combination of the Aesthetic and "the Clue." But since the need to restrict the speculative or theoretical scope of the categories to objects of possible experience presupposes that they necessarily apply to such objects, it would seem that the Transcendental Deduction is absolutely essential for that task, which was the view of the *Critique*. In other words, there appears to be an ambiguity in Kant's formulation of the *that* issue, since it can be taken in either an inclusive or an

---

[45] It is noteworthy that Schultz does not express any of the concerns regarding the Deduction contained in his review of Ulrich in his brief treatment of the Deduction in his 1784 commentary on the *Critique*. See Schultz (1968).

[46] Although it is not evident from the text of the Note, Kant's reference to the *speculative* use of reason is crucial here, since it was during this time that he was articulating the essential features of his moral theory, which required a practical use of pure reason and with it of the categories, particularly freedom, which Kant regarded as a mode of causality. Thus, it was essential for Kant to be able to argue that, even though cognition through the categories is restricted to possible experience, their non-empirical origin allowed for their extension (for practical purposes) beyond the domain of experience. As we shall see in Chapter 9, this was also a crucial part of the distinction between thinking and cognizing through the categories that Kant emphasized in the B-Deduction. For a discussion of this issue in connection with Kant's views on the Deduction, see Thöle (1991), esp. 31–5.

exclusive sense. Taken in the former sense, the task of the Deduction is to demonstrate *that* the categories make experience possible, and therefore necessarily apply to objects of possible experience and only to such objects. Taken in the latter sense, it has only the second of these tasks. Although it seems evident that Kant wished the task to be understood in the inclusive sense, the little that he says in the Note that bears on that issue suggests that he assigns the positive part of the task to the Analytic of Principles rather than to the Deduction. At least this is the location of the source of the second of the three essential propositions that Kant takes for granted; viz., that the understanding contains synthetic a priori principles through which it subjects all objects that may be given to it to the categories. Moreover, this accords with Kant's procedure both in the *Prolegomena*, where, rather than including a special section for the Deduction, he incorporates its argument into the more general question of the possibility of a pure science of nature, and in the *Metaphysical Foundations of Natural Science*, where Kant's explicit concern is with the application of the Transcendental Principles of the Analytic to the empirical concept of matter.

What Kant says in the Note about the Deduction is reminiscent of what he had said about its subjective side in the A-Preface. Just as he there downplayed the significance of the latter with respect to the central concern of the *Critique*, though not the Deduction itself, which he described in positive terms as establishing and making comprehensible the objective validity of the understanding's a priori concepts (Axvi), so he now downplays the significance of the Deduction with respect to the main goal of the system of the *Critique*, which he characterizes in negative terms as restricting the speculative use of the categories to objects of possible experience. And just as in the A-Preface he had assigned to the subjective side of the Deduction the task of resolving a how-question, so he now attributes such a task to the Deduction as a whole. To be sure, the how-questions that are addressed in the two places are not the same: that to which Kant refers in the A-Preface is "How is the **faculty of thinking** itself possible" (Axvii), and that in the Note is how the categories make experience possible. But if, as was argued in Chapter 5, Kant is concerned with the real use of the understanding, then the difference between the two questions is more one of formulation than of substance.

This still leaves us with the question of why Kant expressed himself as he did in the Note, leaving the deeply misleading impression that in the *Critique* he did not assign to the Deduction the essential task of demonstrating *that* the categories are necessary conditions of the possibility of experience, or at least leaving the issue somewhat murky. In my view, the most likely explanation is that Kant expressed himself as he did in the Note for largely strategic reasons. In other words, while still unsatisfied with his initial formulation of the Deduction, and perhaps its replacement in the *Prolegomena* as well, and deeply disappointed by Schultz's failure to challenge Ulrich's main point (the extendibility of the categories and principles beyond possible experience), he takes upon himself the task of doing what he had expected

Schultz to have done, without having at the same time to mount a defense of the Deduction in its current imperfect form.

This view of Kant's intent finds further support in both the remainder of the Note and in his response to a query regarding it by Reinhold. I shall begin with the latter, which is contained in a letter to Kant dated October 12, 1787. In this letter, Reinhold, newly ensconced in Jena, introduces himself to Kant as the admiring author of *Letters on the Kantian Philosophy*; requests that if he finds his interpretation of Kant's philosophy in this work correct, he make a public announcement of this fact; informs him that Ulrich is attacking Kant's philosophy; and asks Kant to resolve a "seeming difficulty" that he had found in the Note. Speaking of the latter, Reinhold remarks: "[Y]ou [Kant] write very pointedly that the main foundation of your system is secure 'even without a complete deduction of the categories'—on the other hand in both the first and second editions of the *Critique of Pure Reason* [...] 'the indispensable necessity of that deduction is asserted and demonstrated.' "[47]

In response to Reinhold's understandable perplexity regarding Kant's declaration in the Note that, while important, the deduction is "yet not extremely necessary, after insisting upon its indispensability in the *Critique*," Kant replies in the last paragraph of his 1788 essay "On the Use of Teleological Principles in Philosophy" that,

One can easily see that in the former work [*The Metaphysical First Principles of Natural Science*] the deduction was considered only with a *negative* intention, namely in order to prove that with the categories *alone* (without sensible intuition) *no cognition* of things could come about—which becomes clear already if one turns only to the **exposition** of the categories (as logical functions applied merely to objects in general). Yet since we also engage in a use of the categories in which they actually pertain to the *cognition* of objects (of experience), the possibility of an objective validity of such concepts *a priori* in relation to the empirical had to be proven separately, so that they would not be judged to be without meaning or to have *originated* empirically. And that was the *positive* intention with respect to which the *deduction* is indeed indispensably necessary.   (GTP 8: 184_{13-25}; 218)

Although technically correct in its depiction of what he had said in the Note regarding the Deduction, Kant's account is again misleading. This is because in framing the issue in this way he glosses over what appears to have been the real source of Reinhold's perplexity; viz., Kant's failure even to mention the positive goal for which the Deduction is indispensably necessary, which I have suggested is to be understood as strategically motivated. As is generally recognized, Kant was engaged in a two-front war in the *Critique*, with the opponents being a skeptical empiricism, on the one hand, and a dogmatic rationalism, on the other. Since Ulrich's critique stemmed from the latter direction, Kant pointed his "critical" weapons there; thereby ignoring for the moment the other, equally significant, if not even more important front. Nevertheless, Kant does not totally ignore the positive side of the Deduction in

---

[47] Br 10: 500; 266.

the Note. In fact, what he says about it is its most important feature with respect to the understanding of Kant's view at the time regarding the still-unfinished work of the Deduction. Thus, immediately after formulating the three above-mentioned propositions, he claims that it follows from them that all use of pure reason extends only to objects of experience and "since nothing empirical can be the condition of *a priori* principles, the latter can be nothing more than principles of the possibility of experience in general." And from this he concludes that,

This alone is the true and sufficient basis for the determination of the limits of pure reason, but not the solution of the problem **how** experience is now possible by means of these categories, and only through these categories alone. The latter problem, although without it the structure still stands firm, has great importance nonetheless, and, as I now understand it [it can be solved with] just as much ease, since it can almost be accomplished through a single inference from the precisely determined definition of a *judgment* in general (an action through which given representations first become cognitions of an object). The obscurity that attaches to my earlier discussions in this part of the deduction (and which I do not deny), is to be attributed to the common fortunes of the understanding in its investigations, in which the shortest way is not the first way that it is aware of. Therefore, I shall take up the next opportunity to make up for this deficiency (which concerns only the manner of presentation, and not the ground of explanation, which is already stated correctly there).   (MAN 4: 475_{30}–6_{18}; 190)

Although Kant here acknowledges the truth of Schultz's obscurity charge, he ignores the latter's substantive claim regarding an equivocation in the use of the term "experience." Instead, he indicates that and how he intends to provide the much-needed clarity at the next opportunity, which turns out to be the second edition of the *Critique*, published the following year. Thus, the reader who has struggled through the twists and turns of the A-Deduction, with its preparatory and systematic sections, its arguments from above and below, is here informed that Kant now envisions the Deduction as accomplished "almost . . . through a single inference from the precisely determined definition of a *judgment* in general (an action through which given representations first become cognitions of an object)." Unfortunately, Kant's cryptic remark provides no clue regarding the nature of this "single inference" and the "almost" cries out for an explanation that Kant does not provide. Indeed from what Kant says here it remains unclear whether he had already worked out the structure of what was to become the B-Deduction or merely had a general idea of how it would proceed. Speaking for the latter alternative is the fact that the second part of the B-Deduction, where Kant supposedly will show how the categories make experience possible, cannot plausibly be regarded as based on a single inference (or even "almost" such an inference, whatever that may mean) from the definition of judgment that is provided in the first part.

We shall deal with these issues in Chapters 8 and 9, which are concerned with the B-Deduction. Our immediate concern, however, is with the final segment of the Note, in which Kant discusses Schultz's tentative proposal to replace the view that the understanding, through its categories, prescribes laws to nature with the postulation of a pre-established harmony between the order of representations in the mind and the course of nature. Referring to Schultz as "the perceptive reviewer," Kant writes:

This remedy would be much worse than the disease it is supposed to cure, and, on the contrary, actually cannot help at all. For the *objective necessity* that characterizes the pure concepts of the understanding (and the principles of their application to appearances), in the concept of cause in connection with the effect, for example, is still not forthcoming. Rather, it remains only subjectively necessary, but objectively merely contingent, placing together, precisely as Hume has it when he calls this mere illusion from custom. No system in the world can derive this necessity from anywhere else than the principles lying *a priori* at the basis of the possibility of *thinking itself*, through which alone the cognition of objects whose appearance is given to us, experience, becomes possible. Even if we suppose, therefore, that the explanation of **how** experience thereby becomes possible in the first place could never be sufficiently carried out, it still remains incontrovertibly certain **that** it is possible solely through these concepts, and, conversely, that these concepts are capable of meaning and use in no other relation than to objects of experience. (MAN 4: 476$_{23-40}$; 190)

This dismissive response to Schultz's proposal is not surprising. As we have already seen, Kant's fundamental objection to the appeal to such an hypothesis to account for the cognitive fit between the understanding and the order of nature, which in the A-Deduction he refers to as a transcendental affinity, is that it reduces the objective necessity requisite for cognition to a merely subjective necessity concerning the capacities and operations of the mind, which, as such, has no normative import. In short, like the more sophisticated naturalistic variants offered by Guyer and Westphal, it is a non-starter.

III

The final part of this chapter is concerned with a set of *Reflexionen* (R5923–35), which are attached to Baumgarten's discussion of causation in Kant's copy of the *Metaphysica*.[48] According to Adickes, they stem from 1783–84; but they were clearly composed during the period between the first and second editions of the *Critique*, since they are closely related to the accounts of the Deduction in the *Prolegomena* and the Note. The discussion is divided into three parts: the first contains an analysis of R5923, which is the most substantive of these *Reflexionen* and the one to which some of the others appear to be directly related; the second considers as a group the remaining *Reflexionen*, with a focus on what, if anything, each of them adds to our understanding of Kant's emerging conception of the aim and proof-structure of the Transcendental Deduction during the interlude period; the third provides an assessment of Kant's position at this point in time and contrasts it with that of the B-Deduction.

---

[48] Baumgarten (1926, 94–6; §307–18).

A) *R 5923*: Kant gives this *Reflexion* the heading: "Deductions of pure cognitions *a priori*" (18: 385$_7$; 305). It consists of eight paragraphs, each of which constitutes a distinct step in the argument.

(1) Kant begins with a statement of the restriction thesis with respect to concepts, as distinguished from "mere ideas," which, as in the *Critique*, are evidently considered as concepts in the broad sense.[49] The basic claim is that, inasmuch as concepts can be given "fully *in concreto*" only in experience, it is only there that their objective reality can be "fully exhibited." Accordingly, concepts the objective reality of which cannot be so given, i.e., ideas, are not assigned objective reality; though Kant adds that they can be assumed as hypotheses (18: 385$_{7-14}$; 305).[50]

(2) Having restricted the scope of cognition to possible experience, Kant replaces the initial question regarding the possibility of pure cognition a priori with one concerning the nature of experience; viz., "whether experience contains merely cognition that is given only *a posteriori*, or whether something is also encountered in it which is not empirical and yet contains the ground of the possibility of experience" (18: 385$_{16-19}$; 305). Kant's reasoning appears to be based on the assumption that the restriction allows for the replacement because it entails that a priori cognition is possible only if it concerns conditions of possible experience. Although this is not strictly true, since Kant neglects mathematical cognitions, he rectifies this in the next *Reflexion*, where, after denying that synthetic propositions a priori are possible from mere concepts, he asserts that they are possible either through the construction of concepts or "from rules that contain the possibility of experience and through perceptions become objective cognitions" (R 5924 18: 387$_{8-11}$; 306).

(3) Kant's next canvasses the contents of experience in which he finds two ingredients: immediate representations of the senses, i. e., intuitions, and consciousness. He stipulates that if this consciousness is immediately combined with the former it is called empirical consciousness and, following the definition in the *Critique*, states that if these representations are combined with consciousness they are called perceptions. The main point, however, is that "If experience were nothing more than a heap [*Anhäufung*][51] of perceptions, then nothing would be found in it which is not of empirical origin" (18: 385$_{23-6}$; 305), from which it follows that the required non-empirical element is not contained in the contents of empirical consciousness.

(4) This initial negative result leads Kant to analyze further the concept of experience and he notes that, in addition to the consciousness of perceptions, experience also involves cognition of sensible objects (18: 386$_{5-6}$; 305). Kant thus introduces the normative conception of experience, which is presupposed by the entire account.

---

[49]   At A320/B277 Kant refers to ideas as concepts of reason.

[50]   In the Doctrine of Method Kant discusses "transcendental hypotheses" and while denying them any explanatory import assigns them a function with respect to the practical use of reason (A772–82/B800–10).

[51]   I have substituted "heap" for Guyer's "agglomeration" as the rendering of Kant's *Anhäufung*.

Prior to doing so, however, he provides two reasons why the consciousness of perceptions does not yield cognition: (a) such consciousness (empirical consciousness) relates representations "only to our self as modifications of our condition;" and (b) "they are in this case separated among themselves, and are above all [*vornehmlich*][52] not cognition of any things and are related to no object" (18: 386₁₋₄; 305).

(5) The question thus shifts to the nature of cognition, which leads Kant to reflect further on the nature of concepts. He writes:

> [A] concept (or sum of them) is a representation that is related to an object and that designates [*bezeichnet*] it; and insofar as we connect (separate) one concept with another in a judgment, then we think something about the object that is designated through a given concept, i.e., we cognize it by judging it. All cognition, hence also that of experience, accordingly consists of judgments; and even concepts are representations that are prepared for possible judgments, for they represent something in general that is given as cognizable through a predicate.[53]
>
> (18: 386₉₋₁₇; 305)

Since Kant's reasoning here is straightforward and familiar, it requires little comment. Basically, the claim is that, as discursive, human cognition consists in relating concepts to an object in a judgment, from which it follows that all such cognition has the form of a judgment.

(6) Kant concludes from this that, since experience is a form of cognition, it is possible only through judgments, in which perceptions constitute the empirical element. But, as he also notes, the merely empirical consciousness that perception involves does not suffice for the relation to an object, and therefore cognition (18: 386₁₈₋₂₁; 305–6). Thus, at this point the deduction purports to have established two important claims: (a) that experience requires a non-empirical condition of its possibility; and (b) that this condition must have something to do with judgment. It has not, however, shown either what feature of judgment provides this non-empirical condition or how it is to be understood. These are the concerns of the final two steps.

(7) Kant responds to the first of these concerns by distinguishing between the form and matter of judgment. He reasons that, since the matter (or content) of an empirical judgment consists of the perceptions that are brought together in empirical consciousness, it cannot be the source of the non-empirical element required for cognition. This leaves as the only viable candidate the form, which Kant claims "consists in the objective unity of the consciousness of the given concepts, in the consciousness that these **must** belong to one another, and thereby designate an object in whose (complete) representation they are always to be found together" (18: 386₂₂₋₆; 306). Since this formulation reflects the conception of judgment that Kant

---

[52] I have substituted "above all" for Guyer's "especially" as the rendering of Kant's "*vornehmlich*."

[53] I have modified Guyer's syntax from "something that is given in general" to "something in general that is given."

introduced in the Note, it indicates that he here gave it a pivotal role in his new conception of the proof-structure of the Deduction. Apart from this there are two noteworthy features in this step. First, Kant introduces the missing ingredient of necessity, which in the form of a **must** (*müssen*) has a normative sense, since it expresses the condition under which alone the representations unified in consciousness can relate to an object. Second, the relation to an object is claimed to involve not merely necessity but a *consciousness* of this necessity, which reinforces the point that a judgment for Kant is an inherently self-conscious act in which the cognizer knows what it is doing.

(8) In the final step Kant claims that this consciousness of necessity "presupposes a rule that must be given *a priori*, i.e., a unity of consciousness, which takes place *a priori*. This unity of consciousness is contained in the moments of the understanding in judging, and only that is an object in relation to which unity of consciousness of the manifold representations is thought *a priori*" (18: 387_{1-6}; 306). Kant here appeals to his rule theory of objectivity and insists upon the a priori status of the rules in question, which is required to ground the necessity built into the representation of an object. Since Kant here says that the unity of consciousness "takes place [*statt* findet] *a priori*," he presumably means the act of unification, i.e., synthesis, rather than the unified consciousness that is a product of this act; and, as in the A-Deduction, "*a priori*" must be taken to refer to the governing rule rather than to the act. Although Kant does not mention the categories, he implies that these rules are derived from "the moments of the understanding in judging," which can only mean the categories. And this licenses the conclusion, which Kant does not explicitly draw, that the categories are necessary conditions of the possibility of experience.

B) *R 5924–35*: Since these *Reflexionen* do not require the detailed analysis given to R 5923, their discussion will be much briefer and will focus on the ways in which they fill in the sketch of Kant's emerging view of the Transcendental Deduction. Taking them in order, R 5924 and R 5925 (18: 387_8–8_2; 306) do not really add very much. As already noted, R 5924 corrects an omission in R 5923 by adding mathematical propositions to the class of legitimate synthetic a priori propositions; while R 5925 notes that synthetic a priori cognitions from concepts (without intuitions), by which Kant evidently understands those involving the concept of the noumenon in the negative sense, though not capable of determining objects of experience, nevertheless have a legitimate limiting function with respect to the determination of the bounds of experience.

By contrast, R 5926 (18: 388_{4-21}; 306–7) introduces an element that will play a crucial role in the second part of the B-Deduction; viz., the characterization of space and time as "forms of the composition of objects of sensation." Although the text is none too clear and Kant's main point is that, as mere forms, if one removed all composition from space and time, nothing would remain, by identifying "the unity of consciousness in this combination, insofar as it is considered as universal, with the concept of the understanding," and claiming that "this unity belongs to experience as objective cognition," Kant appears to be suggesting that the unifying activity of the understanding, qua governed by its pure concepts, conditions the possibility of experience by determining space and time as well as the manifold represented therein.

R 5927 is noteworthy for two reasons. First, it contains the initial use of the term "category" in this set of *Reflexionen*; second, it shows us Kant seemingly experimenting with his terminology regarding the unity and universality of consciousness. It consists of four paragraphs. Of these, the first contains the familiar denial that we can have synthetic a priori cognition of things in themselves, on the grounds that such cognition requires pure intuitions as well as pure concepts, and the positive claim that such intuitions are only possible as forms of sensibility, which apply merely to appearances (18: 388_{19}–9_5; 307); while the fourth reiterates the point that the two a priori elements of cognition are intuitions (presumably as forms of sensibility) and the unity of consciousness of the manifold of intuitions, by which Kant here evidently understands the unifying activity, i.e., synthesis, since he claims that it "constitutes the form of experience as objective empirical cognition" (18: 389_{14-15}; 307). But our main interest in this text concerns its second and third paragraphs, where Kant writes:

A category is the representation of the relation of the manifold of intuition to a universal consciousness (to the universality of consciousness, which is properly objective). The relation of representations to the universality of consciousness, consequently the transformation of the empirical and particular unity of consciousness, which is merely subjective, into a consciousness that is universal and objective, belongs to logic. This unity of consciousness, insofar as it is universal and can be represented *a priori*, is the pure concept of the understanding. This can thus be nothing other than the universal [*allgemeine*] of the unity of consciousness, which constitutes the objective validity of a judgment.

The manifold, insofar as it is represented as belonging necessarily to one consciousness (or also to the unity of consciousness in general), is thought [crossed out: as belonging] through the concept of an object: the object is always a something in general. The determination of it rests merely on the unity of the manifold of its intuition, and indeed on the universally valid unity of the consciousness thereof. (18: 388_{29}–9_{11}; 307)

We find here a mixture of the terminology of the *Prolegomena* with that of the A-Deduction, as well as that which will appear in the B-Deduction. Accordingly, it presents us with a Kant who is in *medias res*, at least as far as terminology is concerned. Four points are particularly germane. The first is the introduction of the phrase "universal consciousness" and its equation with the universality of consciousness regarded as the source of objectivity, which apparently corresponds to the "consciousness in general" of the *Prolegomena*.[54] The second is the distinction between a subjective and an objective (universally valid) unity of consciousness. While absent from the A-Deduction and expressed in terms of the distinction

---

[54] Although there is no reference to a universal self-consciousness in the A-Deduction, Kant does use the term at B132.

between the connection of perceptions in a particular consciousness and in consciousness in general in the *Prolegomena*, it will play a significant role in the B-Deduction. The third is the parenthetical reference to "the unity of consciousness in general" (combining the unity of consciousness of the *Critique* and the consciousness in general of the *Prolegomena*) and its apparent identification with the one consciousness to which the manifold is represented as necessarily belonging insofar as it is regarded as related to an object. Finally, Kant indicates that it is the universalizing function of the category (with respect to the community of cognizers) that grounds objectivity, which shows that, even though we find him shifting away from the terminology of the *Prolegomena*, the basic thought linking objective validity with a subjective universality-cum-normative necessity remains firmly in place.

Apart from one detail, R 5928 (18: 389_{17-23}; 308-9) is of little significance for our purposes, since it reiterates in slightly different terms the point in R 5924 that, while synthetic a priori cognitions through concepts are not possible, such propositions through either the construction of concepts or in connection with possible experience are not only possible but necessary. The detail is the introduction of the term "formal intuition" as that in which concepts are constructed, which likewise will play a pivotal role in the B-Deduction.[55]

More than the other *Reflexionen* in this series, R 5929 (18: 389_{25}–90_{14}; 308) is directly related to the text of Baumgarten to which they are all attached. Its overall concern is with what is involved in thinking something through the understanding alone, without reference to sensible intuition, and the concept with which Kant is concerned is that of contingency. In agreement with Baumgarten, Kant acknowledges that in thinking something through the understanding as "contingent in itself," where "in itself" presumably means with respect to the understanding, one cannot think of it as existing without a cause. But whereas Baumgarten's analysis stops at this point, Kant goes on to ask why we must think of the contingent as existing through the understanding and what the term "contingency" signifies. Rather than addressing these questions, however, Kant devotes the remainder of the *Reflexion* to reasserting the familiar thesis that sensible intuition is the condition under which our thoughts have application and significance.

In R 5930 (18: 390_{15-29}; 308-9) Kant distinguishes between two forms of the objective unity of the consciousness of the manifold of representations. He suggests that it can refer either to the distributive unity that representations possess as falling under the same concept, as, for example, the representations of distinct men all fall under the general concept "man," in which case it is termed "logical," or to the unity that a manifold of representations possesses insofar as they are regarded as representations of the same thing and constitute the concept of that (kind of) thing, in which case it is termed the "synthetic or transcendental unity of consciousness."

---

[55] Kant here refers to "sensible formal intuition in general," but since all human intuition for Kant is sensible and the "in general" presumably refers to both space and time, this is equivalent to the formal intuition of the B-Deduction, which will be discussed in Chapter 9.

This corresponds to the distinction that Kant will draw in the B-Deduction between the analytic unity of apperception, which pertains to all concepts, and the synthetic unity of apperception, which Kant there claims is "the highest point to which one must affix all use of the understanding, even the whole of logic and, after it, transcendental philosophy" (B133–4). More specifically, what Kant here calls the "logical unity of the manifold of representations" corresponds to the analytic unity of consciousness and what he terms the "synthetic or transcendental unity" to the synthetic unity of apperception.[56]

Since R 5931 and R 5932 (18: 390_{30}–2_{21}; 309–10) are both concerned with the concept of a category it will be convenient to consider them together. In the former Kant defines a category as "the necessary unity of consciousness in the composition of the manifold of representations (intuition), insofar as it makes possible the concept of an object in general (in distinction from the merely subjective unity of the consciousness of the perceptions)" (R 5931 18: 390_{30}–1_2; 309). The focus is on the necessity involved in the application of a category and, anticipating what he will say in the B-Deduction, Kant indicates that it concerns the way in which the concepts based upon the perceptual data must be thought in order to yield the cognition of an object.[57] In the case of a categorical proposition, as far as its propositional form is concerned, either concept can function as subject or as predicate; but if the unification of the concepts is considered with reference to an object in a judgment, one of the concepts is conceivable only as subject and the other only as predicate, which is achieved by subsuming them under the relational category of substance and accident. Although he does not develop the point, Kant also suggests that a similar story can be told with respect to the other categories. In short, the categories tie down given perceptions by bringing them to the unity of consciousness in a determinate order and with a determinate structure, e.g., as extensive magnitudes, and it is through this determination that the unified perceptions are related to an object.

R 5932 continues this line of thought. Explicitly appealing to the reflexive formulation, which is implicit throughout, Kant states that, "Through the category I represent to myself an object as such as determined with regard to the logical functions of judgments: of the subject (not predicate), of the consequence as ground, of the multiplicity in its representation" (18; 391_{14-17}; 309). He proceeds immediately, however, to pose a further question, which leads the enquiry in a new direction; viz., "[W]hy must I always represent every object as **determined** with regard **not only**

---

[56] Despite terminological similarities, this distinction is not to be equated with either the one drawn in B-12 and considered in Chapter 3 between the analytic and synthetic unity of apperception or the distinction between a transcendental and an objective unity drawn at A107 and discussed in Chapter 5. In the former case the distinction refers to the contrast between the productive and the reproductive functions of the imagination. In the latter case it is between the *unity of consciousness* (as transcendental ground) and the *consciousness of unity* (as an objective unity). By contrast, the present distinction is between two forms of the consciousness of an objective unity and does not *directly* involve the unity of consciousness.

[57] See B128–9. This passage was discussed in Chapter 4.

to one, but rather to **all the logical functions** of judgment?" To which Kant answers: "Because only thereby is objective unity of consciousness possible, i.e., a universally valid connection of perceptions, hence experience as the only reality of cognition" (18: 391_{18-22}; 309). Moreover, Kant returns to this point later in *Reflexion*, noting that "All objects that we are to think must be determined with regard to all of the logical functions of the understanding, for **thereby alone can we think**" (18: 392_{7-10}; 309).

These remarks indicate that the need to determine whatever we represent to ourselves as an object under *all* of the logical functions is a consequence of the nature of thinking as judging. Although it does not seem plausible to take Kant as claiming literally that every judgment involves all twelve of the logical functions, since many of them are mutually exclusive, e.g., a judgment must be either categorical, hypothetical, or disjunctive, not all of these at once, it makes better sense if we take him to mean one function from each of the four titles.[58] In short, a judgment, and therefore a thought, must have a quantity, a quality, a relation, and a modality.

After contrasting a judgment, defined as "[t]he **unity of the consciousness** of the manifold in the representation **of an object** as such," with a category, defined as [t]he representation of an object as such insofar as it is determined with regard to this objective unity of consciousness (logical unity) (18: 392_{23-7}; 310), Kant returns in R 5933 to the unity of consciousness, distinguishing between an empirical and a logical unity, which corresponds to the contrast between a subjective and an objective one. He attributes the former to the imagination, which is the only mention of this faculty in the entire set of *Reflexionen*, and suggests that this unity is requisite for concepts and the latter for judgments (18: 392_{28-34}; 310). Thus, while Kant assigns an empirical function to the imagination, presumably along the lines of the reproductive function given to it in the A-Deduction, there is no hint of it having a transcendental function.

R 5934 (18: 393_{6-33}; 310–11) provides what amounts to a complete sketch of a deduction of the categories, albeit in a more abbreviated form than R 5923. It contains four paragraphs. The first makes a series of assertions from which conclusions are drawn in the second. Since the argument largely overlaps with that of R 5923, it would be redundant to discuss it in the detail with which the former was considered. Thus, a summary of Kant's claims and the order in which they are made should suffice to indicate the structure of the proposed deduction. And inasmuch as the last two paragraphs contain elements that are not found in R 5923, they will be considered as well.

---

[58] Nevertheless, this seems to differ from what Kant says in both the first and second editions of the *Critique*. Thus, at A245 he states merely that the manifold of representations "must be thought through one or another of these logical functions;" and in (nominally) defining the categories at B128 he states that through them the intuition of an object is "regarded as determined with regard to one of the **logical functions** for judgments."

The first paragraph begins with a definition of experience as a posteriori cognition, with the a posteriori elements characterized as sensations, which are here considered as equivalent to perceptions. After claiming that sensations cannot of themselves yield empirical cognition or experience, since they cannot account for the requisite element of necessity, Kant asserts that an a priori ingredient is required and that it must be in the form of concepts (a priori intuitions are already assumed as forms of sensibility, but are insufficient of themselves to constitute experience). Finally, Kant claims that the a priori concepts in question must be concepts of connection or synthesis, as contrasted with concepts of comparison.[59]

In the second paragraph Kant concludes from this that "[A]ll perceptions are with regard to their connection in one consciousness determined *a priori*," which he refers to as "the universal formal principle of possible experience," and he claims it to be grounded in the objective unity of consciousness (18: 393_{14-18}; 310). Kant then connects this objective unity of consciousness with the form of judgment, character-ized as "the objective unity in the consciousness of different representations." This, in turn, enables him to conclude that "all perceptions, insofar as they are to constitute experience, stand under the formal conditions of judgments in general" (18: 393_{20-1}; 310–11), which leaves as the remaining task connecting these conditions with the categories. This is obviously a key move and its viability depends upon an under-standing of the relation between these formal conditions of judgment in general (presumably the logical functions or forms of judgment) and the corresponding categories. Unfortunately, Kant here is typically cryptic, since he simply states that the determination of perceptions "through this function is the concept of the understanding" (18: 393_{22-3}; 311). But assuming that by "this function" Kant under-stands the logical functions of judgment and by "the concept of the understanding" the categories, he can be taken as restating the point made in R 5931 to the effect that the categories tie down given perceptions by bringing them to the unity of con-sciousness in a determinate manner, through which the unified perceptions are related to an object. And from this Kant concludes that "All experiences as possible perceptions stand *a priori* under concepts of the understanding, through which alone they can become empirical cognition, i.e., representation of objects (*a posteriori*)" (18: 393_{23-6}; 311).

---

[59] Kant's reference to "concepts of comparison" suggests the contrast drawn in the Amphiboly chapter in the *Critique* between the categories and the concepts of reflection (also referred to as concepts of comparison), as two distinct kinds of a priori concepts, which are distinguished by the fact that what is exhibited through the former is "the object in accordance with what constitutes its concept (magnitude, reality)," whereas the latter are concerned only with "the comparison of representations in all their manifoldness, which precedes the concepts of things" (A269/B325). It is also possible, however, that Kant here had in mind the contrast between the categories as concepts of synthesis and the comparison of concepts, which he held in the *Prolegomena* to be insufficient to constitute cognition. Indeed, inasmuch these two characterizations of the possible alternatives complement rather than compete with one another, it is possible that Kant had both in mind.

In the single-sentence third paragraph Kant claims that "All appearances are *a priori* determinable with regard to their connection in conformity with the unity of consciousness in all judgments in general, i.e., they stand under categories" (18: 393_{28-31}; 311). What is new here is the shift from talking about *perceptions* (perceivings) standing under the categories to talking about *appearances* (the objects perceived) standing under them, which amounts to the assertion of the objective reality of the categories. As such, it corresponds to the dictum of the A-Deduction that, "The *a priori* conditions of a possible experience in general are at the same time conditions of the possibility of the objects of experience" (A111). It is also what the Deduction must show, if it is to exorcize the specter that "appearances could . . . be so constituted that the understanding would not find them in accord with the conditions of its unity." As in both versions of the Deduction in the *Critique*, Kant's rejection of this possibility appears to turn on the distinction between the conditions under which objects are given and those under which they are thought, i.e., brought to an objective unity of consciousness. Accordingly, Kant's point is that, while it is logically possible that appearances might be so constituted, it is not possible that the understanding could find them as such because it would violate the conditions of the unity of consciousness.

The final paragraph states that "Space and time are the forms of combination in intuition and serve to apply the categories *in concreto*" (18: 393_{33-4}; 311). Although this adds nothing to the argument sketched above, it has a possible two-fold significance with respect to the broader implications of Kant's views. First, the claim that space and time are conditions for the application of the categories *in concreto* suggests the doctrine of the Schematism to which Kant explicitly refers in R 5933 and perhaps even the possibility that he was considering including space as well as time within his account of it.[60] Second, by characterizing space and time as "forms of *combination*" (my emphasis) rather than as forms of receptivity, Kant may have been hinting at the line of thought that he will develop in the second part of the B-Deduction with the introduction of a figurative synthesis.[61] But, given the crypticness of Kant's claim, this conclusion is highly speculative.

R 5935 (18: 394_{2-11}; 311), which is the final *Reflexion* in this group, consists of two brief paragraphs. The first merely reiterates the familiar point that all our synthetic cognition from concepts reaches only to things as appearances, never to things in themselves. The second adds a new element, however; for rather than being concerned with what we can cognize, it considers what we can represent to ourselves, i.e.,

---

[60] Eckart Förster (2012), 56, 66–8 has argued that Kant came to recognize the need for something like a schematism of outer sense in order to establish the objective validity of the categories and that this underlies the argument of the *Metaphysical First Principles of Natural Science*. Moreover, in the "General Note on the System of Principles" added in the second edition of the *Critique*, Kant insists that in order to establish the objective reality of the categories "we do not merely need intuitions, but always **outer intuitions**" (B291). It should also be noted, however, that Kant does not either integrate this line of thought into the argument of the B-Deduction or revise the Schematism chapter in light of it.

[61] In R 5926 (18: 388_{4-5}; 306) Kant refers to space and time as "forms of the composition of objects of sensation."

think, a priori, which depends upon our power of representation. Moreover, in this context Kant distinguishes between what the understanding can represent to itself theoretically, through determining the unity of consciousness, and what reason, in conformity with the understanding, can determine practically with respect to possible acts. Although this *Reflexion* (like R 5929) stands apart from the others in this set in that it does not seem to have anything directly to do with the problematic of the Deduction, the cryptic reference to reason and the practical accords with Kant's concern in the B-Deduction to allow for the possibility of a practical use of the categories.[62]

C) *Concluding reflections*: As previously noted, these *Reflexionen* show us a Kant in *medias res* with regard to the formulation of the argument of the Deduction. First and foremost, they indicate that Kant had distanced himself from the "subjective side" of the A-Deduction with its appeal to the three-fold synthesis as its organizing principle, replacing it with a focus on the nature of judgment as defined in the Note ("an action through which given representations first become cognitions of an object"). Second, they suggest that Kant had taken to heart Schultz's point about an equivocal use of "experience," since he here uses it consistently in the strong sense as equivalent to objectively valid empirical cognition.[63] Third, as is required by this conception of judgment, Kant no longer appeals to the distinction drawn in the *Prolegomena* between judgments of perception and judgments of experience, replacing it with the distinction between a subjective and an objective unity of consciousness, which reappear in the B-Deduction. Fourth, despite rejecting the distinction between the two species of empirical judgment, Kant retains the closely related contrast between the unification of perceptions in an individual consciousness and in a universal consciousness (consciousness in general), with only the latter governed by the categories and claimed to be objectively valid, which is the main contribution of the *Prolegomena* to the problematic of the Deduction. Finally, we have seen that at one point Kant introduced the notion of a formal intuition, which, as distinguished from a form of intuition, will play an important role in the second part of the B-Deduction.

Nevertheless, one would be hard pressed to find in these *Reflexionen* an indication of how they shed light on Kant's bold claim in the Note that the completion of the Deduction, which requires showing how the categories make experience possible, could "almost be accomplished through a single inference from the precisely

---

[62] The most prominent example of a practical use of the pure categories (apart from their schemata) in Kant is his extremely obscure account of the categories of freedom in the second *Critique* (KpV 5: 66–7; 193–4).

[63] Actually, we have seen that Kant typically takes the term in this sense in the A-Deduction; since it is presupposed in the project of demonstrating that the categories are necessary conditions of the possibility of experience. But, on occasion, he does sometimes use it in the looser sense that is characteristic of the British empiricists, particularly Locke. For a discussion of the contrast between the Lockean and Kantian conceptions of experience, see Beck (1978), esp. 40–1.

determined definition of a *judgment* in general." Assuming the correctness of
Adickes' dating (1783–84), one might explain this on the grounds that they antedate
the composition of the Note, which leaves open the possibility that Kant only arrived
at this shortcut after their composition. But, quite apart from the dating issue, the
main point is that Kant did not achieve this in the B-Deduction, on which he was
presumably already at work at the time of the composition of the Note, at least not if
it takes the form of anything like a single inference from the definition of judgment.[64]
In Chapters 8 and 9, which deal respectively with the two steps in the proof of the
B-Deduction, I shall endeavor to show that and why this is the case.

---

[64] For a defense of the single inference claim as the key to understanding the B-Deduction and a critique
of my treatment of the issue in Allison (2004), see Pollok (2008), 332 note 30. As Pollock correctly points
out, the differences between our views concerns our interpretations of the relation between the two parts of
the B-Deduction. Whereas I emphasize a sharp distinction between the two steps of the proof, he insists
upon their closeness.

8

The B-Deduction (1)

§§15–20

The distinctive feature of the B-Deduction is its division into two parts, with the conclusion drawn at the end of the first part that the manifold in a given intuition necessarily stands under the categories (B143) constituting only "the beginning of a deduction of the pure concepts of the understanding" (B144); while the argument of the second part concludes with the claim that "the categories are conditions of the possibility of experience, and are thus also valid *a priori* of all objects of experience" (B161). Accordingly, though the final conclusion is the same as that of the A-Deduction, the manner in which Kant arrives at it is quite distinct. Rather than two complementary and self-contained proofs of the objective validity of the categories, such as was supposedly provided by the arguments from above and from below in section 3 of the A-Deduction, the two parts of the B-Deduction constitute two distinct steps in a single proof. Moreover, this proof-structure is not what one would have been led to expect on the basis of Kant's comments on the Deduction in the Note and the *Reflexionen* analyzed in Chapter 7; for while the conception of judgment plays a pivotal role in the first step of the B-Deduction, the second step, in which Kant endeavors to answer both the *that* and the *how* questions with regard to the categories and possible experience, can hardly be regarded as consisting in "almost a single inference" from it.

Although he ignores the complications stemming from the Note and the *Reflexionen*, the exegetical problem has been given its definitive formulation by Henrich, who in his classical paper on the B-Deduction writes: "The interpretation must show that, contrary to the initial impression that the two conclusions merely define the same proposition . . . sections 20 and 26 offer arguments with significantly different results, and these together yield a single proof of the transcendental deduction. We shall call this task the problem of the two-steps in one proof."[1] While Henrich's own attempt to meet this challenge has been widely criticized, his account of the conditions of a successful interpretation of the B-Deduction has determined the direction

---

[1] Henrich (1982), 67–8.

of all subsequent analyses of the text, including my own.[2] Assuming that the overall goal of the Deduction is to remove the worry that what is given in sensible intuition might not conform to the categories, which I have characterized as a specter, Henrich claims that Kant's preliminary conclusion in §20 accomplishes this for a range of sensible intuitions; viz., those that already possess unity; while the final conclusion in §26 affirms this for all intuitions that can be brought to consciousness. In short, on Henrich's reading, the second part of the Deduction removes a restriction on the scope of the applicability of the categories that is left in place by the argument of the first part.[3]

Against this, I have argued that it is counter-intuitive to regard the first part of the Deduction as containing a restriction that is removed in the second. Since the first part maintains that the manifold of sensible in general, i.e., *any* sensible intuition, stands under the categories, while the second makes this claim with respect to the manifold of *human* sensible intuition, which is structured by space and time as its a priori forms, it seems rather that the former claim is broader. In fact, inasmuch as human sensible intuition is a species of sensible intuition in general or as such, the real problem confronting an interpretation of the B-Deduction is to explain why the conclusion of the second part is anything more than a trivial inference from genus to species, as it is sometimes taken to be.[4]

My answer, for which I shall argue in this chapter and in Chapter 9, is that, rather than differing merely with respect to the range over which a single unifying function is exercised, which is the central feature of Henrich's interpretation, the two steps of the B-Deduction are concerned with two distinct epistemic functions of the categories; and since the first does not entail the second, while the second presupposes the first, both steps are necessary. The first step argues that the categories are rules for the

---

[2] I analyze the B-Deduction in detail in Allison (1983), 133–72, and (2004), 159–201, and more succinctly in (1996), 27–40. For an analysis of Henrich's interpretation and a survey of its reception up to about 1990 see Baumanns (1991), 329–48 and 436–55.

[3] A frequently voiced criticism of Henrich's account concerns the suggestion that intuitions could possess unity independently of their relation to the understanding, since this would appear to obviate any need for the understanding as the source of this unity and with it of the categories. Subsequently, however, Henrich (1984), 41–2, has clarified his position, claiming that his view is merely that intuitions contain a unity insofar as they are related to apperception, but that this relation cannot without further argument be affirmed of everything given in sensibility. For a discussion of this issue see Evans (1990), 554–60.

[4] Among those making the triviality claim are Baum (1986), 7–11 and Bird (2006), 310. It might be argued that Kant himself considered the second step a trivial, or at least unproblematic, inference from the first step, when he claims in the Note that the Deduction can be completed by an "almost single inference" from the definition of judgment. In fact, though he does not refer to the argument of the second step as trivial or unproblematic, its contribution to the overall Deduction appears to be downgraded by Pollok (2008), esp. 332, note, who rejects my sharp separation of the aim of the two steps. Citing as evidence for his reading Kant's reference to empirical intuition in the conclusion of the first part (B143), Pollok states that the task of the second step is to "cash out" what the determining synthesis of the manifold to which Kant refers amounts to. Nevertheless, I find it a stretch to take the reference to empirical intuition at this point as a sign that Kant thought that he had already connected the categories with human experience. Rather, I think that Kant is here using "empirical" as synonymous with "sensible," which is the term that he generally uses in the first part of the B-Deduction to characterize the kind of intuition with which he is concerned; viz., sensible intuition as such.

thought of an object of sensible intuition in general, which is to say that they function as discursive rules for the determination of the manifold of an intuition with respect to one of the logical functions of judgment (B128). Accordingly, in this part of the Deduction Kant abstracts from the spatial and temporal forms of human sensibility and focuses instead on the concept of an object of sensible intuition in general. The aim is to show that any representation that is brought to the objective unity of apperception is thereby also related to such an object and necessarily stands under the categories. Although this might be thought sufficient for Kant's purposes, we shall see that it is not. The essential point, which necessitates a second part, is that the Deduction aims to show that the categories are conditions of *experience*, which requires more than discursive thought. Specifically, it requires that the categories relate to the manifold of human sensibility through their relation to space and time as its a priori forms, which involves attributing a pre-discursive function to them as conditions of perception. But that is a long and complex story, which must be reserved for Chapter 9. The present chapter is concerned with the first part of the Deduction, which consists of §15–§20. Following the text, I shall analyze each section in turn, considering both its inherent claims and its relation to the argument as a whole.

I

§15 *On the possibility of a combination in general* (B129–31): Although the principle of the synthetic unity of apperception is the focal point of the first part of the B-Deduction and that from which the move to the categories begins, it is not the actual starting point of its argument. This is provided by the claim in §15 that, while the manifold of representation can be given in a sensible intuition with an a priori form, its combination (*Verbindung*) must be the product of an act of spontaneity. Kant terms this act "synthesis" and, in contrast to the A-Deduction, where it was assigned to the imagination, he here attributes it to the understanding. Moreover, whereas in the A-Deduction Kant affirmed that a synthesis is required in order to represent the manifold of intuition as a manifold because of the successive nature of the manner in which it is given in inner sense, Kant now claims that a synthesis is required in order to represent a manifold as unified (combined) simply in virtue of the fact that it is given, quite apart from its manner of giveness. As Kant puts it,

[A]ll combination, whether we are conscious of it or not, whether it is a combination of the manifold of intuition or of several concepts, and in the first case whether of empirical or non-empirical intuition,[5] is an action of the understanding, which we would designate with the

---

[5] I am here following Mellin, who was in turn followed by Erdmann and Kemp Smith, in emending the text to read "empirical and non-empirical" rather than the original "sensible or non-sensible." Although we have already seen that in the B-Deduction (as elsewhere) Kant is concerned to contrast our sensible intuition with a problematic non-sensible or intellectual intuition, he is also quite clear that the analysis of the understanding, which he is here providing, is our discursive understanding for which a sensible

general title **synthesis** in order at the same time to draw attention to the fact that we can represent [to ourselves] nothing as combined in the object without having previously combined it ourselves, and that among all representations **combination** is the only one that is not given through objects but can be executed only by the subject itself, since it is an act of its self-activity. One can here easily see that this action must originally be unitary [*einig*] and equally valid for all combination, and that the dissolution (**analysis**) that seems to be its opposite, in fact always presupposes it; for where the understanding has not previously combined anything, neither can it dissolve anything, for only **through it** can something be given to the power of representation as combined.   (B130)

This passage contains a number of important points. First and foremost is the scope of the claim as encompassing *all* combination, which Kant carves up in three distinct ways: (1) between conscious and unconscious acts of combination; (2) between those in which the items combined are contained in the manifold of an intuition and those in which they are distinct concepts; and (3) in the case of the former whether the intuition be empirical or non-empirical. In addition, there is (4) the characterization of the understanding as spontaneity; and (5) the proposition that analysis presupposes synthesis. I shall discuss each in turn.

1) *Conscious and unconscious acts of composition*: Although Kant does not explicitly refer to the imagination in this passage, it is clearly what he has in mind by an unconscious combination. This is evident from the important and previously discussed passage, where, contrary to the one currently under consideration, Kant ascribes synthesis to the imagination and characterizes the latter as "a blind though indispensable function of the soul, without which we would have no cognition at all, but of which we are seldom even conscious" (A78/B103). Despite the retention of this passage in the second edition, by attributing such unconscious (or mainly unconscious) combination to the understanding rather than to the imagination, Kant appears to be making a sharp break with his view in the A-Deduction. Whereas he had there regarded the imagination, together with sensibility and apperception (not the understanding), as one of the three original or fundamental cognitive faculties, we shall see that he now characterizes the transcendental synthesis of the imagination as an "effect of the understanding on the sensibility" (B152); claims that it is the understanding, "under the designation of a transcendental synthesis of imagination," that determines inner sense (B153); and maintains that "It is one and the same spontaneity that, there under the name of imagination, and here under the name of understanding, brings combination into the manifold of inner sense" (B162n).[6]

---

intuition is required. See, for example, B148. Moreover, the empirical–non-empirical contrast makes perfect sense in this context, since Kant will argue, as he did in the A-Deduction, that both empirical and pure (sensible) intuitions are subject to synthesis.

[6] It is clear from the first sentence of this note that "there" refers to the empirical synthesis of apprehension and "here" to what Kant calls the "synthesis of apperception," which is the intellectual synthesis of the first part of the B-Deduction.

2) *Composition of the manifold of a sensible intuition and of distinct concepts*: Since by "the combination of distinct concepts" Kant is presumably referring to the act of judgment, the claim that the same combinatory act is operative there as in the combination of the manifold of a sensible intuition suggests that he has in mind the act of thinking at whatever level it occurs, a reading which is confirmed by Kant's claim at the beginning of the next sentence that it is easy to see that "this action must originally be unitary and equally valid for all combination." This also accords with Kant's previous claim that "The same function that gives unity to the different representations **in a judgment** also gives unity to the mere synthesis of different representations **in an intuition**, which, expressed generally, is called the pure concept of the understanding" (A79/B104–5). And since this assertion is likewise present in both editions, it indicates that, despite the apparent absorption of the imagination into the understanding, there is no substantive difference between Kant's views on the matter in the two editions.

3) *Combination of both empirical and non-empirical intuition*: The claim that this combinatory act operates with respect to both empirical and non-empirical intuition is also not an innovation of the second edition; for we have seen that in his account of the three-fold synthesis in the A-Deduction Kant claims that apprehension and reproduction have both an empirical and an a priori dimension, with the former consisting in its application to empirical and the latter to pure intuition. Moreover, though Kant no longer refers to a three-fold synthesis in the B-Deduction, replacing it with the distinction between an intellectual (*synthesis intellectualis*) and a figurative synthesis (*synthesis speciosa*), he connects the latter with the imagination and attributes to it both an a priori function (as transcendental synthesis of the imagination) and an empirical function (as synthesis of apprehension), with the latter being the vehicle through which the categories are linked to perception and through this to experience.

4) *Spontaneity*: The notion of spontaneity or self-activity is not absent from the first edition of the *Critique*. Indeed, Kant introduces it on the very first page of the Introduction to the Transcendental Logic, where the understanding is characterized as the "spontaneity of cognition" and contrasted with the receptivity of sensibility (A51/B75). And we have seen that in the A-Deduction Kant reiterates this characterization in the context of a catalogue of various descriptions that he has given of the understanding before settling on his preferred characterization of it as the "faculty of rules" (A126). It plays a far more prominent role in the B-Deduction, however, where, in addition to the above-cited passage, it appears five times.[7] Nevertheless, it seems reasonable to surmise that this increased prominence is due not to a doctrinal change but to the revised structure of the argument. The essential point is that by

----

[7] See B132, B151, B157n, 162n, 167n.

abstracting from the contribution to cognition of human sensibility and its a priori forms, thereby isolating the understanding as the Aesthetic isolated sensibility, Kant is able to argue that the need for a combinatory act, i.e., synthesis, is a consequence of the discursive nature of the human understanding, and is therefore independent of how the sensible manifold may be presented to the mind in intuition.[8] In other words, while the focus on the temporality of consciousness in the A-Deduction suggested that the need for synthesis is a function of how the sensible manifold presents itself to consciousness in inner sense (successively), the present account indicates that this is not the case. As Kant succinctly puts it in the crucial portion of the passage, "we can represent to ourselves nothing as combined in the object without having previously combined it ourselves, and that among all representations **combination** is the only one that is not given through objects but can be executed only by the subject itself, since it is an act of its self-activity."[9]

By composing Kant does not mean literally creating, as if discursive thought somehow generates the world, since that would require an originary or intellectual intuition. What is composed or brought about by the subject through its cognitive activity is rather the representation or thought of something as composite, which underscores the point that compositeness cannot be simply passively registered, but must be taken as such by the subject. It also bears reiteration at this point that the claim that the combinatory act involves *representing to oneself* sensible data as combined in the object is not a detail that can be omitted from Kant's account. As was already clear from the analysis of apperception in the A-Deduction (and even from the earlier accounts from the "Silent Decade"), thinking for Kant, as contrasted with the "blind" and (largely unconscious) operation of the imagination, is an inherently reflexive, self-conscious activity. It is not simply something that the subject does, but that it does for itself in the sense of being aware of what it is doing. This was already implicit in the account of the synthesis of recognition in a concept in the A-Deduction, where recognition consists in taking as (x as an a or a manifold as a manifold), and we shall revisit this point below in connection with an analysis of Kant's insistence in §16 not only on a need for synthesis, but also for a *consciousness* of synthesis.

5) *Analysis and synthesis*: Kant's final claim in the initial paragraph of §15 is that analysis, understood as dissolution, presupposes synthesis, understood as composition. Since analysis presupposes that there is something composite to analyze, and it

[8] This is not to suggest, however, that the nature or coherence of the sensible manifold is irrelevant for Kant. On the contrary, this will be shown to be crucial in the second part of the B-Deduction. The present point is rather that this does not come into play in the recognition of the need for synthesis. And it should also be kept in mind that Kant is here concerned with the nature of discursive thought as such and the issue of whether and under what conditions such thought yields cognition does not arise at this point.

[9] As Kant later put it in a letter to J. S. Beck from 1792: "The composition itself is not given; on the contrary, we must produce it ourselves: we must *compose* if we are to represent to ourselves [*wir uns vorstellen*] something as composite (even space and time)" (Br 11: 515$_{15-18}$; 482).

has been claimed that the representation of compositeness presupposes an act of synthesis, this claim is hardly surprising. As we shall see in connection with the analysis of §16, however, it is of considerable importance to Kant's overall account, since it underlies the proposition that the analytical unity of apperception presupposes its synthetic unity, with the latter being the supreme condition of all thought.

In the second paragraph of §15 Kant engages in a further bit of conceptual analysis. It contains three claims centering on the concept of unity (*Einheit*). The first two of these focus on the relation between the concepts of unity (as applied to a manifold) and combination; whereas the third contrasts this unity with the category of unity. Once again, I shall discuss each in turn.

1) *The concept of combination entails (bei sich führt) the concept of the unity of the manifold*: As the text indicates, the analysandum is the concept of combination (*Verbindung*), and in addition to the concepts of the manifold and its synthesis, which presumably were already shown to be contained in it in the first paragraph of §15, Kant here adds to it that of the unity of this manifold. In justification of this he notes simply that "Combination is the representation of the synthetic unity of the manifold" (B130–1). Unfortunately, as is all too often the case, in his analysis Kant seems to gloss over the ambiguity inherent in terms like "*Verbindung*" (and the English "combination"), which can be understood as referring either to an act or to the product of an act. Accordingly, Kant could be read here as intending either or perhaps both alternatives. Taking "combination" as referring to the act, i.e., synthesis, as he clearly did in the first paragraph of §15, Kant is claiming that the act of combining a manifold consists in representing to oneself its synthetic unity; whereas taking it as referring to the product of an act, the claim is that the representation of a manifold as combined just is the representation of it as constituting a synthetic unity. Although both readings are possible, I shall argue below in favor of the former.

In a note attached to this claim Kant points out that this has nothing to do with whether the unified representations are themselves analytically connected, i.e., constitute an analytic judgment, since "The **consciousness** of the one, as far as the manifold is concerned, is still always to be distinguished from the consciousness of the other, and it is only the synthesis of this (possible) consciousness that is at issue here" (B131n). This must be understood in light of Kant's claim in the first paragraph of §15 that combination, as an act of the subject, is required whether the elements of the manifold in question are of an intuition or distinct concepts. Nevertheless, it is the latter type of composition to which Kant is here referring, and his point is that, quite apart from the logical relation of the concepts unified in a judgment, the latter, qua combinatory act, unifies phenomenologically distinct items.

2) *The priority of the representation of unity to the concept of combination*: Kant next claims that it follows from the preceding that the representation of the unity of a manifold cannot arise from the combination, but by being added to the representation of a manifold, first makes possible the concept of combination. Here it seems

evident that by "combination" is to be understood the product rather than the act; for the claim that the representation of a synthetic unity cannot arise from the combination because it makes the latter possible cannot refer to the act, since Kant had already claimed that this representation is the product of an act of combination. Accordingly, Kant must here mean that the representation of a synthetic unity cannot be derived by abstraction from the representation of a combination (as product), since that would mean that it is passively received, which would contradict the spontaneity thesis. Moreover, as suggested above, if this is correct, it indicates that "combination" should be taken in the sense of the act in the preceding claim; otherwise it is hard to see why Kant would indicate that the second claim is derived from it.

3) *Synthetic unity and the category of unity*: The final issue with which Kant deals in §15 is the nature of the synthetic unity, which by being added to the representation of the manifold first makes possible the concept of combination. His concern is to differentiate this unity from the category of unity, which, together with the other categories, was introduced in §10; and his point is that this category, like the others, already presupposes combination (presumably in the sense of the act of combining), since they are grounded in the logical functions of judgment, which are themselves the forms of combining. Accordingly, Kant notes that we must look higher (than the category) for this unity and he characterizes this higher ground as "that which itself contains the ground of the unity of different concepts in judgments, and hence of the possibility of the understanding, even in its logical use" (B132). This "higher ground" is the synthetic unity of apperception, to which Kant turns abruptly in §16, without explicitly noting that it was the unity sought in §15.

A further noteworthy feature of this discussion is that Kant refers parenthetically to this higher unity as "qualitative." But rather than explaining what he means by this he points the reader to §12, where the notion of a qualitative unity was introduced. In this section, which like §11 was added in the second edition, Kant discusses the scholastic principle: "*quodlibet ens est unum, verum, bonum*," with the aim of showing that the concepts of the one, the true, and the good (understood as perfection, i.e., completeness, rather than moral goodness), though "pure," i.e., a priori, are not to be reckoned among the categories, since they are not concepts of objects. As Kant puts it, evidently with Baumgarten in mind, "These supposedly transcendental predicates of **things** are nothing other than logical requisites and criteria of all **cognition of things** in general."[10] And he makes it clear that by unity, so construed, which he refers to as "**qualitative unity**," Kant understands "the **unity** of the concept, which is required for every cognition of an object," and which he likens

---

[10] In *Metaphysica* §73 Baumgarten writes: "The ONE is that whose determinations are inseparable, and indeed the TRANSCENDENTALLY ONE is that whose determinations are inseparable *per se. Therefore, every being* is transcendentally *one*." Baumgarten (2013), 113. Kant's claim seems to have been directed at Baumgarten's ontological conclusion.

to the unity of the theme in a play, a speech, or a fable (B114). Moreover, this comparison seems apt, since grasping a concept, especially when understood as a rule, is much like recognizing a thematic unity, which holds together the items (partial representations) thought in the concept.[11]

II

§16 *On the original synthetic unity of apperception*: Kant begins this segment with the oft-discussed proposition that "The **I think** must **be able** to accompany all my representations; for otherwise something would be represented in me that could not be thought at all, which is as much as to say that the representation would either be impossible or at least would be nothing to me" (B131–2). The most striking feature of this proposition is its complex modality. Rather than simply claiming that the "I think" must (necessarily) accompany all my representations, which might be justified on the grounds that to have a representation just means to think it, Kant maintains that it must be possible, for the "I think" to accompany them, even if it does not always actually do so. In short, Kant affirms the necessity of a possibility.

Although this doubly modalized thesis is not new to the second edition, the prominence that he attaches to it is.[12] Moreover, it must be understood in light of two essential aspects of Kant's account of cognition, which are present in both editions but more sharply formulated in the second. The first is the sensibility-understanding distinction, which, though fundamental to the architecture of the *Critique* as a whole, is used by Kant to structure the B-Deduction in a way that differs significantly from the structure of the initial version. Given this distinction, Kant cannot simply argue straightforwardly that the "I think" must (necessarily) actually accompany all my representations, since these include sensible intuitions that are not thought. Instead, he opts for the weaker proposition that it must be *possible* for it to accompany them, since that is the only way in which these representations can be something for me qua *res cogitans*.

The second aspect is Kant's view of the nature and function of the imagination, particularly in the second edition account, where he denies it the status of a distinct and fundamental faculty that he gave it in the first. Since the imagination (in both editions) is a "blind though indispensable function of the soul (or understanding) . . . of which we are seldom even conscious," its activity (synthesis) is, *ex hypothesi*,

---

[11] Kant also refers to a qualitative unity and distinguishes it from a quantitative unity in R 5733 18: 339 and R 5736 18: 340. In the latter he frames the contrast as between the unity of the object (quantitative) and the unity of the manifold in the object.

[12] The most explicit A-Deduction statement of the modality thesis is at A117n, where Kant states that "All representations have a necessary relation to a possible empirical consciousness." It is interesting that this is consigned to a note, albeit a very important one, in the A-Deduction, whereas its counterpart in the B-Deduction is located at a prominent place, which makes it evident that it is central to the ensuing argument.

seldom, if ever, connected with an actual "I think;" but we have also seen that if it is to yield cognition "in the proper sense," it must be "brought to concepts" by the understanding, which is say accompanied by an "I think." Accordingly, if this activity could not be brought to concepts, it would remain blind and of no cognitive import.

While I cannot claim that this is what Kant actually had in mind, his formulation of this proposition suggests that it can be seen as an attempt to mediate between the views of Descartes and Locke, each of whom maintained, albeit on radically distinct grounds, that the mind must be aware of all of its occurrent representations (ideas), and of Leibniz, who in the *New Essays* and other later writings, offered a number of arguments (both a priori and empirical) for the contrary view that the mind possesses a multitude of *petites perceptions*, of which it is not conscious (at least not individually).[13] So considered, Kant holds with Leibniz (and against Descartes and Locke) that the "I think" need not actually accompany all one's representations, while insisting (against Leibniz) that it must be able to accompany them, at least insofar as these representations are to enter into cognition. In short, though denying that every cognitively significant representation must be *apperceived*, he maintains that it must be *apperceivable*.[14]

After articulating in the first sentence of §16 the principle of the necessary apperceivability of all cognitively significant representations, Kant applies it in the next to intuitions. He writes: "That representation that can be given prior to all thinking is called **intuition**. Thus all manifold of intuition has a necessary relation to the **I think** in the same subject in which this manifold is to be encountered" (B132). With this reference to a manifold and its necessary relation to the same subject, Kant introduces the second essential aspect of his conception of the "I think"; viz., its numerical identity. As Kant had already made clear in the A-Deduction, it must not only be possible for an "I think" to accompany each of my representations, if they are to be anything to me (cognitively speaking), but it must be the *same* "I think," if the representations are collectively to constitute the representation of a manifold rather than merely a heap of disconnected representations, which once again means if they are to function cognitively.

---

[13] The situation is complicated by the fact that Locke's position was itself developed partly as a critique of Descartes', which concerned both the innateness thesis and the conception of the soul as an immaterial thinking substance, whose essence consists in thinking. Meanwhile, Leibniz., though defending both the conception of the soul as an immaterial substance and the innateness thesis against Locke, also criticizes the latter's quasi-Cartesian view that, though the soul does not always think, insofar as it does it is necessarily conscious of its thoughts, which Locke uses against the innateness thesis. For an analysis of this three-sided debate see Jolley (1984), esp. 102–24.

[14] I am assuming that Leibniz would have rejected this Kantian view because he held that the perceptions of which we are aware, i.e., apperceive, are composed of the small perceptions of which we are unaware as such. In other words, we are aware of the perceptions en mass but not of all the elements of which it is composed. See, for example, Leibniz (1981), 134. Leibniz also held that innate ideas function dispositionally in an unconscious manner, but he presumably maintained that such ideas are apperceivable.

We have seen from our examination of the A-Deduction that this already entails the need for synthesis; but before proceeding to that Kant devotes the remainder of the first paragraph of §16 to a series of terminological pronouncements, which are essential to understanding the subsequent argument. First, referring back to §15, he characterizes the representation "I think" as an act of spontaneity, thereby also indicating that he regards it as *both* an act *and* a representation, whereas it initially appeared to have been taken merely as an act. Nevertheless, it is a peculiar sort of representation, since from what Kant says about it in the Paralogisms and elsewhere it is evident that he considers it neither an intuition nor a determinate concept. Rather, he describes it as "a form of representation in general, insofar as it is to be called a cognition" (A346/B404), a formulation which, despite its vagueness, indicates that Kant considered it an ineliminable component of cognition.

Kant next announces that he will call this act/representation "pure" or "original apperception," both of which were used in the first edition. Although the "or" suggests that Kant regarded these terms as logically equivalent, he indicates that he assigns to them somewhat different functions. In the case of the first, it is to distinguish it from empirical apperception, which in the A-Deduction was equated with empirical consciousness (A115 and117n). In the case of the second, to which Kant appears to attribute greater significance, he characterizes it as: "that self consciousness which, because it produces the representation **I think**, which must be able to accompany [*begleiten*] all others and which in all consciousness is one and the same, cannot be derived [*abgeleitet*] from any other" (B132).

There are two noteworthy features of this passage. The first is that original apperception, though described as a form of self-consciousness, is not identified with the representation "I think." Rather, the latter is characterized as the product of the former, which suggests that Kant understood original apperception as a power or faculty that is exercised through the act of thinking. Accordingly, it is the "I think" qua act of thinking that is one and the same in all cognition and that accompanies all our representations. Although one could also say this about apperception qua power or faculty this would be trivially true and it is hard to see why Kant would bother pointing it out. The second, which is a purely textual matter, concerns the reading of the last cause. At issue is whether Kant intended to write "*begleiten*" (accompanied by), which is what is contained in the original text, or this is a misprint for "*abgeleitet*" (derived from). The Academy and Schmidt editions follow the original text in opting for the former, as do the standard English translations. The Cassirer edition, however, contains the latter and this reading is advocated by Paton, who claims that the original contains an obvious misprint since it makes nonsense of the text.[15] While I hesitate to go as far as Paton in dismissing the possibility of the standard reading, I do think that the proposed alternative makes better sense of the

---

[15] See Paton (1936a), 512, note 1.

text.[16] For one thing, it brings out the contrast between "original" and "derived," which lay behind Kant's characterization of apperception, in contrast to the understanding, as an original faculty in the A-Deduction. For another, as Paton points out, it is difficult to see how Kant could say both that the "I think" must be able to accompany all my representations and that it is not accompanied by any.

Kant then turns from apperception to its unity, noting that he calls the latter "the **transcendental** unity of self-consciousness in order to designate the possibility of *a priori* cognition from it" (B132). This echoes the use of "transcendental" with respect to the Transcendental Exposition of the concepts of space and time in the Aesthetic in the second edition. And, explaining why he applies this term to the unity of apperception, Kant writes:

For the manifold representations that are given in a certain intuition would not all together be **my** representations if they did not all together belong to a self-consciousness; i.e., as my representations (even if I am not conscious of them as such) they must yet necessarily be in accord with the condition under which alone they **can** stand together in a universal self-consciousness, because otherwise they would not throughout belong to me.   (B132–3)

Contrary to what Kant suggests with the use of the term "transcendental," this explanation can hardly be regarded as showing how the unity of apperception can be a source of a priori cognition; but it could be considered as a first step in such an account, which is perhaps all that Kant intended. The main point is already familiar from the A-Deduction; viz., that in order to be my representations in the sense of collectively representing something for me it is not sufficient that they be given in an intuition, it is also necessary that they accord with the condition under which they can be grasped together in a single self-consciousness. Presumably, by the parenthetical remark "even if I am not conscious of them as such" Kant means even if I do not reflectively attach the "I think" to them, as long as I am capable of doing so. Although Kant does not explain what he means by characterizing the self-consciousness involved as "universal," he would seem to be insisting upon its all-inclusive nature. In other words, it must encompass all the representations that a single cognizer could have because all of its cognitions must refer to a single phenomenal world or, as Kant put it in the A-Deduction, constitute a single experience (A110).[17]

Kant concludes the first paragraph of §16 by noting that much can be inferred from this "original combination," i.e., the transcendental unity of apperception, and he devotes the second paragraph to spelling out these consequences. To begin with, he contends that,

[T]his thoroughgoing identity of the apperception of a manifold given in intuition contains a synthesis of the representations, and is possible only through the consciousness of this synthesis. For the empirical consciousness that accompanies different representations is by

---

[16] This is also claimed by Bennett (1966), 109.
[17] See Paton (1936), 511, note 2.

itself dispersed and without relation to the identity of the subject. The latter relation therefore does not yet come about by my accompanying each representation with consciousness, but rather by my **adding** one representation to the other and being conscious of their synthesis. Therefore it is only because I can combine a manifold of given representations **in one consciousness** that it is possible for me to represent [to myself] **the identity of the consciousness in these representations** itself, i.e., the **analytical** unity of apperception is only possible under the presupposition of some **synthetic** one.   (B133)

Kant here makes three distinct claims, all of which are essential to his account: (1) that the thoroughgoing identity of the apperception of the manifold given in intuition contains a synthesis; (2) that it is possible only through a consciousness of this synthesis; and (3) that the analytical unity of apperception presupposes a synthetic one. Although Kant presents these as closely connected, for analytic purposes I shall consider each separately.

1) *The identity of apperception contains a synthesis*: Kant's point is clear from the A-Deduction and relatively straightforward.[18] As he here puts it, it turns on the dispersed nature of different episodes of empirical consciousness, as a result of which the I's consciousness of its identity with respect to its distinct representings (episodes of empirical consciousness) is only possible through a synthesis of these representings by means of which they are attributable to the same thinking subject. In other words, in order for the I that thinks *a* to be able to identify with the I that thinks *b* it must first combine them in a single consciousness, which means that a capacity to synthesize its distinct representings is a necessary condition of its becoming conscious of its identity.

2) *The I's consciousness of its identity requires a consciousness of this synthesis*: In view of the ambiguity of "synthesis" (it can refer either to the act or the product of the act) this claim is more complex, particularly since Kant evidently intended it in both senses. Understood in the second sense, it is unproblematic, since it follows immediately from the preceding claim. Assuming again the simplest case in which there are only two representations (*a* and *b*), the consciousness of the identity of the I that thinks *a* with the I that thinks *b* obviously requires an awareness of both *a* and *b* together. As Kant puts it, apart from such consciousness "I would have as multicolored, diverse a self as I have representations of which I am conscious [to myself]" (B134). Thus, not only is a consciousness of the identity of the I only possible by means of the combination of its representations; it is itself a consciousness of the product of this combination and in this sense a consciousness of synthesis.

The claim seems somewhat more problematic, however, if the consciousness of synthesis is taken to refer to the activity rather than merely its product. First, there is the question of its compatibility with what Kant says elsewhere. For example, we have

---

[18] In a parallel passage in the A-Deduction (A118) Kant claims that the synthetic unity of apperception presupposes or includes a synthesis.

seen that in §15 Kant refers in passing to "all combination, whether we be conscious of it or not," which suggests that not all synthesis involve a consciousness of the act (as opposed to the product).[19] Second, though it is often ignored, the proposition that the mind must be conscious of its acts of synthesis strikes some critics as a wildly implausible thesis in cognitive psychology.[20]

With regard to the first point, it must be noted that, even though Kant does not refer specifically to a consciousness of synthesis in the A-Deduction, the conception is clearly present. For example, we have seen that in a key passage Kant states that,

[T]he mind could not possibly think of the identity of itself in the manifoldness of its representations, and indeed think this *a priori*, if it did not have before its eyes the identity of its action, which subjects all synthesis of apprehension (which is empirical) to a transcendental unity, and first makes possible their connection in accordance with *a priori* rules.

(A108)

We have also seen that when Kant refers in §15 to a combination (synthesis) of which we might *not be conscious* he likely had in mind the synthesis of the imagination rather than that of the understanding, which he referred to in the A-Deduction as the "synthesis of recognition in the concept" and in the B-Deduction as the "intellectual synthesis." Accordingly, Kant is not claiming that *all* synthesis is a self-conscious act, which would be a blatant contradiction to what he says in §15 and elsewhere, but only that through which the I can become conscious of its own identity, i.e., the synthesis involved in bringing a manifold of representations to the unity of apperception. This is because the contentlessness of the "I think" means that there is nothing apart from the identity of its action in unifying a manifold of representations through which the thinking subject, considered as such, could become aware of its own identity qua thinking subject.[21] Expressed schematically, the consciousness of the identity of the I that thinks *a* with the I that thinks *b* could only consist in the consciousness of the identity of its action in thinking together *a* and *b* as its representations. That is why a consciousness of synthesis (considered as activity as well as product) is a necessary condition of apperception, even though the latter requires merely the *possibility* of the self-ascription of one's representations.

Turning to the second point, in response to the charge that the necessity of a consciousness of synthesis in the sense of an awareness of the act rather than merely its product is an implausible thesis in cognitive psychology, it must be emphasized that this results from the erroneous assumption that Kant means by such consciousness a

---

[19] See also A78/B103.

[20] Thus, Kitcher (1990), 111, 126-7, dismissively refers to it as "synthesis watching" and regards it as an embarrassment to be explained away rather than an integral part of Kant's account of cognition. I discuss her view in Allison (1996), 53-66. In her more recent book, however, she has abandoned this line of criticism and adopted a reading closer to the one advocated here. See Kitcher (2011), 138-9.

[21] I have added the qualifier "qua thinking subject" to underscore the point that Kant is not here concerned with the question of personal identity.

bit of introspection, as if we are supposed to have to be able to observe ourselves synthesizing in order to engage in the activity at all. But this is not what Kant claims. As already noted, his point is rather that discursive cognition is an inherently self-conscious activity, since I cannot take *x* as *a*, without being aware of what I am doing; though this does not mean either that I must somehow watch myself doing it (indeed, how could I?), or be aware that I (Henry Allison) am doing this. Otherwise expressed, the consciousness of synthesis, is not another thing that one does when one is thinking (a second-order thinking that one is thinking); it is rather an ineliminable component of the first-order activity itself.[22]

3) *The analytical unity of apperception presupposes a synthetic unity*: This is a direct consequence of the claim in §15 that the act of analysis (dissolution), which is the process through which an analytical unity is produced, presupposes synthesis, which is the act through which a synthetic unity is created. In the second paragraph of §16 Kant applies this claim to the unity of apperception. Here the analytical unity of apperception is the unity of the I with respect to its manifold of representations, i.e., that they are all representations for the same I. Correlatively, the synthetic unity of apperception is the unity of the representations in virtue of which they can all be taken by the I as its representations. Accordingly, the claim that the analytical unity of apperception presupposes or is only possible on the basis of a synthetic unity means that it is only insofar as the I unifies its representations that it can become conscious of its own identity, which is to say that "Synthetic unity of the manifold of given intuitions, as produced [*hervorgebracht*] a priori is thus the ground of the identity of apperception itself, which precedes *a priori* all my determinate thinking" (B134).[23] And since the analytical unity of apperception is the unity of the I of the "I think," which, according to the first paragraph of §16, must be able to accompany all my representations, and since, as Kant now claims, this analytical unity presupposes a synthetic unity, he concludes that this "principle [of the synthetic unity of apperception] is the supreme one in the whole of human cognition" (B135).

Kant attempts to clarify this claim in yet another important note, where he links the synthetic unity of apperception to the possibility of forming and applying concepts. The thrust of the argument, which is implicit in the note, goes roughly as follows: since (1) all concepts are analytical unities; and (2) all analytical unities presuppose a synthetic unity; and (3) all synthetic unity is grounded in the synthetic

---

[22] The point is suggested in a critique by Ameriks and Dieter Sturma of what Henrich called the "reflection theory," which, following what he termed "Fichte's original insight," Henrich attributed to Kant. Basically, this theory maintains that self-consciousness is to be explained as the result of a subject making an object of itself, which Henrich, following Fichte, claims is viciously circular. See Henrich (1966). In response to Henrich, Ameriks and Sturma argue convincingly not only that Kant was not committed to such a theory, but that he anticipated Fichte's claim that consciousness is "primitively self-referential." See Sturma (1985) and Ameriks (2000), 244–9.

[23] Following the Kemp Smith translation I am accepting Vaihinger's emendation of "*hervorgebracht*" for "*gegeben*" (given), since the latter makes no sense.

unity of apperception; it follows that (4) the possibility of forming and applying concepts presupposes the synthetic unity of apperception. Although Kant here assumes rather than argues for the proposition that concepts are analytical unities, it can easily be seen to follow from his understanding of such unity and his conception of concepts. As we have seen, Kant understands by an analytical unity a one contained in a many, as contrasted with a synthetic unity, which is a many contained in a one. And a concept is such a unity because it contains within a single representation the thought of what is common to a multitude of distinct representations.[24]

Kant illustrates the connection between concepts as analytical unities and a synthetic unity by focusing on two features of concepts, each of which presupposes that a concept stands in a synthetic unity with other representations. The first is their nature as partial representations or marks, i.e., representations of properties of an object. The point is that in order to predicate a property, say redness, of an object, it must be possible to predicate other properties of it as well, e.g., size and shape. As Kant puts it, "If I think of **red** in general, I thereby represent to myself a feature that (as a mark) can be encountered in anything, or that can be combined with other representations; therefore only by means of an antecedently conceived possible synthetic unity can I represent to myself the analytical unity" (B133n). The second relevant feature of a concept to which Kant alludes is its generality. The point here is that in order to grasp a concept I must recognize its generic nature, the fact that it is predicable of different objects, which share different properties, and this again requires that it stand in a synthetic unity, this time with the representations of objects with different properties. Kant writes:

A representation that is to be thought of as common to **several** must be regarded as belonging to those that in addition to it also have something **different** in themselves; consequently they must antecedently be conceived in synthetic unity with other (even if only possible representations) before I can think of the analytical unity of consciousness in it that makes it into a *conceptus communis.*   (B133–4n)

Although Kant does not call attention to the matter, it seems that the first of the forementioned features of a concept (its being a partial representation or mark) is that in virtue of which it can have an intension; while the second (its generality) is that in virtue of which it can have an extension. And if this is the case, it seems possible to tease out of the text of the note an argument to the effect that standing in a synthetic unity is a necessary condition of a concept having either an intension or an extension. Setting that speculation aside, however, the main point is that the analytical unity that constitutes a concept is closely related to, if not actually modeled upon, the analytical unity of apperception. In fact, the analytical unity of apperception may be characterized as the form or prototype of the unity that pertains to all general

---

[24] As was noted in Chapter 6, note 28, concepts are both analytical and synthetic unities for Kant: the former with respect to their extension and the latter with respect to their intension.

concepts, which differ from the latter only by containing a determinate content that is provided by sensible intuition.[25]

Kant concludes from his brief analysis of the connection between the possibility of concepts and the synthetic unity of apperception that the latter is "the highest point to which one must affix all use of the understanding, even the whole of logic and, after it, transcendental philosophy; indeed this faculty is the understanding itself" (B134). This is a consequence of the combination of the discursive nature of human cognition and the conception of the understanding as the faculty of concepts (A65–6/B90–1). Since human cognition is discursive, the supreme principle or condition of its possibility must lie in the condition of the possibility of concepts, which is grounded in the synthetic unity of apperception. Moreover, this is a condition of the possibility of logic because, as Kant understood it, logic is concerned with the rules of discursive thinking as such, which effectively means the use of concepts in judgments and inferences.[26] Similarly, insofar as the synthetic unity of apperception is a condition of logic it is a condition of transcendental philosophy, since Kant defines the latter as a system of concepts through which cognition of objects is possible a priori (B25).

The analyticity of the principle of the synthetic unity of apperception: In the third and final paragraph of §16 Kant states that "this principle of the synthetic unity of apperception is, to be sure, itself identical, thus an analytical proposition, yet it declares as necessary a synthesis of the manifold given in an intuition, without which the thoroughgoing identity of self-consciousness could not be thought" (B135). The seemingly paradoxical nature of this proposition, particularly when considered in the context of Kant's view that analytic judgments cannot extend our knowledge beyond what is already thought (however obscurely) in a given concept, is that Kant seems to be claiming that this proposition entails the doctrine of an a priori synthesis, which, in turn, plays a key role in grounding synthetic a priori knowledge involving the categories as conditions of the possibility of experience. Similarly, in § 17, Kant reiterates that this proposition

is ... itself analytic, although to be sure it makes synthetic unity a condition of all thinking; for it says nothing more than that all **my** representations in any given intuition must stand under the condition under which alone I can ascribe them to an identical self as **my** representations, and thus can grasp them together, as synthetically combined in an apperception through the general expression **I think**.   (B138).

The first step in analyzing this contention is to determine precisely what proposition Kant claims to be analytic and why. Since Kant equates the analytic proposition with

---

[25] In the words of Klaus Reich (1992), 32, "[E]very concept is, in a restricted way, what the 'I think' is unconditionally." See also Stuhlmann-Laeisz (1976), 81–3, and Carl (1997), 147–63.

[26] In the *Critique* Kant defines logic, in contrast to aesthetic, as "the science of the rules of understanding in general" (A52/B76). Similarly, in the *Jäsche Logic* he defines it as "the science of the necessary laws of the understanding and of reason" (9: 13; 528).

the principle of the synthetic unity of apperception, which is the subject matter of §16, perhaps the most obvious option is the initial claim of this section; viz., that "The **I think** must be able to accompany all my representations." Given the modalized nature of the claim, this proposition has at least one necessary condition of analyticity, namely, apriority. But since Kant recognizes the possibility of synthetic cognitions that are also a priori, this is not sufficient. Moreover, the justification that Kant provides for it further muddies the waters. As we have seen, he claims that "otherwise something would be represented in me that could not be thought at all, which is as much as to say that the representation would either be impossible or at least nothing for me." The problem here, which has been previously noted and applies to Kant's other formulations of the apperception-principle as well, concerns his characterization of the negation of this principle; viz., that a representation that could not be accompanied by the "I think" would either be impossible or nothing to me. On the assumption of the first disjunct, the proposition would clearly be analytic, at least if the impossibility to which Kant refers is understood as logical. It is not clear, however, that this would hold if the negation of the proposition entails simply that representations that did not conform to the apperceivability condition would "be nothing to me;" for we have seen that this means only that such representations could play no cognitive role, though they might well exist and even affect our feelings, desires, and behavior, which Kant acknowledged is a real possibility.

Accordingly, we must qualify the principle as Kant initially formulated it to capture the representational function that he clearly intended, which can be done by giving it a conditional form. So construed, it maintains that the "I think" must be able to accompany all my representations, *if* I am to be able to represent anything through them, i.e., if they are to be capable of functioning as representations for me. Such a proposition seems to be analytic because it would be contradictory to claim that something functions as a representation for me, even though it is not possible for me to become conscious of it as mine. Like a Leibnizian small perception, it might well be a representation *in me*, but not a representation *for me*.

Nevertheless, it is not clear that this is what Kant actually meant, or at least not all that he meant, by the analyticity of the principle of synthetic unity. For one thing, the principle, so described, does not appear to be a principle of *synthetic unity*, i.e., one affirming the necessity of a many in a one. For another, it ignores Kant's emphasis on identity in both §16 and §17. Beginning with the latter, it seems that Kant misspoke in §16 when he characterized the principle of the necessary unity of apperception as itself an identical and therefore analytic proposition. This suggests that he considered it a simple tautology ($a = a$), whereas it appears that what he intended to say is that it asserts an identity, which, as the much discussed identity of the morning star and the evening star indicates, is not at all the same thing. And since it is evident from what Kant says in §17 about the analyticity claim that he intended it as a reiteration in somewhat different terms of what he had said in §16, it seems reasonable to take it as a further articulation of the point that he was there trying to make. In fact, the passage from §17 adds two previously neglected elements to Kant's initial account: (1) that it applies to all my representations in a given intuition (though not all my representations as such) and (2) that the identity at issue is that of the I for whom these function as representations. In other words, it is not simply that it must be possible for an "I think" to accompany each of a subject's representations, if they are to function as representations for that subject; it is rather that it must be the *same* (numerically identical) subject whose thought must accompany each of these representations, if this subject is to think of them as collectively constituting the representation of the manifold of an intuition.

This is clearly a principle of synthetic unity and as such entails a synthesis; but it still leaves us with the question of whether the principle, so construed, is analytic. In order to resolve this question it is necessary to return to a previously discussed feature of Kant's account in both editions; viz., its reflexive dimension, by which I mean the notion that representing is understood as representing something *to oneself*. I have argued repeatedly that this locution is not an incidental feature of Kant's account, but reflects an essential aspect of the conception of thinking as an act of spontaneity; viz., a conscious taking of an *x* as *a*, which, as such, necessarily involves an awareness of what one is doing (a consciousness of synthesis). The present point is only that, given this conception of cognition, the analyticity of the principle of synthetic unity follows, because in order to represent to myself a manifold of representations as a manifold I must consider myself as the identical subject of the representations that I am taking together. In other words, I am claiming that the principle of the synthetic unity of apperception is at bottom a conceptual claim about how a thinking subject, considered merely as such, must regard itself in the act of thinking.

Moreover, that this is how Kant viewed the matter is indicated by his revised account of the Paralogisms in the second edition, where the focus is on the analyticity of claims regarding the I. Thus, in his discussion of the Second Paralogism (concerning simplicity) he writes:

That the I of apperception, consequently in every thought, is **a single thing** [*ein Singular sei*] that cannot be resolved into a plurality of subjects, and hence a logically simple subject, lies already in the concept of thinking [*des Denkens*], and is consequently an analytic proposition: but that does not signify that the thinking I is a simple **substance**, which would be a synthetic proposition. (B407–8)

Kant here not only insists upon the analyticity of the principle, but also presents it as grounded in the concept of thinking. Applying Kant's own criterion of analyticity, the concept in which the predicate is "contained" and from which it follows by means of the principle of contradiction is that of discursive thinking.[27] It is because such

---

[27] Paton, who was highly skeptical about Kant's attribution of analyticity to the principle of the synthetic unity of apperception, claimed that "The proposition can be analytic only if it is made by an analysis of human knowledge" (1936a), 518.

thinking consists in bringing a manifold of representations under a concept, i.e., judging, that it cannot be conceived apart from a numerically identical subject. Or, putting it in the first-person mode, I cannot conceive of myself as thinking without also conceiving of myself as the abiding subject of the thoughts that I ascribe to myself. But since, as Kant also points out against the rational psychologist, this concerns merely how the thinking subject must regard itself, it cannot be taken as yielding a synthetic a priori proposition regarding the nature of this subject.[28]

Despite its clear presence in the text, the analytic nature of the principle of the synthetic unity of apperception has met with resistance in the literature, partly because of the seemingly paradoxical nature of the claim that the principle of synthetic unity could be analytic and partly because of the difficulty of reconciling it with some current views about what the Transcendental Deduction is supposed to accomplish. A case in point is the view of Guyer, who raises two basic objections to this reading.[29] The first is his contention that if the apperception-principle were analytic, it could yield only the conditional necessity that I must be able to synthesize my representations, *if* I am to be conscious of them as belonging to my identical self. Against this Guyer contends that for the argument of the Deduction to succeed, Kant must establish the *unconditional* necessity that all my representations are synthesizable and ascribable to a single self, the numerical identity of which can be determined a priori. The second consists in an appeal to a previously discussed passage in the A-Deduction, where Kant appears to affirm that the principle of the synthetic unity of apperception is synthetic, which Guyer uses as evidence for Kant's uncertainty regarding his own first principle.

As far as Guyer's first point is concerned, I agree that Kant's analytic principle asserts a merely conditional necessity, since it expresses the condition under which the I can be conscious of its own identity; but I reject the conclusions that he draws from this. First, given the fact that the argument fails under Guyer's own preferred (synthetic) reading of it, its purported failure on the assumption that the principle in question is analytic hardly constitutes a sufficient ground for dismissing it as a reading of the text. Moreover, Guyer's alternative reading is itself deeply problematic. But having already discussed my difficulties with his reading at various junctures I shall not rehash them now. Instead, I shall simply point out that Guyer fails to

---

[28] Kant underscores the first-person nature of his claim in the Third Paralogism (concerning personal identity), where already in the first edition version (A361–6) he frames the issue in terms of how the thinking subject is constrained to think itself, which Kant uses to bring out the fallacious nature of the argument from this to personal identity by noting that the inference does not hold from a third-person standpoint. Moreover, he there also alludes to the analycity of the claim made from the first-person standpoint by claiming that from this standpoint "the personality [personal identity] of the soul must be regarded not as inferred but rather as a completely identical proposition of self-consciousness in time" (A362). In the more succinct second-edition version of this paralogism Kant notes that "The proposition of the identity of myself in everything manifold is equally one lying in the concepts themselves, and hence an analytic proposition" (B408).

[29] See Guyer (1987), esp. 133–40.

contextualize Kant's analyticity claim, by which I mean its location in the first part of a two-step proof, which, *ex hypothesi*, does not entail the desired conclusion. In what follows I shall attempt to show that the entire argument of the first part of the B-Deduction should be seen as Kant's effort to spell out the major implications of this analytic principle, which means that its conclusion must likewise be seen as analytic in a broad sense.

The viability of Guyer's second point depends entirely upon the correctness of his claim that the expressly synthetic proposition from the A-Deduction to which he refers is logically equivalent to the proposition in the B-Deduction, which Kant characterizes as analytic. In the passage in question Kant states that, "The synthetic proposition, that every different empirical consciousness must be combined into a single self-consciousness is the absolutely first and synthetic principle of our thinking in general" (A117n); whereas the proposition in the B-Deduction, which Kant claims to be analytic, states that, "all **my** representations in any given intuition must stand under the condition under which alone I can ascribe them to an identical self as **my** representations, and thus can grasp them together, as synthetically combined in an apperception through the general expression **I think**" (B138).

Although these propositions are similar, since each makes a necessity claim with regard to the unity of apperception, a closer inspection indicates that they are not equivalent. The fundamental difference is that the first-edition passage concerns the necessary combinability of different episodes of empirical consciousness (of a particular cognizer) in a single self-consciousness, which Kant identifies with transcendental consciousness; whereas the second-edition account concerns the necessary unification of all of a subject's representations *in a given intuition*. Accordingly, in order to claim that these propositions are equivalent it must be assumed that by the combinability of representations in a given intuition Kant understands the same thing as the combinability of distinct episodes of empirical consciousness, which is manifestly not the case. On the contrary, we have seen that by "empirical consciousness" Kant understands something like a perceptual awareness, which implies that by the combination of different episodes of empirical consciousness Kant means the combinability of different states of perceptual awareness. By contrast, the combinability of representations in a given intuition is best understood as their combinability in a single perception or perceptual state. Thus, it does not follow that because the former proposition is synthetic that the latter must be also.

In order to clarify the matter, we must see why Kant regarded the former proposition as synthetic and the latter as analytic. With regard to the former, the essential point is that a synthesis of perceptions, such as is required for the possibility of experience, involves the unification of temporally successive items, which for Kant means that it involves a consideration of the specific nature of human sensibility. And it is this that makes the proposition regarding the combinability of perceptions synthetic. In fact, we have seen that at the very beginning of the preparatory section of the A-Deduction Kant makes the general remark on which he claims that everything that follows is grounded; viz., that all our representations, whatever their source or origin, as modifications of the mind, belong to inner sense and are therefore "subjected to the formal condition of inner sense, namely time, as that in which they must all be ordered, connected, and brought into relations" (A98–9).

By contrast the analytic nature of the proposition from the B-Deduction must be understood in light of the procedure that Kant adopts in the first part of this Deduction, which he presents as a counterpart to the Aesthetic. Just as in the Aesthetic he abstracted from all contribution of the understanding so as to isolate sensibility, Kant here abstracts from the specific nature of sensibility in order to isolate the contribution of the understanding. Moreover, in abstracting from the nature of sensibility Kant is also abstracting from the conditions required to ground synthetic judgments. As Kant consistently maintains, such judgments require relating concepts to sensible intuitions, a requirement which in the present case cannot be met. To be sure, Kant here continues to insist that, as discursive, human cognition must relate to sensible intuition; but what such cognition is actually related to in the first part of the B-Deduction is the *concept* of "sensible intuition in general," which means that the entire account must be seen as a highly complex exercise in conceptual analysis.

Kant also points out that his analysis applies only to the concept of an understanding that thinks, i.e., a discursive understanding for which a sensible manifold must be given to it in order for it to have something to think. And in order to give meaning to this scope limitation Kant contrasts it with the concept of an intuitive (non-discursive) intellect, which would have no need for synthesis in order to bring the manifold of its representations to the unity of consciousness because through its self-awareness "the manifold of intuition would at the same time be given" and "through whose representation the objects of this representation would at the same time exist" (B138–9).[30] Although Kant viewed the conception of an intuitive intellect as a merely problematic idea, he held that the mere conceivability (logical possibility) of such an "understanding" suffices to drive a "critical" wedge between the conditions of human, i.e., discursive, cognition and the conditions of any conceivable cognition.

III

§17 *The principle of the synthetic unity of apperception is the supreme principle of all use of the understanding* (B136–9): Although the section contains five paragraphs, since the last two, which reiterate the claims regarding the analyticity and restriction to a discursive understanding of the principle of the synthetic unity of apperception, have already been considered, the present discussion will focus on the first three,

[30] See also B135.

which speak directly to the heading and significantly develop the analysis of the synthetic unity of apperception begun in §16.

Inasmuch as the specific concern of this section is with the understanding and, like the whole of the first part of the B-Deduction, it supposedly abstracts from the nature of sensibility, it is somewhat surprising that Kant begins the section with a reflection on the conditions of the possibility of *intuition*. He claims that there are two such conditions. One, which concerns its relation to sensibility, is that "all the manifold of sensibility stands under the formal conditions of space and time." The other, which Kant characterizes as "the supreme principle of all intuition in relation to the understanding," is that "all the manifold of intuition stand under conditions of the original synthetic unity of apperception." The manifold of intuition stands under the former insofar as its elements are given and under the latter "insofar as they must be capable of being **combined** in one consciousness" (B136). In support of the latter, Kant points out that, "without that [the capability of being combined in a single consciousness] nothing could be thought or cognized through them, since the given representations would not have in common the act of apperception, **I think**, and thereby would not be grasped together in one consciousness" (B137).

In a note attached to the claim that in relation to the understanding the manifold of intuition stands under the conditions of the synthetic unity of apperception, Kant remarks that,

Space and time and all their parts are **intuitions**, thus individual [*einzelne*] representations along with the manifold that they contain in themselves (see the Transcendental Aesthetic), thus they are not mere concepts by means of which the same consciousness is contained in many representations, but rather are contained in one and in the consciousness of it; they are thus found to be composite, and consequently the unity of consciousness, as **synthetic** and yet as original, is to be found in them. This singularity [*Einzelnheit*] of theirs is important in its application (see §26).[31]   (B136)

Since the claim that the representations of space and time are intuitions rather than concepts is a central claim of the Transcendental Aesthetic, this again leads one to wonder about the location of this note in the portion of the B-Deduction that supposedly abstracts from any considerations concerning the specific nature of sensibility. But since Kant remarks in the main text that the manifold of sensible intuition is subject to the formal conditions of space and time as well as the synthetic unity of apperception, it does seem appropriate for him to say something about the former, even though his present concern is with the latter. And since the latter, though intrinsically important, is peripheral to the argument of this part of the Deduction, it was also appropriate for Kant to place the discussion in a note rather than in the main body of the text.

---

[31] Although the text refers to §25 it is generally regarded as a misprint for §26, where the discussion to which Kant refers is actually to be found.

Nevertheless, in view of its intrinsic importance and the fact that Kant located this note in §17 it also seems appropriate to say something at this point about its significance. To anticipate what will be discussed in greater detail in Chapter 9, I take Kant to be here posing the problem of the relation between the unity of apperception and the unity of space and time, which will be a central issue of the second part of the B-Deduction. Appealing to the results of the Aesthetic, Kant points out that the unity of space and time consists in the fact that, as intuitions rather than concepts, they are representations of individuals: there is a single space and a single time of which particular spaces and times are conceived as delimited portions. Accordingly, each contains a many (actually an infinitely many) in one.[32] The problem, however, is that this seems to make them into synthetic unities, which, given what Kant says about synthesis and synthetic unity in §15 and §16, implies that they are products of an act of synthesis, which contradicts his fundamental tenet that space and time are forms of receptivity and, as such, *given* rather than *made*. Since Kant will address this issue in §26 in terms of the distinction between forms of intuition (which are the contribution of sensibility) and formal intuitions (which are products of the determination of sensibility under these forms by the understanding), he here seems to be alluding to this later discussion.

The second paragraph of §17 is pivotal because it introduces the concept of an object and with it the whole question of objective validity and its conditions. After defining the understanding as the faculty of cognitions and stipulating that these consist in the determinate relation of given representations to an object, Kant states:

An **object** [*Object*] ... is that in the concept of which the manifold of a given intuition is **united**. Now, however, all unification of representations requires unity of consciousness in the synthesis of them. Consequently the unity of consciousness is that which alone constitutes the relation of representations to an object, thus their objective validity, and consequently is that which makes them into cognitions and on which even the possibility of the understanding rests.   (B137)

Kant's definition of an object in terms of its concept in the first sentence can be compared with a similar, though more expansive treatment of the issue in the A-Deduction. Once again, the fundamental difference stems from the fact that the A-Deduction assumes from the beginning the results of the Aesthetic, while the first part of the B-Deduction abstracts from these results. Consequently, the A-Deduction formulates the problem of objectivity in terms of appearances, asking how (as "mere representations") their relation to an object is to be understood and explained, which immediately places the discussion in an idealistic framework. By contrast, the first part of the B-Deduction eschews any reference to appearances and

---

[32] I have argued elsewhere that Kant's claim in the Aesthetic that space and time are "infinite given magnitudes" is not to be taken as an assertion that they consist of an infinite number of parts but rather that they are boundless or limitless in that every determinate magnitude of space or time (no matter how great) is only conceivable as a limitation of the single space or time. See Allison (2004), 110–12.

poses the question in more general terms, asking simply what is to be understood by an object for a discursive understanding.

More germane to our present concerns are two closely related passages from the A-Deduction, which were discussed in Chapter 5. In the first Kant assumes that it has already been established in the Aesthetic that the objects of human cognition are appearances, which he here characterizes as "nothing but sensible representations, which must not be regarded in themselves, in the same way, as objects (outside the power of representation)," and he asks: "What does one mean, then, when one speaks of an object corresponding to and therefore also distinct from the cognition?" And we saw that in response to this question Kant wrote that, "this object must be thought of only as something in general=X, since outside of our cognition we have nothing that we could set over against this cognition as corresponding to it" (A104).

In the second passage, which is separated from the first by an introductory account of the unity of apperception as an objectifying ground in the guise of a "formal unity of consciousness" and the account of concepts as rules governing this unity, Kant develops the point by appealing to the dual nature of representations, i.e., the fact that, though qua representations (representings) they necessarily have an object, they can themselves also become objects of other representations (representeds). We saw that applying this account to appearances on the grounds that they are themselves representations, Kant maintained that, qua intuiteds, appearances are the immediate objects of representation, but qua intuitings must have their object, which, since it cannot itself be intuited, Kant dubbed "the non-empirical, i.e., transcendental object=X" (A109). And by this line of reasoning the indeterminate thought of the object of cognition as "something in general=X" is transmuted into the "transcendental object=X."

Although this might appear to be a distinction without a difference, it was argued that there is a significant difference between the two formulations and that it lies in the intervening account of the objectifying function of apperception as the formal unity of consciousness. In light of this account, it was suggested that the transcendental object = X should be regarded as the correlate of the formal unity of consciousness. As such, it is not the concept of a special sort of non-sensible object, but, rather, a special sort of concept of an object, which can be more appropriately termed a "transcendental concept of an object" because it concerns the objectivity of the "object," i.e., that in virtue of which any empirical object is an object. Accordingly, its function is to set the stage for the introduction of the categories as the a priori rules through which the formal and objective unity of consciousness is determined.

Nevertheless, if one sets aside the differences stemming from the contrasting methodologies of the A and B Deductions and compares Kant's second-edition characterization of the concept of an object with the first-edition account, one sees that there is a notable similarity; for common to both is the view that by an object is to be understood that which is thought through and corresponds to the conscious unification of the manifold of intuition by and for a single consciousness. Although

Kant no longer refers to the transcendental object, this could also be described as the transcendental *concept of an object*, since it constitutes the thought of an object as such.

Kant concludes from this that "the unity of consciousness is that which alone constitutes the relation of representations to an object, thus their objective validity (B137)," which he attempts to illustrate by the example of the cognition of a line as a determinate portion of space. As in a parallel discussion in the A-Deduction, Kant's point is that the cognition of a line involves drawing it, thereby producing a synthetic unity of the manifold, with the unity of consciousness understood as the unity of the action in the conception of the line. And from this he concludes that,

> The synthetic unity of consciousness is therefore an objective condition of all cognition, not merely something I myself need in order to cognize an object but rather something under which every intuition must stand **in order to become an object for me**, since in any other way, and without this synthesis, the manifold would **not** be united in one consciousness.   (B138)

While it is more evident in the first of these passages, where Kant claims that the synthetic unity of consciousness alone constitutes the relation of representations to an object, the clear implication of both is that the synthetic unity of consciousness is not only a necessary condition of the possibility of the representation of an object but also a sufficient one.

In the second passage, the first part of the sentence might be taken as simply reinforcing the claim that this unity is a necessary condition of the cognition of an object, since it states that it is a condition apart from which an intuition cannot be cognized as an object. But if, as seems plausible, we take an "objective condition" to mean an *objectivating* condition, it can be read as implying that it is a sufficient condition as well. The second part, however, seems to require taking it as also a sufficient condition, since it effectively maintains that the synthesis through which an object is cognized is itself a necessary condition of the synthetic unity of consciousness, which is logically equivalent to the claim that the latter is a sufficient condition of the former. Otherwise expressed, Kant is here affirming a reciprocity between the synthetic unity of consciousness and the cognition of an object.[33]

Not surprisingly, the claim that the synthetic unity of consciousness is not merely a necessary but also a sufficient condition of the representation of an object has met with significant skepticism among commentators. The basic objection is that the most that Kant is entitled to claim on the basis of the argument of §16 and §17 is that it is a necessary condition and the claim that it is also a sufficient condition is a

---

[33]   A similar claim is made by Schulting (2012), 53–61, who likewise attempts to defend Kant's argument against the objections here considered. The difference between us with respect to this issue is that whereas his concern is to defend an updated version of Reich's view that the categories are derived from an analysis of the analytic unity of apperception, my focus is on the relation between the two parts of the B-Deduction.

non-sequitur of the type that Kant has frequently been found guilty by critics.[34] Even worse, it seems that the stronger claim has the untoward consequence of ruling out the very possibility of non-objective modes of awareness, such as dreams and hallucinations, since these presumably also presuppose a synthetic unity of consciousness as a necessary condition of their possibility.[35]

In dealing with this problem it is essential to become clear about what is meant by "object" (*Objekt*) and "cognition" (*Erkenntnis*) in this context. If one understands by the former an actual empirical object (an object in the "thick" sense) and by the latter empirical knowledge or experience (cognition in the "thick" sense), then the proposition that the unity of consciousness is a sufficient condition of the cognition of an object is a *non-sequitur* and leads to the consequence described above. Accordingly, it is appropriate to ask if these consequences can be avoided by interpreting these terms in a weaker or "thin" sense and if so, whether there is any textual justification for doing so. To begin with, by "object" in the thin sense I understand an object of thought or intentional object, which may, though need not be, something actual in the sense of being empirically real. Correlatively, by "cognition" in the thin sense I understand the act of thinking by a discursive intellect or, more simply, discursive thinking.

It seems evident that if these terms are to be taken in their thin senses the *non-sequitur* and untenable consequences charges no longer hold. With respect to the former, the key point is the above-mentioned reciprocity between the synthetic unity of consciousness and the cognition (in the thin sense) of an object. Since on this view the cognition of an object is a necessary condition of the unity of consciousness, the claim that the latter is a sufficient as well as a necessary condition of the former is logically in order.[36] With respect to the latter, while it is true that on this reading the objects for which the synthetic unity of consciousness would be a sufficient as well as a necessary condition include dream and hallucinatory objects as well as genuine

---

[34] Prominent among those who criticize Kant's argument on these grounds are Hossenfelder (1978), 128–30, Guyer (1987), 117, Thöle (1991), 260–3, and Bird (2006), 320. Carl (1998), 197–8 notes the problem, but finds its solution in the specification of the unity of consciousness as an objective unity in §18.

[35] Thus C. I. Lewis famously remarked: "Did the sage of Konigsberg have no dreams!" (1929), 221. Although Lewis posed the problem in terms of the categories rather than the unity of apperception, it is obvious that the same problem arises with respect to the latter, since Kant maintained that the validity of the categories is grounded in their connection with the unity of apperception. The classical response to this line of objection is by Beck (1978), 38–60, who defended Kant by appealing to a thin sense of object, according to which dreams and hallucinations involve the categories (and therefore the transcendental unity of apperception) without losing their subjective status. My own analyses of these issues has been significantly influenced by Beck's; though I believe that I go further in exploring the ambiguities in Kant's account and in linking it to the methodology of the B-Deduction. I shall say more about this issue in the Conclusion.

[36] I take Kant's position here to be essentially unchanged from that of the A-Deduction, where he effectively affirmed a reciprocity between the unity of consciousness and the consciousness of unity, with the latter being understood as the consciousness of an object.

empirical ones, the fact that these are all considered merely as objects in the thin sense rules out the worry about its implications.

Accordingly, it appears that everything turns on the textual question of whether it is plausible to claim that in the first part of the B-Deduction Kant understood "cognition" and "object" in the manner suggested. And my contention is that, given Kant's avowed methodology in the first part of the B-Deduction, such a reading is not merely plausible but required. Let us consider first cognition in its thick and thin senses. Typically, Kant contrasts the former with thought. This contrast is crucial for him, since it underlies his concern to restrict cognition to the realm of possible experience, without thereby also restricting thought, which is the means through which he finds conceptual space for the thought of freedom and, more generally, for a practical use of reason. Thus, while admitting that we can *think* things as they are in themselves, Kant denies that we can *cognize* them, so considered. Indeed, we shall see in Chapter 9 that in §22 Kant explicitly denies the equivalence of thinking and cognizing an object on the familiar grounds that the latter, unlike the former, requires that the object be given in intuition (B146). We also saw in Chapter 7 that Kant used the thinking-cognizing distinction in the *Prolegomena*, albeit not in precisely these terms, to explicate the distinction between judgments of perception and judgments of experience. Whereas the former are instances of judging, and *a fortiori* of thinking, because they involve the logical functions of judgment, they are not cognitions in the thick sense because they supposedly do not appeal to the categories, and therefore lack objective validity. By contrast, the latter are cognitions in this sense because they predicate the categories of sensible data, and are deemed objectively valid.

We have also seen, however, that in explicating the principle of the synthetic unity of apperception at the beginning of §17 Kant states that without the capability of being combined in a single consciousness "nothing could be thought or cognized" through our representations (B137). Kant here seems to regard thought and cognition as equivalent acts, which means that the latter is understood in the thin sense.[37] Moreover, lest this be considered merely a lapse on Kant's part, it should be noted that in §24 he claims that considered as related "through the mere understanding to objects of intuition in general," which is how they are regarded in the first part of the B-Deduction, the pure concepts of the understanding or categories are "mere **forms of thought**, through which no *determinate* [my emphasis] object is yet cognized" (B150). Although the categories are not yet introduced in §17, the understanding has been and the clear implication is that, apart from its relation to the particular nature of human sensibility, its concepts, as mere forms of thought, can only ground the cognition of an "indeterminate object." Assuming that the latter is equivalent to the "object in general=X" of the first edition, it seems evident that it is an object in

[37] See B137. This point was noted by Schulting (2012), 60.

the thin sense and that the cognition of an object, so understood, can consist in nothing other than its thought.

Nevertheless, quite apart from its plausibility as a reading of the text, this line of interpretation, which can be characterized as attributing to Kant a deflationary account of "object" and "cognition," appears to open him up to another powerful objection, albeit from the opposite direction; viz., that the resulting account is far too weak to serve the ends of the Deduction. Since this requires demonstrating that the categories are necessary conditions of the possibility of experience, its concern is with both objects and cognition in the thick sense. Thus, if this is really all that Kant's argument shows, it is of little philosophical interest and would hardly reward the labor required to understand it.[38]

As already suggested, I believe that this line of objection can be dealt with by insisting that Kant's account be understood contextually, where the context is the first part of the B-Deduction, in which Kant is attempting to analyze the contribution of the understanding to cognition (in the thick sense) in abstraction from the equally necessary contribution of sensibility. Once again, the point is that an analysis of the understanding that proceeds independently of the nature of sensibility is, at bottom, an essay in conceptual analysis, which is reflected in Kant's claim that the principle of the synthetic unity of apperception is analytic, even though it entails the necessity of a synthesis of the manifold given in intuition. While such a procedure obviously cannot provide sufficient conditions of the cognition (in the thick sense) of objects (in the thick sense), it can provide both necessary and sufficient conditions from the side of the understanding, which, as I have argued, are conditions of the cognition (in the thin sense) of objects (in the thin sense). To reduce a complex issue to a formulaic statement: the synthetic unity of apperception is both a necessary and sufficient condition of the cognition (in the thin sense) of an object (in the thin sense) and a necessary, but not a sufficient condition of the cognition (in the thick sense) of an object (in the thick sense). And, as I have tried to show, the necessity of distinguishing between these two senses of "object" and "cognition" is a consequence of Kant's methodology in the B-Deduction.

IV

§18 *What objective unity of self-consciousness is*: In what the heading suggests is an effort to clarify the problematic thesis of §17 that "the unity of consciousness is that

---

[38] This line of objection has been sharply expressed by Thöle (1991), 86–9 and 260–3. In the first of these places Thöle addresses this objection to Beck's appeal to a similar weak conception of an object in response to C. I. Lewis' critique of Kant (see note 44). In the second he addresses my initial treatment of the problem in Allison (1983), 144–6. A similar objection has also been raised by Guyer (1992), 151–2, who emphasizes the insufficiency of a deflationary account of objectivity on the grounds that what Kant must show is that the categories are necessary conditions of the cognition of objects distinct from the self.

which alone constitutes the relation of representations to an object," in §18 Kant draws the distinction between an objective and a subjective unity of consciousness, thereby implying that this claim pertains only to the former. Although this distinction was not present in the A-Deduction, we saw that Kant made repeated appeal to it in *Reflexionen* 5923–35, where he appeared to treat it as the replacement for the *Prolegomena*'s distinction between judgments of perception and judgments of experience. We shall see, however, that Kant's account of the subjective unity of consciousness is ambiguous and that this raises questions about both the nature and viability of his post-*Prolegomena* position. Since this section is both brief and opaque, I shall cite the text in full, once again numbering the sentences for ease of reference.

(1) The **transcendental unity** of apperception is that unity through which all of the manifold given in an intuition is united in a concept of the object. (2) It is called **objective** on that account, and must be distinguished from the **subjective unity** of consciousness, which is a **determination of inner sense**, through which that manifold of intuition is empirically given for such a combination. (3) Whether I can become **empirically** conscious of the manifold as simultaneous or successive depends on the circumstances, or empirical conditions. (4) Hence the empirical unity of consciousness, through association of the representations, itself concerns an appearance, and is entirely contingent. (5) The pure form of intuition in time, on the contrary, merely as intuition in general, which contains a given manifold, stands under the original unity of consciousness, solely by means of the necessary relation of the unity of the manifold of intuition to the one **I think**, thus through the pure synthesis of the understanding, which grounds *a priori* the empirical synthesis. (6) That unity alone is objectively valid; the empirical unity of apperception, which we are not assessing here, and which is also derived only from the former, under given conditions *in concreto*, has merely subjective validity. (7) One person combines the representation of a certain word with one thing, another with something else; and the unity of consciousness in that which is empirical is not, with regard to that which is given, necessarily and universally valid.   (B139–40)

Although the question posed in the heading concerns the objective unity of consciousness, only the first sentence and the initial clause of the second are directly concerned with it. The objective unity is identified with the transcendental unity of apperception, which is characterized as objective in virtue of its epistemic function; viz., uniting the manifold given in an intuition in the concept of an object. We have seen that in the above-mentioned *Reflexionen* Kant had equated this unity with that of a judgment and he will do likewise in §19. His aim in the present section is to prepare the way for this equation by contrasting it with a subjective unity of consciousness. If, as Kant states, an objective unity of consciousness is one in which "all of the manifold given in an intuition is united in a concept of the object," then a subjective unity must be one in which this unification does not occur. But since this characterization is purely negative, telling us merely what a subjective unity is not, Kant owes the reader an explanation of what it is and how one is to understand its relation to an objective unity.

Kant initially describes a subjective unity as a "**determination of inner sense**, through which that manifold of intuition is empirically given for such a combination." As de Vleeschauwer has pointed out, Kant uses the verb "*bestimmen*" (to determine) and the corresponding noun "*Bestimmung*" (determination) in both an active and a passive sense.[39] Understood in the latter sense, a determination is a mental state that is produced in a subject by external factors.[40] By contrast, when used in the active sense "to determine" means to make determinate, i.e., to fix or order the elements of a manifold in a specific way by subjecting them to a rule. Correlatively, a determination in the active sense is the product of an act of determining, as when we make an intuition determinate by subsuming it under a rule or recognizing it in a concept.

It is clear that "determination" cannot here be understood in the active sense, since that would make a determination of inner sense into an objective rather than a subjective unity. Moreover, this characterization does not accord with the description that Kant actually provides of a determination of inner sense, as that "through which the manifold of intuition is empirically given for such a combination." This indicates that such a determination refers to a mental state in which a cognizer finds itself rather than one produced by that cognizer. In Kantian terms, it is attributed to the receptivity rather than the spontaneity of the cognizer, which appears to be supported by Kant's explanatory remark in the third sentence that, "Whether I can become **empirically** conscious of the manifold as simultaneous or successive depends on the circumstances or empirical conditions" (B139).

This strongly suggests the identification of the subjective unity of consciousness with the unity of empirical consciousness. Assuming that Kant is using "empirical consciousness" in his usual manner to designate a *merely* empirical consciousness, i.e., one without any a priori elements or conditions, we are to understand by it one that pertains to perception or apprehension as contrasted with cognition.[41] In other words, it is a form of consciousness that is dependent upon the reproductive imagination; though the methodology of the B-Deduction prevents Kant from appealing to the latter at this juncture.

Focusing on Kant's claim in the third sentence that the empirical consciousness of the manifold as simultaneous or successive depends on the circumstances or empirical conditions, Longuenesse attempts to illustrate what Kant understands by such consciousness through the examples of the perceived simultaneity of the shining of the stars in the night sky (even though the reality behind their apparent simultaneity may be a difference of millions of light years), and the perceived successiveness of the

---

[39] See de Vleeschauwer (1937), 135.

[40] We shall see in Chapter 9 that in §24 Kant speaks of a self-affection, through which inner sense is determined by the understanding. This does not appear to be at issue in the present context, however, since the determination is by external factors.

[41] See, for example, A122–3, B133, B134, B144, B160, B164, A162/B202, B207.

different positions of the sun and of the sound of thunder to the sight of lightening (even though the phenomena that seem to be successive are actually simultaneous).[42] And she correctly notes that these appearings are dependent upon "circumstances and empirical conditions" and that the "appearance" at issue here is to be understood in the empirical rather than the transcendental sense.[43]

There is, however, one problem with Longuenesse's lucid and informed account; viz., that, while it succinctly expresses what Kant was apparently trying to say, it glosses over the question of its compatibility with the conception of a subjective unity of consciousness, understood as one in which the manifold in a given intuition is *not united* in the concept of the object. This is because, like Kant, Longuenesse fails to disambiguate the conception of a subjective unity. As Longuenesse shows through her examples, the forms of empirical consciousness involving the perception of seemingly simultaneous and successive states of affairs are clearly subjective in the sense that these temporal determinations depend upon contingent factors and conditions, which cannot be projected onto the phenomena. Accordingly, they hold only from the standpoint of an observer on Earth and due to factors such as the speed of light, cannot be said to hold for *any* observer. In short, these empirical unities are subjective in precisely the same sense and for the same reason as the judgments of perception in the *Prolegomena*, which is to say that they hold only for the consciousness of particular perceivers, and therefore cannot lay claim to the (subjective) universality and necessity that attaches to objectively valid judgments of experience. The problem is that it does not follow from this that the unity of empirical consciousness, so understood, is also a subjective unity in the sense of one not involving the unification of the manifold given in intuition in the concept of an object. On the contrary, even though Kant does not refer to an empirical unity of consciousness as a judgment, it seems to involve more than the purely passive recording of the sensible data as given or as impressed upon inner sense as its determinations. Rather, it appears to require something like an interpretation of the data, taking them as simultaneous or successive on the basis of what appears to be the case. And if this is the case such empirical unities would involve acts of thought, which by Kant's stipulated criterion makes them objective unities.

The problem is exacerbated by Kant's shift in the fifth and sixth sentences from the empirical unity of consciousness, which is presumably equivalent to the unity of empirical consciousness, to the empirical unity of apperception, which he contrasts with the original unity of consciousness, i.e., the transcendental unity of apperception. Evidently taking this as a further elucidation of the distinction between the objective and the subjective unity of consciousness, Kant states that only the latter is objectively valid, while the former, which he purports not to be considering here, is

---

[42]   See Longuenesse (1998), 184. Although Longuenesse does not explicitly draw the contrasts between the appearance and the (empirical) reality that I do, I assume that it underlies her account.
[43]   Ibid.

claimed to be derived from the latter "under given conditions *in concreto*" and to have "merely subjective validity." It is understandable why Kant chose not to consider empirical apperception and its unity here, since it would have required a lengthy digression from the task of the first part of the B Deduction. It is also unfortunate, however, since the little that he says about it elsewhere further clouds the situation. For example, at A107 Kant appears to indentify empirical apperception with inner sense. But later in the A-Deduction, after specifying the faculties of sense, imagination, and apperception as the three subjective sources of cognition and claiming that each can be considered empirically "in application to given appearances" (as well as transcendentally), he states that (empirical) apperception represents appearances empirically "in the **empirical consciousness** of the identity of these reproductive representations with the appearances through which they were given, hence in **recognition**" (A115). Accordingly, empirical apperception, as Kant here construes it, is manifested in acts of conceptual recognition, which implies that it pertains to the spontaneity of the understanding rather than the receptivity of sense and as such involves an objective rather than a subjective unity of consciousness. Apart from the passage under consideration, the only other reference to empirical apperception in the B-Deduction (B132) is made in passing and is of no help, since Kant says merely that he calls the conception of apperception with which he is there concerned "pure" in order to distinguish it from the empirical variety, about which nothing further is said.[44]

The main issue, however, is what Kant meant by the claim that the empirical unity of apperception is derived from the transcendental unity under given conditions *in concreto*. There seem to be two possible ways to interpret this claim. One, which assumes the identification of empirical apperception and inner sense, is that since the order in which perceptions occur in inner sense is determined by causal laws it is subject to the transcendental conditions of experience, and in this attenuated sense is derived from the transcendental unity of apperception as the ultimate ground of

---

[44] Kant's most extensive account of empirical apperception is in the *Anthropology*, but it cannot be said that he there provides a clear and unambiguous account of it either. First, in a note attached to the section on self-observation, after distinguishing between the act of spontaneity or reflection, by which a thought becomes possible, and receptivity or apprehension, through which an empirical intuition becomes possible, Kant states that "consciousness of oneself (*apperceptio*) can be divided into that of reflection and that of apprehension. The first is a consciousness of understanding, *pure* apperception; the second a consciousness of inner sense (*empirical* apperception)" (A 7: 134n; 246). Then, in a section on inner sense, Kant states that "Inner sense is not pure apperception, a consciousness of what the human being *does*, since this belongs to the faculty of thinking. Rather, it is a consciousness of what he undergoes, so far as he is affected by the play of his own thoughts" (A 7: 161; 272). And, finally, in a marginal note that is not contained in the published text, where Kant is attempting to defend his thesis that we can cognize ourself only as we appear to ourself through inner sense, not as we are in ourself, he states that, "This difficulty rests entirely on a confusing of *inner sense* (and of empirical self-consciousness) with *apperception* (intellectual self-consciousness")" (A 7 H 141; 253). Thus, while Kant is emphatic on the distinction between inner sense and *pure* apperception, he does not seem to draw a sharp distinction between inner sense and the empirical variety.

these conditions.[45] Assuming the identification of empirical apperception with inner sense, which A115 shows to be problematic, this reading is possible, though not terribly appealing. Among its problems is that it seems unmotivated, since it does not appear to further our understanding of what is meant by the subjective unity of consciousness. Why should Kant make such a claim at this point? And if he thought it important why did he not help the reader by simply noting that by *empirical* apperception he meant simply inner sense?[46] Moreover, it makes no sense to claim that a causally determined order of perceptions is subjectively valid, since the notion of validity is out of place.

The other possible reading accords with what Kant says about empirical apperception at A115, and therefore distinguishes it from inner sense.[47] It also construes the derivation of the empirical unity of apperception from the original or transcendental unity in a normative rather than a causal (or logical) sense, which, unlike the alternative sketched above, makes it possible to attribute to the empirical unity a subjective validity. On this reading, it is not that the content of an empirical unity can be derived from the transcendental unity, since the latter is purely formal and, as such, lacking in content. It is rather that the transcendental and formal unity imposes constraints on whatever content is brought under the former, i.e., empirically apperceived or brought to empirical consciousness.

If the latter, or something like it, is what Kant is claiming in the fifth and six sentences, which I believe to be the most plausible reading of the text, then, apart from the fact that he does not refer to it as involving judgment, his account of the subjective unity of empirical consciousness is essentially in accord with his accounts of judgments of perception in the *Prolegomena* and of provisional judgments in the various versions of his logic lectures. In particular, it meshes nicely with Kant's claim that all judgments of experience are at first judgments of perception, which appears to be the point to which Longuenesse was alluding through her examples.[48] Once again, however, the problem is that, though subjectively valid in the sense that the unity it contains pertains only to a particular subject (or set thereof) and is dependent upon particular empirical conditions, e.g. the comparative velocities of light and sound, it is also an *objective* unity of consciousness according to Kant's definition, which, as such, fails to provide an unambiguous conception of a merely subjective unity.

---

[45] This interpretation is suggested by Paton (1936), 520.

[46] At B153 Kant does distinguish between apperception and inner sense, but he evidently construes the former in the transcendental rather than the empirical sense.

[47] Although I am sure that neither interpreter would agree with all of the specifics of this account, I believe that the reading formulated below is at least roughly in accord with those of Prauss (1971), 284–5, and Longuenesse (1998), 184–5. In fact, much of what I say about the text in question is said with the latter's view directly in mind.

[48] These examples reflect Longuenesse's strongly teleological view of judgments of perception, according to which "[T]he empirical unity of consciousness is that initial unity produced in our representations with a review to reflecting them under concepts in empirical judgments," Longuenesse (1998), 185. I discuss this aspect of her position in Allison (2012), esp. 33–4.

Against this it might be objected that this negative conclusion is premature, since in the fourth and seventh sentences of §18 Kant also points to what appears to be a different account of subjective unity in terms of association.[49] Here again, however, the issue is complicated by the fact that, though each of these sentences connects association with the subjective unity of consciousness, they do not seem to understand association in the same sense. In the fourth sentence, Kant concludes from the preceding account of subjective unity that "the empirical unity of consciousness, through association of the representations, itself concerns an appearance, and is entirely contingent." But in the seventh and final sentence he remarks: "One person combines the representation of a certain word with one thing, another with something else; and the unity of consciousness in that which is empirical is not, with regard to that which is given, necessarily and universally valid."

Beginning with the latter, which Kant seems to have included as an afterthought rather than as an essential ingredient in his account, the association between word and thing reflects the traditional view of the association of ideas, where the focus is on the arbitrary nature of the association, stemming from the lack of any intrinsic connection between the associated items. As such, the association is the by-product of a particular experience, which is why different subjects associate the same word with different things. An anomalous feature of Kant's discussion of this sort of association is his denial that it is necessarily and universally valid. While certainly correct, this is misleading, since it suggests that we are to regard the associative connection as subjectively valid in accordance with the model of judgments of perception, rather than as one to which the normative notion of validity simply does not apply.

Nevertheless, it appears that it is the association to which Kant refers in the fourth sentence in which he is really interested, since he connects it directly with the empirical unity of consciousness and presents it as a conclusion from the account in the first three sentences. According to this view of association, which is clearly Humean, the constant conjunction of representations ("perceptions" in Hume's sense) in past experience produces in the mind a custom or habit to reproduce one of a set of representations when presented with the other (or at least some of the other) members of the set. In Kant's terms, the resulting unity of consciousness is a product of the reproductive imagination, which he links closely with association in the A-Deduction. Here "appearance" is understood in the empirical sense as referring to the appearing of the associated representations in empirical consciousness; while the contingency refers to the "circumstances and empirical conditions" on which this association is based. Although association, so construed, is not itself a determination of inner sense, it can be regarded as the result of such a determination by the reproductive activity of the imagination. Moreover, it meets Kant's criterion

---

[49] Kant also refers to laws of association in §19 (B142), but I shall reserve my discussion of this important passage for the analysis of that section.

for a subjective unity, since, unlike that of a judgment of perception, it does not involve the concept of an object.

The problem, however, is that if this is what Kant meant and the distinction between a subjective and an objective unity of consciousness is understood as between an association of perceptions, which does not involve the representation of an object (not even an object in the thin sense) because it does not involve an act of thought, and an objective unity, understood as one through which an object (in the thick sense) is cognized (in the thick sense), then we are back to the situation with which we began. First, with an objective unity, so construed, we are confronted again with both the *non-sequitur* objection and the worry about what to do with non-veridical subjective "experiences," which cannot be reduced to mere associations. Second, and perhaps even worse, this dichotomy leaves no room for either judgments of perception or preliminary judgments, which not only play an important positive role in Kant's overall account of cognition but also seem to be required by Kant's identification of thinking and judging.

This identification is crucial, since it entails the necessity of distinguishing between the two senses of a subjective unity of consciousness with which Kant operates and which in various contexts he juxtaposes to the objective unity that is his central concern. One of these, which is exemplified in judgments of perception and preliminary judgments, is, like the objective unity found in judgments of experience, the product of an act of thought. As such, it is located in the logical space of reasons and has validating grounds. What makes it merely subjectively valid is the nature of these grounds. Rather than being objectively sufficient, which would justify the thought for any cognizer, thereby bringing with it a normative demand for agreement, they are merely subjectively sufficient, since they stem from the way in which something appears to a particular subject under certain conditions.[50] The other is the kind of unity of consciousness that is produced by an association. This is a unity in the sense that the associated representations are connected in a single consciousness; but since the unification is the product of the mechanism of the reproductive imagination, without any role for thought, it is located in the logical space of causes rather than reasons, and therefore lacks a normative dimension.[51] So described, these two unities

---

[50] I am here using "subjectively sufficient" in a way that differs from Kant's own use of the expression. In his discussion of opining, knowing (*Wissen*), and believing (understood in the sense of practical belief) in the Canon of the *Critique*, Kant says that having an opinion is neither objectively nor subjectively sufficient, while believing can be subjectively sufficient, and knowing is both objectively and subjectively sufficient (A822–5/B850–3). But whereas Kant here understands sufficiency in terms of its capacity to produce conviction, I am merely considering it in connection with entertaining a thought.

[51] A third case, which also involves a unity for consciousness, is a judgment of inner sense about one's mental state. Presumably, this would be an objectively valid judgment yielding empirical self-knowledge. The places where Kant discusses this issue include §24 and §25 of the B-Deduction (to be considered in Chapter 9), the Refutation of Idealism of the second edition, together with the many *Reflexionen* connected therewith, and the *Anthropology*. I analyze Kant's account of inner sense and its relation to empirical self-knowledge in Allison (1983), 255–71 and (2004), 275–85.

are quite distinct and it would seem that there is no reason to conflate them. It appears, however, from Kant's cryptic discussion of association in §18, as well from what he will say in §19, that the conflation arises because of a slide from a consideration of an association as such to a judgment that is based upon this association. Whereas the former, as an event in one's mental history, lacks any normative element, the latter may be assigned a subjective validity in the sense designated above. And while we have seen that non-rational animals are capable of the former for Kant only rational beings are capable of the latter.

Moreover, it cannot be objected that appealing to this distinction introduces an unnecessary complication into Kant's account because he does not refer to judgments of perception, much less preliminary judgments, in the B-Deduction. Although this is correct, it is beside the point, since we have seen that the distinction between the two kinds of subjective unity is necessary to deal with the *non-sequitur* objection and the worry about subjective "experiences" such as dreams and hallucinations. And it should also be kept in mind that references to judgments of perception and preliminary judgments are found in Kant's lectures and *Reflexionen* that post-date the second edition of the *Critique*. Rather, it seems that the more likely explanation for the absence of judgments of perception (preliminary judgments were discussed only in Kant's lectures and *Reflexionen*) is the difficulty of integrating them into the structure of the Deduction, since this would require showing how they involve the categories. But while this would be a complex task, it would by no means be an impossible one. Indeed, we have already seen that Kant would have had no difficulty in regarding judgments of perception as involving the mathematical categories.

V

§19 *The logical form of all judgments consists in the objective unity of the apperception of the concepts contained therein* (B140–2): In this two-paragraph section, Kant ties the analysis of the objective unity of consciousness developed in §17 and §18 together with a characterization of the nature of judgment, which paves the way for the introduction of the categories via their connection with the logical forms of judgment in §20. Accordingly, §19 is the pivot on which the argument of the first part of the B-Deduction turns.

In the initial paragraph of this section, Kant expresses his dissatisfaction with the traditional definition of judgment as "the representation of a relation between two concepts."[52] This dissatisfaction has three grounds, the first two of which Kant notes only in passing, since they are not directly relevant to the argument of the Deduction. The first is that it is too narrow, since it applies only to categorical judgments, thereby

---

[52] Authors with whom Kant can assume to have been familiar and who define judgment in this way include C. Wolff (1965), 156, G. F. Meier (1924), 624, and Tetens (1777a), 328–9.

ignoring the hypothetical and disjunctive forms.[53] The second, which Kant explains in a note appended to the paragraph, is that the narrowness of this view of judgment has adverse consequences within logic, since it leads to the widespread but misguided doctrine of the four syllogistic figures, which Kant had already criticized in his 1762 essay on the subject. The third ground, which is the one on which Kant focuses and which, unlike the first two, is the concern of transcendental rather than general logic, is that it is incomplete because it fails to explain in what this relation consists.[54]

In the second paragraph, Kant specifies this relation through his definition of judgment as "nothing other than the way to bring given cognitions to the **objective** unity of apperception" (B141). In other words, the relation at issue is between the cognitions connected in a judgment and the objective unity of apperception. Or, more precisely, since Kant regards the traditional definition as incomplete rather than as wrongheaded, in a judgment the component cognitions (concepts) are related to each other through their mutual relation to this objective unity. In an attempt to clarify the point, Kant contrasts this relation with the relation "in accordance with laws of the reproductive imagination (which has only subjective validity)" (B141).[55] Although it might not seem obvious at first glance, this definition accords with the one provided in the Note as "an action through which given representations first become cognitions of an object." Both focus on the act of judging, and the difference is only in the direction in which this action is viewed. Whereas the definition in the Note characterizes the act in the familiar manner as one in which a cognizer relates its representations to an object; this one describes the relation as to the objective unity of apperception. The essential point, however, is that we have seen from the argument of §16–§18 that these are two sides of the same coin, since it maintains that

[53]   Kant himself was, of course, also frequently guilty of this, perhaps most notably in this formulation of the distinction between analytic and synthetic judgments at A6–7/B10–11. Moreover, for Kant hypothetical and disjunctive judgments are composed of categorical ones.

[54]   Kant seems to be somewhat disingenuous here, since the logicians referred to in note 51 did state what they take this relation to consist in; viz., the agreement or disagreement, identity or difference of the representations that are related in the judgment. Moreover, we have seen that Kant himself adhered to this view in the writings of the 1760s. I believe that his real objection, which he does not mention here, is that this effectively makes all judgments analytic.

[55]   This is, however, only one of two definitions of judgment contained in the *Critique*. According to the other, which is found in both editions, "Judgment is...the mediate cognition of an object, hence the representation of a representation of it" (A68/B93). As was noted when initially discussing this definition in Chapter 4, it reflects the account of judgment as discursive cognition, which underlies Kant's distinction between analytic and synthetic judgments. Once again, the basic idea is that discursive cognition occurs in and through acts of judgment and yields a representation of an object only under a certain description, which is also applicable to other objects and which in order to link up with a determinate object (or set thereof) must ultimately be related to a representation that is in immediate relation to an object, i.e., an intuition. Although this differs significantly from the definition in §19, the fact that Kant repeated it unchanged in the second edition suggests that he did not see it as conflicting with the latter. Moreover, there is in fact no conflict, since these accounts consider judgment from different points of view. The one contained in both editions considers judgment with respect to its structure and function and thus pertains to general logic; whereas the one from §19 considers it with regard to its normativity and thus pertains to transcendental logic.

to relate one's representations to an object just is to relate them to the objective unity of self-consciousness (the original synthetic unity of apperception).

Kant attempts to clarify the point with a reflection on the meaning of the word "is," understood in its copulative function linking the subject and predicate concepts in a judgment. According to Kant, "[T]his word designates the relation of the representations to the original apperception and its **necessary unity**, even if the judgment itself is empirical, hence contingent" (B142). As an example of such a judgment, Kant cites "Bodies are heavy," and explaining how this example fits the account of the copula, he writes:

> By that, to be sure, I do not mean to say that these representations **necessarily** belong **to one another** in the empirical intuition, but rather that they belong to one another **in virtue of the necessary unity** of the apperception in the synthesis of intuitions, i.e., in accordance with principles of the objective determination of all representations insofar as cognition can come from them, which principles are all derived from the principle of the transcendental unity of apperception. Only in this way does there arise from this relation a **judgment**, i.e., a relation that is **objectively valid**, and that is sufficiently distinguished from the relation of these same representations in which there would be only subjective validity, e.g., in accordance with laws of association.   (B142)

This passage contains three important points: (1) the attribution of a kind of necessity to empirical judgments in virtue of their grounding in the necessary unity of apperception; (2) the claim that every judgment as such is objectively valid; and (3) the suggestion that a judgment can contain the same content as an association. I shall discuss each in turn.

1) *Empirical judgments and necessity*: This is not a new topic, since we have seen that it played a central role in both the A-Deduction and the *Prolegomena*. Indeed, we saw that in a note to §22 of the latter work Kant, realizing its seemingly paradoxical nature, attempted to explain what he meant by attributing necessity to such judgments. We also saw, however, that here, as elsewhere, he confuses matters by choosing as his example a causal judgment, thus failing to distinguish between the kind of necessity attributed to every judgment of experience and the causal necessity affirmed in a causal claim. It was argued that the former kind of necessity is best understood as normative, since it concerns how one ought to think and that this is intimately linked with Kant's conception of concepts as rules, which have a built-in normative force. Consider his example: "Bodies are heavy." Here the concept of body functions as a first-order rule requiring one to predicate weight of anything that is brought under this concept. The necessity is normative in the sense that it imposes a requirement on anyone who applies the concept in a judgment.

Although in the case of empirical concepts the rule is not derived directly from the original and synthetic unity of apperception, it is nonetheless grounded in it, since, like any concept, it is an analytical unity, which, as such, is grounded in the principle of the synthetic unity of apperception. In the passage cited, Kant further contends that this necessity is mediated by "the principles of the objective determination of all representations insofar as cognition can come from them." These are the Principles of Pure Understanding, particularly the Analogies, which are themselves grounded, together with the categories on which they are based, in the synthetic unity of apperception. Accordingly, they are second-order rules or rules for the formation of the first-order rules contained in empirical concepts. It was argued in Chapter 7 that the normative nature of the necessity pertaining to judgments of experience is expressed more perspicaciously in the *Prolegomena* with its distinction between the unification of representations in consciousness in general and in a particular consciousness and its equation of objective validity and necessary universal validity. Moreover, having also claimed that it was already present in the A-Deduction, I can see no reason not to view the account presently under consideration as making essentially the same point, albeit in somewhat different terms.

2) *The objective validity of judgment as such*: The claim that objective validity is a constitutive feature of judgment as such rather than a value attributable to some judgments is the most frequently noted feature of §19 and it raises two questions. The first concerns what Kant understands by "objective validity." If it is taken as equivalent to "true," Kant must be read as affirming the deeply paradoxical thesis that every judgment is true. Although Kant is not completely consistent on the point, I have argued that he is best read as meaning by "objective validity" having a truth value, i.e., a capacity to be either true or false, which would both allow for false judgments and mark a distinction between a judgment and an association.[56]

The second and more pressing question concerns the relation between this account of judgment and that of the *Prolegomena*. Since Kant there distinguished between two species of empirical judgment, only one of which is objectively valid, there appears to be a direct contradiction between the two accounts. The standard responses to this conundrum take one of two forms. It is claimed either that Kant only introduced the distinction for didactic purposes in the *Prolegomena* and did not there seriously intend it, a view which is motivated by the assumption that the "critical" Kant could not acknowledge the possibility of judgments without the categories, or that, he did take it seriously at the time, but abandoned it in the B-Deduction in light of his new account of judgment.[57] As was noted in Chapter 7, however, though it seems evident that the distinction has a didactic function in the *Prolegomena*, indicating what empirical judgments would be like on the assumption that they do not presuppose any a priori conditions, it cannot be maintained that this

---

[56] Those who maintain a similar view include Prauss (1971), 86–7, Thöle (1991), 69–72, and Longuenesse (1998), 82.

[57] As was noted in Chapter 7, the view that judgments of perception have a merely didactic function in the *Prolegomena* was held by Cassirer (1953), 255–6. A recent commentator who argues for the view that Kant simply abandoned the conception of a judgment of perception in the *Prolegomena* is Pollok (2008), 308.

is its *only* function, since this is belied by Kant's claim that all judgments of experience were first judgments of perception.

Accordingly, the problem is to reconcile Kant's denial of objective validity to judgments of perception with the claim that judgment as such is objectively valid. This seems, however, to confront us with the choice of denying either that judgments of perception are judgments, which is difficult to do in light of Kant's identification of thinking with judging, or that all judgments have objective validity. But while the latter alternative initially seems compelling, it has the untoward consequence of undermining Kant's strategy in the B-Deduction of grounding the application of the categories to the manifold of sensibility as such in its connection with the logical functions of judgment. And given this state of affairs, it seems that the best hope for avoiding this dilemma, without totally abandoning the proof structure of the B-Deduction, involves a further examination of the underlying conception of object-ive validity. Specifically, what is needed is a way to assign a kind of objective validity to judgments of perception, which preserves their distinction from judgments of experience, yet also brings them under the categories. Since Kant does not consider judgments of perception in the B-Deduction, he does not deal with this problem; but if, as has here been claimed, such judgments have a significant place in Kant's account of cognition, it is necessary to account for their possibility.

Fortunately, the prospects for such an endeavor are not as blight as they might initially appear. First, we have already seen the necessity of rejecting Kant's claim in the *Prolegomena* that the categories have no role in judgments of perception, since they clearly involve at least the mathematical categories. Second, inasmuch as judg-ments of perception evidently have a truth value, they are objectively valid in the sense of §19. Third, as such these judgments arguably involve an objective rather than a subjective unity of consciousness in the sense in which these are understood in §18. Fourth, for this very reason, such judgments have an object; indeed, not merely one in the thin sense of an intentional object, but an actual empirical object such as the stone on which the sun shines or the air of which elasticity is provisionally predi-cated. Otherwise they could not be transformed into judgments of experience.

Nevertheless, it is obvious that judgments of perception cannot be considered objectively valid in the same way as judgments of experience, since there would then no longer be grounds for distinguishing between them. But this does not preclude the possibility of their being objectively valid in a different, perhaps weaker sense, which reflects the normative dimension that they possess qua judgments.[58] And though no

---

[58] While I do not claim that there is an equivalence, it should be noted that Kant appeals to an extremely broad sense of objective validity when he claims in the Appendix to the Dialectic that the principles of systematic unity (homogeneity, specificity, and affinity) have an "objective but indeterminate validity" (A663/B691). See also A664/B692 and A669/B697. The basic difference is that these principles purport to be synthetic a priori, whereas judgments of perception are empirical; but the point is that this shows that Kant was willing to entertain a nuanced or layered view of objective validity, which arguably could be extended to judgments of perception, even though Kant himself evidently did not do so. For my analysis of Kant's argument in the Appendix, see Allison (2004), 423–48.

such distinction is explicitly drawn by Kant, I believe that one is both called for by the exigencies of the situation and compatible with the main elements of his account of judgment. The fundamental idea is that judgments of perception, like judgments of experience, are objectively valid in the sense that every judgment, qua judgment, is objectively valid according to Kant's definition in §19. I shall call this the "formal" sense of objective validity, for which the unity of apperception is both a necessary and a sufficient condition. But judgments of perception, unlike judgments of experience, are not objectively valid in the sense of laying claim to a "necessary universal validity."[59] I shall call this the "material" sense of objective validity and it is this sense that is operative in the *Prolegomena* and for the most part in the *Critique*.[60] Moreover, one cannot object to this distinction on the grounds that the formal conception of objective validity is vacuous, since, as will be discussed below, Kant uses it in §19 to distinguish between the objective unity in a judgment and a subjective one brought about through association.

3) *Judgment and association*: Just as in the *Prolegomena* Kant maintained that a judgment, e.g., "The air is elastic," can serve either as a judgment of perception or a judgment of experience, so he now claims that the same representations that are related in a judgment possessing objective validity can also be related in accordance with empirical laws of association, in which case the relation would have merely subjective validity. Appealing to the judgment "Bodies are heavy," Kant contrasts it with the corresponding association-based relation: "If I carry a body, I feel a pressure of weight." According to Kant, the difference between them is that in the case of the former, but not the latter, we "would be able to say that these two representations are combined in the object, i.e., regardless of any difference in the condition of the subject, and are not merely found together in perception (however often as that might be repeated)" (B142). Otherwise expressed, the same elements constitute an objective unity in the former case and a merely subjective one in the latter, depending upon how the relation between them is understood.

By way of comment, I shall briefly note three points regarding this claim, which complement what has already been said. First, Kant's reference to the same representations being related in a judgment and an association is a bit misleading, since we have seen that a judgment involves the relation between concepts (as cognitions); whereas an association consists in a relation between intuitions or sensations (perceptions in Hume's sense). Second, as also appears to have been the case in §18,

---

[59]   Since Kant claims in the *Prolegomena* (4: 298$_{28-9}$; 93), that "objective validity and necessary universal validity (for everyone) are . . . interchangeable concepts" this proposal obviously involves a rejection of that view.

[60]   A similar view has been offered by Hoppe (1983), esp. 5–8 and 45–58, who distinguishes between two senses of objectivity and subjectivity, which he calls "categorial" (*kategorial*) and "factual" (*faktisch*). For a concise summary of Hoppe's position see Longuenesse (1998a), note 32, 183–4.

Kant's characterization of association is ambiguous between the expectation, based on a constant conjunction in past experience of a sensation of pressure whenever one lifts or carries a body, which, as previously noted, can be had by an animal without the capacity for thought, and the *thought* that whenever I carry a body, I shall have a corresponding sensation, which, since it is based solely on my own past experience, does not justify the predication of a property (weight or, more precisely, the capacity to produce the sensation in question) unto the object (a body). Although much of what Kant says here, particularly the attribution of a subjective validity to this association, suggests that he understood it primarily in the latter sense, as was noted above, the contrast that Kant intends to draw with judgment requires taking it in the former sense. Third, if taken in the latter sense the contrast coincides with the *Prolegomena*'s distinction between a judgment of experience and a judgment of perception. Indeed, if taken in this sense, the associative connection that Kant depicts just is a judgment of perception in the sense of the *Prolegomena*, which suggests that he continued to recognize the act of thought that he had previously characterized as a judgment, and merely refrained from continuing to call it one because it would unnecessarily complicate the main point that he was trying to make.

VI

§20: *All sensible intuitions stand under the categories, as conditions under which alone their manifold can come together in one consciousness* (B143): As already noted, this brief section introduces the categories via their relation to the logical functions of judgment and constitutes the conclusion of the first part of the B-Deduction. Once again, I shall cite the text in full, numbering its five sentences, each of which marks a step in what constitutes a polysyllogism.

(1) The manifold that is given in a sensible intuition necessarily belongs under the original synthetic unity of apperception, since through this alone is the **unity** of the intuition possible (§ 17). (2) That action of the understanding, however, through which the manifold of given representations (whether they be intuitions or concepts) is brought under an apperception in general, is the logical function of judgments (§19). (3) Therefore all manifold, insofar as it is given in **One** [*Einer*] empirical intuition, is **determined** in regard to one of the logical functions for judgment, by means of which ... it is brought to a consciousness in general.[61] (4) But now the **categories** are nothing other than these very functions for judging, insofar as the manifold of a given intuition is determined with regard to them (§13). (5) Thus the manifold in a given intuition also necessarily stands under the categories.   (B143)

---

[61] I have here modified the Guyer and Wood translation. The German text reads: "*Also ist alles Mannigfaltige, sofern es in* **Einer** *empirischen Anschauung gegeben ist, in Ansehung einer der logischen Funktionen zu urteilen bestimmt, durch die es nämlich zu einem Bewusstsein überhaupt gebracht wird.*"

1) In stating that it is alone through belonging under the original synthetic unity of apperception that the unity of intuition is possible Kant is maintaining that the former is both a necessary and a sufficient condition of the latter. Accordingly, it is closely related to the claim in §17 that the unity of apperception is both a necessary and sufficient condition, which is presumably why Kant refers to that section as the basis for the present claim. These claims do not appear to be equivalent, however, since they do not state that the unity of apperception is a necessary and sufficient condition of the same thing. As we have seen, Kant maintains in §17 that this unity is both a necessary and sufficient condition of the representation of an object; whereas the present claim is that it is both a necessary and sufficient condition of a unified intuition, by which I take Kant to mean the representation of an intuitively given manifold *as a manifold*. Nevertheless, if we understand "object" in the sense of §17 as the correlate of the synthetic unity of apperception and add the implicit premise that the objects of human cognition must be given in sensible intuition, these claims can be considered as equivalent, as is indicated by Kant's appeal to §17 in support of it.

2) The second step calls for little comment, since it reiterates the thesis of §19 that judgment is the unity-producing act of the understanding. This reflects Kant's characterization of the understanding as "a faculty for judging" (*ein Vermögen zu urteilen*) (A69/B94), which Longuenesse renders as "the capacity to judge" and which lies at the very heart of her interpretation of the *Critique*.[62] It should also be noted, however, that Kant explicitly states that this operation acts upon *both* intuitions and concepts, which might be seen as an attempt to underscore the connection between §17 and §19.

3) The third step contains the conclusion of a syllogistic inference for which the first two steps constitute the premises. Simply put, if the manifold given in sensible intuition necessarily belongs under the unity of apperception (as the sole source of its unity) and the unifying act of the understanding through which a manifold is brought under the unity of apperception is judgment, then it follows that, insofar as this manifold is given in one (a unified) intuition, it must be determined by one of the logical functions of judgment, since they are the forms of unification through which the elements of the manifold are brought to the unity of consciousness. There are, however, several complexities in Kant's conclusion, which this restatement of it glosses over and which call for further discussion.

Perhaps the most contentious of these is Kant's restriction of the claim regarding a manifold to it "insofar as it is given in **One** [*Einer*] empirical intuition." In addition to the need to explain the double emphasis on "*Einer*" (both the capitalization and the boldface (*Fettdruck*)), which Kant repeats in his reiteration of the claim in §21 (B144), the problem is that the most natural reading of the text is impossible. This is because on this reading the manifold given in an intuition only falls under the unity

---

[62] See Longuenesse (1998), 7–8 and passim.

of apperception (and by implication the logical functions and categories) insofar as it already possesses unity, which directly contradicts the fundamental premise (argued for in §15) that without the activity of the understanding there is no unity for consciousness. Accordingly, if this is what Kant intended to say, it would mean that *nothing* given in sensibility could be brought to the unity of apperception, which would undermine the entire project of the Deduction.

How, then, are we to understand this claim? I believe that in order to make sense of the text we must take Kant to be claiming that, *up to this point*, the necessary unity of the manifold of intuition has only been established insofar as this manifold is considered as having already been brought under the unity of apperception. In addition to leaving open the question of the extent to which the manifold given in sensible intuition is capable of being brought under this unity, which is Henrich's central contention about the first part of the argument, this enables us to understand Kant's strong emphasis on the unity or oneness of the intuition, considered as brought under the principle of the synthetic unity of apperception, which has already been claimed to be both a necessary and a sufficient condition of this unity. In the terms that were used in the analysis of the A-Deduction, Kant is attempting to underscore the point that the understanding, operating under the principle of the synthetic unity of apperception, is the ground of the representation of a manifold *as a manifold*, i.e., as a synthetic unity. The difference is that, whereas in the A-Deduction this unifying function is assigned to the imagination, it is here attributed to the understanding.

Also calling for clarification is Kant's claim that the unification of the elements of the manifold of a sensible intuition is produced by their being "**determined** in regard to one of the logical functions for judgment." I take this to mean being made determinate according to a rule, which specifies how the elements of a manifold are to be represented through a judgment, e.g., as subject rather than predicate, or as ground rather than consequent.[63] The claim that the representation of a unified manifold is determined with regard to *one* of these functions could well be Kant's attempt to correct his statement in R5932 that it must be considered with regard to *all* of them; though clearly neither is correct, since, as was noted in considering this

---

[63] This is to be seen in connection with Kant's previously discussed claim at B128–9 that the function of a category is to determine the manifold of a sensible intuition with regard to one of the logical functions. Using the categorical judgment "All bodies are divisible" as an illustration, Kant notes that, with respect to the merely logical use of the understanding, it is undetermined which of these concepts will function as subject and which as predicate and that it is only by subsuming the empirical concept of body under the concept of substance that its place in the empirical intuition is determined. The problem is that since he has not yet introduced the categories, Kant can refer only to the manifold as being determined through the logical functions, even though his complete view is that the functions are themselves made determinate of fixed through the categories. As we shall see below, however, once we include the account of the relation between the logical functions and the categories given in the Metaphysical Deduction, which Kant appears to ignore at this point, we can see that these determinations are two sides of the same coin.

text in Chapter 7, Kant's official view is that it must be considered as determined with regard to one function from each of the titles in order to constitute a judgment.

It is also striking that Kant here states that it is by being determined with regard to one of these functions (or one from each of the four titles) that the manifold "is brought to a consciousness in general," since this is the only appearance of this expression in the *Critique*. But assuming that he here means by it what he had meant in the *Prolegomena*, it indicates that Kant is claiming that it is by being determined with regard to the logical functions that the representation of the manifold of a sensible intuition attains objective validity. This accords with the argument of §19, though it differs from the view of the *Prolegomena*, where judgments of perception, while supposedly having a merely subjective validity, are likewise determined with regard to the logical functions.

4) *From the functions of judgment to the categories*: We here find the belated introduction of the categories via the logical functions of judgment, a move through which Kant evidently attempted to fill a major lacuna in the A-Deduction. The problem is that he seems to fill it by fiat, since he simply refers to his earlier explanation of the categories as "concepts of an object in general, by means of which its intuition is regarded as **determined** with regard to one of the functions for judgments" (B128). If this is what the categories are and do, then Kant appears to be entitled to transfer what he claimed about the logical functions in §19 to the categories, which is what he effectively does here. But some justification for this pivotal claim is required beyond referring the reader back to his earlier one. In order to provide this justification, Kant should perhaps have referred to his initial account of the relation between the logical functions in §10 on which the claims in both §13 and §18 are based. In the relevant passage, which is also contained in the first edition, Kant writes:

The same function that gives unity to the different representations **in a judgment** also gives unity to the mere synthesis of different representations **in an intuition**, which, expressed generally, is called the pure concept of understanding. The same understanding, therefore, and indeed by means of the very same actions through which it brings the logical form of a judgment into concepts by means of the analytical unity, also brings a transcendental content into its representations by means of the synthetic unity of the manifold of intuition in general, on account of which they are called pure concepts of the understanding that pertain to objects *a priori*; this can never be accomplished by general logic.   (A79/B104–5).

When initially examining this passage, it was noted that it affirms an isomorphism between the unifying function of the understanding at two levels: that of concepts in a judgment and of intuitions in the representation of an object; the former being the domain of general and the latter of transcendental logic.[64] It is evident that the

---

[64] See Chapter 4, pages 164–96.

passage currently under consideration presupposes this isomorphism, since it under-lies the move from logical function to category. It was also noted, however, that the argument for this isomorphism, as Kant there presented it, was anticipatory or conditional, with the implicit assumption being that the understanding has such a distinct unifying function, which is to say that, through its application to the manifold intuition, it introduces a "transcendental content," understood as relation to an object of intuition. And if this is correct, it follows that this isomorphism between the logical functions and their corresponding categories does not, of itself, suffice to justify Kant's claim regarding the categories in §20. What still remained to be determined is whether the capacity to introduce a transcendental content is to be attributed to the understanding.

In the B-Deduction, this is the task of §16 through §18, which provides an argument from the synthetic unity of apperception to the representation of an object. If successful, this argument would show that the understanding injects a transcen-dental content as Kant characterized it in §10, thereby justifying the isomorphism that he there provisionally assumed. Having already analyzed and attempted to defend this line of argument, albeit with major caveats regarding the sense of "object" (and related terms) to which it appeals, I have nothing further to add at present. I do wish, however, to re-emphasize the point that it turns crucially on the premise that the conformity of the manifold of a given intuition to the synthetic unity of apperception, understood as the objective unity of self-consciousness, is both a necessary and a sufficient condition of the representation of an object. For without this premise the understanding could not be claimed to introduce a transcendental content (so understood) and its function would be merely logical. Accordingly, with regard to this issue we cannot help Kant by weakening his claim, as many critics have done, since virtually the entire weight of his argument is based upon it.

5) *"Thus the manifold in a given intuition also necessarily stands under the categor-ies."* This proposition constitutes the conclusion to both the polysyllogism of §20 and the entire first part of the B-Deduction. It is the former because it follows from the characterization of the categories in step four. It is the latter because it constitutes the ultimate conclusion of an analytic argument based upon the analytic principle of the synthetic unity of apperception. And, as has already been noted on several occasions, it is for this reason that Kant claims that with it only a beginning is made in the deduction of the categories. Indeed, when considered in this light, what is remarkable is not that Kant makes the deflationary claim that the argument is *only* a beginning, but, rather, that it *is a beginning*. What still remains to be shown is that appearances, qua given under the forms of space and time, necessarily conform to these categories, which is the concern of the second part of the B-Deduction and of Chapter 9.

9

The B-Deduction (2)

§§21–7

Whereas apart from §15, which effectively functions as an introduction to the argument as a whole, the first part of the B-Deduction (§16–§20) has the form of a linear argument from the unity of apperception to the necessary applicability of the categories to the manifold of an intuition in general, insofar as it is capable of being brought to this unity, the structure of the second part (§21–§27) is more complex. §21 serves as a transition between the two parts. §22 and §23 together restrict the scope of the categories to what can be given in empirical intuition. §24 is divided into two parts: the first introduces the transcendental synthesis of the imagination under the title of a "figurative synthesis" or "*synthesis speciosa*," which is the basis for relating the categories to the forms of human sensibility; while the second part of §24 and all of §25 deal with the relation between inner sense and apperception. Although it constitutes a digression, this two-pronged discussion is of central importance for understanding Kant's views on self-knowledge and self-consciousness. In §26 Kant introduces the empirical synthesis of apprehension to complement the transcendental synthesis of the imagination, thereby linking the categories to both perception and experience. Finally, §27 summarizes the results of the Deduction as a whole and adds further reflections on its method. Following the usual procedure, I shall devote a section of this chapter to each of these segments of Kant's account.

I

§21 *The transition* (B144–6): As noted above, this two-paragraph section, which Kant labels simply "Remark" (*Anmerkung*), provides a bridge between the two parts of the B-Deduction. Kant begins by recapitulating the results of the preceding argument and stipulating what remains to be done. He tells us that it has been shown that "a manifold that is contained in an intuition that I call mine is represented as belonging to the necessary unity of self-consciousness through the synthesis of the understanding, and this takes place by means of the category" (B144). It is curious that Kant characterizes this as the accomplishment of the first part of the Deduction, rather than describing the latter as the demonstration that the manifold in a given intuition necessarily stands under the categories, which is the conclusion of §20. But it appears that Kant viewed these as equivalent, and that he presented the result in this manner because it enabled him to draw an analogy between the way in which "the empirical consciousness of a given manifold of one [*Einer*] intuition stands under a pure *a priori* self-consciousness" and the way in which "empirical intuitions stand under a pure sensible one" (B144).

In a note added to the sentence containing the proposition that he refers to as the beginning of the Deduction, Kant indicates that its ground of proof "rests on the represented **unity of intuition** through which an object is given, which always includes a synthesis of the manifold that is given for an intuition, and already contains the relation of the latter to the unity of apperception" (B144n). This note is of interest for two reasons. First, it provides further evidence that Kant viewed the argument of the first part of the Deduction as turning on the reciprocity between the unity of consciousness and the consciousness of unity, which entails that the unity of apperception is both a necessary and a sufficient condition of the representation of an object. Second, Kant here uses the term "given" (*gegeben*) in two radically distinct senses. In the first it signifies an object for consciousness and the point is that the given in this sense is already the product of a synthesis through which the manifold is unified. In the second the given is just the sensible manifold as such, which is not given as a unity. Accordingly, if one is to make any sense of Kant's argument it is essential to keep these two senses of the term in mind.[1]

In the initial paragraph of §21 Kant also points out that, since his intent in the first part of the Deduction was merely to explicate "the unity that is added to the intuition through the understanding by means of the category," he had to abstract "from the way in which the empirical intuition is given in sensibility" (B144). This sets the agenda for the rest of the Deduction, which Kant describes as showing "from the way in which the empirical intuition is given in sensibility that its unity can be none other than the one the category prescribes to the manifold of a given intuition in general" (B145). The claim is that this would account for the a priori validity of the categories for all objects of our senses, thereby completing the task of the Deduction. Here again, we encounter the ambiguity of "given," which can be taken to refer to either the spatial and temporal forms in which an empirical intuition is given in sensibility or to the manner of its apprehension by consciousness. This time, however, it appears that Kant intended the term to be taken in both senses.

In the second paragraph of §21, Kant notes that, while the argument of the first part abstracted from the particular nature of human sensibility, it could not abstract from the necessity of some sensory input. This reflects Kant's view of the discursivity of the human intellect, which he illustrates by contrasting it with a putative intuitive intellect, for which cognition would not be dependent upon data being given. The

---

[1] The point is noted by Paton (1936a), 525–6.

paragraph concludes with a sentence that has been the subject of a fair amount of controversy. Kant writes:

But for the peculiarity of our understanding, that it is able to bring about the unity of apperception *a priori* only by means of the categories and only through precisely this kind and number of them, a further ground may be offered just as little as one can be offered for why we have precisely these and no other functions for judgment or why space and time are the sole forms of our possible intuition.   (B145–6)

The problem posed by this statement concerns Kant's oft-criticized claim for the systematic completeness of the table of the forms of judgment from which the categories are derived; and it stems from the analogy that he draws between these forms of judgment and the corresponding categories, on the one hand, and space and time as the forms of our sensible intuition, on the other. Since he had acknowledged the logical possibility of other forms of intuition and effectively treated the spatial and temporal forms of human sensibility as inexplicable brute facts, Kant here seems to be implying that a similar status should be given to the forms of judgment and categories, which would contradict his claim to have grounded their necessity in the very nature of the understanding as the capacity to judge.[2]

Although the issue remains controversial, I do not believe that this passage and its companions need be read as a retreat on Kant's part from his completeness claim with respect to the forms of judgment and the categories. The key point is that he does not deny that these claims have *any* ground, but merely any *further* ground. In the case of the categories, with which Kant is primarily concerned in the passage before us, what he denies is the possibility of providing a further ground beyond the one just offered; viz., the synthetic unity of apperception. In the case of the forms of judgment, the claim would be that one can provide no further ground for them beyond the analysis of what is required for the capacity to judge provided in §9.[3]

II

§22–§23 *The restriction thesis* (B146–9): The close connection between these two sections is indicated by the fact that they share the same heading; viz., "The category has no other use for the cognition of things than its application to objects of experience" (B146). To begin with, it is noteworthy that, rather than claiming simply that the category, meaning thereby any of the categories, has no use other than its application to objects of experience, Kant states that it has no other use *for the*

---

[2] The classical argument for this thesis was formulated by Krüger (1968), 333–5 and the reply by Michael Wolff (1995), esp. 177–81. What follows is based largely on Wolff's account.

[3] In other places where he makes the same claim, Kant states that the reason why no further ground is possible is that, because of their foundational role, any attempt to explain why our sensibility and our understanding have the forms they do would require using these very faculties, thereby making the account circular. See *Prolegomena* 4:318; 111 and B 11: 51; 313–14.

cognition of things, thereby leaving room for a non-cognitive use. Although Kant does not here specify what this non-cognitive use is, he makes it clear elsewhere in the *Critique* that he understands by it a morally practical use.[4] And he lays the foundation for this use by distinguishing between thinking and cognizing. In fact, this distinction, which turns on the discursivity thesis, is the central topic of §22. In accordance with this thesis, Kant notes once again that cognition contains two components: a concept through which an object is thought, which he refers to as "the category," and an intuition through which it is given. And he further points out that, lacking a corresponding intuition, the concept would have the form of a thought but would be without any object, which means that it could not amount to a cognition, since "as far as I would know nothing would be given nor could be given to which my thought could be applied" (B146).

All of this is familiar and does not require further discussion. But Kant does introduce an important new element, at least as a matter of emphasis, by claiming that in order to yield cognition, the categories need to be applied not simply to sensible intuition as such, but to *empirical* intuition. It is not that Kant denies that the categories and, more broadly, a priori concepts, are applicable to a priori intuitions, since this is precisely what takes place in mathematics. It is rather that through the application of such concepts to pure intuition we only acquire cognition of the forms of objects, which leaves open the question of whether there are any objects given in experience that conform to these forms. In the case of mathematics, this means that pure intuition suffices to ground the possibility of pure mathematics, but we need empirical intuition if mathematics is to be applied to nature. Extending this principle to the categories, Kant concludes that they likewise only yield cognition through their possible application to empirical intuition, and therefore serve only for the possibility of empirical cognition (B147–8). Accordingly, Kant's goal in the remainder of the Deduction is to link the categories to empirical intuition.

In §23 Kant's concern is to draw out the consequences of this prioritizing of empirical intuition for the determination of the boundaries for the (theoretical) use of the categories, which he does by comparing them with space and time as analyzed in the Aesthetic. His basic point is that, while there is a significant *prima facie* difference in the scope of the two sets of a priori representations, this does not result in a corresponding difference in the extent to which they allow for the possibility of cognition. In the case of space and time, Kant claims that it is clear from the Aesthetic that beyond objects of the senses, of which they constitute the forms, space and time "do not represent anything at all, for they are only in the senses and outside of them have no reality" (B148). By contrast, Kant suggests that the pure concepts of the understanding (as concepts of an object in general) extend to objects of intuition in general, with the only proviso being that the intuition is sensible rather than

---

[4] See, for example, Bxxvi–xxxi and B424–6.

intellectual. But he further notes that this extension does not bring with it a corresponding extension of cognition, since the latter is inseparably linked to our sensible intuition, through which alone objects are given to us. And from this Kant concludes, in confirmation of what he had already claimed in §22, that "**Our** sensible and empirical intuition alone can provide them [the categories] with sense and significance [*Sinn und Bedeutung*]" (B149).

In the second paragraph of §23 Kant takes up the counter-factual issue of the application of the categories to objects of a non-sensible intuition, i.e., noumena. He notes that if one assumes that such an object is given, one could represent it through all the predicates that are implied by its *not being* an object of sensible intuition, which Kant illustrates by stipulating that it would not be "extended, or in space, that its duration is not a time, that no alteration (sequence of determinations of time is to be encountered in it), etc." (B149). Once again, however, the point is simply that such purely negative predication would not constitute cognition, since there could be no way of determining whether such an object is even possible.

III

§24 (the first part) *The relation of the categories to the forms of sensible intuition through the transcendental synthesis of the imagination* (B150–2): Although §24 is divided into two quite distinct parts, Kant gives it a heading ("On the application of the categories to objects of the senses in general") that does not adequately reflect the concern of either part. We shall see in the sequel that it does not apply to the second part at all and it will become immediately apparent that it only relates obliquely to the first. Moreover, the latter is itself divided into two parts, which, though intimately related, call for separate discussion, since they refer to two distinct syntheses.

1) *The intellectual synthesis*: This is the name that Kant assigns to the first of these syntheses. He means by it the action of the understanding analyzed in the first part of the Deduction, which was considered in abstraction from the nature of the sensible intuition on which it operates, and it here functions largely as a point of contrast to the figurative synthesis with which he is now primarily concerned and which is directly related to the nature of human sensibility. Although Kant does not characterize it in this way, he effectively begins this section by combining the results of the first part of the Deduction with the conclusion of §23 that the categories only attain sense and significance through their relation to empirical intuition. This enables him to claim that,

The pure concepts of the understanding are related through the mere understanding to objects of intuition in general, without it being determined whether this intuition is our own or some other but still sensible one, but they are on this account mere **forms of thought**, through which no determinate object is yet cognized. The synthesis or combination of the manifold in them was related merely to the unity of apperception, and was thereby the ground of the possibility of cognition *a priori* insofar as it rests on the understanding, and was therefore not only transcendental but also merely purely intellectual. (B150)

These two sentences contain Kant's clearest explanation of why the conclusion of §20 only constituted a beginning of the deduction. The first sentence stipulates that what the first part of the Deduction showed is that through their connection with the "mere understanding" the categories relate to objects of intuition in general, which, due to the argument of §§22 and 23, we can now recognize establishes only that they are merely "**forms of thought**, through which no determinate object is cognized." And since the aim of the Deduction is to demonstrate that the categories are necessary conditions of the cognition of *determinate* objects, i.e., phenomena located in space and time, it is evident that more work needs to be done.[5]

The second sentence provides further clarification of what Kant thought was lacking in the first part of the Deduction. The key factor is the dual appearance of the term "merely" (*bloss*). Kant says first that the synthesis or combination of the manifold is related "merely to the unity of apperception," implying thereby that something more is needed to account for the cognition of a determinate object. And then he says that, as a result of this, the synthesis that produces this unity is not only transcendental but also "merely purely intellectual." That it is transcendental is clear, since the unity of apperception is transcendental and the synthesis is at least a necessary condition of this unity. It is also clear that it is "purely intellectual," since, *ex hypothesi*, it is governed by the categories and contains no sensible features. But what is striking is the claim that the synthesis is *merely* purely intellectual, since this again indicates that something essential is lacking. In short, the point is that in order to generate cognition of a determinate object the synthesis of the manifold given in intuition must relate to the unity of apperception, *but not merely to this unity*; and the transcendental synthesis itself must be intellectual, but evidently not purely, i.e., *merely*, such.

Setting aside for the moment the nature of this transcendental synthesis, there appears to be a significant difference between the view of apperception and its synthetic unity that Kant here provides and his initial account of it in §17. Whereas he there maintained that it is both a necessary and a sufficient condition of the cognition of an object, he now suggests that it is merely a necessary condition. The appearance of an inconsistency depends, however, on the assumption that Kant understands the same thing by "object" in both accounts, which, if the analysis of Kant's reasoning in §17 is correct, is clearly not the case. We saw that Kant there understood "object" in an extremely broad sense, according to which "[a]n **object** . . . is that in the concept of which the manifold of a given intuition is **united**" (B137). Expressed in the terms of the A-Deduction, the concept of an object, so understood, is the thought of "something in general=X," which was there referred to as the "transcendental object." Alternatively, expressed in the terms that Kant uses in §24 of the B-Deduction, it would be an "indeterminate object" or, more precisely, an

---

[5] For a similar view of the function of the second part of the Deduction see Thöle (1991), 280–5.

indeterminate concept of an object.[6] And we also saw that the synthetic unity of apperception is both a necessary and sufficient condition of an object in this sense; though it is only a necessary condition of a determinate object, understood as an empirically real, phenomenal object.

In the final sentence of the extraordinarily dense first paragraph of §24 Kant considers the tools available for bridging the gap between these two conceptions of an object, which is evidently necessary in order to complete the argument of the Deduction. And, not surprisingly, Kant finds them in the Transcendental Aesthetic, which for reasons already noted had been left out of the story in the first part of the Deduction. He notes:

> But since in us a certain form of sensible intuition a priori is fundamental [*zum Grunde liegt*], which rests on the receptivity of the capacity for representation (sensibility), the understanding, as spontaneity, can determine inner sense through the manifold of given representations, in accord with the synthetic unity of apperception, and thus think a priori synthetic unity of the apperception of the manifold of **sensible intuition**, as the condition under which all objects of our (human) intuition must necessarily stand, through which the categories, as mere forms of thought, acquire objective reality, i.e., application to objects that can be given to us in intuition, but only as appearances; for of these alone are we capable of intuition a priori.[7]   (B150–1)

This sentence contains two claims, which jointly provide the bases for the subsequent argument of the Deduction. The first is that the understanding, through its spontaneous activity, i.e., synthesis, determines inner sense with respect to its form (time). Accordingly, it is by means of this that the understanding acquires a sensible content a priori, albeit a merely formal one. Moreover, this leads to what might be considered a "thickened" conception of the synthetic unity of apperception, according to which what is apperceived brings with it an a priori dimension of its own to which the act of apperception must conform, if it is to yield cognition of a determinate object. In other words, there is a normative constraint placed upon apperception, and therefore the human understanding, by the nature of human sensibility in virtue of its a priori form. For example, the necessity of representing all phenomena as existing in a single

---

[6] Kant uses two terms that are translated as "object": "*Object*" or "*Objekt*" and "*Gegenstand*." Noticing that he generally uses the former in the first part of the B-Deduction and the latter in the second, in the original version of *Kant's Transcendental Idealism* I suggested that Kant's use of these terms could be taken as mirroring the above distinction between the two senses of "object." See Allison (1983), 135–6. In response to philologically oriented criticisms, which point to a certain randomness in Kant's use of these terms, I ceased placing any weight on the terminology; but I have continued to insist upon the importance of distinguishing between the two senses of "object" for understanding the B-Deduction. It must be emphasized, however, that the distinction is between two conceptions of an object rather than between two kinds of object. One conception (that with which the first part of the B-Deduction is concerned) is that of an object considered qua thought by a discursive understanding; the other (which is the concern of the second part) is an object of possible experience. Although anything falling under the latter conception also falls under the former, the converse does not hold. Thus the former conception is wider; whereas, since it encompasses the sensible as well as the conceptual conditions of cognition, the latter is thicker.

[7] I have here modified the Guyer and Wood translation, which omitted the crucial reference to inner sense.

time, which plays a pivotal role in the arguments of the Analogies, is not derived from the "pure" (or "mere") understanding, since there is no logical contradiction in the thought that there is more than a single time (and/or space); but it is nonetheless precluded for Kant because it contradicts the intuition arguments in the Aesthetic, which show that all spaces and times must be thought as parts of a single space and a single time.[8] Thus, while one may without contradiction think of objects as existing in different times and spaces, one cannot form a determinate concept of such a state of affairs, which is required to establish its real possibility.

An additional noteworthy feature of this first claim is the reference to inner sense. Rather than maintaining simply that it is by determining sensibility with respect to its form (which would include outer as well as inner sense) that the categories relate to a determinate object, Kant limits the claim to inner sense and its a priori form (time), thereby apparently ignoring space. And to confuse matters further, this privileging of inner sense seems difficult to reconcile with what Kant says in the General Note to the System of Principles added in the second edition, where he remarks that in order to establish the objective reality of the categories, we need not merely intuitions but outer intuitions (B291).[9] Since the question here parallels that of the Schematism, with respect to which it is frequently asked why Kant appears to ignore the role of space in supplying schemata for the application of the categories, the same answer suffices for both questions.

To begin with, in the Aesthetic time is characterized as "the *a priori* formal condition of all appearances in general," whereas space is merely "the pure form of all outer intuitions" (A34/B50). And since all appearances, as "modifications of inner sense," are in time, while only outer appearances are in space, it follows that time has a greater universality than space. Thus, if, as Kant insists, the categories apply universally within the field of possible experience, then their application-conditions must have reference to time. Moreover, it is necessary to distinguish between the sphere of objects to which the categories apply and the conditions under which they apply. Although Kant clearly holds that they apply to objects of outer as well as inner sense, he insists that they apply to the former in virtue of their temporality. When Kant fully develops this line of thought in the Schematism, he does so largely on the basis of the above claim. And we shall see below that this also underlies Kant's account of the transcendental synthesis of the imagination, which is the vehicle through which the understanding relates to time as the form of inner sense.

---

[8] In arguing for the proposition that our representation of space is an intuition rather than a general concept in the Aesthetic, Kant notes that "one can only represent a single space, and if one speaks of many spaces, one understands by that only parts of one and the same unique space" (A25/B29). And, in the case of time, after making a similar claim, he also notes that "The proposition that different times cannot be simultaneous cannot be derived from a general concept;" from which he concludes that it is synthetic and, as such, "immediately contained in the intuition and representation of time" (A31–2/B47). This is an important point and I shall return to it below in connection with Kant's account of the figurative synthesis.

[9] Kant makes a similar claim in MAN 4: 478; 192.

Before turning to that, however, we must consider the second significant claim in the passage before us; viz., that it is through its relation to inner sense that the categories first obtain objective reality, understood as an "application to objects that can be given to us in intuition." The key term here is "objective reality" (*objektive Realität*) and at issue is its relation to "objective validity" (*objektive Gültigkeit*), which is the term that Kant generally used to characterize the goal of the Deduction of the categories in the A-Deduction. Unfortunately, the matter cannot be decided simply by inspecting Kant's definitions or use of these terms, since these are varied and at least partially overlapping, with the predicable result that there is a decided lack of agreement in the literature on the topic. In fact, the views range from those that affirm a fundamental difference between Kant's use of these terms to those who claim that he treats them as virtual synonyms and that his use of one rather than the other in a given context is merely a matter of stylistic variation and should not be assigned any philosophical import.[10] Nevertheless, while acknowledging the difficulty of providing anything like an overarching account of Kant's use of these terms in the first *Critique*, not to mention the "critical" writings as a whole, I think it possible to show that there is a significant difference between what Kant understands by "objective reality" in the present context and his account of "objective validity" in the first part of the Deduction.[11]

As noted, Kant here equates the objective reality of a concept with its applicability to an object that can be given in intuition, which accords with his usual connection of objective reality with real rather than merely logical possibility. Mere lack of contradiction is the criterion of the latter; but it is not sufficient for the former, since that requires conformity with the conditions of intuition as well as the understanding. For present purposes, however, the crucial point is that objects are "given," i.e., brought to consciousness or apperceived, as conditioned by their sensible form. Moreover, as was noted above, this imposes a formal a priori constraint upon the unifying activity of the understanding that first makes possible its relation to a determinate object.[12]

In order to appreciate how this claim differs from Kant's claims regarding objective validity in the first part of the Deduction, it is necessary to revisit his reference to objective validity at B137. To cite once again the passage that was a focal point of

---

[10] Those who insist upon a significant difference in Kant's understanding of these terms include Heidegger (1965), 183–4, Meerbote (1972), 51–8, and Zöller (1984), esp. 132–40. Those who deny any systematic import to the distinction and regard it largely as a stylistic variation include Förster (1985), 366–7, Howell (1992), 363, note 11 and 366, note 39, and Longuenesse (1998a), 110–11, note 14.

[11] As has been noted by Zöller (1984), nowhere in §15–§20 does Kant refer explicitly to the objective validity of the categories, much less claim to have shown that they are objectively valid. He does, however, refer to it as something that needs to be demonstrated at A91/B123 and A93/B126.

[12] As previously noted, Kant's point here is essentially the one that he made at the end of the Schematism, where he remarks that the significance (*Bedeutung*) of the categories, meaning their capacity to represent a determinate object, as opposed to being merely functions of the understanding for concepts, "comes to them from sensibility, which realizes the understanding at the same time as it restricts it" (A147/B187).

Chapter 8: "[T]he unity of consciousness is that which alone constitutes the relation of representations to an object, thus their objective validity, and consequently is that which makes them into cognitions and on which even the possibility of the understanding rests." If we compare this with what Kant is claiming in the second part of the Deduction, the difference should become immediately apparent. Specifically, he no longer speaks either of the unity of consciousness, or, more precisely, the synthetic unity of apperception, as constituting both a necessary and a sufficient condition of the representation of an object. Instead, this unity is considered merely as a necessary condition, since its relation to a *determinate* object is now seen to depend upon a contribution of sensibility, apart from which it contains merely the empty form of the *thought* of an object as such. And since we have also seen that the relation between the unity of apperception and the categories that is affirmed in this segment of the B-Deduction ultimately turns on the former relation, via the connection of both to judgment, it seems reasonable to maintain that the aim of the first part of the B-Deduction is to establish the objective validity of the categories and the second their objective reality.[13]

Nevertheless, this should not be taken as indicating either that the second part of the Deduction contradicts the first by demoting what was both a necessary and sufficient condition of objectivity into a merely necessary one or that it amounts to a change of subject through the introduction of a substantially different conception of an object. The former is not the case because we have seen that the argument of the second part presupposes and purports to build upon that of the first by introducing an additional factor; viz., the relation to the nature of human sensibility, from which the first part abstracts. And the latter is not the case either because, though Kant does introduce a new conception of an object in the second part, it should be seen as a thickening (through the inclusion of sensible conditions) rather than a replacement of the conception operative in the first part.[14] In other words, both parts of the Deduction are concerned with the relation between the categories and objects of possible experience, since these are the only objects of human cognition for Kant. But while the first part considers such objects merely from the side of the understanding, and therefore *qua* correlates of the synthetic unity of apperception, which we have seen is both a necessary and sufficient condition of the representation of an object, so considered, the second part is concerned with them *qua* objects of possible experience, and therefore as they appear clothed in their spatial and/or temporal forms.

---

[13] As was the case with the contrast between "*object*," and "*Gegenstand*," in the original version of *Kant's Transcendental Idealism* I used this distinction to indicate the difference between Kant's aim in the first and second parts of the B-Deduction and was criticized on the grounds that Kant sometimes appears to consider them as interchangeable. And once again I acknowledge the philological point but reaffirm my original thesis on the substantive grounds that, regardless of the nomenclature, the two parts of the B-Deduction deal with two conceptions of an object and make a distinct claim with respect to each conception.

[14] See note 6.

2) *The transcendental synthesis of the imagination*: The second and third paragraphs of the first part of §24 are concerned with the synthesis of the manifold of inner sense through which the representation of a determinate object is brought about. Kant refers to this synthesis as "figurative," or as the "*synthesis speciosa*," because of its relation to the forms of sensibility. He also attributes it to the imagination and contrasts it with the "*synthesis intellectualis*" which he states "would be thought in the mere category in regard to the manifold of an intuition in general." And he further claims that both syntheses are transcendental because they are not only a priori but ground the possibility of other a priori cognition (B151).

Thus, just as the understanding, and with it the categories, made a belated entrance in the A-Deduction, following the detailed analysis of the role of the imagination, the latter first appears in the second act of the two-act drama that constitutes the B-Deduction. And whereas in the A-Deduction it is the imagination that plays the lead role as a fundamental faculty, with the understanding relegated to the seemingly subordinate part of mediator between the synthesis of the imagination and apperception, in the B-Deduction it is the understanding that assumes the lead role from the beginning, with the transcendental synthesis of the imagination described as "an effect of the understanding on sensibility," to which Kant adds that it is "its [the understanding's] first application (and at the same time the ground of all others) to objects of the intuition that is possible for us" (B152).[15]

While the initial portion of this description of the transcendental synthesis of the imagination suggests its subordination to the understanding, the remainder indicates that Kant assigns it a central role in the second part of the Deduction. As we shall see, this role consists in making possible the transition from the categories as mere forms of thought, lacking in objective reality, to their true epistemic function as a priori conditions of possible experience. But, as is suggested by Kant's claim that it is the first application of the understanding to sensibility, this transition proceeds in two steps. The first consists in connecting the understanding to time as form of inner sense through the transcendental synthesis of the imagination. This is its first application. In the second step, which involves the second application, this transcendental synthesis grounds the empirical synthesis of apprehension, through which the categories are related to empirical intuition. I shall consider the first step below; but since Kant separates his accounts of the two syntheses with an analysis of the relation between inner sense and apperception in the second part of §24 and §25, I shall examine his account of the latter before proceeding to the analysis of the synthesis of apprehension in §26.

---

[15] See also B153 and B162, note. In the former Kant refers to the understanding as affecting inner sense "[u]nder the designation of a transcendental synthesis of the imagination." In the latter, referring to the necessary agreement between the empirical synthesis of apprehension and the intellectual synthesis of apperception, he states that "It is one and the same spontaneity that there under the name of the imagination and here under the name of understanding, brings combination into the manifold of intuition."

Kant defines the transcendental synthesis of the imagination stipulatively as the figurative synthesis, "if [i.e., insofar as] it pertains merely to the original synthetic unity of apperception, i.e., this transcendental unity, which is thought in the categories" (B151). And he defines the imagination as "the faculty for representing an object even **without its presence in intuition**" (B151). Although Kant fails to provide an argument linking the imagination, so construed, with the determination or, more precisely, the determinate representation of time, one can easily be constructed on the basis of his account of time in the Aesthetic. The argument, which is implicit in Kant's typically cryptic account, turns on the premise that each determinate extent of time is intuited as part of a single all-inclusive time, which is itself represented as an infinite given magnitude.[16] It follows from this that the representation of a determinate time involves the awareness of it as a delimited portion of this single time. But, as with space, the whole is not itself actually given in intuition as an object. Rather, time is, as it were, given only one moment at a time. Accordingly, in order to represent to oneself a determinate time one must also be able to represent past and future times that are not "present" and ultimately the single time of which they are delimited parts, which requires the imagination as defined above.

Kant notes that he occasionally assigns this task to the productive imagination, as distinguished from the reproductive imagination, and claims that only the former is connected with the spontaneity of the understanding, and therefore with transcendental philosophy; while the latter, which is governed by empirical laws of association, is the concern of psychology (B152). We have seen, however, that Kant is inconsistent on this score, since in section 2 of the A-Deduction he connects the determination of time (and space) with the reproductive synthesis and does not mention a productive synthesis. But setting Kant's shifting terminology aside, the main point is that the determination of time requires not only the retention of past times, which in the A-Deduction he characterized as "reproduction," but also the projection or protention of future times, both of which are functions of the imagination on Kant's view.

Even though in the Schematism Kant characterizes time as "[t]he pure image... for all objects of our senses in general" (A142/B182), it is evident that the representation of a single all-inclusive time cannot consist in an image. Rather, as counterintuitive as it may initially appear, applying the previous analysis of the function of the imagination in connection with perception, it seems plausible to construe this representation as a kind of interpretation.[17] Consider Kant's own account of how we represent time in the B-Deduction. After noting that we cannot think a line without drawing it in thought and a circle without describing it, or represent the three

---

[16] Since Kant assigns a parallel mereological structure to space, the same applies to it, *mutatis mutandis.* By the infinitude of space and time Kant understands the unlimited nature of their divisibility into parts rather than the infinite number of their parts. For my analysis of this see Allison (2004), 110–12.

[17] See Chapter 6, pp. 243–86.

dimensions of space without placing three lines perpendicular to each other at a point, Kant remarks that we cannot represent time "without, in **drawing** a straight line (which is to be the external figurative representation of time), attending merely to the action of the synthesis of the manifold through which we successively determine inner sense, and thereby attending to the succession of this determination in inner sense" (B154). This indicates not only that the imaginative representation of time presupposes a figurative synthesis, as in the case of drawing a line, but also that it involves an interpretation of the line as an image of time. Moreover, the need for such an interpretation stems from the fact that inner sense has no manifold of its own. Accordingly, the materials for the intuitive representation of time must be borrowed from outer sense, from which it follows that time is necessarily represented or "interpreted" in spatial terms. In the apt terms of Michael Young, the line is taken "as something more or other than it is perceived as being."[18]

This still leaves us, however, with questions concerning the relation between the synthetic unity of apperception, the categories, and the figurative synthesis that determines time. Although one might expect an expansive account of this matter, perhaps along the lines of the three-fold synthesis in the A-Deduction, Kant simply asserts, without further argument, that the figurative synthesis is an expression of the spontaneity of the understanding; that it determines inner sense a priori in respect of its form; and that this determination is in accord with the unity of apperception (B151–2). Kant here seems to have assumed that simply pointing out that the spontaneity of the understanding underlies the figurative synthesis would be enough to address these questions. But, while given the argument of the first part of the Deduction this might suffice to show that if the figurative synthesis necessarily accords with the unity of apperception it must also accord with the categories, it is not yet clear why this synthesis must conform to the unity of apperception. Indeed, it might be claimed that it is not yet clear why Kant thought that a distinct figurative synthesis is required at all. To be sure, such a synthesis was central to the A-Deduction; but we have seen that there is not a hint of it in either the *Prolegomena* or R5923–35, and the need for one seems to be denied by Kant's brief remarks in the Note. Since the second is more fundamental, I shall consider these questions in reverse order.

We have seen that Kant said in §21 that in order to complete the Deduction it must be shown "from the way in which the empirical intuition is given in sensibility that its unity can be none other than the one the category prescribes to the manifold of a given intuition in general" (B145). And we have also seen that this was not accomplished in the first part of the Deduction because the argument abstracted from the specific nature of human sensibility and assumed only that some data must be given, if the understanding is to have something to unify. But now we might ask why this

---

[18] Young (1988), 142.

additional factor should change matters in the fundamental way that Kant suggests, particularly since human sensible intuition is a species of the sensible intuition in general with which the first part of the Deduction is concerned. Otherwise expressed, what is it about the way in which the sensible data are given to us that requires a distinct figurative synthesis?

Inasmuch as Kant is here primarily concerned with inner sense and its form time, it can safely be assumed that it must have something to do with the representation of time. Although this is also true of the A-Deduction, there is a subtle difference between the two accounts, which bears directly on the difference in the structure of the argument in the two versions. We saw in Chapter 5 that it was the successive nature of our representations as modifications of inner sense that underlay the need for the synthesis of apprehension-cum-reproduction; but we also saw that the initial focus was on the synthesis of the successively given data, which is empirical, and only subsequently did Kant claim that there is a corresponding a priori synthesis. By contrast, in the present case the focus from the beginning is on time as a priori form of inner intuition. As the intuition arguments of the Aesthetic indicate, however, the fundamental feature of time for Kant is not its successive nature, but (as is also the case with space) its singleness or unity, which entails that successive moments must be intuitively represented as delimited portions of the same time. In other words, the manifold of inner sense is not simply given, but *given as* parts of a single all-inclusive time. And this requires that the synthesis through which particular times are represented as parts of a single time must be figurative rather than merely intellectual because the singleness of time is presupposed by rather than constituted through this synthesis.[19]

If this is acknowledged, there should be no further difficulty in seeing why the synthesis through which time is represented must conform to the conditions of the unity of apperception and with it to the categories. With regard to the former, it follows from Kant's account of apperception that the *representation* of time through the drawing of a line must conform to the conditions of its synthetic unity. Not merely the intuitive representation of the line as such, but also the "interpretation" of its successive synthesis as the pure image of time presupposes a single subject conscious of its identity throughout the generative process. In short, even though time itself is an intuition and as such not composed of preexisting parts, its determinate representation requires a synthetic unity of consciousness, which necessitates bringing it under the principle of the synthetic unity of apperception. And, assuming

---

[19] Kant suggests this at B136n, which is appended to §17 in the first part of the B-Deduction. Also relevant to the issue is the distinction that Kant draws in a remark on the thesis of the Second Antinomy between a *compositum* and a *totum* (A438/B467), which Kant elsewhere refers to as a *totum syntheticum* and a *totum analyticum*, respectively (R 3789 17: 293). The former is a whole composed of parts that are given separately (at least in thought). Accordingly, it is conceived as the product of the combination or synthesis of its parts. The latter, by contrast, is a whole, the parts of which are only possible with reference to this whole. Thus, space and time for Kant are *tota* or *tota analytica*.

the soundness of the argument of the first part of the Deduction linking the unity of apperception with the categories, it follows that if the transcendental synthesis of the imagination is subject to the principle of the synthetic unity of apperception, it is subject to the categories as well.

This is not the end of the story, however, since not only is the transcendental synthesis of the imagination subject to the conditions of the synthetic unity of apperception, but the latter is also subject to the conditions of the former. At least this is the case if what is brought to an objective unity of consciousness is to yield cognition of a determinate object. In other words, we once again encounter a reciprocity between the unity of consciousness and the consciousness of unity; though now the latter is understood as the consciousness of the manifold as unified in a single time. As we have seen, this is because the necessity of representing entities and occurrences as occupying determinate positions in a single time, unlike unifying them on the basis of the categories alone, is not imposed upon them by the nature of the understanding, but by the nature of time as a formal condition of human sensibility. Moreover, this is essential for understanding the proof-structure of the B-Deduction, since it explains why the argument does not proceed in a linear fashion, as it would if there were a straight path from the unity of consciousness to the unity or singleness of time, which would be the case if the latter were a product of a purely intellectual synthesis.

IV

§24 (the second part) and §25 *Inner sense and apperception* (B152–9): Although the topics dealt with in these pages may be peripheral to the main concern of the Deduction, they are central to Kant's views on the nature and conditions of the self's awareness and cognition of itself. A distinctive feature of Kant's account is the distinction between inner sense and apperception as two modes of self-awareness, only the first of which yields cognition of oneself. Kant deals with the former in the remaining portion of §24 and with the latter in §25. The discussion is divided into three parts: an examination of the seemingly paradoxical nature of inner sense as Kant depicts it in the second part of §24; an analysis of Kant's account of apperception as a form of self-consciousness in §25 and related texts; and an assessment of Kant's position in light of some of the major criticisms in the literature.

A) *The paradox of inner sense* (B152–6): Upon completing his argument connecting the categories to the form of inner sense by way of the transcendental synthesis of the imagination, Kant turns in the second part of §24 to what he describes as

the paradox that must have struck everyone in the exposition of the form of inner sense (§6): namely how this presents even ourselves to consciousness only as we appear to ourselves, not as we are in ourselves, since we intuit ourselves only as we are internally **affected**, which seems to be contradictory, since we would have to relate to ourselves passively; for this reason it is customary in systems of philosophy to treat **inner** sense as the same as the faculty of **apperception** (which we carefully distinguish).   (B152–3)

The text to which Kant is here referring is a second-edition addendum to the Transcendental Aesthetic (B66–9), which is intended to confirm the doctrine of the ideality of both outer and inner sense. Its relevance to our present concerns stems from its attempt to account for the phenomenal nature of the cognition of ourselves attainable through inner sense. Although Kant adhered to this view of inner sense in the first edition of the *Critique*, he evidently did not really attempt to explain it because he did not regard the mind's empirical cognition of itself through inner sense as a separate transcendental problem distinct from that of the possibility of experience in general.[20]

Kant did, however, recognize the need to explain this aspect of his position in the second edition and the focal point is the notion of affection. In fact, there are two problems of affection for Kant. The most famous one was given its classical expression by Jacobi. It primarily concerns outer affection and pertains to the status of the object that affects us: is it the thing in itself or an appearance, or, in the later formulations of the issue, which introduce the notion of a double affection, or both?[21] But it is the second problem, which concerns inner or self-affection, that evidently most bothered Kant. The problem is rooted in his insistence on the connection between sensibility and receptivity, which entails that the subject is affected by the object being cognized. Setting aside Jacobi's question, Kant evidently regarded the situation as non-problematic in the case of outer affection; but he came to recognize a special problem regarding inner sense and its object to which he points in the passage cited above. As the passage indicates, the problem concerns the connection between affection and passivity. This does not arise in the case of outer sense, since, *ex hypothesi*, the affecting object is external to the self and the latter is purely receptive. But Kant notes that the same cannot be said of inner sense, since there the self both is the affecting agent and that which is affected, which requires attributing two apparently incompatible properties to the self in its relation to itself.

In his initial discussion of the problem to which he alludes in §24, Kant wrote:

Now that which, as representation, can precede any act of thinking something is intuition and, if it contains nothing but relations, it is the form of intuition, which, since it does not represent anything except insofar as something is posited in the mind, can be nothing other than the way in which the mind is affected by its own activity, namely this positing of its representation, thus the way in which it is affected through itself, i.e., it is an inner sense as far as regards its form. Everything that is represented through a sense is to that extent always appearance, and an inner sense must therefore either not be admitted at all or else the subject, which is the object of this sense, can only be represented by its means as appearance, not as it would judge of itself if

[20] The issue is discussed in detail by Prauss (1971), 254–321.
[21] For my analysis of this see Allison (2004), 64–73.

its intuition were mere self-activity, i.e., intellectual. Any difficulty in this depends merely on the question how a subject can internally intuit itself; yet this difficulty is common to every theory.   (B67–8)

In addition to the characterization of self-affection as the mind's act of positing its representations in itself, what is particularly noteworthy is Kant's depiction of the limited options to which his analysis restricts any account of a supposed inner sense; viz., either deny that there is such a thing as an inner sense or admit that it can provide only representations of the self as it appears to itself. Accordingly, Kant's task is to explain how the conception of self-affection provides the key to understanding the thesis that through inner sense the self cognizes itself only as it appears to itself, rather than as it might judge of itself, if it had intellectual as opposed to merely sensible intuition of itself. He attempts to accomplish this through a deeper analysis of self-affection, which connects it directly with the transcendental synthesis of the imagination. Kant claims that what determines inner sense is the understanding through its characteristic combinatory act and notes that it does this "[u]nder the designation of a **transcendental synthesis of the imagination**," from which he immediately concludes that it "exercises that action on the **passive** subject, whose **faculty** it is, about which we rightly say that the inner sense is thereby affected" (B153–4). Kant's thus proposes to resolve the above-mentioned paradox by distinguishing between two aspects of the self: one with respect to which it is active (doing the affecting) and the other with respect to which it is passive (being affected). And he supports this proposal by appealing to the previously discussed drawing of a line. Once again, the point is that the understanding (still under the designation of a transcendental synthesis of the imagination) does not find a combination of the manifold of inner sense but produces it by affecting inner sense (B154–5).

Although this is a clear illustration of how Kant thought that the figurative synthesis determines inner sense, it is far from apparent that it sheds much light on the issue of self-cognition through inner sense. Proceeding as if it were a natural continuation of the line of thought he had just provided, Kant reflects,

But how the I that thinks[22] differs from the I that intuits itself (for I can represent other kinds of intuition as at least possible) and yet be identical with the latter as the same subject, how therefore I can say that **I** as intelligence and **thinking** subject cognize my self as an object that is **thought**, insofar as I am also given to myself in intuition, only, like other phenomena, not as I am for the understanding but rather as I appear to myself, this is no more or less difficult than how I can be an object for myself in general and indeed one of intuition and inner perceptions.
(B155–6)

This convoluted sentence contains three how-questions. (1) How can the I that thinks be distinguished from the I that intuits itself and yet be the same subject?

---

[22] Following Kemp Smith, Pluhar, and Renault's French translation, who themselves follow Vaihinger, I read *das Ich, das denkt* for *das Ich, der Ich denke*. The latter is chosen by Guyer and Wood.

(2) How can I say that I as thinking subject cognize myself as an object that is thought, insofar as I am given to myself in intuition, and therefore, like other phenomena, as I appear to myself rather than as I am for the understanding? (3) How can I be an object for myself at all (in general), particularly an object of inner perception? It is clear from Kant's syntax that he views the second question as an alternative formulation of the first rather than as a distinct question; and while Kant does not explicitly identify the last question with the first (in either of its forms), instead saying merely that it has the same degree of difficulty, it also seems clear that this is because he regards it as essentially the same question. Accordingly, rather than providing an explication of the self's cognition of itself, these turn out to be three ways of expressing the mysterious nature of self-cognition.

Nevertheless, Kant proceeds as if he had answered rather than merely reformulated his initial question regarding self-affection and its relation to self-cognition through inner sense. Thus, in an even lengthier sentence of which I shall quote only the conclusion and which begins with the reminder that space is a mere form of outer appearances, Kant points to two factors regarding the representation of time that he regards as supporting his view: (1) that time can only be represented through the image of a line; and (2) that we can only derive the length or position in time of inner perceptions from alterations that are exhibited in outer things. And from this he concludes first that we must order the determinations of inner sense in time in the same way in which we order those of outer sense in space, i.e., that the latter order is both parallel to and dependent upon the former, and second that,

[I]f we admit about the latter [determinations of outer sense] that we cognize objects by their means only insofar as we are externally affected, then we must also concede that through inner sense we intuit ourselves only as we are internally affected **by our selves**, i.e., as far as inner intuition is concerned we cognize our own subject only as appearance but not in accordance with what it is in itself.   (B156)

Both of the factors to which here Kant appeals concern the dependence of temporal upon spatial representation and stem from his core thesis that inner sense has no manifold of its own but depends for its content on materials provided by outer sense. The first has already been considered and no further discussion of it is required at this point. Although this cannot be said of the second, which is directly related to the new Refutation of Idealism added in the second edition, I shall refrain from considering it here, since doing so would require an extended digression.[23] Moreover, this does not bear directly on the main point, which is that, even if we accept Kant's premises, it is not clear that they suffice to establish the phenomenal status of the object of inner sense.

---

[23] I analyze their connection and the argument of Kant's Refutation of Idealism in Allison (2004), 275–303.

To begin with the obvious, the argument explicitly assumes the view of outer sense expounded in the Aesthetic. Although it is perfectly reasonable for Kant to proceed in this way, it has the unintended consequence of depriving his argument of any force against a critic who would challenge the latter view, of which there were many in Kant's own time, not to mention our own. For present purposes, however, the salient point is that, even assuming the soundness of Kant's account of space and its relation to outer sense in the Aesthetic, its application to inner sense remains problematic. As Kant presents his argument in the addendum to the Aesthetic and §24, it contains two strands, which, though not clearly distinguished, can be considered apart for analytic purposes.[24] The first, which I call "the materials argument," has roughly the following form: (1) since the materials of inner sense are all derived from outer sense; and (2) since (as Kant argues at B66–7) our representations of outer things contain nothing but relations; and (3) since a thing as it is in itself (by which Kant here understands a thing considered merely with respect to its intrinsic, non-relational properties) cannot be cognized through mere relations; (4) it follows that we cannot cognize ourselves through inner sense as we are in ourselves. I call the second strand of Kant's analysis "the self-affection argument." The basic idea is that in apprehending its contents as they appear in inner sense the mind must somehow affect itself. From this, taken in connection with the ideality of time as the form of inner sense, it is inferred that the mind can cognize itself only "as it appears to itself, not as it is" (B69).

Taken as self-standing arguments, neither is very convincing and the combination of two weak arguments seldom produces a strong one. Indeed, the materials argument is particularly weak. First, even assuming that sensible intuition contains only relations and nothing "absolutely inner," it does not follow that it yields a representation of its object only as it is in relation to the subject and not as it is in itself. Kant here seems to conflate two distinct claims about the relational character of what is sensibly intuited: (1) that because of the spatiotemporal form of intuition we can sensibly intuit only *the relational properties of things*; and (2) that we can sensibly intuit objects *only in their relation to the subject*. Second, the argument seems to conflate two senses of "thing in itself": the Leibnizian conception of a simple substance or monad, which serves as the non-sensible ground of relations and is more properly characterized as a noumenon, and the transcendental conception of a thing considered as it is apart from its epistemic relation to the cognizing subject. Although the aim of the argument is to deny the possibility of sensible intuition of a thing as it is in itself in the second sense, the most that it can do is to deny its possibility with respect to the first.

---

[24] What follows is a condensed and modified version of the analysis of Kant's argument for the phenomenal nature of empirical self-cognition originally given in Allison (1983), 263–71 and reformulated in (2004), 280–5.

The argument from self-affection is based upon the connection between affection and receptivity; the assumption that the receptivity of sensible data is conditioned by an a priori form; and a presumed analogy between inner and outer affection.[25] But since the first two elements were formulated by Kant with respect to outer sense, virtually the entire weight of his argument falls on the analogy. The problem, however, is that it does not appear that it can bear this weight. As was pointed out by Paton, the function of affection by external objects is to supply the raw materials for cognition, while that of self-affection is to combine these materials in accordance with the conditions of time-determination.[26] Accordingly, in contrast to outer affection, self-affection cannot be understood as the source of the sensible data presented to the understanding; rather, it only operates upon what is already given, which appears to undercut the use for which the analogy is intended.

Kant's use of the analogy appears to be further undercut, if one considers his characterization of self-affection in §24 as the determination of inner sense by the understanding, qua transcendental synthesis of the imagination. First, since there is little in common between the influence of objects on outer sense and "the synthetic influence of the understanding on the inner sense" (B154), the identification of self-affection with the latter serves to accentuate the difference between them rather than their commonality. Second, the latter, in the form of the transcendental synthesis of the imagination, is supposedly a transcendental condition of *all* experience, not simply of *inner* experience, and since Kant does not purport to ground the phenomenal status of all objects of experience upon it, there seems to be no reason why it should have that function with respect to inner experience.

Nevertheless, further consideration suggests that, given the arguments of the Aesthetic and the preceding account of the transcendental synthesis of the imagination, Kant has provided the materials for a defensible account of the phenomenal status of the object of inner sense, albeit one in which the nature of this object turns out to differ from what one might initially assume. An essential ingredient is Kant's

---

[25] Following Strawson's exegetical thesis that Kant's denial of the possibility of knowledge of things in themselves, to which she refers as "Kantian humility," is supposed to be a consequence of the mind's receptivity with respect to its sensible data, Langton (1998) has developed an argument for their connection, which supposedly bypasses any need to appeal to a priori forms of sensibility, and therefore to idealism. On her reading, in which the previously discussed addendum to the Aesthetic in the second edition plays a major role, Kant's humility regarding objects of outer sense (she ignores inner sense) turns on three metaphysical theses: (1) that sensibility, in virtue of its receptive nature, can only provide awareness of the relational properties of things; (2) that things in themselves (modeled on the Leibnizian monad) are distinguished by their intrinsic (non-relational) properties; and (3) that relations and the relational properties of things are not reducible to intrinsic properties. And from this she claims that, contrary to Kant's express declarations, the denial of the possibility of cognition of things in themselves is not a function of the thesis that sensibility has a priori forms in accordance with which sensible data are received. In short, she separates receptivity from the notion of a *form* of receptivity. For my critique of this view, a central point of which is that Langton ignores the discursivity thesis, see Allison (2004), 9–11 and 17–19.

[26] See Paton (1936b), 238–40.

previously cited claim that the transcendental synthesis of the imagination, as an effect of the understanding on sensibility, is the first but not the only application of the understanding to sensibility. In initially considering this claim it was suggested that the second application was the empirical synthesis of apprehension through which perception is constituted. But it now appears that there is also a third application through which a specifically inner experience is constituted and which Kant refers to as "attention" (*Aufmerksamkeit*) (B156–7n). The second of the above-mentioned applications, which is the central concern of §26, will be considered in the next segment; our present concern is with the third.

Attention, so considered, may be characterized as an act of "self-objectification."[27] It is a second-order, reflective act of the understanding, through which one's first-order representings are themselves taken as objects of cognition rather than being related as representations to external phenomenal objects. This amounts to a change in epistemic focus, which requires an act of attention and which, as conditioned by the form of time, yields the cognition of a segment of one's mental history through an experience in which this segment is, as it were, injected into the history of the phenomenal world. Although this line of thought is largely implicit in the scanty treatment of the topic in the *Critique*, Kant provides a somewhat fuller picture of his view in the discussions of self-cognition in the *Nachlass*, which are connected with Kant's further thoughts regarding the Refutation of Idealism. One such text is R 5655 (18: 313–16; 286–8). Its importance lies in its focus on the dual nature of time or, more precisely, on the self's relation to time. As Kant succinctly puts it, "time is in me, and I am in time" (18: 314_{9-10}; 286). Starting with this duality, Kant sketches an argument for the phenomenal nature of the self qua cognized through inner sense. He notes that while, on the one hand, "I must presuppose my existence...in order to be able to think of time as the determination of my existence and that of all things outside me" (18: 315_{23-8}; 287), on the other hand, I must presuppose time in order to determine my existence in it (18: 315_{28-30}; 287).

Kant concludes from this that if my existence is understood in the same way in both cases there is a contradiction, which can only be avoided by distinguishing between the characterizations of my existence in these two cases. In short, I exist in time qua appearance; whereas time exists in me qua supersensible, but not theoretically cognizable being (18: 316_{3-5}; 287) or, as Kant also puts it, as "pure I" (18; 316_{16-17}; 288). This parallels the argument of the *Critique* in that both take the form of an assertion of what must be assumed in order to avoid a contradiction, but they differ in their depictions of the terms of the contradiction. Whereas in the *Critique* it concerns the need to consider one and the same subject as both affecting and affected, in this *Reflexion* it concerns the necessity of assuming that one and the same subject exists in two seemingly incompatible relations to time. In the end they

---

[27] The terminology is borrowed from Zöller (1984), 267.

come to much the same thing, however, since the self in which time exists is the spontaneous affecting self and the self that exists in time is the affected and therefore determined self. Thus, the issue concerns the unifiability of these two conceptions of the self, both of which are required: one to characterize the act of cognizing and the other to depict the nature of the object cognized through this act.

In suggesting that, despite the initial impression, Kant's account of inner sense and its connection with self-affection provides the materials for a broadly defensible argument (i.e., one which assumes the phenomenal status of the object of outer sense, the connection between sensibility and affection, and the spontaneity of the understanding) for the merely phenomenal status of the object of inner sense, it was noted that this object will turn out to be somewhat different than one might assume. Given Kant's insistence on the parallel between inner and outer sense, one would expect him to maintain that, just as the objects of outer sense are cognized in terms of the manner in which they appear, so the object of inner sense is cognized in terms of the manner in which it appears to itself in inner sense. But since inner sense has no manifold of its own and derives its data from outer sense, it has no content that it can be regarded as representations of the self in the way in which outer intuitions are regarded as intuitions of body. Accordingly, the self cannot be said to appear to itself through inner sense; rather what appears to it are its representations of outer objects, which through a reflective act are taken as its representations in the possessive sense of *belonging to itself* rather than in the intentional sense as representations *of itself.*

As a result, Kant's account of inner sense turns out to be surprisingly close to Hume's, who famously denied that he had any impression of the self, claiming instead that "when I enter most intimately into what I call *myself,* I always stumble upon some particular impression...I never catch *myself* at any time without an impression, and can never perceive anything but the impression."[28] In a similar vein, Kant could say that when he introspects he finds only his representations (the counterpart of Hume's impressions), and never the subject whose representation they are. Nevertheless, there is a fundamental difference between the two philosophers in this respect, since Kant, unlike Hume, distinguishes between inner sense and apperception. Thus, the failure to find an inner intuition of the self does not lead Kant to the rejection of the *thought* of the self, which is why he turns in §25 directly from inner sense to apperception.

B) *§25: Apperception or intellectual self-consciousness* (B157–9): Although Kant affirms the epistemic significance of the consciousness of synthesis in both versions of the Deduction, his main focus is on the unity or identity of apperception and the consequent necessity of the possibility of the "I think" accompanying all my representations. But having argued that inner sense yields only a consciousness of the self as it appears to itself and that the inability to recognize this stems from the failure to

---

[28] Hume (2007), 165.

distinguish between it and apperception in the second part of §24, Kant turns in §25 to apperception as a distinct mode of self-consciousness, which is linked specifically to the spontaneity of thinking. He begins by claiming that in the transcendental synthesis of the manifold of representations, i.e., the exercise of the spontaneity of the understanding, "I am conscious of myself not as I appear to myself, nor as I **am** in myself, but only **that** I am. This **representation** is a **thinking**, not an **intuiting**" (B157). Kant here affirms three seemingly incompatible propositions: (1) that through inner sense we can only cognize ourselves as we appear to ourselves rather than as we are in ourselves; (2) that through apperception we have a consciousness of ourselves as active, spontaneous subjects, which does not constitute cognition; and (3) that this consciousness, though not sufficient for a cognition of the self, either as it appears to itself or as it is in itself, nevertheless provides an awareness of the *existence* of the self. Accordingly, our task is to see how Kant uses the distinction between thinking and intuiting to reconcile these claims.

It is clear from Kant's account of inner sense why he denied that the consciousness of thinking is a consciousness of the self as it appears to itself. Since the latter is dependent on conditions of time and, as such, yields the cognition of a conditioned series of mental occurrences in the phenomenal world, it cannot provide cognition of the *act* of thinking.[29] And since Kant held that it would require a capacity for an intellectual intuition, it is also clear why he denied that it yields a cognition of the self as it exists in itself. But what remains to be explained is why, given the dichotomy between these two manners in which something can be considered as existing, Kant maintained that apperception yields an awareness of the existence of the self that falls under neither of these alternatives.

Underlying Kant's account is the principle that the cognition of any object, whether it be oneself or an object distinct from oneself, and whether it be cognized as it appears or as it is in itself, requires a determinate representation, and therefore an intuition as well as a concept. And since the inner sensible intuition with which we are equipped does not provide this cognition and we lack the intellectual intuition, which supposedly could provide it, it follows that the consciousness of spontaneity does not amount to a cognition of the self as it is in itself. Kant's clearest statement of his position is in a note attached to his discussion of the necessity of a determinate representation of oneself in order to have what would count as a cognition of oneself. He writes:

The **I think** expresses the act of determining my existence. The existence is thereby already given, but the way in which I am to determine it, i.e., the manifold that I am to posit in myself as belonging to it, is not yet thereby given. For that self-intuition [*Selbstanschauung*] is required, which is grounded in an *a priori* given form, i.e., time, which is sensible and belongs

---

[29] Kant's fullest statement of this point is in a *Reflexion* with the heading "Answer to the question: is it an experience that we think?" (R 5661 18: 318–19; 289–90). For my analysis of this text see Allison (1983), 276–8.

to the receptivity of the determinable. Now I do not have yet another self-intuition, which would give the **determining** in me, of the spontaneity of which alone I am conscious, even before the act of **determination**, in the same way as time gives that which is to be determined, thus I cannot determine my existence as that of a self-active being, rather I merely represent the spontaneity of my thought, i.e., of the determining, and my existence always remains only sensibly determinable, i.e., determinable as the existence of an appearance. Yet this spontaneity is the reason I call myself an **intelligence**.   (B157–8n)

Since "existence" for Kant is not a real predicate or determination, to determine the existence of something is not a matter of determining *that* it exists, i.e., that existence can be predicated of it. Rather, it consists in attributing a determinate nature to something that is already taken as an existent because it is given in intuition. And since time is the form of inner sense or, as Kant here puts it, self-intuition, this means that I can only have a determinate representation, i.e., cognition, of my existence as a being in time, which precludes the cognition of myself as a spontaneous, self-active being. The latter, Kant suggests, would require a kind of meta-intuition of my self-activity, i.e., an intuition of the act of determining my existence in time, which would have to be intuited in a meta-time, etc., thereby generating an infinite regress.[30] Nevertheless, Kant also insists that through the apperceptive consciousness "I think" I am aware of my spontaneity as exercised in every act of thought, which is why I can call myself an intelligence. In short, through apperception I have a consciousness of my existence as a self-active being, which, due to Kant's constraints on what constitutes cognition, cannot be characterized as such.

Kant elaborates upon both aspects of this complex claim in the second-edition version of the Paralogisms. With respect to the existential nature of the claim about the I of the "I think," in commenting on the organization of his critique of rational psychology, Kant notes that if one follows the "**analytic** procedure," i.e., that of Descartes in the *Meditations*, the set of paralogistic inferences that constitute the subject matter of rational psychology begins with "the 'I think' given as a proposition that already includes existence in itself," and therefore "not from the concept of a thinking being in general but from an actuality [*Wirklichkeit*]" (B418).[31] And, later, in the context of a discussion of the Second Paralogism, Kant remarks that "apperception is something real [*Reales*], and its simplicity lies already in its possibility" (B419). Moreover, in three different places in the B-Paralogisms Kant claims that "I think" is not only an existential but also an empirical proposition. In the most important of these he writes:[32]

The "I think" is, as has already been said, an empirical proposition, and contains within itself the proposition "I exist." But I cannot say "Everything that thinks exists"; for then the property

---

[30] For a more developed formulation of this argument see R 5661 18: 319$_{26-31}$; 289.

[31] Kant contrasts this with a synthetic procedure, which begins with the concept of a thinking being. The latter is the procedure of Wolffian rational psychology.

[32] The others are B420 and 428. The latter will be discussed below.

of thinking would make all beings possessing it into necessary beings. Hence my existence also cannot be regarded as inferred from the proposition "I think," as Descartes held ... but rather it is identical with it. It expresses an indeterminate empirical intuition, i.e., a perception (hence it proves that sensation, which consequently belongs to sensibility, underlies [*zum Grunde liege*] this existential proposition),[33] but it precedes the experience that is to determine the object of perception through the category in regard to time; and here existence is not yet a category, which is not related to an indeterminately given object, but rather to an object of which one has a concept, and about which one wants to know whether or not it is posited outside this concept. An indeterminate perception here signifies only something real, which was given, and indeed only to thinking in general, thus not as appearance, and also not as a thing in itself (a noumenon), but rather as something that in fact exists and is indicated as an existing thing in the proposition "I think." For it is to be noted that if I have called the proposition "I think" an empirical proposition, I would not say by this that the I in this proposition is an empirical representation; for it is rather purely intellectual, because it belongs to thinking in general. Only without any empirical representation, which provides the material for thinking, the act I think would not take place, and the empirical is only the condition of the application, or use, of the pure intellectual faculty.   (B422n)

I have cited this lengthy note in virtually its entirety because, quite apart from its discussion of Descartes and its connection with the overall argument of the Paralogisms, it is essential for understanding what Kant says in §25 of the B-Deduction.[34] For present purposes four points call for discussion: (1) the claim that existence is already assumed in the proposition "I think;" (2) that this existence is not that which is thought through the category of existence; (3) that this existence is neither of the I as it exists in itself nor as it appears to itself in inner sense; and (4) that "I exist" is an empirical proposition.

1) *"I think" and "I exist"*: Although Kant's account of the connection between these propositions is formulated with Descartes in mind, it can be understood independently of Kant's problematic interpretation and critique of the *cogito* argument.[35] The main point is that rather than being an inference from "I think," "I exist" is already assumed in it. Otherwise expressed, "I think," "I am thinking," and "I exist thinking" are logically equivalent. Moreover, though similar claims are also to be found in Spinoza and Leibniz, for Kant this seems to follow directly from the conception of apperception as a consciousness of the activity of thinking.[36] Since there can be no

[33] Following Kemp Smith and Pluhar I am translating "*zum Grunde liege*" as "underlies" rather than "grounds," which is the rendering of Guyer and Wood because it makes better sense of the text.

[34] For a fuller discussion of this note from which much of what I say here is extracted see Allison (2004), 352–6.

[35] Kant here treats Descartes' argument as a syllogistic inference in which "I exist" is considered as a conclusion from the major premise "Everything that thinks exists" and the minor premise "I think," a reading that is widely rejected by Descartes' scholars. For my discussion of the issue, see Allison (2004), 355–6 and 501, note 39.

[36] See Spinoza (1985), 234 and Leibniz (1981), 411.

activity without an agent, to recognize the existence of an activity is to assume the existence of something that acts.

2) *"I think" and the category of existence*: Kant's denial that the existence built into the proposition "I think" is the category must be understood in connection with his view that, as a modal category, existence, is not a real predicate or determination.[37] Thus, as Kant here points out, in order to predicate the category of existence of something one must first have a determinate concept of the entity in question. One might think that this condition is met in the present case, since it involves a thinker of whom an understanding with the property of spontaneity is attached. But Kant quickly disabuses the reader of any such thought, when he notes that, "Through this I, or He, or It (the thing), which thinks, nothing further is represented than a transcendental subject of thoughts =x, which is recognized only through the thoughts that are its predicates, and about which, in abstraction, we can never have even the least concept" (A346/B404).[38] Accordingly, rather than a determinate concept of a thinking being we have only a "mere consciousness that accompanies every concept" (A346/B404).

3) *The existence of the I of the "I think"*: Kant claims that this I is to be considered neither as appearance nor as thing in itself, which transcends the familiar Kantian dichotomy between ways of existing or, more precisely, between ways in which the existence of something can be considered. We have seen that Kant had already made this claim in §25 and he will reiterate it at B429. Moreover, it follows from his analysis of the conditions of predication. Once again, to consider something as it appears or as an appearance presupposes a determinate empirical intuition, which is the source of the description under which it is taken and which allows for the predication of it of the category of existence.[39] But Kant denies that this is the case with the I of the "I think" on the grounds that the only representation of it that we have is an "indeterminate intuition" or perception.[40]

In light of this one might ask why we should predicate existence of this I at all, since it seems that the only grounds for doing so is an indeterminate intuition, which hardly seems to have much evidentiary value. The answer is that it is wrong to think of the latter as evidence from which the existence of this I is to be inferred. Inasmuch as existence is presupposed or built into the act of thinking, Kant's appeals to the

[37] For Kant's account of the distinctness of the modal categories, which underlies his famous denial that "existence" is a real predicate or determination, see A74/B99–100. I discuss this issue in Allison (2004), 138–9 and 413–17.

[38] This claim is the subject of a classical paper by Sellars (1971), 5–31.

[39] At B429 Kant suggests that this claim can be extended from the modal categories to all the categories, when he states that in representing myself as subject of thought or ground of thinking I am not applying the categories of substance and cause, since these presuppose a sensible intuition. Given the distinction between pure and schematized category, however, I do not see how he can be taken as denying the former.

[40] In the *Prolegomena* (4: 344n; 125) Kant says of the I of apperception that, rather than being a concept, "it is nothing more than a feeling of an existence without the least concept, and it is only a representation of that to which all thinking stands in relation (*relatione accidentis*)."

indeterminateness of this intuition or perception is to underscore the impossibility of providing any content to the thought of this I, which is why he claims that from it I can only know *that* I am, not *what* I am beyond the vacuous thing that thinks.

4) *"I think" as an empirical proposition*: Since Kant makes this claim three times in the B-Paralogisms, it is evident that he attached considerable importance to it. It is also evident, however, that it is a very peculiar kind of empirical proposition; for, on the one hand, it lacks what would normally be considered an essential feature of any such proposition; viz., the concept of an empirical subject of which properties are predicated; while, on the other, its predicate (spontaneity or self-activity) is, *ex hypothesi*, not something empirical. Clearly, part of what Kant meant by characterizing the proposition as empirical is that it expresses a contingent rather than a necessary truth. Here he is in agreement with Leibniz, for whom it is a "proposition of fact, founded on immediate experience, and is not a necessary proposition whose necessity is seen in the immediate agreement of ideas."[41] But the cited passage indicates that this is not all that Kant had in mind in emphasizing the empirical nature of this proposition. In fact, it seems that he assigned two distinct roles for the empirical. One is to provide the proposition with a sensible referent, albeit an indeterminate one. The other, which is suggested by the claim that without an empirical representation to provide the material for thinking the act of thinking would not take place, implies that the empirical functions as the trigger or occasion of the act of thinking rather than the source of its empirical content. But regardless of whether Kant meant one or both of these, it is clear that the representation of the I in this proposition is intellectual rather than empirical. Thus, while the empirical nature of the proposition "I think" precludes taking it as referring to a noumenal thinking being, its indeterminate nature precludes basing any substantive claims upon it.

C) *An Assessment*: In order properly to assess Kant's account of apperception, inner sense, and the relation between them in the second edition of the Transcendental Deduction and related texts we must first determine what he was trying to do. And despite the complexity and obscurity of this account, Kant's main concern is relatively clear, namely, to answer the question: how can the thinking subject cognize itself as object, particularly as an object given in intuition? Although Kant suggests that this is a question confronting any theory of self-knowledge, there are two factors that make his treatment of it more complex and seemingly problematic. One is that it requires integrating two distinct elements: apperception and inner sense, between which Kant claims competing theories fail to distinguish, thereby evading the real problem, which concerns precisely this integration. The other is that by denying that inner sense has a manifold of its own, he raises a fresh question concerning the object of inner sense.

---

[41] Leibniz (1981), 411.

With respect to the first point, while demonstrating that Kant was correct in this global charge against competing theories would require examining at least a representative sample of these theories, the main point can be expressed concisely in a manner that should suffice for present purposes.[42] Simply put, a failure to distinguish between apperception and inner sense, like the more general failure to distinguish between understanding and sensibility of which it is an instance, can take two forms: either the theory effectively (if not in so many words) reduces apperception to inner sense or, conversely, it effectively reduces (again not necessarily in so many words) inner sense to apperception. The former characterizes the Cartesian approach (broadly construed), for which the self has an intuitive certainty of itself, and the latter the Leibnizian approach, especially in its Wolffian form in which rational psychology constitutes a branch of special metaphysics, the tenets of which are supposedly derived from an analysis of the concept of a thing that thinks.[43]

With respect to the second point, it should be noted that either form of reduction presupposes that inner sense has a content of its own, since it requires that there be something given in inner intuition that is either reducible to the I of apperception or to which the latter is reducible. But we have seen that for Kant what is actually so given does not fall under that description, from which it apparently follows that the close parallelism between outer and inner sense on which Kant's account is based breaks down. Thus, while this account avoids reductionism, it might also seem that it amounts to the abandonment of any cognitive role for inner sense as the ground of a genuinely inner experience under the form of time.

We have also seen, however, that this is not the case; for rather than concluding that inner sense has no content at all, which would be tantamount to rejecting the notion of such a sense, Kant maintains that its content is provided by outer sense. This not only allows for the possibility of an inner experience, understood as a second-order, reflective cognition of one's mental history, but since this involves the injection of this history into the course of the phenomenal world, it also helps to explicate Kant's claim in the A-Deduction that, just as there is only one space and one time of which particular spaces and times are parts, so "[t]here is only **one** experience, in which all perceptions are represented as in thoroughgoing and lawlike connection."

Nevertheless, these considerations could hardly constitute a defense or even a mitigation of Kant's account, if the latter were deemed incoherent, which is precisely what Kant's critics have frequently claimed. The basic problem can be traced back to the critiques by Lambert, Mendelssohn, and Schultz of Kant's claim in the *Inaugural Dissertation* that time, like space, is merely a subjective form of sensibility. Within the

---

[42] For comprehensive and detailed accounts of these theories, which have informed my own discussion, see Wunderlich (2005) and Thiel (2011).

[43] As Kant puts it at one point: "I think is the sole text of rational psychology...from which it is to develop its entire wisdom" (A343/B401).

"critical" period, one of Kant's more perceptive critics, Hermann Andreas Pistorius, in a lengthy and largely respectful review of the *Prolegomena*, while expressing some sympathy with Kant's account of the ideality of space, confessed an inability to understand his claim that the object of inner sense, like that of outer sense, is merely phenomenal. Taking Kant's use of the term "appearance" (*Erscheinung*) as equivalent to "seeming" or "illusion" (*Schein*) and evidently assuming that this status applied both to the perceiving self and the self inwardly perceived, Pistorius noted that an appearance requires something (or someone) to which it appears and if this, in turn, is itself taken as an appearance, there remains nothing real in which the original seeming can exist.[44]

Moreover, this line of objection is also found in present-day Kant criticism. For example, Strawson, as part of his wholesale dismissal of transcendental idealism, asks:

[W]hat sort of truth about ourselves is it, that we appear to ourselves in a temporal guise? Do we really so appear to ourselves or only appear to ourselves so to appear to ourselves? It seems that we must either choose the first alternative at once or uselessly delay a uselessly elaborated variant of it. Then is it a temporal fact, a fact about what happens in time, that we really so appear to ourselves? To say this would be to go back on our choice; for all that occurs in time belongs on the side of appearances. So it is not a fact about what happens in time that we really appear to ourselves in a temporal guise. I really do *appear* to myself temporally; but I do not really *temporally* appear to myself. But now what does "really do appear" mean? The question is unanswerable; the bounds of intelligibility have been traversed on any standard.[45]

Although Pistorius' focus is on the nature of the self to which appearances appear and Strawson's on the temporality of their appearing, both challenge the intelligibility of Kant's account on essentially the same grounds; viz., the assumption that Kant's transcendental distinction between things as they appear and as they are in themselves is to be understood as a straightforward application of the traditional distinction between appearance and reality. Admittedly, Kant's language provides some support for this, since he all too often refers to "mere appearances" and characterizes them as "representations in us." But he also took pains, particularly in the *Prolegomena* and the second edition of the *Critique* in response to critics of his first-edition account, to make it clear that this is not how he wished to be understood. A well-known example of this is Kant's clearly expressed distinction between "*Erscheinung*" and "*Schein*" (B69–71). More to the present point, however, is a remark appended to the second-edition version of the Paralogisms, which was apparently intended as a response to Pistorius, but which can serve as an anticipatory rejoinder to Strawson and the many others who raise similar criticisms. Kant there writes:

The proposition "I think," or "I exist thinking," is an empirical proposition. But such a proposition is grounded on empirical intuition, consequently also on the object thought, as an appearance; and thus it seems as if, according to our theory, the whole, even in thinking, is

[44] See Pistorius (1991), 101–2.   [45] Strawson (1966), 39.

completely transformed into appearance [*Erscheinung*], and in such a way our consciousness itself, as mere illusion [*Schein*], would in fact come down to nothing.   (B428)[46]

If we examine Strawson's unintelligibility charge in light of these considerations, it seems less than compelling. He asks what does "'really do appear' mean," as if Kant's defense against the charge of advocating a form of subjective idealism consisted largely in the claim that objects really do appear to us as in space and time, as contrasted with merely appearing, i.e., seeming to appear. Such a claim may well be unintelligible, but it is not Kant's. The appearance of unintelligibility is the product of a conflation of empirical and transcendental claims, where the latter concern conditions of human cognition and not some supersensible world. One can certainly question the adequacy of Kant's arguments for the claims that space and time are merely forms of human sensibility and as such cannot be predicated of objects in general or as such; but this is quite distinct from Strawson's contention that such claims are literally unintelligible. Indeed, if this were the case, the proposition that space and time are empirically real and transcendentally ideal would be not simply unfounded but self-contradictory, which makes one wonder how Kant could have argued (even inadequately) for it.

Strawson's critique, however, is not limited to Kant's account of inner sense. In fact, his main target is Kant's account of the relation between the active I of the "I think" and the passive I ("the me") that it cognizes through inner sense. On Strawson's reading, Kant's fundamental concern is to establish a connection "by way of identity" between the natural or empirical subject and the "real" or supersensible subject. Appealing to a passage where Kant states that it is through apperception that we become conscious of possessing understanding and reason, which cannot be ascribed to sensibility, he takes Kant to be claiming that it is through apperception that the empirical subject recognizes its identity with the transcendental subject that it "really" is.[47] In short, apperception on this view is not only a

---

[46] Similarly, in the *Anthropology*, after reprising his account of self-cognition through self-affection in terms close to that of the B-Deduction, from which he concludes that one only cognizes oneself as one appears to oneself, Kant laments that this proposition is "often so maliciously twisted as if it said that: it only *seems* to me...that I have certain ideas and sensations, indeed it only seems that I exist at all" (7: 142; 255). This passage is cited in response to Strawson's objection by Bird (2006), 384. Although I express it in somewhat different terms, my response to Strawson's and similar objections is substantially the same as Bird's.

[47] The passage that Strawson cites reads: "Man...who knows all the rest of nature through the senses, knows himself also through pure [*blosse*] apperception; and this, indeed, in acts and inner determinations which he cannot regard as impressions of the senses. He is thus to himself, on the one hand phenomenon, and the other hand, in respect of certain faculties which cannot be ascribed to sensibility, a purely [*bloss*] intelligible object. We entitle these faculties understanding and reason" (A546–7/B574–5). Following Strawson, I have cited the Kemp Smith translation. The most problematic feature of this passage is Kant's claim that one *knows* (*erkannt*) oneself through apperception, since this contradicts his thesis that cognition requires intuition as well as thought. But given the many places where Kant denies this, I think it reasonable to assume that Kant here misstates his view, perhaps because of his desire to contrast the consciousness of the spontaneity of the self in apperception with the sensible nature of our cognition of nature. Moreover, if "knows himself" is replaced by "is conscious of

consciousness of the "real" or noumenal self, but also of its identity with the phenomenal self.

According to Strawson, this doctrine is incoherent on two counts. First, both the consciousness of the activity of thinking and the thinking of which the self is conscious take place in time. Thus, both this consciousness and its object must be assigned to a being who, in Strawson's terms, "has a history and hence is not a supersensible being, not the subject in which the representation of time has its original ground."[48] Second, by identifying the self-conscious subject, who has a history, with a supersensible subject Kant commits himself to the absurd doctrine that the empirical self *both appears to* and is an appearance of the "real," supersensible self. Once again, the problem stems from the presumed atemporal nature of the latter. On the one hand, this entails that the appearing to it of the successive states of the empirical subject, with which it is supposedly identical, cannot be regarded as an occurrence in time, while, on the other, any attempt to put a non-temporal construction on "to appear" leads immediately to unintelligibility. And from this Strawson concludes with a rhetorical flourish:

> Repeated like spells, these pronominal incantations are as inefficacious as spells. In the dictum regarding knowledge of oneself (empirical self-consciousness) the identity which has to be explained—the identity of the empirically self-conscious subject and the real or supersensible subject—is simply assumed without being made a whit more intelligible. If the appearances of *x* to *x* occur in time, they cannot be assigned to the transcendental, supersensible subject, for that being has no history. That is to say, they cannot justifiably be described as appearances *to* myself as I (supersensibly) am in myself, nor—since what they are appearances *to* they are also appearances *of*—as appearances *of* myself as I (supersensibly) am in myself. The reference to myself as I (supersensibly) am in myself drops out as superfluous and unjustified: and with it goes all ground for saying that, in empirical self-consciousness, I appear to myself as other than I really am.[49]

While there is no question that the view that Strawson depicts transcends the bounds of intelligibility (as well as sense), there is once again ample room for denying that it is Kant's. The basic issue is the claim that the empirical self both appears to and is the appearance of a supersensible and real self. Even though there are passages that suggest such a reading, I believe that attributing it to Kant is again the result of a conflation: this time between two distinctions. One is the familiar transcendental distinction between things as they appear and as they are in themselves, which Kant applies to the self. As I have argued at length elsewhere, this is to be understood as a distinction between two ways of considering one and the same entity: as it is when thought in relation to human sensibility and its a priori conditions and as it would be

---

himself," "conceives of himself," or some such locution, what Kant claims in this passage is perfectly compatible with the "critical" view on this matter.

[48] Strawson (1966), 248.   [49] Ibid., 248–9.

for some putative pure intelligence, which cognizes it as it is in itself independently of these conditions.[50] Although our dependence upon sensible conditions precludes cognizing things so considered, we can think them through the pure categories. Applied to the self, this takes the form of a distinction between the self as it is for itself when cognized through inner sense and as it would be from a non-sensible God's eye view, which is inaccessible to us. Granted, both this transcendental distinction in general and its application to the self in particular involve well-known and frequently discussed difficulties, but these are not our present concern.

The other, which is our present concern, is the self's cognition of itself, where the distinction is an epistemological one between the cognizing self, i.e., the I of the "I think," and the cognized self, qua apprehended through inner sense and brought under the categories. While Kant asserts that "apperception is something real," he denies that the apperceiving I is to be identified either with the self as it is in itself, which is what Strawson understood by the "real" self, or with the self as it appears to itself. And though some of what Kant says seems to suggest the contrary, we have seen that the latter cannot be regarded as the appearance *of* the apperceiving I. Once again, this is a consequence of the fact that inner sense has no manifold of its own, which means that it provides no specifically inner qualities that could be predicated of the self as its qualities.[51]

This still leaves us, however, with the cognizing self, which Kant evidently distinguished from the self as it is itself. Thus, we need to ask why Kant not only denies that we can *cognize* this self, which on "critical" grounds is obvious, but why he also denies that we can even *think* it, which we presumably could, if, like Strawson, we understood by it the "real" self. The answer is that we lack what would be necessary to think it; viz., a concept. Moreover, on this point at least Kant is quite clear. For example, in a previously cited passage he notes that, "Through this I, or He, or It (the thing), which thinks, nothing further is represented than a transcendental subject of thoughts =x, which is recognized only through the thoughts that are its predicates, and about which, in abstraction, we can never have even the least concept" (A346/B404). And in a later passage in the B-Paralogisms, he explains that this is because "the subject of the categories cannot by thinking them obtain a concept of itself as an object of the categories; for in order to think them, it must take its pure self-consciousness, which is just what is to be explained as its ground" (B422). In other words, we cannot form a concept, much less have an intuition, of what must be presupposed in any act of conceptualization, which means that unlike our incapacity to cognize things as they are in themselves, this is a limitation that could not be overcome even if, *per impossibile*, we had an intellectual intuition.

---

[50] For my most recent discussion of this topic see Allison (2004), 50–64 and (2006), 1–28, or (2012), 67–83.

[51] Kant excludes feelings on the grounds that they lack cognitive content. See KU 5: 206; 92, and Anthro 7: 153; 265.

Finally, although the preceding does not constitute a full-scale defense of Kant's account of self-cognition, I believe that it demonstrates the misguided nature of critiques such as those of Pistorius and Strawson, which are examples of a widespread line of criticism that extends from Kant's contemporaries to the present day. In particular, it shows that, while Kant's account may be obscure in spots and insufficiently developed, which accounts for certain inconsistencies, particularly with respect to the relation between the I of apperception and the noumenal self, it is not incoherent.[52] Moreover, the incoherence charge is rooted in an ingrained antipathy to transcendental idealism, which reflects a tacit commitment to the transcendental realism with which Kant contrasts it and which invariably leads to a distortion of Kant's "critical" position.

V

§26 *Apprehension, perception, and experience* (B159–65): If the first major step in the B-Deduction was to relate the categories to pure intuition through the transcendental synthesis of the imagination, as the "first effect of the understanding on sensibility," which was the task of the first part of §24, the second, which is the task of §26, is to relate them to empirical intuition and through this to perception and experience. The argument proceeds by linking the categories to the empirical synthesis of apprehension, which is supposedly governed by the transcendental synthesis of the imagination. Accordingly, with the principle of the synthetic unity of apperception remaining in the background as the supreme condition of the use of the understanding, the second part of the B-Deduction as a whole is structured on the transitivity of the "necessary condition of" relation. In other words, since the categories are necessary conditions of the unity of conscious attained through the transcendental synthesis of the imagination, and the empirical synthesis of apprehension must conform to the conditions imposed by the transcendental synthesis; viz., the unification of appearances in a single time and space, the empirical synthesis must likewise conform to the rules of unification prescribed by the categories.

The analysis of this section is complicated, however, by two factors. The first is Kant's inclusion in his discussion of the synthesis of apprehension of a perplexing note, which in view of the direct bearing that it has on the interpretation of the B-Deduction as a whole and the wide variety of interpretations it has received calls for special consideration. The second is that since Kant here continues to distinguish between perception and experience an additional step, beyond linking the categories to perception through the synthesis of apprehension, is required in order to connect them also with experience. But whereas in the *Prolegomena* this distinction was the organizing principle of Kant's account, in §26, after arguing that the categories are

---

[52] I have discussed this issue in detail in Allison (1983), 272–93.

related to perception through the empirical synthesis of apprehension, he seems to treat their further connection to experience, understood as "cognition through connected perceptions" (B161), almost as a matter of course. In an attempt to deal with these complicating factors and present a comprehensive account of §26 the discussion is divided into four parts: (A) a consideration of Kant's introductory paragraph, which contains a succinct formulation of his view of the various parts of his project; (B) an analysis of the note and its significance for the argument of the Deduction; (C) a step-by-step examination of Kant's argument linking the categories to perception through the synthesis of apprehension; (D) an assessment of Kant's attempt to connect the categories with experience as distinct from mere perception.

A) *Kant's introductory overview* (B259–60): In the opening paragraph of §26 Kant provides an overview of his deduction project as he conceived it in 1787. It is divided into three parts. The first, which he now refers to as the "**metaphysical deduction**," is described as concerned with demonstrating the a priori origin of the categories by showing their "complete coincidence with the logical functions of thinking." As previously noted, this is Kant's only use of the label and it corresponds to what he also refers to (even in the second edition) as the "Clue [or "Guiding Thread] to the Discovery of all Pure Concepts of the Understanding." Apart from the change in labeling, there are two points to note. One is an apparent shift from a concern to identify and determine the completeness of the list of pure concepts of the understanding to that of ensuring their a priori status. Although both are supposedly achieved by the same means; viz., grounding these concepts in the forms of judgment or discursive thinking as delineated in general logic, they are clearly distinct goals. The other, which appears to be closely related to the first, is a greater integration of the derivation of the categories into the overall justificatory project.

   The last two parts of Kant's tripartite division of labor correspond to the two parts of the B-Deduction proper as he distinguished them in §21. Kant confuses matters, however, by referring to the first part as *the* (my emphasis) "**transcendental deduction**," claiming that in it the possibility of the categories "as *a priori* cognitions of objects of an intuition in general was exhibited." And he states that the remaining task is to explain "The possibility of cognizing *a priori* **through categories** whatever objects **may come before our senses**, not as far as the form of their intuition but rather as far as the laws of their combination are concerned, thus the possibility of as it were prescribing the law to nature and even making the latter possible" (B159–60). Moreover, Kant adds that, "[I]f the categories did not serve in this way, it would not become clear why everything that may ever come before our senses must stand under laws that arise *a priori* from the understanding alone" (B160).

   Setting aside the labeling confusion, which appears to be due to simple carelessness on Kant's part, this account of the aim of the first part of the Deduction corresponds fairly closely to the one given in §21. In fact, it helps to clarify further why the argument of the first part is not sufficient. Since there is no such thing as "intuition in general" and no "objects of an intuition in general" to be cognized through the categories, this could hardly be considered anything more than a preliminary, albeit indispensable step. More specifically, to speak of the possibility of cognizing objects of an intuition in general through the categories is to consider cognition solely from the side of the understanding, abstracting from the complementary contribution of sensibility, which we have seen is precisely what Kant does in the first part of the B-Deduction.

There does, however, seem to be a significant difference between Kant's two characterizations of the task of the second part of the Deduction. Whereas in §21 Kant claimed merely that completing the Deduction required showing "from the way in which the empirical intuition is given in sensibility that its unity can be none other than the one that the category prescribes to the manifold of an intuition in general" (B144-5), the claim is now that completing the Deduction requires demonstrating the possibility of the categories prescribing the law to nature and even making the latter possible. Since Kant made a similar claim regarding the relation between the categories and the a priori laws of nature in the A-Deduction (A127-8), this is nothing new. Indeed, the proposition that the human understanding is the lawgiver to nature is the fundamental claim of the Analytic in both editions of the *Critique* and the second part of the *Prolegomena*. Nevertheless, there is a question concerning the relation between this claim and the earlier one in §21, which bears directly on the broader question of just what Kant claims to have established in the B-Deduction. The problem is that though the later formulation of the task of the second part of the B-Deduction entails the first, the converse does not seem to hold. In other words, assuming that the laws that the understanding supposedly prescribes to nature through the categories are universal, as Kant obviously did, it follows that one cannot accept this claim without also accepting the claim that the categories apply necessarily to the manifold of empirical intuition; but one might well accept the latter claim and question the former. Moreover, we shall see that this issue is inseparable from the previously mentioned move from the categories as conditions of perception to conditions of experience.

B) *Forms of intuition and formal intuitions* (B160-1n): Kant here once again exercises his penchant for locating a key element of his argument in a note rather than integrating it into the main body of the text. Although the topic with which it explicitly deals; viz., the distinction between a form of intuition and a formal intuition, might seem to be peripheral to the discussion of the empirical synthesis of apprehension to which it is appended, we shall see that in addition to serving as a bridge between the initial account of the transcendental synthesis of the imagination in §24 and the argument linking the categories to both perception and experience, it plays a key role in clarifying the factors underlying the structure of the B-Deduction. It states:

Space represented as **object** (as is really required in geometry), contains more than the mere form of intuition, namely the **comprehension** [*Zusammenfassung*] of the manifold given in accordance with the form of sensibility in an **intuitive** representation, so that the **form of intuition** merely gives the manifold, but the **formal intuition** gives unity of the representation. In the Aesthetic I ascribed this unity merely to sensibility, only in order to note that it precedes all concepts, though to be sure it presupposes a synthesis, which does not belong to the senses but through which all concepts of space and time first become possible. For since through it (as the understanding determines the sensibility) space or time are first **given** as intuitions, the unity of this *a priori* intuition belongs to space and time, and not to the concept of the understanding.   (§24)

Because of the various tensions and at least seeming contradictions it contains, this note has been read in a number of different ways and received wildly different assessments. The problem has been expressed in its sharpest form by Lorne Falkenstein, who in his discussion of the relation between the form and matter of intuition in Kant refuses even to consider it on the grounds that,

[I]t is so obscure that it can be made to serve the needs of any interpretation whatsoever. From a contradiction, anything follows, and any text that contains two assertions like (a) 'this unity [of space and time] . . . presupposes a synthesis . . . through which all concepts of space and time are first made possible,' and (b) 'the unity of this intuition [of space and time] belongs a priori to space and time and not to the intellectual concept' is close enough to exhibiting a contradiction that it makes it possible to get virtually any conclusion one pleases out of this passage.[53]

Although Falkenstein is correct to wonder how Kant could in the same note affirm both of these propositions, he is too hasty in his summary dismissal of it. In fact, the putative near contradiction to which he alludes is not confined to the note but concerns the relation between the conceptual and non-conceptual elements of Kant's account of cognition, which is an issue that lies at the heart of the Transcendental Deduction as a whole and particularly the second part of the B-Deduction. Accordingly, the note calls for close consideration.

   Taken by itself, its first sentence is relatively unproblematic. We have seen that the proposition that unity is produced by an act of understanding, as opposed to being received by sensibility, is present from the very beginning of the B-Deduction (§15) and Kant here seems to be simply applying this principle to the representation of space. This representation is referred to as a "formal intuition" and is contrasted with space as a "form of intuition."[54] Whereas the latter is the form or manner in which the elements of the pure manifold of outer sense are "given," i.e., passively received by a cognizing subject, e.g., as arranged three dimensionally, the former is the same manifold qua conceptually determined, and thereby "represented as **object**," as occurs, for example, in geometrical cognition. Elsewhere, I have characterized these

---

[53] Falkenstein (1995), 91.
[54] In the *Critique* Kant also distinguishes between a form of intuition and a formal intuition at B207, A268/B324, and A429/B457.

as an indeterminate and a determinate pure intuition respectively, with the essential point being that the latter has a hybrid character involving both a sensible and a conceptual component.[55]

The problem, however, is to reconcile this with what Kant says in the remainder of the note. For instance, in the second sentence he states that in the Aesthetic he had attributed this unity (that contained in a formal intuition) to sensibility in order to indicate that it "precedes all concepts," even though he now informs us that it presupposes a synthesis. Although this might be taken as an admission on Kant's part that the account in the Aesthetic was misleading (the result of the isolation of sensibility) and must be corrected by appealing to the role that is given to the understanding in the Analytic, this reading is belied by the claim in the third sentence that the unity of the a priori intuition belongs to space and time rather than to the concept of the understanding. If, rather than being a product of the understanding, the unity pertains to space and time themselves, it would indeed "precede all concepts." But how can it then presuppose a synthesis, which, even if assigned to the imagination, must be regarded as the effect of the understanding on sensibility? Conversely, if the unity presupposes a synthesis, how can it precede *all* concepts (not merely those of space and time) and be attributed to space and time rather than to the understanding, which is supposedly the source of all unity? And how, as Kant also claims in the third sentence, can the determination of sensibility by the understanding account for the *givenness* of space and time as intuitions, when this is supposedly the function of sensibility itself? Unless these puzzles can be resolved, it is difficult to avoid Falkenstein's harsh assessment of the contents of this note.

Moreover, a survey of the literature of the note does not appear to yield a viable solution to these puzzles. As Christian Onof and Dennis Schulting point out in their in-depth and highly informative treatment of the topic, these interpretations fall neatly into two camps, which they label "conceptualist" and "non-conceptualist."[56] The former emphasizes Kant's claim that the unity of space and time presupposes a synthesis and that it is through the determination of sensibility by the understanding that space and time are first given as intuitions, while having little or nothing to say about the claims that this synthesis precedes all concepts and that the unity belongs to space and time rather than to the concept of the understanding. Conversely, the latter camp attributes this unity either to space and time themselves or to the imagination, considered as an autonomous faculty. In short, each camp finds in the note ample material to support its position, while encountering great difficulty in dealing with the aspects of the note that are highlighted by the opposing camp.

An important attempt to meet this challenge has been mounted by Longuenesse. Although as Onof and Schulting note, her highly nuanced reading belongs in the conceptualist camp broadly construed, she endeavors to do justice to the non-

---

[55] See Allison (2004), 112–16.
[56] See Onof and Schulting (2015), esp. 4–8.

conceptualist features of the note as well.[57] Unlike many interpretations, Longuenesse's is embedded in a highly sophisticated and systematic interpretation of the B-Deduction as a whole, which gives to this note a central place. Having discussed her views in detail elsewhere, I shall here be brief, focusing mainly on aspects that are directly relevant to the interpretation of the note.[58] At the heart of her interpretation is a strongly teleological view of the cognitive process in which the categories operate at both ends. At the lower end they function in a pre-conceptual manner guiding the *synthesis speciosa* in its endemic quest to unify the sensible manifold in such a way as to make possible its eventual subsumption under concepts in judgments; while at the upper end they govern the actual subsumption of the unified intuitions under concepts, thereby producing what Kant calls "cognition in the proper sense." Given this view, she takes Kant's claim that this synthesis precedes *all* (or on her reading *any*) concepts to refer merely to concepts (particularly the categories) in their fully reflected, predicative function, which leaves in place a role for the understanding, as "the capacity to judge," and with it the categories operating in a pre-conceptual manner in connection with the *synthesis speciosa*.

Although I am sympathetic to Longuenesse's claim that the categories function at a pre-conceptual level, I cannot accept her further contention that, as products of a synthesis governed by the categories functioning at this level, space and time are *entia imaginaria*. Admittedly, Kant does characterize them as such, but the place and the manner in which he does this does not support her interpretation. It occurs in his discussion of the various senses of the concepts of something and nothing, which he considers as the division of the highest concept (that of an object in general) and which he introduces at the very end of the Analytic for the sake of the completeness of his system of transcendental concepts. In this context Kant writes: "The mere form of intuition, without substance, is in itself not an object, but merely the formal condition of one (as appearance), like pure space and pure time, which are to be sure something as the forms of intuiting, but are not in themselves objects that are intuited (*ens imaginarium*)" (A291/B347).

As I read this passage, Kant's target is the Newtonian conception of absolute space and time considered as transcendentally real objects. His two-fold claim is that, *so considered*, space and time are merely *entia imaginaria* and that they must therefore be reconceived as forms of intuiting things, i.e., forms of intuition or sensibility, rather than objects that are intuited. Accordingly, Kant is *not claiming* that space and time, as he considers them in the Aesthetic, are *entia imaginaria*, but merely that this status is applicable to the Newtonian conception of them as absolute realities.[59] By contrast, for Longuenesse space and time, as considered in the Aesthetic, are *entia imaginaria* because they are products of the figurative synthesis and this insight is said to result from a re-reading

[57] Ibid., 26.   [58] See Allison (2012), 31–48.
[59] Kant is here echoing Leibniz's critique of the Newtonian view in his correspondence with Clarke. See Leibniz (1956), 38 and 69–72.

of the Aesthetic in light of the note.[60] Although this proposal is indeed "radical" as Longuenesse maintains, it is also problematic in at least three respects.

First, by connecting the synthesis directly with the form of intuition, her reading fudges, if not totally eliminates, Kant's seemingly sharp distinction between a form of intuition and a formal intuition, wherein the former refers to the form of intuiting and the latter to a determinate formal object that is intuited, e.g., a triangle.[61] Second, it calls into question the distinctive contribution of sensibility to cognition and with it the qualitative distinction between sensibility and understanding, which we have seen was a centerpiece of Kant's thought since the "great light" of 1769. After all, if the synthesis upon which Longuenesse correctly places great weight is defined as an "effect of the understanding on sensibility," it would seem that sensibility must play a significant role in the process, particularly if it is assumed to have an a priori form.[62] Third, and most important, Longuenesse misconstrues the sense of unity at issue in Kant's concluding claim that "the unity of this *a priori* intuition belongs to space and time, and not to the concept of the understanding." According to Longuenesse, there is at bottom only one unity involved, namely, the unity of apperception and all further unities, including those of space and time, must be understood in relation to it.[63] Although this is the appropriate conceptualist response, it fails to explain the above claim. As Onof and Schulting emphasize, the unity of space or time consists in their singleness, i.e., in the fact that there is only one space and one time of which all determinate spaces and times are parts. And to underscore the point, they refer to this sense of unity as "unicity" and characterize it as a mereological property that belongs to space and time as *given*.[64]

Nevertheless, this cannot be the whole story, since Kant also claims that this unity presupposes a synthesis, which brings us back to the apparent contradiction noted by Falkenstein. How can the same unity be both given and produced by a synthesis? The short answer is that it cannot and that a careful reading of the note indicates that this is not what Kant claims. Rather than a single conception of unity about which incompatible claims are made, the note is concerned with two distinct conceptions: one that pertains to space and time themselves as "given," i.e., as forms of sensibility, and one that pertains to the *representation* of their unity by the cognizing subject. The former is the unicity of space and time as described above; the latter, as a product of a transcendental synthesis, is a synthetic unity and, as such, grounded in the unity

---

[60] Longuenesse (1998a), 305.

[61] See Longuenesse (1998a), esp. 216–25. In these pages Longuenesse argues that the space and time of the Aesthetic, considered as products of the figurative synthesis, encompass both the form of intuition and the formal intuition of the note. In fact, she denies that there is any sharp distinction between a form of intuition and a formal intuition in Kant. For my criticism of this claim see Allison (2012), esp. 38–40.

[62] Longuenesse is aware of the problem and attempts to deal with it by characterizing a form of intuition as a "potential form," which is actualized by the figurative synthesis. See Longuenesse (1998a), 220–4. For my criticism of this move see Allison (2012), 40–1.

[63] See Longuenesse (2000), 103.   [64] Onof and Schulting (2015), 9–11 and passim.

of apperception. Whereas the former pertains to space and time as forms of intuition; the latter pertains to them as formal intuitions.

The difficulty in interpreting the note appears to be rooted not only in an ambiguity in its use of the term "unity" but also the term "given." As already noted, depending on the context, it can refer either to what is given by sensibility apart from any operation of the understanding and/or the imagination, i.e., the sensible manifold, or to what is given in experience, which requires the operation of these faculties.[65] The first sense of the term is found in the claim that "the **form of intuition** gives the manifold" and the second in the claim that "the **formal intuition** gives unity of the representation" and the claim in the last sentence that it is through the synthesis whereby the understanding determines sensibility that "space or time are first **given** as intuitions." And once "given" is disambiguated in this manner the contradiction disappears, since the unity that is *given* in the latter sense must, within Kant's account of cognition, also be considered as *taken*, i.e., represented, which, like all representings, is a product of the spontaneity of the cognizing subject.

Moreover, this reading of the note complements the analysis of the first part of §24 and explains Kant's apparent allusion to that section. As we saw in initially examining this text, where the focus is on time, the unifiability of all appearances in a single time cannot be regarded as a logical consequence of the unity of apperception, since there is no contradiction in the thought that appearances are located in distinct times (or spaces). Equipped with the account of the unity of space and as unicity, the note enables us see that this is because unicity is a property of space and time as forms of sensibility to which the unity of apperception must conform rather than the reverse. And we also saw that the fact that the Deduction is concerned with two distinct unities rather than only one is what prevents it from proceeding in a linear fashion from the unity of apperception and makes the second step more than a trivial inference from the conclusion of the first. While the goal of the first part of the Deduction was to demonstrate that the synthetic unity of apperception is both a necessary and sufficient condition of the representation of an object of intuition in general, the first part of §24 and the note indicate that, because of the nature of the forms of human sensibility, particularly their unicity, it is only a necessary condition of the cognition of objects of human intuition, and therefore of experience.

C) *The synthesis of apprehension*: As already noted, Kant's concern at this point is to link the categories to empirical intuition and through this to experience as necessary conditions of its possibility. The vehicle for this linkage is the empirical synthesis of apprehension, which is stipulatively defined as "the composition [*Zusammensetzung*] of the manifold in an empirical intuition, through which perception, i.e., empirical consciousness of it (as appearance), becomes possible" (B160).[66] It turns out to be a

[65] See note 1.

[66] This differs in two respects from the accounts of apprehension contained in the A-Deduction. First, Kant there viewed it in a somewhat narrower fashion as the act of "running through" or surveying a given manifold and it is paired with a "holding together" or reproduction as two inseparable aspects of the act

somewhat imperfect vehicle, however, since even though Kant links this synthesis directly with perception, he continues to distinguish between perception and experience. Moreover, this is reflected in the extremely unbalanced structure of the argument, which can be broken down into six steps crammed into a single paragraph (B160–1). Of these, the first five are concerned explicitly with perception; while the move from perception to experience is presented in the sixth as if it were merely a matter of course rather than the problematic extension that it really is. Accordingly, I shall first examine the five-step argument connecting the categories with perception via the synthesis of apprehension and then consider separately the sixth step in which Kant moves from perception to experience.

Step 1: We have **forms** of outer as well as inner sensible intuition *a priori* in the representations of space and time, and the synthesis of the apprehension of the manifold of appearance must always be in agreement with the latter, since it can only occur in accordance with this form.

(B160)

Kant here assumes both the account of space and time in the Aesthetic and the actuality of a synthesis of apprehension. The claim is that the latter must conform to the former, which reinforces the thesis that the forms of sensibility impose a priori constraints on the exercise of the human understanding. Its relevance to the current argument is that it entails that whatever turns out to be a necessary condition for the determinate representation of space and time will also be a necessary condition of the apprehension or perception of appearances in space and time.

Step 2: But space and time are represented *a priori* not merely as **forms** of sensible intuition, but also as **intuitions** themselves (which contain a manifold), and thus with the determination of the **unity** of this manifold in them (see the Transcendental Aesthetic).   (B160)

This is the passage to which Kant attaches the note. The claim that space and time are both forms of sensible intuition and themselves intuitions corresponds to the distinction drawn in the note between a form of intuition and a formal intuition. The systematic function of this step is to underscore the point, already made in §24 and reinforced in the note, that a determinate representation of the manifold of such an intuition requires its unification. Although Kant does not refer explicitly to it in the text and only alludes to it in the note, it is clear that the transcendental synthesis of the imagination is the vehicle for this unification.

Step 3: Thus even **unity of the synthesis** of the manifold, outside or within us, hence also a **combination** with which everything that is to be represented as determined in space or time

_____

through which a manifold is unified by the imagination and as together constituting the first two aspects of the three-fold synthesis (A98–102); whereas now apprehension is understood as a single act embodying both of these aspects. Second, it was claimed to be exercised both empirically, with respect to the manifold of an empirical intuition and a priori with respect to space and time as pure intuitions (A99–100); whereas now it is considered merely as empirical, with the a priori dimension assigned to the transcendental synthesis of the imagination.

must agree, is already given *a priori*, along with (not in) these intuitions, as condition of the synthesis of all **apprehension**.   (B161)

This step consists essentially in a combination of the first two. The point is that the conditions of the representation of space or time are also conditions of the apprehension of anything in space or time. The key conception here is that of representing something as determined in space or time. Although Kant does not explain what he understands by this, it seems reasonable to assume that in the case of space it involves perceiving a manifold as having a size and shape and in the case of time as ordered in inner sense, which in both cases results from the unification of the elements of this manifold. The claim that this unity is "given *a priori* along with (not in) these intuitions" reflects Kant's underlying thesis that the representation of unity requires a synthetic activity and cannot be passively received through sensibility.

Step 4: But this synthetic unity can be none other than that of the combination of the manifold of a given **intuition in general** in an original consciousness, in agreement with the categories, only applied to our **sensible intuition**.   (B161)

Despite being the key step in the argument, since it links the synthesis of apprehension with the categories, Kant offers no argument for it. Instead, he simply asserts that the synthetic unity involved in apprehension is an application to human sensibility of the unity of the manifold in general that is required for apperception, which licenses the claim that the former, like the latter, is governed by the categories. Nevertheless, we can easily construct such an argument by combining the claim of §24 that the transcendental synthesis of the imagination is governed by the categories with step 3 of the present argument. Or, more precisely, it follows if, as seems reasonable, we take this step as implying that the empirical synthesis of apprehension, which is concerned with the unification of empirical manifolds given in space and time, is subject to the conditions of the transcendental synthesis of the imagination, which is charged with the unification of the pure manifold of space and time.[67]

Step 5: Consequently all synthesis, through which even perception itself becomes possible, stands under the categories.   (B161)

This is the result at which the first segment of the argument aims. Perception stands under the categories because the synthesis through which it is constituted (the synthesis of apprehension) does; while the latter stands under the categories because it is governed by the transcendental synthesis of the imagination, which likewise stands under the categories because it is an application to human sensibility and its a priori forms of an intellectual synthesis of the manifold of an intuition in general, which was shown in the first part of the Deduction to stand under them. But even if we accept both the validity of the inferences and its long list of premises, which

---

[67] This is the B-Deduction's replacement for the A-Deduction's thesis that there is both an empirical and a pure synthesis of apprehension. See the preceding note.

include the accounts of space and time in the Aesthetic, the analytic argument of the first part of the Deduction, and the claims regarding the roles of the imagination (the two syntheses), it remains unclear just what the argument is supposed to show and, perhaps equally important, not show.

In an attempt to elucidate the main points at issue, I shall break them down into three questions. (1) Is not the claim that the categories are conditions of perception too strong? Even leaving aside the elusive issue of animals and infants, who have perceptions but not thoughts in Kant's sense, it has seemed evident to many critics of Kant and even to some defenders that we can have perceptions without concepts. Indeed, it might be argued that, inasmuch as the categories are concepts of an object in general, and therefore operative in the relation of perceptions to objects, they cannot be applied to perceptions themselves. (2) If, despite this, the categories are already involved at the level of perception, *how* are they involved, and does their function differ from their role as conditions of experience? (3) Are *all* of the categories involved at the level of perception or only *some* of them, and, if the latter, which ones?

Before addressing these questions, it is necessary to determine more precisely what Kant understands by "perception" (*Wahrnehmung*).[68] According to the above-cited characterization of the synthesis of apprehension, perception is the empirical consciousness of the manifold in an empirical intuition as appearance, which is in basic agreement with the other accounts in the *Critique*.[69] As we have seen, by "empirical consciousness" Kant understands a discrete episode of sensible awareness, which in the A-Deduction he contrasts with a "transcendental consciousness" or "original apperception" (A117n). Kant's basic point there was that these discreet awarenesses must conjointly belong to a single thinking subject, if they are to constitute a single cognition. This discreteness is reflected in the claim that what is apprehended in an episode of empirical consciousness is the manifold of an empirical intuition, which implies that the synthesis of apprehension unifies the manifold in *an intuition* rather than connecting distinct intuitions. The qualification "as appearance" is to be understood in terms of the definition of the term in the Aesthetic as the "undetermined object of an empirical intuition" (A20/B34). While we perceive determinate objects, e.g., tables, houses, trees, we do not strictly speaking perceive them as such, since recognizing them in this way requires an act of conceptualization that is not contained in perception.

This brings us, then, to our first question: How could Kant claim that the synthesis of apprehension stands under the categories? Since the categories are concepts, it seems to follow that where there is no conceptualization, there can be no role for

---

[68] In the *Stufenleiter* passage Kant uses the Latinate term "*perception*" rather than the Germanic "*Wahrnehmung*," which Kant appears to have regarded as synonyms, and he defines it simply as "representation with consciousness" (A320/B376).

[69] See A120 and A123.

them, which is why Sellars insisted upon attributing a minimally conceptual content to the products of the imagination in Kant and conceptualists of all stripes affirm some version of this view. But we have seen that the problem with a conceptualist reading, even one as nuanced as Longuenesse's, is its inability to deal with the unicity of space and time as forms of sensibility, rather than as products of a figurative synthesis; while the difficulty confronting a non-conceptualist reading is accounting for the role that Kant gives to synthesis, which includes the synthesis of apprehension. Given these considerations, it seems that an effort to defend the coherence of Kant's account of perception is left with only two options: either attribute to Kant a form of non-conceptualism that does justice to the essential role that he assigns to the synthesis of apprehension or show how the categories can guide this synthesis in a proto-conceptual manner.

The first alternative has been chosen by Peter Rohs, who affirms the non-conceptual nature of perception and presents his account as an attempt to reconcile two fundamental claims of Kant that have often been considered contradictory: that intuitions relate directly to objects and that intuitions without concepts are blind.[70] He does so by distinguishing between seeing something, which is supposedly a matter of intuition involving a singular reference, and seeing *that* something is the case, which has the form of a proposition, and therefore presupposes concepts. In light of this distinction, Rohs makes two major claims that bear directly on our present concern. The first is that the "blindness" of intuitions pertain only to the latter and that single objects are "seen," i.e., given in intuition, without being brought under concepts. In fact, Rohs insists that this non-conceptual seeing is necessary in order to provide a content of which concepts can be predicated in propositions.

Rohs' second claim is that the non-conceptual content of perception presupposes a synthesis, which he equates with the syntheses of apprehension and reproduction in the A-Deduction and the figurative synthesis in the B-Deduction. Such a synthesis is necessary on his view because sense impressions, apart from their unification in an image, do not relate to an object.[71] Accordingly, since the conceptual counterpart of this imaginative synthesis is also necessary for cognition, Rohs attributes to Kant the view that there are two distinct syntheses: one operating at the level of intuition forming images of individual objects without using concepts; the other operating at the conceptual level forming propositions under the direction of the categories. And since Rohs follows Kant in asserting that the former involves an exercise of spontaneity, he attributes to him the view that there are two kinds of spontaneity: an intuitive one of the imagination and an intellectual one of the understanding.[72]

---

[70] Rohs (2001), 214–28. My view of Rohs' paper has been informed by the analysis of its central argument by Wenzel (2005), esp. 407–10.

[71] Rohs (2001), 223–4.   [72] Ibid., 222.

Given this analysis, it is not surprising that Rohs finds the argument of §26, indeed the whole of the B-Deduction, incompatible with the account in the A-Deduction. The problem, on his view, can be traced back to §15, where Kant mistakenly equates an act of spontaneity with an act of the understanding, which leads to a misguided view of the transcendental synthesis of the imagination as an effect of the under-standing on sensibility, thereby precluding the possibility of a genuinely intuitive synthesis, understood as an act of the imagination issuing in an image of a particular object, without the use of any concepts.[73] Rohs finds this equation not only ungrounded but in clear contradiction to other assertions of Kant, including the general definition of synthesis as an effect of the imagination, with the understanding assigned the task of bringing the synthesis to concepts (A78/B103), and the previ-ously examined claim that the imagination (not the understanding) is a necessary ingredient in perception, which indicates that Kant assigned to the imagination a distinct and essential function; viz., providing a determinate content (a "this") of which concepts can be predicated, but that does not itself depend upon concepts.[74]

Setting aside Rohs' identification of the product of an intuitive synthesis with an image (*Bild*), which was called into question in Chapter 6, there is much in his account that is correct. Clearly, Kant makes claims regarding the imagination and its relation to the understanding in both editions of the *Critique* that are notoriously difficult to reconcile with each other. In addition, Rohs is warranted in insisting upon a distinct and indispensable role in cognition for the imagination. The problem, however, is that his non-conceptualist account of the synthesis of apprehension comes at a high price; viz., the failure of the argument of the Deduction. Moreover, this failure applies not only to the argument of §26 but to the A-Deduction as well; for in both versions it is essential to link the categories with perception, which on Rohs' reading becomes impossible. Although this does not, of course, suffice to rule out Rohs' reading, since the Deduction may well fail for the reasons he suggests, it does call for a consideration of alternative interpretive possibilities, which in the present case is that the categories govern perception in a proto-conceptual manner.

By a proto-conceptual function of the categories is here understood one in which rather than being predicated of objects in a judgment, as they are, for example, in the judgments of experience in the *Prolegomena*, the categories govern the apprehension of the sensible manifold in a merely empirical consciousness, which is how they would function if, pace the *Prolegomena*, they were operative in judgments of perception. So considered, the categories can be considered rules of apprehension.[75] They are *rules* because they function normatively to specify how the manifold must be unified in order to conform to the dual requirements of the unity of apperception

---

[73] Ibid.   [74] Ibid., 222–3.
[75] In viewing the function of the category here as that of a "rule of apprehension" I am following the lead of Longuenesse (1998a), esp. 116–18, who emphasizes the importance of this conception. For Kant's use of the expression "*Regel unserer Auffassung*" see R 2880 16: 557.

and the unicity of space and time as forms of sensibility. They are rules of *apprehension* because they govern the apprehension, i.e., intuition, of an object rather than its cognition or experience. Accordingly, the answer to the second of our three questions is that this is how the categories must function, insofar as they are viewed as conditions of perception as contrasted with experience.

In order to test this interpretive hypothesis, let us briefly revisit the five-step argument in §26 in which Kant purports to demonstrate that the categories condition the possibility of perception. The focal point is the third step, itself a product of the first two, where Kant claims that "everything that is to be represented as determined in space or time" must conform to the conditions of the representation of the unity of space and time. Since the fourth step maintains that these conditions are provided by the categories, from which Kant concludes in the fifth step that perception stands under the categories, the operative questions become what is meant by being represented as determined in space or time and whether this determination can be said to involve the use of the categories as described above. Unfortunately, Kant does not there indicate in precisely what such determination consists, but it was suggested that in the case of an outer perception it should be taken to mean that what is perceived (a unified manifold) is apprehended as having size and shape. In other words, while we do not strictly speaking perceive a house *as* a house, since that requires subsuming what is perceived under the concept of a house (and other concepts as well), we perceive it as determined in space, which is to say as a three-dimensional something with *some* size and shape. Accordingly, this may be considered as a rule for the apprehension of an object of outer sense.

Although this does not yet specify which categories are required for this determination, Kant makes this clear in the first of the two illustrations of the function of a particular category that he provides in this section. Using as his example the perception of a house, which tokens an object of outer sense, he writes:

Thus if, e.g., I make the empirical intuition of a house into perception through apprehension of its manifold, my ground is the **necessary unity** of space, and of outer sensible intuition in general, and I as it were draw its shape in agreement with this synthetic unity of the manifold in space. This very same synthetic unity, however, if I abstract from the form of space has its seat in the understanding, and is the category of the synthesis of the homogeneous in an intuition in general, i.e., the category of **quantity**, with which that synthesis of apprehension, i.e., the perception must therefore be in thoroughgoing agreement.   (B162)

The twin foci of this passage are the necessary unity of space and the synthetic unity of the manifold in space. If the interpretation of the note on B160–1 is correct, the former refers to the unicity of space, since this is the sense in which space is considered a unity. And this unity is necessary because it pertains to the a priori form of outer sense (space as form of intuition). As such, however, it is not a synthetic unity. The latter pertains to the determinate representation, i.e., perception, of the house, which is made determinate through the determination of the space it occupies.

Accordingly, the claim is that by abstracting from the spatial form of this determination (not the form of space, which is just its unicity) that we arrive at a category, which has its seat in the understanding and functions as the rule governing the empirical synthesis of apprehension.

Kant attempts to clarify his view in a note appended to this passage in which he states:

In such a way it is proved that the synthesis of apprehension, which is empirical, must necessarily be in agreement with the synthesis of apperception, which is intellectual and contained in the category entirely *a priori*. It is one and the same spontaneity that there under the name of imagination and here under the name of understanding, brings combination into the manifold of intuition.   (B162n)

Although this is an accurate statement of what the passage to which it is appended purports to show, its account of how it supposedly shows it is misleading because it is incomplete. Moreover, what it omits is also not made explicit in the passage itself; viz., the fact that the necessary agreement between the intellectual synthesis according to a category and the empirical synthesis of apprehension resulting in the perception of a house is mediated by the relation of both to the transcendental synthesis of the imagination through which the spatial parameters of the house are represented. The note's importance, however, lies in the asserted identity of the spontaneity attributed to the imagination and the understanding; for this suggests that, pace Rohs, rather than distinct syntheses, Kant is claiming that there is a single combinatory act with an intellectual and a figurative, as well as an a priori and an empirical, function. Considered with respect to its function of unifying the manifold of sensible intuition in general it is an intellectual synthesis; while the same act considered in relation to the specific forms of human sensibility is termed the transcendental synthesis of the imagination and in relation to the sensible content intuited under these forms it is the empirical synthesis of apprehension. Moreover, this explains why Kant can claim that the empirical synthesis *necessarily* agrees with both the intellectual synthesis and the transcendental synthesis of the imagination. Since these syntheses pertain to one and the same act considered from different points of view they necessarily agree; whereas if they were distinct acts their agreement would be contingent, leaving in place the dreaded specter of a possible non-agreement of appearances with the requirements of the understanding.

Assuming that this shows why Kant claims that the empirical synthesis of apprehension stands under a category functioning as a rule of apprehension, we still need to explain the identification of this category as quantity (*Grösse*).[76] The explanation lies in the nature of the synthesis from which the category is abstracted. In this case, it is the synthesis of the pure manifold of space, which Kant claims in the Aesthetic is

[76]   Strictly speaking, *Grösse* is not a category for Kant but the term that he uses to refer to the heading for the three categories of quantity (*Quantität*): unity, plurality, and totality in the table of categories (A80/B106).

represented as an infinite given magnitude (*Grösse*) (A25/B39). In other words, it is because what is synthesized is considered in purely quantitative terms that the rule governing the synthesis is characterized as the category of quantity. But in order to understand Kant's point here and in other texts in which he discusses *Grösse*, it is essential to keep in mind that he uses it to translate two distinct Latin terms: *quantum* and *quantitas*.[77] By a *quantum*, which is best rendered in English as "magnitude," Kant understands a single entity that can be quantitatively determined; while a *quantitas* is a determinate *quantum*, i.e., one of a certain size, e.g., six feet high, or as containing a specific number of parts, e.g., a dozen apples. Accordingly, an object of outer sense for Kant is a *quantum*; though, as perceived, it does not have a determinate *quantitas*. In other words, whatever is apprehended as located in space is apprehended as having a magnitude, but not a specific one, since that requires a further determination through a conceptual act of measurement or counting. As Kant puts it in his discussion of the mathematically sublime in the third *Critique*: "That something is a magnitude (*quantum*) may be cognized from the thing itself, without any comparison with another; if that is, a multitude of homogenous elements together constitute a unity. But **how great** it is always requires something else, which is also a magnitude as its measure" (KU 5: 248; 132). To say that something being or having a magnitude may be cognized from the thing itself, without any comparison, is to say that it is a matter of perception rather than judgment. It pertains to a thing, qua immediately perceived, apart from any conceptualization, such as would be required for measurement. Kant argues in the Axioms of Intuition, where he attempts to demonstrate that all appearances are extensive magnitudes, that having such a magnitude is what makes appearances measureable or, perhaps better, numerable, and that this in turn is a transcendental condition of the application of mathematics to nature (A165–6/B206–7).[78] For present purposes, however, the key point is that, since this property is claimed to apply to appearances simply qua intuited or perceived, it suggests that the deduction of the category of quantity takes the form of a demonstration that it is a necessary condition of perception.

This is not the only kind of magnitude with which Kant is concerned, however, since a parallel claim is made in the Anticipations of Perception, where he argues that "In all appearances the real [*das Reale*], which is an object of sensation, has intensive magnitude, i.e., a degree" (B207). This principle applies to the sensed properties of things, particularly, but not exclusively, to their secondary qualities, such as color and heat.[79] The claim is that all such properties are necessarily perceived as having an

[77] See Longuenesse (1998a), 263–71.
[78] It should be kept in mind that in the Schematism chapter Kant claims that number is the schema of magnitude (*Grösse*) (A142/B182).
[79] For a discussion of the nature of the properties or qualities to which this principle is supposed to apply see Paton (1936b), 135, note 3.

intensive magnitude, which as such is capable either of increase or diminution to 0. Thus, when I sense, for example, the warmth or brightness of the sun I immediately perceive them as having a degree (though not a specific one) and it is built into the perception itself that this sensation is not only capable of increase but also encapsulates, as it were, all lesser degrees of heat or brightness within it. Kant's argument for this principle is notoriously obscure and cannot be further considered here; but, fortunately, this is not necessary, since for present purposes the salient point is merely that the categories under quality, which supposedly underlie the synthesis through which sensible qualities are endowed with intensive magnitude, are, like extensive magnitude, "deduced" by showing that they function as rules of apprehension.[80]

Moreover, in the second edition of the *Critique* Kant introduced a distinction between the mathematical and the dynamical categories, which parallels the one he had already drawn in the first edition between their corresponding principles.[81] Thus, in commenting on the table of categories Kant notes that its four classes can be split into two divisions, which he refers to as mathematical and dynamical; and he cites as the principle of division the fact that the first is concerned with objects of intuition (both pure and empirical), while the second is concerned with the existence of objects (either in relation to each other or to the understanding) (B110). Although Kant does not refer to any of these categories by name, it is clear that by the former are meant those that fall under the headings of quantity and quality and the latter are those of relation and modality. And it also seems that the first five steps of the argument of §26 are best read as a deduction of the mathematical categories, since these directly concern objects qua perceived rather than qua existing, either in relation to each other or to the understanding.

Against this interpretation of Kant's intent it might be argued that, rather than focusing only on the mathematical categories, he is endeavoring to provide a global deduction of all of the categories. And in support of this view it could be pointed out that Kant's second illustration of the functioning of a category involves the dynamical category of causality (B162–3), which suggests that he chose one from each group in order to emphasize the global nature of the argument.[82] But while I do not deny that Kant's overall intent is to provide a deduction of all of the categories, I also maintain that both the distinction that he draws between perception and experience and the structure of the argument that he offers in §26 point to a division of labor that is not evident in the A-Deduction. Once again, the main point is that only the mathematical categories can plausibly be claimed to condition perception and that this is the most that the first five steps of the argument can show. Accordingly, if we are to find

---

[80] For a comprehensive analysis of Kant's argument for this principle see Guyer (1987), 196–205.
[81] For the latter distinction see A160–2/B199–202.
[82] This illustration will be discussed below.

an argument that applies to the dynamical categories, it must be in the sixth step in which Kant's concern shifts to experience.[83]

D) *From perception to experience*: In what amounts to the sixth step in the argument of §26, which consists of a clause in the fifth sentence that has the appearance of being a mere afterthought, Kant states that "since experience is cognition through connected perceptions the categories are conditions of the possibility of experience, and are thus also valid *a priori* of all objects of experience" (B161). Assuming that the argument up to this point is sound, Kant is entitled to conclude that at least the mathematical categories are necessary conditions of the possibility of experience, since experience, as cognition through connected perceptions, obviously requires perception. But since experience, so defined, involves more than simply perception, and the argument of the *Prolegomena* indicated that the conversion of perceptions into experience through their connection in consciousness in general, i.e., the synthetic unity of apperception, is the epistemic task of the relational categories, it is difficult to see how the preceding argument could be considered as demonstrating that result. Instead, it seems that Kant attempts to complete the Deduction by fiat rather than argument, suggesting that after showing that the categories are conditions of perception there is no further serious work to be done.

Unfortunately, Kant further obfuscates matters by his second illustration of a category at work, which, not surprisingly, concerns the relational category of causality. His example is the familiar one of the perception of the freezing of water. Kant notes that the perception of such an event involves the apprehension of the succession of two states of the water: as fluid and as solid. Thus, the problem is to explain how such apprehension is possible and to this end he writes:

But in time, on which I ground the appearance as **inner intuition**, I represent [to myself] necessary synthetic **unity** of the manifold, without which that relation could not be **determinately** given in an intuition (with regard to temporal sequence). But now this synthetic unity, as the *a priori* condition under which I combine the manifold of an **intuition in general**, if I abstract from the constant form of **my** inner intuition, time, is the category of **cause**, through which if I apply it to my sensibility, I **determine everything that happens in time in general as far as its relation is concerned**. Thus the apprehension in such an occurrence, hence the occurrence itself, as far as possible perception is concerned, stands under the concept of the **relation** of **effects and causes**, and so in all other cases.   (B162–3)

The basic point of this illustration appears to be that the representation of a determinate sequence in time (in this case the succession in the states of the water) presupposes the representation of the synthetic unity of time and thus a synthesis governed by a category, which, since it concerns a succession of states, is identified with causality. In short, this category is claimed to be a necessary condition of such

[83] This is to be contrasted with the view of Leppäkoski (1998), 107–16, who argues that the two parts of the B-Deduction are concerned with the mathematical and dynamical categories, respectively.

apprehension, via its connection with the transcendental synthesis of the imagination. The problem is that on Kant's official account a succession of states is not something that can be simply apprehended or perceived. We can have successive apprehensions or perceptions, i.e., successive episodes of empirical consciousness, the contents of which are intuitions of water at different times, in one of which it is in a fluid state and in another a solid one, but we do not, strictly speaking, apprehend or perceive their succession. Instead we *experience* it, which presupposes the category of causality (as well as substance).

One might object at this point that such quibbling is out of place, since Kant is here concerned merely to provide an illustration of his view rather than an argument for the validity of the concept or principle of causality, that being reserved for the Second Analogy. Thus, it could be argued that one should allow Kant a certain looseness in his use of terms and not endeavor to make too much of it. But the problem does not lie simply in Kant's terminology, which is often loose and perplexing. It lies rather in the combination of the two examples and the reasoning operative in the illustration of the function of the category of causality. Given Kant's introduction of the distinction between the mathematical and the dynamical categories in the second edition, it seems reasonable to assume that he chose quantity and causality in order to provide an example from each class, thereby suggesting that his argument applies to all of the categories. The manner in which he characterizes the operation of causality, however, not only conflicts with the account in the Second Analogy, it also works against this end by ignoring the fact that the dynamical categories are supposed to function as rules for the empirical thought of an object rather than as rules for apprehension, which is the task assigned to the mathematical categories.[84]

Of greater import, however, is the previously noted fact that in order to complete the Deduction Kant needs an argument showing that the categories are not only necessary conditions of perception but also of experience, *as distinguished from mere perception*. And since experience differs from mere perception in consisting in cognition through the connection of perceptions, this requires showing that they function as rules for the connection (synthetic unity) of perceptions in a single consciousness. Moreover, inasmuch as this is a function that could only be accomplished by the relational categories, it appears that the task of the sixth step of the argument of §26 can be fairly described as providing a deduction of these categories,

---

[84] At A160/B199 Kant states that, as conditions of possible intuition of objects, the mathematical principles are unconditionally necessary, whereas the necessity of the dynamical principles holds only under the condition of the empirical thought of an object. I take this as implying that the dynamical categories, at least the relational categories, are to be taken as such rules. Evidently driven largely by architectonic considerations, Kant placed the modal categories and principles (the Postulates of Empirical Thought) in the dynamical group; but in view of the significantly different function that Kant assigns to the modal forms, it might also be argued that they stand apart from the other categories. Moreover, since, unlike the other categories, they are not claimed to be objectively valid, it is not clear how the argument of §26 is supposed to apply to them.

which complements the deduction of the mathematical categories contained in the first five steps.

One might dismiss this demand on the grounds that the sought-for argument is contained in the Analogies. But while there is some truth to this, it should also be kept in mind that a parallel argument could be made that the deduction of the mathematical categories is contained in the Axioms of Intuition and the Anticipations of Perception, and perhaps that the Postulates of Empirical Thinking contains a deduction of the modal categories, which would have the unsettling consequence that the Transcendental Deduction, supposedly the crown jewel of the *Critique*, is largely redundant. And though we have examined some texts of Kant that seem to come close to expressing such a view, I have suggested that these should be considered more as signs of frustration on Kant's part with the willful misinterpretations of his critics and dissatisfaction with the clarity of his exposition, than as his considered view. Moreover, as has often been the case, I think that Kant has provided the materials for the essential sixth step of the argument of §26; though formulating it takes us beyond the confines of what he explicitly claims in this section. Kant expressed the essential point in the context of his argument for affinity in the A-Deduction, where in a previously cited passage he states that,

[E]ven though we had the faculty for associating perceptions, it would still remain in itself entirely undetermined and contingent whether they were also associable; and in case they were not, a multitude of perceptions and even an entire sensibility would be possible in which much empirical consciousness would be encountered in my mind, but separated, and without belonging to **one** consciousness of myself, which, however, is impossible.   (A121–2)

We saw in our initial consideration of this passage that it is embedded in a rejection of the possibility that the associability of appearances, i.e., the uniformity of nature, might be a merely contingent matter, as was claimed by Hume. And we also saw that Kant had to reject this possibility because it contradicts the central thesis of the Deduction that appearances necessarily conform to the categories, if they are to be anything to me qua cognizer. Considered in the context of the argument of §26, where by "experience" is understood cognition through the connection of perceptions, this entails the rejection of the possibility of a scenario in which there would be "much empirical conscious," and therefore perceptions subject to the mathematical categories, without any experience, and therefore without any use of the dynamical categories, because it would violate the conditions of the unity of apperception. In other words, despite (or perhaps because of) their distinct epistemic functions, the two classes of categories turn out to be interdependent; for without the mathematical categories there would be no perceptions to connect through their dynamical counterparts (at least the relational counterparts), while without the latter the distinct perceptions constituted through the application to the manifold of an empirical intuition there could be no unification of these perceptions in a single consciousness.

Since it appeals to the unity of apperception this line of argument goes beyond the resources provided by §26, which is perhaps why Kant does not explicitly formulate it in the text. Nevertheless, it can be seen as the product of the combination of the argument of this section with the account of apperception developed in the first part of the B-Deduction. Moreover, such a combination is what we should expect, if we take seriously the view that its two parts are to be considered as two steps in a single proof. And in light of this we can sketch the missing sixth step in the argument of §26, which would presumably take roughly the following form:

1. It follows from the first five steps that all perceptions, as contents of an empirical consciousness, fall under the mathematical categories.
2. It follows from the principle of the synthetic unity of apperception that episodes of empirical consciousness that are not connected in a single self-consciousness would be nothing to me qua cognizer, i.e., I could not even be aware of them as jointly mine.
3. As was argued in the *Prolegomena* and will be shown in the Analytic of Principles, this connection is the work of the dynamical (or at least the relational) categories.
4. Therefore, all perception and all empirical consciousness must also fall under these as well as the mathematical categories.

E) *The categories and the laws of nature* (B163–5): The final two paragraphs of §26 constitute an appendix in which Kant first poses and then attempts to resolve a riddle regarding the prescription of a priori laws to nature defined as "the sum total of appearances or *natura materialiter spectata*." The riddle arises from the character-ization of the categories as "concepts that prescribe *a priori* laws to appearances" (B163), which Kant here appears to regard as an immediate inference from the conclusion that the categories are conditions of the possibility of experience. In other words, it is assumed that prescribing laws to nature a priori is not another thing that the categories do besides making experience possible, but is rather the means whereby they exercise their transcendental function.[85] Accordingly, the riddle is how to explain the possibility of such prescription. Since the argument is essentially a repetition, albeit in somewhat different terms, of what Kant had claimed at the end of the A-Deduction (A127–8), it does not require extensive discussion at this point. We shall see, however, that it raises questions concerning the relationship between the transcendental laws prescribed by the understanding and the empirical laws of nature, which do call for consideration.

In essence, Kant reiterates his "Copernican" turn, which was explicitly enunciated in the B-Preface (Bxvi–xviii). Since these laws cannot be derived from experience because of their apriority, he concludes that they must have their seat in the

---

[85] Kant makes this explicit in *Prolegomena* §36 4: 319; 111.

understanding. And since the understanding cannot prescribe laws to things in themselves, it follows that if the understanding prescribes laws to nature at all, it must prescribe them to nature construed as the sum-total of appearances or *natura materialiter spectata*. But whereas in §13 Kant had emphasized the peculiar difficulty of a deduction of the categories *vis à vis* one of space and time as a priori forms of sensibility on the grounds that, while it is evident that appearances must conform to the conditions under which they are given, "that they must also accord with the conditions that the understanding requires for the synthetic unity of thinking is not so easily seen" (B123), he here glosses over that difficulty, suggesting instead that, "It is by no means stranger that the laws of appearances in nature must agree with the understanding and its *a priori* form, i.e., its faculty of combining the **manifold** in general, than that the appearances themselves must agree with the form of sensible intuition *a priori*" (B164). The main point, however, is that transcendental idealism is a necessary condition of both the success of the Deduction and the necessary lawfulness of nature, or "*natura formaliter spectata*" (B165), since the latter is only conceivable as the result of the legislation of the understanding. As in the A-Deduction, Kant limits this legislation to the a priori laws of nature and, while denying that empirical laws can be derived directly from the understanding, he affirms their partial dependence upon the laws that are so derived. As Kant here puts it, "Particular laws, because they concern empirically determined appearances, **cannot** be **completely derived** from the categories, although they all stand under them" (B165).

This indicates that Kant affirmed an indirect and partial dependence of the empirical laws of nature on the transcendental laws legislated by the understanding.[86] Simply put, the latter are necessary but not sufficient conditions of the former. So far there is universal agreement among commentators concerning Kant's intent, if not the cogency of his arguments. But the non-sufficiency condition contains an ambiguity, which, when spelled out, gives rise to two distinct lines of interpretation regarding the relation between the transcendental and empirical laws. On what might be termed the standard view, which seems to be supported by Kant's account of the relation between transcendental affinity and empirical affinity in the A-Deduction, the lawfulness of nature at the transcendental level guarantees its lawfulness at the empirical level and the insufficiency of the transcendental laws consists merely in the fact that they underdetermine the particular laws that constitute this system.[87] This insufficiency, however, can also be taken in a stronger sense, as indicating not merely that transcendental laws underdetermine any empirical laws that fall under them, but also that they do not, of themselves, guarantee that nature

---

[86] See also A159/B198 and *Prolegomena* §36 4: 318–20.

[87] A strong version of this view has been affirmed by Guyer (1990a), 29–34 and (1990b), 224–8, who maintains that in the first *Critique* all of the genuinely transcendental work is supposed to be accomplished in the Analytic, by which is meant that it is intended to show (not that it succeeds in showing) that the categories and the principles based upon them are sufficient to ground the unity of experience, even at the empirical level.

embodies an intelligible order according to empirical laws, such as might, for example, justify inductive procedures. On this reading, there is what Gerd Buchdahl termed a "looseness of fit" between the transcendental and empirical levels for Kant, which is filled by reason in its regulative use in the first *Critique* and reflective judgment in the third.[88]

Pursuing this issue in any detail would take us well beyond the scope of a commentary on the Transcendental Deduction of the categories in the first *Critique*; but, since it bears directly on the question of what the Deduction is intended to prove, it cannot be completely ignored. Accordingly, I shall conclude the discussion of §26 with a brief statement of what I have argued for in detail elsewhere.[89] Like Buchdahl and others who argue for the second of the above-mentioned alternatives, I believe that a proper understanding of Kant's position requires a sharp distinction between what is supposedly established in the Transcendental Deduction and, indeed, in the Transcendental Analytic as a whole, and his views on topics such as empirical concepts, empirical knowledge, empirical laws, and induction. In all of these matters, Kant's transcendental account provides the necessary framework in terms of which their consideration is approached, but it does not guarantee any outcome.

Although Kant raises the issue in the Appendix to the Dialectic in the first *Critique* with the assignment of a transcendental status to reason's principle of systematicity, his definitive account of the matter is in the Introduction to the third *Critique* with its appeal to the principle of the formal purposiveness of nature.[90] The latter, which Kant classifies as a transcendental principle of the reflective power of judgment, states that,

[S]ince universal laws of nature have their ground in our understanding, which prescribes them to nature (although only in accordance with the universal concept of it as nature), the particular empirical laws, in regard to what is left undetermined in them by the former, must be considered in terms of the sort of unity they would have if an understanding (even if not ours) had likewise given them for the sake of our faculty of cognition, in order to make possible a system of experience in accordance with particular laws of nature.   (KU 5: 180$_{18-26}$; 67–8)

The reason why Kant assigns a transcendental status to this principle is that it expresses a normative necessity regarding how we ought to reflect upon nature when engaged in the business of empirical enquiry. And such a principle is deemed necessary because,

[I]t may certainly be thought that, in spite of all of the uniformity of things in nature in accordance with the universal laws, without which the form of an experiential cognition in general would not obtain at all, the specific diversity of the empirical laws of nature together

---

[88]   See Buchdahl (1969a), 651–65; (1969b), 187–208; (1974), 128–50.
[89]   See Allison (2001), 35–42; (2004), 423–37; and (2012), 165–88.
[90]   Despite its clear presence in the text (see A650–4/B678–82) the claim that Kant attaches transcendental significance to the principle of systematicity is controversial. Prominent among those arguing against it are Horstmann (1989), esp. 165–8; Guyer (1990a), 29–34 and (1990b), 224–8; and Walker (1990), 255–6.

with their effects, could nevertheless be so great that it would be impossible for our under-standing to discover in them an order we can grasp, to divide its products into genera and species in order to use principles for the explanation and the understanding of one for the explanation and comprehension of the other as well, and to make an interconnected experi-ence out of material that is for us so confused (strictly speaking, only infinitely manifold and not fitted for our power of comprehension).   (KU 5: 185$_{23-34}$; 72)

For present purposes, what is particularly noteworthy here is that Kant describes a specter that is both reminiscent of and distinct from the one underlying the problem-atic of the Transcendental Deduction of the categories. We have seen that the worry there was that "Appearances might very well be so constituted that our understanding should not find them to be in accordance with the conditions of its unity" (A90/B123), or, more graphically, that our perceptions might constitute no more than "unruly heaps," which would preclude bringing them under empirical concepts and laws (A121). These specters are similar in that each concerns the possibility of a cognitive chaos that would undermine the possibility of empirical cognition of nature, but they differ in that the chaos has radically different grounds. In the one case, it stems from a total lack of order in appearances; in the other from the complexity of the order, which the human understanding is not equipped to comprehend. Adopting a phrase from Leibniz, one might say that it would require eyes as discerning as those of God to grasp this order and thus to link distinct appearances under empirical concepts and laws. I have termed the former "transcendental chaos" (chaos at the level of the categories and principles) and the latter "empirical chaos" (chaos at the level of empirical concept formation and the discovery of empirical laws).[91]

The exclusion of the former is the task of the Transcendental Deduction of the categories in the first *Critique*. It proceeds by denying the unifiability in a single consciousness, of the transcendentally chaotic scenario. Accordingly, such a scenario is ruled out on the grounds that it would be nothing to us qua cognizers. The principle of the logical purposiveness of nature is assigned the task of excluding the possibility of empirical chaos. But since this possibility remains in place even if the former is excluded, it obviously cannot function in the same manner. In fact, inasmuch as an empirically chaotic situation is not inconceivable and the principle of purposiveness is merely a subjective principle governing our reflection on nature rather than an objective one that prescribes laws to nature, it cannot exclude its possibility. Instead, it renders it idle by requiring that in our reflection on nature we proceed as if it possesses a cognizable order. Although this raises questions in its own right, for present purposes the important point is that the exorcism of the first specter (transcendental chaos), even if successful, would leave the latter in place. And the moral to be drawn from this is that, given the complexity, obscurity, and problematic nature of some of its moves, one should not compound its difficulties by saddling the

---

[91] See Allison (2001), 38 and (2011), 184.

Transcendental Deduction of the categories with an inflated view of what it is supposed to accomplish.

VI

§27 *A recapitulation* (B165–9): Kant devotes the final section of the B-Deduction to a brief statement of what he takes it to have shown and an explanation of his procedure. The statement of accomplishment is contained in the first paragraph:

> We cannot **think** any object except through the categories; we cannot **cognize** any object that is thought except through intuitions that correspond to these concepts. Now all our intuitions are sensible, and this cognition, so far as its object is given, is empirical. Empirical cognition, however, is experience. Consequently **no** *a priori* cognition is possible for us except solely of objects of possible experience.   (B165–6)

Kant here succinctly expresses both the positive and the negative results of the Deduction in terms of the distinction between thinking and cognizing. That there can be no thinking, i.e., judging, without the categories can be taken as a summary statement of the result of its first part. Correlatively, the limitation of cognition through the categories to objects of possible experience is the negative result established by its second part. Although Kant fails to note the point, it is evident that he also regarded the Deduction as a whole as establishing the positive conclusion that through the categories we do have (synthetic) a priori cognition of objects of possible experience. Moreover, in a note attached to this paragraph, which looks forward to the imminent appearance of the second *Critique*, Kant appeals to the thinking–cognizing distinction to underscore the point that, even absent sensible intuition, "the thought of the object can still have its true and useful consequences for the **use** of the subject's **reason**…for it [the subject's reason] is not always directed to the determination of the object, thus to cognition, but rather also to that of the subject and its willing" (B166n).[92]

In the remainder of the section Kant uses the then-current biological concepts of epigenesis and preformation, which underlay the competing theories of the origin of life at the time, to frame the problem of the Deduction.[93] As Kant had already noted

---

[92]   As Kant famously put it in the B-Preface, in order to allow for the practical extension of pure reason, he found that he "had to deny **knowledge** [*Wissen*] in order to make room for faith" (Bxxx).

[93]   The theory of epigenesis or generic preformation, which Kant favored in his own work on the subject and frequently used in a metaphorical sense in his discussions of cognition, was initially formulated by Aristotle, but reinvented, as it were, in the eighteenth century by vitalists such as Casper Friedrich Wolff and Johann Blumenbach. Although it took many forms, the basic idea is that an embryo is a new being jointly produced by both parents, which therefore inherits traits from both. It was contrasted both with mechanistic theories, associated primarily with Cartesians such as Malebranche, in which the organic stems from the inorganic (through an act of God) and with individual preformation, which had Leibnizian roots and likewise took many forms. In its essentials, it held that the germs of individuals of all future generations were already contained in those of the first being; so that the generation of new individuals is seen as the unfolding or "evolution" of what was already there implicitly from the beginning rather than

in §14 (B124–5), what requires explanation is the possibility of a *necessary* agreement of experience with concepts of objects, since this is what is assumed to be the case in claims of cognition a priori. Kant notes that there are two possibilities: "either experience makes these concepts possible or these concepts make the experience possible" (B166). He rules out the former, which he suggests might be regarded as a kind of *generatio aequivoca*, on the grounds that it is incompatible with the already established apriority of the concepts involved. This leaves, as the surviving alterative, the view that Kant characterizes as "a system of the **epigenesis** of pure reason," which maintains that "the categories contain the grounds of the possibility of all experience in general from the side of the understanding" (B167). In short, rather than experience making the categories possible in the sense of accounting for their origin, it is the categories that make experience possible.

As has been noted at several points, the endemic problem with an argument by elimination is the possibility of neglected alternatives. But while Kant is frequently charged with this neglect, he here faces it squarely by characterizing the alternative as a putative "middle way" between the previously mentioned ones: that the categories are **self-thought** (*selbstgedachte*) a priori first principles (epigenesis) or that they are derived from experience (*generatio aequivoca*). The proposed middle way is that the categories are "subjective predispositions for thinking, implanted in us along with our existence by our author in such a way that their use would agree exactly with the laws of nature along which experience runs" (B168). In addition to its utter arbitrariness, Kant's chief objection to such a proposal with regard to the categories is its inability to account for the necessity that pertains to their very concept. Appealing yet again to causality, he notes that,

[T]he concept of cause, which asserts the necessity of a consequent under a presupposed condition, would be false if it rested only on a subjective necessity, arbitrarily implanted in us, of combining certain empirical representations according to such a rule of relation. I would not be able to say that the effect is combined with the cause in the object (i.e., necessarily), but only that I am so constituted that I cannot think of this representation otherwise than as so connected; which is precisely what the skeptic wishes most, for then all our insight through the supposed objective validity of our judgments is nothing but sheer illusion, and there would be no shortage of people who would not concede this subjective necessity (which must be felt) on their own; at least one would not be able to quarrel with anyone about that which merely depends on the way in which his subject is organized.   (B168)

Although Kant had already rejected the appeal to such a harmony in its Crusian form on the grounds that it constitutes a *deus ex machina* in the 1772 letter to Herz, it

the creation of anything new. In the "critical" period Kant's systematic discussion of these competing theories and his preference for the first is contained in §81 of the third *Critique*. See KU 5: 422–9; 290–7. For an illuminating study of the controversy itself in eighteenth-century biological thought, which traces Kant's concern with the issue from his earliest writings through the "critical" period and analyzes his use of the contrast in his accounts of cognition, see Mensch (2013).

is clear from both his formulation of the proposed alternative and the grounds adduced for rejecting it that his target this time is closer to home, namely, Johann Schultz. We have seen that Schultz proposed this option in his review of Ulrich's *Institutiones Logicae et Metaphysica* as a means of avoiding the dilemma that he (Schultz) found in Kant's Transcendental Deduction in the first edition of the *Critique* and the *Prolegomena*. To reiterate, the alleged dilemma resulted from what Schultz took to be an equivocation in Kant's understanding of "experience." Appealing to the distinction between judgments of perception and judgments of experience, Schultz claimed that Kant took the term to apply to both species of judgment and that, despite Kant's explicit statement to the contrary, he was committed by his analyses of objective succession and simultaneity in the Second and Third Analogies to the view that the categories are conditions of experience in both senses. The alleged dilemma is that, if "experience" is taken in the first sense the claim that the categories are necessary conditions of its possibility is false, since it would mean that an empirical judgment presupposes an a priori one; whereas if taken in the second sense it is trivially true, since it claims only that a priori concepts, i.e., categories, are required to make a priori judgments.

We also saw that in the Note in which he referred to Schultz's review Kant dismissed the latter's proposal as a case of the cure being worse than the disease, albeit without discussing the nature of the disease. In other words, seemingly ignoring the alleged dilemma, Kant dismissed Schultz's proposal on the grounds that by denying any genuine necessity, it would open the door to the skeptic, there identified as Hume, by undermining the very possibility of attributing objectivity to empirical cognition. And though in the *Critique* Schultz's proposal is repackaged as a possible alternative to two contrasting views concerning the origin of the categories rather than as a cure for an unnamed "disease," Kant's critique of it is substantially the same. Nevertheless, without mentioning it, Kant effectively addresses Schultz's dilemma by calling attention to the fact that his claim is that empirical *cognitions* presuppose a priori concepts, i.e., the categories, not that empirical *judgments* presuppose a priori ones, which was the view that Schultz had attributed to him. Once again, the essential point is that the necessity to which Kant appeals as foundational of objectivity is normative in nature and is grounded in the categories in virtue of their status as rules for the unification of the manifold given in accordance with space and time as forms of sensibility in a single "universal" consciousness. But given Schultz's critical remarks about the Deduction it seems likely that he was misled by Kant's penchant for using causality to illustrate his general thesis about the objectivating function of categories to conflate the necessity affirmed in causal claims with the normative necessity attributable to all empirical judgments qua objectively valid cognitions. And if a reader of Kant as sympathetic as Schultz could misunderstand him on this fundamental point, it is not surprising that many less sympathetic readers have done so as well.

Conclusion

In his typically provocative manner, Jonathan Bennett claimed that the Transcendental Deduction "is not a patchwork but a botch;" though he condescendingly added that, "Since it contains some good things ... it is not a negligible botch."[1] I agree with Bennett that it is not a patchwork: either in the original sense claimed by Adickes, Vaihinger, and Kemp Smith, according to which the A-Deduction consists of various strands of argumentation stemming from different periods, which they purport to date with some precision and which Kant allegedly stitched together at the last minute, or in the more modern sense affirmed by Guyer and others, who ignore the unresolvable issue of dating but insist that at least the A-Deduction, if not both versions, consists of a hodge-podge of loosely linked argumentative strategies rather than a coherent line of argument. Instead, following the lead of Paton, I have tried to show that, despite its obscurity at key points and a manifestly inadequate account of the categories, which often appear to be almost an afterthought, the A-Deduction contains a carefully designed, if not elegantly executed, line of argument, the intent of which is to introduce the reader, step by step, to a radically new philosophical project. But I have also expressed a strong preference for the B-Deduction because its two-step-in-one proof-structure, in which the first step isolates the understanding in order to analyze its contribution to cognition and the second relates the formal structure of thinking stemming from the understanding to the content furnished by sensibility. My claim is that this provides a more perspicacious view of the problematic with which the Deduction in both versions is concerned; viz., the nature of the connection between what is given in sensibility in accordance with its a priori forms and the requirements of the understanding, which are themselves grounded in the synthetic unity of apperception as the supreme principle of discursive thinking.

Although it would not be practical at this point to consider in detail the reasons why Bennett regards the Transcendental Deduction as a botch, I believe it fair to say that they are quite similar to those expressed by Strawson and others; viz., the entanglement of a core analytic and anti-skeptical argument linking self-consciousness, understood

---

[1] Bennett (1966), 100. In reality, however, Bennett does seem to have some sympathy for the patchwork theory of Vaihinger and Kemp Smith, since at one point he states that it "throws some light on these passages about imagination; and it may even be possible to discover precisely and in detail lie behind the neurotically inept exposition of the Transcendental Deduction;" though he proceeds to add that, "Such a discovery would probably not be worth the trouble" (Bennett (1966), 138).

as the attribution of mental states or the awareness of a mental history, and the consciousness of an orderly objective world that is distinct from a subject's awareness of it, which is paramount among the "good things," with the twin bogeymen of a transcendental psychology and a subjective idealism. Having endeavored in the body of this work and my previous writings on Kant to dispel these bogeymen I shall not say anything further regarding these matters at present. I do believe, however, that, in addition to blurring the line between the tasks of the Transcendental Deduction and the Refutation of idealism, this view of what is salvageable in the former, though widely shared, reflects an anachronistic and exceedingly narrow conception of Kant's project. The problem is not in the endeavor to relate Kant's argument to contemporary concerns, but rather in a failure to consider seriously the relation of these concerns to those of the historical Kant.

Nevertheless, this is not to suggest that all is smooth sailing when Kant's project is considered contextually and developmentally as I have attempted to do here. On the contrary, we have seen that Kant himself was sufficiently dissatisfied with the A-Deduction to suggest that his readers replace it with the surrogate that he provided in the *Prolegomena* and that in the note to the Preface to the *Metaphysical First Principles of Natural Science* he appears to distance himself from it further by minimizing its significance for his overall "critical" project. In addition, we have seen that, even in the favored B-Deduction, Kant's account suffers from numerous ambiguities involving key terms such as "object," "necessity," "subjective validity," as well as considerable unclarity concerning crucial issues, including the analyticity of the apperception principle, the relation between the two steps of the proof, the interpretation of the note to B160–1, the status of judgments of perception in light of the definition of judgment as involving objective validity in §19, the role of the categories with respect to perception and experience, as well as other issues discussed in the preceding chapters.

In order to determine whether the Transcendental Deduction is a botch, it is necessary to become clear about what it is supposed to accomplish. And though we have seen that Kant formulates this goal in a number of ways, not all of which are obviously equivalent, I believe that a fair statement of its aim is to demonstrate the *necessary* conformity of appearances to the categories, which would establish their a priori objective validity for all appearances and *only* for appearances. Otherwise expressed, it is to provide a restricted warrant for the use of the categories, which answers to the *quid juris*. Moreover, I take it as non-controversial that an essential element of this project is to demonstrate that "The a priori conditions of a possible experience in general are at the same time conditions of the possibility objects of experience" (A111). In explicating this proposition, which he reiterates in slightly different terms in the Analytic of Principles (A158/B197), Kant stipulates that the categories "are nothing other than the **conditions of thinking in a possible experience**," which he compares with space and time as containing "the **conditions of intuition** for the very same thing [i.e., possible experience]." And from this he concludes that they are "fundamental concepts for thinking objects in general for the appearances, and they therefore have *a priori* objective validity," which Kant notes, "was just what we really wanted to know" (A111). In short, the categories are valid a priori of appearances because they make possible the cognition of appearances as objects. The argument for this claim rests upon the following premises:

1. That experience (understood as empirical cognition) requires both intuition and thought. This is a direct consequence of the discursivity thesis, according to which synthetic cognition requires the cooperation of sensibility and understanding.
2. That the thought of particular objects presupposes the thought of an object in general or, better, of an object as such. This rests upon the assumption that the representation of something as an object of a particular kind presupposes the recognition of it as an object *simpliciter.*
3. That such thought requires the use of the categories, understood as the concepts of an object as such. This is presumably established in "The Clue" or Metaphysical Deduction. What the latter does not show is how such thought becomes cognition.
4. That the particular objects cognized on the basis of these categories are appearances, i.e., objects given in accordance with the forms of sensibility, rather than objects as such or as they are in themselves. This is based upon the argument of the Aesthetic and is the point at which the Deduction presupposes the results of the latter.
5. If (as was argued) the categories are conditions of the possibility of experience, then by that very fact they must also be conditions of the possibility of objects of experience. The claim is that conditions of cognizing, i.e., epistemic conditions, are conditions of what is cognized, qua cognized.

If one accepts these propositions, the argument can be taken as having shown that both experience and its objects necessarily stand under the categories. Accordingly, it suffices to defeat a concept empiricism such as Locke's, which maintains that we have experience, so understood, but no a priori concepts such as the Kantian categories. And this would seem to be enough for those interpreters who maintain that the Deduction assumes that we do have experience in the sense of empirical cognition of an objective phenomenal world and that, unlike the Refutation of Idealism, it is not concerned with addressing a radical, external world skepticism. But the problem is that this relatively modest characterization of the task of the Deduction ignores the specter that it is supposedly intended to exorcize. Moreover, this appears to pose something of a dilemma. Simply put, one can either construe the Deduction as starting with the "fact" of experience and regressing to the a priori conditions of its possibility, much as in the *Prolegomena,* or as attempting to exorcize the specter of a possible radical non-conformity of what is given in sensibility to the requirements of the understanding but not both. Or, if perchance one wishes to claim that Kant maintains both, it becomes difficult to avoid concluding that the Deduction is *both* a patchwork *and* a botch.

Nevertheless, it is clear that Kant did intend to establish both claims; for, as we saw in initially examination this portion of the text in Chapter 5, rather than ending his analysis with the claim that the categories are necessary conditions of the possibility of both experience and the objects of experience, he proceeds to maintain that,

[T]he possibility, indeed even the necessity of these categories rests on the relation that the entire sensibility, and with it also all possible appearances, have to the original apperception, in which everything is necessarily in agreement with the conditions of the thoroughgoing unity of self-consciousness, i.e., must stand under universal functions of synthesis, namely of the synthesis in accordance with concepts, as that in which alone apperception can demonstrate *a priori* its thoroughgoing and necessary identity.   (A111–12)

And, after illustrating the thesis of the necessary unity of apperception with the category of causality, he concludes that, absent this unity, our perceptions "would . . . belong to no experience, and would consequently be without an object, and would be nothing but a blind play of representations, i.e., less than a dream" (A112).

Eliminating this possibility, which is another description of the specter, requires two additional steps. Expressed in the terms used in the body of this work these are:

6. The categories are grounded in the unity of apperception, which entails that whatever does not conform to them cannot be brought to this unity, i.e., would not be apperceivable.
7. Whatever is not apperceivable would be "nothing to me," qua cognizer.

By supplementing the first five steps of the argument with these additional steps we arrive at a conclusion that purports to exorcize this specter, not by demonstrating that the scenario it depicts is logically impossible, but by showing that it is epistemically null (it would be nothing to us qua cognizers, even "less than a dream"), and therefore does not designate a really possible state of affairs that we would ever recognize as such. The question, however, is whether this is really necessary to achieve the goal of the Deduction. As Kant's argument has here been reconstructed, the function of these steps is to eliminate the worry that appearances might not conform to the conditions of apperception, i.e., the categories. But if the analysis of this elimination given here is correct, that is to say, if the actual occurrence of such a state of affairs is not a real possibility, why is it necessary to worry about it at all? Indeed, exorcizing the specter in this way seems to undermine the rationale for introducing it in the first place to characterize the problematic of the Deduction.

The short answer is that the logical possibility of the non-conformity of appearances to the apperceivability condition is sufficient to make its exorcism necessary. Moreover, this is not, as critics often assume, because Kant is engaged in the Deduction in a misguided attempt to refute a radical Cartesian skepticism. It is rather that the view that the conformity of appearances to this condition opens the door to a Humean-style skepticism that calls into question the normativity of empirical cognition by effectively reducing the conformity of appearances to the conditions of apperception to a matter of epistemological luck. Accordingly, it is to counter this challenge that Kant found it necessary to show that the concepts of a categorically structured experience and the unity of apperception reciprocally imply each other, which is another manifestation of the reciprocity between the unity of consciousness and the consciousness of unity that we have seen is the pivot on which the Deduction turns in both editions.

We have also seen, however, that this reciprocity is one of the more problematic features of Kant's argument and the focus of a good deal of criticism, particularly insofar as it implies that the unity of consciousness is not merely a necessary but also a sufficient condition of the cognition of objects, a proposition which of itself might be sufficient to characterize the Deduction as a botch. And, in light of this, I shall devote the remainder of this conclusion to a further discussion of three central issues that have been addressed in the main body of this work and are closely related to this problem. The first, which was touched upon in Chapter 8, is the objection that, in view of this presumed reciprocity, if the Deduction proves anything at all, it proves too much. The second, which is almost the converse of this, is that the Deduction claims too much, since all that it is either required or able to establish is the conditional necessity: if we have experience it necessarily conforms to the categories. And since the latter is closely related to the issue of whether the Deduction presupposes transcendental idealism, I shall conclude with a final reconsideration of it as well.

A) *The Deduction proves too much*: The objection that if the Transcendental Deduction proves anything at all it proves too much was given its classical expression by C. I. Lewis, who asked rhetorically: "Did the sage of Königsberg have no dreams!"[2] Underlying this question is the worry that Kant's argument entails that everything that is brought to consciousness must conform to the a priori laws stemming from the human understanding, which leaves no room for "subjective experiences" such as dreams and hallucinations. And the problem, as Lewis saw it, lies in Kant's virtual identification of "experience" with the cognition of physical reality. As he put it, "*A priori principles of categorial interpretation are required to limit reality; they are not required to limit experience.*"[3]

Despite the erroneous nature of the claim that Kant identified experience with the cognition of physical reality, Lewis seems to have struck a nerve.[4] For if, as Kant appears to argue, conformity to a priori laws, as specified through the categories, is a necessary condition for what is sensibly given to be brought to consciousness, then

---

[2] Lewis (1929), 221. See also Chapter 8, notes 34 and 37.   [3] Lewis (1929), 222.

[4] Lewis' claim is erroneous because we have seen in Chapter 9 that in the second edition Kant discusses in detail the nature and conditions of a specifically inner experience, where the object is one's mental states.

there seems to be no place for an awareness of recalcitrant data. And, even worse, to admit the possibility of the latter, which "belong to no experience" and are "without an object," is to leave in place the very specter that the Deduction was supposed to exorcize. Otherwise expressed, Kant's account seems to lead to a dilemma: either admit that not all "experience" is "objective," and therefore counts as experience in Kant's sense, which accords with common sense but appears to come at the high cost of undermining a central aim of the Deduction; or stick to its core principle and assert that all conscious representation is experience in the strict sense, which seems to lead to the implausible scenario depicted by Lewis in which there is no room for purely "subjective experiences" such as dreams and hallucinations.[5]

Although it is not clear that Kant recognized this dilemma in the stark form in which it is here described, he was neither completely oblivious to the problem nor totally without resources to deal with it. This much is evident from his appeal in the *Prolegomena* to the much maligned distinction between judgments of perception and judgments of experience, and the distinction between the objective unity of self-consciousness and a subjective unity of consciousness that Kant draws in the B-Deduction. But having already discussed these topics in some detail, our present concern will be limited to other materials from the *Critique* (outside of the Deduction) that bear on the issue.

A good place to begin is with a look at what Kant there says about dreams. Apart from the passing reference to non-apperceivable appearances as amounting to "less than a dream," which likely inspired Lewis' formulation of his objection, there are three such places in the *Critique*, all in the *Dialectic*.[6] The first is from the Fourth Paralogism, which contains the first edition's version of the Refutation of Idealism. Dreams are there viewed as deceptive (*trügliche*) representations resulting from a semblance (*Blendwerke*) of the imagination, and Kant suggests that their deceptiveness can be avoided by appealing to the postulate of empirical thinking: "**Whatever is connected with a perception according to empirical laws is actual**" (A376). Inasmuch as it suggests that dreams are not connected with perceptions according to empirical laws, and therefore are not occurrences in the phenomenal world, this is perplexing. But Kant's point becomes understandable if we keep in mind that he is arguing that the skeptic cannot appeal in Cartesian fashion to the existence of dreams as grounds for doubting the mind's capacity to distinguish between veridical experience and illusion because this distinction is made in terms of the connection of perceptions according to empirical laws. In other words, Kant is not denying that the

---

[5] The definitive response to Lewis' critique is to be found in Beck (1978), 38–60, where he distinguishes between "L-experience," where experience is equated with conscious awareness of any kind, and "K-experience," where experience is equated with objectively valid empirical cognition. Although I differ from Beck on a number of details, my own account of the issue is greatly indebted to his.

[6] Texts outside of the *Critique* in which Kant discusses dreams and dreaming include VKK 2: 264 and A 7: 189–90. In both of these works Kant treats dreams as natural phenomena, and therefore as a part of rather an exception to the natural order of things.

occurrence of dreams can be explained in terms of empirical laws; rather, he is simply pointing out that the content of a dream can be distinguished from an actual experience on the basis of empirical criteria.[7] Moreover, by way of a supplemental argument against the Cartesian skeptic, Kant also points out that fictions and dreams presuppose actual perceptions (A377), a move which will become the focal point of the radically revised Refutation of Idealism in the second edition.

Kant's two other references to dreams are in the Antinomy chapter and both focus on the notion of "empirical truth." The first of these is from the remark on the antithesis to the Third Antinomy and is merely incidental. Assuming the voice of the critic of the conception of transcendental freedom, Kant notes that to attribute such a faculty to intermundane entities would conflict with the universal laws of nature, thereby effectively undermining the criterion of empirical truth, which consists in conformity to these laws and which serves to distinguish experience from dreaming (A451/B479). Like the preceding, this suggests that, while dreams and other subjective phenomena, such as hallucinations, lack empirical truth, they are nonetheless part of the phenomenal world and their occurrence is explicable in terms of empirical laws, in contrast to transcendental freedom, which, as transcendent, contradicts the conditions of a possible experience.

The final reference is in section 6 of the Antinomy chapter, where Kant proposes transcendental idealism as the key to the resolution of the antinomial conflict. After affirming the transcendental ideality of space and time and denying that the inner and sensible intuition of our mind as object of consciousness is "the real self as it exists in itself, or the transcendental subject,"[8] Kant insists that "In space and time... the empirical truth of appearances is satisfactorily secured and sufficiently distinguished from its kinship [Verwandtschaft] with dreams if both [appearances and dreams] are correctly and thoroughly connected up according to empirical laws in one experience" (A492/B520–1).[9] The importance of this text for our purposes consists in the fact that it indicates Kant's adherence to the view that one would expect him to hold; viz., that dreams (and again presumably other "subjective experiences") are objects of the "one experience" and, as such, connected according to empirical laws with the physical world. Once again, even though the contents of dreams do not contain empirical truth, there is an empirical truth about their occurrence and their contents.

---

[7] Kant makes essentially the same point in two places in Met M (29: 815 and 860–1).

[8] This is the only occurrence of the term "transcendental subject" in the Critique; but we saw in Chapter 3 that Kant used it in the Duisburg Nachlass in a very different sense to refer to the x that is conceptually determined in cognition, that is, the subject of the judgment or object judged about.

[9] The text is grammatically ambiguous, since "both" (beide) could refer either to space and time of dreams and appearances. As is their wont, Guyer and Wood leave the ambiguity, but in their renderings both Kemp Smith and Pluhar remove it in favor of the latter reading. I am following their reading because on the alternative it is difficult to make philosophical sense of the passage.

Nevertheless, this is not sufficient to avoid the dilemma sketched above. For that concerned the actual contents of dreams of which the dreamer is presumably conscious and which according to Kant's theory must accord with the conditions of the unity of apperception, and therefore with the categories. Thus, the question becomes how Kant can acknowledge this, while still maintaining the distinction between dreams and veridical experience that is essential to his response to skeptical idealism. And, of course, the same problem arises in the case of hallucinations and other forms of non-veridical experience.

In dealing with this issue I follow the lead of Lewis White Beck, who has provided the fullest Kantian response to it. In discussing Lewis' objection, Beck cites the latter's claim that "The subsumption of the given under the heading 'dream' or 'illusion' is itself a categorial interpretation by which we understand certain experiences."[10] Beck concurs with this and suggests that Kant would also, with the proviso that he held to a much narrower view of what counts as "categorial" than Lewis. As Beck notes, "The difference between seeing Paris and dreaming that one sees Paris is not a categorial difference, but an empirical difference;" and he goes on to add: "The categories do not differentiate veridical from non-veridical experience; they make the distinction between dumbly facing chaos without even knowing it . . . and telling a connected story, even if it is false."[11]

Although Beck's analysis is spot on, it is incomplete. What needs to be added is that, though not categorial (in Kant's sense), differentiating veridical from non-veridical experience is a matter of interpretation. Kant expresses this nicely in a well-known passage in the *Critique*, where he characterizes the task of the human understanding as that of "spelling out appearances according to a synthetic unity in order to be able to read them as experience" (A314/B370–1). To "read as" (*buch-stabieren*) is to interpret, i.e., to "take as" something or other and "experience" here clearly has the distinctively Kantian sense of empirical cognition of an objective phenomenal world. But the essential point is that we can only speak of an interpret-ation (and the same applies to the metaphorical expression "read as") when there are available alternatives, which in this case means taking a synthetic unity of appear-ances as something other than an experience in Kant's sense. Moreover, it is difficult to imagine what this could be other than taking it as not constituting an experience, i.e., as a dream or hallucination, which for Kant must be on the basis of empirical laws that are grounded in the categories. And if this is correct, it indicates that there is room in Kant's scheme for dreams and hallucinations.

B) *The necessity issue*: We have seen that it is frequently objected that Kant claimed a stronger form of necessity regarding the conformity of objects to the categories than his argument either allows or requires. Rather than being content with the merely conditional or hypothetical necessity that objects must conform to the categories, if

---

[10] Lewis (1929), 225; cited by Beck (1978), 355–78.   [11] Beck (1978), 54.

experience of them is to be possible, which presumably would suffice to demonstrate that the categories are necessary conditions of the possibility of experience, Kant allegedly insisted, without justification, upon the unconditional necessity of such conformity, which, in turn, led him down the disastrous path to transcendental idealism.[12] My response to this prevalent line of objection consists of three parts, which reiterate and further develop points already made in the main body of this work: a restatement of the case for the non-contingency thesis; a critique, based upon my defense of this thesis, of Guyer's claim that the Transcendental Deduction, as contained in the *Critique*, is vitiated by a crude modal fallacy and his consequent separation of what he considers Kant's "transcendental theory of experience" from any connection with transcendental idealism; and a final defense of the thesis that the Transcendental Deduction is in fact inseparable from transcendental idealism.

1) *The non-contingency thesis*: In reconstructing Kant's argument for this thesis, it is convenient to begin with his claim that "our thought of the relation of all cognition to its object carries something of necessity with it" (A104). Since "all cognition" includes empirical cognition, this indicates that Kant attributed "something of necessity" to empirical cognitions, which has sometimes led to the objection that he illicitly collapsed empirical into a priori cognitions or, what amounts to the same thing, maintained that empirical judgments are necessarily true.[13] In addressing this issue in Chapter 5, I suggested that the necessity in question should be understood as normative in the sense of stemming from a rule. To reiterate, the basic idea is that in predicating a property or set of properties of some object *x*, I am implicitly expressing an epistemic ought, claiming that the predication holds not only for me in my present perceptual situation but for any observer, which makes it objectively valid. And, as textual support for attributing this view to Kant, I pointed to the account of objective validity in the *Prolegomena* as equivalent to a necessary universality (4: 288; 93).

Although I have refrained from doing so in the main body of this work in order to avoid introducing undue complexity into what is already an extremely complex story, I believe that it may be useful at this point to note the significant parallels between Kant's analysis of judgments of experience in the *Prolegomena* and his account of judgments of taste in the third *Critique*. The main differences are that, as aesthetic, judgments of taste are based upon feeling rather than concepts and that they are all singular with respect to logical form ("This rose is beautiful" but not "All [or even some] roses are beautiful"). But these differences, though crucial for Kant's account of judgments of taste, do not obviate their significant similarities. In particular, Kant

[12] For a particularly clear formulation of this line of thought see Cassam (1987), 355–78. Finding it totally obvious that transcendental arguments such as Strawson's objectivity argument do not depend upon transcendental idealism and require only a conditional necessity, Cassam wonders what could conceivably have led Kant to the contrary view and he speculates that it must lie in his misguided view of synthesis.

[13] This appears to have been the case with Schultz in his review of Ulrich. See Chapter 7, notes 41 and 42.

maintains that when judging an object of nature or art to be beautiful one takes oneself to be speaking with a "universal voice" (KU 5: 216; 101), by which is understood an aesthetic counterpart of Rousseau's conception of a general will; and, as such, one demands the agreement of others with one's verdict. In other words, the necessity involved in judgments of taste, like that pertaining to empirical cognitive judgments, is normative in nature and like all oughts, requires an a priori ground or principle, which in his deduction of pure judgments of taste Kant identified with "the subjective principle of the power of judgment as such" (KU 5: 286; 167). It is not possible here to analyze either what Kant understood by this principle or the argument that he provided in support of it; but it is also not necessary to do so.[14] For present purposes what is crucial is simply the fact that Kant modeled his deduction of the principle of taste on the Transcendental Deduction in the first *Critique*, changing things only to the extent necessary to deal with the aesthetic nature of judgments of taste.[15]

Nevertheless, the parallel with judgments of taste should not be pushed too far, since it ignores an essential feature of cognitive judgments, which accounts for both their normative necessity in Kant's account and the fact that they can possess a logical as well as a subjective universality (apply to every x as well as to a particular x for every cognizer); viz., the claim that the concepts, which function as predicates in such judgments, are to be understood as rules. As was noted in Chapter 5, concepts function as rules in two distinct, though closely related ways for Kant: as rules of unification governing a synthesis and as rules of recognition, which enable us to determine what counts as the instantiation of a concept. But the crucial point is that, as rules, empirical concepts have a built-in normativity in the sense that their use presupposes something like an epistemic right to expect that whatever objects fall under the rule contain the properties that are expressed in the concept and to require that other cognizers, who possess the concept, will agree with one's judgment. Returning to the example there used, if some perceived x is judged to fall under the concept of gold, one assumes a warrant to predicate of this x certain properties deemed essential to gold, e.g., a yellow color, a metallic nature, malleability, and solubility in *aqua regia*, etc.

Moreover, it cannot be countered that this is a matter of analyticity, which concerns merely what is contained in the definition of a term, and that any necessity involved is therefore logical. Although the issue was briefly touched upon in Chapter 5, the naturalness of this line of objection calls for further discussion at this point.[16] To begin with, since Kant understood by a definition "a sufficiently distinct and precise concept (*conceptus rei adequatus in minimis terminis, complete*

---

[14] For readers interested in my account of Kant's subjective principle of taste and its deduction, see Allison (2001), 160–92.

[15] See especially KU 5: 287–9; 168–9.

[16] The following discussion is indebted to the account of Beck (1965b), 61–73.

determinatus)" (JL 9: 140; 631), he contended that empirical concepts cannot be defined because it is always possible to find in experience further marks of the concept (JL 9: 141–2; 632). But the main point, as Kant also notes obliquely, is that even if, *per impossibile*, empirical concepts could be defined, the definition would be a synthetic judgment (Kant refers to it as a "synthetic definition") because the synthesis through which the unification of marks thought in the definition is produced would be empirical (JL 9: 141; 632). In Kant's schematic rendering, it would be a definition in which an *x* taken under *a* also has the property *b*: e.g., if *x* is a body it necessarily has weight or mass. Thus, though Kant denies that this can be considered a matter of definition, the propositions that bodies are heavy and that gold is soluble in *aqua regia* are synthetic judgments and as such involve a necessity claim, which cannot be regarded as logical and is best understood as normative.

Accordingly, this claim requires a warrant or justifying ground, which is provided by the non-contingent, i.e., necessary, uniformity of nature. In other words, it is because nature is assumed to be non-contingently uniform in the sense that there are natural laws, which ensure, for example, that yellow, malleable metals are also found to be soluble in *aqua regia*, that one has the "right" to assume that this will hold in the future and that one is therefore entitled to claim that gold *is* soluble in *aqua regia* and not merely that this solubility has been found in conjunction with the aforementioned qualities in the past. Clearly, any such empirical claims are fallible and might be falsified by future discoveries, which prevents one from claiming that they are necessarily true. But the essential point is that the empirical truth of this and similar claims, i.e., judgments of experience, presuppose that nature as a whole (*natura formaliter spectata*) is governed by universal laws, which ground the possibility (though not the empirical truth) of such projections and warrant requiring the assent of others.

Moreover, in order to preclude the contingency that would undermine normativity as such, and not merely the validity of a particular judgment or candidate for empirical law, these universal laws must have a transcendental ground, which we have seen Kant locates in the categories and ultimately in the principle of the synthetic unity of apperception. And we have also seen that this principle does this by imposing the apperceivability condition on whatever can be thought together by a single "I think," which precludes, as a performative, though not a logical impossibility, the "experience" of a chaotic scenario, which would have to be regarded as possible, if, as Kant's critics assume, the uniformity of nature were regarded as merely contingent.

In sum, Kant's account of the conditions of the possibility of empirical cognition rests upon the conception of the empirical concepts that function in such cognition as rules; that, as such, they purport to express a normative necessity; that this necessity requires that the uniformity of nature, which these rules presuppose, cannot be merely contingent, a matter of epistemic luck, because these rules would then lose their normative status; and that this status is preserved by subjecting the uniformity of nature to the unity of apperception as its transcendental condition. Accordingly, whatever may be the case with present-day "Kantian" transcendental arguments, Kant's Transcendental Deduction cannot make do with a merely conditionally necessary uniformity of nature, which is once again why exorcizing the specter of the non-conformity of appearances to the conditions of the understanding is an essential part of the Deduction.

2) *Guyer's argument for the separability thesis*: It is no coincidence that those who accuse Kant of conflating a merely conditional with an unconditional or absolute necessity with regard to the conformity of experience to the categories, or otherwise maintain that a viable transcendental argument, if not Kant's actual Deduction, would be satisfied by the conditional necessity that objects of experience conform to some weaker analogue of Kant's categories and principles, e.g., an orderly course of nature, closely coincide with those who argue for the separability of whatever positive results Kant's argument achieves from its idealistic underpinnings. In fact, in addition to a generic antipathy to idealism, which includes Kant's transcendental version, this is the main argument advanced by proponents of the separability thesis.[17] Accordingly, in order to argue for the thesis that the argument of the Transcendental Deduction, if not some sanitized simulacrum thereof, is inseparably tied to transcendental idealism it is necessary to address this familiar line of objection in some detail.

Although my concern is with this general line of objection, I shall address it through an examination of Guyer's account, since, despite some idiosyncratic features, he is the most thorough and systematic of the anti-idealists and can be considered as representative of the broader view. Guyer's generic argument for the separability thesis can be broken down into the following claims: (1) Kant's self-defined task is to account for the possibility of synthetic a priori cognition. (2) As a priori, such cognition requires necessity. (3) Kant assumed incorrectly that the required necessity must be unconditional or *de re*. (4) This entails that the unconditionally necessary conditions must be imposed by the mind. (5) This, in turn, leads to transcendental idealism, understood as a dogmatically metaphysical imposition theory, according to which the mind stamps its forms of sensibility (space and time) and the categories onto whatever is given in experience. (6) But a *de dicto* or conditional necessity, properly understood, is sufficient to account for the possibility of synthetic a priori cognition. (7) Moreover, there is textual evidence indicating that at one time Kant entertained this view, only to be "seduced" into preferring the imposition view "by some very bad arguments."[18]

---

[17] As was noted in Chapter 6, an exception to this is the interpretation of Lucy Allais.

[18] Guyer (1987), 342. Guyer devotes the last three chapters of his book to analyzing these "bad arguments" for transcendental idealism. I discuss his critique in my review of *The Claims of Knowledge*, Allison (1989), 214–21.

The claim that Kant was fundamentally concerned in the *Critique* with accounting for the possibility of synthetic a priori cognition can hardly be gainsaid. It is also clear that Kant grounded the possibility of such cognition in the cognitive capacities of the human mind and regarded its conditions as imposed upon objects rather than derived from them. As Kant succinctly put it, "we can cognize of things *a priori* only what we ourselves have put into them" (Bxviii). Similarly, it is correct that Kant appeals to transcendental idealism in order to understand the mind-dependence of such cognition; though as I have argued elsewhere and shall suggest again below, this does not take the unpalatable form that Guyer assumes. Accordingly, the key issue is whether, as Guyer and other anti-idealists maintain, Kant's account turns on a crude modal fallacy, which leads him to the dead end of transcendental idealism. I have contended that, at least with respect to the Transcendental Aesthetic, the modal fallacy that Guyer purports to find is a consequence of an extraordinarily unsympathetic reading of the text. But since I agree that in the Transcendental Deduction Kant is concerned to establish an unconditional necessity in the form of a denial of the contingency of the conformity of appearances to the requirements of the understanding, I shall limit the present discussion to a consideration of Guyer's argument for the sufficiency of a merely conditional necessity and his claim to find at least a hint of such a view in Kant.

We have seen that, on Guyer's preferred view, rather than being imposed by the mind upon the given, the forms of sensibility and the categories function as gatekeepers, which prevent representations that do not conform to them from entering consciousness; thereby ensuring that everything that we perceive will accord with these conditions. Thus, assuming that space, qua form of sensibility, is one of these gatekeepers and that it has a Euclidean structure, we are entitled to the conditional claim that "Necessarily, if we are to perceive an object, then it is spatial and euclidean. But instead of this Kant affirms the proposition: "If we perceive an object, it is necessarily spatial and euclidean."[19] And whereas the former is compatible with the transcendentally realistic view that things as they are in themselves exist in a Euclidean space, the latter is not.

Setting aside his highly idiosyncratic exegesis of Kant's arguments in the conclusions from his expositions in the Aesthetic, the problematic feature of Guyer's account is his claim that it explains how a form of sensibility, so understood, could account for the possibility of a priori cognition of space.[20] Guyer's argument for this explanatory thesis apparently consists in the claim that "it seems at least possible to imagine that we could know, *because of certain constraints on our ability to perceive*

[19] Guyer (1987), 364.
[20] For my criticism of Guyer's idiosyncratic reading of Kant's conclusions from the metaphysical and transcendental expositions of the concepts of space and time in the Aesthetic, see Allison (1989), 220 and (1996), 22–4.

that any object we perceive must have a certain property."[21] This may well be true, but the question is what bearing it has on a priori knowledge. In fact, Kant had reason to reject any reliance on this kind of necessity, since it is not only conditional but subjective. Consequently, from Kant's standpoint the problem with a conception of a priori knowledge based on this foundation is not that it applies only contingently to objects, which is why Guyer thinks that Kant rejects it, but that it does not apply at all because it would lack objective reality. At best it yields cognition of the "natural constitution" of our cognitive powers, of the sort provided by Tetens, but not of the world, either as it is in itself or as it appears.

In an effort to underscore this point, let us assume that the mind is structured so as to allow only green objects to be perceived. Guyer is correct in claiming that this would yield only the conditional necessity: necessarily, if something is perceived it is green, and not the unconditional necessity: everything perceived is necessarily green. Accordingly, it would be a contingent matter that everything we perceive happens to be green; for had we been differently constituted, perhaps everything we per-ceive would be some other color or even without color altogether. But I dare say that we would not wish to conclude from this that we know a priori that everything that we perceive will be green. Part of the problem would be that, unless we had ideas of other colors it would be impossible to form the concept of greenness and thus predicate it of everything we perceive. The major point, however, is that if this were the case, all that we would be entitled to claim is that things necessarily *seem* green to us in virtue of the nature of our sensory apparatus. Thus, far from yielding a priori knowledge of *things*, it would not provide even empirical knowledge of them, but at best of our sensory apparatus. In Kantian terms, it would yield a subjective but not an objective necessity.[22]

Guyer's critique of the Transcendental Deduction follows a similar path; though his account has added complexity due to the role played by the principle of the synthetic unity of apperception. As we have seen, Guyer, following Henrich, takes Kant's key move in the Deduction to be his "new argument from the *a priori* certainty of apperception," which maintains that the cognizing subject can have a priori certainty regarding its own identity, which, as Kant puts it, supposedly ensures that all appearances must be "associable in themselves and subjected to universal rules of thoroughgoing connection" (A122).[23] Guyer's modal conflation charge is directed against this conclusion. On his reading, rather than being content with the merely conditional necessity "that I must synthesize my several representations if I am to be conscious of them at all," Kant posits "the existence of [an] absolutely necessary connection among them that can be explained only by an *a priori* synthesis

[21]   Guyer (1987), 363.

[22]   It should also be noted that, pace Guyer, in the Aesthetic the necessity that appearances are given in space and time is only conditional, since for Kant other forms of sensibility are logically possible.

[23]   Guyer (1987), 132.

according to *a priori* concepts."[24] In other words, according to Guyer, in the Transcendental Deduction Kant ends up affirming the dogmatically metaphysical and manifestly untenable thesis that the understanding imposes a categoreal structure on appearances on the seemingly flimsy grounds that this is necessary in order to account for the possibility of the self's synthetic a priori knowledge of its own identity. And he further claims that Kant takes this as requiring not merely a synthesis governed by a priori rules, but a literally a priori synthesis, understood as a noumenal act of metaphysical constitution, in order to account for the possibility of the Cartesian certainty of the self's knowledge of its numerical identity with respect to all of its possible representations, which is the fundamental premise of Kant's actual argument in the Deduction.[25]

Since I have already rejected the thesis that Kant is concerned with securing anything like a Cartesian certainty regarding the self's cognition of its own identity in the Deduction, there is no need to say anything further on the matter. Instead, I shall consider Guyer's claim that Kant actually entertained the view, which he believes that Kant ought to have held. The text in question is the *Duisburg Nachlass*, where at one point Kant writes:

The *principium of analysis*: a rule of thought in general. The principles of thinking, insofar as it is restricted [*reststringiert*] by the condition of the subject or determined to the subject, are not fundamental principles [*Grundsätze*] but rather restrictions [*restrictionen*]. (1. Of the possibility of empirical *synthesis* in general.) Cognition is determined a priori to an object if it 1. pertains to the condition by means of which an object is given (construction), and the cognition only represents it through concepts of appearance. 2. if it pertains to [*crossed out*: conditions of apprehension in general, through which] appearance, insofar as it contains the conditions for forming a concept of it, 3. if it pertains to apprehension in general, insofar as it contains the condition of the unity of perception as well as intellection, i.e., of the consensus [*Einstimmung*] of appearances among one another and with the unity of the mind, consequently of exposition.   (R 4678 17: 661$_{13-26}$; 169–70)[26]

Expressing an appropriate tentativeness, Guyer states that "In this passage, Kant *seems* [my emphasis] to suggest that there is a conditional or hypothetical necessity that objects of experience conform to the rules under which a unified experience or "exposition of them, and indeed under which a unified self-consciousness itself is possible."[27] But since Guyer acknowledges that the impositional view is also present in the *Duisburg Nachlass*, he sees in these jottings a tension between two models of the mind: one in which it imposes its rules (as conditions of self-consciousness) upon

---

[24] Guyer (1987), 140.

[25] For Guyer's strongest statement of what he takes to be the metaphysically constitutive nature of Kant's idealism insofar as it arises from the conception of apperception see his early paper (1980), 205–6. It seems clear, however, that he retains this dismissive view in his later treatments of the issue.

[26] I am here citing Guyer's revised translation of this passage, which differs significantly from his earlier version in (1987), 54. I do not believe, however, that the difference bears on the point at issue.

[27] Guyer (1987), 55.

objects, thereby constituting experience, the other in which these same rules function merely to restrict the sorts of things that we can experience.[28]

I have but two things to say about Guyer's account. First, I find it tenuous on textual grounds, since, as was argued in Chapter 3, the most natural reading of Kant's references to "restrictions" on the use of the understanding, even in the *Duisburg Nachlass*, is as designating a scope restriction on the legitimate use of the categories to objects of possible experience, rather than that the categories somehow do the restricting. Second, as has also been already noted, I question the adequacy of Guyer's "modest proposal" to accomplish its supposed task, i.e., to account for the possibility of a priori cognition, without appealing to transcendental idealism by showing the sufficiency of a merely conditional necessity. In fact, I think that, *mutatis mutandis*, the objection raised against Guyer's proposal regarding a priori knowledge of space and of things, qua spatial, is applicable here as well.

Finally, I believe that the most fundamental mistake committed by Guyer and others who take a similar anti-idealist line regarding the Deduction is that they tend either simply to ignore or merely pay lip service to the normative dimension of Kant's account, particularly insofar as it concerns empirical propositions. To be sure, Kant's transcendental project is concerned with the possibility of metaphysics, and therefore of a priori knowledge. But the focus of the Transcendental Deduction is on the conceptual conditions of the possibility of experience, i.e., empirical cognition, and it is with the a priori status of these conditions that Kant is primarily concerned. Moreover, in analyzing the Deduction, particularly in the first-edition version, which formulates the issue in terms of the notion of affinity, thereby apparently addressing Hume's skeptical reflections regarding the uniformity of nature, I have placed considerable weight on the necessity that Kant attributes to contingent empirical cognitions. To reiterate, the claim is that this necessity must be understood as normative and that Kant attempts to show that and how the categories make experience possible by demonstrating that, through their relation to the synthetic unity of apperception, they ground this normative necessity.

C) *The Transcendental Deduction and transcendental idealism*: These concluding remarks are intended to supplement the analysis of the issue given at the end of Chapter 6 by linking the indispensability of transcendental idealism for the Deduction to the notion of a normative necessity as considered above. Although the issues are complex, the connection between this conception of a normative necessity and transcendental idealism is relatively straightforward. First, the normative necessity, i.e., objective validity, of empirical propositions requires that the conformity of experience to the categories is not, as the anti-idealists, a.k.a. transcendental realists, maintain, a contingent matter, which would not require any commitment to a form of idealism. Second, this non-contingent, i.e., unconditionally necessary, conformity requires a

---

[28] Guyer (1987), 69. Guyer here frames the issue in terms of models of the mind.

transcendental ground because "every necessity has a transcendental ground as its condition" (A106). Third, Kant locates this ground in the transcendental unity of apperception. Fourth, this grounding function presupposes transcendental idealism.

As one would expect from what has been said previously, the key steps here are the first and the fourth. Since the central contention of the anti-idealists is that a contingent, de facto agreement of experience with the requirements of the understanding is sufficient to demonstrate (presumably through something like Strawson's objectivity argument) that a self-conscious experience requires an orderly course of nature with re-identifiable objects and that this demonstration does not require an appeal to idealism of any sort, in order to establish the dependence of the Transcendental Deduction on transcendental idealism, it is essential to show that experience requires something more than what the anti-idealists assume. Although Kant characterizes this as something more in various ways, e.g., as a single universal experience to which all particular experiences belong (A110), as "a **transcendental affinity** of which the **empirical** affinity is a mere consequence" (A114), as the necessary unity of nature in the connection of appearances (A125), as the necessary lawfulness of nature (as *natura formaliter spectata*) (B165), I believe that they all amount to essentially the same thing, namely, that nature, so considered, is governed by necessary transcendental laws in virtue of which everything that can fall within a possible experience constitutes a universal order. And since these laws stem from the understanding, and in this respect depend on us, this conception of experience presupposes transcendental idealism.

Admittedly, this is not the whole story, since we have seen that both versions of the Deduction refer to the Aesthetic, where Kant locates his direct proof for transcendental idealism. In the A-Deduction this occurs at the very beginning, where Kant appeals to the temporal nature of consciousness, and therefore to time as the form of inner sense, in his account of the three-fold synthesis. And the connection is more explicit in the B-Deduction, which distinguishes between an intellectual and a figurative synthesis and links the latter specifically with human sensibility. But for present purposes I shall set aside these considerations and focus instead on the connection between Kant's account of apperception and transcendental idealism. It is not that this conception, or what has been referred to as the apperceivability condition, either presupposes or entails transcendental idealism, since a transcendental realist could accept the claim that non-apperceivable perceptions would be "nothing to me" in the sense that they could not lead to any cognition and would amount to "less than a dream." But such a realist would also insist that, while exceedingly unfortunate for our cognitive aims, a matter of epistemic bad luck, such a state of affairs is conceivable because the coherence of our experience is not something that depends on us. Moreover, we have seen that Kant cannot deny the logical possibility of such a chaotic scenario, since its conception does not involve a contradiction. Rather, he denies its *performative* possibility, i.e., the possibility of representing it to oneself. But it seems evident that this would not satisfy the transcendental realist. Again, such a realist, e.g., Westphal's "realist *sans phrase*," could acknowledge the point but deny its import by claiming that it merely indicates a limitation of our cognitive or imaginative capacities and, as such, is without any idealistic implications. Thus, it appears that nothing that has been said so far is sufficient to dislodge the committed transcendental realist.

This ignores, however, the previous course of argument, which endeavored to show that the realist's confidence in the sufficiency of a contingently orderable nature for the establishment (through a transcendental argument) of necessary conditions of the possibility of a self-conscious experience was misplaced. To reiterate, the main point was that a merely de facto or contingent conformity of appearances to the categories cannot account for the normative necessity (the epistemic ought) that is built into claims of empirical cognition as the mark of their objective validity. And if this is the case, inasmuch as the transcendental realist is committed to the real (not merely the logical) possibility of a fully chaotic experience, it follows that such a realist must admit that no such argument can be successfully mounted on the basis of a merely contingent conformity, at least not one that claims to establish against the skeptic the objective validity of empirical cognition. Even worse, it seems that the transcendental realist will have no answer to the Humean challenge to the norma-tivity (as opposed to the psychology unavoidability) of the belief in the uniformity of nature or, more simply, that the future will resemble the past, which is necessary to license any inference "beyond the present testimony of our senses, or the records of our memory."

Although these considerations do not establish transcendental idealism or, what amounts to the same thing, refute transcendental realism, they go a long way toward confirming two complementary points: (1) that transcendental realism is unable to provide a viable account of the conditions of the possibility of experience; and (2) that if an account of these conditions is to be forthcoming, it can only be on an idealistic basis, understood as one in which there are conditions of cognition that depend on us in the sense that they are grounded in the conditions of apperception and the nature of the understanding, rather than merely conditions that may or may not be met by reality, if it is to be cognizable, as transcendental realism would have it.[29]

The problem, then, is to understand such an idealism and in an effort to clarify my view I have appealed at various points in this commentary to the notion of a transcendental internalism, as a characterization of the epistemological stance from which the Transcendental Deduction proceeds. Although "internalism" and "exter-nalism" are defined in a variety of ways in present-day discussions, despite

---

[29] This transcendentally realistic conception of an epistemic condition has been affirmed by Westphal (2004), 70 in opposition to my idealistic conception. I acknowledge that there was some ambiguity in my earlier appeals to this conception, particularly in Allison (1983), but I have tried to rectify this in my subsequent discussions, especially Allison (2004), where I have characterized such conditions as "objecti-vating" in order to underscore their subjective nature.

Westphal's provocative characterization of Kant as a mental content and justificatory externalist, I think it clear that he is more appropriately located in the internalist camp. There are a number of reasons for this, but the main one is that the problematic of the Deduction is defined in terms of the relation between two species of representation (sensible intuitions and concepts) rather than between representations and a reality that exists *an sich*. In fact, we have seen that this is what differentiates the Kantian specter, as a worry about cognitive dissonance, from the more familiar Cartesian specter and its present-day successors. And we have also seen that the distinctive feature of this form of internalism, that in virtue of which it is termed "transcendental," is that it regards cognition as an act of taking some *x* both as an object *simpliciter* and as a determinate object of a certain kind by subsuming the intuition of *x* under rules which warrant this ascription.

Moreover, transcendental internalism, so understood, is inseparable from transcendental idealism. Indeed, it is transcendental idealism considered as a methodological stance. This is because of the norm-grounding capacity with respect to empirical cognition attributed to the synthetic unity of apperception, which Kant identifies with "the understanding itself" (B134n). As we have seen, this unity is norm grounding, or what amounts to the same thing, transcendental, because, as Kant argues most fully in the first part of the B-Deduction, it is the source of the conditions, insofar as they stem from thought, which must be met by any unification of representations that is to count as objective. And it is transcendentally idealistic because it assumes that the objects for which it provides the normative ground of judgment are objects qua subject to the conditions of our cognition, i.e., epistemic conditions, rather than either objects as such or as they are in themselves.[30]

I have also distinguished this transcendental from a psychological form of internalism, which characterizes the cognitive stance of Tetens and, more generally, classical empiricism. The defining feature of the latter, in virtue of which it is both an internalism and psychological in nature, is its adherence to what is often referred to as "the veil of perception," i.e., the view that the immediate objects of consciousness are internal to the mind in the form of Lockean ideas. With respect to the question of dependence of the Transcendental Deduction upon transcendental idealism, this contrast is crucial for at least two reasons. First, only the transcendental form of internalism is capable of addressing the normative question as Kant formulates it in the Deduction; viz., "how **subjective conditions of thinking** should have **objective validity**, i.e., yield conditions of the possibility of all cognition of objects"

---

[30] It might be objected at this point that, while this way of characterizing Kant's view as a transcendental internalism shows that it involves an idealistic commitment, it does not suffice to show that it presupposes transcendental idealism, since Kant characteristically defines that in terms of the theory of sensibility presented in the Aesthetic rather than the account of the understanding contained in the Analytic. This ignores, however, the crucial point that this account of the understanding presupposes what I have termed Kant's "discursivity thesis," which involves the theory of sensibility. For my analysis of this thesis and its relation to transcendental idealism see Allison (2004), esp.12–16, 27–8.

(A89–90/B122). This is not to deny that the psychological internalist worries about the objective validity of subjective conditions of thinking, since the worry is built into the metaphor of a veil of perception. Indeed, we have seen that Tetens had just a concern, which he expressed in terms of a contrast between a subjective and an objective necessity, which may well have influenced Kant's own formulation of the issue. But we have also seen that such a position cannot understand this as Kant did because this requires regarding these conditions as not only objectively valid but as *objectivating*, i.e., as epistemic conditions. Second, just as transcendental internalism is inseparable from transcendental idealism, so psychological internalism is a form of transcendental realism because it assumes that what lies beyond the veil of perception are the "real things," which correspond to things in themselves for Kant.[31]

Finally, at the risk of mixing metaphors, it can be argued that the manifestly transcendentally realist gatekeeper analogy to which Guyer and other Kantian anti-idealists appeal in support of their reading, can itself be regarded as a form of the veil of perception doctrine, albeit a veil with leaks. Moreover, as such, it is subject to the same difficulties as the presumably impregnable veil of the empiricists. Simply put, the "gate," which for Guyer and others who adopt this view supposedly corresponds to Kant's subjective conditions of cognition (forms of sensibility and categories), only allows "real things" and their relations to enter consciousness insofar as they serendipitously conform to these conditions. The problem, however, is that this not only blocks out those real things and their relation that happen not to conform, which reflects Guyer's understanding of "restriction," but, as far as I can see, makes it impossible to distinguish between the representation of real things that make it through the gate and merely subjective representations, which necessarily conform to these conditions. In short, I fail to see how the approach that Guyer recommends helps to achieve any of the goals of the Transcendental Deduction, including accounting for the possibility of a priori cognition, which leads me to believe that if, as Guyer suggests, Kant really did entertain such a view during the "Silent Decade," it is a good thing that he abandoned it.

Accordingly, I conclude that Kant's project of a Transcendental Deduction is inseparable from his transcendental internalism, and therefore from transcendental idealism. Moreover, if this is true, it follows that, short of an extended debate concerning the adequacy of various forms of internalism and externalism, the most that can reasonably be asked regarding the success of the Deduction, which is perhaps the most that can be asked of any groundbreaking philosophical project, is whether it succeeds in its self-defined task. And while we have encountered considerable obscurity, much wavering on Kant's part, and a number of significant loose ends, I think that judged by this criterion, the Transcendental Deduction, particularly in the second edition, must be judged at least a qualified success. At the same time,

---

[31] Kant clearly expresses this point in the first-edition version of the Fourth Paralogism (A369), when he points out that it is the transcendental realist who assumes the role of the empirical idealist.

however, I am aware that insistence on the inseparability of the Deduction from transcendental idealism is likely to have the unintended consequence of leading some to dismiss it on these grounds alone. But here I find myself in agreement with Kierkegaard, who, in response to Hegelian efforts to present a version of Christianity without the element of paradox, chose as the motto for one of his main treatments of the topic the line from Shakespeare's *Twelfth Night*: "Better well hung than ill wed."[32]

---

[32] Kierkegaard (1962), 2.

Bibliography

Allais, Lucy. "Transcendental Idealism and the Transcendental Deduction," *Kant's Idealism: New Interpretations of a Controversial Doctrine*, edited by Dennis Schulting and Jacco Verburgt, New York: Springer (2011), 91–107.

Allison, Henry E. *The Kant-Eberhard Controversy*, Baltimore, MD: Johns Hopkins University Press (1973a).

Allison, Henry E. "Kant's Critique of Berkeley," *Journal of the History of Philosophy* (11) (1973b), 43–63.

Allison, Henry E. "The Critique of Pure Reason as Transcendental Phenomenology," in *Selected Studies in Phenomenology and Existential Philosophy*, edited by R. Zaner and D. Ihde, Volume 5, Boston, MA: Martinus Nijhoff (1974a), 136–55.

Allison, Henry E. "Transcendental Affinity: Kant's Answer to Hume," in *Kant's Theory of Knowledge: Selected Papers from the Third International Kant Congress*, edited by Lewis White Beck. Boston, MA: D. Reidel (1974b), 119–27.

Allison, Henry E. *Kant's Transcendental Idealism*: *An Interpretation and Defense*, New Haven, CT: Yale University Press (1983).

Allison, Henry E. "Incongruence and Ideality Reflections on Jill Buroker's *Space and Incongruence*: *The Origin of Kant's Idealism*," *Topoi* 3 (1984), 169–75.

Allison, Henry E. "The Originality of Kant's Distinction between Analytic and Synthetic Judgments," *The Philosophy of Immanuel Kant*, *Studies in Philosophy and the History of Philosophy* Volume 12, edited by Richard Kennington, Washington, DC: Catholic University of America Press (1985), 15–38.

Allison, Henry E. "Review of Paul Guyer, *Kant and the Claims of Knowledge*," *Journal of Philosophy*, LXXXVI (1989), 214–21.

Allison, Henry E. *Idealism and Freedom: Essays on Kant's Theoretical and Practical Philosophy*, Cambridge: Cambridge University Press (1996).

Allison, Henry E. *Kant's Theory of Taste*: *A Reading of the Critique of Aesthetic Judgment*, Cambridge: Cambridge University Press (2001).

Allison, Henry E. *Kant's Transcendental Idealism*: *An Interpretation and Defense*, New Haven, CT: Yale University Press (2004).

Allison, Henry E. "Kant and the Two Dogmas of Rationalism," in *A Companion to Rationalism*, edited by Alan Nelson, Oxford: Blackwell Publishing (2005), 343–59.

Allison, Henry E. "Transcendental Realism, Empirical Realism and Transcendental Idealism," *Kantian Review* (2006), 1–28.

Allison, Henry E. *Custom and Reason in Hume: A Kantian Reading of the First Book of the Treatise*, Oxford: Clarendon Press (2008).

Allison, Henry E. *Kant's Groundwork for the Metaphysics of Morals: A Commentary*, Oxford: Oxford University Press (2011).

Allison, Henry E. *Essays on Kant*, Oxford: Oxford University Press (2012).

Ameriks, Karl. "Kant's Transcendental Deduction as a Regressive Argument," *Kant-Studien* 69 (1978), 273–87.

Ameriks, Karl. *Kant's Theory of Mind: An Analysis of the Paralogisms of Pure Reason*, Oxford: Clarendon Press (1982).

Ameriks, Karl. "Kant, Fichte and Apperception," in *Kant and the Fate of Autonomy: Problems in the Appropriation of the Critical Philosophy*, Cambridge: Cambridge University Press (2000), 234–64.

Amrhein, Hans. *Kants Lehre vom "Bewusstsein überhaupt" und ihre Weiterbildung bis auf die Gegenwart, Kantstudien Ergänzungshefte*, 10, Berlin: Verlag von Reuther and Reichard (1909).

Anscombe, G. E. M. "'Whatever Has a Beginning of Existence Must Have a Cause': Hume's Argument Exposed," in *From Parmenides to Wittgenstein: The Collected Philosophical Papers of G. E. M. Anscombe*, Volume 1, Minneapolis, MN: University of Minnesota Press (1981), 93–9.

Banham, Garry. "Transcendental Idealism and Transcendental Apperception," in *Kant's Idealism, New Interpretations of a Controversial Doctrine*, edited by Dennis Schulting and Jacco Verburgt, New York: Springer (2011), 109–25.

Baum, Manfred. *Deduction und Beweis in Kant's Transzendental-Philosophie*, Königstein: Athenäum Verlag (1986).

Baumanns, Peter. "Kants transzendentale Deduktion der reinen Verstandesbegiffe (B): Ein kritischer Forschungsbericht," *Kant-Studien* 82 (1991), 328–48 and 455.

Baumgarten, Alexander Gottlieb. *Metaphysica*, reprinted in *Kant's gesammelte Schriften*, herausgegeben von der Preussischen Akademie der Wissenschaften, Berlin: Walter de Gruyter and Co. (1926), Band 17, 6–206.

Baumgarten, Alexander Gottlieb. *Metaphysics, A Critical Translation with Kant's Elucidations, Selected Notes, and Related Materials*, translated and edited with an introduction by Courtney D. Fugate and John Hymers, London: Bloomsbury (2013).

Beck, Lewis White. "Can Kant's Synthetic Judgments Be Made Analytic?" *Studies in the Philosophy of Kant*, Indianapolis, IN: Bobbs-Merrill (1965a), 74–91.

Beck, Lewis White. "Kant's Theory of Definition," *Studies in the Philosophy of Kant*, Indianapolis, IN: Bobbs-Merrill (1965b), 61–73.

Beck, Lewis White. *Early German Philosophy: Kant and His Predecessors*, Cambridge, MA: Belknap Press (1969a).

Beck, Lewis White. "Kant's Strategy," in *The First Critique: Reflections on Kant's Critique of Pure Reason*, edited by Terrence Penelhum and J. J. MacIntosh, Belmont, CA: Wadsworth Publishing Company (1969b), 4–17.

Beck, Lewis White. *Essays on Kant and Hume*, New Haven, CT: Yale University Press (1978).

Beck, Lewis White. *Kant's Latin Writings, Translations, Commentaries and Notes*, in collaboration with Mary G. Gregor, Ralf Meerbote, and John A. Reuscher, New York: Peter Lang (1986).

Beck, Lewis White. "Two Ways of Reading Kant's Letter to Herz: Comments on Carl," *Kant's Transcendental Deductions, The Three "Critiques" and the "Opus postumum,"* edited by Eckart Förster, Stanford, CA: Stanford University Press, (1989), 21–6.

Beiser, Frederick. *The Fate of Reason, German Philosophy from Kant to Fichte*, Cambridge, MA: Harvard University Press (1987).

Beiser, Frederick. "Kant's Intellectual Development: 146–1781," *The Cambridge Companion to Kant*, edited by Paul Guyer, Cambridge: Cambridge University Press (1992), 26–61.

Bennett, Jonathan. *Kant's Analytic*, Cambridge: Cambridge University Press (1966).

Berkeley, George. *A Treatise Concerning the Principles of Human Knowledge: The Works of George Berkeley Bishop of Cloyne*, Volume 2, edited by T. E. Jessop, London: Thomas Nelson (1949a), 19–113.

Berkeley, George. *Three Dialogues between Hylas and Philonous: The Works of George Berkeley Bishop of Cloyne*, Volume 2, edited by T. E. Jessop, London: Thomas Nelson (1949b), 167–263.

Bird, Graham. *Kant's Theory of Knowledge*, London: Routledge and Kegan Paul (1962).

Bird, Graham. *The Revolutionary Kant: A Commentary on the Critique of Pure Reason*, La Salle, IL: Open Court (2006).

Borowski, Ludwig Ernst. *Darstellung des Lebens und Charakters Immanuel Kants*, in *Immanuel Kant sein Leben in Darstellungen von Zeitgenossen*, edited by Felix Gross. Reprinted by Darmstadt: Wissenschaftliche Buchgesellschaft (1698).

Brandt, Reinhard. "Review of Lothar Kreimendahl, *Kant-Der Durchbruch von 1769*," *Kant-Studien* 83 (1992), 100–11.

Brandt, Reinhard. *The Table of Judgments: Critique of Pure Reason A67–76/B92–101*, translated by Eric Watkins, Atascadero, CA: Ridgeview Publishing (1995).

Brook, Andrew. *Kant and the Mind*, Cambridge: Cambridge University Press (1994).

Buchdahl, Gerd. *Metaphysics and Philosophy of Science*, Cambridge, MA: MIT Press (1969a).

Buchdahl, Gerd. "The Kantian 'Dynamic of Reason' with Special Reference to the Place of Causality in Kant's Cystem," in *Kant Studies Today*, edited by L. W. Beck, La Salle, IL: Open Court (1969b), 187–208.

Buchdahl, Gerd. "The Conception of Lawlikeness in Kant's Philosophy of Science," in *Kant's Theory* of Knowledge, edited by L. W. Beck, Dordrecht: Reidel (1974), 128–50.

Buroker, Jill Vance. *Space and Incongruence: The Origin of Kant's Idealism*. Dordrecht, Holland, Boston, and London: D. Reidel Publishing Company (1981).

Caranti, Luigi. *Kant and the Scandal of Philosophy: The Kantian Critique of Cartesian Scepticism*, Toronto: University of Toronto Press (2007).

Carl, Wolfgang. "Kant's First Drafts of the Deduction of the Categories," *Kant's Transcendental Deductions, The Three "Critiques" and the "Opus postumum,"* edited by Eckart Förster, Stanford, CA: Stanford University Press (1989a), 3–20.

Carl, Wolfgang. *Der schweigende Kant, Die Entwürfe zu einer Deduktion der Kategorien vor 1781*, Göttingen: Vanderghoeck and Ruprecht in Göttingen (1989b).

Carl, Wolfgang. *Die Transzendentale Deduktion der Kategorien in der ersten Auflage der Kritik der reinen Vernunft, Ein Kommentar*, Frankfurt am Main: Vittorio Klostermann (1992).

Carl, Wolfgang. "Apperception and Spontaneity," *International Journal of Philosophical Studies* 5 (1997), 147–63.

Carl, Wolfgang. "Die B-Deduktion," in *Immanuel Kant: Kritik der reinen Vernunft*, edited by Georg Mohr and Marcus Willaschek, Berlin: Akademie-Verlag (1998), 189–216.

Cassam, Quassim. "Transcendental Arguments, Transcendental Synthesis and Transcendental Idealism," *Philosophical Quarterly* 37 (1987), 355–78.

Cassirer, Ernst. *Das Erkenntnisproblem in der Philosophie und Wissenschaft der neueren Zeit*, Volume 2, Berlin: Verlag Bruno Cassirer (1911).

Cassirer, Ernst. *Substance and Function*, translated by W.C. Swabey and M.C. Swabey, New York: Dover (1953).

Cassirer, Ernst. *Kant's Life and Thought*, translated by James Haden, New Haven, CT: Yale University Press (1981).

Chipman, Lauchlin. "Kant's Categories and Their Schematism," *Kant-Studien* 63 (1972), 36–49.

Cicovacki, Predrag. "An Aporia of a priori Knowledge, On Carl's and Beck's Interpretation of Kant's Letter to Markus Herz," *Kant-Studien*, 82 (1991), 349–60.

Cohen, Hermann. *Kants Theorie der Erfahrung*, Berlin: Ferd, Dümmlers Verlagsbuchhandlung (1885).

Cohen, Hermann. *Die Systematischen Begriffe in Kants vorkritischen Schriften*, Berlin: F. Dümmler (1926).

Cohen, Hermann. *Kommentar zu Immanuel Kants Kritik der reinen Vernunft*, 5, Zürich: Georg Olms Verlag (1989).

Crusius, Christian August. *Entwurf der nothwendigen Vernunft=Wahrheiten, wiefern sie den zufälligen entgegen gestetzt* (1745), Reprinted in *Christian August Crusius Die philosphischen Hauptwerke*, Volume 2, herausgeben von Gorgio Tonelli, Hildesheim: Georg Olms Verlagsbuchhandlung (1964), 3–344.

Crusius, Christian August. *Weg zur Gewissheit und Zuverlässigkeit der mensclichen Erknntniss*, Leipzig: Johann Friedrich Gledich (1747). Reprinted in *Christian August Crusius Die philosphischen Hauptwerke*, Volume 3, herausgeben von Gorgio Tonelli, Hildesheim: Georg Olms Verlagsbuchhandlung (1965).

de Vleeschauwer, H. J. *The Development of Kantian Thought*, London: Thomas Nelson and Sons (1962).

de Vleeschauwer, H. J. *La Déduction Transcendantale dans L'Oeuvre de Kant*, 3 Volumes, Antwerp: De Sikkel (1934, 1936, 1937). Reprinted by Garland Publishing, New York (1976).

DeRose, Keith. "Epistemic Possibilities," *Philosophical Review*, 100 (1991), 581–605.

Descartes, René. *The Philosophical Writings of Descartes*, Volume 2, translated by John Cottingham, Robert Stoothoff, and Dugald Murdoch, Cambridge: Cambridge University Press (1984).

Dyck, Corey W. *Kant and Rational Psychology*, Oxford: Oxford University Press (2014a).

Dyck, Corey W. "Spontaneity *before* the Critical Turn: Kant's Views on the Spontaneity of the Mind in Context," available online at: <http://philpapers.org/rec/DYCTRO> (2014b).

Erdmann, Benno (editor). *Reflexion Kants zur Kritik der reinen Vernunft*, Leipzig: Fues's Verlag (R. Reisland) (1882).

Evans, Joseph Claude. "Two-Steps-in-One-Proof: The Structure of the Transcendental Deduction of the Categories," *Journal of the History of Philosophy* 28 (1990), 553–70.

Falkenstein, Lorne. *Kant's Intuitionism: A Commentary on the Transcendental Aesthetic.* Toronto: University of Toronto Press (1995).

Fischer, Kuno. *Geschichte der neuern Philosophie: Immanuel Kant und seine Lehre*, Heidelberg: Carl Winter's Universitätsbuchhandlung (1889).

Förster, Eckart. "Review of Allison's *Kant's Transcendental Idealism* (1983)," *Journal of Philosophy* 82, 734–8 (1985).

Förster, Eckart. "Kant's Selbstsetzungslehre," in *Kant's Transcendental Deductions: The Three "Critiques" and the "Opus postumum*, edited by Eckart Förster, Stanford, CA: Stanford University Press (1989), 216–38.

Förster, Eckart. *The Twenty-Five Years of Philosophy: A Systematic Reconstruction*, translated by Brady Bowman, Cambridge, MA: Harvard University Press (2012).

Freudiger, Jürg. "Zur Problem der Wahrnehmungsurteile in Kants theoretische Philosophie," *Kant-Studien* 82 (1991), 414–35.

Friedman, Michael. *Kant and the Exact Sciences*, Cambridge, MA: Harvard University Press (1992a).

Friedman, Michael. "Causal Laws and Natural Science," in *The Cambridge Companion to Kant*, edited by Paul Guyer, Cambridge: Cambridge University Press (1992b), 161–99.

Gardner, Sebastian. *Kant and the Critique of Pure Reason*, London: Routledge (1999).

Garve, Christian. *Uebersicht der vornehmsten Principien der Sittenlehre: von dem Zeitalter des Aristoteles an bis auf unsern Zeiten*, Breslau (1798), reprinted in Aetas Kantiana, Brussels: Culture et Civilisation (1968).

Gassendi, Pierre. "Fifth Set of Objections to Descartes' Meditations," *The Philosophical Writings of Descartes*, translated by John Cottingham, Robert Stoothoff, and Dugald Murdoch, Cambridge: Cambridge University Press, Volume 2 (1984), 179–240.

George, Rolf. "Kant's Sensationism," *Synthese* 47 (1981), 229–55.

Gibbons, Sarah. *Kant's Theory of the Imagination: Bridging Gaps in Judgment and Experience*, Oxford: Clarendon Press (1994).

Gotz, Gerhard. "Kants 'grosses Licht' des Jahres 69." *Kant und die Berliner Aufklärung, Akten des IX. Internationalen Kant-Kongresses*, edited by Volker Gerhardt, Rolf-Peter Horstmann, and Ralph Schumacher, Berlin (Volume 2, 2001), 19–26.

Gram, S. Moltke. *The Transcendental Turn: The Foundations of Kant's Idealism*, Tampa, FL: University Presses of Florida (1984).

Grier, Michelle. *Kant's Doctrine of Transcendental Illusion*, Cambridge: Cambridge University Press (2001).

Guéroult, Martial. "Canon de la raison pure et critique de la raison pratique," *Revue Internationale de Philosophie* 8 (1954), 331–57.

Guyer, Paul. "Review of Henrich's *Identität und Objectivität*," *Journal of Philosophy* 76 (1979), 151–67.

Guyer, Paul. "Kant on Apperception and a priori Synthesis," *American Philosophical Quarterly* 17 (1980), 205–12.

Guyer, Paul. "Kant's Tactics in the Transcendental Deduction," in *Essays on Kant's Critique of Pure Reason*, edited by J. N. Mohanty and Robert W. Shahan, Norman, OK: University of Oklahoma Press (1982), 157–99.

Guyer, Paul. *Kant and the Claims of Knowledge*, Cambridge: Cambridge University Press (1987).

Guyer, Paul. "Reason and Reflective Judgment: Kant on the Significance of Systematicity," *Noûs* 24 (1990a), 17–43.

Guyer, Paul. "Kant's Conception of Empirical Law," *Proceedings of the Aristotelian Society* 64 (1990b), 220–42.

Guyer, Paul. "The Transcendental Deduction of the Categories," in *The Cambridge Companion to Kant*, edited by Paul Guyer, Cambridge: Cambridge University Press (1992), 123–60.

Guyer, Paul. *Kant*, Abingdon: Routledge (2006).

Guyer, Paul. "Guyer on Allison," in *Debating Allison on Transcendental Idealism, Kantian Review* (2007), 10–23.

Guyer, Paul and Allen Wood (editors and translators). *Critique of Pure Reason: The Cambridge Edition of the Works of Immanuel Kant*, Cambridge: Cambridge University Press (1998).

Guyer, Paul (editor and translator with Curtis Bowman and Frederick Rauscher). *Notes and Fragments: The Cambridge Edition of the Works of Immanuel Kant*, Cambridge: Cambridge University Press (2005).

Haering, Theodor. *Der Duisburgsche Nachlass und Kants Kritizismus um 1775*, Tübingen: J. Mohr (1910).

Hamann, Johann Georg. *Briefwechsel*, Volume 4, edited by Arthur Hinkel, Weisbaden: Insel Verlag (1959).

Harrison, Ross. "Transcendental Arguments and Idealism," in *Idealism Past and Present*, edited by Godfrey Vesey, Cambridge: Cambridge University Press (1982), 211–24.

Heidegger, Martin. *Kant und das Problem der Metaphysik*, Third Edition, Frankfurt am Main: Vittorio Klostermann (1965).

Henrich, Dieter. "Fichtes ursprüngliche Einsicht," in *Subjectivität und Metaphysik: Festschrift für Wolfgang Cramer*, edited by Herausgegeben von Dieter Henrich and Hans Wagner, Frankfurt: Klostermann (1966), 188–232.

Henrich, Dieter. "Kants Denken 1762/3 über den Ursprung der Unterscheidung analytischer und synthetischer Urteile," in *Studien zu Kants philosophischer Entwicklung*, edited by Herausgegeben von Heinz Heimsoeth, Dieter Henrich, and Gorgio Tonelli, Hidesheim: Georg Olms Verlagsbuchhandlung (1967), 9–38.

Henrich, Dieter. "The Proof-Structure of Kant's Transcendental Deduction," in *Kant on Pure Reason*, edited by Ralph C. S. Walker, Oxford: Oxford University Press (1982), 66–81.

Henrich, Dieter. "Die Beweisstruktur der transzendentalen Deduktion der reinen Verstands-begriffe-eine Diskussion mit Dieter Henrich," *Probleme der "Kritik der reinen Vernunft,"* edited by Burkhard Tuschling, Berlin: Walter de Gruyter (1984), 34–96.

Henrich, Dieter. "Kant's Notion of a Deduction and the Methodological Background of the First *Critique*," *Kant's Transcendental Deductions: The Three "Critiques" and the "Opus postumum"*, edited by Eckart Förster, Stanford, CA: Stanford University Press (1989a), 29–46.

Henrich, Dieter. "The Identity of the Subject in the Transcendental Deduction," in *Reading Kant*, edited by Eva Schaper and Wilhelm Vossenkuhl, Oxford: Oxford University Press (1989b), 250–80.

Henrich, Dieter. "Identity and Objectivity: An Inquiry into Kant's *Transcendental Deduction*," translated by Jeffrey Edwards, in *The Unity of Reason: Essays on Kant's Philosophy*, edited by Richard Velkley, Cambridge, MA: Harvard University Press (1994), 123–208.

Herz, Markus. *Betrachtungen aus der spekulativen Weltweisheit*, edited by Elfriede Conrad, Heinrich P. Delfosse, and Birgit Nehren, Hamburg: Felix Meiner Verlag (1990).

Hintikka, Jaako. "Cogito, Ergo Sum: Inference or Performance," *Philosophical Review* 71 (1962), 3–32.

Hoppe, Hansgeorg. *Synthesis bei Kant*, Berlin: de Gruyter (1983).

Horstmann, Rolf P. "The Metaphysical Deduction in Kant's Critique of Pure Reason," *Philosophical Forum*, 18 (1981), 225–40.

Horstmann, Rolf P. "Why Must There Be a Transcendental Deduction in Kant's *Critique of Judgment*?" in *Kant's Transcendental Deductions: The Three "Critiques" and the postumum*, edited by Eckart Förster, Stanford, CA: Stanford University Press (1989), 157–76.

Hossenfelder, Malte. *Kants Konstitutions-Theory und die Transzendentale Deduktion*, Berlin: de Gruyter (1978).

Howell, Robert. *Kant's Transcendental Deduction: An Analysis of Main Themes in His Critical Philosophy*, Dordrecht/Boston/London: Kluwer Academic Publishers (1992).

Hume, David. *An Enquiry Concerning Human Understanding*, edited by Tom L. Beauchamp, Oxford: Oxford University Press (1999).

Hume, David. *A Treatise of Human Nature*, Volume 1, edited by David Fate Norton and Mary J. Norton, Oxford: Clarendon Press (2007).

Husserl, Edmund. "Philosophy as a Rigorous Science," translated by Quentin Lauer, in *Edmund Husserl: Phenomenology and the Crisis in Philosophy*, New York: Harper Torchbook (1965).

Jacobi, F. H. *Werke*, Volume 2, edited by F. Roth and F. Köppen, Darmstadt: Wissenschaftliche Buchgesellschaft (1968).

James, William. *The Principles of Psychology*, Volume 1, New York: Henry Holt and Co. (1890).

Janke, W. *Historisches Wörterbuch der Philosophie*, edited by Joachim Ritter, Band 1: A-C, Darmstadt: Wissenschaftliche Buchgesellschaft (1975), 448–50.

Jolley, Nicholas. *Leibniz and Locke: A Study of the New Essays on Human Understanding*, Oxford: Clarendon Press (1984).

Kemp Smith, Norman. *Translation of* Critique of Pure Reason, New York: St Martin's Press (1958).

Kemp Smith, Norman. *A Commentary to Kant's "Critique of Pure Reason,"* Second Edition, New York: Humanities Press (1962).

Kierkegaard, Søren. *Philosophical Fragments*, translated by David F. Swenson and revised by Howard V. Hong, Princeton, NJ: Princeton University Press (1962).

Kitcher, Patricia. *Kant's Transcendental Psychology*, New York: Oxford University Press (1990).

Kitcher, Patricia. *Kant's Thinker*, New York: Oxford University Press (2011).

Klemme, Heiner R. *Kant's Philosophie des Subjeckts*, Hamburg: Felix Meiner Verlag (1996).

Kobusch, Theo. "Intuition," *Historisches Wörterbuch der Philosophie*, edited by Joachim Ritter and Karlfried Gründer, Band 4:I-K, Darmstadt: Wissenschaftliche Buchgesellschaft (1976), 524–40.

Kreimendahl, Lothar. *Kant-Der Durchbruch von 1769*, Köln: Dinter (1991).

Kreimendahl, Lothar and Gawlick, Günter. *Hume in der Deutschen Aufklärung: Umrisse einer Rezeptionsgeschichte*, Stuttgart: Frommann-Hoolzboog (1987).

Krouglov, Alexi N. "Tetens und die Deduktion dr Kategorien bei Kant," *Kant-Studien* 104 (2013), 466–89.

Krüger, L. "Wollte Kant die Vollständigkeit seiner Urteilstafel beweisen?" *Kant-Studien* 59 (1968), 333–55.

Kuehn, Manfred. "Kant's Conception of Hume's Problem," *Journal of the History of Philosophy* 21 (1983a), 175–93.

Kuehn, Manfred. "Hume's Antinomies, *Hume Studies* 9 (1983b), 25–45.

Kuehn, Manfred. "Hume and Tetens," *Hume Studies* 15 (1989), 365–75.

Kuehn, Manfred. "The Wolffian Background of Kant's Transcendental Deduction," in *Logic and the Workings of the Mind*, edited by P. A. Easton, Atascadero, CA: Ridgeview (1997), 229–50.

Kuehn, Manfred. *Kant: A Biography*, Cambridge: Cambridge University Press (2001).

Kulstad, Mark. *Leibniz on Apperception, Consciousness, and Reflection*. München, Hamden, Wien: Philosophia Verlag (1991).

Lambert, Johann Heinrich. *Neues Organon, oder Gedanken Über die Erforschung und Bezeichnung des Wahren und dessen Unterscheidung vom Irrthum und Schein*, Band 1, Leipzig: Johann Wendler (1764).

Landau, Albert (editor). *Rezensionen zur kantischen Philosophie 1781–87*, Bebra: Albert Landau (1991).

Langton, Rae. *Kantian Humility: Our Ignorance of Things in Themselves*, Oxford: Oxford University Press (1998).

Laywine, Alison. *Kant's Early Metaphysics and the Origins of the Critical Philosophy*, Volume 3, Atascadero, CA: Ridgeview Publishing Company (1994).

Laywine, Alison. "Kant's Reply to Lambert on the Ancestry of Metaphysical Concepts," *Kantian Review* 5 (2001), 1–48.

Laywine, Alison. "Kant on Sensibility and the Understanding in the 1770s," *Canadian Journal of Philosophy* 33 (2003), 443–82.

Laywine, Alison. "Kant on the Self as Model of Experience," *Kantian Review* 9 (2005), 1–29.

Laywine, Alison. "Kant's Metaphysical Reflections in the Duisburg Nachlass," *Kant-Studien* 97 (2006), 79–113.

Leibniz, G.W. *The Leibniz-Clarke Correspondence*, edited by H. G. Alexander, Manchester: Manchester University Press (1956).

Leibniz, G. W. *New Essays on Human Understanding*, translated and edited by Peter Remnant and Jonathan Bennett, Cambridge: Cambridge University Press (1981).

Leibniz, G. W. *Philosophical Essays*, edited and translated by Roger Ariew and Daniel Garber, Indianapolis, IN: Hackett Publishing Company (1989).

Leppäkoski, Markku. "The Two Steps of the B-Deduction," *Kantian Review* 2 (1998), 107–16.

Lewis, Clarence Irving. *Mind and the World Order Outline of a Theory of Knowledge*, New York: Dover Publications (1929).

Locke, John. *An Essay Concerning Human Understanding*, edited by Peter H. Nidditch, Oxford: Clarendon Press (1975).

Longuenesse, Béatrice. *Kant and the Capacity to Judge*, translated by Charles Wolfe, Princeton, NJ: Princeton University Press (1998a).

Longuenesse, Béatrice. "The Divisions of the Transcendental Logic and the Leading Thread," in *Immanuel Kant: Kritik der reinen Vernunft*, edited by Georg Mohr and Marcus Willaschek, Berlin: Akademie-Verlag (1998b).

Longuenesse, Béatrice. "Kant's Categories and the Capacity to Judge: Responses to Henry Allison and Sally Sedgwick," *Inquiry* 43 (2000), 91–110.

Lovejoy, Arthur. "Kant's Antithesis of Dogmatism and Criticism," in *Kant: Disputed Questions*, edited by Moltke S. Gram, Chicago, IL: Quadrangle Books (1967), 105–30.

Makkreel, Rudolf A. *Imagination and Interpretation in Kant: The Hermeneutical Import of the Critique of Judgment*, Chicago, IL: University of Chicago Press (1990).

McRae, Robert. *Leibniz: Perception, Apperception, and Thought*, Toronto: University of Toronto Press (1976).

Meerbote, Ralf. "Kant's Use of the Notions 'Objective Reality' and 'Objective Validity,'" *Kant-Studien* 63 (1972), 51–8.

Meier, Georg Friedrich. *Auszug aus der Vernunftlehre*, in *Kant's gesammelte Schriften*, herausgegeben von der Preussischen Akademie der Wissenschaften, Berlin: Walter de Gruyter, Volume 16 (1924), 3–872.

Melnick, Arthur. *Kant's Analogies of Experience*, Chicago, IL: University of Chicago Press (1973).

Mensch, Jennifer. *Kant's Organicism*. Chicago, IL: University of Chicago Press (2013).

Naragon, Steve. "Kant on Descartes and the Brutes," *Kant-Studien* 81 (1990), 1–23.

Oeser, Stephan. "Symbol," in *Historisches Wörterbuch der Philosophie*, edited by Joachim Ritter and Karlfried Gründer, Band 10: St-T, Darmstadt: Wissenschaftliche Buchgesellschaft (1998), 710–23.

Onof, Christian and Schulting, Dennis. "Space as Form of Intuition and as Formal Intuition. On the Note to B160 in Kant's *Critique of Pure Reason*," *Philosophical Review* 124 (2015), 1–39.

Paton, H. J. *Kant's Metaphysic of Experience*, New York: Macmillan, 2 Volumes (1936a and 1936b).

Paton, H. J. "Is the Transcendental Deduction a Patchwork?" Reprinted in *Kant: Disputed Questions*, edited by Moltke S. Gram, Chicago, IL: Quadrangle Books (1967), 62–91.

Pinder, Tillman. "Kants Begriff der transzendentalen Erkenntnis," *Kant-Studien* 77 (1986), 1–40.

Pippin, Robert, B. *Kant's Theory of Form, An Essay on the Critique of Pure Reason*, New Haven, CT: Yale University Press (1983).

Pippin, Robert, B. *Hegel's Idealism: The Satisfaction of Self-Consciousness*, Cambridge: Cambridge University Press (1989).

Pistorius, Hermann Andreas. "Review of Kant's *Prolegomena*," in *Resenzionen zur Kantischen Philosophie*, edited by Albert Landau, Bebra: Albert Landau Verlag (1991).

Pluhar, Werner. Translation of the *Critique of Pure Reason*, Indianapolis, IN: Hackett Publishing (1996).

Pollok, Konstantin. "'An Almost Single Inference': Kant's Deduction of the Categories Reconsidered," *Archiv für Geschichte der Philosophie* 90 (2008), 323–45.

Pollok, Konstantin. "*Wie sind Erfahrungsurteile möglich?*" in *Kants Prolegomena Ein kooperativer Kommentar*, edited by Holger Lyre and Oliver Schliemann, Frankfurt am Main: Klostermann (2012), 103–26.

Prauss, Gerold. *Erscheinung bei Kant*. Berlin: de Gruyter (1971).

Prauss, Gerold. *Kant und das Problem der Dinge an sich*, Bonn: Bouvier (1974).

Pritchard, Duncan. *Epistemic Luck*, Oxford: Clarendon Press (2005).

Reich, Klaus. *The Completeness of Kant's Table of Judgments*, translated by Jane Kneller and Michael Losonsky, Stanford, CA: Stanford University Press (1992).

Renault, Alain (translator and editor). *Critique de la raison pure*, Paris: Aubier (1997).

Rescher, Nicholas. *Conceptual Idealism*, Oxford: Basil Blackwell (1973).

Rescher, Nicholas. "Conceptual Idealism Revisited," *Review of Metaphysics* 44 (1991), 495–523.

Rohs, Peter. Review of *Identität und Objektivität* by Dieter Henrich, *Zeitschrift für philosophische Forschung* 32 (1978), 303–8.

Rohs, Peter. "Bezieht sich nach Kant die Anschauung unmittelbar auf Gegenstände?" in *Kant und die Berliner Aufklärung, Akten des IX. Internationalen Kant-Kongresses*, edited by Volker Gerhardt, Rolf-Peter Horstmann, and Ralph Schumacher, Berlin: de Gruyter (2001), 214–28.

Sassen, Brigitte (editor). *Kant's Early Critics: The Empiricist Critique of the Theoretical Philosophy*, Cambridge: Cambridge University Press (2000).

Schönfeld, Martin. *The Philosophy of the Young Kant, The Precritical Project*, Oxford: Oxford University Press (2000).

Schopenhauer, Arthur. *The World as Will and Idea*, Volume 1, translated by E. F. J. Payne, Indian Hills, CO: Falcon's Wing Press (1958).

Schulthess, Peter. *Relation und Funktion: eine systematische und entwicklungsgeschichtliche Untersuchung zur theoretischen Philosophie Kants*, Berlin: de Gruyter (1981).

Schulting, Dennis. Kant's Deduction and Apperception: Explaining the Categories, London: Palgrave (2012).

Schultz, Johann. "Review of J. A. H. Ulrich's *Institutiones Logicae et Metaphysicae*," in *Allgemeine Literatur-Zeitung* (1785); reprinted in *Rezensionen zur kantischen Philosophie* (1781–87), edited by Albert Landau; Bebra: Albert Landau Verlag (1991), 243–8. English translation by Briggitte Sassen in *Kant's Early Critics: The Empiricist Critique of the Theoretical Philosophy*, translated and edited by Briggitte Sassen, Cambridge: Cambridge University Press (2000), 210–14.

Schultz, Johann. *Erläuterungen über des herrn Professor Kant Critik der reinen Vernunft*; reprinted in Aetas Kantiana, Bruxelles (1968). English translation: *Exposition of Kant's Critique of Pure Reason*, translated with an introduction by James C. Morrison, Ottawa: University of Ottawa Press (1995).

Schultz, Johann. "Review of Kant's *Inaugural Dissertation*," Appendix B in *Exposition of Kant's Critique of Pure Reason*, translated by James C. Morrison, Ottawa: University of Ottawa Press (1995), 163–7.

Sellars, Wilfrid. *Science and Metaphysics: Variations on Kantian Themes*, London: Routledge and Kegan Paul, and New York: Humanities Press (1968).

Sellars, Wilfrid. "... This I or He or It (the Thing) which Thinks...," *Proceedings and Addresses of the American Philosophical Association* 44 (1971), 5–31.

Sellars, Wilfrid. "The Role of the Imagination in Kant's Theory of Experience," in *Categories: A Colloquium*, edited by Henry W. Johnstone, Jr., University Park, PN: Pennsylvania State University Press (1978).

Sellars, Wilfrid. *Kant and Pre-Kantian Themes: Lectures by Wilfrid Sellars*, edited by Pedro Amaral, Atascadero, CA: Ridgeview Publishing (2002).

Serck-Hanssen, Camilla. *Kant und die Berliner Aufklärung: Akten des IX. Internationalen Kant-Kongresses*, Volume 2, edited by Volker Gerhardt, Rolf-Peter Horstmann, and Ralph Schumacher, Berlin: de Gruyter (2001), 59–68.

Spinoza, Benedict de. "Descartes' 'Principles of Philosophy,'" in *The Collected Works of Spinoza*, edited and translated by Edwin Curley, Volume 1, 224–336, Princeton, NJ: Princeton University Press (1985).

Stern, Robert. *Transcendental Arguments and Scepticism, Answering the Question of Justification*, Oxford: Oxford University Press (2000).

Strawson, P. F. *The Bounds of Sense: An Essay on Kant's Critique of Pure Reason*, London: Methuen (1966).

Strawson, P. F. "Imagination and Perception," in *Kant on Pure Reason*, edited by Ralph C. S. Walker, Oxford: Oxford University Press (1982), 82–99.

Stuhlmann-Laeisz, Rainer. *Kants Logik*, Berlin: de Gruyter (1976).

Sturma, Dieter. *Kant über Selbstbewusstseins*, Hildesheim: Georg Olms Verlag (1985).

Svendson, Lars. *Kant's Critical Hermeneutics: On Schematization and Interpretation*, Dissertation, Oslo: Unipub Forlag/Akademia AS (1999).

Tetens, Johann Nicholas. *Philosophische Versuche über die menschliche Natur and ihre Entwicklung*, 2 Volumes, Leipzig: Weidemanns (1777a and 1777b).

Thiel, Udo. "Between Wolff and Kant: Merian's Theory of Apperception," *Journal of the History of Philosophy* 34 (1996), 213–32.

Thiel, Udo. *The Early Modern Subject: Self-Consciousness and Personal Identity from Descartes to Hume*, Oxford: Oxford University Press (2011).

Thöle, Bernhard. *Kant und das Problem der Gesetzmässigkeit der Natur*, Berlin: Walter de Gruyter (1991).

Tonelli, Giorgio. "Die Umwälzung von 1769 bei Kant," *Kant-Studien* 54 (1963), 399–473.

Tonelli, Giorgio. "Analysis and Synthesis in XVIIIth Century Philosophy Prior to Kant," *Archiv für Begriffsgeschichte*, Band XX (1976), 178–213.

Treash, Gordon (translator). "Introduction," *The One Possible Basis for a Demonstration of the Existence of God*, New York: Abaris Books (1979).

Tuschling, Burkhard. "Apperception and Ether: On the Idea of a Transcendental Deduction of Matter in Kant's *Opus postumum, Transcendental Deductions*, the Three *Critiques* and the *Opus postumum*," edited by Eckart Förster, Stanford, CA: Stanford University Press (1989), 195–216.

Uebele, Wilhem. *Johann Nicolaus Tetens nach seiner Gesamtentwicklung betrachtet mit besonderer Berürksichtigung des Verhältnisses zu Kant*, Berlin: Reuther and Reichard (1912).

Vaihinger, Hans. *Commentar zu Kants Kritik der reinen Vernunft*, Stuttgart: W. Spemmann, Volume 1 (1881), Volume 2 (1892).

Vaihinger, Hans. "The Transcendental Deduction of the Categories in the First Edition of the Critique of Pure Reason," translated by Moltke S. Gram in *Kant: Disputed Questions*, edited by Moltke S. Gram, Chicago, IL: Quadrangle Books (1967), 23–61.

Walford, David (editor and translator with Ralf Meerbote). *Theoretical Philosophy, 1755–1770, The Cambridge Edition of the Works of Immanuel Kant*, Cambridge: Cambridge University Press (1992).

Walker, Ralph. "Kant's Conception of Empirical Law: II," *Proceedings of the Aristotelian Society*, 64 (1990), 243–58.

Walsh, W. H. *Kant's Criticism of Metaphysics*, Edinburgh: Edinburgh University Press (1975).

Watkins, Eric (editor and translator). *Kant's Critique of Pure Reason Background Source Materials*, Cambridge: Cambridge University Press (2009).

Weldon, T. D. *Kant's Critique of Pure Reason*, Second Edition, Oxford: Clarendon Press (1958).

Wenzel, Christian. "Spielen nach Kant die Kategorien schon bei Wahrnehmung eine Rolle?" *Kant-Studien* 96 (2005), 407–26.

Werkmeister, W. H. *Kant's Silent Decade*, Tallahassee, FL: University Presses of Florida (1979).

Werkmeister, W. H. *Kant the Architectonic and Development of his Philosophy*, La Salle, IL: Open Court Publishing Company (1980).

Westphal, Kenneth R. "Affinity, Idealism, and Naturalism: The Stability of Cinnabar and the Possibility of Experience," *Kant-Studien* 88 (1997), 130–89.

Westphal, Kenneth R. "Freedom and the Distinction between Phenomena and Noumena: Is Allison's View Methodological, Metaphysical, or Equivocal?" *Journal of Philosophical Research* 26 (2001), 593–622.

Westphal, Kenneth R. *Kant's Transcendental Proof of Realism*, Cambridge: Cambridge University Press (2004).

Wittgenstein, Ludwig. *Philosophical Investigations*, translated by G. E. M. Anscombe, Oxford: Basil Blackwell (1963).

Wolff, Christian. *Vernünfftige Gedancken von Gott, der Welt und der Seele des Menschen, Auch allen Dingen überhaupt, Den Leibhabern der Wahrheit mitgetheilet* (1751), reprinted Ann Arbor, MI: UMI (2005).

Wolff, Christian. *Vernünftige Gedanken von den Kräften des menschlichen Verstandes und ihrem richtigen Gebrauche in Erkenntnis der Wahrheit*, edited by Hans Werner Arndt, Hildesheim: Georg Olms Verlagsbuchhandlung (1965).

Wolff, Michael. *Die Vollständigkeit der kantischen Urteilstafel*, Frankfurt am Main: Vittorio Klostermann (1995).

Wolff, Robert Paul. *Kant's Theory of Mental Activity, A Commentary on the Transcendental Analytic of the Critique of Pure Reason*, Cambridge, MA: Harvard University Press (1963).

Wunderlich, Falk. *Kant und die Bewusstseinstheorien des 18. Jahrhunderts*. Berlin: Walter de Gruyter (2005).

Wundt, Max. *Kant als Metaphysiker*, Stuttgart: Enke (1924).

Young, J. Michael. "Kant's View of Imagination," *Kant-Studien* 79 (1988), 140–64.

Young, J. Michael (editor and translator). *Lectures on Logic: The Cambridge Edition of the Works of Immanuel Kant*, Cambridge: Cambridge University Press (1992).

Zocher, Rudolf. "Kants Transzendentale Deduktion der Kategorien," *Zeitschrift für philosophische Forschung* 8 (1694), 161–94.

Zöller, Günter. *Theoretische Gegenstandsbeziehung bei Kant*, Berlin: Walter de Gruyter (1984).

Index

Printed in Great Britain
by Amazon

63156553R00296